From Suffrage to the Senate

From Suffrage to the Senate: America's Political Women

An Encyclopedia of Leaders, Causes & Issues

Volume 1: A–N

Suzanne O'Dea

Forewords by Ann W. Richards
and
Susan M. Collins

Grey House
Publishing

PUBLISHER:	Leslie Mackenzie
EDITORIAL DIRECTOR:	Laura Mars-Proietti
PRODUCTION EDITOR:	Toby Raymond
EDITORIAL ASSISTANT:	Jane Murphy
MARKETING DIRECTOR:	Jessica Moody

AUTHOR:	Suzanne O'Dea
COPYEDITOR:	Elaine Alibrandi
COMPOSITION & DESIGN:	ATLIS Systems

Grey House Publishing, Inc.
185 Millerton Road
Millerton, NY 12546
518.789.8700
FAX 518.789.0545
www.greyhouse.com
e-mail: books @greyhouse.com

Publisher's Cataloging-In-Publication Data
(Prepared by the Donohue Group, Inc.)

O'Dea, Suzanne
   From Suffrage to the Senate: America's Political Women / An Encyclopedia of Leaders, Causes & Issues /
   Suzanne O'Dea / forewords by Ann W. Richards and Susan M. Collins
      2.v. : ill. ; cm.

   Originally published: Santa Barbara, Calif.: ABC-CLIO, 1999.
   Includes biographical references and index.
   Contents: v. 1. A–N—v. 2. O–Z

   ISBN-13: 978-1-59237-117-4
   ISBN-10: 1-59237-117-5

Hardcover

1.   Women in politics—United States—Encyclopedias.   I. Title

QQ1236.5.U6 S32 2006
320/.082/0973

Contents

From Suffrage to the Senate

Volume 2: O–Z

Appendix 1: Documents

Setting Political Agendas

Woman Suffrage

Equal Rights Amendment

Women, Campaigns, and Political Parties

Women of Sovereign Nations

Confronting Racism and Discrimination

Foreword*
by Ann W. Richards

The big story in American politics, the narrative that runs through our history, is the expansion of power from the few to the many. When they left Europe for the New World, our ancestors were leaving nations where they had little or no influence over politics or political action. Their religion or their poverty or their failure to be born into the nobility kept them from having any real power in government. So, from the beginning in America, it was fundamentally important to ensure that ability to participate and the power that goes with it.

American women have been petitioning for equal rights since colonial times. When the founding fathers were debating the Constitution, Abigail Adams wrote her husband John and told him to be sure to "remember the ladies."

Looking back to the beginning of the organized movement for suffrage, we remember founding mothers like Elizabeth Cady Stanton, Susan B. Anthony, and Carrie Chapman Catt. Anthony is especially vivid in my mind because she worked so long and so hard. She was there when the organized movement began in 1848, and she was the symbolic leader until she died in 1906. And, I especially admire the work of African American women like Mary Church Terrell who supported suffrage in spite of the fact that they were often discriminated against in order to reduce Southern political objections. We share the legacy of these strong women and we add to it with every day of our lives.

But when we look back to find our past, it is not always easy to do. I know because I worked for years on the Women in Texas History Project. In fact, that project was born because of a question my daughter Ellen asked. I had taken my kids to San Antonio to see an exhibit about Texas history at the Institute of Texan Cultures. And after we had seen most of the presentation, Ellen, who was about 12 at the time, turned to me and said, "Mama, where are the women?" Several years and a lot of work later, we opened "Texas Women: A Celebration of History" at the Institute of Texan Cultures.

* Reprinted from the First Edition.

So I understand what is required to reclaim our history and I know how valuable the work of reclamation is to all of us.

Finding the women from our past helps us know who we are and where we came from. Those of us who grew up looking at history textbooks that contained few pictures of strong women know how much it means to have those pictures in this book for our children and grandchildren.

We have come a long way from the days when, for all we knew, Clara Barton, Florence Nightingale, Jane Addams, and Amelia Earhart were the only women who ever worked outside the home. Only one of them dared to take on a "man's job" like flying. And we know what happened to her.

There was a time when the history books told us by their omissions that women should know their place and keep their silence. Thanks to the efforts of historians like Suzanne O'Dea Schenken and thoughtful publishers like ABC-CLIO,* we've made considerable progress.

I hope that every young person who opens this encyclopedia finds inspiration in its pages and determines to go into public service—if not in elective office, then by working for candidates and issues of your choice and volunteering to help your community. And, I hope many of you will become entries in later editions of *From Suffrage to the Senate: An Encyclopedia of American Women in Politics.*

Ann W. Richards
Austin, Texas
September, 1999

* Publisher of the First Edition.

Foreword

by Susan M. Collins

"But we'll have our rights; see if we don't; and you can't stop us from them; see if you can."—Sojourner Truth

With those words—determined, even defiant—the great reformer and evangelist faced down an angry mob of protestors at the Women's Rights Convention of 1853 in Cleveland. To many, the message of equality for all Americans was disturbing, and the messenger was despised: a black born into slavery, and a woman. All of the insults that could be dredged from color and gender were hurled at her; none made even the slightest scratch in her armor of dignity, intellect, and righteousness.

From our high vantage point a century and half later, it may seem that the path to equality is one unbroken trail of progress, of impediments cleared and obstacles surmounted by a succession of such resolute women as Sojourner Truth. We enjoy such a view here in the early 21st Century because we stand on the shoulders of giants.

This invaluable encyclopedia takes us down to the ground level, where we can see that the trail was difficult—at times seemingly impassable—that the impediments and obstacles were formidable, and that the way was cleared by mere mortals building on the efforts of those who came before, all combining to do the work of giants. Although it is arranged in the traditional format of the encyclopedia—discrete entries on people and events in alphabetical order—these volumes tell one great story, a moving saga of vision and principles, of striving and failure, of determination and eventual success.

It has often been said, as Emerson put it, that "there is properly no history; only biography." The biographies contained in these pages are inspiring, in part because of the accomplishments they describe, in greater part because the setbacks experienced in one generation did not deter those who came later, but gave them the strength to persevere. The earliest entry in this set belongs to Margaret Brent, who in 1647 demanded a seat in the Maryland Assembly by virtue of her status as a landowner. She was denied, but the seed she planted took root.

Abigail Adams' admonition to her husband, John, that the new nation he was helping to form must "remember the ladies" was not heeded, but it was never forgotten.

Sojourner Truth's call for the abolition of slavery would not be answered for a decade, universal suffrage took nearly seven, but her words continued to resonate.

Most of us, when we browse through an encyclopedia, turn initially to those subjects we know and care about. I am proud that Maine, my home and the state I am honored to represent in the United State Senate, offers some truly inspiring entries. Dorothea Dix, born in Hampden, Maine, in 1802, was a pioneer in the movement to provide humane care for those with mental illness and, at age 60, was the tireless organizer of the Army Medical Corps during the Civil War. Harriet Beecher Stowe lived in Brunswick when she wrote *Uncle Tom's Cabin*, the book that brought the horror of slavery into parlors across America and that turned abolition from a political issue into a moral imperative. Margaret Chase Smith, the great "Lady from Maine" and my role model in public service, was the first woman elected to both the House and Senate, and the first woman to have her name entered into nomination by a major party for President. She was the woman who gave other women the right to careers in the military. Women of such firsts, of such accomplishments, fill these stimulating pages.

Thanks to those who are found on these pages, American women today enjoy unprecedented opportunity. We are leaders in business. We are university presidents, scientists, and astronauts. We are governors, state legislators, Supreme Court justices, cabinet members, and members of Congress. We have come a long way, and we owe much to these trailblazers.

We have farther to go. Here at home, glass ceilings have cracked but still prevent too many women from realizing their full potential. In other places around the world, far too many women are still denied the most basic human rights. It is my hope that the great story told here will give us the strength and commitment to meet the challenges that lie ahead. As Sojourner inspired us, "see if we don't!"

Susan M. Collins
United States Senator from Maine
October, 2006

Preface

In this updated and expanded edition of *From Suffrage to the Senate: America's Political Women / An Encyclopedia of Leaders, Causes & Issues*, you will find new categories of women in politics, including journalists, commentators and columnists. Women political pollsters, campaign advisers, and campaign managers are also extensively covered. The number of Documents in Appendix 1 has nearly doubled to 51, and now covers 13 topics, including the following new subject areas:

- Sustainability
- Presidential Appointees
- The Justice System and Women
- Political Commentators

Users will also find that the Documents in Appendix 1 are now referenced at the end of relevant entries, making it easy to use them as supplemental material.

All entries from the first edition have been updated, as well as Facts & Statistics in Appendix 2, the Chronology and the Bibliography. This second edition has a total of 832 entries, 144 more than the first edition of the work. There are 543 biographies and 289 that cover court cases, legislation, organizations, movements and social issues that are relevant to the topic. When possible, updated photos replace older ones, and we have added to the number of overall images.

The story of American women and politics covers a wide range of topics. In selecting entries for this volume, consideration was given to several factors depending on the nature of the entry. Biographical sketches can be found for women who served in Congress, as governors, and in presidential Cabinets. Also included are sketches of women mayors of cities with populations over one million people. Women heads of organizations or agencies who influenced policies related to women are also included, as are women leaders in political parties. Women's organizations have been limited to those that seek to influence public policy. With the increasing attention on women's health, more of the organizations that lobby for women's health issues are included in this edition. Only a few decades ago, few women held visible positions in the media, but today women are working in every area of reporting. The journalists, columnists, and commentators in this edition include those who focus on national politics and have a national audience. Although women have worked on political campaigns for more than a century, most did not hold influential positions. In the last 10 years, however, women have held increasingly powerful positions as pollsters, campaign advisors, and campaign managers. In this edition, women representing these areas are those who have worked on the presidential level.

Selecting the legislation to include presented some challenges because women have been involved in so many areas of public policy and because every policy from tax rates to war and peace affects women. To narrow the selections, those measures are included that more specifically address issues related to women. Court decisions pose a similar problem, and the same criteria were used. Some broad topics, such as the civil rights movement, were narrowed to women's roles in them.

The entries in this volume include subjects of intense controversy and heated debate. In an effort to present information on the topic without prejudice, the practice has been to use the vocabulary chosen by a group to describe itself and its positions on issues. Using abortion as an example, those who support reproductive rights call themselves pro-choice; that is the term used in this work. Those opposed to abortion call themselves pro-life, the term used here.

The Biographical Directory of the U.S. Congress has been used as the source for the dates women served in Congress. It has also been used for determining the names under which women who have served in Congress are listed. For example, Senator Nancy Kassebaum married after leaving the Senate and changed her name to Nancy Kassebaum Baker. In the *Biographical Directory of the U.S. Congress* she is listed under Kassebaum, as she is here. Enid Greene Waldholtz was elected with that name, divorced her husband while she was in office, and changed her name to Enid Greene, the name under which she is listed. Jacqueline Bouvier Kennedy Onassis, however, was not an officeholder, and the entry for her is Onassis, Jacqueline Bouvier Kennedy.

Acknowledgments

My deepest gratitude goes to the women who have wanted fuller lives for themselves, their daughters, and their neighbors; the women who have challenged the status quo and raised their voices in protest; the women who have articulated the fundamental human needs for dignity, justice, and equality; and the women who have run for public office, whether they won or lost. Conservative, moderate, liberal, and radical women have enriched this nation and have offered a range of perspectives for evaluating its past actions and planning its future. Their energy, commitment, and courage have made researching and writing this volume a rewarding adventure.

Next, my thanks to the scholars who believed that women's actions deserved attention, preservation, and analysis; created the field of women's studies; and established it as a legitimate area of scholarly pursuit. Their work provided the foundation for this volume. Thank you to Elizabeth M. Cox, whose guide, *Women in Modern American Politics: A Bibliography, 1900–1995,* led me to sources that otherwise would have remained hidden and left this work impoverished. Thank you to the librarians and staff at the West Des Moines Public Library for finding the many items I have requested through interlibrary loan. Your patience and goodwill have made it a pleasure to work with you.

My thanks to Grey House Publishing for publishing this updated and expanded edition of *From Suffrage to the Senate*. I appreciate Richard Gottlieb's vision for ways to improve this second edition over the first. Thank you to production editor Toby Raymond's enthusiasm for the project and to copy editor Elaine Alibrandi for her diligent work.

Editorial director Laura Mars-Proietti receives a round of applause for her valiant work in the last weeks of this project. I am grateful for her ability to make things happen, almost magically.

Suzanne O'Dea

Introduction

As this second edition of *From Suffrage to the Senate* goes to the printer, Nancy Pelosi (D-CA) holds the highest leadership position achieved by a woman in Congress, House Democratic Leader. Another woman, Senator Hillary Rodham Clinton (D-NY), the former first lady, is running for re-election, laying the groundwork for a presidential bid in 2008. Clinton is the first woman who has a viable chance to become a major party's presidential nominee. Fourteen women senators serve in the 109th Congress (2005-2006), compared to the one woman who served in the 96th Congress (1979-1981) and the nine women senators in the 106th Congress (1999-2001), when the first edition of this book was published. Sixteen women served in the U.S. House of Representatives in the 96th Congress, 56 in the 106th Congress, and 67 in the 109th Congress. Eight states have women governors in 2006, compared with only one woman governor in 1979, and three at the end of 1999.

Women's political participation has additional dimensions. Since the 1980s when Susan Estrich became the first woman to manage a presidential campaign in one of the two major parties, other women have held an increasing number of high-level positions in presidential and congressional campaigns. They have also become pollsters and consultants at the national level. Some of these female pollsters have focused attention on the issues that most concern women, regarding both current events and concerns specific to women. The combined effects of women in these positions heighten women's political visibility, regardless of their location on the conservative/liberal spectrum.

Women have also gained increased visibility as political commentators and columnists, articulating strong views on both the political right and left. While their opinions cover the full range of issues, and they are not expressed as women's views, they nonetheless bring women's voices into the political arena in a significant way, whether the topic is women's health or foreign policy or one of the other issues important to Americans.

In the last decade, sustainability has emerged as an increasingly significant part of the national debate. Global warming, energy conservation, environmental protection and renewal, and the business and personal practices that contribute to preserving life on Earth all come under the umbrella term sustainability. Human rights, peace, and economic and social justice are also part of the sustainability movement. Unlike the woman's rights movement, which had a narrow agenda, identifiable leadership and affiliated organizations, the sustainability movement is a grass-roots movement with leaders and ad hoc groups addressing local issues and developing new approaches to old problems within established disciplines. Examples range from shrimper Diane Wilson's work to stop industrial pollution in the Texas Gulf Coast to economist Hazel Henderson's advocacy for socially responsible business practices. These women follow in the tradition of scientist Rachel Carson, whose research on insecticides initiated some of the most significant environmental protection legislation in the nation's history.

Women in public office, women consultants to candidates, women reporting on the nation's politics, and women in the sustainability movement are all beneficiaries of the legacy granted them by generations of foremothers with vision and courage. The stories of these foremothers are testimonies to their patriotism and their beliefs in the grand premises of the Declaration of Independence and the promises of the United States Constitution.

One of the most fascinating stories in American history has been women's acquisition of political power and the ways that they have used it to change the nation's perceptions of government's roles and responsibilities. Like all captivating dramas, the story includes heroines, detractors, courage, frustration, confrontation, passion, failures and successes. Throughout the story, women and men grapple with the questions of citizenship, democracy and freedom, and struggle to determine who benefits from them and how to grant and obtain them.

During the first century that Europeans lived in North America, survival consumed colonists' time and energy, but two women attempted to assert themselves in the public realm. In Boston, Anne Hutchinson led discussions of the weekly sermon in her home and offered a theology that differed from that espoused by the local clergy. Tried and convicted of heresy, she was banished in 1638. A decade later, in 1648, landowner and lawyer Margaret Brent sought to vote in the Maryland assembly, a right granted to other landowners, but was refused.

As words of liberty, equality and freedom filled the air and as conflicts with England developed, the Daughters of Liberty, a loosely defined group, joined in the support of the Nonimportation Agreement in 1769. Most memorable from that era, however, is Abigail Adams's 1776 admonition to her husband John Adams to "remember the ladies" while forming the new government. The Congress did not remember the ladies, nor did the state governments that were being created. Only New Jersey granted women suffrage rights, in 1783, but the state disenfranchised women in 1807.

One could argue that the story of women and power in America begins in the early nineteenth century. It was a time when women, especially married women, had virtually no legal existence. Their status had a name, "coverture," meaning "covered," which was a part of English common law that had emigrated to this continent with other laws and traditions. Under common law, when a woman and a man married, they became one and that one was the man. From the mid-nineteenth century through the mid-twentieth century, women's rights activists sought to shed the forced invisibility imposed upon them by coverture.

The early nineteenth century imposed other burdens on women. Few educational opportunities beyond the elementary levels existed for girls. Almost 200 years after Harvard College opened in 1636, the first women's college-level institution, Troy Female Seminary, opened in 1821. Mount Holyoke Seminary, the first women's college, was founded in 1837, and the first coeducational college, Oberlin College, was founded in 1833. Women yearned for formal education, and a few satisfied themselves with independent and unguided efforts, but most lived with the limitations that their poor education placed on them.

Society imposed another limit on women. They were not to speak in public before mixed audiences, that is, audiences of women and men. When Frances Wright addressed mixed audiences in 1828 or 1829, newspapers and ministers attacked her for her brazenness. Even though many obstacles confronted women's participation in the nation's life, women attempted to change their society. In the 1830s, women formed temperance societies and abolitionist societies but discovered that social and legal constraints greatly reduced their effectiveness.

The legal inequities inhibiting women's freedom of action and the exercise of their rights as citizens gained formal expression in 1848, at the first women's rights convention. Organized by Elizabeth Cady Stanton and Lucretia Mott, the Seneca Falls, New York, gathering endorsed the *Declaration of Sentiments and Resolutions,* a document modeled after the Declaration of Independence. Word of the convention spread, and women organized other conventions throughout the 1850s, launching the women's rights movement.

The luxuries of gathering together, protesting their status, and organizing to change laws and society were reserved for white women. Native American women and men had no rights that the government of the United States or Anglo Americans honored. Their land, their homes, and their very lives were unprotected and vulnerable to the depredations of Anglo Americans. African American women living in slavery coped with the daily threats of rape and other violence, separation from loved ones, and oppression without end. For these women, married women's property rights, voting rights and educational opportunities were too implausible for contemplation. Two African American women, however, grace the era with their courage, dedication and devotion to freedom: Sojourner Truth and Harriet Tubman. Sojourner Truth denounced slavery and slaveowners with fierce and compelling rhetoric. Tubman conducted slaves on the Underground Railroad into freedom.

The women's rights movement receded into the background during the Civil War but reappeared with a vengeance over the exclusion of women from the Fourteenth and Fifteenth Amendments. Controversy over the amendments spawned the American Woman Suffrage Association and the National Woman Suffrage Association, both in 1869. The two groups merged into the National American Woman Suffrage Association (NAWSA) in 1890, and the concentrated effort to pass the woman suffrage amendment became less fractured. Suffragists' unity, however, ended in the 1910s, when a militant organization, the Congressional Union, split from NAWSA. The Congressional Union staged demonstrations, picketed the White House, and frustrated

NAWSA's attempts to conduct a refined campaign. After Congress passed in 1919 and the states ratified in 1920 the Nineteenth Amendment granting voting rights to women, NAWSA reorganized itself into the League of Women Voters (LWV), and the Congressional Union reorganized itself into the National Woman's Party (NWP).

The LWV's initial mission was to educate newly enfranchised women on voting, issues, and related matters. It joined other women's groups to pass measures that established a woman's citizenship independent of her husband's and created a maternal and infant health program, among others. Politicians passed the laws because they believed that women would vote as a bloc, but that phenomenon did not materialize until the 1980s in what became known as the gender gap.

The National Woman's Party drafted and presented the Equal Rights Amendment (ERA), a measure that was introduced in 1923 and in every subsequent session of Congress until 1972, when it passed. The ERA languished for almost fifty years and is an important part of the drama of women's acquisition of political power, even though it was not ratified. From the 1920s into the 1960s, social reformers opposed the ERA because they believed that it would make protective labor legislation unconstitutional. Protective legislation included limits on the number of hours women could work, the hours of the day they could work, and the weight they could lift. The NWP viewed the legislation as barriers to women's employment options, whereas social reformers viewed it as safeguarding women's health and well-being. The ERA and other women's issues moved to the forefront in the 1960s and 1970s as the feminist movement developed. Feminists were inspired, in part, by the civil rights movement.

For African Americans living in the South, slavery ended in 1865, but oppression did not, and civil rights were only an illusion. Periods of lynching in the 1890s, 1920s, and 1940s wreaked havoc across the South. Outraged by the injustice and further angered by civil authorities' failure to intervene, black women led anti-lynching crusades throughout the South and carried the stories into the North. Their efforts from the grassroots level to the congressional level significantly contributed to reducing the incidence of the crime. Violations of voting rights and other civil rights, however, continued unabated. African American women across the South risked their jobs, their homes and their lives to end the tyranny of segregation and denigration that intruded on every aspect of their days. Some became icons of the civil rights movement. Rosa Parks, Daisy Bates, and Fannie Lou Hamer stand among the nation's patriots for their passionate commitment to the country's fundamental beliefs in equality, liberty and freedom. They, the hundreds of women and men who followed their leadership, the men whose stories are better known, and the young people who shared their beliefs presented the story of racism and violence in words and images so potent that the nation responded. The Civil Rights Act of 1964, the Voting Rights Act of 1965 and other measures are part of their legacy.

The belief in equality that civil rights leaders espoused resonated with women, who considered their status and found it unacceptable. For most women, however, Betty Friedan's 1963 book *The Feminine Mystique* crystallized their discontent. Her articulation of the barriers between women and their full participation in the nation's political, social and economic life gave women a guidebook for examining their own lives.

Also in 1963, the President's Commission on the Status of Women released its report itemizing the laws and policies that stood between women and equality.

The Civil Rights Act of 1964, however, served as one of the most powerful catalysts for motivating women into action. The act primarily addressed discrimination on the basis of race. Title VII prohibits discrimination in employment on the basis of race, but unlike other sections of the act, it also prohibits discrimination on the basis of sex. Title VII also created the Equal Employment Opportunity Commission (EEOC) to enforce the law. The EEOC's resistance to responding to sex discrimination complaints led to the founding of the National Organization for Women (NOW) in 1966. In addition to NOW, dozens of local and regional groups sprang up, independent of each other, across the country. Energetic and committed women formed rape crisis centers and child care centers, identified domestic violence as a legal problem, and coined phrases like "displaced homemaker." Women lobbied Congress and their state legislatures to enact new policies to remedy these and other problems. Solutions that seemed obvious to these women appeared radical to other women, men and policymakers.

In some ways, the proposals that feminists offered did have radical aspects to them. Claiming that the personal is political, feminists sought to change the distribution of power and to make matters that had traditionally been considered private or personal issues into public ones. They sought equality and visibility. Their agenda included the legalization of abortion; lesbian rights; and equality in education, employment, and every other aspect of life. They challenged religious beliefs and practices, and they objected to the use of gender-based nouns and pronouns. Two major successes came within a year of each other: Congress passed the ERA in 1972, and it went to the states for ratification; and the U.S. Supreme Court legalized abortion in 1973.

The changes overwhelmed many women and men. To preserve the status quo, halt the progress of the ERA, and reverse the legalization of abortion, new groups formed. Phyllis Schlafly fought ratification of the ERA for almost ten years and succeeded. The amendment failed to be ratified by the required thirty-eight states and died in 1982. Pro-life groups sought passage of the Human Life Amendment and failing to do that, effectively limited access to abortion through state and federal laws. Abortion remained legal, but legal restrictions and social pressures constricted its availability. Progress in fulfilling the feminist agenda in other areas stagnated as well in the 1980s.

Also in the 1980s, however, increasing numbers of women ran for public office and won. In 1981, there were 912 women in state legislatures; a decade later, there were 1,359. In 1981, there were twenty-one women in the U.S. House of Representatives and two women in the U.S. Senate; in 1991, there were twenty-eight women in the House and four women in the Senate. The increases continued in the 1990s, with 1,652 women serving in state legislatures in 1999, fifty-six women in the U.S. House, and nine women in the U.S. Senate that year. Some of the women in state legislatures and Congress held feminist beliefs, but not all. Conservative women who opposed the feminist agenda entered the political arena to gain political power.

The political power that women have obtained as officeholders, lobbyists and voters has transformed issues considered radical or marginal in the 1970s and 1980s into matters of national debate. Initially articulated by feminists and identified as women's issues, many of these issues have lost their gender labels and taken their places in candidates' and policymakers' lists of priorities.

In 1971, for example, Republican President Richard Nixon vetoed a $2 billion child care package because he felt it might encourage mothers to enter the paid workforce. Child care programs were an issue in the 1988 presidential election and in 1990, Republican President George Bush signed a package of more than $22 billion in tax credits and new grant programs. In another example, Bush's veto of a measure to require employers to permit their employees to take leaves for childbirth, adoption or family illness was a campaign issue in 1992. Democratic presidential candidate Bill Clinton promised to sign the policy into law if Congress again passed it. After women voters gave him the margin of victory in the election, Clinton signed the Family and Medical Leave Act of 1993. Child support enforcement offers a third example. Custodial parents, generally women, had sought help collecting delinquent child support payments for years but with few results, until members of Congress realized that a significant number of the families were on welfare. The Personal Responsibility and Work Opportunity Reconciliation Act of 1996 and the Deadbeat Parents Punishment Act of 1998 significantly increased government involvement in collecting delinquent child support.

In the almost 400 years since European women became permanent settlers on this continent, American women have transformed their status from invisible and silenced observers into policymakers and leaders. Throughout the process, men at every level have been their partners by sharing the vision of full citizenship for all Americans, extending voting rights to women, supporting legislation, and contributing in dozens of other small and large ways. The story of women's political involvement and leadership has not ended. It continues to develop new plotlines and themes as the nation explores the meanings of freedom, liberty and equality.

From Suffrage to the Senate

Abbott, Grace (1878–1939)

One of the many social reformers influenced by Chicago's Hull House and its founder Jane Addams, Grace Abbott worked to improve the lives of immigrants and children, using her skills as a researcher to investigate and report the conditions in which they lived and worked. She began her career as the first director of the Immigrants' Protective League, conducting research on immigrants' lives and writing a series of articles published as "The Immigrant and the Community" (1917). Based on her research, Abbott concluded that immigrants needed protection from aggressive employment agencies, and she proceeded to successfully lobby the Illinois legislature for a measure to regulate them. In 1913, she directed an investigation into the exploitation of immigrants in Massachusetts and again recommended proposals for the legislature's consideration.

In 1917, Julia Lathrop, who was director of the Children's Bureau in the U.S. Department of Labor, invited Abbott to join her staff and direct the implementation of the Keating-Owen Child Labor Reform Act. The next year, however, the U.S. Supreme Court found the law unconstitutional. Abbott, who had observed the abuses of child labor, became a dedicated advocate for a child labor amendment, which was passed by Congress in 1923 but was not ratified by the states.

Abbott succeeded Lathrop as head of the Children's Bureau in 1921 and had as her first mission the implementation of the Sheppard-Towner Maternity and Infancy Protection Act of 1921, which provided federal grants-in-aid to states for maternal and infant health programs. Under Abbott's leadership, approximately 3,000 child health and prenatal health clinics opened across the country. Despite the program's demonstrated success and the protests of Abbott and other social reformers, Congress ended it in 1929. During the 1930s, Abbott directed several studies on the Depression's impact on children, describing the nutritional deficiencies, educational losses, and health hazards that threatened children's well-being. Neither the research findings nor Abbott's pleas convinced President Herbert Hoover that children were suffering. After Franklin Roosevelt's election to the presidency, Abbott's proposals for a mother's pension and emergency food and medical care for the neediest children gained acceptance.

Abbott resigned from the Children's Bureau in 1934 to recover from tuberculosis, but she remained involved in the agency as an adviser, helping develop sections of the Social Security Act of 1935 that related to maternal and child health, aid to dependent children, children with special needs, and crippled children. From 1934 until her death, Abbott was professor of public welfare administration at the University of Chicago School of Social Service Administration.

Born in Grand Island, Nebraska, Grace Abbott earned her bachelor's degree from Grand Island College in 1898, studied at the University of Nebraska, and earned her master's degree in political science from the University of Chicago in 1907.

See also Addams, Jane; Child Labor Amendment; Children's Bureau; Lathrop, Julia; Sheppard-Towner Maternity and Infancy Protection Act of 1921

References Lindenmeyer, "A Right to Childhood": The U.S. Children's Bureau and Child Welfare, 1912–1946 (1997).

Document Florence Kelley, "Child Labor and Woman Suffrage," 1905

Abel, Hazel Pearl Hempel (1888–1966)

Republican Hazel Abel of Nebraska served in the U.S. Senate from 8 November 1954 to 31 December 1954. Abel had run for the office for a very specific reason: "To me it was more than a short term in the Senate. I wanted Nebraska voters to express their approval of a woman in government. I was a sort of guinea pig."

Born in Plattsmouth, Nebraska, Abel graduated from the University of Nebraska in 1908. A high school mathematics teacher and a high school principal from 1908 to 1916, she left teaching to marry George Abel and moved to Lincoln, Nebraska, in 1916. She joined his construction company, and following his death in 1936, she became company president. She was also a Girl Scout leader, treasurer of the Nebraska League of Women Voters, and active in the Nebraska Republican Party, serving as vice chairwoman in 1954. Her many activities in Lincoln earned her the nickname "Hurricane Hazel."

In the summer of 1954, Abel, a Republican, became a candidate for the U.S. Senate to complete an unexpired term that would have only two months left at the time of the election. A technicality in Nebraska law prevented candidates from running for both the unexpired term and the full six-year term that would be filled in the election. During her short time in office, Abel held the distinction of being the only senator to listen to all of the debate to censure Senator Joseph McCarthy. She voted with the majority to censure him.

Abel was a delegate to the White House Conference on Education in 1955 and a member of the Theodore Roosevelt Centennial Commission from 1955 to 1959. In 1960, she unsuccessfully ran in the Republican primary for governor.

See also Bowring, Eva Kelly; Congress, Women in

References "Lady from Nebraska," *Newsweek*, 20 December 1954, 20; Office of the Historian, U.S. House of Representatives, Women in Congress, 1917–1990 (1991); Treese, ed., *Biographical Directory of the American Congress 1774–1996* (1997).

Abolitionist Movement, Women in the

In the 1830s, African American and white women from the North and the South entered the men's political world to crusade against slavery. Outraged by slavery's inhumanity, they founded anti-slavery societies, broke social taboos by making public speeches before audiences of women and men, and petitioned Congress. The honor of their cause did not protect them from public acrimony and derision or from threats of violence, and in the process they carved new public spaces for themselves and laid the groundwork for a women's rights movement.

Women encountered their first significant obstacle to participating in the abolitionist movement in 1833 at the founding meeting of the American Anti-Slavery Society in Philadelphia. The meeting organizers permitted women to attend the meeting but refused to let them speak from the floor or join the society. After the meeting, a group of black women and white women organized the Philadelphia Female Anti-Slavery Society. In 1832, a group of African American women had already moved on to the public stage when they formed the Female Anti-Slavery Society of Salem, Massachusetts, one of the first abolitionist groups. Groups formed in Boston, New York, and other communities, particularly in New England. When the National Female Anti-Slavery Society convened in New York in 1837, delegates from twelve states attended.

Participating in the abolition movement required courage as well as commitment. Some courageous women, Harriet Tubman being a notable example, served the abolitionist movement as conductors on the Underground Railroad, and others housed and fed fugitive slaves as they made their way North. Even attending abolitionist meetings could be dangerous. For example, at a Boston Female Anti-Slavery Society meeting in 1835, William Lloyd Garrison was scheduled to speak, but after an angry mob gathered, the mayor ordered the women in the convention hall to leave. In order to provide some level of safety to the African American women in the audience, each white woman accompanied a black woman out of the building. Garrison did not escape—he was dragged through the streets on a rope. At the second Anti-Slavery Convention of American Women, held in Philadelphia in 1838, a mob gathered outside the convention and later burned the meeting hall.

Without voting rights, women were limited in the ways that they could influence political decisions, but they conducted petition drives and gathered thousands of signatures. In 1836, after abolitionist women had flooded Congress with petitions to end slavery, Congress responded to their pleas by passing a gag rule prohibiting the petitions from being read or considered.

The commitment to ending slavery compelled some women to break the social prohibition against women speaking in public. Frances Wright, Maria Stewart, and Angelina and Sarah Grimké all suffered criticism from the public, the press, and the pulpit for publicly addressing mixed audiences of women and men in the late 1820s and 1830s. In the next decade, however, it became more common for women, including Susan B. Anthony, Lucy Stone, Lucretia Mott, and Sojourner Truth, to use their oratorical skills on behalf of the abolition movement.

Women writers used their pens to expose the wretchedness of slaves' lives and to decry the injustice of slavery. For example, in 1833 Lydia Maria Child wrote the first anti-slavery book by a northern abolitionist calling for the immediate emancipation of the nation's two million slaves. Harriet Beecher Stowe's *Uncle Tom's Cabin* humanized slavery for thousands of readers, solidifying their antipathy to slavery.

As women continued to seek the end of slavery, they became increasingly frustrated by the limits on their effectiveness as abolitionists and their rights as citizens. One of the most historically significant examples occurred at the 1840 World Anti-Slavery Convention held in London. Despite objections and heated debate, the convention ruled that only male delegates could be seated. Among the women relegated to the convention hall galleries were U.S. delegates Lucretia Mott and Elizabeth Cady Stanton. Excluded from active participation, the two women spent hours discussing women's status and the need for change. Eight years later, they organized the first U.S. women's rights convention and launched the nineteenth-century women's rights movement.

See also Child, Lydia Maria Francis; Grimké, Angelina Emily and Sarah Moore; Mott, Lucretia Coffin; Stanton, Elizabeth Cady; Stowe, Harriet Elizabeth Beecher; Suffrage; Truth, Sojourner; Tubman, Harriet

References Evans, *Born for Liberty: A History of Women in America*

Abortion

The issue of a woman's right to decide whether to continue a pregnancy or to terminate it became one of the United States' most challenging political questions in the last three decades of the twentieth century. Debates on abortion have taken place in front of abortion clinics, in state legislatures, on the floors of the U.S. House and Senate, and in the U.S. Supreme Court, but the nation has not found a common ground on which to rest the range of issues related to abortion. It has prompted men and women to organize, run for political office, and perform acts of civil disobedience. Violence, including murder, has been committed in the name of protecting fetuses.

Those who support reproductive rights insist that women must have the right to control their own bodies and that the state has no role in the decision regarding whether a woman continues a pregnancy. Calling themselves pro-choice, they argue that no one favors abortion, but that circumstances, including a woman's health, the fetus's health, the pregnant woman's ability to care for a child, and other factors such as rape or incest make the decisions so intimate that only the pregnant woman can make them. Those who oppose abortion call it infanticide and insist that abortion is murder. Identifying themselves as pro-life, they argue that life begins at conception, that all life must be protected, and that abortions must stop.

In 2002, about 1.29 million abortions occurred in the United States, down from about 1.36 million in 1996. Between 1973 (the year abortion was legalized in the United States) through 2002, more than 42 million abortions were performed. More than half (52 percent) of the women obtaining abortions are under the age of 25. Two-thirds of all abortions are among women who have never married. Hispanic women are two and a half times more likely to have an abortion than white women, and African American women are four times more likely to have an abortion than white women.

In 1821, Connecticut became the first state to enact abortion legislation, making it illegal after quickening (first recognizable movement of the fetus). In 1860, Connecticut made all abortions illegal, a policy followed by every state by the end of the nineteenth century. By 1930, an estimated 800,000 illegal abortions were performed annually, and between 8,000 and 17,000 women died every year from them.

In addition to prohibitions against abortion, access to birth control information and devices was also limited in some states and illegal in others. The first step in the legalization of abortion occurred in 1965, when the U.S. Supreme Court decided *Griswold v. Connecticut*. The case centered on a Connecticut law that made it illegal for anyone, including married couples, to obtain birth control drugs and devices. The Court found that the ban on contraception violated the constitutional right to marital privacy. In 1972, the Court extended the right to use contraceptives to all people, regardless of their marital status.

As the second wave of the feminist movement developed increasing visibility in the 1960s, reproductive rights, including the right to abortion, became one of the demands. Feminists initiated a wide range of projects to make abortions available, from teaching women how to self-abort to establishing referral services to presumably safe practitioners. In some communities, physicians and Protestant ministers established abortion referral services or worked together to provide abortions by disguising the procedure in their records and reports. Between 1967 and 1971, seventeen states decriminalized abortion, reflecting a change in public opinion: 15 percent of Americans favored legal abortions in 1968, and by 1972, 64 percent did.

In 1973, the U.S. Supreme Court made its landmark decision in *Roe v. Wade*, invalidating restrictive abortion laws across the country and making abortion legal. The Court found that the right to privacy "is broad enough to encompass a woman's decision whether or not to terminate her pregnancy." The Court also recognized two compelling state interests that would justify restricting a woman's right to choose. During the second trimester (fourth to sixth months) of a pregnancy, the abortion procedure could be regulated to protect a woman's health. After fetal viability (approximately the twenty-fourth to twenty-eighth weeks), a state could pass legislation prohibiting abortions to protect the life of the fetus. The Court also stated that abortions could be performed at any time during the pregnancy to save the life of the mother.

To some, the decision meant that women would no longer need to seek illegal abortions and that women's lives would be saved. To others, the decision meant that more pregnancies would be terminated. A Roman Catholic bishop called the decision "an unspeakable tragedy." Those opposed to the decision organized to seek ways to make abortion illegal again. On both sides, existing organizations began defining their stands, and new organizations were formed to preserve *Roe v. Wade* or to reverse it. More than two dozen resolutions to overturn the decision by constitutional amendment were introduced in Congress following the announcement of the Court's decision in 1973. Several pro-life groups supported, and members of Congress introduced, the Human Life Amendment that stated that life begins at conception and that ending it was murder.

One of the early questions that arose centered on the issue of whether tax dollars could be used to pay for poor women's abortions. In 1974, Medicaid programs in forty-three states and the District of Columbia paid for first-trimester abortions without restrictions for women who were covered by the program. In addition, Medicaid programs in thirty-nine states and the District of Columbia paid for all legal abortions. In 1976, Republican Congressman Henry Hyde of Illinois passed a measure prohibiting the use of federal funds for abortions. Known as the Hyde Amendment, the measure excluded coverage for abortions under Medicaid except to save the life of the mother. In subsequent years, Congress permitted the use of Medicaid funds for abortions for pregnancies resulting from rape or incest and pregnancies that two doctors agreed would cause the mother to suffer "severe and long-lasting physical health damage." Pro-choice advocates promptly began looking for test cases with which to challenge the policy. In 1980, the U.S. Supreme Court decided in *Harris v. McRae* that the Hyde Amendment was constitutional. Justice Stewart Potter wrote: "...The Congress has neither invaded a substantive constitutional right or freedom, nor enacted legislation that purposefully operates to a detriment of a suspect class, the only requirement of equal protection is that congressional action be rationally related to a legitimate governmental interest." In 2003, seventeen states used public funds to pay for abortions for some poor women, usually under conditions requiring a court order to obtain the funding.

Pro-life groups also sought ways to limit access to abortion by establishing a variety of conditions and restrictions before the procedure could be performed. Several states passed legislation requiring minors seeking abortions to notify one or both parents or to obtain a judicial waiver. Beginning in 1976, the U.S. Supreme Court considered a variety of different approaches. The Court rejected requirements that both parents be notified, but permitted the minor woman to obtain an abortion with the notification of one parent. In addition, the Court insisted that minor women must have an option beyond telling a parent and approved a system that allowed a minor woman to bypass her parent(s) and obtain permission from a judge to obtain an abortion. In 2006, thirty-four states required parental consent or notification for minors seeking an abortion.

Another approach to limiting access to abortion developed in 1988, when President Ronald Reagan's administration issued new regulations for federally supported family planning programs. Under what became known as the "gag rule," 4,000 federally funded health clinic medical personnel were prohibited from discussing abortion with their clients. The U.S. Supreme Court upheld the regulations in *Rust v. Sullivan* (1991), but in 1993 President Bill Clinton eliminated them.

The availability of physicians trained and willing to perform abortions also became an obstacle to women seeking abortions. By 2000, 87 percent of counties in the United States had no trained, qualified doctors willing to perform abortions, requiring some women seeking abortions to travel great distances. Thirty-four percent of all women ages 15 to 44 lived in counties without abortion providers. In South Dakota and North Dakota, for example, only one physician in each state performed abortions. Some physicians stopped performing abortions because they did not want to be harassed by pro-life demonstrators or because they feared for their safety.

Violence at abortion clinics first appeared in the 1970s, when groups including Operation Rescue physically blocked clinic entrances and destroyed clinic property and equipment. Between 1977 and April 1993, there were thirty-six bombings, eighty-one arsons, eighty-four assaults, and two kidnappings at abortion clinics or involving abortion providers. In 1993 and 1994, abortion opponents killed two doctors, two clinic workers, and one volunteer escort. The National Organization for Women (NOW) initiated a lawsuit contending that the violence was part of a nationwide conspiracy that used violence to attain its goal of closing abortion clinics. NOW argued that trespassing, arson, the theft of fetuses, physical attacks, and threats against abortion clinics and abortion providers constituted extortion and came under the Racketeer Influenced and Corrupt Organizations (RICO) statute. In *NOW v. Scheidler* (1994), the U.S. Supreme Court agreed and held that RICO could apply to anti-abortion protesters. The U.S. Supreme Court revisited *NOW v. Scheidler* two more times, in 2003 and in 2006, ultimately concluding that RICO could not be used to sue anti-abortion organizations because economic extortion was not involved.

Congress, however, passed the Freedom of Access to Clinic Entrances Act of 1994 to help protect women seeking abortions and the facilities and professionals providing the service. The law prohibits the use of force, threats of force, physical obstruction, and property damage intended to interfere with people seeking or providing reproductive health services.

In the mid-1990s abortion opponents focused on making a specific abortion procedure illegal, one they named "partial birth abortion," which is not a medical term. Several states passed measures prohibiting partial birth abortions and Congress twice passed bills prohibiting partial birth abortions, but President Bill Clinton vetoed the bill both times. Congress again passed a ban on the procedure in 2003, which President George W. Bush signed. The first federal law restricting abortion practice, it was immediately challenged in three federal courts on the basis that it endangers the lives of women. The U.S. Supreme Court plans to review the legislation in its term beginning October 2006.

Congress passed, and President George W. Bush signed, "conscience clause" legislation in 2004. It was an expansion of earlier conscience clause policies that protected health care providers who refused to perform abortions based upon their personal opposition to the procedure. The measure, passed in 2004, denies federal aid to states and localities that require health care providers, hospitals and other facilities, or health insurance companies to fund, provide, or refer abortion services.

By the 1980s, abortion had become a delineating issue between the Republican Party, with its adamant insistence on opposing abortion, and the Democratic Party, with its strong support for abortion rights. The issue may have determined the 1992 presidential election between pro-life Republican incumbent President George Bush and pro-choice Democratic challenger Bill Clinton and the 1996 race between pro-life Republican Robert Dole and incumbent Clinton. Polls suggest that abortion played a key role in both years and that women who support abortion rights may have provided the winning margins for Clinton, who promised to support those rights. Clinton kept his pledges to pro-choice supporters. He overturned the gag rule that prohibited abortion counseling in federally funded family planning clinics, lifted the ban on fetal tissue research, and ended a ban on abortions at overseas military medical facilities. In addition, Clinton ended the Mexico City Policy, which denied United States aid to international family planning organizations that provided abortion services. President George W. Bush reinstated the policy immediately after taking office in 2001.

Preventing unwanted pregnancies has been a goal of both reproductive rights supporters and abortion opponents. In 1970 Congress created the family planning program, offering birth control information, devices, and prescriptions through hospitals, health departments, Planned Parenthood affiliates, and other agencies. Then in 1981, Congress passed the Adolescent Family Life Program (AFLP) designed to discourage teenagers from being sexually active and to encourage pregnant teens to carry their pregnancies to term and put their babies up for adoption. The AFLP sponsors demonstration projects designed to encourage abstinence and to provide health, education, and social services to pregnant adolescents, adolescent parents, and their infants, male partners, and families. The AFLP also supports research on adolescent sexuality, pregnancy, and parenting.

Groups that support abortion rights include the American Association of University Women, American Civil Liberties Union, NARAL Pro-Choice America, National Council of Jewish Women, National Organization for Women, National Women's Political Caucus, Planned Parenthood, and Religious Coalition for Reproductive Rights.

Groups that oppose abortion rights include the American Life League, Concerned Women for America, Eagle Forum, Feminists for Life of America, National Right to Life Committee, Operation Rescue, and Pro-Life Action League.

See also *Akron v. Akron Center for Reproductive Health*; American Association of University Women; American Civil Liberties Union; American Life League, Inc.; *Bellotti v. Baird*; *Bray v. Alexandria Clinic*; *Colautti v. Franklin*; Concerned Women for America; *Doe v. Bolton*; Eagle Forum; Feminists for Life of America; *Griswold v. Connecticut*; *Harris v. McRae*; *Hodgson v. Minnesota*; Hyde, Henry John; National Council of Jewish Women; National Organization for Women; National Right to Life Committee; National Women's Political Caucus; *NOW v. Scheidler*; Operation Rescue; Planned *Parenthood Association of Kansas City, Mo. v. Ashcroft*; *Planned Parenthood of Central Missouri v. Danforth*; *Poelker v. Doe*; Religious Coalition for Reproductive Choice; *Roe v. Wade*

References Congressional Quarterly Almanac, 93rd Congress, 1st Session . . . 1973 (1974); Congressional Quarterly Almanac, 103rd Congress, 1st Session. . . 1993, vol. 49 (1994); Congressional Quarterly Almanac Plus, 108th Congress, 2nd Session. . . 2004, vol. 60 (2005); Guttmacher Institute, Facts in Brief, 4 May 2006; Harrison and Gilbert, eds., Abortion Decisions of the United States Supreme Court: The 1970s (1993); Abortion Decisions of the United States Supreme Court: The 1980s (1993); Abortion Decisions of the United States Supreme Court: The 1990s (1993); www.aclu.org; www.all.org; www.feminist.org; www.hhs.gov; www.naral.org; http://www.whitehouse.gov/infocus/achievement/chap15.html; http://www.ayottevplannedparenthood.org./statements/pr-060118-ayotte-ruling.php.

Documents Margaret Sanger, "Birth Control–A Parents' Problem or Woman's?" 1920; Faye Wattleton, "Reproductive Freedom: Fundamental to All Human Rights," 1990; Frederica Matthews-Green, "Abortion and Women's Rights"; Helen Chenoweth, "Statement to Feminists for Life of America," 1997; Gloria Feldt, "So Much We Can Do: A Nation of Leaders," 1998

Abzug, Bella Savitzky (1920–1998)

Democrat Bella Abzug of New York served in the U.S. House of Representatives from 3 January 1971 to 3 January 1977. The first Jewish woman to serve in Congress, she was an outspoken, flamboyant feminist, who once said: "We don't so much want to see a female Einstein become an assistant professor. We want a woman schlemiel to get promoted as quickly as a male schlemiel."

Born in New York City, Bella Abzug earned her bachelor of arts from Hunter College in 1942 and entered Columbia University School of Law, but left to work in a shipbuilding factory to aid the war effort. She resumed her legal studies at the end of World War II and received her law degree in 1947 from Columbia University. She also did graduate work at the Jewish Theological Seminary of America.

In her legal practice, Abzug specialized in labor and civil rights cases, representing fur workers, restaurant workers, longshoremen, and civil rights workers. She defended people accused of subversive activities by Senator Joseph McCarthy in the 1950s and was a lawyer for the Civil Rights Congress and the American Civil Liberties Union. From 1961 to 1970, she was national legislative director for Women Strike for Peace, an organization she helped found.

Early in her legal career, Abzug began wearing her trademark hats. She explained: "When I was a young lawyer, I would go to people's offices and they would always say, 'Sit here. We'll wait for the lawyer.' Working women wore hats. It was the only way they would take you seriously." She added: "When I got to Congress, they made a big deal of it. So I was watching—did they want me to wear it or not? They didn't want me to wear it, so I did."

Abzug challenged the incumbent Democratic member of Congress in the 1970 primary, running as an anti–Vietnam War candidate. With the campaign slogan, "This woman belongs in the House–the House of Representatives," she promised to work for better housing, a reduced defense budget, equal rights for women, and an end to the war in Vietnam.

A leading opponent of the war, she introduced a measure on her first day in office to withdraw troops from Vietnam by 4 July 1971. It failed, as did her other attempts to end U.S. involvement in Vietnam. She supported the Equal Rights Amendment, child care, women's credit rights, pay equity for women, and welfare reform. She introduced the measure that created Women's Equality Day in 1973, which celebrated the fifty-third anniversary of woman suffrage. She helped organize the Congresswomen's Caucus, but in part because some did not want to be identified with Abzug's outspoken feminism, it did not formally organize until she left Congress. She wrote the bill that created the National Women's Conference, which was held in 1977 and which she chaired. Following the conference, President Jimmy Carter appointed Abzug co-chair with Carmen Delgado Votaw of the National Advisory Committee for Women. Six months later, Abzug criticized the president's economic policies, charging that they adversely affected women, and Carter dismissed her. Abzug ran unsuccessfully in the Democratic primary for United States senator in 1976, for mayor of New York in 1977, and for a seat in the U.S. House of Representatives in 1978 and 1986.

A founding member of the National Women's Political Caucus, she also founded the Women U.S.A. Fund in 1980. With an initial agenda of increasing women's involvement in politics through voter education and registration programs, the Women U.S.A. Fund worked to involve more women in foreign and environmental policy-making.

Abzug presided at the World Women's Congress for a Healthy Planet in 1991 and was a member of the 1992 International Facilitating Committee of Nongovernmental Organizations and Independent Sectors for the United Nations Conference on the Environment and Development, held in Rio de Janeiro, Brazil. She also founded the Women's Environment and Development Organization (WEDO), which served as one of the main coordinators of the nongovernmental forum held in coordination with the 1995 United Nations Fourth World Conference on Women in Beijing, China.

She wrote *Bella! Ms. Abzug Goes to Washington* (1972), and co-authored *Gender Gap: Bella Abzug's Guide to Political Power for American Women* (1984), as well as other works relating to women and politics.

See also Congress, Women in; Congressional Caucus for Women's Issues; Equal Rights Amendment; National Women's Conference; National Women's Political Caucus; Pay Equity; Women Strike for Peace

References H. W. Wilson, *Current Biography Yearbook, 1971* (1971); *The New York Times*, 12 September 1995; Office of the Historian, U.S. House of Representatives, *Women in Congress, 1917–1990* (1991); Schoenebaum, ed., *Political Profiles: The Nixon/Ford Years* (1979).

Adams, Abigail Smith (1744–1818)

Patriot Abigail Adams established herself as an early advocate for women's rights with a letter she wrote to her husband John Adams in 1776, asking him to "remember the ladies" as he helped construct a new nation. A dedicated correspondent with her husband and other revolutionary leaders and thinkers, she shared her husband's commitment to American independence. When John Adams was elected president of the United States in 1797, Abigail Adams became first lady.

Born in Massachusetts, Abigail Adams was largely self-educated, primarily because educational opportunities for females in colonial America were nonexistent. The lack of educational opportunities for women was a continuing disappointment to her and one that she saw as an unnecessary limitation on her sex, an early indicator of her awareness of women's status. In 1764, she married John Adams, who deeply influenced the depth of her patriotism and her commitment to separation from England. When John Adams was elected to serve in the First Continental Congress in 1774, the couple began decades of extended separations as he accepted a variety of assignments at home and abroad. Abigail Adams remained at home with their growing family, managing their farm and educating their children. Her business acumen may have saved the family from the financial ruin that many other patriots experienced.

In addition, she provided John Adams with reports on local political developments through their extensive correspondence. In her letters she expressed her concerns about proposals for taxation and trade policies as well as her opposition to slavery. Of her many letters, the one dated 31 March 1776 has received the greatest attention. In it, Abigail Adams wrote to John Adams:

I long to hear that you have declared an independency–and by the way in the new Code of Laws which I suppose it will be necessary for you to make I desire you would Remember the Ladies, and be more generous and favourable to them than your ancestors. Do not put such unlimited power into the hands of the Husbands. Remember all Men would be tyrants if they could. If particular care and attention is not paid to the

Ladies we are determined to foment a Rebellion and will not hold ourselves bound by any Laws in which we have no voice, or Representation.

That your Sex are Naturally Tyrannical is a Truth so thoroughly established as to admit of no dispute, but such of you as wish to be happy willingly give up the harsh title of Master for the more tender and endearing one of Friend. Why then, not put it out of the power of the vicious and the Lawless to use us with cruelty and indignity with impunity. Men of Sense in all Ages abhor those customs which treat us only as the vassals of your Sex. Regard us then as Beings placed by providence under your protection and in imitation of the Supreme Being make use of that power only for our happiness.

In this historic letter, Abigail Adams's request is modest. She does not ask for political rights such as suffrage rights or political equality; she only sought legal protection for women. Under English common law, married women had no legal existence and from that status were vulnerable to abuse by their husbands.

When John Adams replied on 14 April 1776, he compared women to other dependent groups:

As to your extraordinary Code of Laws, I cannot but laugh. We have been told that our Struggle has loosened the bands of Government everywhere. That Children and Apprentices were disobedient–that schools and Colleges were grown turbulent–that Indians slighted their Guardians and Negroes grew insolent to their Masters. But your Letter was the first Intimation that another Tribe more numerous and powerfull than all the rest were grown discontented.

Abigail Adams repeated her pleas for women in later letters, including one in which she described to John Adams the frustrations of women patriots, who could not vote, serve in the government, own property, or have a voice in legislation. As she explained, women patriots had also made significant sacrifices in the quest for independence, but they were limited in the ways that they could contribute to their country or could benefit from its potential. In a letter to another woman, Abigail Adams contemplated sending a petition to Congress calling for women's independence. In other letters, Abigail Adams expressed her concern about the inequality of educational opportunities for boys and girls and married women's lack of rights.

In the context of the American and French Revolutions in which the ideals of freedom, liberty, and equality were being sought in new ways, Abigail Adams's plea for women's rights could be viewed as a reasonable extension of the philosophies supported by her husband and other American patriots. Abigail Adams's letters testify to one woman's interest in women's status, but she did not begin a woman's movement or provide the basis for later women's rights efforts.

See also Coverture; Suffrage

References Levin, *Abigail Adams: A Biography* (1987).

Adams, Annette Abbott (1877–1956)

In 1914, Annette Adams became U.S. attorney for the northern district of California, the highest judicial position any woman in the world had ever held. In 1920, she became the first female U.S. assistant attorney general.

Born in Prattville, California, Annette Adams graduated from the State Normal School in Chico, California, in 1897 and taught school for five years. She returned to college and earned her bachelor of law degree in 1904 and her juris doctor degree in 1912, both from Boalt Hall.

In 1912, Democratic Congressman John Raker recruited Adams to join presidential candidate Woodrow Wilson's campaign. After Wilson won the election, Raker believed that Adams deserved a reward for her labors and began to work for her appointment as an assistant U.S. attorney, the kind of post that generally went to young men with political potential. Raker brought her to the attention of President Wilson, the U.S. attorney general, and other decision-makers, developing strategies to make the novel choice of a woman an acceptable one. Raker worked for more than a year and finally won Adams's appointment in 1914. Adams became the first female federal prosecutor when she was appointed assistant U.S. attorney for the northern district of California. Her first cases involved U.S. neutrality laws in the early days of World War I, a group of cases that other prosecutors had not successfully pursued, but Adams developed a strategy for prosecuting the cases that succeeded where others had failed. President Wilson appointed her special U.S. attorney in San Francisco in 1918.

In 1920, she became the first woman to hold the position of assistant attorney general. Assigned to enforce the Volstead Act, her first case required defending the constitutionality of the Eighteenth Amendment, which she successfully did before the U.S. Supreme Court. After Democrats lost the presidency in the 1920 elections, Adams stayed with the Justice Department until the summer of 1921, when she was replaced by Mabel Walker Willebrandt.

Adams unsuccessfully ran for a seat on the San Francisco Board of Supervisors in 1923 but remained active in the Democratic Party. She persuaded the California Democratic Party that 50 percent of its delegates to the party's 1924 national convention should be women. She also worked for Franklin D. Roosevelt's 1932 presidential campaign. She was appointed presiding justice of California's intermediate appellate court in 1942, the year she was elected to a full twelve-year term. She retired in 1950, four years before her term expired.

See also Democratic Party, Women in the; Willebrandt, Mabel Walker
References Jensen, *Annette Abbott Adams* (1966).

Addams, Jane (1860–1935)

A leader in the settlement house movement, Jane Addams founded Hull House in Chicago in 1889, perhaps the best known of the settlement houses in the United States. Addams created an environment at Hull House that nurtured the development and activities of immigrants, political activists, artists, union organizers, children, and young adults. A social reformer, Addams supported education and labor reform, woman suffrage, improvements in municipal government, and other aspects of the progressive social agenda.

Born in Cedarville, Illinois, Jane Addams graduated from Rockford Seminary in 1881. She enrolled in the Women's Medical College of Pennsylvania in 1881, but poor health and the realization that she was not suited to be a doctor contributed to her decision to leave the college. In 1883, Addams went to Europe, where exposure to London's slums and the wretched conditions in which poor people lived introduced her to the type of environment in which she would eventually live and work. She began to consider living in a poor neighborhood with other like-minded women and through it test the concepts she had learned in school. A visit to London's Toynbee Hall gave her a model for the institution she wanted to establish.

With her friend Ellen Gates Starr, Addams found the abandoned Hull mansion in a neighborhood of 5,000 Greek, Italian, Russian, German, and other immigrants. They moved into it in 1889, invited the neighbors to visit them, and began the traditions of Hull House. Over the decades, programs grew to include child care, children's activities, youth activities, social events for women and men, English-language classes, cultural activities, health care, and dozens of other programs and projects. Hull House's success rested in Addams's ability to attract talented and dedicated residents to it, her skill at raising money from wealthy Chicago women, and the program innovations that sustained interest in the settlement and helped it grow. In an attempt to gain a better understanding of the neighborhood and thereby address its fundamental problems, the settlement residents embarked on a study of it. *The Hull House Maps and Papers*, published in 1895, provided a survey of the housing, sweatshops, and child labor in Chicago's 19th Ward. Pressure from Addams and other Hull House residents helped pass Illinois's first factory inspection law and contributed to the establishment of the nation's first juvenile court. Addams and other Hull House activists led crusades for trash removal, recognition of labor unions, protective legislation for immigrants, and many other reforms.

Beginning in 1907, Addams took an active part in the Chicago woman suffrage effort and was an officer of the National American Woman Suffrage Association from 1911 to 1914. In 1912, she seconded Theodore Roosevelt's nomination at the Progressive Party convention and campaigned for him. Also active in the peace movement, she headed the Woman's Peace Party in 1915 and served as the first president of the Women's International League for Peace and Freedom from 1919 to 1928. In 1931, she shared the Nobel Peace Prize with another recipient.

Addams wrote *The Spirit of Youth and the City Streets* (1909), *Twenty Years at Hull-House* (1910), *A New Conscience and an Ancient Evil* (1912), and *The Second Twenty Years at Hull-House* (1930), among other works.

> **See also** Abbott, Grace; Balch, Emily Greene; Lathrop, Julia; National American Woman Suffrage Association; Progressive Party, Women in the; Suffrage; Women's International League for Peace and Freedom
>
> **References** Addams, *Twenty Years at Hull-House* (1911); Lasch, ed., *The Social Thought of Jane Addams* (1965).

Adkins, Bertha Sheppard (1906–1983)

Undersecretary of Health, Education, and Welfare from 1958 to 1960, Bertha Adkins began her political career as representative to the Republican National Committee for Maryland in 1948 and served as director of the Republican Party's Women's Division from 1950 to 1953, when the division closed. Adkins then became assistant to the chair of the Republican National Committee, serving until 1960.

One of presidential candidate Dwight Eisenhower's earliest supporters, Adkins played a central role in organizing women to support him in 1952. The effectiveness of her efforts appears in the significant amount of support he received from women: Eisenhower won with one of the earliest identified gender gaps, about 6 percent. To maintain women's support for President Eisenhower, Adkins established a series of "for ladies only" breakfasts with him to provide women with access to him and to introduce him to potential presidential appointees. She also organized annual conferences for Republican women that drew between 1,500 and 1,800 women to hear Cabinet members, Vice President Richard Nixon, and Eisenhower speak; to attend classes on political organization; and to share information on political strategies.

Born in Salisbury, Maryland, Adkins earned her bachelor of arts at Wellesley College in 1928 and her master of arts degree from Columbia University. Adkins taught at a private school from 1928 to 1932, when she became a secretary. She served as dean of women at Western Maryland College from 1934 to 1942 and dean of residence at Bradford Junior College from 1942 to 1946.

She was headmistress of the Foxcroft School in Middleburg, Virginia, from 1961 until her retirement in 1967. In 1970, she served as special assistant on President Nixon's Advisory Committee on Social Security and, in 1972, was executive vice chair of the Older Americans Advisory Committee. She chaired the National Council on Aging from 1974 to 1978.

See also Gender Gap; Republican Party, Women in the

References H. W. Wilson, *Current Biography 1953* (1953); http://redbud.lbjlib.utexas.edu/eisenhower/fa7317.txt; *The New York Times*, 14 August 1958, 15 August 1958, 15 January 1983.

Adkins v. Children's Hospital (1923)

In *Adkins v. Children's Hospital*, decided in 1923, the U.S. Supreme Court found unconstitutional a 1918 law providing a minimum wage for women workers in the District of Columbia. Similar to laws passed in several states to protect women workers, the District of Columbia law created a three-member board charged with determining the wages for women and minors, depending upon the occupation and upon the board's determination of the amount necessary to maintain workers' good health and to protect their morals.

The Court acknowledged that several states had enacted comparable laws and that women's wages were higher with the policies, but questioned whether minimum wage laws were the reason for the improvements. In finding the law unconstitutional, the Court explained that if the legislation were legally justified, "the field for the operation of the police power will have been widened to a great and dangerous degree." Because the law considered only the needs of the employee and not those of the employer, the Court expressed concern that some employers' "bargaining power may be as weak as that of the employee" and that the employer could be left "without adequate means of livelihood." The Court concluded that the minimum wage unduly restricted the freedom to contract and that no reasonable relationship existed between pay and health and morals. Social reformers criticized the decision as guaranteeing women's constitutional right to starve.

See also Employment Discrimination; *Muller v. Oregon*; Protective Legislation

References *Adkins v. Children's Hospital*, 261 U.S. 525 (1923); Baer, *The Chains of Protection: The Judicial Response to Women's Labor Legislation* (1978).

Affirmative Action

Affirmative action seeks to remedy past discrimination against women and minorities through education, employment, and contractual policies. The primary strategies used in affirmative action employment programs are increased recruitment, promotion, retention, and on-the-job training opportunities. Affirmative action in education includes removing admissions barriers to educational institutions and providing grants and graduate fellowships in nontraditional careers, for example, in engineering, math, and the physical sciences. Women's rights and civil rights groups have supported affirmative action plans and programs as demonstrations of the United States' commitment to equal opportunity. Conservative groups have opposed affirmative action, arguing that it leads to reverse discrimination.

Within the civil rights context, affirmative action had its earliest roots in presidential orders, beginning with President John F. Kennedy's 1961 Executive Order 10925, which referred to efforts to end racial discrimination. In 1965, President Lyndon Johnson's Executive Order 11246 required federal contractors to take affirmative action to ensure equality in employment as it related to race, religion, and national origin. Explaining his concept of affirmative action to Howard University's 1965 graduating class, President Johnson said: "You do not take a person who, for years, has been hobbled by chains and liberate him, bring him up to the starting line of a race and then say, 'You are free to compete with all the others,' and still justly believe that you have been completely fair." President Johnson expanded the scope of his 1965 executive order to include women in his 1967 Executive Order 11375. The order covered employment, upgrades, demotions, transfers, employee recruitment and advertising for employees, pay rates, layoffs and termination, and training opportunities. President Richard Nixon significantly expanded federal involvement in affirmative action in 1969 when he announced the Philadelphia Order, which instructed federal construction contractors to establish goals and timetables for affirmative action. In 1970, he included nonconstruction federal contractors in the policy.

In addition to presidential actions, Congress contributed to the concept of equal opportunity by passing the Civil Rights Act of 1964, which included prohibitions against employment discrimination and created the Equal Employment Opportunity Commission (EEOC) in Title VII. The EEOC was given enforcement responsibilities for private employers, and the Office of Federal Contract Compliance enforced the law for federal contractors and subcontractors. By 1968, the government had developed goals and timetables for affirmative action programs and recognized that discrimination could be systemic and unintentional. The Equal Employment Opportunity Act of 1972 expanded coverage of the 1964 act and increased the EEOC's enforcement powers. In addition, one of the more persistent advocates of affirmative action, Congresswoman Yvonne Brathwaite Burke, passed a measure that required that contracts for the construction of the Alaskan pipeline be awarded on an affirmative action basis, and she placed amendments that required any project receiving federal funding to implement an affirmative action plan. Eventually, the measures became known as the Burke Amendment.

Although the U.S. Supreme Court has never defined affirmative action as a legal term, it has decided several cases related to it. The Court has decided that affirmative action programs are permissible when there is evidence of continuing discrimination. The plans must not use quotas, must be flexible, cannot require the selection of unqualified candidates, must not last longer than necessary to remedy the discrimination, and must not replace incumbent white male employees or businesses.

The most widely publicized affirmative action case was probably *Bakke v. Regents of the University of California* (1978). Bakke was a white male who applied to the University of California Medical School but was denied admission, even though minority students with lower scores were admitted. The U.S. Supreme Court decided that race could be a factor in admissions policies, that universities could design affirmative action programs to increase the enrollments of minority students, and that those policies must be the least intrusive available. The Court decided that the University of California did not meet the criteria, and Bakke won his case, but the Court also concluded that affirmative action programs are constitutional. In *Gratz v. Bollinger* (2003), the U.S. Supreme Court concluded that affirmative action strategies for college admissions that treated race as a determining factor were unconstitutional. In a related case, however, *Grutter v. Bollinger* (2003), the U.S. Supreme Court decided that college admissions policies that treated race as one consideration among many considerations were constitutional.

Strategies used by affirmative action opponents have included ballot initiatives. Voters passed measures in California in 1996 and Washington in 1998 that ended affirmative action programs and policies in those states. In 2006, Michigan voters will decide the fate of a similar measure.

Although women are the largest group of Americans to benefit from affirmative action, the only affirmative action case to reach the Supreme Court that dealt specifically with women was *Johnson v. Transportation Agency of Santa Clara County*, decided in 1987. The Court approved the county's affirmative action program, which set goals that would have a workforce of women, minorities, and people with disabilities in proportion to their population in the county.

Affirmative action supporters point to persistent inequities that could be remedied by continuing the policies. For example, according to a report published in 2000, white men are 43 percent of the workforce at *Fortune 2000* companies, but they hold 95 percent of the senior management positions. In 2002, women were 10.8 percent of all engineers, 1.4 percent of all auto mechanics, and 1.8 percent of all carpenters, all jobs that pay more than jobs traditionally held by women.

See also *Bachur v. Democratic National Committee*; Burke, Perle Yvonne Watson Brathwaite; Civil Rights Act of 1964, Title VII; Equal Employment Opportunity Commission; *Johnson v. Transportation Agency of Santa Clara County*

References Taylor, *Affirmative Action at Work: Law, Politics, and Ethics* (1991); *Washington Post*, 23 June 2003; www.aclu.org; www.civilrights.org; www.feminist.org; www.whitehouse.gov.

Akron v. Akron Center for Reproductive Health (1983)

In *Akron v. Akron Center for Reproductive Health*, the U.S. Supreme Court considered five aspects of an Akron, Ohio ordinance relating to abortion and found all of them unconstitutional. The Court rejected the requirement that after the first trimester of pregnancy all abortions had to be performed in a hospital, saying that it "unreasonably infringes upon a woman's constitutional right to obtain an abortion." It turned down the requirement that before performing an abortion on an unmarried minor under the age of fifteen, a physician had to obtain either the consent of one of her parents or the minor had to obtain a court order. The Court disagreed with the stipulation that the attending physician had to inform the woman about the status of her pregnancy, the development of the fetus, the likely date of viability, the physical and emotional complications that could result from an abortion, sources of assistance for pregnant women, and information about childbirth and adoption. The Court also disallowed the mandatory twenty-four-hour waiting period after a woman had signed the informed consent form, saying that no legitimate state interest had been demonstrated in defense of it. The last section considered by the Court required physicians performing abortions to ensure the humane and sanitary disposal of fetal remains or risk punishment for a misdemeanor. The Court decided that the provision violated the due process clause because it failed to give a physician fair notice that he or she could be breaking the law. The Court considered several of these issues in earlier and subsequent cases.

See also Abortion; *Bellotti v. Baird*; *Planned Parenthood of Southeastern Pennsylvania v. Casey*

References *Akron v. Akron Center for Reproductive Health*, 462 U.S. 416 (1983).

Albright, Madeleine Jana Korbel (b. 1937)

The first woman U.S. secretary of state, Madeleine Albright served from her appointment by President Bill Clinton in 1997 until 2001. Upon taking the post, Albright became the highest-ranking woman in the U.S. government in the nation's history. After she left office, she explained that as a woman, the personal relationships she had established had "mattered in terms of what I was able to get done. And I did bring women's issues to the center of our foreign policy." During the first Clinton administration, she was the U.S. permanent representative to the United Nations and a member of the National Security Council.

Born in Prague, Czechoslovakia, Albright was the daughter of a member of the Czechoslovak diplomatic service. Her father's career played a significant role in Albright's life, beginning in 1938 when her family had to flee their home to escape the Nazis. When Communists took over the Czech government in 1948, Albright, her siblings, and her parents became refugees and were granted political asylum in the United States. These experiences greatly influenced Albright's views of the United States' responsibilities to refugees and its relationships with totalitarian governments.

A naturalized U.S. citizen, Albright graduated from Wellesley College in 1959 and earned her master of arts in 1968 and her Ph.D. in 1967, both from Columbia University. Albright began her career as a professor and researcher, developing and implementing programs designed to enhance women's professional opportunities in international affairs. She entered politics by working for Senator Edmund Muskie's 1972 presidential campaign and later became his chief legislative assistant. In 1974, she became congressional liaison for national security adviser Zbigniew Brzezinski, one of her former professors. Foreign policy adviser to Democratic vice presidential candidate Geraldine Ferraro in 1984, Albright held the same position in presidential candidate Michael Dukakis's campaign in 1988. She then taught international relations at Georgetown University in the School of Foreign Service until 1992.

President Bill Clinton appointed Albright the U.S. permanent representative to the United Nations in 1993. After her appointment, she explained her perspective on the United States' role in international affairs: "For me, America is really, truly the indispensable nation. I've never seen America as an imperialist or colonialist or meddling country." Her belief in the central role the United States plays in international affairs includes the use of military power, which is exemplified by her active efforts in two areas. She worked for United Nations authorization to use military force in Haiti in 1994, which led to the legally elected president of that nation being restored to power. In addition, she worked with several nations in developing the UN plan to use force to quell the war in Bosnia in 1995 and was a leading voice in the creation of a war crimes tribunal in that country. During her tenure as U.S. ambassador to the United Nations, Albright inspected peacekeeping operations and United Nations initiatives in twenty-four countries.

When Clinton began his second term in 1997, he appointed Albright secretary of state. On her first day as secretary, Albright learned that her ancestry was Jewish and that three of her grandparents had died at the hands of the Nazis. News stories abounded, some of them openly skeptical that she could have been ignorant of her ancestry. Albright, however, steadfastly maintained that she had not known and that she was proud of her parents for making the decisions they had to protect their children. She also expressed pride in her heritage.

As secretary of state, Albright worked to convince the American public that the country's foreign policy should be important to them, even in the post-Cold War era. Albright worked to expand the North Atlantic Treaty Organization (NATO), obtained Senate approval of the International Chemical Weapons Treaty, and gained congressional approval of the State Department reorganization plan.

Albright published her memoir, *Madame Secretary*, in 2003.

See also Cabinets, Women in Presidential; Ferraro, Geraldine Anne

References Blood, *Madam Secretary: A Biography of Madeleine Albright* (1997); *The New York Times*, 5 February 1997; "10 Questions for Madeleine Albright," *Time*, 22 September 2003, p. 8.

Alexander, Sadie Tanner Mosell (1898–1989)

Lawyer and civil rights advocate Sadie Alexander led desegregation efforts in Philadelphia, Pennsylvania, in the 1930s by helping draft Pennsylvania's public accommodation law prohibiting discrimination in hotels, restaurants, and theaters. She and her husband Raymond Alexander, also a lawyer, tested the law by attempting to enter a theater. When the manager refused to admit them, he was arrested for violating the law, and the Alexanders won their point. They continued their crusade at hotels and restaurants.

Born in Philadelphia, Sadie Alexander received her bachelor's degree in education in 1918, her master's degree in economics in 1919, and her doctorate in economics in 1921. She was the first African American woman in the United States to earn a doctoral degree and the first to earn one in economics. She completed her law degree in 1927, receiving all of the degrees from the University of Pennsylvania. Alexander entered private law practice and served as Philadelphia assistant city solicitor from 1927 to 1931 and from 1936 to 1940.

In the late 1940s, Sadie Alexander was "Woman of the Year" in the comic book *Negro Heroes*. She served on the President's Committee on Civil Rights, which reported in 1948 that the United States had a substantial gap between its ideals and practice. In the 1960s, she headed Philadelphia's Commission on Human Rights. President Jimmy Carter appointed her chair of the White House Conference on Aging in 1981.

Alexander was the first national president of Delta Sigma Theta, a black woman's sorority. She was also active in the American Civil Liberties Union, Americans for Democratic Action, and the National Urban League's national board.

> **See also** American Civil Liberties Union; Civil Rights Movement, Women in the; Delta Sigma Theta Sorority
>
> **References** Hine, ed., *Black Women in America: An Historical Encyclopedia* (1993); *The New York Times*, 3 November 1989.

Allen, Maryon Pittman (b. 1925)

Democrat Maryon Allen of Alabama served in the U.S. Senate from 8 June 1978 to 7 November 1978. While working as women's editor for the *Birmingham News*, she interviewed Alabama lieutenant governor James B. Allen in the spring of 1964 and married him that summer. Following James Allen's death while serving in the U.S. Senate, Governor George Wallace appointed Maryon Allen to fill the vacancy, with the understanding that hers would be an interim appointment, ending when another person was elected in the fall. Instead, she announced her candidacy to complete the unexpired term. When a newspaper article quoted Maryon Allen criticizing Governor Wallace and his wife, her support dwindled, despite her contention that her comments had been distorted. Allen won more votes than any of the other primary candidates, but not a large enough percentage of votes cast to win the primary. She lost in the runoff election.

Born in Meridian, Mississippi, Allen attended the University of Alabama from 1944 to 1947 and the International Institute of Interior Design in 1970. After serving in Congress, Allen wrote a column for the *Washington Post* from 1978 to 1981. She returned to Birmingham in 1993 and opened Cliff House, a clothing restoration and design company.

> **See also** Congress, Women in
>
> **References** *The New York Times*, 6 March 1971; Office of the Historian, U.S. House of Representatives, *Women in Congress, 1917–1990* (1991).

Allred, Gloria Rachel (b. 1941)

Feminist lawyer Gloria Allred serves as an advocate for women through her work in the courtroom. She has argued family law, sexual harassment, employment discrimination, and sex discrimination cases. Some of her cases have been considered trivial–for example, one challenging the higher rates that dry cleaners charged for laundering women's shirts than for men's–but she notes that she has never had a case dismissed for being frivolous or without merit.

Founder and president of the Women's Equal Rights Legal Defense and Education Fund, Allred became an activist lawyer as a result of personal experience. She explained that it developed from "being married as a teenager, giving birth to a child, getting divorced, not receiving child support, basically having to raise a child by myself, getting paid less than a man in my first job for what I consider to be equal work and equal experience, having been raped, having to have an abortion when abortion was illegal and unsafe, almost dying from it."

Although Allred has generally used litigation as the method for seeking justice, she has also used other techniques. She once gave a chastity belt to a California state senator who supported a constitutional amendment to outlaw abortions, and she led a group of women who hung diapers in a governor's office to impress upon him the importance of a bill to allow payroll deductions to enforce child support. On another occasion, she organized a picket outside a courthouse after a judge made a sexist comment during a rape trial.

Allred has hosted a daily radio talk show in Los Angeles and provided commentary on television news programs.

Born in Philadelphia, Pennsylvania, Allred received her bachelor's degree from the University of Pennsylvania in 1963, her master's degree from New York University in 1966, and her law degree from Loyola University in 1974.

References Evory and Gareffa, eds., *Contemporary Newsmakers, 1985* (1985); Klapper, "Activist Lawyer" (1985).

Alpha Kappa Alpha Sorority

Founded at Howard University in 1908, Alpha Kappa Alpha (AKA) was the first African American women's Greek letter society. Begun by nine women, it has grown into an organization of over 170,000 members in 930 chapters in the United States, West Africa, the Bahamas, Germany, Korea, Japan, and the Caribbean.

During the Depression of the 1930s, AKA entered into an era of social action, developing plans for teacher education, lobbying to end lynching, and working with the National Association for the Advancement of Colored People. It also established a program to address health problems on the Mississippi Delta, where people suffered from malnutrition, diphtheria, smallpox, and syphilis and other venereal diseases. Beginning in 1935 and continuing for eight years, AKA sponsored mobile health units staffed by doctors and nurses that traveled throughout Holmes County, Mississippi, providing medical services. Known as the Mississippi Health Project, it received national attention for its contributions to public health.

Working with other groups in the 1940s, AKA's political agenda included the elimination of discrimination, ending disenfranchisement, supporting anti-lynching legislation, establishing a permanent Fair Employment Practices Commission, and ending racial inequities in federal programs. During World War II, the sorority also worked with the National Council of Negro Women to convince the U.S. Navy to admit African American women into the newly formed Women Accepted for Voluntary Emergency Service (WAVES) and to end discrimination and segregation in the Women's Army Corps (WAC).

AKA established "ON TRACK," an acronym for organizing, nurturing, team building, achieving, character building, and knowledge, targeting at-risk elementary school students to help them prepare for middle school. It has worked with the U.S. Department of Health to promote women's health, and with the U.S. Department of Transportation to increase seat belt use among minority populations. In 2000, it established a school in South Africa.

Providing educational and employment opportunities, making grants for medical research and education, honoring black families, and supporting black businesses are among the many areas in which AKA has provided leadership in the United States. On the international level, it has helped improve life in several African nations by providing training, improved water supplies, assistance to refugee children, and relief.

See also Anti-lynching Movement; National Association for the Advancement of Colored People, Women in the; National Council of Negro Women

References Hartmann, *The Home Front and Beyond: American Women in the 1940s* (1982); Hine, ed., *Black Women in America: An Historical Encyclopedia* (1993); http://www.aka1908.com

Alpha Suffrage Club

Organized in 1913 by writer and activist Ida B. Wells-Barnett, Alpha Suffrage Club of Chicago worked to politicize black women and to support woman suffrage. Wells-Barnett formed the club out of her commitment to woman suffrage and because the dominant woman suffrage organization, the National American Woman Suffrage Association, held racist views and excluded African American women. Members registered and organized voters, and offered political education programs. Their most visible success came with Oscar DePriest's 1915 election as the first black alderman in Chicago.

See also National American Woman Suffrage Association; Suffrage; Wells-Barnett, Ida Bell

References Hine, ed., *Black Women in America* (1993).

Alvarez, Aida (b. 1949)

A member of President Bill Clinton's Cabinet, Aida Alvarez was administrator of the Small Business Administration (SBA) from 1997 to 2001. She was the first Hispanic woman and the first person of Puerto Rican heritage to hold a position in a president's Cabinet. As head of the SBA, Alvarez shaped the policies for federal programs that provide financial and business development assistance to entrepreneurs. Alvarez's priorities included improving access to capital and credit for a diverse population. She said: "Small business is the heart and soul of the American economy. It has always been, and it will always be."

Reflecting on her tenure as administrator, she believed that she had "captured an opportunity because we really zeroed in on the fact that women and minorities were starting up businesses at a faster pace than the general population. And we worked with our lenders and with our district offices to set goals to create more lending activity. We've seen a tripling in the number of SBA loans for women, and a near tripling of the loans for minority-owned businesses."

Born in Aguadilla, Puerto Rico, Alvarez earned her bachelor's degree from Harvard University in 1971. A television and print journalist from 1973 to 1984, she worked for the New York City Health and Hospitals Corporation from 1984 to 1985 and was an investment banker in San Francisco and New York from 1986 to 1993. Appointed the first director of the Office of Federal Housing Enterprise Oversight in 1993, she established regulatory oversight of Fannie Mae and Freddie Mac, the nation's two largest housing finance corporations.

See also Cabinets, Women in Presidential

References "The SBA's Outgoing Boss: 'We Captured an Opportunity,'" *BusinessWeek Online*," 28 December 2000, www.businessweek.com/print/smallbiz/content/dec2000/sb20001228_74.htm?chan=sb; www.sba.gov/alvarez/.

American Association of University Women

The American Association of University Women (AAUW) promotes equity for all women and girls, lifelong education, and positive societal change. With over 100,000 members, it is the oldest national organization working for equity and the advancement of women through education. Founded in 1881 by seventeen college women who wanted to form a national organization of women college graduates, AAUW was originally known as the Association of Collegiate Alumnae (ACA), which merged with the Western Association of College Alumnae and finally with Southern Association of College Women in 1921 to form AAUW.

The early purposes of ACA members were to help other women obtain higher education and to help educated women fit into their communities. So few women held college degrees in the nineteenth century that several myths surrounded educated women and the effect their education had on them. In addition to society scorning women who sought higher education, some people thought that women who obtained college degrees would become infertile or lose their minds. These questions led the association to begin its long tradition of research related to women and women's education. One of the organization's first studies, in 1885, investigated the effects of a college degree on women and resulted in the conclusions that women with college degrees could bear children and did not lose their minds.

The organization's 1992 study, *The AAUW Report: How Schools Shortchange Girls*, showed that systemic sex discrimination or gender bias has placed schoolgirls at a disadvantage in the classroom. A subsequent study, *Girls in the Middle: Working to Succeed in School* (1996), focused on girls in middle school and the strategies they have used to meet the challenges of adolescence. Through its research, AAUW also identified the prevalence of sexual harassment in schools, which prompted the publication of *Hostile Hallways: The AAUW Survey on Sexual Harassment in America's Schools*

(1993). Other publications have examined gender equity programs in the sciences, women learning online, sex discrimination in academia, and sexual harassment on campuses.

In addition to conducting research, AAUW has lobbied Congress and state legislatures. As a charter member of the Women's Joint Congressional Committee in 1920, AAUW helped pass the Sheppard-Towner Act, the Cable Act, and several other measures. In the decades since, AAUW has supported the appointment of women to public offices, environmental conservation and protection, public broadcasting, the Equal Pay Act of 1963, Title IX of the Education Amendments of 1972, the Equal Credit Opportunity Act of 1974, consumer protection, accessibility to housing, drug abuse prevention, and many other issues. AAUW, along with several other women's organizations, initially opposed adding the Equal Rights Amendment (ERA) to the U.S. Constitution, was neutral on the amendment in the 1950s and 1960s, but in 1971 became a strong and committed supporter of the ERA.

AAUW's current public policy goals include promoting educational and economic equity, and expanding and defending civil rights. In the area of educational equity, AAUW supports adequate and equitable funding for public education, increased support for and access to higher education, enforcement of Title IX, and education for women and girls for career preparation. AAUW opposes using public funds for non-public elementary and secondary education. In the area of economic equity, AAUW supports equitable access and advancement in employment; enforcement of employment anti-discrimination laws; fairness in compensation; access to high-quality, affordable dependent care; and programs that provide women with education, training, and support for success in the workforce. Its civil and constitutional rights priorities include freedom from violence in homes, schools, workplaces, and communities and expansion of women's health care rights.

Because of the emerging power of far-right politicians who opposed much of AAUW's public policy agenda, it has worked to elect candidates who support its views. For example, AAUW's 1996 Voter Education Campaign distributed voter guides and other policy information material, contacted nearly one million women who had not voted in 1994, and conducted get-out-the-vote drives. In addition to participating in elections, AAUW has a paid lobbyist whose work focuses on influencing members of Congress. The lobbyist's work is supported by AAUW members, who also lobby their members of Congress in person, through the mail, and with faxes and e-mail. AAUW keeps its members informed of congressional activities through its print and electronic publications.

AAUW provides financial support to women through the Educational Foundation and the Legal Advocacy Fund. The Educational Foundation uses money raised by local and state branches to support fellowships for advanced study and research grants. It awards over $2.5 million a year to women for graduate education, community projects, and international academic exchanges. The Legal Advocacy Fund helps women in higher education fight discrimination and harassment.

See also Abortion; Cable Acts; Domestic Violence; Education Amendments of 1972, Title IX; Education, Women and; Equal Credit Opportunity Act of 1974; Equal Pay Act of 1963; Equal Rights Amendment; Pay Equity; Sexual Harassment; Sheppard-Towner Maternity and Infancy Protection Act of 1921; Women's Joint Congressional Committee

References Chipley, comp., *AAUW: Historic Principles 1881–1989* (1989); "Election '96: Deciding the Vote" (1997); Levine, *Degrees of Equality: The American Association of University Women and the Challenge of Twentieth-Century Feminism* (1995); www.aauw.org.

American Civil Liberties Union

Founded in 1920, the American Civil Liberties Union (ACLU) is a nonpartisan public interest organization dedicated to protecting the basic civil liberties of all Americans and extending them to those who have been denied them. The ACLU's mission is to safeguard First Amendment rights, equal protection of the law, due process of law, and the right to privacy. In addition to litigating cases and supporting other groups litigating issues in which it believes civil rights are involved, the ACLU lobbies Congress.

The ACLU has national projects that focus on a specific area, including acquired immunodeficiency syndrome (AIDS), arts censorship, capital punishment, children's rights, education reform, lesbian and gay rights, immigrants' rights, reproductive freedom, and women's rights. The Women's Rights Project, which seeks full equality for women, provides an example of the work done by these special projects. It took the sex discrimination case *Reed v. Reed* (1971) to the U.S. Supreme Court, and for the first time the Court held that a classification based on sex was unconstitutional. The Women's Rights Project has also been involved in cases related to pregnancy, employment, pay equity, and insurance benefits.

See also Abortion; *Craig v. Boren*; *Frontiero v. Richardson*; Ginsburg, Ruth Joan Bader; Lesbian Rights; *Reed v. Reed*; *Weinberger v. Wiesenfeld*

References www.aclu.org.

American Life League, Inc.

Founded by Judie Brown in 1979, the American Life League (ALL), first known as the American Life Lobby, has 300,000 supporters and a network of 5,000 activists. ALL's mission statement says, in part: "American Life League exists to serve God by helping to build a society that respects and protects individual innocent human beings from inception to natural death–without compromise, without exception, without apology."

ALL works to educate its members and the public about abortion, using the group's interpretations of biblical writings. ALL opposes abortion without any exceptions, including rape, incest, and fetal deformity. ALL also opposes the use of most contraceptives, including birth control pills, intrauterine devices (IUDs), RU-486, and other chemical contraceptives, arguing that these contraceptive methods are abortifacients, which means they cause abortions. ALL opposes using public funds, facilities, or employees to perform abortions; providing abortion coverage in public employees' health insurance plans; and using fetal tissue transplants from induced abortions in medical experiments, also known as stem cell research.

ALL opposes in vitro fertilization, arguing that all of the embryos are human life. ALL objects to freezing embryos (a method for storing them until needed), the disposal of unwanted or unuseable embryos, and the loss of embryos through the procedures involved in transferring them into a woman's womb. ALL considers these losses of embryos as losses of human life.

In 1999, ALL issued a proclamation against violence, including acts against abortion clinic personnel and others involved in providing abortions. The proclamation called on "Every pro-lifer to reject violence and those who commit violent acts."

ALL advocates passage of the Human Life Amendment, which states: "The paramount right to life is vested in each human being at fertilization." The organization supports passage of "fetal homicide" legislation and conscience clauses for doctors, health care workers, facilities, and police officers that would allow them to refuse to participate in abortions or abortion-related activity. It supports crisis pregnancy centers that do not perform abortions or make referrals to abortion facilities.

See also Abortion; Brown, Judie

References www.all.org.

American Woman Suffrage Association

Founded in 1869, the American Woman Suffrage Association (AWSA) developed out of a division between two factions in the women's rights movement and in response to Elizabeth Cady Stanton and Susan B. Anthony's new organization, the National Woman Suffrage Association (NWSA), also founded in that year. Conflicts had appeared three years earlier between those who insisted that any constitutional amendments related to citizenship and voting rights for freed slaves must also include women and those who believed that the post-Civil War years demanded those rights for former slaves, even if the provisions did not include women. Other events exacerbated the differences, leading to the creation of the NWSA.

AWSA members, led by Lucy Stone and her husband Henry Blackwell, supported the Fifteenth Amendment, which granted suffrage to all males regardless of color and advocated state amendments for woman suffrage rather than a federal amendment. AWSA, the more conservative of the two groups, limited its focus to woman suffrage and avoided other controversial topics embraced by NWSA, such as divorce or critiques of organized religion.

By the late 1880s, AWSA's more conservative views better reflected the nation's conservatism than NWSA, but NWSA had organized more affiliates. The necessary components for uniting the two groups existed, needing only a leader to help bring them together. In 1887, Alice Stone Blackwell, daughter of Stone and Blackwell, and Harriot Eaton Stanton Blatch, daughter of Elizabeth Cady Stanton, began the process of uniting the two groups in negotiations that took more than two years. In 1890, the AWSA and NWSA became the National American Woman Suffrage Association.

See also Anthony, Susan Brownell; Blackwell, Alice Stone; Blatch, Harriot Eaton Stanton; Fifteenth Amendment; Fourteenth Amendment; National American Woman Suffrage Association; National Woman Suffrage Association; Stanton, Elizabeth Cady; Stone, Lucy

References Flexner and Fitzpatrick, *Century of Struggle: The Woman's Rights Movement in the United States* (1996).

American Women Presidents

Founded in 2000, American Women Presidents (AWP) is a political action committee (PAC) that works to elect a woman president, with the goal of seeing a woman inaugurated in 2009. A bipartisan group of women and men, AWP endorses and financially supports women running for governor and the United States Senate, offices that occasionally lead to the presidency. In 2004, it attempted to recruit several women, including Senators Hillary Rodham Clinton and Kay Bailey Hutchison and others, to run for the presidency. The group helped launch former Senator Carol Moseley Braun's 2004 candidacy.

Reference http://www.americanwomenpresidents.org/

Ames, Jessie Harriet Daniel (1883–1972)

Founder of the Association of Southern Women for the Prevention of Lynching (ASWPL), Jessie Daniel Ames worked to end lynching by dispelling the myths surrounding it. Ames's central arguments were that lynching was not in retaliation for black men raping white women but was a form of racial control and a means of perpetuating sexual exploitation of women–the arguments that African American women had earlier articulated. Ames contributed to the anti-lynching cause by bringing white women into the crusade.

Born in Palestine, Texas, Ames graduated from Southwestern University in 1902. Married in 1905, she had three children before she became a widow. To support her family, she managed a local telephone company that her mother owned.

Ames became involved in politics through the suffrage movement in 1916, organized a county suffrage association, and became treasurer of the Texas Equal Suffrage Association in 1918. Through her writing and speaking on behalf of the cause, she helped make Texas the first southern state to ratify the Nineteenth Amendment granting women voting rights. In 1919, Ames organized and became the founding president of the Texas League of Women Voters and through it organized citizenship schools. She also worked to give women equal rights to custody of their children, to ensure married women's property rights, and to expand educational opportunities for girls.

As Ames pursued an agenda for women's rights, she concluded that fundamental barriers to achieving her goals were the power of racism and the domination of the Ku Klux Klan in southern politics. During the time she was developing these ideas, she attended a meeting hosted by the Council on Interracial Cooperation (CIC). The CIC had been formed to help ease the racial tension that had developed after World War I, with an emphasis on addressing the tragedy of lynching. In 1924, Ames became a CIC fieldworker in Texas, conducted an educational and legislative campaign against lynching, and investigated lynchings. In 1929, Ames moved to Atlanta, Georgia, where she became director of women's work for CIC.

In 1930, with financial support from CIC, Ames founded the ASWPL, which organized white women through existing groups, particularly Protestant missionary societies. For many traditional southern women, involvement in politics was seen as degrading, but Ames's approach permitted them to become political under the guise of their churches. Her primary strategy was to convince women that lynchings did not occur in response to attacks on or rapes of white women. Instead, she demonstrated that mob violence and racial hatred motivated the crimes. In addition, she attacked the paternalism of chivalry, which asserted that white women needed white men's protection from the threat of sexual violence from black men. Ames argued that these distortions of the motives behind lynching served to keep women submissive.

ASWPL members circulated anti-lynching pledges, obtaining more than 43,000 signatures. They also publicized their findings, printed pamphlets, organized speaking tours, and intervened to prevent lynching in their own communities. By 1935, there were affiliates in all of the former Confederate states plus Kentucky and Oklahoma.

Ames eventually became estranged from other leading anti-lynching advocates because she insisted that the states must be responsible for stopping mob violence and lynching, and opposed any federal measure, which many other leaders supported. Although an anti-lynching law passed the House in 1921, the Senate refused to act upon it and no federal measure against lynching ever became law. In 1942, ASWPL closed its doors, and Ames returned to her work with CIC, retiring in 1944.

> **See also** American Association of University Women; Anti-lynching Movement; Association of Southern Women for the Prevention of Lynching; League of Women Voters; Suffrage
>
> **References** Hall, *Revolt against Chivalry* (1979).

Anderson, Amalia (b. 1974)

Community organizer and educator, Amalia Anderson works on every level from local activism to international policy. Born in Guatemala City, Guatemala, Anderson earned her bachelor of arts degree at Macalester College in 1996 and her JD at Hamline University School of Law in 2003, concentrating on social justice. A self-described Maya/Latina organizer, she has worked as director of a teen dating violence program, a battered women's legal advocate, and program director for the Indigenous Peoples' Human Rights Project. A field representative for the American Indian Treaty Council, she participates in U.N. meetings, including the Working Group on Indigenous Populations and the Permanent Forum on Indigenous Issues. A co-founder of Fourth World Rising, an indigenous youth leadership program, Anderson seeks to bridge the gap between local issues and the international Indigenous Peoples' movement. She also is a representative on the National Media Justice Network. Director of political education and action for the League of Rural Voters, Anderson created the Latino Leadership Project, working to identify, recruit, and support emerging Latino leaders.

Anderson's work emerges from her belief system. She explained: "I believe in people, in the ability of regular folks to guide their lives, to speak for themselves, to learn the world and make it better." She added: "I am specific and intentional about not only the type of work I do, but the ways in which I work. I believe *ethical leadership* means building collective power and working in ways, which value people!" [Emphasis as indicated in original.] Her work also comes from her identity, as she explained: "As a Mayan woman I am *responsible* for honoring the identity of First Nations Peoples and our inherent right to self-determination. I understand our custodial relationship to the land and I believe that traditional knowledge is a way of life and that we must maintain its continuity for our survival." [Emphasis in original.]

> **References** Amalia Anderson, email to author, 18 November 2005.

Anderson, Eugenie Moore (1909–1997)

Democrat Eugenie Moore Anderson served as U.S. ambassador to Denmark from 1949 to 1953 and to Bulgaria from 1962 to 1964. She was the first female U.S. ambassador and the first woman to sign a treaty between the United States and another nation. Her interest in international issues developed during a trip to Germany in 1937 that exposed her to the country's totalitarian government and prompted her to speak on foreign affairs when she returned to the United States. As a representative of the League of Women Voters, Anderson spoke against isolationist policies and changed her party affiliation from Republican to Democrat because of her opposition to the isolationist views of people living in her area. Anderson helped Hubert H. Humphrey remove a Communist faction in Minnesota's Democratic Party and helped form the Democratic-Farmer Labor Party in 1944. She became Democratic national committeewoman for Minnesota in 1948, the same year she helped Harry S. Truman win the state for his presidential candidacy.

When Truman appointed her ambassador, she said: "I know that he intended my appointment to signify to all women that he recognizes our growing assumption of mature responsible citizenship, our work for the public good, not simply as women and mothers, but as citizens and as people." In order to facilitate her work as ambassador, Anderson learned Danish and traveled throughout Denmark. Through her work, Anderson helped reach an agreement in the Treaty of Friendship, Commerce and Navigation in 1951 and negotiated an arrangement with Denmark that brought Greenland into the North Atlantic Treaty Organization's (NATO's) defense authority. She also negotiated the creation and maintenance of U.S. military bases in Greenland. When Truman's term ended in 1953, Anderson returned to the United States. She ran for the U.S. Senate in 1958 but lost in the primary.

President John F. Kennedy appointed her head of the U.S. delegation to Bulgaria in 1962, an assignment very different from her previous one. A strong anti-Communist, Anderson found the censorship and surveillance there difficult to accept. She negotiated the settlement of World War II claims and related matters, but repeated demonstrations at the U.S. embassy protesting U.S. espionage activities led Anderson to resign in 1964.

Anderson was U.S. representative to the United Nations General Assembly from 1965 to 1967, served on the United Nations Trusteeship Council from 1965 to 1968, and then was a special assistant to the secretary of state.

Born in Adair, Iowa, Anderson taught piano lessons in 1926 and 1927 and worked for Northwestern Bell Telephone Company to pay for her college tuition. She attended Stephens College, Simpson College, Carleton College, and the Julliard School.

> **References** *The New York Times*, 3 April 1997; Stineman, *American Political Women* (1980).

Anderson, Marian (1902–1993)

A classical vocalist, Marian Anderson became a symbol for the civil rights movement in the 1930s and an inspiration to other African American musicians. Despite her artistic accomplishments, Anderson suffered the full range of racism's indignities, including being denied admission to a music school and the use of performance halls, experiencing the insults of being refused service at white restaurants, and being refused lodging in white hotels. By focusing on her art, however, Anderson brought attention to the problems of racism in the United States.

Born in Philadelphia, Marian Anderson began singing in church choirs when she was six years old and offering solo performances when she was eight. She studied music under several teachers until 1925, when she entered a New York Philharmonic Orchestra voice competition, making her debut with that orchestra the same year. Over the next several years, she continued her studies and toured the United States, particularly the South, where segregation laws significantly complicated her travels and performances.

Wanting to expand her skills and seeking new performance opportunities, Anderson went to Europe in 1930, where she was warmly received. In 1935, she returned to the United States at the encouragement of her manager, impresario Sol Hurok, who created performance opportunities for her and shielded her from some of the more blatant expressions of racism.

Hurok, however, could not protect Anderson from the Daughters of the American Revolution's (DAR's) racial prejudice in an incident that made her a national civil rights figure. When Hurok attempted to schedule a concert at the DAR's Constitution Hall, he was told that all dates were taken. Convinced that racism was the true problem, Hurok took the matter to the public. In response, Eleanor Roosevelt resigned from the DAR, and Secretary of the Interior Harold Ickes offered the Lincoln Memorial on Easter Sunday, 1939, for a concert site. More than 75,000 people attended the concert, and millions more listened to it on the radio. In addition, newspapers and other publications printed pictures of Anderson singing in front of Abraham Lincoln's statue, an image that became a symbol for the civil rights movement. At the invitation of the DAR, Anderson sang at Constitution Hall in December 1942 and on subsequent occasions.

The first African American to sing with the New York Metropolitan Opera, Anderson debuted with the opera company in 1955, an event that received front-page coverage in *The New York Times* for its significance in race relations. Anderson sang at inaugurations for President Dwight D. Eisenhower in 1957 and President John F. Kennedy in 1961. Eisenhower appointed her an alternative representative in the U.S. delegation to the United Nations Human Rights Committee in the late 1950s.

See also Civil Rights Movement, Women in the; Roosevelt, Eleanor

References Anderson, *My Lord, What a Morning* (1956); *The New York Times*, 14 April 1993.

Anderson, Mary (1872–1964)

Head of the federal Women's Bureau from 1920 to 1944, Mary Anderson began her working life as a laborer, developed organizational skills as a union recruiter, and became a powerful advocate for protective labor legislation. As an advocate for improving women's working conditions, Anderson opposed the Equal Rights Amendment, believing that it would make protective labor legislation unconstitutional and leave working women vulnerable to unsafe and harmful working conditions.

Born near Lidköping, Sweden, Anderson and one of her sisters migrated to the United States in 1889. Upon her arrival, she worked as a dishwasher, as a domestic, in a garment factory, and in a shoe factory. In 1899, she joined the International Boot and Shoe Workers Union and was elected president of the women's stitchers' local union the next year. She served on the union's national executive board from 1906 to 1919 and became active in the Women's Trade Union League (WTUL). In 1910, she became a full-time organizer for the WTUL and also developed expertise as an industrial arbitrator, preventing and ending wildcat strikes.

Anderson began her career in public service in 1918, when she joined the staff of the Women in Industry Service, a temporary agency in the Department of Labor established to monitor women's employment during World War I. Anderson crusaded for equal pay for women, but formulating an enforceable policy eluded her and others committed to the concept. She did, however, contribute to eliminating one form of pay discrimination and opening more employment opportunities to women. Under civil service rules, women were prohibited from taking 60 percent of the exams, and women's entry-level pay was lower than men's. Negotiating with the Civil Service Commission, Anderson reached an agreement in which all civil service exams were opened to women in 1919. When qualifications and salaries were established for federal jobs, Anderson successfully worked to establish pay grades that did not discriminate on the basis of sex or age.

After World War I, women active in the labor movement pressured Congress to make the agency permanent. In 1920, Congress created the Women's Bureau in the Department of Labor, and President Woodrow Wilson appointed Anderson to head it. The bureau's primary tasks included researching women's status as workers, reporting the research, coordinating efforts on behalf of women workers, and serving as their advocate. Anderson's background in the labor movement made her a devoted supporter of protective labor legislation for women and an equally strong opponent of the proposed Equal Rights Amendment (ERA). Anderson viewed the ERA as an "absurd theoretical pronouncement." Her antipathy to the amendment emerged from her belief, one shared by amendment supporters and opponents, that it would void protective labor legislation for women.

During World War II, Anderson believed that her biggest challenge was to convince employers that women could competently perform a wide range of jobs. Anderson retired from public life in 1944, when she left the Women's Bureau.

See also Equal Pay Act of 1963; Equal Rights Amendment; National Committee to Defeat the UnEqual Rights Amendment; Protective Legislation; Women's Bureau

References Anderson, *Woman at Work* (1951); Harrison, *On Account of Sex* (1988).

Andrews, (Leslie) Elizabeth Bullock (1911–2002)

Democrat Elizabeth Andrews of Alabama served in the U.S. House of Representatives from 4 April 1972 to 3 January 1973. Andrews first entered politics in 1944, when her husband George Andrews ran for Congress while serving in the Navy, and she campaigned as his surrogate. Following Congressman George Andrews's death, the Alabama Democratic Executive Committee selected Elizabeth Andrews to be the party's nominee to fill the vacancy. She did not have a Republican opponent in the special election. During her nine months in office, she introduced amendments to protect medical and Social Security benefits and cosponsored a bill to make Tuskegee Institute a national historical park. She did not run for a full term in 1972.

Born in Geneva, Alabama, Andrews earned her bachelor of arts at Montevallo College in 1932 and then taught home economics.

See also Congress, Women in

References Office of the Historian, U.S. House of Representatives, *Women in Congress, 1917–1990* (1991).

Angelou, Maya (b. 1928)

Teacher, poet, dancer, writer, actress, and civil rights organizer Maya Angelou has revealed the life experiences of one African American woman through the volumes of her autobiography. In 1960, Angelou cowrote the stage production *Cabaret for Freedom*, which was produced in New York City to raise funds for civil rights activities in the South. Following her work with the cabaret, she became increasingly involved with civil rights activists, among them Martin Luther King, Jr. At his request, Angelou served as northern coordinator for the Southern Christian Leadership Conference from 1959 to 1960.

Born in St. Louis, Missouri, Maya Angelou, who was first named Marguerite Johnson, studied dance and drama. Angelou began performing as an actor, singer, and dancer in the 1950s and toured with the U.S. State Department production of *Porgy and Bess*.

Angelou's books include *I Know Why the Caged Bird Sings* (1970); *Just Give Me a Cool Drink of Water 'Fore I Die* (1971); *On the Pulse of Morning: The Inaugural Poem* (1992), which she wrote for and read at President Bill Clinton's 1993 inauguration; and *Lessons in Living* (1993). Since 1981, she has been the Reynolds Professor of American Studies, a lifetime appointment, at Wake Forest University.

References H. W. Wilson, *Current Biography Yearbook, 1974* (1974).

Anthony, Susan Brownell (1820–1906)

A charismatic leader, Susan B. Anthony used her organizational ability and her political acumen to help gain suffrage and other rights for women. With her political partner Elizabeth Cady Stanton, she carried the women's rights message across the country, educated women about the legal and constitutional barriers to their full citizenship, and organized the National Woman Suffrage Association.

Born in Adams, Massachusetts, Anthony, a Quaker, attended Deborah Moulson's Seminary for Females when she was seventeen years old. After teaching and serving as a headmistress at other schools for several years in her twenties, she left teaching to manage her family's farm in 1849. Her parents had created a gathering place for temperance activists and abolitionists, including Frederick Douglass, William Lloyd Garrison, and Wendell Phillips. In addition, her parents and younger sister had attended the 1848 women's rights convention in Seneca Falls, New York.

Anthony entered politics through the temperance movement, making her first speech as president of the local Daughters of Temperance in 1849. It was through her temperance work that Anthony met Amelia Bloomer in 1851 and through her, Elizabeth Cady Stanton, who had helped organize the 1848 Seneca Falls Convention. At a Sons of Temperance meeting in 1852, Anthony stood up to speak but was told that women were supposed to listen and learn and was denied permission to speak. When she walked out of the meeting, it was her first spontaneous protest action. In response, she organized the Woman's State Temperance Society, with Stanton serving as president.

Anthony attended her first women's rights convention in 1852 in Syracuse, New York, where she became convinced that without the right to vote or to independently own property, women had virtually no political power. She had found the issue to which she devoted the rest of her life–women's rights.

Anthony and Stanton began their cooperative reform efforts in 1854, working to expand married women's legal rights. They sought to secure for married women the rights to own their wages and to have guardianship of their children in cases of divorce. Anthony organized door-to-door campaigns throughout New York, soliciting signatures on petitions for these causes. The Married Women's Property Act, passed in 1860, gave a married woman control over her wages, the right to sue, and the same rights to her husband's estate as he had to hers.

The partnership that developed between Anthony and Stanton resulted in some ways from their personal circumstances and strengths. Stanton, who was married and had children, had little freedom to travel and organize, but she could develop arguments to support women's rights and write speeches and articles. Anthony, who was single, did not have the same responsibilities, and her strengths included organizing and publicity. Through their work, the two women challenged the assumptions that confined women to the private sphere. They argued that women's sex did not limit their ability to think, that women were not made to serve men, and that women and men should receive the same education in coeducational settings.

In addition to working for women's rights, Anthony was active in the abolitionist movement. By 1856, Anthony was the principal agent for the American Anti-Slavery Society in the state of New York. With the creation of the Republican Party, Anthony began advocating the inclusion of a plank in the party platform for the immediate emancipation of slaves, a proposal that provoked angry responses. Lecture halls she had reserved were denied to her, effigies of her were burned, and violent mobs threatened her. To further the cause of emancipation, Anthony and Stanton founded the Woman's National Loyal League in 1863, advocating the freedom of all slaves and constitutional guarantees for their rights. Under the auspices of the league, Anthony led a national petition drive for emancipation, obtaining 400,000 signatures in support of the cause. After Congress passed the Thirteenth Amendment to the U.S. Constitution in 1865, the Woman's National Loyal League disbanded.

After the Civil War, Anthony opposed the wording of the proposed Fourteenth Amendment to the U.S. Constitution, which guaranteed citizenship to the newly freed slaves. Her objection to the amendment was that it used the word "male" in connection with citizenship, raising the question of whether or not women were citizens. Anthony and Stanton recognized that passage of the Fourteenth Amendment as it was drafted would require another constitutional amendment to give women the vote in federal elections. Both women pledged to oppose the amendment if it did not include women. Abolitionist and Republican leaders, who had long worked with them in the abolitionist and women's rights causes, however, were committed to the amendment with the word "male" in it, saying that it was "the Negro's hour" and that freed slaves needed the protections created by it. Anthony and Stanton were outraged by what they considered a betrayal by their colleagues. In 1866, the two women joined abolitionists and other Republicans in organizing the American Equal Rights Association to work for universal suffrage rights, but the association ultimately decided to work for the Fourteenth Amendment with the word "male" in it, and Anthony and Stanton left the association.

In 1867, Anthony and Stanton went to Kansas, where referenda on African American and woman suffrage amendments were being held. Republican leaders supported African American suffrage but were silent on woman suffrage, which convinced Anthony and Stanton that the party would not promote the woman suffrage measure. During the campaign, Anthony and Stanton met George Francis Train, an eccentric, wealthy Democrat, whose racist and pro-slavery views were well known. Train campaigned for woman suffrage and against the measure for blacks, often appearing onstage with Anthony. Her alliance with Train created a scandal among Republicans and abolitionists, who ridiculed and discredited Anthony as a woman suffrage leader. Kansas voters defeated both amendments.

Anthony's involvement with Train continued, however, when he offered to finance a newspaper for woman suffrage, and Anthony and Stanton accepted it. In 1868, Anthony published the first issue of *The Revolution*, but Train's financial support ended when he left for Europe and abandoned the financial commitment he had made. Anthony continued publishing the paper until 1870, when its indebtedness made continuing it impractical. She turned the paper over to another woman and worked as a lecturer for several years to pay the debts she had incurred publishing it.

A constitutional amendment for woman suffrage was introduced in Congress for the first time in 1868, as was the proposed Fifteenth Amendment, which granted suffrage to male former slaves, but not to women. The next year, Anthony and Stanton organized the National Woman Suffrage Association (NWSA) to develop support for the woman suffrage amendment and opposition to the Fifteenth Amendment as long as it excluded women. In addition to its call for woman suffrage, NWSA advocated divorce reform and working women's rights. In response, two other suffrage leaders, Lucy Stone and her husband Henry Blackwell, organized the American Woman Suffrage Association (AWSA), which supported the ratification of the Fifteenth Amendment and advocated working for state woman suffrage amendments. The two groups competed for more than twenty years.

Seeking alternative strategies for voting rights, Anthony and other suffragists began reconsidering the Fourteenth Amendment as a route to the voting booth. Some suffragists believed that the amendment's identification of citizens as male and the Fifteenth Amendment's provision that citizens were voters combined to exclude women from voting. Other suffragists argued that the Constitution permitted states to define the qualifications for voting. Anthony concluded that she was a citizen and that the Constitution did not specifically prohibit women from voting. She cast her ballot in the 1872 presidential election in New York state. Fifteen other women joined her, and all of them were arrested. Charges were dropped against all but Anthony. Her trial was scheduled for early in 1873, time she used to travel the state of New York, lecturing on the reasons that she believed women could legally vote. Using the Declaration of Independence, the Preamble to the U.S. Constitution, and the Fourteenth Amendment, she argued:

It was we, the people, not we, the white, male citizens, nor we the male citizens; but we, the whole people who formed this Union. We formed it not to give the blessings of liberty but to secure them; not to the half of ourselves and the half of our posterity, but to the whole people–women as well as men. It is downright mockery to talk to women of their enjoyment of the blessings of liberty while they are denied the only means of securing them provided by the democratic-republican government–the ballot.

She continued her argument by asserting that women were people, people were citizens, and citizens could vote. Convicted and fined $100, she refused to pay, but she was not ordered to jail and the matter died. The judge's decision to drop the matter denied her the opportunity to appeal the decision in a higher court.

Anthony continued to campaign for woman suffrage, speaking on the topic, organizing supporters, and working for bills in state legislatures and in campaigns for state constitutional amendments. She traveled the country for more than thirty years on behalf of woman suffrage. She also joined the effort to record the events in which she had played such a significant part. With Matilda Joslyn Gage, Anthony and Stanton wrote *History of Woman Suffrage*, a three-volume work that was published over several years, the first volume in 1881 and the last in 1886. Anthony and Ida Husted Harper published a fourth volume in 1902 and Harper published two additional volumes in 1922.

In 1890, Anthony helped with the merger of the National Woman Suffrage Association and the American Woman Suffrage Association into the National American Woman Suffrage Association. Stanton served as NAWSA's first president from 1890 to 1892. Anthony was vice-president-at-large those years and succeeded Stanton as president from 1892 until 1900. Anthony made her last public statement in 1906, at a gathering of suffragists celebrating her eighty-sixth birthday. After expressing her appreciation to her friends and colleagues and after noting that suffrage had not been won, she said, "with such women consecrating their lives, failure is impossible." Her declaration, "failure is impossible," became a motto for suffragists and for feminists who followed later in the twentieth century. The Nineteenth Amendment granting women the vote was ratified in 1920, fourteen years after Anthony's death.

In 1979, Anthony's leadership was recognized with the issuance of the Susan B. Anthony dollar coin, the first coin intended for general circulation with the image of an American woman on it.

> **See also** Abolitionist Movement, Women in the; American Woman Suffrage Association; Bloomer, Amelia Jenks; Douglass, Frederick; Fifteenth Amendment; Fourteenth Amendment; Gage, Matilda Joslyn; Married Women's Property Acts; Minor v. Happersett; National American Woman Suffrage Association; National Woman Suffrage Association; Nineteenth Amendment; Stanton, Elizabeth Cady; Stone, Lucy; Suffrage; Temperance Movement, Women in the; Woodhull, Victoria Claflin

References Barry, *Susan B. Anthony: A Biography of a Singular Feminist* (1988).
Document Susan B. Anthony, "Speech after Being Convicted of Voting in the 1972 Presidential Election," 1873

Anti-lynching Movement

In the 1890s, African American women organized efforts to focus national attention on the crime of lynching and the racial hatred and mob violence that surrounded it. The crime most frequently occurred in the South, its victims were most frequently African American men, and its perpetrators were most frequently white men. The dominant myth surrounding lynching was that it was a form of vigilante justice exacted to punish a black man who had raped a white woman. Through the efforts of African American women, the myth was exposed and the truth that lynching and rape were unrelated was revealed.

African American journalist Ida B. Wells-Barnett, for example, researched the circumstances of more than 700 lynchings and publicized the lies and distortions used to justify the crime. Wells-Barnett's work, combined with that of Josephine St. Pierre Ruffin, Mary B. Talbert, Mary Church Terrell, and others, resulted in a decline in lynching that began in 1893 and continued for several years.

In 1921, the U.S. House of Representatives passed a federal anti-lynching bill, but the U.S. Senate refused to act on the measure. Talbert organized the Anti-Lynching Crusaders in 1922, an effort sponsored by the National Association for the Advancement of Colored People (NAACP), to involve one million women and raise $1 million. They did not reach their goals, but the publicity generated by the campaign may have contributed to the reduction in the number of lynchings after 1924.

For decades, African American women had tried to enlist white women in the crusade against lynching, but their pleas went largely unheeded. In 1930, however, Texan Jessie Daniel Ames emerged as a leader in the crusade. Her arguments against lynching echoed those that Wells-Barnett had made more than thirty years earlier. Ames explained that mob violence and lynching were not in retaliation for a black man raping a white woman but were an expression of racial hatred. Ames founded the Association of Southern Women for the Prevention of Lynching, mobilizing Southern women in the campaign. Unlike African American women, however, Ames opposed federal anti-lynching measures. Although a federal anti-lynching law was not passed, the efforts of these groups significantly altered public opinion. A 1942 Gallup poll showed that whites in the North and the South supported making lynching a federal crime.

See also Alpha Kappa Alpha Sorority; Ames, Jessie Harriet Daniel; Association of Southern Women for the Prevention of Lynching; National Association of Colored Women; Ruffin, Josephine St. Pierre; Terrell, Mary Eliza Church; Wells-Barnett, Ida Bell

References Giddings, *When and Where I Enter: The Impact of Black Women on Race and Sex in America* (1984).

Armstrong, Anne Legendre (b. 1927)

Republican feminist Anne Armstrong served as the first woman counselor to the president from 1973 to 1974, a Cabinet-level position in President Richard Nixon's administration. Armstrong established the first White House Office of Women's Programs, which served as a liaison between the Nixon administration and women's organizations and recruited women to high-level positions in the federal government. Armstrong also chaired the Federal Property Council, a group that reviewed policies regarding federal property and conflicting land use claims. She served on the Council on Wage and Price Stability and on the Domestic Council.

Born in New Orleans, Louisiana, Anne Armstrong earned her bachelor's degree from Vassar College in 1949, majoring in English. Following college, she worked for *Harper's Bazaar* as an assistant editor. She left the magazine when she married Tobin Armstrong, a Texas rancher.

Armstrong entered politics to support Democrat Harry Truman's 1948 presidential campaign and became a Republican after her marriage. She served as vice chair of the Texas Republican Party in 1966 and as national committeewoman for Texas from 1968 to 1973. In 1971, she became the Republican National Committee's first female co-chair, a position she used to encourage other feminists to become active in the party. At the party's 1972 national convention, she and other feminists obtained an agreement with the party that it would work to increase the number of women delegates to the 1976 Republican National Convention.

As the Watergate scandal developed in 1973 and 1974, Armstrong staunchly defended President Nixon. Only after the most incriminating evidence regarding Nixon's involvement in the cover-up became public did Armstrong join Senator Barry Goldwater in encouraging Nixon to resign. Armstrong retained her position when President Gerald Ford took office, but she resigned in December 1974 because of family health problems and returned to Texas. From 1976 to 1977, Armstrong was U.S. ambassador to the United Kingdom and chaired the president's Foreign Intelligence Advisory Board from 1981 to 1990.

See also Cabinets, Women in Presidential; Equal Rights Amendment; Republican Party, Women in the

References *The New York Times*, 6 January 1976; Schoenebaum, ed., *Political Profiles: The Nixon/Ford Years* (1979); Stineman, *American Political Women* (1980); www.lbjlib.utexas.edu/ford/library/faintro/armstro1.htm.

Ashbrook, (Emily) Jean Spencer (b. 1934)

Republican Jean Ashbrook of Ohio served in the U.S. House of Representatives from 29 June 1982 to 3 January 1983. Her husband, John M. Ashbrook, had served eleven terms in the U.S. House when he died in April 1982. At the request of Ohio governor James M. Rhodes, Jean Ashbrook entered the special primary to complete her husband's term and won the primary and general elections. Because reapportionment and redistricting following the 1980 census eliminated the district, Jean Ashbrook did not run for re-election.

Born in Cincinnati, Ohio, Jean Ashbrook earned her bachelor of science degree at Ohio State University in 1956.

See also Congress, Women in

References Office of the Historian, U.S. House of Representatives , *Women in Congress, 1917–1990* (1991).

Association of Southern Women for the Prevention of Lynching

Founded by Jessie Daniel Ames in 1930, the Association of Southern Women for the Prevention of Lynching (ASWPL) linked mob violence and racial hatred to the concerns of women and helped reduce occurrences of the crime. The ASWPL emerged from and was financed by the Council on Interracial Cooperation, a group that worked to end lynching. The crime had declined until 1929, but escalated in 1930.

In November 1930, twenty-six women representing several civic and religious organizations from seven Southern states met to discuss the resurgence of lynching and ways that women could end the crime. Eleven of the women agreed on the following statement: "Lynching is an indefensible crime, destructive of all principles of government, hateful and hostile to every ideal of religion and humanity, debasing and degrading to every person involved. Though lynchings are not confined to any section of the United States, we [Southerners] are aroused by the record which discloses our heavy responsibility for the presence of this crime in our country."

The ASWPL had two primary strategies. One involved disseminating facts and information about lynching, particularly to refute the myth that the crime was committed in retribution for an attack on a white woman, especially rape. The ASWPL also sought pledges from private citizens, governors, sheriffs, and other government officials that they opposed lynching and would act against it. The 37,267 people who had signed cards by 1937 provided notice to potential lynchers that the crime would no longer be ignored. In addition, when ASWPL members learned of a potential lynching, they notified public officials and members in the area with the hope of preventing the crime.

The southern women who endeavored to stop lynching worked in a culture that accepted lynching and rejected women's political activism. Jessie Daniel Ames sidestepped these obstacles by developing the ASWPL through traditional women's organizations, particularly Protestant missionary societies. By involving women in this way, the ASWPL provided a path for Southern women's political activism in an era when many Southerners considered it degrading for women to be openly political.

Ames refused to support federal anti-lynching legislation, which was seen as one of the most direct approaches to ending lynching. A strong states' rights advocate, Ames believed moral persuasion was the preferred approach. Her adamant stand on the issue separated the ASWPL from African American organizations working to end lynching. Some ASWPL state affiliates, however, supported a federal measure. Although no federal measure was ever signed into law, lynching decreased in the 1940s, and ASWPL dissolved in 1942.

See also Ames, Jessie Harriet Daniel; Anti-lynching Movement

References Miller, *The Ladies and the Lynchers: A Look at the Association of Southern Women for the Prevention of Lynching* (1978).

Atkinson, Ti-Grace (b. 1939)

In the 1960s and 1970s, radical feminist theorist Ti-Grace Atkinson repeatedly challenged feminists to structure organizations and to conduct themselves in ways that did not perpetuate women's oppression of other women. A leader in the National Organization for Women (NOW), a founder of the Feminists, and an active member of other feminist groups, she resigned from them when she concluded that they were not ful-filling feminist goals.

Born in Baton Rouge, Louisiana, Atkinson grew up in an affluent family that trav-eled extensively. As a result of her family's mobility, she attended more than fifteen different schools in the United States and Europe by the time she married at the age of seventeen. When her husband entered military service, Atkinson enrolled at the Uni-versity of Pennsylvania, where she earned her bachelor of fine arts degree. She became a critic for *Art News* and, in 1964, a founder and the first director of the Institute of Contemporary Art in Philadelphia.

Having read Simone de Beauvoir's *The Second Sex* in 1962, she sought to expand her understanding of the ideas offered in it. She wrote to de Beauvoir, who suggested she contact Betty Friedan, who had published *The Feminine Mystique* in 1963. With Friedan's encouragement, Atkinson joined NOW in 1967, serving as president of the New York chapter and as fundraiser for the national organization. Her insistence that NOW discuss the controversial issues of abortion and the inequalities in marriage made members uncomfortable. In 1968, Atkinson left NOW when the New York group refused to accept her recommendations for reorganizing its structure. She an-nounced that some feminists wanted to create the opportunity to become oppressors, whereas others wanted to end oppression.

Later in 1968, Atkinson helped found the Feminists, a radical group that shared her belief in sharing skills and rotating creative and routine assignments. In 1971, how-ever, the group decided that individual members should not speak to the press with-out consent from all the members. In protest, Atkinson resigned from the Feminists.

Atkinson published *Amazon Odyssey* in 1974. The collection of speeches and essays included her thoughts on abortion, the myth of vaginal orgasm, lesbianism, feminism, prostitution, pornography, and violence. By then, the radical feminist movement in the United States was suffering from internal dissension and had begun to splinter.

Atkinson taught women's studies at Western Washington University from 1976 to 1978 and then for a year at the University of Washington. Next, she taught at Parsons School of Design for ten years. Atkinson has written about 200 papers and has worked with other women on a project collecting material on radical feminism.

See also Beauvoir, Simone Lucie Ernestine Marie Bertrand de; *The Feminine Mystique*; Friedan, Betty Naomi Goldstein; National Organization for Women

References DeLeon, ed., *Leaders from the 1960s: A Biographical Sourcebook of American Activism* (1994).

Avery, Byllye Yvonne Reddick (b. 1937)

"It took the death of a person I loved and thought was healthy to turn my attention to the issue of health," Byllye Avery wrote. The founding president of the National Black Women's Health Project, Avery began her professional career as an occupational and recreational aide, later working with emotionally disturbed children and as a teacher in a children's mental health unit.

Born in Waynesville, Georgia, Avery had earned her bachelor of arts degree in psy-chology at Talladega College in 1959 and her MEd degree in special education at the University of Florida in 1969. Following the death of her husband in 1970, she turned her attention to health issues, particularly black women's health. She acted on her interest in 1976, taking out personal loans and soliciting donated equipment to found, with a small group of women, the Gainesville Women's Health Center, and served as its director of education. Two years later, she was a cofounder and director of public relations for Birthplace: An Alternative Birth Environment.

Avery led the planning for the first National Health Conference on Black Women's Health Issues, held in 1983. Avery identified the oppressions that affected black women's health, including racism, sexism, and classism. She wrote: "In this way, we saw that our efforts to promote our health–to take control of our lives and support each other to do the same–were clearly political in nature."

Avery promotes the importance of women taking one hour a day for themselves, and of walking, saying that walking enhances health and provides time for solitude. She received a MacArthur Foundation "Genius" Fellowship Award in 1989, and wrote *An Altar of Words: Wisdom, Comfort and Inspiration for African American Women* in 1998.

References Byllye Avery, "Who Does the Work of Public Health?" *American Journal of Public Health*, April 1, 2002; *The New York Times*, June 13, 1999; http://medstat.med.utah.edu/symposium/speakers/curriculumvitaebyllye.pdf.

B

Baca, Pauline Celia (Polly) (b. 1941)

Hispanic American civil rights activist Pauline Baca has served as special assistant to President Bill Clinton, director of the U.S. Office of Consumer Affairs from 1993 to 1994, and regional administrator of the General Services Administration, Rocky Mountain Region VII, from 1994 to 1998. Baca entered politics in 1967 as public information officer for the Interagency Committee on Mexican Americans, the first Cabinet-level committee on opportunities for Spanish-speaking people. From 1968 to 1970, Baca served as director of research services and information for the Southwest Council of La Raza, which later became the National Council of La Raza. She next worked as the first director of the Democratic National Committee's Division of Spanish-Speaking Affairs and special assistant to the party's chair.

Baca won a seat in the Colorado House of Representatives in 1974 and served until 1979. She introduced and passed legislation related to housing, consumer protection, bilingual and bicultural education, child abuse, and other areas. She became the first Hispanic American elected to the Colorado State Senate in 1978, where she served until 1987, and when she was elected chair of the Colorado Senate Democratic Caucus, she became the first Hispanic woman to serve in a leadership position in any state senate in the United States. In 1980, she was also the first Hispanic woman nominated by a major party for the U.S. House of Representatives, but she lost that election as well as one in 1986. She served on the Democratic National Committee (DNC) from 1973 to 1989 and was vice chair of the DNC from 1981 to 1989.

Born in La Salle, Colorado, Baca was orphaned when she was a teenager, leaving her to raise her three younger brothers alone. With the help of a scholarship, she earned her bachelor's degree from Colorado State University in 1962 and did postgraduate work at American University from 1966 to 1967.

See also Democratic Party, Women in the; State Legislatures, Women in

References Baca, "Seasons of a Life" in Nancy Neuman, ed., *True to Ourselves* (San Francisco: Jossey-Bass Publishers, 1998), pp. 154–168; Hardy, *American Women Civil Rights Activists* (1993).

Bachur v. Democratic National Committee (1987)

Beginning in the late 1960s, the Democratic Party sought ways to encourage more women to become delegates to its national conventions and established guidelines for affirmative action to accomplish the goal. Several commissions studied the problem of women's underrepresentation at the national conventions, resulting in the adoption of the Equal Division Rule at the 1976 Democratic National Convention to promote affirmative action in the selection of delegates for the 1980 national convention. The same rules applied for the selection of delegates for the 1984 and 1988 conventions.

Maryland Democrat Nicholas Bachur challenged the rule in 1987, saying that its requirement that he allocate his votes based on the candidates' sex infringed on his fundamental right to vote. The district court that heard the case agreed with Bachur and placed an injunction on the implementation of the rule. The appeals court, however, decided that the rule did not unconstitutionally infringe on the right to vote for delegates, saying that the Equal Division Rule had a rational purpose–to broaden the base of the party.

See also Affirmative Action; Democratic Party, Women in the

References *Bachur v. Democratic National Committee*, 836 F.2d 837 (4th Cir. 1987); Boyle, "Affirmative Action in the Democratic Party: An Analysis of the Equal Division Rule" (1991).

Baker, Ella Josephine (1903–1986)

African American civil rights organizer Ella Baker played key roles in the National Association for the Advancement of Colored People (NAACP), the Southern Christian Leadership Conference (SCLC), the Student Nonviolent Coordinating Committee (SNCC), and the Mississippi Freedom Democratic Party (MFDP). Throughout her years of activism, Baker envisioned the development of civil rights organizations that arose from the grassroots and became mass organizations without a structured hierarchy. She protested the moderate, charismatic, and male leadership of NAACP and SCLC, believing it limited the ability of poor people, women, and youth to influence those organizations. She saw an opportunity in 1960 to create a grassroots democratic organization and guided the founding of SNCC.

Born in Norfolk, Virginia, the granddaughter of slaves, Ella Baker earned her bachelor's degree from Shaw University in Raleigh, North Carolina, in 1927. Baker's commitment to grassroots organizations emerged from her work as a writer on and teacher of consumer issues and as a founder of the Young Negroes Cooperative League in the early 1930s. Working in the New Deal's Works Progress Administration in New York, Baker encountered a wide range of radical ideas, reinforcing her belief in achieving social change through organizing people to solve their problems for themselves.

In 1938 she joined the NAACP as an assistant field secretary, traveling thousands of miles a year, primarily in the South, where she encountered the indignities of segregation, particularly when she traveled on trains. She believed that by working together, African Americans could improve their lives; told local NAACP branches that they needed to focus their efforts on local issues; and suggested that they form neighborhood units in order to take the NAACP's message closer to the people for whom it was intended. Director of all of the NAACP's branches from 1943 to 1946, she resigned out

Ella Jo Baker, founder of the Southern Christian Leadership Conference (University of Mississippi)

of frustration with the NAACP's refusal to transform its hierarchical structure into a more democratic one. She also felt that the organization fell short of its potential and that the staff's abilities, including her own, were not adequately used. Baker continued her work speaking at NAACP branch meetings, working for school desegregation, and raising money for the Urban League and the Salvation Army.

In 1956, Baker went to Montgomery, Alabama, to help with the bus boycott and saw the opportunity to make further progress toward the end of racial injustice. Calling on Southern black leaders to expand their desegregation efforts, she convinced such leaders as Martin Luther King, Jr. to participate in the development of the SCLC, which was founded in 1957 in large part due to her efforts. She hoped to create a mass organization and was disappointed when there were not leadership roles in it for women, even those who had been leaders and organizers in the bus boycott. Baker became acting executive director of SCLC in 1959, a post she held until 1961.

Early in 1960, when students at several traditionally black colleges protested segregation through sit-ins, Baker saw an opportunity to organize them and called a meeting of the student leaders to help coordinate their efforts. The meeting led to the formation of SNCC, a grassroots, democratic, decentralized organization based on the principles she had advocated for almost three decades. She explained her philosophy: "Most of the youngsters had been trained to believe in or to follow adults if they could. I felt they ought to have a chance to learn to think things through and to make decisions." Serving as mentor and teacher, Baker worked to develop new leaders from the local populace, organizing workshops, study groups, and training institutes. When SNCC activists were jailed and refused bail, Baker made sure they had necessities such as toothbrushes and that they had told their parents where they were.

As the 1964 Democratic National Convention approached, members of SNCC, Baker, Fannie Lou Hamer, and other civil rights leaders formed the MFDP to counter

Mississippi's all-white delegation to the convention. Confronting the Democratic Party with the discrimination evident in the white delegation, Baker and others urged the party to replace the all-white delegation with the MFDP group. Although unsuccessful at the convention, their efforts contributed to the Democratic Party's subsequent reforms in its delegate selection process. She described her role: "You didn't see me on television, you didn't see news stories about me. The kind of role that I tried to play was to pick up the pieces or put together pieces out of which I hoped organization might come. My theory is, strong people don't need strong leaders." In the 1970s, SNCC slowly withered away as its activists grew tired from the intense work they had done for years. Baker remained active in social justice issues, particularly prison reform.

See also Civil Rights Movement, Women in the; Hamer, Fannie Lou Townsend; Parks, Rosa Louise McCauley

References Grant, *Ella Baker: Freedom Bound* (1998).

Baker, Irene Bailey (1901–1994)

Republican Irene Baker of Tennessee served in the U.S. House of Representatives from 10 March 1964 to 3 January 1965. She entered politics by working in her husband Howard Baker's congressional campaigns. In 1960, she became the Republican National Committeewoman for Tennessee, serving until 1964. Following her husband's death, Baker won the special election to fill the vacancy. Congresswoman Baker advocated cost-of-living increases for Social Security recipients and criticized Democratic spending policies, arguing that they risked causing inflation. She did not run for re-election. After leaving Congress, Irene Baker moved to Knoxville, Tennessee, where she was director of public welfare from 1965 to 1971.

Born in Sevierville, Tennessee, Baker attended public schools and studied music. She was first deputy county court clerk and then deputy clerk for Sevier County, Tennessee, from 1918 to 1924.

See also Congress, Women in

References Office of the Historian, U.S. House of Representatives , *Women in Congress, 1917–1990* (1991).

Balch, Emily Greene (1867–1961)

Emily Greene Balch's careers included social work, a position teaching economics at the college level, and international political leadership. She opposed the use of force and proposed nonviolent ways to resolve conflicts. She proposed replacing traditional governments with authorities, as she called them, to administer international waterways, the polar regions, defense bases, and other territories and facilities. In recognition of her efforts, she was one of two co-winners of the Nobel Peace Prize in 1946.

Born in Jamaica Plain, Massachusetts, Balch earned her bachelor's degree from Bryn Mawr College in 1889 and then studied economics and the French social welfare system in Paris. A social worker with the Children's Aid Society in Boston for a short time, Balch cofounded Boston's Denison House Settlement in 1892, was a founder of the Women's Trade Union League, worked with the National Consumers League, and helped draft the first minimum wage bill ever presented to a U.S. legislature.

In the 1900s and 1910s, Balch taught economics, political science, and social science at Wellesley College. She was dismissed for her opposition to World War I, defense of conscientious objectors' civil liberties, and other anti-war activities. Balch viewed World War I as "a tragic interruption of what seemed to me the real business of our times–the realization of a more satisfactory economic order.... Now all the world was at war, one hardly knew for what–for reasons of ambition, prestige, mutual fear, of frontiers and colonies." In 1915, she joined Jane Addams in calling a conference that resulted in the creation of the Woman's Peace Party, which later became the U.S. affiliate of the Women's International League for Peace and Freedom (WILPF). She also went to a meeting of European and American women at The Hague to discuss options for mediating a peaceful settlement of the war. Balch was a member of one of the two delegations that called on leaders of both neutral and belligerent nations to ask if they wanted a mediated settlement of the war.

A leader in the creation of the WILPF in 1919 and its first secretary-treasurer, she developed many of WILPF's initial priorities and guidelines. Through WILPF, she influenced the development of the League of Nations. After retiring in 1922, Balch continued to be involved in peace issues as a volunteer, traveling, speaking, writing, serving on committees, organizing conferences, and accompanying international missions investigating conflicts. She was president of the U.S. section of WILPF from 1928 to 1933.

As World War II developed in Europe, Balch's responses were somewhat different than they had been to World War I. Her work with Jewish refugees convinced her that German leader Adolf Hitler needed to be stopped. She later explained: "When the war broke out in its full fury in 1939, and especially when, after the disaster at Pearl Harbor, the U.S.A. became a belligerent, I went through a long and painful mental struggle, and never felt that I had reached a clear and consistent conclusion." She thought that any government "would have found it impossible to refuse to fight" after the Japanese attack on Pearl Harbor and believed that the answer would have been to have an effective "technique for constructive nonviolent action, such as Gandhi aimed at."

Balch's writings include *Public Assistance of the Poor in France* (1893); *A Study of Conditions of City Life, with Special References to Boston* (1903); *Our Slavic Fellow-Citizens* (1910); *Approaches to the Great Settlement* (1918); and *The Miracle of Living* (1941).

See also Addams, Jane; National Consumers League; Women's International League for Peace and Freedom; Women's Trade Union League

References Alonso, "Nobel Peace Laureates, Jane Addams and Emily Greene Balch" (1995); H. W. Wilson, *Current Biography 1947* (1947); Randall, *Beyond Nationalism: The Social Thought of Emily Greene Balch* (1972).

Baldwin, Tammy (b. 1962)

Democrat Tammy Baldwin of Wisconsin entered the U.S. House of Representatives on 3 January 1999. She is the first woman elected to Congress who has publicly stated that she is a lesbian, and was the only one of four lesbians running for Congress in 1998 who won. She is also the first woman to represent Wisconsin in Congress. Baldwin's congressional priorities include health insurance coverage for all children; a patient's

Congresswoman Tammy Baldwin is the first woman to serve in the
House of Representatives from Wisconsin
(Courtesy Office of Tammy Baldwin)

bill of rights that health insurance companies and health maintenance organizations (HMOs) would be required to follow; strengthening enforcement of equal pay laws; and education, including nutrition programs, expansion of Head Start, and increased use of computer technology.

Congresswoman Baldwin has worked to expand programs to end violence against women, to enact bankruptcy protection for farmers, and to implement changes in the USA PATRIOT Act to protect civil liberties. She has also introduced legislation to guarantee health care for all. Her other priorities include reducing the price of prescription drugs for seniors, protecting the environment, supporting and assisting veterans, and creating a balanced energy program. In the 106th Congress (1999–2001), Baldwin worked with a Republican colleague on the Violence Against Women Act to gain approval of $10 million to assist disabled victims of domestic violence. In the 108th Congress (2003–2005), she worked with another Republican colleague to extend the Chapter 12 farm bankruptcy law.

Born in Madison, Wisconsin, Baldwin earned her bachelor's degree from Smith College in 1984 and her law degree from the University of Wisconsin in 1989. A member of the Dane County Board of Supervisors from 1987 to 1993, she established and chaired the Dane County Task Force on acquired immunodeficiency syndrome (AIDS). Baldwin served in the Wisconsin legislature from 1993 until her election to Congress.

See also Congress, Women in; Lesbian Rights; State Legislatures, Women in

References *Congressional Quarterly*, "Politics in America 2006" (2005); "Tammy Baldwin" (1998); www.tammybaldwin.com; http://www.ksg.harvard.edu/citizen/Nov01/acei1101.html.

Bañuelos, Romana Acosta (b. 1925)

Appointed by President Richard Nixon in 1971, Romana Bañuelos was the first Mexican American to serve as treasurer of the United States. The highest-ranking Mexican American in the Nixon administration, she held the position until 1974.

Born in Miami, Arizona, Romana Bañuelos was the daughter of undocumented Mexican citizens who were forced to return to Mexico in 1931. Bañuelos returned to the United States when she was nineteen years old. In 1949, she started a tortilla factory in Los Angeles with $400 and developed it into a business with annual sales of $12 million. She helped establish the Pan American National Bank in 1965, and served as chair of its board of directors.

References Telgen and Kamp, eds., *Notable Hispanic American Women* (1993).

Barnard, Catherine (Kate) Ann (1875–1930)

Corrections reformer and advocate for Native Americans, Catherine Barnard is often identified as the first woman elected to statewide office in the nation, but that distinction belongs to Laura J. Eisenhuth of North Dakota, who was the state superintendent of public instruction in the 1890s. Barnard served as Oklahoma commissioner of charities and corrections from 1908 to 1912.

Barnard entered the political arena in 1903, working as assistant to the chief clerk of the Democratic caucus of the Oklahoma territorial legislature. Through her job, she came to know many of the territory's leading politicians and learned the legislative and political processes, knowledge that later helped her influence the development of the Oklahoma state constitution.

In 1904, Barnard was the hostess and secretary for the territory's pavilion at the St. Louis World's Fair, an experience that exposed her to the problems of urbanization, including child labor and unsafe working conditions. As Oklahoma territory prepared to write its state constitution, Barnard saw an opportunity to protect children and workers through the new document. She worked with social reformers and unions to include mandatory school attendance and prohibitions against child and convict labor. In 1906, she organized the Oklahoma City Child Labor League, as well as similar groups in other communities, to create a broad base of support for the constitutional agenda. With this informal coalition of reformers, unions, and child labor groups, Barnard coordinated a campaign to obtain pledges of support from candidates seeking to be constitutional convention delegates. Barnard's coalition succeeded in electing their candidates, with seventy of the 112 convention delegates supporting their agenda. The proposed constitution included the prohibition against child labor as well as provisions sought by unions.

Barnard also successfully lobbied for the inclusion of an elected commissioner of charities and corrections in the proposed constitution. In 1907, when Oklahoma women could not vote, Barnard sought the position, campaigned for it, and won it in the general election.

As commissioner, Barnard investigated the treatment of Oklahoma convicts who were incarcerated in Kansas and reported the appalling conditions in which they lived, resulting in prison reform in Kansas and the construction of prisons in Oklahoma. Barnard also investigated reports that Native American orphans had been defrauded by their white guardians, resulting in the return of $950,000 to 1,361 minors. Her success in such a politically unpopular endeavor cost her significant support and essentially ended her political career. Her political friends deserted her, and the legislature reduced the appropriations to her agency. During her two terms in office, Barnard also instituted reforms in mental health care, widows' pensions, union blacklisting, labor legislation, prison reform, and compulsory education. She did not run for a third term. Despite her successes as a candidate and politician, Barnard did not support woman suffrage, arguing that she had not needed it to accomplish her goals.

Born in Geneva, Nebraska, Catherine Barnard graduated from St. Joseph's Academy, a parochial high school in Oklahoma City, and later took a business course.

> **References** Bryant, "Kate Barnard, Organized Labor, and Social Justice in Oklahoma during the Progressive Era" (1969); Hardy, *American Women Civil Rights Activists* (1993).

Barshefsky, Charlene (b. 1949)

Charlene Barshefsky served as U.S. trade representative (USTR) from 1997 to 2001. She held the rank of ambassador extraordinary and plenipotentiary and was a member of President Clinton's Cabinet. She had earlier served as deputy U.S. trade representative in 1993 and as acting trade representative from 1996 to 1997. A key policymaker in and negotiator of an agreement with Japan to increase U.S. business opportunities in that country, Barshefsky also negotiated landmark intellectual property rights agreements with China that required it to close illegal compact disc and software factories. In addition, she opened markets for U.S. agricultural products, boosting beef exports to South Korea and fresh produce exports to Japan and China. Barshefsky has also worked to increase world trade in technology.

Born in Chicago, Charlene Barshefsky graduated from the University of Wisconsin in 1972 and received her law degree from the Columbus School of Law at Catholic University in 1975. Barshefsky specialized in international trade law and policy for eighteen years while working for a private law firm.

> **See also** Cabinets, Women in Presidential
> **References** www.ustr.gov/people/Ambassador/barshefsky.html.

Bass, Charlotta Spears (1880–1969)

Newspaperwoman Charlotta Spears Bass was the first African American woman candidate for vice president of the United States, running on the Progressive Party ticket in 1952. Bass entered politics in the 1910s as a civil rights advocate in Los Angeles, crusading through the pages of *The California Eagle*, the newspaper for which she was managing editor and that her husband Joseph Bass edited. She battled against the movie *Birth of a Nation*, the Ku Klux Klan, employment discrimination, and housing restrictions that prohibited African Americans from living in certain neighborhoods. She supported a permanent fair employment practices committee, and efforts to organize waterfront workers. She also supported the nine African American boys accused of raping two white girls in 1931 in Scottsboro, Alabama. One girl later said that she had not been raped, but trials, appeals, and retrials lasted from 1931 to 1937 and prompted protests across the nation.

An active Republican, she unsuccessfully ran as an Independent for the Los Angeles City Council in 1945. As racial violence erupted after World War II, Bass concluded that neither of the two major parties intended to effectively address racial issues, and in 1948, she joined Henry A. Wallace's Progressive Party as a founding member. She unsuccessfully ran for Congress on the Progressive ticket in 1950 and was the party's vice presidential nominee. In the campaign in 1952, she advocated the end of the Cold War, a ceasefire in Korea, equal rights for minorities, and ending poverty in the United States.

Born in Sumter, South Carolina, Bass wrote her autobiography, *Forty Years: Memoirs from the Pages of a Newspaper*, in 1960.

See also Civil Rights Movement, Women in the; President and Vice President, Women Candidates for

References Sicherman and Green, eds., *Notable American Women: The Modern Period* (1980).

Bates, Daisy Lee Gatson (1920–1999)

African American journalist and civil rights activist Daisy Bates became a national figure in the 1950s as she worked to integrate the Little Rock, Arkansas public schools. Her courage and leadership helped sustain nine high school students and their families as white segregationist mobs attempted to defy the U.S. Supreme Court's 1954 directive in *Brown v. Board of Education of Topeka, Kansas* to integrate public schools. Despite violent episodes, including bombs thrown at her house and being hanged in effigy, that continued for years, Bates and the students ultimately prevailed and integrated the city's schools.

Born in Huttig, Arkansas, Daisy Bates attended segregated public schools and as an adult attended Shorter College and Philander Smith College. After she married L. C. Bates, the couple founded and edited a weekly newspaper, *Arkansas State Press*, in Little Rock in 1941. The next year, when a police officer murdered an African American soldier from a nearby military base, Daisy Bates reported the story and challenged local authorities to investigate it. Displeased with the article, white business owners withdrew their advertising from the newspaper, but Bates persisted, and the paper continued to expose police brutality. She added other issues to her list of objections to the community's racism, including muddy streets, slum housing, menial job opportunities, and injustice in the courtroom. The crusade resulted in the city's hiring of black police officers to patrol black neighborhoods and a reduction in police brutality. As the African American community came to realize that it had a voice in the newspaper, readership grew, and the paper survived.

Elected president of the Arkansas State Conference of the National Association for the Advancement of Colored People (NAACP) in 1952, Bates became involved in integration efforts in Little Rock following the 1954 U.S. Supreme Court decision making public school segregation illegal. The school board delayed implementation of integration plans but finally approved a three-phase plan that would first integrate high schools and then junior high schools, followed by elementary schools. The school district selected high school students to enroll in Central High School in the fall of 1957. To prepare them to attend an integrated school, Bates met with the students throughout the summer.

As the date for enrolling the students neared, racial tension in Little Rock increased. On 22 August 1957, a rock was thrown through the Bateses' living room window with a note saying: "Stone this time. Dynamite next." The following week, a court granted a temporary injunction to stop the proposed integration plan, but a higher court overturned the injunction. Arkansas governor Orval Faubus created the next obstacle to integration when he ordered the Arkansas National Guard to surround Central High on 2 September 1957, announcing that African American students were prohibited from entering it. On 3 September 1957, with a mob of white segregationists gathered at the school, white students entered Central High, but with the National Guard barring their entrance, the nine black students did not. Later in the day, a federal district judge ruled that desegregation would begin the next day. The presence of the mobs, however, alarmed Bates and others, who became even more concerned when school officials told the children's parents that they could not accompany their children to school. Fearing for the students' safety, Bates enlisted the help of area ministers, asking them to escort the students. Some ministers declined out of fear for their own safety, but two white and two black ministers agreed to help, even though they, too, were fearful. The plan was that the students would meet at the Bateses' home and then go to the school with the ministers. After the arrangements were finalized late at night, Bates called the students' parents, but Elizabeth Eckford's family did not have a phone. Bates planned to go to her home early in the morning, but other complications kept her from making the trip.

In the morning, eight of the students gathered, but Elizabeth Eckford, who did not know about the arrangements, went directly to Central High. A mob of 500 white segregationists surrounded her, yelling racist epithets at her and threatening her. Her dignity and courage camouflaged the intense fear she felt as she looked for an entrance through the line of National Guardsmen. Seeing some white students make their way through the line of guards, Eckford tried that route, but the guards held up their bayonets and prevented her from entering the grounds. As she sought refuge elsewhere, the mob surrounded her and continued to threaten her. A reporter helped her escape to a city bus. The other eight students accompanied by the ministers were also refused entrance.

On 20 September, the National Guard left Central High. On 23 September, the nine students met at the Bateses' home accompanied by the Little Rock police, who got the children into Central High. When the mob of 1,000 people that had once again gathered attacked the building, the children locked themselves in a schoolroom until they could safely leave. The mob spread throughout the city and randomly attacked any African American they found. With reporters and others, the Bateses waited out the night at their home, armed to protect themselves. On 24 September, President Dwight D. Eisenhower federalized the Arkansas National Guard to protect the children, accompany them from the Bateses' home to Central High, and return them to the

Bateses' home after school. The Guard remained on duty protecting the children until the spring of 1958. On 27 May 1958, one of the boys Daisy Bates had shepherded became the first African American to graduate from Central High.

Racists continued to harass and threaten Daisy and L. C. Bates, burning crosses in their yard and bombing their home. In addition, on 31 October 1957, the Little Rock City Council had ordered the arrest of Daisy Bates and other NAACP officials for their refusal to relinquish the organization's membership lists. Convicted, Bates appealed her case, and in 1960 the U.S. Supreme Court overturned her conviction in *Bates v. Little Rock*. The problems also extended to the Bateses' newspaper: their carriers were harassed and advertisers were threatened with violence. When white businesses refused to advertise in it, the Bateses closed their newspaper in 1959.

Bates continued her civil rights work, focusing on voter registration. In 1972, she founded "Bootstraps," which built a sewage system and improved health and educational services in Mitchelville, Arkansas. In 1984, Bates resumed publishing the *Arkansas State Press*, selling it in 1988.

At the ceremony commemorating the fortieth anniversary of the integration of Central High, Bates said: "I'm happy about what's happened, not just because of school integration but because of the total system."

In 2001, the Arkansas legislature honored Daisy Bates by designating the third Monday in February as a state holiday. Her home in Little Rock, Arkansas, is a National Historic Landmark.

See also Civil Rights Movement, Women in the

References Bates, *The Long Shadow of Little Rock* (1962); "Late Daisy Bates Honored by Arkansas with State Holiday," *Jet*, 12 March 2001, p. 34; *Los Angeles Times*, 5 November 1999.

Beal v. Doe (1977)

In *Beal v. Doe*, the U.S. Supreme Court decided that Pennsylvania's Medicaid program did not have to pay for nontherapeutic abortions, explaining that the program did not require the payments as a condition of participating in it. The Court noted that the state has a strong interest in encouraging normal childbirth and that it is reasonable for the state to further that interest by covering childbirth expenses and discouraging nontherapeutic abortions by refusing to cover them in the program. It also said that when Congress created Medicaid, nontherapeutic abortions were illegal in most states, thus refuting the idea that Congress intended to require states to pay for them.

See also Abortion; *Harris v. McRae*

References *Beal v. Doe*, 432 U.S. 438 (1977).

Bean, Melissa (b. 1962)

Democrat Melissa Bean of Illinois was sworn in as a member of the U.S. House of Representatives on 4 January 2005. When she won in 2004, she defeated 17-term incumbent Phil Crane by a margin of 9,043 votes in Illinois' most Republican congressional district. The 2004 race was the second time she had challenged Crane, who had defeated her in 2002.

Congresswoman Melissa Bean being sworn into office on January 4, 2005 (Courtesy U.S. House of Representatives)

Bean's congressional priorities include reducing health care costs and making it easier for small businesses to provide health care to their employees, attracting new businesses to her district, and opposition to oil drilling the Arctic National Wildlife Refuge. Pro-choice, she was endorsed by EMILY's List, the League of Conservation Voters, and other groups.

"My primary reason for entering politics was to create a better future for my children," Bean said referring to her two daughters. "Quality education, a safe environment, a growing economy, and affordable health care became even higher priorities for me after my children were born."

Before entering politics, Bean was a high-tech consultant, forming her own company in 1995. She earned her associate of arts degree from Oakton Community College in 1982 and her bachelor of arts degree in political science from Roosevelt University in 2002.

> **References** http://www.vote-smart.org/bio.php?can_id=MIL20905; https://secure1.emilyslist.org/; *Washington Post*, 4 November 2004; *Washington Times*, 14 March 2005.

Beauvoir, Simone Lucie Ernestine Marie Bertrand de (1908–1986)

French existentialist philosopher Simone de Beauvoir inspired the modern international feminist movement with her 1949 book, *The Second Sex*. Translated into seventeen languages, the book made her the most widely read feminist author in the world and brought her both acclaim and condemnation for its challenges to accepted roles for women. Published in the United States in 1953, *The Second Sex* had its greatest influence among U.S. feminists. A member of the French intellectual elite, de Beauvoir wrote: "One is not born, but rather becomes a woman. No biological, psychological or economic fate determines the figure that the human female presents in society; it is civilization as a whole that produces this creature, intermediate between male and eunuch, which is described as feminine." Arguing that men saw themselves as the subject and were the actors in their own lives and that women were objects and acted upon, she identified men as the normative human beings, "the One," and women as "the Other," or the second sex.

Although de Beauvoir's work did not spark the modern U.S. feminist movement, it influenced several U.S. feminists, including Kate Millett, Ti-Grace Atkinson, Gloria Steinem, and Betty Friedan. Widely read and debated at the time of its publication, *The Second Sex* did not attain its position as a fundamental feminist work for several years, when it became a basic text for women's studies programs.

Born in Paris, France, de Beauvoir graduated from the Sorbonne and then taught philosophy at French educational institutions. She left teaching in 1943 to write, producing both fiction and nonfiction. De Beauvoir and French philosopher Jean-Paul Sartre were lifelong partners in their intellectual pursuits and in their personal lives, although they never married.

See also Atkinson, Ti-Grace; Feminist Movement; Friedan, Betty Naomi Goldstein; Millett, Katherine (Kate) Murray; Steinem, Gloria Marie

References Francis and Gontier, *Simone de Beauvoir* (1987); *The New York Times*, 2 June 1974, 6 May 1984, 15 April 1986.

Bellamy, Carol (b. 1942)

Director of the Peace Corps from 1993 to 1995, Carol Bellamy was the first returned volunteer to head the Corps. She was executive director of the United Nations International Children's Emergency Fund (UNICEF) from 1995 to 2005, holding the rank of undersecretary-general. She restructured the organization for greater efficiency and cost-effectiveness the year she began serving as director of UNICEF. She also worked with governments to improve data collection, to provide measures of progress, and to identify needs.

Born in Plainfield, New Jersey, Bellamy received her bachelor's degree from Gettysburg College in 1963. A member of the Peace Corps from 1963 to 1965, she volunteered in Guatemala. In 2005, she said about her service in Guatemala: "I think that was the most important thing I ever did." While there, she decided she wanted to become involved in government and that she needed credentials, which led her to earning her law degree from New York University in 1968. Following law school, she became a corporate finance attorney. Bellamy served in the New York State Senate from 1973 to 1977 and was New York City Council president from 1978 to 1985, when she returned to the private sector.

See also State Legislatures, Women in

References David Arnold, "Beyond the Basics," *Worldview*, 1 April 2005, p. 11; *The New York Times*, 20 September 1977, 15 October 1993.

Bellotti v. Baird (1976, 1979)

Both *Bellotti v. Baird* decisions center on the state of Massachusetts's attempts to find a constitutionally acceptable avenue for requiring unmarried minor women to obtain parental consent before obtaining an abortion. In the first *Bellotti v. Baird* (1976), the U.S. Supreme Court decided that the district court had erred in ruling on the constitutionality of the Massachusetts law requiring parental consent because it should have waited until the state court had interpreted the law. The Court said that, in some circumstances, states may require a minor woman to obtain parental consent before having an abortion.

In the second *Bellotti v. Baird* (1979), the U.S. Supreme Court considered a Massachusetts law requiring an unmarried woman under the age of eighteen to obtain parental consent before she could have an abortion. If one or both parents refused, she could request an order from a superior court judge "for good cause shown." The Court said that the abortion decision differs from other decisions minors face and that the state needs to be particularly sensitive when it legislates parental involvement in the decision. The Court rejected the law. Four justices said it was not constitutional because a minor found to be mature and fully competent to make the decision independently could still be denied judicial authorization for an abortion and because the law required parental consultation or notification, whether or not it was in the minor's best interests. Four other justices rejected the law because no minor, regardless of her maturity and ability to make decisions, could obtain an abortion without the consent of either both parents or a judge, "thus making the minor's abortion decision subject in every instance to an absolute third-party veto."

See also Abortion; *Akron v. Akron Center for Reproductive Health*

References *Bellotti v. Baird*, 428 U.S. 132 (1976); *Bellotti v. Baird*, 443 U.S. 622 (1979).

Belmont, Alva Erskine Smith Vanderbilt (1853–1933)

President of the National Woman's Party (NWP) from its founding in 1921 until her death in 1933, Alva Belmont was a wealthy socialite who joined the suffrage movement in 1909 after hearing Anna Howard Shaw speak at a tea party. Two years later, she donated a house for the use of suffrage speakers and provided a building that allowed the National American Woman Suffrage Association (NAWSA) to move its headquarters from Ohio to New York City, a better location for a national political campaign. In addition, she made other substantial financial contributions to woman suffrage. Her homes in New York and Newport, Rhode Island, became centers of suffrage activity, the sites of meetings and planning retreats.

Introduced to the Congressional Union (CU) by Crystal Eastman, Belmont found the militant organization more suited to her personality than the NAWSA, joined the CU, and provided it with financial support. When the CU began its campaign to send women to suffrage states to organize women to vote against Democratic candidates in 1914, Belmont donated $5,000 to carry it out. In all, Belmont contributed over $1 million to the woman suffrage campaign.

After ratification of the Nineteenth Amendment in 1920, Belmont continued her commitment to women's rights through the NWP, the successor to the CU. Elected the first president of the NWP, Belmont held the position for the rest of her life. She purchased a mansion for the National Woman's Party's headquarters in Washington, D.C. Later named for her, it is now a national historic site.

Born in Mobile, Alabama, Belmont received most of her education in private schools in France.

See also Congressional Union; National American Woman Suffrage Association; National Woman's Party; Nineteenth Amendment; Paul, Alice; Suffrage

References Buell, *Alva Belmont: From Socialite to Feminist* (1990).

Benjamin, Medea (b. 1952)

Social activist and antiwar organizer Medea Benjamin cofounded Global Exchange in 1988 with her husband Kevin Danaher, and Code Pink in 2002 with Jodie Evans and Gael Murphy.

Through Global Exchange, Benjamin has conducted Reality Tours to Mexico, Cuba, Indonesia, Haiti, and other countries. The tours expose Americans to the working conditions of laborers in these countries, with the goal that the tourists will lobby their lawmakers, write letters to newspaper editors, and take other actions to remedy the low wages, unsafe working conditions, and other labor issues.

In 1999, Benjamin was an organizer for the Seattle, Washington protests against the World Trade Organization. She ran in California for the U.S. Senate as the Green Party's candidate in 2000.

On November 17, 2002, in Code Pink's first action, Benjamin and about 100 other women began a four-month vigil in front of the White House to protest the pre-emptive strike against Iraq. The organization's name plays on the Bush Administration's use of color-coded terrorism alert levels.

Benjamin's protests took another form during the 2004 Republican National Convention and the Democratic National Convention. With the intention of demonstrating against the war in Iraq, she found ways to gain access to the floors of both conventions, unfurl banners and interrupt the proceedings. She was arrested both times. She explained: "I felt that the issue of the war had to be brought up at both the Democratic and Republican conventions in any way we could."

Benjamin holds a master's degree in public health from Columbia University and a master's degree in economics from the New School for Social Research.

Benjamin has written several books, including *No Free Lunch: Food & Revolution in Cuba Today* (1986), *Bridging the Global Gap: A Handbook Linking Citizens of the First and Third Worlds* (1989), and *The Peace Corps and More: 175 Ways to Work, Study, and Travel at Home & Abroad* (1997). In addition, she is the coauthor of several books, including *Stop the Next War Now: Effective Responses to Violence and Terrorism* (2005).

References Los Angeles Times, June 23, 1997, February 15, 1998; *The Progressive*, December 1, 2004; http://www.codepink4peace.org/article.php?list=type&type=3.

Bentley, Helen Delich (b. 1923)

Republican Helen Bentley of Maryland served in the U.S. House of Representatives from 3 January 1985 to 3 January 1995. She entered politics as an adviser on maritime issues to 1968 Republican presidential candidate Richard Nixon. After his election, Nixon appointed Bentley chair of the Federal Maritime Commission, making her the highest-ranking woman in his administration at the time of her appointment. She held the chair until 1975, when she resigned and became a shipping company executive.

In 1980 and again in 1982, she unsuccessfully ran for the U.S. House of Representatives on the Republican ticket, winning in 1984. Congresswoman Bentley began her tenure in office emphasizing trade issues and the need for harbor dredging, especially to deepen Baltimore's harbor. In 1989, she volunteered her services as a mediator during a difficult strike at the Baltimore port and succeeded in helping resolve the differences between waterfront management and dockworkers.

In the late 1980s, Bentley became an adamant critic of Japan's trading practices, regularly lambasting that country. Blaming the loss of factory and harbor jobs on Japan's policies, she expressed frustration over the flood of Japanese imports. Her targets included the 1989 purchase of Columbia Pictures by Sony Corporation and the Japanese purchase of Pebble Beach golf course. In the early 1990s, Bentley, the daughter of Yugoslav immigrants, became an advocate for Serbia, her parents' native land. In 1991, she helped form SerbNet, a pro-Serb lobbying group, and served as its president until 1992. She did not run for re-election in 1994 but instead was a candidate for governor of Maryland. She was defeated in the Republican primary. Bentley unsuccessfully ran for Congress in 2002.

Born in Ruth, Nevada, Bentley wanted to be a lawyer, but the years of education seemed too long, and she chose her second interest, journalism. She attended the University of Nevada from 1941 to 1942, George Washington University in 1943, and received her bachelor's degree in journalism from the University of Missouri in 1944. Throughout high school and college, she gained experience in her field, working for various newspapers and United Press International.

In June 1945, she went to work for the *Baltimore Sun*, covering maritime, transportation, and labor stories. In addition to her newspaper work in the 1950s and 1960s, she produced weekly local television shows with maritime themes in Baltimore, Washington, D.C., and Philadelphia.

See also Congress, Women in

References *Congressional Quarterly, Politics in America 1994* (1993); H. W. Wilson, *Current Biography Yearbook, 1971* (1972); Office of the Historian, U.S. House of Representatives , *Women in Congress, 1917–1990* (1991); Treese, ed., *Biographical Directory of the American Congress 1774–1996* (1997).

Berkley, Shelley (b. 1951)

Democrat Shelley Berkley of Nevada entered the U.S. House of Representatives on 3 January 1999. She has fought against the proposed nuclear waste storage facility at Yucca Mountain in Nevada. After Congress passed legislation, in 2002, making Yucca Mountain a storage facility for nuclear waste, Berkley and other members of the Nevada delegation continued to fight, this time through the courts. A federal appeals court concluded that the plan for the storage facility was based upon faulty science. Berkley and her colleagues continued to work on the issue, intending to block legislation that would go around the court's decision. Berkley has vowed: "I will line up in front of the railroad ties to keep nuclear waste from going to Yucca Mountain."

Congresswoman Berkley opposes increased regulation or taxation of the gaming industry and has sought federal support for transportation projects and school construction to deal with the rapid population growth in Las Vegas. She supports expanded medical services for senior citizens, improvements in nursing home quality, and full medical services for qualified veterans. She co-chairs the Congressional Stop DUI Caucus, which will identify congressional tools to curb drunk driving. She has proposed federal loan guarantees for renewable energy projects.

Congresswoman Shelley Berkley has been serving Nevada's First Congressional District in the U.S. House of Representatives since 1999 and is currently in her fourth term. (Courtesy Office of Shelley Berkley)

After discovering that she had osteoporosis, Berkley successfully sponsored legislation to fund testing for the disease in Medicare and Medicaid recipients. "The trouble is that so many people don't know that they have the disease until they have a hip or spine fracture. And half of those [elderly people] who suffer fractures will die within a year," Berkley explained. She is working to obtain funding for a model program to demonstrate the benefits of having the testing done.

Born in New York, New York, Berkley earned her bachelor's degree at the University of Nevada at Las Vegas in 1972 and her law degree at the University of San Diego in 1976. She was deputy director of the Nevada State Commerce Department and vice president of government and legal affairs for the Sands Hotel. She served in the Nevada legislature from 1983 to 1985. Appointed to the University and Community College System of Nevada Board of Regents in 1990, she served for two full terms, completing her last term in 1998.

See also Congress, Women in; State Legislatures, Women in

References *Congressional Quarterly, Politics in America 2002* (2001), *Politics in America 2004* (2005), *Politics in America 2006* (2005);; *Las Vegas Review-Journal*, 16 August 2001; Ian Mylchreest, "Congresswoman Still Pushes for Bone Density Testing, *Las Vegas Business Press*, 9 August 2004, p. A5; "New Congressional Caucus to Address Drunk Driving," *NCADD Washington Report*, June 2004, p.1; "Shelley Berkley" (1998); www.shelleyberkley.com.

Berry, Mary Frances (b. 1938)

The first African American woman to serve as chief educational officer of the United States, Berry has protested legal and extralegal forms of racism, war, and racial, gender, and disability discrimination. A devoted advocate of social justice, she has offered thoughtfully reasoned and carefully articulated analyses of it.

Born in Nashville, Tennessee, Berry once described her early years as something close to a horror story, having spent part of her youth in an orphanage where she experienced cruelty and racial prejudice. A high school teacher who became her mentor prodded her to achieve, however, and Berry worked her way through college, often without any financial assistance. She earned her bachelor's degree in 1961 and her master's degree in 1962, both from Howard University. She received her doctoral degree in 1966 and her law degree in 1970, both from the University of Michigan.

Berry held teaching positions at Eastern Michigan University, the University of Michigan, and the University of Maryland, where she was acting director of the Afro-American studies programs from 1970 to 1972. She became the first African American woman to serve as president or chancellor of a major research university in 1976 when she became chancellor of the University of Colorado. Berry's research and writing reflect her academic interests. Her published works include *Black Resistance, White Law: A History of Constitutional Racism in America* (1971); *Military Necessity and Civil Rights Policy: Black Citizenship and the Constitution, 1861–1868* (1977); *Stability, Security, and Continuity: Mr. Justice Burton and Decision-Making in the Supreme Court, 1945–1958* (1978); and *Why ERA Failed: Politics, Women's Rights, and the Amending Process of the Constitution* (1986).

In 1977, Berry became the first African American woman to serve as assistant secretary for education in the U.S. Department of Health, Education, and Welfare. She advocated the creation of a separate department of education, created the Graduate and Professional Opportunities Program to expand opportunities for minorities and women, increased the budget for education of persons with disabilities, and implemented policies to enhance historically black colleges and universities.

In 1980, President Jimmy Carter appointed Berry to the U.S. Commission on Civil Rights, where she served as vice chair from 1980 to 1982. Four years later, President Ronald Reagan attempted to remove Berry and two other commissioners whose viewpoints were in conflict with his. Berry argued that Reagan wanted to change the commission from a "watchdog of civil rights" to "a lapdog for the administration." She explained: "Our job is to investigate and make recommendations to Congress and the President on what should be done to move us toward real economic opportunity.... The Commission is the conscience of the nation on civil rights." She believed that the president had "destroyed" the commission and that "they have taken it over so that they could use the wreckage for their own ends–to do studies that will prove that Blacks are to blame for our social and economic problems, that government has no role to play and that racial discrimination is insignificant." Berry successfully sued in federal court to retain her appointment to the commission. In 1993, President Bill Clinton appointed Berry chair of the Civil Rights Commission. Reappointed to a second six-year term in 1999, Berry resigned in 2004. During her tenure on the commission, it issued reports on several topics, including the 2000 Florida presidential elections, police practices in New York City, environmental justice, affirmative action, and conditions on Indian reservations.

With other civil rights activists, Berry cofounded the Free South Africa Movement (FSAM) in 1984. On the day before Thanksgiving that year, she participated in an anti-apartheid demonstration outside the South African embassy and was arrested. Every day for the next year, a picket line that included celebrities formed in front of the embassy, arrests were occasionally made, and a press conference followed. The organization spread across the country, and colleges, universities, and cities divested themselves of holdings in companies that did business in South Africa. Apartheid ended in that country in the 1990s.

From 1980 until 1989, Berry was a professor of history and law at Howard University. President of the Organization of American Historians from 1990 to 1991, she became the Geraldine R. Segal professor of social thought and professor of history at the University of Pennsylvania in 1991.

Berry's book *The Politics of Parenthood: Child Care, Women's Rights, and the Myth of the Good Mother* (1993) explores the history of families and child care responsibilities. She wrote: "The issue of child care is really an issue of power, resources and control among adults; it is not a battle over who is more suited to care." She argues that, historically, child care was not the sole responsibility of mothers. The central civil rights message Berry worked to articulate is that until mothers are freed from the primary responsibility of raising children, they will not be able to pursue their own economic or other interests.

Berry's deep commitment to social justice can be heard in her statement: "When it comes to the cause of justice, I take no prisoners and I don't believe in compromising."

See also Affirmative Action; Child Day Care

References Barthel, "Mary Frances Berry" (1987); DeLeon, ed., *Leaders from the 1960s* (1994); Hardy, *American Women Civil Rights Activists* (1993); http://www.maryfrancesberry.com; www.usccr.gov.

Bethune, Mary Jane McLeod (1875–1955)

One of the most influential African American women of her time, Mary McLeod Bethune founded the National Council of Negro Women, the Federal Council on Negro Affairs, and Daytona Normal and Industrial Institute, which later became Bethune-Cookman College. In 1936, she became the first black woman to head a federal agency, serving in President Franklin D. Roosevelt's administration.

Born near Mayesville, South Carolina, Mary McLeod Bethune did not attend school until she was about nine years old because there were no schools in the area for African American children. In addition, her parents, who were former slaves, did not read or write. She attended the Presbyterian Mission School, about five miles from her home, until she was twelve, when she left home to study at Scotia Seminary, graduating in 1894. When she completed her studies, she entered the Moody Bible Institute for Home and Foreign Missions in Chicago, Illinois, to prepare to be a missionary. For reasons that are unclear, she was denied an assignment to a mission, but racism may have played a role. The denomination may have had an unwritten policy of not sending African American missionaries to Africa. Instead, Bethune taught at schools in Georgia and Florida.

In 1904, she moved to Daytona Beach, Florida, which had a large black population and no public education for black students. With only $1.50 to start the school, she raised the money needed to open a private school for African American girls by speaking at churches and other gatherings. The Daytona Normal and Industrial Institute for Negro Girls opened on 3 October 1904 with five girls. Within two years, 250 students attended the college and adult evening classes that the school offered. A high school was added later. Bethune supported the school through public appearances and by soliciting funds from friends and philanthropists. As she described it: "I rang doorbells and tackled cold prospects without a lead. I wrote articles for whoever would print them, distributed leaflets, rode interminable miles of dusty roads on my old bicycle; invaded churches, clubs, lodges, chambers of commerce."

In 1923, the school merged with the all-male Cookman Institute and became the Daytona Cookman Collegiate Institute. In 1924, a junior college curriculum was added, which was accredited in 1932. In 1933, the school became Bethune-Cookman College, adding a four-year degree program in 1943, which received accreditation in 1948. Bethune served as president until 1942 and from 1946 to 1947.

In addition to providing educational opportunities for African Americans, Bethune was actively involved in civil rights issues. She was a founder of the Commission on Interracial Cooperation in 1919, and after the passage of woman suffrage in 1920, she headed a voter registration drive despite threats from the Ku Klux Klan.

President of the Florida Federation of Colored Women from 1917 to 1924, the state affiliate of the National Association of Colored Women (NACW), Bethune founded and was president of the Southeastern Federation of Colored Women in 1920 and was president of the NACW from 1924 to 1928. In 1935, she founded the National Council of Negro Women (NCNW), a coalition of twenty-nine black women's organizations. As president of the organization, Bethune testified before congressional committees regarding federal aid to education, the Fair Employment Practices Act, the General Housing Act, and agricultural policies. The organization addressed women's issues, education, health, and international relations. NCNW worked for the integration of black women in the Women's Army Corps during World War II and held employment clinics to address the needs of black women in defense industries. The group held a war bond drive to finance a Liberty ship named for abolitionist Harriet Tubman. Bethune retired from the presidency in 1949. President of the Association for the Study of Negro Life and History from 1936 to 1951, Bethune organized a Museum-Archives Department in the NCNW in 1938. From 1940 to 1944, Bethune was vice president of the National Association for the Advancement of Colored People and of the National Urban League.

At a meeting of the National Council of Women of the United States, Bethune met Eleanor Roosevelt and began a long friendship with her and President Franklin D. Roosevelt. The friendship that developed between the two women became increasingly important as Bethune entered public service during President Roosevelt's administration. Bethune regularly called upon Eleanor Roosevelt to use her influence on the president and on other administration officials on behalf of programs and projects for which Bethune needed support.

Through Eleanor Roosevelt's influence, President Roosevelt appointed Bethune to serve on the National Advisory Committee of the National Youth Administration (NYA) in 1935. Roosevelt appointed her director of the Division of Negro Affairs in the NYA in 1936, making her the only African American woman in Roosevelt's administration and the first to hold a major federal appointment. She served until the National Youth Administration disbanded in 1944. One of the highest-placed African Americans in the Roosevelt administration, Bethune held considerable power and influence.

Through the Federal Council on Negro Affairs, which she founded in 1936, black government officials worked to advance African Americans in government jobs, secure job training funds, and advise the government on racial issues, including support for anti-lynching legislation and voting rights legislation. Known as the Black Cabinet, it provided a conduit for information between African Americans and the Roosevelt administration and influenced legislation. The group worked to end discrimination and segregation in the federal government and played an instrumental role in obtaining Roosevelt's 1941 executive order banning racial discrimination in government jobs and defense industries.

In 1937, Bethune organized the National Conference on the Problems of the Negro and Negro Youth at the Department of Labor. The conference, which brought together the NCNW, the Black Cabinet, and national leaders, called for a federal anti-lynching law, equal access to the ballot in federal elections, open housing, an equitable share of federal education funds, and an end to discrimination in the military. In 1941, she secured seats for African American women on the War Department's advisory council on women, and she served as a delegate to the founding conference of the United Nations in 1945.

Toward the end of her career, Bethune said: "The drums of Africa still beat in my heart. They will not let me rest while there is still a single Negro boy or girl without a chance to prove his worth."

See also Civil Rights Movement, Women in the; National Association of Colored Women; National Council of Negro Women; Tubman, Harriet

References H. W. Wilson, *Current Biography 1942* (1942); Perkins, "The Pragmatic Idealism of Mary McLeod Bethune" (1988); www.ncnw.com.

Biggert, Judith Borg (b. 1937)

Republican Judy Biggert of Illinois entered the U.S. House of Representatives on 3 January 1999. Biggert served in the Illinois House of Representatives from 1993 until she won her congressional race in 1998. While in the Illinois House, Biggert passed the Sex Offender Notification Act, a bill creating boot camps for juvenile and youthful offenders, a measure requiring convicts to pay for their medical expenses while in prison, and another measure that strengthened domestic violence laws. She also sponsored successful bills to reform welfare, protect the environment, and improve education, the business climate, and health care. While in the Illinois House, Biggert became known for her abilities to negotiate and create consensus.

Judy Biggert assists in filling USO care packages for U.S. soldiers (Courtesy Office of Judy Biggert)

Co-chair of the Congressional Caucus on women's Issues in the 107th Congress (2001–2002), Congresswoman Biggert advocated funding for women's health research, victims of dating violence, and child care assistance for low-income families. She passed a measure making it easier for homeless children to enroll and remain in school and has worked to help children with eating disorders, among other child-related issues. She has also supported increased funding for homeless education programs and for math and science teacher training. In another area, she has worked to pass "flextime" legislation, which would provide workers with compensatory time off instead of overtime pay, which labor unions and women's groups have successfully opposed.

Born in Chicago, Illinois, Judy Biggert earned her bachelor's degree from Stanford University in 1959 and her law degree from Northwestern University in 1963. She entered politics by serving on the Hinsdale Township High School Board of Education in the mid-1980s.

See also Congress, Women in

References *Congressional Quarterly, Politics in America 2006* (2005); "Judy Biggert" (1998); www.biggert.com; http://judybiggert.house.gov/bio.asp;

Black Women's Health Imperative

The Black Women's Health Imperative (BWHI), founded in 1983 as the National Black Women's Health Project (NBWHP), offers health education, conducts research, and advocates for policies that address African American women's health. The education program ranges from the importance of daily exercise to publications on reproductive health and rights. In collaboration with the Centers for Disease Control and Prevention CDC, NBWHP began a research project to study strategies to reduce the racial disparities in cardiovascular diseases between black women and white women.

Heart disease, according to BWHI, kills black women at four times the rate it kills white women. Another project with CDC investigated issues surrounding domestic violence. In the area of advocacy, NBWHP has conferred with organizations such as the American Heart Association, pointing out that their educational materials did not include images of black women.

Health activist Byllye Avery founded the organization, the only national group devoted solely to black women's health.

See also Avery, Byllye

References "5 Questions for: Dr. Lorraine Cole," *Ebony*, 1 October 2005, p. 26; http://blackwomenshealth.org; *New York Amsterdam News*, February 1998.

Blackburn, Marsha Wedgeworth (b.1952)

Republican Congresswoman Marsha Blackburn of Tennessee entered the U.S. House of Representatives on January 3, 2003. During her first term in office she supported tax cuts, saying: "We need to make the federal income tax codes flatter, fairer, and simpler. We need to continue working on lowering the marginal [tax] rates." She also worked on legislation to help veterans, acquire pay raises for military personnel, make reforms in the Department of Defense personnel system, and obtain a measure prohibiting partial birth abortions.

Blackburn first ran for public office in 1992, an unsuccessful bid for a congressional seat. Six years later, she won a seat in the Tennessee state senate, serving from 1998 to 2002. As a state senator, Blackburn led a successful statewide grassroots campaign to

Tennessee Representative Marsha Blackburn traveled with Defense Secretary Rumsfeld to Fort Campbell in September 2004 to hold a town hall meeting for the community with the Secretary. (Courtesy Office of Marsha Blackburn)

defeat a proposed state income tax, garnering her national attention as an anti-tax advocate. Her anti-tax stands became a key message in her 2002 congressional campaign.

Born in Laurel, Mississippi, Blackburn earned her BA in merchandising and textiles from Mississippi State University in 1973.

References *Congressional Quarterly*, Politics in America 2004 (2003), Politics in America 2006 (2005); http://www.house.gov/blackburn/biography.shtml

Blackmun, Harry Andrew (1908–1999)

U.S. Supreme Court Justice Harry A. Blackmun wrote the majority opinion in *Roe v. Wade* (1973), the decision that legalized abortion as a constitutional right of personal privacy. For those who support reproductive rights, the decision made Blackmun the preeminent champion of women's rights. For those who oppose the decision, it made Blackmun the person most identified with a great moral wrong. More than any other decision related to women's rights, *Roe v. Wade* launched a national debate of intense acrimony, violence, and political controversy that persists more than thirty years later.

Appointed by President Richard Nixon in 1970, Blackmun was regarded as a conservative, but over his tenure on the Court, he emerged as a liberal, supporting women's rights, gay rights, and civil rights and opposing capital punishment.

Reflecting on Roe in 1994, Blackmun said: "I think it was right in 1973 and I think it is right today.... It's a step that had to be taken as we go down the road toward the full emancipation of women." Other people vehemently disagreed with Blackmun's opinion. He received mail in which he was called the "Butcher of Dachau," "Pontius Pilate," "King Herod," and "child murderer." An unidentified person fired a bullet at his apartment, but did not injure Blackmun or his wife Dorothy Blackmun, who was

Supreme Court Justice Harry Blackmun, who authored the opinion in Roe v. Wade, became a strong advocate for abortion rights.

with him. In contrast, feminist Gloria Steinem said: "Justice Blackmun saved more women's lives than any other person in history."

Born in Nashville, Illinois, Blackmun earned his undergraduate degree from Harvard in 1929 and his law degree from Harvard Law School in 1932. Blackmun had a private law practice in Minnesota from 1934 to 1950, served as resident counsel for the Mayo Clinic from 1950 to 1959, and was a federal appeals court judge from 1959 to 1970. Justice Blackmun retired from the U.S. Supreme Court in 1994.

See also Abortion; *Roe v. Wade* (1973); Steinem, Gloria

References *Los Angeles Times*, 5 March 1999, 7 March 1999.

Blackwell, Alice Stone (1857–1950)

Suffragist Alice Stone Blackwell helped unite two major organizations of the woman suffrage movement, the National Woman Suffrage Association (NWSA) and the American Woman Suffrage Association (AWSA), into the National American Woman Suffrage Association (NAWSA) in 1890. Two competing groups had formed in 1869 because of strategy differences between Lucy Stone and Henry Blackwell and their followers and Susan B. Anthony, Elizabeth Cady Stanton, and their followers. Largely through the efforts of Harriot Eaton Stanton Blatch, Stanton's daughter, and of Blackwell, the two groups merged and became the NAWSA. Blackwell served as its recording secretary for most of the next twenty years.

Born in East Orange, New Jersey, Alice Stone Blackwell graduated from Boston College in 1881. The daughter of abolitionist and suffrage leaders Lucy Stone and Henry Brown Blackwell, Alice Stone Blackwell grew up in the center of the suffrage movement. Her parents established the AWSA in 1869 and published its paper, the *Woman's Journal*. Following graduation from college, she became a writer for the *Woman's Journal*, eventually accepting responsibility for the newspaper.

Following ratification of the woman suffrage amendment in 1920, Blackwell helped found the Massachusetts affiliate of the League of Women Voters. Blackwell wrote a biography of her mother, *Lucy Stone: Pioneer in Woman's Rights* (1930), as well as *The Division of Labor* (1906), *Woman and School Vote* (1908), and *Why Should Women Vote?* (1910), among other works.

See also American Woman Suffrage Association; Anthony, Susan Brownell; National American Woman Suffrage Association; National Woman Suffrage Association; Stanton, Elizabeth Cady; Stone, Lucy; Suffrage

References James, ed., *Notable American Women 1607–1950* (1971); Whitman, ed., *American Reformers* (1985).

Blades, Joan (b. 1956)

Joan Blades and her husband Wes Boyd became frustrated in 1998 as impeachment hearings for President Bill Clinton consumed the attention of Congress and the American people. They sent out a petition calling on Congress to "Censure [Clinton] and Move On." Within one week, 100,000 people had signed the petition, and after two weeks, the number had grown to 200,000. The first national rapid-response network, MoveOn.org, was born. "I have a real sense of optimism that we are revolutionizing the way we do politics in this country. Through our site, ordinary citizens who once felt powerless are much more involved in the democratic process in a direct and meaningful way," Blades said.

Following the September 11, 2001, terrorist attacks on the United States, Blades and Boyd published a petition calling for moderate and restrained responses to the attacks. Five hundred thousand people signed the petition. Blades and Boyd have expanded MoveOn.org to include MoveOn Political Action Committee and ActionForum, a place for members to post comments and to suggest MoveOn's priorities. MoveOn has 1.7 million members in the United States and 2.3 million globally.

Born and raised in Berkeley, California, Blades earned her bachelor's degree in history in 1977 at the University of California and her law degree at Golden Gate University School of Law in 1980. A mediator, she wrote *Mediate Your Divorce: A Guide to Cooperative Custody, Property, and Support Agreements* (1985) and *Family Mediation: Cooperative Divorce Settlement* (1985).

Blades married Boyd, a software designer, in 1987. They founded Berkeley Systems, an entertainment software company best known for its flying toaster screen saver. They sold the company in 1997.

> **References** *Current Biography Yearbook*, 2004; Amanda Griscom, "The Internet Insurrection," *Rolling Stone*, 4 March 2004, pp. 30–31; Ellen Hawkes, "Joan Blades," *Ms.*, Winter 2003, pp. 85–86; *The Washington Post*, 1 February 1999; http://moveon.org/.

Blair, Emily Newell (1877–1951)

The first female vice chair of the Democratic National Committee and the second chair of the party's Women's Division, Emily Newell Blair was introduced to politics by her husband, Harry Wallace Blair. She campaigned for some county candidates, but it appears her interest at that time was brief. She began writing short stories that were published in *Cosmopolitan, Harper's Magazine, Women's Home Companion*, and other magazines. In the 1910s, she became involved in Missouri suffrage efforts, using her writing skills as the press and publicity chair of the Missouri Equal Suffrage Association and as editor of *Missouri Woman*, a monthly suffrage publication.

During World War I, she was vice chair of the Missouri Woman's Committee of the Council of National Defense, a civilian agency, and gained recognition that led to an appointment on the executive committee of the Women's Division of the council. She was also an aid to Ida Tarbell, again working in the areas of news and publicity. After the war, she wrote the official history of the Missouri Woman's Committee.

As ratification of the woman suffrage amendment appeared certain in the summer of 1920, the Democratic Party changed its rules to give each state two representatives on its national committee, a national committeeman and a national committeewoman. Blair was in the first group of women to serve on the Democratic National Committee, and in 1921, the committee elected her to be its first female vice chair. The next year, she became the second woman to chair the party's Women's Division and the highest-ranking woman in the party's leadership. Over the next two years, she made more than 200 speeches in twenty-two states and organized more than 2,000 Democratic Women's Clubs. She also helped found the Woman's National Democratic Club, serving as its secretary from 1922 to 1926 and its president in 1928. Throughout those years, she focused on educating women voters through her speeches and the booklets and pamphlets that she wrote.

Blair published several articles in *Woman Citizen* and *Woman's Journal* on feminist issues and the need for women to be active in politics. One of the founders of the League of Women Voters, she later argued that the organization's nonpartisan philosophy did not contribute to the effective use of voting rights and that to develop political power, women needed to be active in one of the political parties. In a 1931 *Woman's Journal* article, she wrote: "There are two ways, and only two ways by which women may become a power in politics, always excepting those who work by the old method of working on and through a man. One is by holding office and the other is becoming effective in political organizations." She insisted that more women needed to run for public office and that other women needed to support their candidacies. She argued that "a new organization of feminists devoted to the task of getting women into politics" might "stir women to action." Forty years later, another generation of women formed an organization with the purposes Blair had in mind, the National Women's Political Caucus.

Blair was appointed to the Consumer Advisory Board under the National Industrial Recovery Act in 1933 and chaired it in 1935. During World War II, she was public relations director of the Women's Army Corps. Throughout the years of her active political life, she also continued her work as a writer. A contributing editor to *Good Housekeeping* from 1925 to 1933, she wrote monthly articles on books and reading. She also wrote *Creation of a Home* (1930) on decorating; *The Letters of a Contented Wife* (1931); and the novel *A Woman of Courage* (1931).

Born in Joplin, Missouri, Emily Blair enrolled in the Women's College of Baltimore and attended classes at the University of Missouri but did not graduate from either school because of family financial difficulties.

See also Democratic Party, Women in the; League of Women Voters; National Women's Political Caucus; Suffrage

References Anderson, "Practicing Feminist Politics: Emily Newell Blair and U.S. Women's Political Choices in the Early Twentieth Century" (1997); Blair, "Putting Women into Politics" (1931).

Blanco, Kathleen Babineaux (b. 1942)

Louisiana's first woman governor, Democrat Kathleen Blanco took office in 2004. Her term began with the usual concerns facing a governor: taxes, economic development, child protection, pay increases for teachers. In late August 2005, all of her attention turned toward the devastation of New Orleans and other coastal areas caused by Hurricane Katrina and the flooding that followed. After addressing the initial catastrophe, assisting the thousands of people displaced by the hurricane and developing plans for rebuilding New Orleans and the surrounding area became the focus of Blanco's work.

Blanco was among the public officials criticized by the press, the public, and a congressional committee for delays in issuing a mandatory evacuation order or failing to issue one in some areas, despite clear and timely warnings of the storm's severity and potential destructive capacity. In addition, the congressional committee criticized Blanco and others for not providing assistance to people in evacuating. Further, the

On January 12, 2004, Kathleen Babineaux Blanco became the first woman to serve as governor of Louisiana. (Courtesy Office of the Govenor of Louisiana)

accommodations for those people who could not or would not evacuate were inadequate. The congressional committee investigating the disaster concluded that "The incomplete pre-landfall evacuation led to deaths, thousands of dangerous rescues, and horrible conditions for those who remained."

Born in Coteau, Louisiana, Blanco earned a degree from the University of Louisiana in 1964. She taught high school business classes and ran her own polling and marketing research business. From 1979 to 1980, she managed the state census office. She served in the state legislature from 1984 to 1989, the year she was elected the first woman to serve on the Louisiana Public Service Commission, chairing it from 1993 to 1994. She next served as the state's lieutenant governor from 1995 to 2003.

When Blanco took office, her priorities were to improve the state's health care and education systems and to improve its business climate.

References H.W. Wilson, *Current Biography Yearbook 2004* (2005); *New York Times*, 8 September 2005; Select Bipartisan Committee to Investigate the Preparation for and Response to Hurricane Katrina, "A Failure of Initiative: Final Report of the Select Bipartisan Committee to Investigate the Preparation for and Response to Hurricane Katrina" (Washington, D.C.: Government Printing Office, 2006), pp. 105–119.

Blatch, Harriot Eaton Stanton (1856–1940)

The daughter of women's rights and woman suffrage crusader Elizabeth Cady Stanton, Harriot Blatch fought for the same causes, helped unite the National Woman Suffrage Association (NWSA) and the American Woman Suffrage Association (AWSA), and worked for the Equal Rights Amendment. Blatch made her first contribution to the suffrage movement in the early 1880s, helping her mother, as well as Susan B. Anthony and Ida Husted Harper compile their *History of Woman Suffrage*, six volumes published between 1881 and 1922. She wrote the section recounting the 1869 split that had resulted in two woman suffrage organizations, the AWSA and the NWSA. Her interpretation of the events eased the merger of the two groups into the National American Woman Suffrage Association (NAWSA) in 1890.

Blatch married British businessman William Henry Blatch in 1882, and the two lived near London, England, for the next twenty years. During those years, Harriot Blatch became deeply involved in the British woman suffrage movement. When the couple moved to New York City in 1902, she concluded that the U.S. movement had become lethargic, saying: "It bored its adherents and repelled its opponents." Seeking ways to reinvigorate it, Blatch began working in New York City's Lower East Side and discovered unexpected support for suffrage among employed women. In 1907, Blatch organized labor and professional women into the Equality League of Self-Supporting Women, which sponsored the first testimony by wage-earning women in support of woman suffrage before the New York legislature.

Blatch continued to recruit working women to testify before legislative hearings, held open-air meetings, and organized parades to bring energy and attention to woman suffrage, gaining increased press attention for woman suffrage and reinforcing Blatch's commitment to militant strategies. When efforts to hold a referendum on woman suffrage in New York succeeded in 1915, Blatch's increasingly militant tactics prompted moderate suffragist Carrie Chapman Catt to form the Woman Suffrage Party. The referendum lost, at least in part as a result of the competing campaigns. When New York voters passed the amendment in 1917, Blatch was in England, settling the estate of her deceased husband.

When the United States entered World War I, Blatch turned her attention to supporting the war effort, serving as a director of the Woman's Land Army and head of the Food Administration's Speakers Bureau. She wrote *Mobilizing Woman Power* (1918), describing European women's efforts in the war and encouraging American women to make comparable contributions. Her next book, *A Woman's Point of View* (1920), described the devastation of war and the ways improved education for all and women's participation in public policymaking could help avoid another war. With the passage of the suffrage amendment in 1920, Blatch supported the National Woman's Party's work for the Equal Rights Amendment.

Born in Seneca Falls, New York, Blatch earned her bachelor's degree in 1878 and her master's degree in 1894, both from Vassar College.

See also American Woman Suffrage Association; Catt, Carrie Clinton Lane Chapman; Congressional Union; Equal Rights Amendment; National American Woman Suffrage Association; National Woman Suffrage Association; National Woman's Party; Nineteenth Amendment; Stanton, Elizabeth Cady; Suffrage

References DuBois, *Harriot Stanton Blatch and the Winning of Woman Suffrage* (1997).

Blitch, Iris Faircloth (1912–1993)

Democrat Iris Faircloth Blitch of Georgia served in the U.S. House of Representatives from 3 January 1955 to 3 January 1963. In Congress, Blitch focused on agricultural issues, passing a measure supporting water conservation on small farms and land drainage programs and working for import limits on jute, which was grown in her area. An environmentalist, she worked to preserve the Okefenokee Swamp. Blitch opposed voting rights legislation and the Supreme Court's 1954 decision in *Brown v. Board of Education of Topeka, Kansas*, which outlawed racial segregation in public schools. Along with other Southern members of Congress, she signed the Southern Manifesto, pledging to seek the reversal of the decision. She did not run for re-election in 1962.

Born near Vidalia, Georgia, Iris Blitch attended the University of Georgia for a short time before her marriage in 1929 and then in 1949 attended South Georgia College. She was active in the Democratic Party in the mid-1930s, serving in the Georgia House of Representatives from 1949 to 1950 and in the state Senate from 1947 to 1948 and from 1953 to 1954. While in the Georgia Senate, she passed a bill to permit women to serve on juries. Blitch served as Democratic national committeewoman for Georgia from 1948 to 1956. She changed her party affiliation from Democrat to Republican in 1964.

See also Congress, Women in; Democratic Party, Women in the; State Legislatures, Women in

References Engelbarts, *Women in the United States Congress, 1917–1972* (1974); Office of the Historian, U.S. House of Representatives , *Women in Congress, 1917–1990* (1991); Tolchin, *Women in Congress: 1917–1976* (1976).

Bloomer, Amelia Jenks (1818–1894)

Temperance advocate and suffragist Amelia Jenks Bloomer founded and edited the first newspaper owned, edited, and published by a woman in the United States, *The Lily: A Ladies' Journal Devoted to Temperance and Literature*. First published in 1849, *The Lily* was also the first newspaper in the United States to espouse women's rights. Bloomer's name was also attached to the alternative clothing she advocated during the nineteenth century. Bloomer entered the public arena as a temperance advocate and expanded her work to include woman suffrage in the hope that women would use their votes to prohibit the sale and consumption of alcohol.

Born in Homer, New York, Bloomer received her education at home and in the local public schools. She began teaching when she was seventeen years old and was a governess from 1837 to 1840, when she married Dexter Bloomer, a young Quaker lawyer. He was a partner in *The Seneca County Courier*, a newspaper in Seneca Falls, New York, to which Amelia Bloomer contributed articles. She also wrote for local temperance newspapers.

Bloomer began publishing *The Lily* to provide a voice for the temperance movement, but within a short time, she began to publish articles on the need for improvements in women's education and on the benefits of physical exercise for women. Bloomer had attended the 1848 Seneca Falls convention organized by Elizabeth Cady Stanton and others, but had not met Stanton until the day in 1849 that Stanton went to Bloomer's office and offered to write for *The Lily*. Although Bloomer and Stanton differed on some issues (Stanton was an abolitionist, but Bloomer felt temperance was the more important issue), Stanton began contributing articles.

Early in 1851, dress reform became a topic in Seneca Falls, and Bloomer became an advocate for it after seeing Stanton wearing the outfit of a knee-length tunic over Turkish pantaloons, which was considerably less confining than the whalebone corsets, layers of underskirts, and voluminous skirts that women usually wore. Newspapers across the country picked up the story from *The Lily* in which Bloomer reported she was wearing it and recommended it for other women. Within a short time, the ap-

Letter witten by Amelia Jenks Bloomer

parel bore Bloomer's name. Lampooned by cartoonists, criticized by clergy, and mocked by editorial writers, the clothing made Bloomer a celebrity. She published a description of it in *The Lily* in response to requests for directions for making it. She dressed in the apparel until some time after 1855.

Bloomer introduced Stanton and Susan B. Anthony in 1851. Although Bloomer and Anthony shared a commitment to temperance work, the relationship between Anthony and Stanton would become a political partnership for women's rights that lasted for decades. Although Bloomer supported women's rights, temperance continued to be her first priority.

In 1853, the Bloomers moved to Ohio, where Amelia Bloomer continued publishing *The Lily*. Two years later, when they planned a move to Council Bluffs, Iowa, Amelia Bloomer found that she could not safely transport her newspaper equipment and sold *The Lily*. The couple moved to Council Bluffs, Iowa, in 1855. Amelia Bloomer continued to work for woman suffrage in Iowa, becoming the first woman to publicly speak on suffrage in the state in 1855. A member of the Nebraska territorial legislature invited her to address that body in 1856. The legislator later introduced a woman suffrage bill that passed the House but was not voted on in the Senate.

After the Civil War, Bloomer renewed her efforts for woman suffrage, serving as vice president in 1870 and president of the Iowa Woman Suffrage Society in 1871. Conflicts within the Iowa suffrage movement ended Bloomer's leadership in the society, but she remained an active advocate for woman suffrage.

> **See also** Anthony, Susan Brownell; Seneca Falls Convention; Stanton, Elizabeth Cady; Suffrage
>
> **References** Noun, "Amelia Bloomer, A Biography: Part I, the Lily of Seneca Falls" (1985), "Amelia Bloomer: Part II, The Suffragist of Council Bluffs" (1985).

Bloor, Ella Reeve Ware Cohen Omholt (Mother Bloor) (1862–1951)

Suffragist, labor organizer, and journalist Ella Bloor was a leader in the Socialist Party and a founder of the U.S. Communist Party. Born on Staten Island, New York, she attended Ivy Hall Seminary, a finishing school, for a year when she was fourteen and the University of Pennsylvania in 1895–1896. She entered the public arena in the 1880s, working in the women's rights and temperance movements. After learning in the late 1890s that women in the weaving trade earned one-quarter of the wages that men earned, she joined the weavers' union so that she could organize women weavers.

Bloor joined the Social Democratic Party of America in 1897, but after a disagreement over the party's future, she switched to the Socialist Labor Party in 1898. Then in 1902, she joined the newly organized Socialist Party, becoming the organization's state labor organizer in Pennsylvania and later in Connecticut. In 1908, Bloor unsuccessfully ran for Connecticut secretary of state. In 1910, she helped create the National Women's Committee in the Socialist Party. After helping to organize the U.S. Communist Party in 1919, she served on its central committee from 1932 to 1948.

In the 1930s, as regional secretary for the National Relief Conference, Bloor focused on the needs of farmers in Iowa, Nebraska, Montana, and the Dakotas. She was also active in the American League Against War and Fascism. She headed the U.S. delegation to the Women's International Congress Against War and Fascism, held in Paris in 1934. Bloor unsuccessfully ran on the Communist Party ticket for governor of Pennsylvania in 1938. That same year, she wrote *Women in the Soviet Union* (1938); *We Are Many* was published in 1940.

> **References** Whitman, ed., *American Reformers* (1985).

Boggs, Marie Corinne Morrison Claiborne (Lindy) (b. 1916)

Democrat Lindy Boggs of Louisiana served in the U.S. House of Representatives from 20 March 1973 to 3 January 1991. Boggs became involved in politics through her husband Hale Boggs's political career, managing his congressional campaigns and working in his congressional office as a paid aide. She was president of the Women's National Democratic Club from 1958 to 1959, the Democratic Wives' Forum in 1962, and the Congressional Club from 1971 to 1972, and she co-chaired President John F. Kennedy's 1961 inaugural committee and President Lyndon Johnson's 1965 inaugural committee.

In October 1972, Hale Boggs was on a campaign trip in Alaska when his plane disappeared. Ever hopeful that rescuers would find her husband, Lindy Boggs refused suggestions that she run for his seat until it was declared vacant following the opening of Congress in January 1973. She ran for office intending to complete her husband's agenda, including international trade, housing, taxes, civil rights, and equal rights.

Congresswoman Boggs advocated economic equality for women, a commitment that developed after her husband's death. Formerly unaware of discrimination against women, she had difficulty getting a credit card in her own name, despite her considerable personal wealth and public visibility. As a member of Congress and as a member of the House Banking and Currency Committee, she worked to guarantee women access to credit through the Equal Credit Opportunity Act of 1974, which specifically barred discrimination on the basis of sex and marital status. She also worked for equal economic rights for women in small business loans, home ownership, and banking. In related areas, Boggs sought better jobs for women in government, equal opportunities to secure government contracts, increased opportunities for women in the workplace, and equal opportunities in higher education.

Boggs also worked to give women educational opportunities in science and math and to provide early childhood education for children in public housing developments. With Barbara Mikulski (D-Maryland), Boggs developed a domestic and family violence bill, seeking to provide assistance to rape and domestic violence victims. She worked to protect Louisiana gas and oil interests, improve the port of New Orleans, and support Mississippi River transportation. She helped create the Congresswoman's Caucus, the National Museum of African Art, and the position of Office of Historian in the House of Representatives. She passed a resolution making the rose the official flower of the United States. In 1984, she passed a measure to defer student loan payments for people in the health professions. Boggs passed legislation to fund the Jean Lafitte Park, a bayou preserve near New Orleans.

Lindy Boggs became the first woman to preside over a major party's national convention when she chaired the Democratic National Convention in 1976. She retired from Congress in 1991. President Bill Clinton appointed Boggs ambassador to the Vatican, a post she held from 1997 to 2001.

Born at Brunswick Plantation, Pointe Coupee Parish, Louisiana, Lindy Boggs earned her bachelor's degree from Sophie Newcomb College of Tulane University in 1935 and then taught high school history and coached the girls' basketball team. Her autobiography, *Washington Through a Purple Veil: Memoirs of a Southern Woman*, was published in 1994.

> **See also** Congress, Women in; Congressional Caucus for Women's Issues; Democratic Party, Women in the; Domestic Violence; Education Amendments of 1972, Title IX; Education, Women and; Equal Credit Opportunity Act of 1974; Mikulski, Barbara Ann

References Boggs, *Washington Through a Purple Veil: Memoirs of a Southern Woman* (1994); Kaptur, *Women of Congress: A Twentieth Century Odyssey* (1996); Lamson, *In the Vanguard: Six American Women in Public Life* (1979).

Boland, Veronica Grace (1899–1982)

Democrat Veronica Boland of Pennsylvania served in the U.S. House of Representatives from 19 November 1942 to 3 January 1943. Boland ran for office to fill the vacancy created by the death of her husband, Patrick J. Boland. She did not run for re-election. Following her term in office, she worked for a Pennsylvania manufacturing company as its executive secretary until her retirement in 1957.

Born in Scranton, Pennsylvania, Veronica Boland attended Scranton Technical High School.

See also Congress, Women in

References Office of the Historian, U.S. House of Representatives , *Women in Congress, 1917–1991* (1991).

Bolton, Frances Payne Bingham (1885–1977)

Republican Frances Bolton of Ohio served in the U.S. House of Representatives from 27 February 1940 to 3 January 1969. Both Frances Bolton and her husband Chester Bolton were active in the Republican Party: she served on the Ohio Republican State Central Committee from 1937 to 1940, and he served in Congress. After his death, Frances Bolton won the special election to fill the vacancy.

Bolton began her congressional career as a critic of New Deal policies and an isolationist, but following the bombing of Pearl Harbor, she supported the war effort and focused her attention on the need for nurses in the military. She helped pass the Bolton Act of 1943, establishing the U.S. Cadet Nurse Corps, which trained nurses in exchange for their pledges to serve in the armed forces. Bolton opposed gender and racial discrimination, called for the end of racial and sexual segregation in military nursing units, and supported drafting women. She opposed the poll tax, which discriminated against African Americans, and fought to include women in anti-discrimination legislation.

As a member and chair of the House Foreign Affairs Committee, she traveled extensively and became familiar with the challenges facing post-World War II Europe, especially the Soviet Union, and the Middle East. She advocated independence for colonial Africa in the late 1940s. In 1953, she became the first woman appointed as a congressional delegate to the United Nations General Assembly. For three terms, her son Oliver Bolton also served in Congress, making them the only mother-son team in the House.

The daughter of a wealthy Cleveland banker and industrialist, Frances Bolton received most of her education from private tutors. Through the Cleveland Debutante Club, she volunteered with visiting nurses in the city's tenements, leading to her lifelong interest in nursing and nursing education. Her philanthropy in 1923 contributed to the founding of the Frances Payne Bolton School of Nursing at Western Reserve University, the first college-level nursing program in the United States. She also helped purchase 485 acres of land near George Washington's Mount Vernon residence in order to preserve the view from it.

> **See also** Congress, Women in; Sex Discrimination

> **References** Engelbarts, *Women in the United States Congress, 1917–1972* (1974); Kaptur, *Women of Congress: A Twentieth Century Odyssey* (1996); Tolchin, *Women in Congress: 1917–1976* (1976).

Bona Fide Occupational Qualification

Title VII of the Civil Rights Act of 1964 prohibits employment discrimination on the basis of race, religion, national origin, and sex. The law permits employers to discriminate on the basis of sex, if sex is a bona fide occupational qualification (BFOQ), for example, for a clothing model. Employers have the burden of proving that the requirements for a job exclude all members of one sex as candidates, and the Equal Employment Opportunity Commission (EEOC) and the courts have narrowly interpreted the attributes that comprise a BFOQ.

The EEOC and the courts have rejected several sex-based job qualifications as BFOQs, including limits on the amount of weight that women could lift (*Bowe v. Colgate-Palmolive Company* and *Weeks v. Southern Bell Telephone and Telegraph Company*), limits on the number of hours in a day women could work, and limits on their working during night hours. Refusing to hire a woman based on the preferences of co-workers, clients, customers, or the employer was also found to be in violation of Title VII. Height and weight requirements that do not have the intention of discriminating are unlawful if statistical evidence shows that the standards exclude most women. Maximum age limits for airline stewardesses were rejected as BFOQs; sex is also not a legal BFOQ for airline attendants (*Diaz v. Pan American World Airways, Inc.*), stenographers, lifeguards, bartenders, race car drivers, car dealers, hunting guides, and several other positions.

> **See also** *Bowe v. Colgate-Palmolive Company*; Civil Rights Act of 1964, Title VII; *Diaz v. Pan American World Airways, Inc.*; Equal Employment Opportunity Commission; *Weeks v. Southern Bell Telephone and Telegraph Company*

> **References** *American Jurisprudence*, 2nd ed., vol. 15 (1976).

Bonney, Mary Lucinda (1816–1900)

Mary Bonney led the first popular movement to reform the U.S. federal government's Native American policies. Bonney first became involved in Native American issues in the early 1850s when she helped found the Women's Home Missionary Committee of First Baptist Church, a group that assisted Native Americans and provided financial assistance to women studying to become missionaries. She also served as an officer of the Philadelphia branch of the Woman's Union Missionary Society of America for Heathen Lands.

Newspaper reports in 1879 of congressional proposals to permit whites to settle in Indian Territory (present-day Oklahoma) outraged Bonney, who believed the federal government should honor its treaties. Bonney and a friend, Amelia Stone Quinton, began circulating petitions to arouse public opinion and to convince Congress to pass legislation favorable to Native Americans. In February 1880, Bonney presented 13,000 signatures on a 300-foot roll to President Rutherford B. Hayes. Bonney and Quinton then organized the Central Indian Committee, which gathered an additional 50,000 signatures. The second petition was presented to the U.S. Senate in 1881 by Henry L. Dawes of Massachusetts, who had become a leader in Native American reform efforts. Bonney and Quinton organized auxiliary groups in other states and changed the name of their organization to the Indian Treaty-Keeping and Protective Association. The next year, the group presented 100,000 signatures on a petition calling for the allotment of tribal lands to individual Native Americans.

The group later changed its name to the National Indian Association, which became the Women's National Indian Association (WNIA). In 1883, Bonney became president of the WNIA and held the office until the next year. The WNIA expanded its mission to provide training and educational programs for Native American women; establish libraries, schools, and missions; build homes; and offer loans. In 1886, the organization had eighty-three affiliates in twenty-seven states. In 1887, the ideas of individual landownership of tribal lands presented by Bonney and the WNIA became part of the Dawes Act, which continued to be the official policy of the U.S. government for almost fifty years.

Born in Hamilton, New York, Mary Bonney graduated from Emma Willard's Troy Female Seminary in 1835. She taught school from 1835 to 1850, when she opened a secondary school for girls in Philadelphia. She moved the school to Ogontz, Pennsylvania, in 1883, and served as its principal until her retirement in 1888.

See also Quinton, Amelia Stone

References Hardy, *American Women Civil Rights Activists* (1993); James, ed., *Notable American Women 1607–1950* (1971); Whitman, ed., *American Reformers* (1985).

Bonnin, Gertrude Simmons (aka Zitkala-Sa, or Red Bird) (1876–1938)

Native American Gertrude Simmons Bonnin lobbied Congress for citizenship for Native Americans and helped expose corruption in the Bureau of Indian Affairs. She consistently advocated and worked for equal educational opportunities for Native Americans while steadfastly endeavoring to preserve Native American culture. Bonnin entered politics in the 1910s through the Society of American Indians (SAI), a lobbying organization that sought political equality for Native Americans, worked to preserve native history and culture, and sought employment for Native Americans. In 1916, she became secretary of the SAI, lectured nationally, lobbied Congress, and worked with the Bureau of Indian Affairs (BIA). From 1918 to 1919, she was editor of the organization's publication, *American Indian Magazine*.

Bonnin became involved with the General Federation of Women's Clubs in 1920, seeking their support for improved education and health care for Native Americans and enlisting their help to expose corruption at the BIA. She persuaded the federation to establish the Indian Welfare Committee, which, with other groups, sponsored an investigation that Bonnin led of the government's treatment of Native Americans in Oklahoma. Bonnin was the primary author of the 1924 report, *Oklahoma's Poor Rich Indians: An Orgy of Graft and Exploitation*, a description of corruption in the BIA and its brutal treatment of Native Americans. The document persuaded President Herbert Hoover to appoint the Meriam Commission, which reported in 1928 on the conditions among Native Americans, leading to the appointment of members of the Indian Rights Association to the top two positions in the Bureau of Indian Affairs.

Bonnin organized the National Council of American Indians in 1926 and served as its founding president. Through the council, Bonnin lectured across the country, lobbied Congress, and testified before congressional committees. She succeeded in attaining many of her goals. Health care improved through the Indian New Deal, limited reforms were made in tribal self-government, and Native Americans gained access to better educational and vocational facilities. In 1924, Congress passed the Indian Citizenship Act, a measure that made all Indians born in the United States citizens of the United States. While Congress declared Indians' status as citizens through legislation, the status did not include voting rights. Since there was never a constitutional amendment for the enfranchisement of Native Americans, as with former slaves in the Fifteenth Amendment and women in the Nineteenth Amendment, the qualifications for voters remained within the purview of individual states. Native Americans have primarily gained voting rights through federal court decisions that continued into the 1990s.

Born at Yankton Sioux Agency, South Dakota, Gertrude Bonnin took the name Zitkala-Sa, or Red Bird, later in her life. When she was about eight years old, she left the reservation to attend White's Indiana Manual Institute. She then studied from 1895 to 1897 at Earlham College in Richmond, Indiana, to become a teacher. An essay she wrote explaining Native Americans' resentment over the disruption created in their lives by whites and the desire of some Native Americans to learn about white culture won second place in the 1896 Indiana State Oratorical Contest.

Gertrude Bonnin, president of the National Council of American Indians, worked for understanding between her people and the American government, 1930

Bonnin taught at Carlisle Indian School in Pennsylvania from 1897 to 1899 and then studied at the New England Conservatory of Music. In the early 1900s, she began writing short stories and autobiographical essays that appeared in *Atlantic Monthly*, *Harper's Magazine*, and other periodicals, making her one of the first Native Americans to present her perspectives to white audiences. Bonnin also wrote *Old Indian Legends* (1901) and *American Indian Stories* (1921). She taught and served on Indian reservations as a clerk.

References Hardy, *American Women Civil Rights Activists* (1993); Johnson and Wilson, "Gertrude Simmons Bonnin" (1988); Whitman, ed., *American Reformers* (1985).

Document Zitkala-Sa, "The School Days of an Indian Girl," 1900

Bono, Mary Whitaker (b. 1961)

Republican Mary Bono of California entered the U.S. House of Representatives on 21 April 1998. She ran in the special election to fill the vacancy created by the death of her husband, Sonny Bono, in a skiing accident. In her campaign, she pledged to continue the work her husband had begun, including obtaining the funding to restore the Salton Sea, a polluted desert lake, an effort that succeeded in late 1998. Mary Bono favors small government, supports abortion rights, and opposes government funding of abortion. Bono owns a gun, but she supports the assault weapons ban.

Congresswoman Bono introduced legislation to expand research on autism, a developmental disorder affecting as many as one child in 166. Bono noted: "Autism is

Representative Mary Bono (R-CA), who took her famous husband's seat after he was killed in a skiing accident, was re-elected to a second term in 1998 (Archive Photos)

the fastest growing developmental disability in our nation." She has also sponsored legislation mandating country-of-origin labeling on imported fruits and vegetables sold at retail. In addition, Bono has worked to pass a measure prohibiting spyware. Bono explained: "This bill aims to empower consumers to help safeguard themselves from nefarious privacy invasions without harming the growth of legitimate technology."

In other areas, Bono passed a measure in 2000 that ratified an agreement to compensate the Torres Martinez Desert Cahulla Indian tribe for the loss of land when the Salton Sea was created. Two years later, she obtained the funds for the settlement. In the 108th Congress (2003–2004), Bono organized the bipartisan Recording Arts and Sciences Caucus.

Born in Cleveland, Ohio, Bono received her bachelor of fine arts degree from the University of Southern California in 1984. Mary Bono worked with her husband Sonny Bono on his mayoral and congressional races. Vice president of Sonny Bono Enterprises, she had also worked with him in his restaurants.

See also Congress, Women in

References Birtel, "New Member Profile: Mary Bono" (1998); *Business Press*, 6 May 2002; *Congressional Quarterly, Politics in America 2006* (2005); "House Sends Anti-Spyware Bill to the Floor," *Techweb*, 10 March 2005; "Neuroscience; Congresswomen Introduce Combating Autism Act of 2005," *Mental Health Business Week*, 18 June 2005, p. 44; www.rci.rutgers.edu/cawp

Bordallo, Madeleine Mary Zeien (b. 1933)

Representative Madeleine Bordallo of Guam entered the U.S. House of Representatives on January 3, 2003. A delegate, Bordallo represents Guam's interests, but is not permitted to vote on legislation. Bordallo, a Democrat, began her public life as First Lady of Guam from 1975 to 1978 and from 1983 to 1986, the years her late husband Ricardo Bordallo served as governor. She held her first public office from 1979 to 1981, serving in the Guam senate. She again served in the Guam legislature from 1987 to 1994.

Following her husband's death, she unsuccessfully ran for governor of Guam in 1990. As lieutenant governor from 1994 to 2002, Bordallo worked to encourage island beautification to enhance Guam's tourism industry.

As the island's congressional delegate, Bordallo has gained passage of measures to create an independent and unified judiciary, to increase federal assistance for expenses related to immigration, and other measures. She advocates changing the tax code to benefit territories. She also wants the Department of Defense to transfer ownership of land that it no longer uses to the territory.

Bordallo served on the Democratic National Committee from 1964 to 2003. Born in Graceville, Minnesota, Bordallo attended St. Mary's College and earned her Associate of Arts degree in music from St. Catherine's College in 1953.

References *Congressional Quarterly*, Politics in America 2006 (2005); http://bioguide.congress.gov/scripts/biodisplay.pl?index=B001245.

Congresswoman Madeleine Z. Bordallo holds the distinction of being the first woman in Guam's history to be elected as Delegate to Congress and twice as Lieutenant Governor (Courtesy Office of Madeleine Bordallo)

Bosone, Reva Zilpha Beck (1895–1983)

Democrat Reva Bosone of Utah served in the U.S. House of Representatives from 3 January 1949 to 3 January 1953. Bosone began her political career in the Utah House of Representatives, where she served from 1933 to 1935, becoming the first woman to serve in that body. She gained national recognition for her role in passing a minimum wage-and-hours law for women and children and for her contribution to Utah's ratification of the Child Labor Amendment to the U.S. Constitution, even though the amendment to limit children's participation in the labor force failed.

Elected a city judge for Salt Lake City in 1936, Bosone heard traffic violations, which was notable because she imposed extraordinarily high fines for drunken driving ($300) and reckless driving ($200). As she heard the cases, she became increasingly concerned about alcoholism and its effects on individuals and the community. She focused the public's attention on the disease, helped establish recovery programs for alcoholics, and from 1947 to 1948, served as the first director of the Utah State Board for Education on Alcoholism. She ended her tenure as city judge when she won her race for Congress in 1948. Another woman, Ivy Baker Priest, challenged Bosone in the 1950 general election, which Bosone won.

As a member of Congress, Bosone developed a Small Water Projects bill that would have created a revolving plan for land reclamation, but did not succeed in passing it. Acutely aware of the need for a national water program from her life in Utah, she unsuccessfully worked for other water projects and land management programs. She ran for a third term in 1952 and again in 1954 but was unsuccessful both times.

Following her defeat, she resumed private law practice until 1957, when she became legal counsel to a U.S. House of Representatives subcommittee. From 1961 to 1968, Bosone was judicial officer and chair of the Post Office Board of Appeals. She retired in 1968.

Born in American Fork, Utah, Reva Bosone graduated from Westminster Junior College in 1917 and received her bachelor's degree from the University of California at Berkeley in 1919. She taught high school for seven years, becoming the head of the public speaking, debating, and dramatic arts department. She left teaching in 1927 to read law at the University of Utah, receiving her law degree in 1929. She had a private law practice in Helper, Utah, from 1931 to 1933 and in Salt Lake City from 1933 to 1936.

See also Congress, Women in; State Legislatures, Women in

References H. W. Wilson, *Current Biography Yearbook: Who's New and Why, 1949* (1949); Office of the Historian, U.S. House of Representatives, *Women in Congress, 1917–1990* (1991); Tolchin, *Women in Congress: 1917–1976* (1976).

Bowe v. Colgate-Palmolive Company (1969)

In *Bowe v. Colgate-Palmolive Company*, the Seventh Circuit Court of Appeals decided that employers could not exclude women from holding a job that required them to lift more than 35 pounds. Colgate-Palmolive, the employer in the case, argued that the weight limit was a bona fide occupational qualification, but Thelma Bowe argued that the policy violated Title VII of the Civil Rights Act of 1964. The court agreed with Bowe, saying that Colgate-Palmolive could retain its 35-pound weight-lifting limit as long as it applied to both men and women, notified employees of the condition for holding certain jobs, gave all employees a reasonable opportunity to demonstrate their ability to meet the job qualification, and permitted all employees who met the test to apply for the position.

See also Bona Fide Occupational Qualification; Civil Rights Act of 1964, Title VII

References Bowe v. Colgate-Palmolive Company, 416 F.2d 711 (1969).

Bowers v. Hardwick (1986)

In 1982, an adult male, Hardwick, was in the bedroom of his home with another adult male engaging in an act of sodomy, when he was charged with violating a Georgia law that criminalized the act. After his conviction, Hardwick challenged the statute, but the U.S. Supreme Court found the law constitutional on the grounds that the Constitution does not grant homosexuals a fundamental right to engage in sodomy. The Court said that prior cases relating to procreation, family relationships, or marriage did not "bear any resemblance" to the right asserted by Hardwick, and the fact that the act occurred in the privacy of the home did not affect the result.

In 1998, the Georgia Supreme Court ruled that the law violated the right to privacy guaranteed by the state's constitution.

See also Lesbian Rights

References *Bowers v. Hardwick*, 478 U.S. 186 (1986).

Bowring, Eva Kelly (1892–1985)

Republican Eva Bowring of Nebraska served in the U.S. Senate from 16 April 1954 to 7 November 1954. Vice chair of the Nebraska Republican Central Committee and director of the state party's Women's Division from 1946 to 1954, Bowring was appointed to fill the vacancy created by the death of U.S. Senator Dwight Griswold. The period for which she was appointed ended at the next general election in the fall of 1954. While in office, Bowring worked for flood control projects in Nebraska. Bowring did not run in the race for the two-month balance of the term, which Hazel Hempel Abel won.

Following her retirement from the U.S. Senate, Bowring served on the national advisory council of the National Institutes of Health from 1954 to 1958 and from 1960 to 1961. She served on the board of parole of the Department of Justice from 1956 to 1964.

Born in Nevada, Missouri, Eva Bowring moved to the Sandhill country of Nebraska when she married her second husband in 1928. While in Nebraska, Eva Bowring became active in the cattle growers association and the local Republican Party.

See also Abel, Hazel Pearl Hempel; Congress, Women in

References Office of the Historian, U.S. House of Representatives, *Women in Congress, 1917–1990* (1991).

Boxer, Barbara Levy (b. 1940)

Democrat Barbara Boxer of California served in the U.S. House of Representatives from 3 January 1983 to 3 January 1993. She entered the U.S. Senate on 3 January 1993. She has held the leadership positions of Senate deputy majority whip in the 103rd Congress (1993–1995), Senate deputy minority whip in the 106th Congress (1999–2001), chief deputy for strategic outlook in the 107th and 108th Congresses (2001–2005), and chief deputy whip in the 109th Congress (2005–2007).

Boxer began her political career in 1974 working on the district staff of her congressman. Two years later, she ran for a seat on the Marin County Board of Supervisors, where she served from 1976 to 1984. Supervisor Boxer actively supported child care centers and programs for the elderly and opposed the movement of nuclear materials through the county. When the congressman for whom she had earlier worked decided to retire, Boxer announced her candidacy for the seat.

During her first term in Congress, Boxer led the fight against military waste, citing a spare part that cost $850 and coffeepots for cargo planes that cost $7,622. Working with other members of Congress, she co-sponsored legislation that opened bidding opportunities and created competitive bidding for spare parts. By 1994, it was estimated that $1 billion had been saved. She has also consistently fought increases in defense spending, repeatedly offering measures to cut it by as much as $6 billion. In 1986, Boxer passed legislation preventing Pentagon officials from working for defense contractors for two years following their departure from government service. She also fought to tie military aid to Guatemala with freedom for human rights groups working in that country. Boxer began her Senate career by introducing legislation to create a "conversion clearinghouse" to assist communities near closed military bases and to make the bases environmentally clean. The measure was particularly important in California, where several military bases were closed. Boxer has also focused on a number of other issues important to her state, including wetlands restoration, improved enforcement of immigration laws, and federal reimbursement to border states for the costs of illegal immigration.

Gender issues have been an important area of concern for Boxer from the time she entered the House of Representatives. For example, the Speaker of the House made frequent references to the "men in Congress." Boxer asked him to say "men and women," a request he granted. She also joined other women in Congress in their objections to the gym to which women were assigned. Although congressmen had a fully equipped gym, congresswomen had only a Ping-Pong table and old-fashioned hood hair dryers in theirs. In protest, the women wrote a humorous song to present their objections and won access to the men's gym.

Boxer wrote the House's Violence Against Women Act in 1991 and, as a senator, worked for its passage, which was accomplished in 1994. She also worked for federal funding for abortions resulting from rape or incest and drafted legislation to punish brokers who arranged surrogate mother agreements, equating it with selling babies.

In 1991, Boxer was one of seven congresswomen who marched to the Senate in an effort to convince that body to delay the confirmation of Clarence Thomas as U.S. Supreme Court justice until hearings could be held on charges of his alleged sexual harassment of Anita Hill. Boxer had been the victim of sexual harassment during her college years and sympathized with Hill. A strong supporter of reproductive rights, Boxer was a leader in the passage of the Freedom of Access to Clinic Entrances Act of 1994 and has supported legalizing the abortion drug RU-486. She has worked to increase federal funding for breast cancer research and prevention and to fight acquired immunodeficiency syndrome (AIDS).

Following the September 11, 2001, attacks on the United States, Boxer wrote laws allowing airline pilots to carry guns in the cockpit and ensuring that air marshals would be on high-risk flights. She has also introduced rail and port security measures.

Senator Boxer has taken controversial positions on several issues. During confirmation hearings for Condoleezza Rice's appointment as U.S. Secretary of State, Boxer emerged as the most aggressive interrogator. She joined Congresswoman Stephanie Tubbs Jones (D-Ohio) in challenging the 2004 presidential vote count in Ohio based upon alleged voting irregularities. She has criticized President George W. Bush's conduct of the war in Iraq, supporting the immediate withdrawal of troops from that country.

In the 2004 election, Boxer received more than 6.9 million votes, the highest total for any Senate candidate in American history.

Born in Brooklyn, New York, Barbara Boxer received a bachelor's degree in economics from Brooklyn College in 1962. A stockbroker from 1962 to 1965 and a journalist from 1972 to 1974, she began her public life helping organize a program to counsel high school dropouts, a successful program that the county school system took over. She is author of *Strangers in the Senate: Politics and the New Revolution of Women in America* (1994) and with Mary-Rose Hayes *A Time to Run: A Novel* (2005).

See also Abortion; Congress, Women in; Feinstein, Dianne Goldman; Freedom of Access to Clinic Entrances Act of 1994; Hill, Anita Faye; RU-486 (Mifepristone); Sexual Harassment; Violence Against Women Act of 1994; Women's Health Equity Act

References Boxer, *Strangers in the Senate* (1994); Center for American Women and Politics, "Women in Congress: Leadership Roles and Committee Chairs," Fact sheet, 2005; *Congressional Quarterly, Politics in America 1994*: The 103rd Congress (1993); H. W. Wilson, Current Biography Yearbook, 1994 (1994); *The New York Times*, 4 June 1992; *New York Amsterdam News*, 13 January 2005; *The New York Times*, 20 January 2005; *San Francisco Chronicle*, 30 November 2005; www.senate. gov/boxer/~ #alphbio/committees; http://boxer.senate.gov/about/index.cfm

Bradwell, Myra Colby (1831–1894)

Myra Colby Bradwell passed the Illinois bar exam in 1869, but the Illinois Supreme Court denied her petition to practice on the grounds that she was a married woman. Bradwell took her case to the U.S. Supreme Court, which upheld the lower court decision.

Born in Manchester, Vermont, Bradwell attended finishing school in Kenosha, Wisconsin, and from 1851 to 1852 attended Elgin Female Seminary in Illinois. In 1852, she married James Bradwell, who was admitted to the Illinois bar in 1855. Myra Bradwell studied the law in order to be able to help her husband in his practice. The Civil War interrupted her law studies, delaying her passage of the Illinois bar until 1869.

In 1868, Myra Bradwell had founded the *Chicago Legal News* (*CLN*), the mostly widely circulated legal newspaper in the country. Because of the common law policy of coverture, married women could not conduct business in their own names. In order to overcome the legal disability created by this tradition, Myra Bradwell had sought and received a special charter from the State of Illinois permitting her to conduct the legal business related to *CLN*. Although the newspaper was not visibly feminist and her purpose was unstated, Bradwell published it to advocate for women's rights. From its beginnings, the *CLN* crusaded to open the legal profession to women.

Bradwell's efforts on behalf of women also had more visible aspects to them. In 1869, she helped organized the first woman suffrage convention in the Midwest, and she later held offices in the American Woman Suffrage Association. In addition, Bradwell took her cause to the Illinois state legislature, drafting, lobbying for, and gaining passage of several bills. One gave mothers equal rights in child custody and guardianship (passed in 1871); others were the married women's earnings act (1872) and the married women's property act (1872). She also drafted and lobbied for legislation related to women's employment, including a bill opening all occupations and professions to anyone regardless of sex, which directly addressed the limitation she had encountered in her failed attempt to gain admission to the Illinois bar. The bill passed the Illinois legislature in 1872, but Bradwell did not reapply for admission to the bar. In 1890, however, the Illinois Supreme Court admitted her. Bradwell's other employment-related legislation, passed in 1873, opened all of the offices in the Illinois public school system to women, and another law making married and single women eligible for appointment as notaries public passed in 1875.

Bradwell is sometimes referred to as the first woman lawyer in America, but that distinction belongs to Englishwoman Margaret Brent, who was a lawyer when she settled in Maryland in 1638. Arabella Babb Mansfield, an Iowa woman, was the first U.S. woman admitted to the bar (in 1869), although she never practiced law.

See also American Woman Suffrage Association; *Bradwell v. Illinois*; Brent, Margaret; Coverture; Employment Discrimination; Married Women's Property Acts

References Friedman, *America's First Woman Lawyer: The Biography of Myra Bradwell* (1993).

Bradwell v. Illinois (1873)

In *Bradwell v. Illinois*, the U.S. Supreme Court decided in 1873 that a married woman could be refused admission to the bar. Myra Bradwell passed the Illinois bar examination in 1869 but was denied admission to the state's bar because she was a married woman. Common law defined a married woman as subject to her husband, and at the time a married woman could not conduct business on her own behalf. Bradwell had earlier encountered the limitation in her profession as founder, chief editor, and president of the *Chicago Legal News*, one of the most important legal publications west of the Allegheny Mountains. To overcome these limits, the State of Illinois had earlier granted her a special charter to conduct the legal aspects of her business.

Claiming that her civil rights had been abridged under the Fourteenth Amendment, she took her case to the U.S. Supreme Court. The Court said that the Fourteenth Amendment did not protect career choices and described the family as a "divine ordinance" that mandated that woman's place was in the home. In addition, it stated: "The harmony, not to say identity, of interest and views which belong or should belong to the family institution, is repugnant to the idea of a woman adopting a distinct and independent career from that of her husband." The paternalistic decision meant that women did not have the constitutional right to pursue the full range of employment opportunities available to men.

Bradwell lost, but in 1872, the year before the Court decided her case, the Illinois legislature had passed a law that made it illegal to deny access to a profession on the basis of sex. Bradwell did not reapply for admission to the Illinois bar, but in 1890 the state's Supreme Court admitted her.

See also Coverture; Employment Discrimination; Fourteenth Amendment

References Johnson, *Historic U.S. Court Cases 1690–1990* (1992).

Brady, Sarah Jane Kemp (b. 1942)

Sarah Brady's dedicated lobbying for gun control resulted in the passage of state and federal gun control laws, including the Brady Bill. In March 1981, her husband James Brady, press secretary to President Ronald Reagan, was wounded in an assassination attempt on the president. Reagan recovered fully from the attempt, but James Brady was left with impaired speech and was unable to walk. As tragic as that event was, it took an incident with her young son who found a handgun and, thinking it was a toy, aimed it at Sarah Brady, to launch her lobbying career.

When Brady learned that Congress was considering a bill to repeal some provisions of the Gun Control Act of 1968, she joined Handgun Control, Inc., and began a public relations and lobbying campaign for a seven-day waiting period for handgun purchasers. She became a member of the board of directors in 1985 and president in 1989. In 1991, she became chair of the Center to Prevent Handgun Violence, the legal advocacy, education, and research organization of Handgun Control.

The measure for the waiting period between applying for a handgun and receiving it became known as the Brady Bill. The primary opposition to the bill came from the National Rifle Association, a powerful lobbying group, but Brady lobbied members of Congress, made speeches across the country, and campaigned for congressional candidates who supported her organization's agenda. During the years she worked for the bill, she expressed her scorn for some members of Congress, calling some of them "gutless." She explained: "My disdain is for the people who don't have the guts to stand up for what's right. We're going to get rid of them."

The U.S. House of Representatives debated and defeated the Brady Bill in 1988. James Brady, who was officially press secretary to Ronald Reagan until 1989, remained silent during his wife's early work. When President Reagan left office in 1989, James Brady joined his wife in her campaign for handgun control. The bill received a substantial boost in 1991, when Reagan spoke in its favor. In 1992, the House passed a bill mandating a five-day waiting period, but the Senate filibustered it.

In 1993, President Bill Clinton included support for the bill in his State of the Union message, and later that year, Congress passed the bill with a waiting period of five working days, which serves as both a cooling-off period for impetuous buyers and time to check the purchaser's background. The act raised licensing fees for gun dealers and requires them to notify police of multiple gun purchases and checks on the person applying to buy a gun. Between February 1994 and December 1997, the Brady Handgun Violence Protection Act stopped 242,000 purchases, or 2.3 percent of handgun purchases. Sarah Brady continues to lobby for the registration of all handgun transfers and other measures. Brady also worked on the 1994 assault weapons ban, which prohibits the manufacture and importation of nineteen types of semiautomatic assault weapons and high-capacity ammunition magazines.

In recognition of Jim and Sarah Brady's contributions to make America safer from gun violence, Handgun Control, Inc. was renamed The Brady Campaign to Prevent Gun Violence, and the Center to Prevent Handgun Violence was renamed the The Brady Center to Prevent Gun Violence in 2001.

Born in Kirksville, Missouri, Brady received her bachelor's degree in education from the College of William and Mary in 1964. She was assistant to the campaign director of the National Republican Congressional Committee from 1968 to 1970 and a congressional aide from 1970 to 1974. Then she served as director of administration and coordinator of field services for the Republican National Committee from 1974 to 1978.

References *Congressional Quarterly Almanac, 103rd Congress, 1st Session . . . 1993* (1994); H. W. Wilson, *Current Biography Yearbook, 1996* (1996); *The New York Times*, 25 May 1990; http://www.bradycenter.org

Bravo, Ellen (b. 1944)

Ellen Bravo served as executive director of 9to5, National Association of Working Women, from 1993 to 2004. In 1982, she and several other women had formed the Milwaukee chapter of 9to5. She became an advocate for flexible work schedules and family leave laws and gained regional and national attention as a spokesperson for workers' rights.

Born in Cleveland, Ohio, Ellen Bravo earned her bachelor's degree from Cornell University in 1968, studied at Cambridge University in England and McGill University in Canada, and earned her master's degree in 1971. She taught women's studies at several colleges. By 1981, Bravo was married, had two sons, and was working when the problems of managing a home, a family, and a job confronted her, leading to her activism in 9to5.

In 1992, Bravo co-authored *The 9to5 Guide to Combating Sexual Harassment: Candid Advice from 9to5, the National Association of Working Women*. The authors explained: "It [sexual harassment] is an exercise of power belonging in the same category of sexual behavior that includes assault and rape."

In 1995, Bravo wrote *The Job/Family Challenge: Not for Women Only*, a guide for managing a job and parenthood that explains worker's rights under the Family and Medical Leave Act, offers suggestions for finding quality child care, and includes strategies for convincing employers to implement policies sympathetic to families.

See also Family and Medical Leave Act of 1993; 9to5, National Association of Working Women; Sexual Harassment

References H. W. Wilson, *Current Biography Yearbook, 1997* (1997); *Milwaukee Journal Sentinel*, 31 August 2004.

Bray v. Alexandria Clinic (1993)

In *Bray v. Alexandria Clinic*, the clinic had sought an injunction against Operation Rescue's anti-abortion demonstrations at abortion clinics in the Washington, D.C. metropolitan area. In the demonstrations, Operation Rescue participants trespassed on the premises of the abortion clinics and obstructed the entrances to them. The question before the U.S. Supreme Court was whether the Civil Rights Act of 1871 included actions in front of abortion clinics. The clinics argued that Operation Rescue's opposition to abortion constituted sex discrimination, but the Court disagreed. The Court said that the federal civil rights law under which the clinics sought to enjoin Operation Rescue from demonstrations did not apply to abortion clinics.

See also Abortion; *NOW v. Scheidler*

References *Bray v. Alexandria Clinic*, 506 U.S. 263 (1993).

Brazile, Donna Lease (b. 1959)

The first black woman to manage a presidential campaign, Donna Brazile began her political life at the age of nine, registering voters in Kenner, Louisiana. The candidate she supported promised to build a playground in the poor neighborhood in which she lived, as well as pave the roads. Her candidate won and built the playground. "I've been involved in campaigns ever since," Brazile said.

Brazile developed her skills working for several presidential candidates, including Jimmy Carter in 1976, Rev. Jesse Jackson in 1984, Walter Mondale in 1984, Dick Gephardt in 1988, Michael Dukakis in 1988, and Bill Clinton in 1992 and 1996. As Democratic presidential candidate Al Gore's campaign manager in 2000, she continued her self-assigned task of trying "to make a difference in the lives of ordinary people" that she had begun in Kenner. From 1990 to 1993, Brazile was chief of staff to Eleanor Holmes Norton, the congressional delegate for the District of Columbia.

Donna Brazile was the first African American to lead a major presidential campaign, for Al Gore and Joseph Lieberman in 2000

Brazile is a political commentator and columnist, chair of the Democratic National Committee's Voting Rights Institute, and founder of Brazile and Associates, which seeks to "empower grassroots advocates and train citizens to participate in the political process."

Born in New Orleans, Louisiana, Brazile earned an undergraduate degree from Louisiana State University in 1981. She is the author of *Cooking with Grease: Stirring the Pots in American Politics* (2004).

References http://www.brazileassociates.com/page.cfm?id=2; http://www.npr.org/programs/npc/2001/010502.dbrazile.html; *Los Angeles Times*, 10 January 2000; *The Washington Post*, 26 January 2003;
Document: Donna Brazile, "Run Sisters Run!," 2005

Brent, Margaret (ca. 1607–ca. 1671)

The first female lawyer in America, Margaret Brent may have been the first woman in the American colonies to seek to vote. Born in England, Brent was a lawyer in 1638 when she settled in Maryland. An astute businesswoman, she received a small land grant that she expanded into thousands of acres. Her strong litigation and negotiating skills served her well as legal counsel to Governor Leonard Calvert. As a freeholder and attorney to the governor, in 1648 she sought two votes in Maryland's House of Burgesses, but the House refused her both votes. Brent then attempted to invalidate the actions the House had taken since the time she had made her request and again failed in her attempt.

Brent's influence in the colony, however, becomes apparent from her roles in two related events in Maryland. Calvert went to England for a time, and when he returned, he found that the government had been taken over. Brent helped Calvert raise a group of soldiers to retake the government and restore his power, but he died soon after that. Before his death Governor Calvert had named Brent executor of his estate. The soldiers, who had not been paid for their services, formed a mob and threatened violence, overwhelming the new governor, who asked Brent to intercede. She negotiated with the soldiers, paying them with food. A severe corn shortage prompted Brent to import corn from Virginia, and she slaughtered some of her own cattle as additional compensation, satisfying the soldiers. The Maryland assembly praised her for preventing a mutiny and protecting public safety.

Brent and the rest of her family moved to Virginia in 1650, where she lived until her death.

See also Bradwell, Myra Colby; *Bradwell v. Illinois*

References Berry, *The 50 Most Influential Women in American Law* (1996).

Brown, Corrine (b. 1946)

Democrat Corrine Brown of Florida entered the U.S. House of Representatives on 3 January 1993. Brown's campaign slogan for her 1992 race for the U.S. House of Representatives was "Corrine Fights, Corrine Works, Corrine Delivers, Corrine Makes It Happen." Her congressional priorities have included the treatment of Haitian refugees in the United States, job creation in Florida, economic development, education, senior citizens' rights, health care, corrections, veterans' issues, and women's issues. She supports expanding reproductive rights, families' access to child care, and health care for young children. Brown voted against the North American Free Trade Agreement, concerned that it would result in the loss of jobs to Mexico.

Defending affirmative action programs, Brown said: "Affirmative action is a thin slice–four percent [of the population]. To tell you the truth, we ought to be going after the other 96 percent." She opposed the many welfare reform bills introduced during the 104th Congress (1995–1997), saying: "Republicans are in a hurry to pay for the tax breaks for the rich at the expense of hungry children, the elderly and veterans."

Florida Congresswoman Corrine Brown participates in press conference with Florida Democrats to protest oil drilling off of Florida's shores. (Courtesy Office of Corrine Brown)

Congresswoman Brown believes that Florida constituents were disenfranchised in the 2000 presidential elections, alleging that the Republican Party and successful presidential candidate George W. Bush had "stolen [the] elections of 2000." With nine other members of Congress, she sent a letter to the United Nations requesting election monitors to guarantee that the 2004 presidential elections would be fair. Despite being censured by the U.S. House of Representatives, Brown said: "I will continue to do everything within my power to ensure that not one voter is denied the right to vote, and our nation does not witness a repeat of the 2000 elections!" Controversial, outspoken, and a persistent critic of President George W. Bush's policies, Congresswoman Brown lost speaking privileges on the House floor in 2004 for accusing some of her colleagues of stealing the 2000 presidential elections, referring to the recounts of Floridians' votes that year.

Born in Jacksonville, Florida, African American Corrine Brown earned her BS in 1969 and her MA in 1971, both from Florida A&M University, and her specialist in education degree from the University of Florida in 1974. From 1977 to 1982, Brown was a college counselor and professor at Florida Community College. From 1983 to 1993, she served in the Florida House of Representatives.

See also Abortion; Affirmative Action; Congress, Women in; State Legislatures, Women in

References *Congressional Quarterly, Politics in America 1996* (1995), *Politics in America 1998* (1997), *Politics in America 2006* (2005); Gill, *African American Women in Congress* (1997); *New York Amsterdam News*, 22 July 2004.

Brown, Elaine (b. 1943)

A member of the Black Panther Party, Elaine Brown served as the party's only female chair from 1974 to 1977. During that time, Brown brought more women into the management of the party, increased its resources, and eliminated much of the intraparty violence. Forced out of the party's leadership, she felt vulnerable to the renewed intraparty violence she had worked to end and left the party.

Born in Philadelphia, Pennsylvania, Elaine Brown attended Temple University and the Philadelphia Conservatory of Music in 1961. She moved to California in 1965 and taught piano to African American girls in the Watts section of Los Angeles. The experience brought back images from her own youth, as she wrote in her memoir *A Taste of Power*: "I recoiled when I beheld their little faces, the blankness in their eyes. It was a look from long ago I knew well. . . . It was me I saw. There was my face, my pain, my nothing-little-nigger-girl expression lingering on their faces and in their eyes."

Brown became active in the Los Angeles Black Congress in 1967 and worked on its newspaper, which led to her involvement with the Black Panther Party (BPP) the next year. Brown's early work with the party included serving as its Los Angeles minister of information, organizing new chapters, leading voter registration drives, and assisting with the party's free breakfast program.

In 1974, she became chairperson of the party, second in command to Huey P. Newton, making her the highest-ranking woman in it. Following Newton's arrest later that year and his subsequent escape to Cuba, he selected Brown as the party's functional leader. Within the party's ranks, the selection became a source of strife because some male party members objected to women's increasing power in the party and to Brown's power in particular. It was a difficult time for her, she explained: "If a black woman assumed a role of leadership, she was said to be eroding black manhood, to be hindering the progress of the black race. She was an enemy of the black people.... I knew I had to muster something mighty to manage the Black Panther Party."

As chair, Brown expanded the party's programs to include electoral politics, education of black youth, civic issues, and the continued elevation of women in the party. In 1975, she unsuccessfully ran for a seat on the Oakland City Council, but that effort further propelled the party into the city's power structure. The voter registration program she organized registered nearly 100,000 new voters and helped elect an African American to the county board of supervisors and African American Lionel Wilson as mayor of Oakland in 1977. She negotiated an agreement with city and state officials to build a freeway extension that helped revitalize Oakland's downtown and created hundreds of jobs. During Brown's tenure, the California State Assembly commended the Panthers for their work in education at their Oakland Community Learning Center.

Brown later recollected: "I loved the commitment. I mean, we were not being paid; here was absolute commitment. I loved the fact that we took it to the wall and that we were willing to die for everything that we said and that some of us did die. Certainly, there were many, many flaws. But this was a group of heroic people, and I was part of a very heroic effort."

When Huey Newton returned to active involvement in the party in 1977, Brown saw that the party's loyalty to her had ended and returned to Newton. In addition, several male party members pressured him to retake control of the party, particularly from powerful women like Brown. After learning that Newton had sanctioned the beating of a woman who was an associate of Brown's, Brown felt threatened. She left Oakland later that year, eventually moving to France. Brown published her autobiography, *A Taste of Power: A Black Woman's Story*, in 1992.

See also Civil Rights Movement, Women in the

References Brown, *A Taste of Power: A Black Woman's Story* (1992); *The New York Times*, 31 January 1993.

Brown, Judie (b. 1944)

Founder of the American Life League (formerly the American Life Lobby) in 1979, Judie Brown became involved in the pro-life movement in 1969, fighting a referendum in Washington state to provide greater access to abortions. She moved to Washington, D.C., with her husband Paul Brown in 1976 and volunteered at the National Right to Life Committee as its office manager.

Through the American Life League, Judie Brown worked to pass a federal constitutional amendment to make all abortions illegal. In addition, Brown opposed all forms of birth control other than abstinence. She also opposes assisted suicide, euthanasia, stem cell research, and cloning.

Born in Los Angeles, California, Judie Brown received her undergraduate degree from the University of California at Los Angeles.

See also Abortion; American Life League, Inc.
References www.all.org.

Brown, Rita Mae (b. 1944)

Author, radical feminist, and lesbian rights activist Rita Mae Brown was a founder of Redstockings and Radicalesbians, and a member of the Furies. She contributed to Radicalesbians' "The Woman-Identified Woman." Her novel *Rubyfruit Jungle*, the story of a lesbian's coming-of-age with hints of autobiography, was first published by a small women's press in 1973 and then was issued by a major publisher and sold more than a million copies.

Born in Hanover, Pennsylvania, Brown grew up in Florida, the adopted daughter of an Amish father. She attended the University of Florida but was dismissed during her sophomore year for her civil rights activism. She earned her bachelor's degree from New York University in 1968 and received a certificate in cinematography the same year from the School of Visual Arts in Manhattan.

See also Lesbian Rights; Radicalesbians; Redstockings; Women's Liberation Movement
References H. W. Wilson, *Current Biography Yearbook, 1986* (1986).

Brown-Waite, Virginia (Ginny) (b.1943)

Republican Virginia Brown-Waite of Florida entered the U.S. House of Representatives on 3 January 2003. She defeated Democratic Representative Karen Thurman in the 2002 elections.

Brown-Waite's priorities have included legislation to guarantee current retirees their full Social Security benefits and policies to improve health care for veterans. She received recognition for her contributions to the passage of the Violence Against

Florida Congresswoman Ginny Brown-Waite listens intently at the Hearing on CBO Analysis of the President's FY 2004 Budget March 25, 2003 (Courtesy U.S. House of Representatives)

Women Act of 2005. She co-chairs the Congressional Women's Caucus during the 109th Congress (2005–2006).

A Hernando County, Florida, commissioner from 1990 to 1992, Brown-Waite served in the Florida state senate from 1992 to 2002, serving as the senate's president pro tempore from 2001 to 2002. Before moving to Florida, Brown-Waite was the legislative director for the New York state senate.

Born in Albany, New York, Brown-Waite earned a bachelor of science degree at the State University of New York in 1976, a labor studies program certificate from Cornell University in 1980, and a master of science degree at Russell Sage College in 1984.

References http://brown-waite.house.gov/biography; http://www.vote-smart.org/bio.php?can_id=BS026279; "Biographies: Florida," *National Journal*, 9 November 2002, p. 3295.

Browner, Carol (b. 1955)

Carol Browner served as administrator of the U.S. Environmental Protection Agency (EPA), a Cabinet-level position in President Bill Clinton's administration, from 1993 to 2001, the longest tenure of any EPA administrator. Browner's priorities included food safety protection, restoring toxic waste sites, and reducing the risks to children's health caused by environmental hazards. During her eight years with the EPA, she worked with Congress to pass the 1996 Food Quality Protection Act, restored 700 toxic waste sites, and created the Office of Children's Health Protection. She also worked for the reauthorization of the Safe Drinking Water Act, reformed administration of the Superfund policies, and implemented new emissions standards for cars, SUVs, diesel trucks, and buses.

She began her political career as an aide in the Florida House of Representatives in 1980, became associate director for the environmental lobbying group Citizen Action in 1983, and entered the national political scene as an aide to Senator Lawton Chiles from 1986 to 1989. After serving as legislative director for Senator Al Gore beginning in 1989, she returned to Florida in 1991 to serve as newly elected Governor Lawton Chiles's secretary of the Florida Department of Environmental Regulations. She negotiated an agreement leading to the restoration of the Florida Everglades, a $1 billion project, and a landmark agreement with the Walt Disney Company, allowing them to develop 400 acres of wetlands in exchange for $40 million to purchase and protect 8,500 acres of wetlands in central Florida.

As administrator for the U.S. Environmental Protection Agency, Browner worked to prevent pollution, improve coordination with other federal regulatory agencies to create more consistent policies, and encourage states to develop their own environmental protection plans. She sought to convince both environmentalists and the business community that economic growth and environmental protection can coexist and received praise and criticism from both groups. During her tenure, Browner collected the largest environmental fines in history while offering new levels of compliance assistance to business owners.

Born in South Miami, Florida, Browner received her bachelor's degree in English in 1977 and her law degree in 1979, both from the University of Florida.

See also Cabinets, Women in Presidential

References Cheryl Hogue, "Browner Leaves her Stamp on EPA," *Chemical and Engineering News*, 15 January 2001, pp. 34–37; H. W. Wilson, *Current Biography Yearbook, 1994* (1994).

Buchanan, Vera Daerr (1902–1955)

Democrat Vera Buchanan of Pennsylvania served in the U.S. House of Representatives from 24 July 1951 until her death on 26 November 1955. Following the death of her husband, Congressman Frank Buchanan, Vera Buchanan was elected to complete his term and then twice won re-election. She introduced bills to combat inflation, increase railroad retirement benefits, provide housing for low-income elderly people, and protect consumers. Her other interests included flood control, labor unions, and laborers' rights.

Born in Wilson, Pennsylvania, Vera Buchanan operated a beauty shop in McKeesport, Pennsylvania.

See also Congress, Women in

References Engelbarts, *Women in the United States Congress, 1917–1972* (1974); Tolchin, *Women in Congress: 1917–1976* (1976).

Burdick, Jocelyn Birch (b. 1922)

Democrat Jocelyn Burdick of North Dakota served in the U.S. Senate from 12 September 1992 to 14 December 1992. Following the death of her husband, Senator Quentin Burdick, Jocelyn Burdick accepted an interim appointment to the U.S. Senate, which she held until a successor was elected.

Born in Fargo, North Dakota, Jocelyn Burdick is the great-granddaughter of suffragist Matilda Joslyn Gage. She attended Principia College and earned her bachelor's degree from Northwestern University in 1943.

See also Congress, Women in; Gage, Matilda Joslyn

References Minot, *North Dakota Daily News*, 13 September 1992.

Burke, Perle Yvonne Watson Brathwaite (b. 1932)

Democrat Yvonne Burke of California served in the U.S. House of Representatives from 3 January 1973 to 3 January 1979. She served in the California Assembly from 1967 to 1973, the first black woman elected to that body, concentrating on child care, prison reform, equal job opportunities for women, and education funding. In the summer of 1972, she served as vice chairperson of the Democratic National Convention, a sometimes unruly event that gave Burke opportunities to demonstrate her ability. The presiding officer of the convention during the debate over the party platform, Burke deftly led the delegates through twenty-one votes in the longest session in U.S. political history, eleven hours.

When California's electoral districts were reapportioned in 1972, a new congressional district was created, and Burke ran to represent it and won. In November 1973, when her daughter Autumn was born, Burke became the first member of Congress to give birth while in office. In 1976, Burke became the first woman to chair the congressional Black Caucus.

Burke sponsored and passed a measure requiring that contracts for the construction of the Alaskan pipeline be awarded on an affirmative action basis. As Burke continued to place amendments that required any project receiving federal funding to implement an affirmative action plan, the measures became known as the Burke Amendment. She passed a measure in 1978 to make displaced homemakers eligible for training and services provided through the Comprehensive Education and Training Act. Burke worked for increases in federal funding for community nutrition programs and funding to help Vietnamese refugee resettlement and fought efforts to increase the price of food stamps. She worked to restrict foreign aid to nations that violated human rights. Civil rights and housing were other areas on which she focused.

She declined to run for a fourth term in 1978, choosing instead to be a candidate for California state attorney general, but she lost that race. She was appointed to the Los Angeles County Board of Supervisors and served from June 1979 to December 1980, when she resigned and resumed her legal practice. She won election to the Board of Supervisors in 1992 and continues to serve there.

Born in Los Angeles, California, Yvonne Burke received her associate's degree from the University of California at Berkeley in 1951, her bachelor's degree in political science from the University of California at Los Angeles in 1953, and her law degree from the University of Southern California School of Law in 1956. She entered private practice, specializing in civil, probate, and real estate law.

> **See also** Affirmative Action; Congress, Women in; Democratic Party, Women in the; Displaced Homemakers; State Legislatures, Women in

> **References** Gill, *African American Women in Congress* (1997); H. W. Wilson, *Current Biography Yearbook, 1975* (1975); Office of the Historian, U.S. House of Representatives, *Women in Congress, 1917–1990* (1991).

Burlington Industries v. Ellerth (1998)

Kimberly Ellerth quit her job as a salesperson at Burlington Industries after 15 months, alleging that her supervisor had subjected her to constant sexual harassment. When she refused to endure his boorish and offensive remarks, he threatened to deny her job benefits. She did not suffer any retaliation; instead she received one promotion. In addition, even though the company had a policy against sexual harassment, Ellerth did not tell anyone in authority about it. After she quit her job, she sued the company.

The U.S. Supreme Court held that under Title VII of the Civil Rights Act of 1964, an employer could be held liable for a sexually hostile work environment, even though the employee did not suffer a job setback. The Court added that an employer could overcome the liability if it took reasonable care to prevent and end the harassment.

> **References** *Burlington Industries v. Ellerth*, 524 U.S. 742 (1998); *Washington Post*, 27 June 1998.

Burton, Sala Galante (1925–1987)

Democrat Sala Burton of California served in the U.S. House of Representatives from 21 June 1983 until her death on 1 February 1987. Following her husband's death, Sala Burton ran to complete his term and then won two full terms. In Congress, Burton advocated social welfare programs, child nutrition assistance, bilingual education, and the Equal Rights Amendment.

Following her re-election in 1986, Burton's health began a rapid decline. Suffering from the effects of surgery for colon cancer, she was unable to attend swearing-in ceremonies on January 6 and was given the oath of office at home the next day. She died on 1 February 1987.

Born in Bialystok, Poland, Sala Burton fled the country with her parents just before the Nazi invasion. She attended San Francisco University, leaving before graduation to marry Phillip Burton. Her interest in politics developed when she was a teenager. She explained: "I saw and felt what happened in Western Europe when the Nazis were moving. You learn that politics is everybody's business."

From 1948 to 1950, she was associate director of the California Public Affairs Institute. During the years that her husband Phillip Burton held offices in the California State Assembly and in Congress, Sala Burton developed her own political skills. She was an organizer of the California Democratic Council and its vice president from 1951 to 1954, worked for the California Public Affairs Institute, served on San Francisco's fair housing board, and chaired the Democratic Women's Forum from 1957 to 1959. She also worked with the National Association for the Advancement of Colored People to end job and housing discrimination. After the couple moved to Washington, D.C., Sala Burton served on the advisory boards of the National Security Committee and the National Council on Soviet Jewry and was legislative chair of the Women's National Democratic Club.

See also Congress, Women in; Equal Rights Amendment

References *The New York Times*, 3 February 1987; Office of the Historian, U.S. House of Representatives, *Women in Congress, 1917–1990* (1991).

Bush, Barbara Pierce (b. 1925)

Barbara Bush was first lady from 1989 to 1993. During the years her husband served as vice president (1981 to 1989) and president (1989 to 1993), Barbara Bush focused on increasing adult literacy. By participating in hundreds of literacy events, she brought national attention to the issue.

Born in Rye, New York, Barbara Bush attended Smith College from 1943 to 1944, when she married George Bush, whom she had first met when she was a teenager. While George Bush pursued careers in business and politics, Barbara Bush raised their family and made a home for them. She served as hostess when he was ambassador to the United Nations and chief of the U.S. Liaison Office to the People's Republic of China.

When George Bush became vice president, Barbara Bush sought ways to raise money to support literacy programs and decided to write *C. Fred's Story* (1984), a collection of stories about the Bushes' late cocker spaniel; later, she wrote *Millie's Book* (1990) about another family dog. Barbara Bush donated the proceeds to literacy organizations, including Literacy Volunteers of America and Laubach Literary Action. In 1989, she established the Barbara Bush Foundation for Family Literacy, a private organization that solicits private and public funds for literacy programs. She served as hon-

First Lady Barbara Bush, January 1989. (Library of Congress Prints and Photographs Division Washington, D.C. 20540 USA LC-USZ62-98303)

orary chair or honorary board member in several literacy organizations, cancer organizations, and children's health groups.

With her white hair, string of pearls, and motherly figure, Barbara Bush endeared herself to Americans, who appreciated her wit, candor, and compassion. For example, she stressed that her husband held the offices and the power that accompanied them, but she would smile as she indicated that she influenced him.

Her son, George W. Bush was elected president in 2000 and re-elected in 2004.

References Bush, *Barbara Bush: A Memoir* (1994).

Bush, Laura (b. 1946)

Laura Bush became first lady in 2001, following her husband George W. Bush's inauguration as president of the United States. In 2001, Laura Bush organized the first National Book Festival in Washington, D.C., co-hosting the event with the head of the Library of Congress. Like her mother-in-law, Barbara Bush, Laura Bush has championed literacy and the pleasures of reading. Also in 2001, Laura Bush became the first wife of a president to deliver the president's weekly radio address.

Laura Bush organized "A Summit on Early Childhood Cognitive Development Ready to Read, Ready to Learn: A Call to Leadership," held in Little Rock, Arkansas, in 2002. In 2005, she became the leader of President Bush's Helping America's Youth program, intended to help children avoid drug and alcohol use. She leads the $150 million program, focusing on boys ages 8 to 17. She explained that she wanted to work with children, particularly adolescent boys, "because I feel like over the last several decades maybe we've neglected boys a little bit." Laura Bush has also worked with the National Heart, Lung, and Blood Institute to publicize the risks heart disease poses for women.

Laura Bush

Laura Bush served as first lady of Texas from 1995 to 2001, the years her husband was governor of the state.

Laura Bush earned a bachelor of science degree in education from Southern Methodist University in 1968. After teaching in public schools, she earned a master of library science degree from the University of Texas and became a public school librarian. She married George W. Bush in 1977.

> **References** http://www.whitehouse.gov/firstlady/fbio.html; *Los Angeles Times*, 3 February 2005; *The New York Times*, 8 September 2001.

Bushfield, Vera Cahalan (1889–1976)

Republican Vera Bushfield of South Dakota served in the U.S. Senate from 6 October 1948 to 26 December 1948. She was appointed to fill the vacancy created by the death of her husband, Harlan J. Bushfield. At the time of her appointment, Congress had recessed, and Vera Bushfield stayed in South Dakota during her brief time in office working on constituent services. She did not take part in debate or receive committee assignments, and she did not run for a full term.

Born in Miller, South Dakota, Vera Bushfield attended Dakota Wesleyan University and the University of Minnesota. She graduated from the Stout Institute in Menominee, Wisconsin, in 1912.

See also Congress, Women in

References Office of the Historian, U.S. House of Representatives, *Women in Congress, 1917–1990* (1991).

Business and Professional Women/USA

Founded in 1919, Business and Professional Women/USA (BPW/USA) promotes equity for women in the workplace through education, information, and advocacy. With 70,000 members in more than 2,000 local groups, BPW/USA has effectively lobbied Congress and state legislatures since its beginning, providing leadership in the passage of several measures.

BPW has its roots in World War I, when the federal government wanted to organize professional women for the war effort. The War Department called on the Young Women's Christian Association (YWCA) to create the National Business Women's Committee and provided a grant of $65,000 to finance the organization. The YWCA's executives provided the initial leadership and helped guide the formation of a permanent organization with state federations.

In its first year, BPW formed twenty-five state federations as well as the New England federation. Its initial legislative agenda in 1919 included ending sex discrimination in civil service appointments and establishing officer rank for army nurses and permanent federal and state employment agencies. The next year, it added support for the woman suffrage amendment and the maternal and infancy health bill, known as the Sheppard-Towner Act. Other BPW priorities in the 1920s included uniform marriage and divorce laws, creation of federal departments of education and health, ratification of the child labor amendment, and the Cable Acts, which gave women independent citizenship.

One of the first mainstream women's organizations to endorse the Equal Rights Amendment (ERA), BPW/USA has supported it since 1937 and opened an office in Washington, D.C., to lobby for the amendment in 1947. The organization took a leading role in gaining congressional approval for it, particularly when Congress considered it in the early 1970s and passed it in 1972. When it appeared that ratification of the amendment would not be as speedy as supporters had initially believed, BPW hired a national political consulting firm to evaluate campaign strategies. At the consultant's recommendation, BPW helped organize an umbrella association comprising groups that supported the amendment. Founded in 1976, ERAmerica eventually included more than 200 organizations in the ERA campaign. The amendment, however, failed to be ratified by the necessary thirty-eight states before the deadline established by Congress.

BPW has been involved in passing several landmark women's and civil rights bills, including the Equal Pay Act of 1963; the Civil Rights Act of 1964; the Education Amendments of 1972, Title IX; the Women's Educational Equity Act of 1974; the

Equal Credit Opportunity Act of 1974; the Family and Medical Leave Act of 1993; and the Violence Against Women Act of 1994. The organization's legislative agenda includes affirmative action, economic equity, reproductive rights, research in women's health care needs, civil rights, pension reform, financial solvency for Social Security, and the elimination of sexual harassment and violence against women.

The Fair Pay Act has been a BPW/USA priority for several years. The Fair Pay Act seeks to eliminate wage discrimination based on sex, race, or national origin by requiring employers to provide equal pay for work of equivalent value. Equivalent value is defined as a composite of skills, effort, responsibility, and working conditions. To publicize the need for pay equity, BPW/USA co-sponsors the annual Equal Pay Day. Held in April, Equal Pay Day signifies how much longer a woman must work into the second year than a man earns in just one year.

In the area of women's health, BPW/USA supports the proposed HEART for Women Act, which calls for improvements in the prevention, diagnosis, and treatment of heart disease, stroke, and other cardiovascular diseases in women. Roslyn Ridgeway, the organization's national president, called the legislation "critical to all women and their families."

In 1980, the organization changed its bylaws to permit men to become members.

> **See also** Abortion; Affirmative Action; Cable Acts; Child Labor Amendment; Civil Rights Act of 1964, Title VII; Education Amendments of 1972, Title IX; Education, Women and; Equal Credit Opportunity Act of 1974; Equal Pay Act of 1963; Equal Rights Amendment; ERAmerica; Family and Medical Leave Act of 1993; Pay Equity; Reproductive Rights; Sheppard-Towner Maternity and Infancy Protection Act of 1921; Violence Against Women Act of 1994; Women's Educational Equity Act of 1974; Women's Health, Office of Research on
>
> **References** Lemons, *The Woman Citizen* (1973); www.bpwusa.org.

Byrne, Jane Margaret Burke (b. 1934)

Democrat Jane Byrne was mayor of Chicago from 1979 to 1983. She was the first woman to lead the nation's second-largest city. Byrne entered politics as a diversion from her grief following the death of her husband, a Marine pilot. Her sister had become involved in John F. Kennedy's 1960 presidential campaign and encouraged Byrne to join her. Byrne refused until she heard Kennedy giving a speech offering sympathy for the families of service members who died in accidents, prompting her to volunteer in Kennedy's campaign. After Kennedy won the election, he invited Byrne to White House events, where she met Chicago Mayor Richard Daley.

Daley appointed Byrne to his Cabinet, became her political mentor, and appointed her to posts within the Cook County Democratic Party and in Chicago government. Following Daley's death in 1976, Michael A. Bilandic became mayor. After engaging in several public battles with him, Byrne decided to run for mayor in 1979. Although Bilandic had the support of the party, Byrne attracted the support of women, minorities, ethnics, and liberals and won the election.

Born in Chicago, Jane Byrne earned her bachelor's degree in chemistry and biology from Barat College of the Sacred Heart in 1955.

> **See also** Public Offices, Women Elected to
>
> **References** H. W. Wilson, *Current Biography Yearbook, 1980* (1980).

Byrne, Leslie Larkin (b. 1946)

Democrat Leslie Byrne of Virginia served in the U.S. House of Representatives from 3 January 1993 to 3 January 1995. Congresswoman Byrne concentrated on transportation, job growth, and family leave policy. A reproductive rights supporter, she also favored a waiting period for handgun purchases. Byrne lost her bid for a second term. In 1996, she became director of the U.S. Office of Consumer Affairs. That year, she unsuccessfully sought her party's nomination for the U.S. Senate.

Before her election, Byrne was president of a business consulting firm, active in the community, and president of the local League of Women Voters. She served in the Virginia House of Delegates from 1985 to 1992, where she focused her attention on transportation issues. She served in the Virginia Senate from 1999 to 2003, after which she unsuccessfully ran for lieutenant governor of Virginia in 2005.

Born in Salt Lake City, Utah, Leslie Byrne attended the University of Utah from 1964 to 1965.

> **See also** Abortion, Congress, Women in; Family and Medical Leave Act of 1993; State Legislatures, Women in
>
> **References** Duncan, *Politics in America 1994* (1993); Treese, ed., *Biographical Directory of the American Congress 1774–1996* (1997); http://www.lesliebyrne.org.

Byron, Beverly Barton Butcher (b. 1932)

Democrat Beverly Byron of Maryland served in the U.S. House of Representatives from 3 January 1979 to 3 January 1993. She became involved in politics in 1962, working for her husband Goodloe Byron's campaign for the Maryland legislature, and remained involved as he moved to the U.S. House of Representatives. When Goodloe Byron died a month before the 1978 elections, Beverly Byron ran for and won his seat. Almost forty years earlier, her mother-in-law, Katharine Edgar Byron, had succeeded her husband following his death. In contrast to her mother-in-law, Beverly Byron won six subsequent elections.

The daughter of an aide to General Dwight D. Eisenhower, Beverly Byron supported the military, opposed the nuclear weapons freeze, worked for funds for a new antitank fighter, and attempted to preserve the Army Veterinary Corps. She went on several test flights of new military planes. A member of the Armed Services Committee and the first woman to chair one of its subcommittees (personnel), she fought for assistance to personnel involuntarily released from the service. She also worked for increased benefits for military personnel, especially those who served in the Gulf War. At one time opposed to women in combat, she supported a measure allowing women to volunteer for air combat duty after she saw women soldiers' accomplishments in the Gulf War.

Chair of the Maryland Commission on Physical Fitness from 1979 to 1989, she promoted physical fitness. Her love of the outdoors prompted her to take a leadership role in protecting and improving the nation's hiking trail system. She was described as "instrumental in passage of the 1984 National Trails System Improvement Act" and was "pivotal in the creation" of the National Parks Trail Assessment program. She sponsored amendments that created the Rails-to-Trails Act, which converts railroad rights-of-way into public hiking trails.

Beverly Byron succeeded in passing measures to ban federal Occupational Safety and Health Administration (OSHA) inspections if state authorities had visited the same workplace in the preceding six months and another to ban routine OSHA inspections in certain industries with fewer than ten employees. She lost her bid for reelection in 1992.

From 1980 to 1987, she served on the U.S. Air Force Academy Board of Visitors and was appointed to the U.S. Naval Academy Board of Visitors in 1995. She also served as a commissioner of the Defense Base Closure and Realignment Commission, beginning in 1993, in addition to other defense-related panels.

Born in Baltimore, Maryland, Beverly Byron attended Hood College from 1963 to 1964.

See also Byron, Katharine Edgar; Congress, Women in; Military, Women in the
References *Backpacker*, May 1990; *Congressional Quarterly, Politics in America 1994* (1993), *Politics in America: The 100th Congress* (1987); Office of the Historian, U.S. House of Representatives, *Women in Congress, 1917–1990* (1991).

Byron, Katharine Edgar (1903–1976)

Democrat Katharine Byron of Maryland served in the U.S. House from 27 May 1941 to 3 January 1943. Following the death of her husband, Congressman William Byron, in an airplane crash, Katharine Byron won the election to complete his term. Both during her campaign and in office, she supported U.S. assistance to countries fighting against the Nazis and worked for U.S. military preparedness. Byron did not run for reelection.

Born in Detroit, Michigan, Katharine Byron moved to Williamsport, Maryland, in 1922, where she was president of the local parent-teachers' association in 1935, chair of the local Red Cross flood disaster committee, and a town commissioner from 1938 to 1940.

See also Byron, Beverly Barton Butcher; Congress, Women in
References Office of the Historian, U.S. House of Representatives, *Women in Congress, 1917–1990* (1991).

Cabinets, Women in Presidential

Frances Perkins, appointed by President Franklin D. Roosevelt in 1933, was the first woman to hold a Cabinet position. Democratic presidents have appointed sixteen women to their Cabinets, including Perkins, and Republican presidents have appointed fourteen women. Since the Roosevelt administration, Presidents Dwight D. Eisenhower, Gerald Ford, Jimmy Carter, Ronald Reagan, George Bush, Bill Clinton, and George W. Bush have appointed women to their Cabinets. Presidents Harry S. Truman, John F. Kennedy, Lyndon Johnson, and Richard Nixon did not appoint women to their Cabinets. Five women, Madeleine K. Albright, Elizabeth Hanford Dole, Patricia Roberts Harris, Carla Anderson Hills, and Laura D'Andrea Tyson, have each held two Cabinet positions. Patricia Roberts Harris was the first African American woman to hold a Cabinet post; Aida Alvarez was the first Latina; and Elaine Chao was the first Asian American woman.

Presidential Cabinets have their roots in tradition and have neither statutory nor constitutional foundations. For this reason, presidents define Cabinet-level positions in their administrations and can make any government official a member of the Cabinet. For example, the position of United Nations ambassador was a Cabinet-level position in Ronald Reagan's and Bill Clinton's administrations. During the Bush administration, the post of special trade representative was Cabinet-level, as was the position of U.S. trade representative in the Clinton administration. Chair of the National Economic Council and administrator of the Environmental Protection Agency were Cabinet-level positions in the Clinton administration.

Presidents have a variety of reasons for expanding their Cabinets beyond the department secretaries. They may want to solicit the advice of specialists, call attention to an issue or an agency, or reward an agency or its head for its achievements. For Cabinet members, the benefits include status, visibility, and access to the president.

The position, the women who have held it, their party affiliation, and the time they held the positions are listed below.

- Secretary of State: Madeleine Albright (D) served from 1997 to 2001; Condoleezza Rice (R) was appointed in 2005

- Attorney General: Janet Reno (D) served from 1993 to 2001
- Secretary of Agriculture: Ann Veneman (R) served from 2001 to 2005
- Secretary of Commerce: Juanita Kreps (D) served from 1977 to 1979; Barbara H. Franklin (R) from 1992 to 1993
- Secretary of Education: Shirley Mount Hufstedler (D) served from 1979 to 1981; Margaret Spellings (R) was appointed in 2005
- Secretary of Energy: Hazel O'Leary served from 1993 to 1997
- Secretary of Health, Education, and Welfare: Oveta Culp Hobby (R) served from 1953 to 1955
- Secretary of Health and Human Services: Patricia Roberts Harris (D) served from 1979 to 1981; Margaret Heckler (R) served from 1983 to 1985; Donna E. Shalala (D) served from 1993 to 2001
- Secretary of Housing and Urban Development: Carla Anderson Hills (R) served from 1975 to 1977; Patricia Roberts Harris (D) served from 1977 to 1979
- Secretary of the Interior: Gale Norton (R) was appointed in 2001
- Secretary of Labor: Frances M. Perkins (D) served from 1933 to 1945; Ann Dore McLaughlin (R) served from 1987 to 1989; Elizabeth Hanford Dole (R) served from 1989 to 1991; Lynn Morley Martin (R) served from 1991 to 1993; Alexis Herman (D) served from 1997 to 2001; Elaine Chao (R) was appointed in 2001
- Secretary of Transportation: Elizabeth Hanford Dole served from 1983 to 1987
- Special Trade Representative: Carla Anderson Hills (R) served from 1989 to 1993
- United States Trade Representative: Charlene Barshefsky (D) served from 1997 to 2001
- United Nations Ambassador: Jeane J. Kirkpatrick served from 1981 to 1985; Madeleine K. Albright (D) served from 1993 to 1997
- Administrator, Environmental Protection Agency: Carol M. Browner served from 1993 to 2001; Christine Todd Whitman (R) served from 1997 to 2003
- Chair of the National Economic Council: Laura D'Andrea Tyson served from 1995 to 1996
- Director of the Office of Management and Budget: Alice Rivlin served from 1994 to 1996
- Chair of the Council of Economic Advisers: Laura D'Andrea Tyson (D) served from 1993 to 1995; Janet Yellen (D) served from 1997 to 1999
- Small Business Administration: Aida Alvarez served from 1997 to 2001
- Director of the Office of Personnel Management: Janice R. Lachance served from 1997 to 2001

See also: Albright, Madeleine Jana Korbel; Alvarez, Aida; Barshefsky, Charlene; Browner, Carol; Dole, (Mary) Elizabeth Hanford; Franklin, Barbara Hackman; Harris, Patricia Roberts; Heckler, Margaret Mary O'Shaughnessy; Herman, Alexis Margaret; Hills, Carla Helen Anderson; Hobby, Oveta Culp; Hufstedler, Shirley Ann Mount; Kirkpatrick, Jeane Duane Jordan; Kreps, Juanita Morris; Martin, Judith Lynn Morley; McLaughlin, Ann Dore Lauenstein; O'Leary, Hazel Rollins; Perkins, Frances (Fanny) Corlie; Reno, Janet; Rivlin, Alice Mitchell; Shalala, Donna Edna; Tyson, Laura D'Andrea; Yellen, Janet

References *Congressional Quarterly, Cabinets and Counselors: The President and the Executive Branch* (1997); Warshaw, *Powersharing: White House-Cabinet Relations in the Modern Presidency* (1996); http://www.cawp.rutgers.edu/Facts/Officeholders/fedcab.pdf

Documents Condoleezza Rice, "Special Briefing on Travel to the Middle East and Europe," 2006; Secretary Margaret Spellings, "Remarks to the First National Summit on the Advancement of Girls in Math and Science"

Cable Acts

The Cable Act of 1922 gave married women citizenship independent of their husband's citizenship. Until 1907, American women (other than Native American women), whether married or not, had independent citizenship, but a law passed that year withdrew the citizenship of women married to aliens, and the U.S. government assigned those women their husbands' nationality. In 1913, the Association of Women Lawyers began working to change the policy and was the only organization involved until 1920, when the League of Women Voters and the Women's Joint Congressional Committee (WJCC) joined the effort.

Passed in 1922, the Cable Act did not apply to all women or all women married to aliens. For example, a female American citizen who married an alien classified as ineligible for citizenship, that is, a Chinese, Japanese, or East Indian immigrant, ceased to be an American citizen. If a woman married a man who could not become a naturalized citizen for any reason, she lost her citizenship and she could not seek repatriation until the termination of the marriage. Native American women did not gain citizenship under the Cable Act; they gained it under the 1924 Indian Citizenship Act. As these and other barriers to women's citizenship became apparent, WJCC persuaded Congress to amend the Cable Act, which it did in 1930, 1931, and 1934. Even after 1934, however, individual women found themselves in circumstances not addressed by the act or subject to interpretation and discovered that their citizenship was threatened.

See also League of Women Voters; Owen Rohde, Ruth Bryan; Women's Joint Congressional Committee

References Bredbenner, *A Nationality of Her Own: Women, Marriage, and the Law of Citizenship* (1998); Lemons, *The Woman Citizen* (1973).

Cahill, Mary Beth (b. 1954)

Called "the miracle worker" by *Time* magazine, Mary Beth Cahill revived Massachusetts Senator John Kerry's 2004 campaign for the Democratic Party's presidential nomination. When Cahill became Kerry's campaign manager in November 2003, Kerry trailed in the polls, but under Cahill's direction, he won the nomination. Cahill placed increased emphasis on Kerry's status as a war hero, eliminated conflicts within the campaign, and clarified the decision-making process. She explained: "We discuss a strategy, decide on it, and then we execute," without revisiting the decision. Kerry lost to George W. Bush in the general election.

Cahill began her political career after graduating from Emmanuel College in 1976. Her first job was answering telephones in Congressman Robert Drinan's (Democrat, Massachusetts) office. In 1980, she worked on Congressman Barney Frank's (Democrat, Massachusetts) campaign. In the 1980s, Cahill served as director of personnel and as director of the Commonwealth of Massachusetts's Washington, D.C. office.

In 1986, Cahill managed Senator Patrick Leahy's (Democrat, Vermont) successful re-election campaign, and in 1990, she managed Senator Claiborne Pell's (Democrat, Rhode Island) successful re-election. Two years later, she managed Representative Les AuCoin's (Democrat, Oregon) unsuccessful senate campaign. Over the years, she also managed several gubernatorial, congressional and other campaigns.

Mary Beth Cahill served as Campaign Manager for the Kerry Campaign Organization. (Courtesy civicactions.org)

Cahill joined the EMILY's List (a political network that supports pro-choice Democratic women candidates) staff in 1993 as political director, later becoming the executive director, a position she held until 1998. President Bill Clinton appointed her Assistant to the President and Director of the Office of Public Liaison in 1999.

Cahill was Senator Ted Kennedy's chief of staff when Kerry recruited her to his campaign. Only two other women, Susan Estrich who was Governor Michael Dukakis's campaign manager and Donna Brazile, who was Vice President Al Gore's, have run major party presidential campaigns.

> **References** "Movers and Shakers," *Campaigns and Elections*, February 1998, p. 10; Garance Franke-Ruta, "Kerry's Women," *American Prospect*, 1 April 2004, p. 34; *The Washington Post*, March 17, 2004; Karen Tumulty, "The Miracle Worker Mary Beth Cahill Used Blunt Talk and Discipline to Bring Back John Kerry," *Time*, March 8, 2004, pp. 34–35.

Calderón, Sila Maria (b. 1942)

Sila Calderón began her political career in 1973, when she served as executive assistant to Puerto Rico's Secretary of Labor. Over the next two decades, she held other positions in government and served on several private corporate boards. From 1997 to 2001, she was mayor of San Juan.

The first woman governor of Puerto Rico, Calderón served from 2001 to 2005. Her campaign promises included ending the U.S. Navy's use of Vieques, a Puerto Rican island, for bombing exercises. Despite forecasts that she would encounter serious resistance from the United States, Calderón achieved her goal, and the use of Vieques for bombing training ended in 2003.

Calderón began her efforts to end the bombing by gaining legislative approval of a noise ordinance that effectively prohibited the bombing exercises. When the navy continued its training exercises, Calderón filed a lawsuit against the navy. The pressure she exerted on President George W. Bush and other United States government officials ended the practice.

Born in San Juan Puerto Rico, Calderón earned her bachelor's degree in political science from Manhattanville College in 1964 and her master's degree in public administration from the University of Puerto Rico in 1972. She did not run for re-election in 2004.

> **References** 2001 *Current Biography Yearbook* (2001); *Financial Times World Desk Reference*, November 1, 2004.

Caldicott, Helen Broinowski (b. 1938)

Helen Caldicott's lectures, books, and leadership alerted citizens, from the local to the international level, to the threat of nuclear arms, facilities, and testing. Caldicott's exposure to the health consequences of nuclear testing convinced her that the nuclear weapons industry threatened life on the planet. Caldicott began her work in Australia, educating residents about the hazards posed by atmospheric nuclear tests on an island in the South Pacific. When she moved to the United States, she continued her crusade, co-founding and leading Physicians for Social Responsibility, an organization of 23,000 doctors committed to educating their colleagues on the dangers of nuclear power, weapons, and war. She described herself as "an anti-nuclear bag lady—three cities a day—churches, ladies' clubs." She explained: "We created a revolution, from 1978, when everyone supported nuclear weapons, to 1983, when one study showed that 80 percent opposed them."

After the Cold War ended, Caldicott continued her crusade, arguing that scientists needed to stop designing new weapons. In addition, she argued: "We're still spending billions on weapons and there's no enemy. The Pentagon's desperately seeking enemies. Now the government is giving away weapons, and companies want to keep building them. Using your tax dollars. That's obscene. They're giving away death."

Caldicott hosted a weekly radio talk show on the Pacifica network in the mid-1990s. She also founded the Women's Party for Survival, which became Women's Action for Nuclear Disarmament, and later became Women's Action for New Direction.

Born in Melbourne, Australia, Helen Caldicott received her bachelor of medicine and bachelor of surgery degrees (equivalent to an MD degree in the United States) from the University of Adelaide Medical School in 1961.

> **References** H. W. Wilson, *Current Biography 1983* (1983); *The New York Times*, 31 October 1996; http://www.helendcaldicott.com.

Califano v. Goldfarb (1977)

In *Califano v. Goldfarb*, the U.S. Supreme Court rejected one of several traditional assumptions about women's roles. Laws written throughout much of American history often assumed that wives stayed home, were not wage-earners, and their husbands provided all or most of the financial resources for the family. Policies related to Social Security reflect that outdated stereotype. Male workers could leave all of their survivors' benefits to their widowed spouses, regardless of their spouses' financial contributions to the family. In contrast, only those female workers who provided 75% of the total family income could leave survivors' benefits to their spouses. About 2.4% of all working women met the criterion.

After Leon Goldfarb's wife died, he was denied survivors' benefits, which he challenged. He argued that his deceased wife, who had worked for 25 years as a secretary, had contributed at the same rate as her male colleagues.

The U.S. Supreme Court agreed with Goldfarb, writing that "the gender-based distinction created by [the law] violates the Due Process Clause of the Fifth Amendment." The Court further wrote: "Such distinctions, which result in the efforts of female workers required to pay Social Security taxes producing less protection for their spouses than is produced by the efforts of male workers, is constitutionally forbidden at least when supported by no more substantial justification than 'archaic and overbroad' generalizations or 'old notions,' such as 'assumptions as to dependency,' that are more consistent with 'the role-typing society has long imposed' than with contemporary reality."

References *Califano v. Goldfarb*, 430 U.S. 199 (1977); Claire Cushman, ed., Supreme *Court Decisions and Women's Rights: Milestones to Equality* (2001).

Califano v. Westcott (1979)

The Aid to Families with Dependent Children, Unemployed Father program provided benefits to families if the father was unemployed. If the mother was the primary earner in the family and she became unemployed, the family did not qualify for the benefits. The U.S. Supreme Court found that the policy rested on "baggage of sexual stereotypes" and that it violated the due process clause of the Fifth Amendment. The Court rejected the gender classification and agreed with a lower court that the benefits should be paid to families in which either the mother or the father was unemployed.

References *Califano v. Westcott, 443 U.S. 76 (1979)*

California Federal Savings and Loan v. Guerra (1987)

In *California Federal Savings and Loan v. Guerra* (1987), the U.S. Supreme Court found that a California law requiring employers to provide leave and reinstatement to employees disabled by pregnancy did not conflict with the Pregnancy Discrimination Act (PDA). The PDA, an amendment to Title VII of the Civil Rights Act of 1964, defines discrimination on the basis of pregnancy as sex discrimination and consequently illegal. The PDA only forbade discrimination, while the California measure went further and required the provision of pregnancy leave and job reinstatement. After having a baby, Lillian Garland sought to return to her job at California Federal Savings and Loan but was told that her old job had been filled and there was not another opening available to her. Garland went to the California Department of Fair Employment and Housing to assert her right to a job, according to state law. The savings and loan filed suit in federal district court, claiming that Title VII preempted the state law because the state law favored pregnant women by giving them preferential treatment. This preferential treatment, California Federal Savings and Loan argued, conflicted with the PDA's prohibition against treating pregnant employees differently than other disabled employees. The Court disagreed, asserting that the PDA and the California law had the same goals and that the PDA established a minimum treatment of pregnant employees, but that it did not establish a limit on the benefits that could be given them.

The case divided the feminist community. The National Organization for Women and the Women's Rights Project of the American Civil Liberties Union argued that the benefit should be extended to all workers disabled for four months or less. Betty Friedan, the International Ladies' Garment Worker's Union, 9to5, the Coalition of Labor Union Women, Planned Parenthood Federation of America, and other groups argued that although the law might violate formal equality, it should be permitted. The Supreme Court decided that the California law was permissible.

See also *Cleveland Board of Education v. LaFleur*; Coalition of Labor Union Women; Employment Discrimination; Friedan, Betty Naomi Goldstein; *Geduldig v. Aiello*; *General Electric v. Gilbert*; National Organization for Women; 9to5, National Association of Working Women; Planned Parenthood Federation of America; Pregnancy Discrimination Act of 1978

References Becker, "Prince Charming: Abstract Equality" (1988); *California Federal Savings and Loan Assn. v. Guerra*, 479 U.S. 272 (1987).

Cammermeyer, Margrethe (b. 1942)

Army nurse Margrethe Cammermeyer challenged her dismissal from the military for being a lesbian and won full reinstatement. While being considered for promotion to national chief nurse and general at the Army War College in 1992, she was asked her sexual preference. Her answer, "I am a lesbian," resulted in her dismissal, making her the highest-ranking officer dismissed on homosexuality charges. After her homosexu-

Retired Army colonel Colonel Margrethe Cammermeyer, who was discharged from service for saying she was lesbian, ran unsuccessfully for the U.S. House from the state of Washington, 1998 (Grethe Cammermeyer)

ality became public, she was the target for verbal attacks and received threatening letters. A bomb was placed in her mailbox. She later said: "I had never felt and heard such hatred before. It comes out of nowhere, because it is so irrational." Cammermeyer described the military's current policy regarding gays and lesbians, "Don't ask, don't tell," as "obscene." She said: "It's the legalizing of discrimination. [It] is based on the denial of speech."

She filed a lawsuit challenging her discharge, and a federal judge found the separation unconstitutional, with the ruling later becoming case law. Cammermeyer was reinstated to the National Guard in 1994 and served as chief nurse of the 164th mobile army surgical hospital (MASH) unit until May 1996. She retired from the military in 1997. In 1998, Cammermeyer was one of four openly lesbian candidates for the U.S. House of Representatives. She lost in the general election.

Born in Norway, Margrethe Cammermeyer earned her bachelor of science degree in nursing from the University of Maryland in 1963. She completed her master's degree in 1976 and her doctoral degree in 1991, both from the University of Washington. She joined the Army in 1961, served as a military nurse in Vietnam from 1967 to 1968, and held other nursing positions in the military.

See also Lesbian Rights

References Collins and Speace, eds., *Newsmakers 1995 Cumulation* (1995); *Harvard Crimson*, 29 April 2005.

Campbell, Bonnie Jean Pierce (b. 1948)

Director of the Justice Department's Violence Against Women Office from 1995 to 2001, Democrat Bonnie Campbell coordinated federal, state, and local efforts to eliminate violence against women. Campbell headed the federal government's Interagency Working Group on Domestic Violence, and she created a national group of law enforcement, health care, media, business, and academic leaders to advise the attorney general and the secretary of health and human services on domestic and sexual violence. She publicized the problems of domestic and sexual violence by speaking throughout the United States and by appearing on television news programs and working with the print media.

Iowa's first woman attorney general, Campbell served from 1991 to 1995. During her term in office, she worked to prevent and end domestic violence, publicizing the problem through a statewide campaign. She convinced the legislature to strengthen Iowa's domestic abuse laws and worked to increase funding for victim compensation and for shelters for abuse victims. In 1992, she drafted the nation's first anti-stalking law. Campbell also used publicity to bring attention to parents who did not meet their child support responsibilities by listing their names in newspaper advertisements. She unsuccessfully ran for governor of Iowa in 1994.

Born in Norwich, New York, Bonnie Campbell earned her bachelor's degree in 1982 and her law degree in 1984, both from Drake University. She clerked for the U.S. Department of Housing and Urban Development from 1965 to 1967 and for the U.S. Senate Subcommittee on Intergovernmental Relations from 1967 to 1969. A caseworker for U.S. Senator Harold Hughes from 1969 to 1974, she served as field representative for U.S. Senator John Culver from 1974 to 1980. Campbell practiced law in Des

Moines, Iowa, from 1984 to 1991 and was chair of the Iowa Democratic Party from 1987 to 1989.

See also Violence Against Women Act of 1994; Violence Against Women Office

References www.usdoj.gov.vawo/bcbio.htm.

Cantwell, Maria (b. 1958)

Democrat Maria Cantwell of Washington served in the U.S. House of Representatives from 3 January 1993 to 3 January 1995 and entered the U.S. Senate in 2001. As a member of the House, Congresswoman Cantwell focused on mass transit and supported reproductive rights, family leave, and notification of plant closings. She believed that a balance needed to be found between reducing the budget deficit and stimulating the economy with health care costs and access. Cantwell was defeated in her bid for a second term.

In the Senate, Cantwell has adamantly opposed plans to allow oil and gas drilling in the Arctic National Wildlife Refuge in Alaska, saying: "Let's not pollute one of the last great refuges of America." She has worked for more stringent rules for oil tankers, hoping to protect Puget Sound from oil spills.

Senator Cantwell, despite being in the minority party, has had success in a range of issues, including legislation to give law enforcement officials tools to help victims of identity theft, to enlarge Mt. Rainier National Park, and to encourage more doctors to work in rural and underserved communities.

Born in Indianapolis, Indiana, Maria Cantwell received her bachelor's degree from Miami University in Oxford, Ohio, in 1981. A political organizer for a Democratic presidential candidate in the early 1980s, Cantwell also built a political base for herself. She started a public relations firm and soon ran for office, serving in the Washington state House of Representatives from 1987 to 1993 and passing legislation to manage the state's growth.

See also Abortion; Congress, Women in; State Legislatures, Women in

References *The Boston Globe*, 4 November 2005; *Congressional Quarterly, Politics in America 1994* (1993); http://cantwell.senate.gov/issues/getting_results.cfm.

Capito, Shelley Moore (b. 1953)

Republican Shelley Moore Capito entered the U.S. House of Representatives on 3 January 2001. Capito has focused much of her attention on health care. "In my home state of West Virginia, 50 of the 55 counties are designated as medically underserved," she said. To address the problem, she has co-sponsored legislation dealing with medical malpractice insurance to limit non-economic damages in medical liability cases. She has also offered proposals for affordable prescription drugs for seniors and took a leading role in designing the plan that passed in 2003. She supports increasing the minimum wage, and protecting the domestic steel industry from foreign imports.

She co-chaired the Congressional Caucus on Women's Issues in the 108th Congress.

After serving as a career counselor at West Virginia State College from 1976 to 1978, Capito became director of the Educational Information Center of the West Vir-

U.S. Secretary of Education Rod Paige and Congresswoman Shelley Moore Capito celebrate National Library Week by reading to children (April 7, 2003). (Courtesy U.S. Department of Education)

ginia Board of Regents from 1978 to 1980. She was a delegate in the West Virginia State House of Delegates from 1997 to 2001.

Born in West Virginia, Capito earned a bachelor of science degree in zoology at Duke University in 1975 and a master's in education at the University of Virginia in 1976. Her father, Arch Alfred Moore, Jr., served in the House from 1957 to 1969 and was governor of West Virginia from 1969 to 1973 and from 1985 to 1989.

References *Congressional Quarterly, Politics in America 2006* (2005); http://capito.house.gov/about_shelley/biography_pf.htm; http://www.vote-smart.org/bio.php?can_id=BS036142; *The State Journal* (Charleston, West Virginia), 14 February 2003.

Capps, Lois (b. 1938)

Democrat Lois Capps of California entered the U.S. House of Representatives on 10 March 1998. When her husband Walter Capps first ran for Congress in 1994, Lois Capps campaigned with him. During the 1996 campaign season, Walter Capps was hospitalized following an automobile accident, and Lois Capps campaigned as his surrogate. After his death from a heart attack in 1997, Lois Capps won the special election to fill the vacancy.

When campaigning for herself, Capps focused on early childhood education, housing at a local Air Force base, and other local issues. Capps opposes an increase in offshore oil drilling and school vouchers. She supports smaller school class sizes, increased classroom access to the Internet and other computer technology, changes in health maintenance organizations that would require physicians to tell their patients about all treatment options, and extending health care coverage to half of the nation's uninsured children through federal legislation. She has sponsored legislation promoting education and awareness of strokes and another measure to clean up MTBE (methyl tertiary butyl ether) sites.

In the 107th Congress (2001–2003), Congresswoman Capps passed legislation to provide federal training, grants, and scholarships to address the national nursing shortage, one of her proudest achievements. When prescription drug coverage under Medicare was debated in 2003, Capps opposed the measure as inadequately addressing availability for people living in rural areas. When the American Association of Retired Persons (AARP) endorsed the plan, Capps resigned from the organization. Some of Capps's successes include measures to stop new offshore drilling, reduce underage drinking, and improve mental health services. She opposed the use of force against Iraq, reflecting both her late husband's commitment to peace and her own religious and family background as the daughter of a Lutheran minister.

Born in Ladysmith, Wisconsin, Lois Capps earned her bachelor of science in nursing from Pacific Lutheran University in 1959, her master's degree in religion from Yale University in 1964, and her master's degree in education from the University of California at Santa Barbara in 1990. She was a school nurse for twenty years and was involved in community organizations.

See also Abortion; Congress, Women in

References "California Representative Introduces Bill to Clean Up MTBE," *Oxy-Fuel News*, 19 February 2001, p.1; Lois Capps, D-California (1998); *Congress Daily*, 15 June 2004; *Congressional Quarterly, Politics in America 2004* (2003), *Poltics in America 2006* (2005); http://fix.net/sldoc/lois-bio.html; http://www.house.gov/capps

Caraway, Hattie Ophelia Wyatt (1878–1950)

Democrat Hattie Caraway of Arkansas served in the U.S. Senate from 13 November 1931 to 2 January 1945. After her husband Thaddeus Caraway died while serving in the U.S. Senate, Hattie Caraway was appointed to fill the vacancy until a special election could be held to elect a person to complete the term. She then won the special election, at least partially with the understanding that she would step down at the end of the term. Louisiana senator Huey Long, whom she had met in 1931 at a cotton conference, however, convinced her to run in the 1932 primary, which already had seven other candidates. In his role as adviser to Hattie Caraway, Long told her to wear black widow's clothing and the same hat throughout the campaign. Long also campaigned for her, using his own sound trucks and making thirty-nine speeches in thirty counties in nine days. Popular in Arkansas, Long attracted some of the largest political gatherings assembled in the state, with some communities planning other events in conjunction with his campaign stops. During his campaign speeches, Long described Caraway as the "little widow woman." Calling her "the true heir to the egalitarian philosophy" of her late husband, he added: "We've got to pull a lot of pot-bellied politicians off a little woman's neck."

When Caraway won in 1932, she became the first woman elected to the U.S. Senate. Rebecca Latimer Felton had served before Hattie Caraway but had been appointed and not elected. When the Senate assigned Caraway the same desk that Felton had used,

Caraway wrote in her journal: "I guess they wanted as few of them [desks] contaminated as possible!"

In the Senate, Hattie Caraway supported President Franklin D. Roosevelt's New Deal programs but seldom entered into debate. She said that she did not have the heart to "take a minute from the men. The poor dears love it so." Despite her resistance to engaging in debate, she passed several economic measures for Arkansas, including $15 million for an aluminum plant, $23 million for the Ozark Ordnance Works, and funds for new military training camps in Arkansas. A rural woman with a farm background, she took great interest in agricultural issues and served on the Agriculture Committee. Her other interests included Prohibition and flood control. Caraway opposed anti-lynching legislation and proposals to end the poll tax. Caraway chaired the Committee on Enrolled Bills from the 73rd to the 78th Congresses (1933 to 1945), the first woman to chair a Senate committee. She was also the first woman to cosponsor the Equal Rights Amendment, the first woman senator to conduct Senate hearings, and the first woman to preside over the Senate.

Hattie Caraway ran for re-election in 1944 but did not campaign, saying that her Senate duties took first priority. Her decision cost her re-election. From 1945 to 1946, Caraway was a member of the U.S. Employees' Compensation Commission, and from 1946 to 1950, she was a member of the Employees' Compensation Appeal Board.

Born in Bakersville, Tennessee, Hattie Caraway graduated from Dickson Normal College in 1896. Following her marriage to Thaddeus Caraway, Hattie Caraway centered her life on raising her family.

> **See also** Anti-lynching Movement; Congress, Women in; Equal Rights Amendment; Felton, Rebecca Ann Latimer
>
> **References** Boxer, *Strangers in the Senate* (1994); H. W. Wilson, *Current Biography 1945* (1946); Malone, *Hattie and Huey: An Arkansas Tour* (1989); Office of the Historian, U.S. House of Representatives, *Women in Congress, 1917–1991* (1991).

Carey v. Population Services International (1977)

In *Carey v. Population Services International*, the U.S. Supreme Court rejected New York laws that made it a crime to sell contraceptives to people under sixteen years old, for anyone other than a licensed pharmacist to distribute contraceptives to people sixteen years old and older, and for anyone to advertise contraceptives. Because the law covered nonprescription contraceptives, the Court said that the law was unconstitutional under the First and Fourteenth Amendments.

> **See also** *Eisenstadt v. Baird*; *Griswold v. Connecticut*
>
> **References** *Carey v. Population Services International*, 431 U.S. 678 (1977).

Carlson, Margaret Mary Bresnahan (b. ca. 1945)

The first female columnist for *Time* magazine, political journalist Margaret Carlson appeared regularly on CNN's *Inside Politics* and *Capital Gang*, both now off the air. Journalism, however, was not her first career choice. After earning a bachelor of arts degree at Pennsylvania State University in 1966, Carlson worked in a federal management program for a year. She next taught in a public school, followed by a year of working for Ralph Nader's campaign to make cars safer. Inspired by Nader's work,

Carlson entered George Washington University Law School, completing her juris doctor degree in 1972. In the late 1970s, she was a lawyer at the Federal Trade Commission.

Carlson began her journalism career in 1981 writing for *Legal Times*, a weekly magazine that covered the practice of law and lobbying. Carlson worked for other publications and did free lance writing until 1988, when she became a White House correspondent for *Time*. As Washington bureau chief for *Time*, she covered the 1988, 1992, 1996, and 2000 presidential campaigns. She began writing her column, "Public Eye," for the magazine in 1993 and became the first woman columnist in the publication's 78-year history. Both conservatives and liberals have praised and criticized Carlson for her columns, attesting to her political independence.

References H.W. Wilson, *Current Biography Yearbook 2003* (2002).

Carnahan, Jean (b. 1933)

Democrat Jean Carnahan of Missouri served in the U.S. Senate from 3 January 2001 to 25 November 2002. Her route to the Senate was uncommon. Her husband, Mel Carnahan, governor of Missouri from 1993 to 2000, had been a candidate for the U.S. Senate in the 2000 elections. Three weeks before the election, Mel Carnahan, his son, and an aide died in a plane crash. Democratic party leaders convinced voters to elect Mel Carnahan, despite his demise, arguing that it would allow his successor to appoint a senator until the 2002 elections. Party leaders also persuaded Jean Carnahan to accept the appointment, should her husband win the election. The deceased Mel Carnahan defeated incumbent Republican Senator John Ashcroft. Jean Carnahan was appointed to the Senate.

Carnahan had a political background as her husband's scheduler, occasionally as his surrogate at events, and as a campaigner and worker. As first lady of Missouri, she worked on early childhood education, day care, and immunization.

Senator Carnahan supported gun control that did not limit gun owners' rights, providing for the economic stability of Social Security, and economic protections for farmers. She was an unsuccessful candidate for election to the balance of the term in 2002.

Born in Washington, D.C., Carnahan earned a bachelor of arts degree at George Washington University in 1955.

References *Congressional Quarterly, Politics in America* 2002 (2003).

Carpenter, Mary Elizabeth (Liz) Sutherland (b. 1920)

Executive assistant to Vice President Lyndon Johnson and press secretary for Lady Bird Johnson, Liz Carpenter campaigned for the federal Equal Rights Amendment as co-chair of ERAmerica. Carpenter entered politics in 1960 to campaign for Democratic presidential nominee John F. Kennedy and vice presidential nominee Lyndon B. Johnson. When fellow Texan Lyndon B. Johnson became vice president of the United States in 1961, Carpenter joined his staff as executive assistant, the first woman to hold the position. After President Kennedy's assassination in Dallas, Texas, in 1963, Carpenter knew that Johnson, who had just been sworn in as president of the United

States, would be expected to speak to the press. She gained national attention with the words she wrote for Johnson to deliver at Andrews Air Force Base that day.

The first professional newswoman to hold the position of press secretary, Carpenter served as staff director and press secretary for Lady Bird Johnson from 1963 to 1969, the years Johnson was first lady. As a member of the first lady's staff, Carpenter lobbied Congress for the highway beautification bill that was a priority of Lady Bird Johnson's.

A founding member of the National Women's Political Caucus in 1971, she traveled across the country campaigning for ratification of the Equal Rights Amendment as co-chair of ERAmerica from 1976 to 1981.

Born in Salado, Texas, Carpenter earned her bachelor's degree from the University of Texas in 1942. After graduating, she moved to Washington, D.C., with Leslie Carpenter, whom she later married. She worked for United Press International, and she and her husband later formed a Washington news bureau, for which she worked from 1945 to 1961.

> **See also** Equal Rights Amendment; ERAmerica; Johnson, Claudia Alta (Lady Bird) Taylor; National Women's Political Caucus
>
> **References** Crawford and Ragsdale, *Women in Texas* (1992).

Carson, Julia May Porter (b. 1938)

Democrat Julia Carson of Indiana entered the U.S. House of Representatives on 3 January 1997. Carson began her political career in 1965 working for a member of Congress. She served in the Indiana House of Representatives from 1973 to 1977 and the state Senate from 1977 to 1991. While in the Indiana legislature, Carson promoted policies that encouraged in-home health care and that eased the collection of child support. A Marion County Center Township trustee from 1991 to 1997, Carson eliminated the $20-million debt that the office had accumulated, lowered the number of people on relief through workfare and other programs, reduced taxes, and left the office with a balance.

Congresswoman Carson passed legislation to honor civil rights leader Rosa Parks with a Congressional Gold Medal in 1999. She has sponsored bills to ensure that veterans have the vote after serving state or federal prison sentences, to regulate the debt consolidation industry, and to address the housing, health, and income needs of homeless people and families at risk of homelessness. She also supports requirements for safety devices on new handguns.

Carson's firsthand experience with heart disease in 1997 has made her a strong advocate for further research on heart disease in women.

Born in Louisville, Kentucky, African American Julia Carson attended Martin University from 1994 to 1995. As a member of Congress, Carson has worked to increase funding for schools, balance the federal budget, regulate managed health care, increase food safety, and block children's access to handguns.

> **See also** Congress, Women in; State Legislatures, Women in; WomenHeart
>
> **References** *Congressional Quarterly, Politics in America 1998* (1997), *Politics in America 2004* (2003; www.house.gov/carson/bio1.htm http://www.juliacarson.house.gov;

Carson, Rachel Louise (1907–1964)

Biologist Rachel Carson's research and writings helped launch the modern environmental movement by transforming technical scientific material into words and images that lay readers could understand and enjoy. She imbued her writing with her appreciation of the natural world's complexity, interconnectedness, and beauty. A U.S. Bureau of Fisheries employee, she wrote pamphlets, radio scripts, and other materials. Her first article for a popular magazine appeared in 1937, when *Atlantic Monthly* published her article "Undersea." Impressed with her work, book publisher Simon and Schuster invited her to write a book-length manuscript, which was published as *Under the Sea-Wind: A Naturalist's Picture of Ocean Life* in 1941.

She continued to work for the bureau, which merged with the Biological Survey and became the U.S. Fish and Wildlife Service, advancing from assistant aquatic biologist in 1942 to biologist and chief editor of publications and booklets, the position she held from 1949 to 1952.

Carson's position at Fish and Wildlife gave her access to scientists, researchers, and explorers, whom she regularly consulted about her own research and writing. The exchange of ideas enhanced her understanding of contemporary research and helped her develop the themes presented in her work. These professionals sometimes also provided her with enriching experiences. For example, as she was writing *The Sea around Us*, she discussed her work with author and explorer William Beebe, who learned that she did not swim, which limited her research. Beebe arranged for her to use a diving helmet and go underwater off the coast of Florida. Although she went only 15 feet below the surface, she saw the colors, vistas, and activity of the sea from within for the first time. *The Sea around Us* (1951), which was on the bestseller list for eighty-six weeks,

Rachel Carson, a marine biologist, became famous as an environmental activist when she challenged the use of the pesticide DDT through her book, Silent Spring, in 1962

describes the oceans, their formation, their living creatures, and their contributions to sustaining life on Earth. The success of the book and support from a Guggenheim Foundation fellowship permitted Carson to leave her government job in 1952 and focus on her research and writing. Her next book, *The Edge of the Sea* (1955), was a study of the seashores of the Atlantic coast.

Carson's greatest impact came in 1962 with the publication of *Silent Spring*. In 1945, Carson had expressed concerns about the chemical DDT, a product used to kill insects. First synthesized in 1874, DDT's potential as an insecticide was discovered in 1939 and it was used to kill lice during World War II. Carson had submitted an article proposal on it to a magazine, but the idea was rejected. She did nothing more about the topic until 1958. The year before, the State of Massachusetts had sprayed the Cape Cod area with DDT, and a woman living in the area had been appalled by the devastation she witnessed, as songbirds died in her yard on the day after the spraying and on the days following. The woman wrote a letter to the *Boston Herald* describing the event, sent a copy to Carson, and provided her with the motivation to write a book about DDT and its dangers.

In *Silent Spring*, Carson described the threats to life from chemicals, questioned the indiscriminate use of poisons, and criticized the abuse of the natural world by an industrial and technological society. Carson faced two challenges in presenting her arguments. She had to translate her scientific research into an understandable and compelling message for the general public. She also had to convince readers that imprudently using chemical pesticides on food crops was not the only remedy for ensuring an adequate food supply. She wrote:

The most alarming of all man's assaults upon the environment is the contamination of air, earth, rivers, and sea with dangerous and even lethal materials. This pollution is for the most part irrevocable; the chain of evil it initiates not only in the world that must support life but in living tissues is for the most part irreversible. In this now universal contamination of the environment, chemicals are the sinister and little-recognized partner of radiation in changing the very nature of the world–the very nature of its life.

The chemical industry, agricultural journals, and agricultural researchers at state institutions attacked the book and attempted to discredit her. The public, however, was outraged at the threat that DDT and other chemicals posed to the environment and expressed this view so clearly that President John F. Kennedy appointed a committee to investigate the findings Carson had presented.

By the time *Silent Spring* was published, Carson's health had deteriorated, leaving her weak and unable to engage in a public debate, but she testified before the president's Science Advisory Committee, the U.S. Senate Committee on Environmental Hazards, and the Senate Committee on Commerce. She also lobbied Congress to protect the environment. Ultimately, her research was endorsed by the scientific community.

Regarded as the patron saint of the environmental movement, Carson's research and writing influenced the creation of the Environmental Protection Agency and the passage of state laws regulating the use of chemicals. Born in Springdale, Pennsylvania, Rachel Carson earned her bachelor's degree in zoology from Pennsylvania College for

Women in 1929 and her master's degree in zoology from Johns Hopkins University in 1932.

References Brooks, *Rachel Carson at Work: The House of Life* (1985).

Carter, Eleanor Rosalynn Smith (b. 1927)

Rosalynn Smith Carter, wife of former U.S. President Jimmy Carter, was first lady from 1977 to 1981. During her years in the White House, she focused attention on mental health by serving as honorary chair of the President's Commission on Mental Health and helped pass the Mental Health Systems Act.

Born in Plains, Georgia, Rosalynn Carter attended Southwestern College in Americus, Georgia, for one year, and in 1946 she married Jimmy Carter, a childhood acquaintance. During their first years of marriage, the couple moved regularly as his assignments in the Navy changed. In 1953, they returned to Plains, Georgia, where he became involved in farming and the family's agricultural business.

When Jimmy Carter began his political career in 1962, Rosalynn Carter began her entry into politics as well. He first served in the state Senate and then as governor of Georgia from 1971 to 1975. During the years she was first lady of Georgia, Rosalynn Carter became involved in mental health issues and served on the Governor's Commission to Improve Services for the Mentally and Emotionally Handicapped, which made recommendations to the governor, many of them implemented by gubernatorial and legislative actions. In addition, Rosalynn Carter worked to improve conditions for imprisoned women, for ratification of the federal Equal Rights Amendment, and for highway beautification projects.

First Ladies Nancy Reagan, Ladybird Johnson, Hillary Rodham Clinton, Rosalyn Carter, Betty Ford, and Barbara Bush sit together at the National Garden Gala, 'A Tribute to America's First Ladies.' By Barbara Kinney, Washington, DC, May 11, 1994 (Courtesy of the White House P015515-28)

Early in her husband's presidency, Rosalynn Carter began attending Cabinet meetings in an effort to better understand issues and to be able to articulate the administration's position on them. The information she gathered helped her as she worked on new issues and accepted new responsibilities. For example, in 1977 she served as an envoy to Latin American nations. In addition, she lobbied Congress for the Age Discrimination Act, the Older Americans Act, and the Rural Clinics Act. President Carter appointed her honorary chair of the President's Commission on Mental Health, a position she used to work for health insurance coverage of mental health services and to increase funding for research on mental health. When she testified before a Senate committee on the topic, she became one of the few incumbent president's wives to appear before a congressional committee. Rosalynn Carter continued to actively support ratification of the federal Equal Rights Amendment, calling state legislators as they considered the measure, and she made speeches in support of it. In addition, she worked to identify women to be appointed to high government positions.

After Jimmy Carter's term in office ended, the couple returned to Plains. In 1982, they founded the Carter Center in Atlanta, Georgia, a private, nonprofit institution. Vice chair of the center, Rosalynn Carter created and chairs its Mental Health Task Force. She initiated the annual Rosalynn Carter Symposium on Mental Health Policy in 1985, and in 1991 established the World Federation for Mental Health Committee of International Women Leaders for Mental Health. In 1991, Rosalynn Carter and Betty Bumpers, wife of a U.S. senator, launched "Every Child by Two," a national campaign publicizing the need for early childhood immunization.

Rosalynn Carter wrote *First Lady from Plains* (1984) and *Helping Yourself Help Others: A Book for Caregivers* (1994). She co-authored *Everything to Gain: Making the Most of the Rest of Your Life* (1987) with Jimmy Carter.

References Carter, *First Lady from Plains* (1984); *The New York Times*, 14 February 1978; www.whitehouse.gov/wh/glimpse/firstladies/html/rc39.html.

Castle Rock v. Gonazales (2005)

Jessica Gonzales had obtained a restraining order to keep her estranged husband away from her and their three daughters. One evening, upon realizing that her daughters had disappeared from the family's yard, she called the Castle Rock police, explaining the situation. The police told her to wait a couple of hours, which she did. When she called the police a second time, they again told her to wait a couple of hours. Finally, around 1 a.m., she went to the police department, hoping to convince the police of the need to enforce the restraining order and to find her daughters. Later that morning, her estranged husband appeared at the police station and opened fire with a semi-automatic handgun. The police killed him. They found the three daughters in his pickup truck, murdered by their father.

Jessica Gonzales sued the Town of Castle Rock under the Fourteenth Amendment's due process clause. The U.S. Supreme Court concluded that domestic violence victims do not have an entitlement to the enforcement of restraining orders.

References *Castle Rock v. Gonzales*, (2005)
http://www.aclu.org/scotus/2004/20938prs20050627.html

Castro, Ida L. (b. 1953)

The first Latina to chair the Equal Employment Opportunity Commission, Ida Castro held the position from 1998 to 2001. During her tenure, she reduced the backlog of cases by almost a quarter, implemented the National Mediation Program and Small Business Initiative, and obtained record financial benefits for victims of workplace discrimination. President Bill Clinton had previously appointed Castro to two other positions in his administration. From 1994 to 1996, she served in the Department of Labor as deputy assistant secretary and director of the Office of Workers' Compensation. From 1996 to 1998, she served as acting director of the Women's Bureau, also in the Department of Labor. Prior to joining the Clinton administration, Castro taught at Rutgers University, served as counsel for public institutions, and had a private law practice.

Born in New York, Castro earned a bachelor of arts degree at the University of Puerto Rico in 1972, a master of arts degree at Rutgers University in 1978, and a juris doctorate degree at Rutgers University in 1982.

References Equal Employment Opportunity Commission, "Ida L. Castro Resigns from Commission," 13 August 2001.

Catholics for a Free Choice

Three Roman Catholic women, all members of the National Organization for Women in New York, organized Catholics for a Free Choice (CFFC) to counter the Catholic Church's opposition to abortion. CFFC members believe that the anti-choice position of Roman Catholic bishops does not reflect the views of the nation's Catholics.

After the state of New York enacted one of the nation's most permissive abortion laws in 1970, the Roman Catholic Church began advocating reinstatement of more restrictive abortion policies. The church's activism prompted this group of Roman Catholic women to counter the church's positions on reproductive and sexual issues.

Established in 1973, CFFC supports the right to legal reproductive health care, including abortion. It also works to reduce the number of abortions by advocating social and economic policies that benefit women, children, and families. CFFC offers training and resources for Catholics, insisting upon the necessity of a moral and ethical framework in deliberations about abortion.

See also Abortion

References www.cath4choice.org.

Catt, Carrie Clinton Lane Chapman (1859–1947)

National American Woman Suffrage Association (NAWSA) president Carrie Chapman Catt reinvigorated the organization, stirred the suffrage movement out of the doldrums, and led one wing of the movement in the final push for the passage and ratification of the Nineteenth Amendment. A skillful political strategist, Catt developed a three-point program that she called the "Winning Plan" to accomplish the goal and in the process created one of the most successful pressure groups in U.S. history. Although she has received credit for her achievements, she has also been criticized for the racist and nativist sentiments she expressed during the campaign for the amendment.

Born near Ripon, Wisconsin, Catt earned her bachelor of science degree from Iowa State Agriculture College (now Iowa State University) in 1880. She became a high school principal in Mason City, Iowa, in 1881 and superintendent of schools in 1883. She married Leo Chapman in 1885, which ended her teaching career because married women were not allowed to be teachers. She began writing for her husband's newspaper, *The Mason City Republican*, including an early column expressing her support for woman suffrage. Also in 1885, she attended her first women's rights conference, a three-day suffrage congress in Des Moines, Iowa, where she heard Lucy Stone speak on equal suffrage. The next year, in what was likely her first public act for suffrage, she circulated a petition supporting it. In 1886, Leo Chapman went to California to buy a larger newspaper, contracted typhoid fever, and died of it. After his death, Catt supported herself by lecturing on woman suffrage.

Catt joined the Iowa Woman Suffrage Association in 1887, became the organization's recording secretary, and was elected state lecturer and organizer in 1889. The next year, she attended the first National American Woman Suffrage Association conference and campaigned for woman suffrage in South Dakota. In 1890, she married George Catt, a man who shared her dedication to women's rights. Their marriage agreement included a contract stipulating that she would be free four months of the year to work for suffrage. George Catt's death in 1905 left her financially secure and free to devote herself to woman suffrage.

Catt saw woman suffrage as more than simply gaining a constitutional right for U.S. women; it was also a way to neutralize what she called a "great danger." She explained in 1894: "That danger lies in the votes possessed by the males in the slums of the cities and the ignorant foreign vote which was sought to be bought up by each party, to make political success." Catt described the solution: "There is but one way to avert the

Carrie Chapman Catt, president of the National American Woman Suffrage Association, with Mrs. Helen Gardener leaving the White House, 1920. (Library of Congress National Photo Company Collection LC-USZ62-110996)

danger–cut off the vote of the slums and give to woman … the power of protecting herself.… Put the ballot in the hands of every person of sound mind in the nation. If that would be too cumbersome, cut it off at the bottom, the vote of the slums."

Catt's nativist beliefs also had racist aspects. She noted that U.S. women "will always resent the fact that American men chose to enfranchise Negroes fresh from slavery before enfranchising American wives and mothers, and allowed hordes of European immigrants totally unfamiliar with the traditions and ideals of American government to be enfranchised … and thus qualified to pass upon the question of the enfranchisement of American women."

Catt first gained national prominence in 1894, when she suggested that NAWSA establish an organizing committee for fieldwork and then worked to put the association on what she called a "sound organizational basis." Her indefatigable efforts and her demonstrated abilities contributed to NAWSA president Susan B. Anthony's choosing Catt to succeed her in 1900. In 1904, Catt resigned, weary from years of working on behalf of suffrage and interested in the international suffrage effort. A founder of the International Woman Suffrage Alliance, Catt was the founding president, serving from 1904 to 1923.

Anna Howard Shaw had succeeded Catt as president of NAWSA in 1904 and held the post until 1915. Over those eleven years, the suffrage movement languished, and NAWSA's organization was in disarray. In addition, militant suffragists who belonged to Alice Paul's Congressional Union had implemented the strategy of holding whatever party was in power responsible for failing to enact suffrage, regardless of the individual party members' views. At the time, Democrats were the party in office, and the Congressional Union sought to defeat even those Democrats who had supported woman suffrage. Catt disagreed with the strategy. She thought it unreasonable to penalize Democrats who had been steadfast supporters and believed it foolish to assume that newly victorious Republicans would enact a suffrage amendment. Suffrage leaders drafted Catt to again serve as president of NAWSA, and she accepted the post in 1915.

Catt's Winning Plan made use of all of NAWSA's resources. The national organization's responsibility was to work on the federal amendment, state organizations were to work on referenda, and suffrage states were to elect suffrage supporters to their state legislatures and to Congress. The plan became NAWSA's official policy in 1916.

Catt also sought President Woodrow Wilson's endorsement of the amendment and offered him the suffrage organization's support in World War I. Despite her pacifist beliefs, Catt served on the Woman's Committee of the Council of National Defense, but she insisted that women must not abandon the suffrage cause.

On 21 May 1919, the House of Representatives passed the amendment, with the Senate following suit on 4 June 1919. On 18 August 1920, Tennessee became the last needed state for ratification. The Nineteenth Amendment was officially included in the U.S. Constitution on 26 August 1920, now known as Women's Equality Day. Catt summarized the effort it had taken:

To get the word male … out of the Constitution cost the women of the country fifty-two years of pauseless campaign. During that time they were forced to conduct fifty-six campaigns of referenda to male voters; 480 campaigns to urge Legislatures to submit suffrage amendments to voters; forty-seven campaigns to induce state constitutional conventions to write woman suffrage into state constitutions; 277 campaigns to persuade state party conventions to include woman suffrage planks; thirty campaigns to urge presidential party conventions to adopt woman suffrage planks in party platforms, and nineteen campaigns with nineteen successive Congresses.

In 1919, Catt had called for the organization of a League of Women Voters in the states that had woman suffrage. She did not take an active part in the organization, saying that younger women should provide its leadership.

Working under the belief that women could not be fully liberated until war was abolished, Catt focused her attention on finding an end to war after 1920. In an effort to develop a unified program for peace and disarmament, she organized the leaders of women's organizations into the National Committee on the Cause and Cure of War, serving as its chair from 1925 to 1932.

> **See also** Anthony, Susan Brownell; Congressional Union; League of Women Voters; National American Woman Suffrage Association; Nineteenth Amendment; Paul, Alice; Shaw, Anna Howard; Stone, Lucy; Suffrage
>
> **References** Ravitch, *The American Reader* (1990); Van Voris, *Carrie Chapman Catt: A Public Life* (1987); Whitman, ed., *American Reformers*
>
> **Document** Carrie Chapman Catt, "The Winning Plan," 1915

Center for the American Woman and Politics

Founded in 1971, the Center for the American Woman and Politics (CAWP) was the first institution to gather information about women in government and politics. A unit of the Eagleton Institute of Politics at Rutgers University in New Jersey, CAWP's mission is to promote greater understanding and knowledge about women and politics and to enhance women's influence and leadership in politics. Since 1975, CAWP has been an information clearinghouse, conducting the first national census and survey of female public officials at the national, state, county, and municipal levels. By collecting data, conducting research, and disseminating its findings, CAWP has become a resource for women at every level of politics as well as for researchers, journalists, government agencies, civic organizations, and political parties.

When CAWP sponsored a conference in 1972 for elected women, it was the first time that elected women in the United States had gathered to gain insight into their own experiences and ideas. At that and subsequent conferences, women in public office learned ways to enhance their effectiveness, gathered information on emerging issues, and discussed strategies that have worked for them. For example, at one conference the idea of forming women's caucuses was discussed, and some attendees developed women's caucuses within their home state legislatures. Research conducted at one conference contributed to Jeane Kirkpatrick's book *Political Women*, a landmark study of women in politics. Through its many studies of women in state legislatures and in Congress, CAWP has provided insight into the significance and importance of women holding public office. CAWP also conducts educational programs to prepare young women for public leadership.

> **See also** Congress, Women in; Kirkpatrick, Jeane Duane Jordan; State Legislatures, Women in
>
> **References** www.rci.rutgers.edu/~cawp.

Chao, Elaine Lan (b. 1953)

The first Asian American woman to hold a Cabinet position, Secretary of Labor Elaine Chao was born in Taiwan, immigrating to the United States when she was eight years old. Her father, James Chao, had immigrated seven years earlier, working three jobs to bring his wife and daughter to the U.S.

After earning a bachelor of arts degree from Mount Holyoke College in 1975 and an master of business administration degree from Harvard University, Elaine Chao began a financial career that lasted until 1986, when President Ronald Reagan appointed her deputy maritime administrator at the U.S. Department of Transportation (USDOT). Reagan appointed her chair of the Federal Maritime Commission in 1988. President George H. W. Bush appointed her deputy secretary of the USDOT in 1989 and director of the Peace Corps in 1991.

Chao was appointed president of the United Way of America (UWA) in 1992, a time when the organization faced a financial and ethical crisis. Through policies she implemented, she helped restore public confidence in the UWA and renewed its financial stability.

A vocal opponent of affirmative action, Chao said: "I think we should heed to the overall core value of this country that equal opportunity applies for all, and that should be the same standard for everyone."

Appointed Secretary of Labor in 2001 by President George W. Bush, Chao noted in 2005 that her greatest accomplishment at that point had been strengthening overtime protection for 6.7 million American workers.

References *Fund Raising Management*, September 1996; *Human Events*, April 18, 2005; *The New York Times*, January 12, 2001, February 26, 2001.

Labor Secretary-designate Elaine Chao answers questions during a news conference in Washington Thursday, Jan 11, 2001 (Doug Mills-AP/Wide WorldPhotos)

Chavez, Linda (b. 1947)

Director of the U.S. Commission on Civil Rights from 1983 to 1985, Linda Chavez was director of the White House Office of Public Liaison in 1985, the highest-ranking woman in President Ronald Reagan's White House and one of the most powerful Hispanic officials in the Reagan administration.

Born in Albuquerque, New Mexico, Chavez earned her bachelor's degree from the University of Colorado in 1970 and did postgraduate work at the University of California at Los Angeles. During her senior year in college, she began her civil rights activism, joining Mexican American and African American students in their demands for affirmative action programs and remedial courses for minority students. She later criticized the remedial classes, calling them "political indoctrination" camps and saying that minority students used them to segregate themselves. In the 1970s, Chavez worked for the Democratic National Committee, the National Education Association, and the Department of Health, Education, and Welfare.

Chavez next worked for the American Federation of Teachers (AFT) as editor of the organization's quarterly publication, *American Educator*. In a series of articles, Chavez argued for a return to traditional values, which gained the attention of conservatives and President Ronald Reagan. In 1981, she became a consultant in the Reagan administration. Two years later, she became staff director of the U.S. Commission on Civil Rights, where she opposed racial preferences. In 1985, Chavez became director of the White House Office of Public Liaison in the Reagan administration and changed her party registration to Republican. She left after ten months, explaining: "My chief reason for wanting to leave the Civil Rights Commission to join the White House staff was to be able to have a greater role in influencing administration policy on a broad array of issues. What I discovered was that the White House was more involved in process than policy." After leaving the White House, Chavez sought the Republican nomination for the U.S. Senate from Maryland, which she won. She lost in the general election.

Chavez became president of U.S. English, an organization that seeks to make English the official national language. She then became a senior fellow at the Manhattan Institute for Policy Research, a conservative think tank. While there, she wrote *Out of the Barrio: Toward a New Politics of Hispanic Assimilation* (1991), which describes her vision of a young Hispanic population more likely than their parents to assimilate and become part of the middle class. In 1995, she founded the Center for Equal Opportunity, a public policy organization that opposes bilingual public education and supports parents and others in their challenges to it. She has also worked on California ballot initiatives to end bilingual education.

References *The New York Times*, 19 August 1998; Telgen and Kamp, eds., *Notable Hispanic American Women* (1993).

Chavez-Thompson, Linda (b. 1944)

Executive vice president of the AFL-CIO, Linda Chavez-Thompson is the first person of color elected to an executive office of the union and is the highest-ranking woman in the labor movement. Chavez-Thompson began her career in the labor movement as a union secretary in 1967 and has risen through the levels of the organization.

Chavez-Thompson was born in Lubbock, Texas, to parents who were sharecroppers, and she began picking cotton when she was ten years old. She dropped out of high school to help support her family. When she was nineteen years old, Chavez-Thompson began working for the labor union as a secretary and then as a union representative because no one else in the office could speak Spanish to the Latino members.

Chavez-Thompson served as an international representative for the American Federation of State, County, and Municipal Employees (AFSCME) from 1971 to 1973, when she became assistant business manager and then business manager for a local San Antonio union. She became executive director of the local union in 1977, holding the position until 1995. She has served as national vice president of the AFL-CIO's Labor Council for Latin American Advancement, international vice president of AFSCME, and national vice president of the AFL-CIO executive council.

References www.aflcio.org/profile/chavez.htm.

Document Linda Chavez-Thompson, Statement on Equal Pay Day, 1998

Chenoweth-Hage, Helen Palmer (1938–2006)

Republican Helen Chenoweth-Hage of Idaho served in the U.S. House of Representatives from 3 January 1995 to 3 January 2001. She served as Helen Chenoweth until her marriage in 1999. Needing a job after a divorce, she entered politics by accident and helped rebuild the Republican Party in Oregon after its losses in the post-Watergate era. From 1975 to 1977, she was state executive director of the Idaho Republican Party and then served as chief of staff to a congressman from 1977 to 1978. Before her election in 1994, she was also a lobbyist and a campaign manager.

Chenoweth-Hage was a nationally recognized advocate for private property rights. She worked to reduce the environmental regulations affecting private landowners and businesses, arguing that conservationists must permit the use of the West's natural resources for commercial ends. She worked for local management of resources, defended recreational use of Hells Canyon Recreational Area, and fought for Idaho's sovereignty over its water. She attacked the 1973 Endangered Species Act because she believed that it denies private landowners their rights and provides the federal government with excessive power. To help her congressional colleagues understand the resource issues she supports, Chenoweth-Hage took members of Congress to visit Idaho and talk to residents. A political conservative, she has voted to balance the budget, lower taxes, and reduce the size of government. She did not seek re-election in 2000 because she pledged to retire after three terms.

Born in Topeka, Kansas, Helen Chenoweth-Hage attended Whitworth College from 1955 to 1958.

See also Congress, Women in

References John Gizzi, "Politics 2000," *Human Events*, 12 May 2000, p. 18; Treese, ed., *Biographical Directory of the American Congress 1774–1996* (1997); www.house.gov/chenoweth/chenbio.htm.

Document Helen Chenoweth, Statement to Feminists for Life of America, 1997

Child Day Care

For single working parents and for families in which both parents work outside the home, finding and paying for adequate, safe, child day care has been a continuing challenge. In 1995, more than 60 percent of all children under the age of six were in child care, which cost low-income families an average of 25 percent of their annual incomes. For decades, advocates for children, educators, and parents have sought government assistance in establishing standards for child day care and subsidies to pay for it. In the 1930s, the federal government offered free nurseries in an effort to provide employment during the Depression as well as to assist low-income workers. Beginning in 1942, these centers accepted the children of defense workers, whom they charged for the services. By the end of World War II, however, the federal government had spent more than $50 million to support child care centers for women employed in defense industries. Although women had been encouraged to work during the war, they were encouraged to return to homemaking after the war, and the federal government essentially ended its involvement in child day care services. In 1962, the federal government appropriated $4 million for child day care, but in 1965 the assistance was eliminated in order to support the war in Vietnam. Another program in the late 1960s provided temporary assistance for women on welfare who were in job training programs. In 1971, Congress passed a $2 billion child care program, but President Richard Nixon vetoed it because he thought it could hurt families by encouraging mothers to work outside the home.

Child care assistance became an issue in the 1988 presidential campaign, with both Republican George Bush and Democrat Michael Dukakis pledging action on the issue. The next year, the Children's Defense Fund and labor unions kept the issue before members of Congress, and both chambers passed child care measures but failed to reconcile differences between them. In 1990, Congress passed and President George Bush signed a child care package that included $18.5 billion in tax credits to help low- and middle-income families with their child care expenses and $4.25 billion for new grant programs to states to improve the quality and availability of child care.

In 1995, the Child Care Bureau was formed within the Administration for Children and Families of the U.S. Department of Health and Human Services. The Child Care Bureau seeks to enhance the quality, affordability, and availability of child care, and it administers the Child Care and Development Fund, which subsidizes child care for low-income families.

See also Children's Defense Fund

References *Congressional Quarterly Almanac, 101st Congress, 2nd Session . . . 1990* (1991); www.acf.dhhs.gov.

Child Labor Amendment

Passing and ratifying the Child Labor Amendment to the U.S. Constitution was an early, although unsuccessful, effort led by women and women's groups in the 1920s. Through the amendment, social reformers hoped to end the employment of children under the age of eighteen, particularly those children working in factories and mines, and to encourage more children to attend school for a longer period of time. Support for the amendment developed after attempts to regulate child labor through federal legislation were determined to be unconstitutional by the U.S. Supreme Court.

Protective child labor legislation emerged as an attempt to protect children from the worst abuses of factory employment. Social reformers, many of them women, who witnessed the low wages, desolate working conditions, and the toll that factory and other labor took on young children, sought to end child labor. They argued that children belonged in school, where they would learn the skills that would improve their lives and enable them to earn living wages.

Research had revealed that in 1910 almost two million children ages ten to fifteen were in the paid labor force, working in coal mines, factories, agriculture, and textile mills. Social reformers actively lobbied for legislation restricting child labor, which passed Congress in 1916 as the Keating-Owen Child Labor Reform Act. The measure prohibited interstate or export shipment of materials produced in mines that employed children under the age of sixteen, of products manufactured in factories employing children under fourteen, and of items produced in workplaces where children between ages fourteen and sixteen worked more than eight hours a day or between the hours of 7:00 p.m. and 6:00 a.m. Two years later, however, the U.S. Supreme Court struck it down, deciding that the restrictions were an unwarranted exercise of the commerce power but noting that child labor was "evil" and should be regulated. The next year, Congress passed a 10 percent tax on the net profit of mills and factories using child labor, using essentially the same restrictions as the Keating-Owen Act. Again, the U.S. Supreme Court rejected the attempt, saying in 1922 that the law was an unconstitutional effort to force people to do what Congress wanted.

By 1923, it had become apparent to opponents of child labor that their only recourse rested in an amendment to the U.S. Constitution. Groups including the Women's Joint Congressional Committee (WJCC), the League of Women Voters, and the Young Women's Christian Association testified on behalf of the proposed amendment. The National Association of Manufacturers, the American Cotton Manufacturers, the Woman Patriots, the Sentinels of the Republic, and the Roman Catholic Church opposed it. Those groups argued that the amendment limited parental rights, violated religious traditions, and would prohibit any gainful employment for children. Newspapers opposed the amendment because they employed boys who sold newspapers.

In 1924, Congress passed the child labor amendment, which stated: "The Congress shall have power to limit, regulate, and prohibit the labor of persons under 18 years of age." When the amendment went to the states for ratification, it encountered intense opposition from the groups listed above. By the late 1920s, only four states had ratified it, with a fifth ratifying in 1932. The passage of New Deal legislation in the 1930s addressed child labor and made the amendment unnecessary.

See also Abbott, Grace; Children's Bureau; League of Women Voters; Spider Web; Women's Joint Congressional Committee; YWCA of the USA

References Breckenridge, *Women in the Twentieth Century* (1933); Brown, *American Women in the 1920s* (1987); Lindenmeyer, "A Right to Childhood": The U.S. Children's Bureau and Child Welfare, 1912–1946 (1997).

Document Florence Kelley, "Child Labor and Woman Suffrage," 1905

Child, Lydia Maria Francis (1802–1880)

An early anti-slavery propagandist, Lydia Maria Child's first work against slavery was *An Appeal in Favor of That Class of Americans Called Africans*, published in 1833. The first anti-slavery book by a northern abolitionist calling for the immediate emancipation of the nation's two million slaves, it provides a history of slavery from the ancient world to the nineteenth-century United States. A major work of propaganda, it influenced the development of other abolitionists' ideas and became required reading for American Anti-Slavery Society agents. The work was so controversial that sales of Child's literary works declined, but she continued to publish anti-slavery books, including *The Oasis* (1834), *Authentic Anecdotes of American Slavery* (1835), *Anti-slavery Catechism* (1836), and *The Evils of Slavery* (1836).

Child opposed annexing Texas because it was a slaveholding state, joined the Boston Female Anti-Slavery Society, and gathered signatures on anti-slavery petitions. In 1840 Child became one of the first three women (with Lucretia Mott and Maria Weston Chapman) appointed to an executive committee of a national anti-slavery society, the American Anti-Slavery Society. From 1841 to 1843, she edited the *National Anti-Slavery Standard* and then essentially retired from the anti-slavery movement for the next sixteen years.

John Brown's 1859 raid on Harpers Ferry prompted Child to send him a sympathetic letter, which, along with other correspondence to him, was published in the *New York Tribune*. Among those who wrote to Child was the wife of a Virginia congressman, Margaretta Mason, who denounced the anti-slavery movement and threatened a boycott of Child's books. Child replied to Mason, writing what she considered her most notable anti-slavery material. The American Anti-Slavery Society published the two women's correspondence and sold more than 300,000 copies of it. Child resumed her role as an anti-slavery propagandist, writing and publishing additional tracts. After emancipation, Child edited an anthology for and about African Americans and became an advocate for freedmen. She also wrote a volume on aging and another on Native Americans.

Born in Medford, Massachusetts, Child completed her education at a local dame school. In addition to her anti-slavery work, she was a novelist, essayist, and author of works for children.

See also Abolitionist Movement, Women in the

References Clifford, *Crusader for Freedom: A Life of Lydia Maria Child* (1992).

Child Support Enforcement

Until the 1990s, Americans generally regarded the enforcement of child support agreements between divorced or separated parents as a private matter. For the custodial parents, usually women, recovering child support owed to them by non-custodial parents often involved expensive lawsuits that they could not afford or other barriers to collection. For example, if the non-custodial parent moved to another state, court orders could not be enforced. The federal government became involved in child support recovery and enforcement as a way to keep women and their dependent children off welfare rolls or to remove them from the rolls. By the 1990s, child support enforcement had become a political issue that involved both divorced or separated parents and parents who had not married.

The first federal child support enforcement legislation, passed in 1950, required state welfare agencies to notify law enforcement officials when they provided Aid to Families with Dependent Children (AFDC) to a child who had been abandoned by a parent. In 1965, legislation passed that permitted welfare agencies to obtain the address and place of employment of a parent who owed child support under a court order. Two years later, another measure allowed states to obtain from the Internal Revenue Service the addresses of non-custodial parents who owed child support, and states were required to work together and with courts and law enforcement officials to enforce child support orders. In 1968, thirty-five states adopted the Revised Uniform Reciprocal Enforcement of Support Act, facilitating child support collections across state lines and citing delinquent parents with contempt.

By 1975, it was clear these measures were inadequate. Forty-four percent of divorced women were awarded child support, less than 50 percent of those awarded it received any money, and the payments covered less than 50 percent of the cost of the child's support. To help remedy the problem, Congress gave the Department of Health, Education, and Welfare responsibility for creating an office dedicated to operating a child support recovery program. The responsibilities included establishing a parent locator service and standards for state programs, approving state programs, certifying cases for referral to federal courts or to the Internal Revenue Service for collection, and related duties. States were given primary responsibility for the Child Support Enforcement Program and were provided with incentive programs for collections made in AFDC cases.

Almost every Congress after 1975 passed a measure related to child support recovery, some of them relatively narrow in scope, whereas others were more aggressive attempts to enforce court-ordered financial obligations and avoid the expenses of welfare. For example, as a condition for receiving federal welfare funds, the Child Support Amendments of 1984 required states to enact several policies to collect child support, including mandatory income-withholding procedures, expedited processes for enforcing child support orders, state income tax refund interceptions, and property liens. The measure, a priority of the Congressional Caucus for Women's Issues (CCWI) and part of its Economic Equity Act, expanded the Child Support Enforcement Program to cover both welfare and non-welfare families. The Parent Locator Service was created to help custodial parents find non-custodial parents who were delinquent in their child support payments. The resources that became available included motor vehicle registration, driver's license records, and Internal Revenue Service records. It was estimated at the time that as many as two million children were entitled to $4 billion in unpaid support.

The Family Support Act of 1988, another CCWI priority, emphasized parental responsibilities to work and support their children and child support enforcement as a primary route to avoiding welfare dependency. Establishing paternity became a priority when the parents had not married.

In the early 1990s, at least partly in response to federal requirements, states became increasingly innovative in their attempts to locate parents who were delinquent. Iowa attorney general Bonnie Campbell, for example, published a list of "deadbeat dads," a top ten list of the state's worst child support offenders. In recognition of the mothers who were delinquent, the list was renamed "deadbeat parents," although women are more likely to be the custodial parent and men more likely to be the non-custodial parent who has not met the assigned financial obligation. The Child Support Recovery Act of 1992 made it a federal crime to willfully fail to pay delinquent child support for a child living in a state other than that of the non-custodial parent.

The Personal Responsibility and Work Opportunity Reconciliation Act of 1996 created new tools for finding parents owing child support, streamlined the process for establishing paternity, and provided new penalties. The Deadbeat Parents Punishment Act of 1998 created felony penalties for egregious failure to pay child support.

The federal Office of Child Support Enforcement, an agency within the U.S. Department of Health and Human Services, works with state and local agencies to assist individuals with child support collection. It has resources to locate noncustodial parents, establish paternity, and create support orders through state courts and administrative procedures. In 2003, Child Support Enforcement agencies collected $21.2 billion, established paternity in 1.5 million cases, and worked with 15.9 million cases. The combined federal/state costs for child support enforcement was $5.2 billion, yielding more than $4 collected for each $1 spent.

> **See also** Congressional Caucus for Women's Issues; Divorce Law Reform; Economic Equity Act; Feminization of Poverty

> **References** *Congressional Quarterly Almanac, 98th Congress, 2nd Session…1984* (1985); http://www.acf.dhhs.gov/opa/fact_sheets/cse

Children's Bureau

Created in 1912, the U.S. Children's Bureau developed out of the reform spirit of the Progressive movement and became the first agency in the world devoted to children's interests. The agency's initial mandate was to investigate the best means to protect "a right to childhood." In the 1990s, the agency assisted states in the delivery of child welfare services, providing grants for child protective services, family preservation, foster care, and adoption.

The National Child Labor Committee first proposed legislation in 1905 for the Children's Bureau, following a plan envisioned by Julia Lathrop and Florence Kelley. Kelley began discussing the need for the bureau in a series of lectures, describing the conditions under which young children were employed in factories, mines, and textile mills and the perceived high levels of infant mortality. A few years later, Lillian Wald organized a group that successfully lobbied President Theodore Roosevelt to support a federal agency devoted to children's interests. A bill for the agency was first introduced in Congress in 1906 and was supported by the National Consumers League, the General Federation of Women's Clubs, the Daughters of the American Revolution, and other women's organizations. Roosevelt agreed to convene the 1909 White House Conference on Child Welfare Standards, which called for a children's bureau, giving added impetus to its creation by Congress in 1912.

Under its first director, Julia Lathrop, the bureau investigated the causes of maternal and infant mortality, developed a child welfare library, published pamphlets on prenatal and infant care, and advocated that states require the registration of every birth. With its appropriations inadequate for its programs, the bureau depended upon volunteers from the groups that had supported its creation to supplement its paid staff. By 1915, for example, 3,000 volunteers conducted door-to-door campaigns across the country registering children and their ages. In 1921, Congress passed the Sheppard-Towner Maternity and Infancy Protection Act, a program administered by the Children's Bureau that provided funding to states for maternal and child health programs from 1921 to 1929.

The Children's Bureau also conducted research in the area of child labor, compiling information on child labor laws in every state, and in the process convincing Lathrop that only federal action would make child labor laws uniform. The Keating-Owen Act, passed in 1916 and administered by Grace Abbott, attempted to discourage child labor, but the U.S. Supreme Court found it and a subsequent child labor law unconstitutional. Those decisions led the bureau and reformers to advocate a child labor amendment, which Congress passed but the states did not ratify. The 1933 National Industrial Recovery Act created minimum ages for employment depending upon the occupation, and following the U.S. Supreme Court's 1935 decision making it unconstitutional, the 1938 Fair Labor Standards Act achieved federal regulation of labor, making the child labor amendment unnecessary.

In 1921, Abbott became head of the Children's Bureau and continued the research projects that Lathrop had begun. The studies included destitute, homeless, and abandoned children, children dependent upon public support, children who begged, children in unfit homes or living in houses of ill fame or other dangerous places, and those who peddled goods to support themselves. Other areas of concern included the causes of juvenile delinquency and the treatment of juvenile delinquents.

Under President Franklin D. Roosevelt's New Deal, the Children's Bureau's work expanded to include aspects of the 1935 Social Security Act, including maternal and child health and assistance to crippled children, children with special needs, and dependent children. The staff grew from 138 employees in 1930 to 438 in 1939, and the budget grew from $337,371 in 1930 to $10,892,797. After the United States entered World War II, the Children's Bureau, along with other federal agencies, suspended all research unrelated to the war effort.

A reorganization of federal departments and agencies resulted in a lowered status for the Children's Bureau in 1946, and its status was further diminished with the bureau's transfer from the Department of Labor to the Department of Health, Education, and Welfare in 1953. In the 1990s, the bureau was part of the Department of Health and Human Services' Administration on Children, Youth and Families. The bureau administers an annual budget of more than $7 billion, covering nine state grant programs and six discretionary grant programs. The program areas include foster care, adoption assistance, independent living for foster children over sixteen years of age, child abuse and neglect prevention and treatment, assistance to abandoned infants, and child welfare research.

See also Abbott, Grace; Child Labor Amendment; General Federation of Women's Clubs; Kelley, Florence; Lathrop, Julia; League of Women Voters; National Consumers League; Sheppard-Towner Maternity and Infancy Protection Act of 1921; Wald, Lillian D.

References Lemons, *The Woman Citizen* (1973); Lindenmeyer, "A Right to Childhood": *The U.S. Children's Bureau and Child Welfare, 1912–1946* (1997); www.acf.dhhs.gov.

Document Florence Kelley, "Child Labor and Woman Suffrage," 1905

Children's Defense Fund

Founded by Marian Wright Edelman in 1973, the Children's Defense Fund (CDF) acts at the local, state, and national levels to advocate programs and legislation for children. Through the information it gathers about children, CDF educates private citizens, other children's advocates, government officials, and members of Congress and their staffs about the status and needs of U.S. children. The data gathered by CDF also serve as a lobbying tool at the state and national levels. CDF's research has revealed that every day in the United States, four children die from abuse or neglect, five children or teens commit suicide, eight children or teens are killed by firearms, 2,447 babies are born into poverty, 2,482 children are confirmed as abused or neglected, and 77 babies die before their first birthday. The organization works to increase public awareness of these statistics and to change them.

CDF was instrumental in increasing Head Start funding during the 1970s, expanding Medicaid eligibility for children and pregnant women, and guaranteeing equal educational opportunities to children with disabilities in the 1980s. CDF has also been successful in the areas of expanding child care assistance for low- and moderate-income working families, increasing the number of children served by Head Start, and expanding the earned income tax credit, which provides a refundable tax credit for low-income families. Child immunizations, job protection for parents needing leaves to care for new or sick children, and community-based programs to prevent child abuse and neglect are additional areas in which CDF has played a key role. Improving children's health, reducing teen pregnancy, protecting children from violence, and keeping children in school are among CDF's continuing areas of focus.

CDF coordinates the Black Community Crusade for Children, which seeks to ensure that every child has a healthy, safe, fair, moral, and head start. It hopes to meet these goals by working to build and renew a sense of community, strengthening the black community's tradition of self-help, rebuilding generational bridges, encouraging black leaders to be advocates for children, and developing a new generation of leaders.

See also Edelman, Marian Wright

References www.childrensdefense.org.

Document Marion Wright Edelman, "Educating the Black Child: Our Past and Our Future," 1987

Chisholm, Shirley Anita St. Hill (1924–2005)

Democrat Shirley Chisholm of New York served in the U.S. House of Representatives from 3 January 1969 to 3 January 1983. She was the first African American woman elected to Congress and the first African American to actively seek the presidential nomination of a major U.S. political party. She served as secretary to the Democratic Caucus, a leadership position, in the 97th Congress (1981–1983).

Born in Brooklyn, New York, Chisholm is the daughter of immigrants, her father from Guyana (formerly British Guiana) and her mother from Barbados. She spent much of her youth in Barbados with her grandmother and sisters, while her parents worked to earn and save for their children's education. Living in Barbados from the time she was three years old until she was nine, Shirley Chisholm acquired her early elementary education in strict British-style schools, but her grandmother was an equally important influence, emphasizing pride, courage, and faith.

Chisholm earned her bachelor's degree from Brooklyn College in 1946 and her master's degree in childhood education from Columbia University in 1952. A nursery school teacher from 1946 to 1953, she was the director of a child care center in New York from 1953 to 1959 and then was a consultant to the city's Bureau of Child Welfare until 1964.

In 1960, she became active in politics, helping form the Unity Democratic Club, a group that defeated the district's party machine and took over the district. She also played an active role in the National Association for the Advancement of Colored People, League of Women Voters, and Bedford-Stuyvesant Political League. In 1964, she successfully ran for the New York State Assembly, where she served until 1968. While in the assembly, Chisholm passed a measure that provided for unemployment compensation for domestic and personal employees.

*Congresswoman Shirley Chisholm announcing her candidacy
for presidential nomination / [TOH]. (Library of Congress,
U.S. News & World Report Magazine Photograph Collection.
LC-U9-25383-33)*

When Chisholm decided to run for Congress, she explained: "I wanted to show the machine that a little black woman was going to beat it." After winning with the motto "unbought and unbossed," she said she had become "the first American citizen to be elected to Congress in spite of the double drawbacks of being female and having skin darkened by melanin."

A recognized feminist, liberal, anti-war activist, and black leader, Chisholm supported the Equal Rights Amendment, reproductive choice, a national commission on Afro-American history and culture, and ending the Vietnam War. She brought together blacks, women, and labor in support of a successful measure to include domestics in the 1974 minimum wage bill. After President Richard Nixon vetoed it, Congress overrode the veto. With another member of Congress, she held hearings to investigate racism in the Army. Chisholm believed that the United States "has the laws and material resources it takes to insure justice for all its people. What it lacks is the heart, the humanity, the Christian love that it would take." She sought to supply them.

She became the first black person and the first woman to seek a major party's presidential nomination in 1972, when she sought to become the Democratic Party's nominee. Gloria Steinem became a delegate for Chisholm, and Betty Friedan and several prominent Washington, D.C. political women worked for Chisholm's candidacy. Although National Organization for Women president Wilma Scott Heide supported Chisholm's candidacy, the organization did not, and neither did the National Women's Political Caucus. Democratic Congresswoman Bella Abzug opposed Chisholm's candidacy because she believed that Chisholm could not succeed and that supporting Chisholm would consume resources that could be better used elsewhere. The effort was doomed from the beginning, but Chisholm said of it: "What I hope most is that now there will be others who will feel themselves as capable of running for high political office as any wealthy, good-looking, white male."

She announced her retirement from Congress in 1982 but continued to be active in politics. Disappointed by the 1984 Democratic National Convention, she gathered other black women together and launched the National Political Congress of Black Women. She also actively supported Jesse Jackson in his 1984 and 1988 presidential campaigns.

Chisholm once said: "I'd like to be known as a catalyst for change, a woman who had the determination and a woman who had the perseverance to fight on behalf of the female population and the black population, because I am a product of both." Chisholm has written two autobiographical works, *Unbought and Unbossed* (1970) and *The Good Fight* (1973).

See also Congress, Women in; Equal Rights Amendment; League of Women Voters; National Association for the Advancement of Colored People, Women in the; National Organization for Women; National Political Congress of Black Women; National Women's Political Caucus; State Legislatures, Women in

References Kaptur, *Women of Congress: A Twentieth Century Odyssey* (1996); H. W. Wilson, *Current Biography Yearbook, 1969* (1969); Schoenebaum, ed., *Political Profiles: The Nixon/Ford Years* (1979); Wandersee, *American Women in the 1970s* (1988).

Documents Shirley Chisholm, "Equal Rights for Women," 1969; Shirley Chisholm, "Women in Politics," 1973.

Christensen, Donna Marie Christian (b. 1945)

Democrat Donna Christensen of the Virgin Islands entered the U.S. House of Representatives as a delegate on 3 January 1997. She served under the name Donna Christian-Green in the 105th Congress. The first female doctor to serve in Congress, her legislative priorities include the environment, child care, and juvenile crime and justice.

Born in Teaneck, New Jersey, Donna Christensen earned her BS from St. Mary's College in 1966 and her medical degree from George Washington University in 1970. A family practitioner for more than twenty years, Christensen was a community health physician for the U.S. Virgin Islands Department of Health, Territorial Assistant Commissioner of Health, and Acting Commissioner of Health for the territory.

Christensen began her political career as vice chairperson of the U.S. Virgin Islands Democratic Territorial Committee in 1980. She served on the Virgin Islands Board of Education from 1984 to 1986 and on the Virgin Islands Status Commission from 1988 to 1992.

See also Congress, Women in
References http://www.house.gov/christian-christensen

Christian Coalition of America

Founded in 1989, the Christian Coalition of America developed out of evangelist Pat Robertson's failed attempt to win the 1988 Republican presidential nomination. It has almost two million members in more than 2,000 chapters located in every state in the nation. The Christian Coalition believes that it is the "largest and most effective grassroots political movement of Christian activists in the history of our nation." Through its programs of training political activists, distributing voter guides, and conducting leadership schools, the Christian Coalition works at the local, state, and federal levels.

The Christian Coalition supports measures that strengthen the family, defend marriage, outlaw pornography, provide for parental and local control of education, permit prayer in public schools, reduce taxes, and prohibit abortions. The organization opposes gay rights.

See also Abortion; Lesbian Rights; Pornography
References www.cc.org.

Church, Marguerite Stitt (1892–1990)

Republican Marguerite Church of Illinois served in the U.S. House of Representatives from 3 January 1951 to 3 January 1963. After her husband Ralph Church's election to Congress in 1934, she moved to Washington, D.C., with him and became involved in his political career. She also began developing her own political skills, working in the 1940 and 1944 Republican presidential campaigns. Following her husband's death, she ran for and won his seat in 1950. As a member of Congress, Marguerite Church introduced a measure to implement recommendations for greater efficiency and economy in government, sponsored a bill for annuities for widows of former federal employees, and passed a bill prohibiting the transport of fireworks into states that outlawed them.

Following her retirement from Congress, Marguerite Church remained active in politics, working on Barry Goldwater's 1964 presidential campaign and Richard Nixon's 1968 run for president. In addition, she served on the Girl Scouts of America national board of directors and the U.S. Capitol Historical Society board.

Born in New York, New York, Marguerite Church earned her bachelor's degree from Wellesley College in 1914 and her master's degree in political science from Columbia University in 1917. She taught psychology at Wellesley College and, during World War I, was a consulting psychologist to the State Charities Aid Association of New York City.

See also Congress, Women in

References Office of the Historian, U.S. House of Representatives, *Women in Congress, 1917–1990* (1991); Treese, ed., *Biographical Directory of the American Congress 1774–1996* (1997).

Citizens' Advisory Council on the Status of Women

Created by Executive Order 11126 on 1 November 1963, the Citizens' Advisory Council on the Status of Women (CACSW) developed from recommendations of the President's Commission on the Status of Women. The council's duties included reviewing and evaluating women's progress toward full participation in American life. Located in the Women's Bureau, the council served as a liaison between government agencies and women's organizations.

CACSW encouraged the Equal Employment Opportunity Commission (EEOC) to prohibit gender-segregated employment ads in 1965, but the EEOC refused, although it banned race-segregated employment ads. The council further recommended revising property laws to protect the interests of married women in common law states, enacting measures to give equal rights to illegitimate and legitimate children, decriminalizing abortion, and repealing laws limiting access to birth control. It also supported the Equal Rights Amendment. CACSW was terminated in 1977.

See also Abortion; Equal Employment Opportunity Commission; Equal Rights Amendment; Health Care, Women and; President's Commission on the Status of Women

References Linden-Ward and Green, *American Women in the 1960s: Changing the Future* (1993); Wandersee, *American Women in the 1970s: On the Move* (1988); www.nara.gov/fedreg/eo1963K.html.

Civil Rights Act of 1964, Title VII

The most comprehensive civil rights legislation enacted since Reconstruction, the Civil Rights Act of 1964 passed Congress as the nation struggled with racial conflict. In the South, three student civil rights workers were murdered in 1964, others were beaten or threatened with violence, and black churches were bombed, and in the North, riots erupted in Harlem and other cities over housing, employment, and other forms of discrimination. The Civil Rights Act of 1964 sought to alleviate the social injustices caused by discrimination on the basis of race, color, religion, or national origin. The act included sections banning discrimination in voting rights and public accommodations, provided for the desegregation of public facilities and public education, and barred discrimination in federally assisted programs. Although amendments were offered to include sex in five sections of the bill, all but one were defeated. Only one section, Title VII on equal employment opportunity, included sex as a classification against which discrimination was banned.

Title VII made equal employment opportunity for women the official national policy of the United States. The Equal Pay Act of 1963 had made it illegal to have different pay rates for women and men doing the same work, but it did not prohibit employers from denying women jobs or advancement on the basis of sex. Before passage of Title VII, it was legal to openly discriminate against women, minorities, people of color, foreign-born people, and people of faith seeking employment or advancement. Title VII also made it illegal for labor organizations to discriminate in their membership policies, classifications of positions, and job referrals. In addition, apprenticeship and training programs came under the prohibitions against discrimination.

The introduction of the amendment to add sex to Title VII has been viewed as an attempt to sabotage the entire bill. A Southern member of Congress and an ardent segregationist, Democrat Howard W. Smith of Virginia introduced the amendment, leading observers to believe that Smith hoped to defeat the entire bill by adding women to the employment section and making the bill unpalatable to other members of Congress who would otherwise have voted for it. That interpretation, however, does not incorporate much of the amendment's history.

Smith had long worked with the National Woman's Party (NWP), a small militant organization that supported the Equal Rights Amendment and as an intermediate measure wanted to add sex to the categories of people covered by the Civil Rights Act of 1964. Congresswoman Martha Griffiths (D-MI) also supported the idea and had considered offering an amendment but hesitated because she was concerned that it would fail. The NWP, Griffiths, and Smith decided that Smith would introduce the amendment because they believed that almost 100 Southern members of the House would vote for the amendment just because Smith introduced it. Griffiths worked to line up the balance of the votes needed to pass the amendment, but with the exception of the NWP, she had little support from women's organizations.

When the House debated the amendment, Smith set the tone of the discussion by making jokes about the amendment, women, and employment, and his colleagues joined him. Amusement, derision, and laughter characterized the day, which became known as Ladies Day in the House. Griffiths took a more serious approach, saying that unless women were added, "you are going to have white men in one bracket, you are going to try to take colored men and women and give them equal employment rights, and down at the bottom of the list is going to be a white woman with no rights at all.... White women will be last at the hiring gate.... A vote against this amendment today by a white man is a vote against his wife, or his widow, or his daughter, or his sister."

In the House of Representatives, only one woman, Democrat Edith Green of Oregon, voted against it. She said that it was neither the time nor the place for the amendment. The amendment passed by a vote of 168 to 133.

When the bill went to the Senate, the sex provision faced significant opposition, but it also benefited from new sources of support. Marguerite Rawalt, a former president of Business and Professional Women/USA (BPW/USA), wrote to members of BPW and Zonta International as well as to lawyers, asking them to lobby for the provision.

She also recruited lawyer Pauli Murray to write a memorandum supporting it and distributed copies of the memo. Senator Margaret Chase Smith (R-ME) convinced the Republican Conference to support the inclusion of sex in Title VII, despite the initial opposition of the Senate majority leader. The bill passed in July 1964, with sex included in Title VII.

The law also created the Equal Employment Opportunity Commission, which heard complaints brought under the law. The commission had little enforcement power, but women presented hundreds of grievances to it in the first year.

See also Business and Professional Women/USA; *County of Washington v. Gunther*; *Dothard v. Rawlinson*; Employment Discrimination; Equal Employment Opportunity Commission; *General Electric v. Gilbert*; Griffiths, Martha Edna Wright; *Harris v. Forklift Systems*; *Hishon v. King and Spaulding*; *Johnson v. Transportation Agency, Santa Clara County*; *Los Angeles Department of Water and Power v. Manhart*; *Meritor Savings Bank v. Vinson*; Murray, Pauli; *Nashville Gas v. Satty*; National Organization for Women; National Woman's Party; Paul, Alice; *Phillips v. Martin Marietta*; President's Commission on the Status of Women; *Price Waterhouse v. Hopkins*; Protective Legislation; Sexual Harassment; Smith, Howard Worth; Smith, Margaret Madeline Chase; Women's Bureau

References *Congressional Quarterly Almanac, 88th Congress, 2nd Session . . . 1964* (1965); Freeman, "How 'Sex' Got into Title VII: Persistent Opportunism as a Maker of Public Policy" (1991); Gabin, *Feminism in the Labor Movement* (1990); Harrison, *On Account of Sex* (1988); Schneir, *Feminism in Our Time* (1994); Stimpson, ed., *Women and the "Equal Rights" Amendment* (1972).

Civil Rights Act of 1991

The Civil Rights Act of 1991 reversed nine U.S. Supreme Court cases to provide increased protection to workers confronting employment discrimination based on race, color, national origin, religion, and sex. In addition, the act permitted limited monetary damages for victims of harassment and other intentional discrimination based on sex, religion, or disability. Racial minorities could receive unlimited monetary damages under a measure passed during Reconstruction. The act also created the Glass Ceiling Commission to study the processes businesses use to fill management and decision-making positions and related matters.

The act allowed workers to challenge an employment decision when race, color, religion, sex, or national origin was a consideration, even if other factors contributed to the same decision. By including bias in the decision, the employer had acted illegally. The provision resulted from the U.S. Supreme Court decision in *Price Waterhouse v. Hopkins*, in which the Court had said that even if bias had been involved in the decision, if there were other factors, it did not violate Title VII.

Another section of the act involved employment factors that appeared neutral but had an adverse impact on a particular group of people. For example, an employer might establish physical tests or academic requirements for a position that a job candidate would have to meet in order to be considered for it. If the qualification excluded more women, for example, than men, then it could have a disparate impact, which could be illegal if the employer could not prove that the qualification was job-related and necessary. In addition, if an employee offered an alternative that met the business goals and the employer refused to adopt it, that could also be illegal.

See also Employment Discrimination; Glass Ceiling Commission; *Price Waterhouse v. Hopkins*

References *Congressional Quarterly Almanac, 102nd Congress, 1st Session . . . 1991* (1992).

Civil Rights Movement, Women in the

African American women's civil rights activism has its roots in the abolitionist movement of the nineteenth century, continued through the suffrage movement, asserted itself in anti-lynching campaigns in the early twentieth century, and persevered through the tragedies and triumphs of the 1950s and 1960s. Many of the women whose leadership significantly enhanced the movement and propelled it forward in the middle of the twentieth century had minimal education and little or no exposure to the leaders of earlier crusades. Other women with professional degrees and greater sophistication formed organizations, taught citizenship schools, and defended female and male leaders in courts from the local level to the U.S. Supreme Court. Equally important were the unnamed women who attended meetings, attempted to register to vote, encouraged others to register, and lodged and fed civil rights organizers, daily risking their safety, their jobs, and their homes. Although African American women and their work in the civil rights movement have been less visible than the work of Martin Luther King, Jr., and other notable male leaders, the contributions women made at every level required courage, determination, stamina, and economic sacrifice.

The 1930s offer several examples of women's early contributions to the incremental recognition of African Americans' civil rights. Sadie Tanner Mosell Alexander helped draft and pass Pennsylvania's public accommodations law and then provoked Philadelphia officials into enforcing it. Daisy Lampkin organized chapters of the National Association for the Advancement of Colored People (NAACP) throughout the South, risking her safety and enduring the humiliations of Jim Crow laws. Classical vocalist Marian Anderson focused the nation's attention on the iniquities of racial prejudice when the Daughters of the American Revolution refused to allow her to perform in their hall, resulting in her 1939 performance at the Lincoln Memorial and her emergence as a symbol of the civil rights movement. As the nation moved toward involvement in World War II, Alpha Kappa Alpha sorority, the National Association of Colored Women, the National Council of Negro Women, and other organizations sought to end segregation of the armed forces and to end racism in the military. Across the country, women like Mary Church Terrell, a former president of the National Association of Colored Women, took action in their communities to enforce existing civil rights laws. In 1949, Terrell was in her mid-eighties when she participated in sit-ins to desegregate lunch counters in Washington, D.C.

Women held center stage in two remarkable dramas of the 1950s, the Montgomery, Alabama, bus boycott and the integration of Central High School in Little Rock, Arkansas. The Montgomery bus boycott resulted from years of planning and preparation by the Women's Political Council, a group that first threatened a boycott in 1950. The December day in 1955 that Rosa Parks refused to surrender her seat on the bus launched a boycott that lasted 381 days, provided the catalyst for the formation of the Southern Christian Leadership Council, and resulted in a U.S. Supreme Court decision that segregation on public transportation was unconstitutional. The boycott's success depended upon the participation of individuals whose sacrifices went unheralded. For example, domestic worker Georgia Gilmore organized the Club from Nowhere (CFN) in 1956 to support the bus boycott. The group's name represents the risks members took by working to end racial segregation and provided assurance to contributors that their donations could not be traced and their support revealed. Gilmore lost her job as a cook at a café and was blacklisted for organizing CFN, but she persisted. She cooked and baked, sold the food door-to-door, and collected donations for the boycott, as did other members. CFN's members, a loosely organized network of neighborhood women, viewed the club as an auxiliary of the male-dominated civil rights movement's organizations. The group dissolved when the boycott ended.

President of the Arkansas NAACP, Daisy Bates fought for the integration of Central High School in Little Rock, Arkansas, seeking to force the city's school system to honor the U.S. Supreme Court's 1954 decision in *Brown v. Board of Education of Topeka, Kansas.* In the fall of 1957, Bates shepherded nine African American high school students through a dangerous ordeal that included mobs and violence. Ultimately, the students enrolled and attended the school under the protection of the Arkansas National Guard, which had been federalized to protect them.

Constance Baker Motley, Marian Wright Edelman, and other members of the NAACP's legal team defended civil rights leaders in the courts. Their ventures into Southern courtrooms clashed with cultural assumptions because they were both black and female. Like the other women and men involved in the civil rights movement, they, too, lived and worked under the threat of violence and in a climate of hatred.

During the 1960s the civil rights movement grew in several directions, and women established themselves as leaders. Ella Baker guided young people in the formation of the Student Nonviolent Coordinating Committee (SNCC). Ruby Doris Smith Robinson and Diane Nash, civil rights activists who had ventured into the Deep South to protest segregation, participated in freedom rides and sit-ins in South Carolina. Their refusal to pay bail-initiated SNCC's "jail, no bail" tactic, and they, along with others, served thirty days in jail. Fannie Lou Hamer's work to register voters and her pleas for justice to the 1964 Democratic National Convention's credential committee presented the nation with the stark brutality of Southern racism. Black Panther Party leaders Kathleen Cleaver and Elaine Brown followed a more radical path, one that accepted violence as part of the process.

Other women lobbied Congress for the Civil Rights Act of 1964 and the Voting Rights Act of 1965. When those bills became law, women continued to register voters and elect public officials who shared their beliefs. African American women and men in Congress continue to press for justice and for compliance with the law and to seek ways to fulfill the vision of equality under the law for all U.S. citizens.

The influence of the civil rights movement extended far beyond the African American community and prompted other groups to consider their status in American law and society. The ideals of freedom and equality resonated with women, gays and lesbians, Hispanic Americans, older citizens, disabled citizens, and others. Groups of people who experience discrimination organized to educate the public regarding the barriers they face and to enact policies to end discrimination against them.

See also Alexander, Sadie Tanner Mosell; Alpha Kappa Alpha Sorority; Anderson, Marian; Angelou, Maya; Anti-lynching Movement; Bates, Daisy Lee Gatson; Brown, Elaine; Civil Rights Act of 1964, Title VII; Cleaver, Kathleen Neal; Hamer, Fannie Lou Townsend; Hurley, Ruby; Lampkin, Daisy Elizabeth Adams; Motley, Constance Baker; National Association for the Advancement of Colored People, Women in the; Parks, Rosa Louise McCauley; Suffrage; Terrell, Mary Eliza Church; Voting Rights Act of 1965

References Barnett, "Black Women's Collectivist Movement Organizations: Their Struggles during the 'Doldrums'" (1995); Crawford, Rouse, and Woods, eds., *Women in the Civil Rights Movement: Trailblazers and Torchbearers, 1941–1965* (1993).

Civil Rights Restoration Act of 1988

The Civil Rights Restoration Act of 1988 reversed the U.S. Supreme Court's 1984 decision in *Grove City College v. Bell* and allowed federally funded institutions to refuse to perform abortions. Prior to the Grove City College decision, Title IX of the Education Amendments of 1972 had been interpreted to ban sex discrimination at educational institutions if any program at the institution received federal money. The Court changed that interpretation and limited the ban on sex discrimination to those programs within the institution that directly received federal funding.

The Civil Rights Restoration Act of 1988 established that if federal funds went to any program in an educational institution, the entire institution had to comply with Title IX, thereby prohibiting sex discrimination at educational institutions receiving federal funds. It also reinstated prohibitions on discriminating on the basis of minority status, disability, and age.

Two provisions in the act related to abortion. One stated that institutions receiving funds could pay for abortion benefits or services, but that those institutions were prohibited from discriminating against individuals seeking benefits or services related to abortion. The other provision stipulated that university hospitals would not lose their funding if they refused to perform abortions.

References *Congressional Quarterly Almanac, 100th Congress, 2nd Session 1988* (1989).

Clark Gray, Georgia Neese (1900–1995)

Democrat Georgia Neese Clark served as treasurer of the United States from 1949 to 1953, the first woman to hold the position. A Kansas bank president, she entered politics in 1936 as Democratic national committeewoman for Kansas, a post she held until her resignation in 1964. Active in President Harry S. Truman's 1948 presidential campaign, Clark received the largely ceremonial post in recognition of her work in the party and for Truman. As treasurer, her signature appeared on $30 billion of the nation's currency.

Born in Richland, Kansas, Georgia Clark attended the College of Sisters of Bethany in 1917 and received her bachelor's degree in economics from Washburn College in 1921. She studied at Sargent's Dramatic School and worked on the stage until 1930. She returned to Richland when her father's health began to fail and she was needed to help run the bank her father had founded. After his death, she became president of the bank.

References H. W. Wilson, *Current Biography: Who's News and Why, 1949* (1949); *The New York Times*, 28 October 1995.

Clark, Septima Poinsette (1898–1987)

African American civil rights leader and teacher Septima Clark began her teaching career and her life as an activist at a black public school on John's Island in South Carolina in 1916. That year, she organized a petition drive to hire black teachers, an effort that attracted 20,000 signatures. Almost thirty years later, while teaching in Columbia, South Carolina, she was instrumental in the 1945 court case that established one salary scale for white teachers and black teachers. She was dismissed from a teaching job in 1956 because she belonged to the National Association for the Advancement of Colored People (NAACP).

Clark remained a teacher but in a new context. Director of education for Highlander Folk School in Monteagle, Tennessee, from 1957 to 1961, she began a program to give African Americans the necessary skills to pass voter literacy tests. Her citizenship schools became the model for programs that spread throughout the southeastern United States. Students learned to write their names, balance their checkbooks, complete a ballot, and understand their rights and duties as citizens. Clark explained: "I just thought that you couldn't get people to register and vote until you teach them to read and write . . . and I was so right." She also taught hundreds of people to teach citizenship schools. Between 1957 and 1970, almost 900 schools were held in kitchens, beauty shops, and any other place that African Americans could gather, often under the threat of violence.

Beginning in 1962, she directed the teacher training project for the Voter Education Project, a cooperative effort of the Southern Christian Leadership Conference, NAACP, the Student Nonviolent Coordinating Committee, and the Urban League. In four years, the project trained 10,000 teachers for citizenship schools. Clark toured the nation giving lectures and gaining national attention for her work. During this period she also published her autobiography, *Echo in My Soul* (1962). After her retirement in 1970, Clark was elected to the Charleston County School Board in 1974.

Born in Charleston, South Carolina, Clark was the daughter of former slaves. She graduated from Avery Normal Institute in 1916, attended Columbia University in 1930 and Atlanta University in 1937, and received her bachelor's degree from Benedict College in 1942 and her master's degree from Hampton Institute in 1946. With Cynthia Stokes Brown, Clark wrote *Ready from Within*, published in 1986.

> **See also** Civil Rights Movement, Women in the; National Association for the Advancement of Colored People, Women in the
>
> **References** Clark, with Cynthia Stokes Brown, *Ready from Within: Septima Clark and the Civil Rights Movement* (1986); *The New York Times*, 17 December 1987.

Clarke, Marian Williams (1880–1953)

Republican Marian Clarke of New York served in the U.S. House of Representatives from 28 December 1933 to 3 January 1935. Following the death of her husband, Congressman John D. Clarke, she won the special election to fill the vacancy. The only Republican woman to serve during the New Deal, Clarke sought tariff protection for the shoe manufacturers in her district and introduced a measure to return the equipment allowance for rural mail carriers to its former level. She did not run for re-election in 1934.

Born in Standing Stone, Pennsylvania, Clarke attended art school at the University of Nebraska and graduated from Colorado College in 1902. She worked for a Colorado Springs newspaper before marrying.

See also Congress, Women in

References Office of the Historian, U.S. House of Representatives, *Women in Congress, 1917–1990* (1991).

Claybrook, Joan (b. 1937)

President of Public Citizen, a nonprofit consumer advocacy organization, Joan Claybrook headed the National Highway Traffic Safety Administration (NHTSA) from 1977 to 1981.

Claybrook worked at the Social Security Administration in the early 1960s, preparing reports for the Commission on the Status of Women, created by President John Kennedy.

Her involvement with automobile safety began when she worked for a freshman member of Congress and met Ralph Nader, who had written a book on auto safety. The meetings that followed contributed to the development of the National Traffic Safety Bureau, the NHTSA's original name. From 1966 to 1970, Claybrook was the special assistant to the bureau's administrator. Claybrook then worked for Public Interest Research Group, created by Nader. She founded and directed Public Citizen's Congress Watch, which she left in 1977 for NHTSA. Claybrook became president of Public Citizen in 1981.

Born in Baltimore, Maryland, Claybrook earned a bachelor of arts degree in history at Goucher College in 1959 and a juris doctor degree at Georgetown Law Center in 1973. She is the author of *Retreat from Safety: Reagan's Attack on American Health* (1984) and *Freedom from Harm: The Civilizing Influence of Health Safety, and Environmental Regulations* (1986).

References Ruth Conniff, "Joan Claybrook," *The Progressive*, March 1999, pp. 33–37; "Joan Claybrook," *Automotive News*, 11 September 2000, p. 30.

Clayton, Eva McPherson (b. 1934)

Democrat Eva Clayton of North Carolina served in the U.S. House of Representatives from 3 November 1992 to 3 January 2003. She held the leadership position of co-chair of the House Democratic Policy Committee in the 104th and 105th Congresses (1995–1999). Following Hurricane Floyd in 1999, which devastated large areas of North Carolina, Clayton sought federal assistance to rebuild her state. She and Charles Rangel (D-NY), also organized over 500 volunteers to help clean up. Clayton first ran for Congress in 1968 but lost in the primary. She succeeded, however, in her campaign for the Warren County Board of Commissioners, serving from 1982 to 1990. In 1992, she ran simultaneously to complete the term of the incumbent who had died in office and for a full term, winning both elections, becoming the first African American from North Carolina elected to Congress since Reconstruction. Elected president of the Democratic freshman class of the 103rd Congress (1993–1995), she was the first woman and the first African American to hold the office.

Reflecting the interests of her district, Clayton focused on agricultural issues, supporting the peanut subsidy and opposing the Freedom to Farm bill because it reduced farm subsidies. She wrote in 1998: "I am disturbed by the continuous loss of small farms, particularly those owned by African Americans. I am outraged that part of the problem is the result of discriminatory practices by agents of our government against minority farmers seeking loans." Some of her other congressional interests included rural health care, housing, job training, nutrition programs, and teen pregnancy.

Clayton did not seek re-election in 2002.

Born in Savannah, Georgia, Eva Clayton received her bachelor of science degree from Johnson C. Smith University in 1955, and her master of science degree from North Carolina Central University in 1962.

See also Congress, Women in

References *Congressional Quarterly, Politics in America 1994* (1993), *Congressional Quarterly, Politics in America 1998* (1997); Gill, *African American Women in Congress* (1997); Neuman, ed., *True to Ourselves: A Celebration of of Women Making a Difference* (1998); www.house.gov/clayton/bio.htm.

Cleaver, Kathleen Neal (b. 1945)

Black Panther Party leader Kathleen Cleaver began her activism in the civil rights movement as a member of the Student Nonviolent Coordinating Committee (SNCC) in 1966. At a black student leadership conference in 1967, she heard Black Panther Party leader Eldridge Cleaver speak. She left SNCC and joined the Black Panther Party, and the two married later that year. Kathleen Cleaver served as the party's national communications secretary and was the first woman member of its decision-making body. Kathleen Cleaver later described her experience with the Black Panther Party: "It was thrilling to be able to challenge the circumstances in which blacks were confined; to mobilize and raise consciousness, to change the way people saw themselves; blacks could express themselves."

In 1968, Eldridge Cleaver left the country to avoid being arrested for a parole violation from an earlier conviction. Kathleen Cleaver joined him in Algiers, Algeria, in 1969, returning to the United States in 1973 to raise money for her husband's defense. In 1980, Eldridge Cleaver's legal problems were resolved. The couple divorced in 1987 and Kathleen Cleaver returned to college.

Born in Dallas, Texas, Kathleen Cleaver attended Oberlin College and Barnard College. She received a bachelor's degree from Yale University in 1983 and her law degree from Yale Law School in 1988 and joined the faculty of Emory University in 1992.

See also Civil Rights Movement, Women in the

References Smith, ed., *Notable Black American Women, Book 2* (1996).

Cleveland Board of Education v. LaFleur (1974)

In *Cleveland Board of Education v. LaFleur*, the U.S. Supreme Court considered the mandatory pregnancy leave policies of the Cleveland Board of Education and of Chesterfield County, Virginia. The Cleveland policy required a pregnant schoolteacher to take unpaid maternity leave five months before her due date and did not permit her to return to teaching until the beginning of the next semester after her child was three months old. Chesterfield County required a pregnant teacher to leave work at least four months before her due date and to give notice at least six months before her due date. The Court found that both maternity leave policies violated the due process clause of the Fourteenth Amendment because they presumed that every pregnant teacher is physically incapable of performing her duties after a certain point, even though any one teacher's ability to work after a fixed period in her pregnancy is an individual matter. The Court decided that Cleveland's provision requiring that a teacher wait three months after childbirth before returning to work was arbitrary and irrational but said that Chesterfield County's policy for women returning to teaching after childbirth was acceptable because it did not have any unnecessary presumptions.

> **See also** *California Federal Savings and Loan v. Guerra*; Employment Discrimination; Fourteenth Amendment; *Geduldig v. Aiello*; *General Electric v. Gilbert*; *Nashville Gas Co. v. Satty*; Pregnancy Discrimination Act of 1978
>
> **References** *Cleveland Board of Education v. LaFleur*, 414 U.S. 632 (1974).

Clift, Eleanor (b. 1940)

Political journalist Eleanor Clift began her career working at *Newsweek* magazine as a secretary in 1963. After a stint as a researcher at the magazine, she became a correspondent at the Atlanta bureau. Her route to covering the White House began in Atlanta. Clift explained: Jimmy Carter launched his 1976 campaign for the presidency: "I was assigned to cover Carter at a time when no one thought he had a chance to win." After Carter won the presidency, Newsweek assigned Clift to cover the White House during the Carter administration, six years of the Reagan administration, and the first two years of the Clinton administration. During the George H. W. Bush administration, Clift covered Congress and politics for *Newsweek*. Since 1994, Clift has been a contributing editor to *Newsweek*, covering the political power structure, the influences of women, and related issues. From 1985 to 1986, Clift was with the *Los Angeles Times* Washington, D.C. bureau. She is also a regular panelist on *The McLaughlin Group*, a syndicated political television program, and a political analyst for Fox News Network.

Born in Brooklyn, New York, Clift attended Hofstra University and Hunter College.

> **References** Eleanor Clift, email message to author, 28 February 2006; http://eleanorclift.com; http://msnbc.msn.id/id/4900886/site/newsweek/#storyContinued

Clinton, Hillary Diane Rodham (b. 1947)

Democrat Hillary Clinton of New York entered the U.S. Senate on 3 January 2001. Senator Clinton was chair of the Democratic Senate Steering and Coordination Committee in the 108th and 109th Congresses (2003-2007). She is the first former first lady elected to the U.S. Senate.

As a senator for New York, one of her first priorities became obtaining federal assistance for New York City after the terrorist attacks on September 11, 2001. Other priorities include ensuring the safety of prescription drugs for children, strengthening the Children's Health Insurance Program, and lowering the cost of prescription drugs. She sponsored legislation to improve the recruitment and retention of nurses, to protect the food supply from bioterrorism, and to increase the nation's efforts against AIDS on a global level. A supporter of abortion rights, she has worked to reduce the number of unwanted pregnancies. She introduced the Count Every Vote Act of 2005, calling for verified paper ballots for every vote cast in electronic voting machines, as well as other provisions.

Clinton voted to permit President G.W. Bush invade Iraq. In 2006, she called for an exit strategy to withdraw troops from Iraq. She also called for the resignation of Secretary of Defense Donald Rumsfeld, primarily for his conduct of the war.

By 2005, Hillary Clinton had become widely recognized as a potential candidate for president of the United States. She ran for re-election to her Senate seat in 2006.

Hillary Rodham Clinton became first lady in 1993, when her husband Bill Clinton was elected president of the United States. Born in Park Ridge, Illinois, Hillary Clinton graduated from Wellesley College in 1969 and received her law degree from Yale Law School in 1973. That same year, she became a staff attorney for the Children's Defense Fund and served on the impeachment inquiry staff of the House Judiciary Committee in 1974. She married Bill Clinton in 1975, and then both Clintons taught on the law faculty of the University of Arkansas.

Hillary Clinton became first lady of Arkansas when her husband won his race for governor in 1978. He lost his bid for re-election in 1980 and then won in 1982, serving until 1992. During those years, she chaired the Arkansas Education Standards Committee, initiated the Home Instruction Program for Preschool Youth, served on the Southern Governors' Association Task Force on Infant Mortality, and helped establish the state's first neonatal nursery. In addition, she founded the Arkansas Advocates for Children and Families and served on the Arkansas Children's Hospital board of directors.

Following Bill Clinton's election as president of the United States, he appointed his wife to head a task force on health care reform. The twelve-member task force worked

New York Senator Hillary Clinton. (Courtesy: Hillary Clinton)

from February through September 1993, when its report was released. It recommended insurance coverage for mammograms, pap smears, and abortions, all priorities of the Congressional Caucus for Women's Issues. Controversy surrounded the task force's proposals and the process used for developing them. Congress did not vote on the recommended plan, and efforts to reform health care reform were set aside.

Throughout most of Bill Clinton's presidency, an investigation of Whitewater land deals dominated. Perhaps the more trying scandal for Hillary Rodham Clinton was the U.S. House of Representatives' approval of two articles of impeachment for perjury related to sexual misconduct. The U.S. Senate narrowly voted against removing him from office.

Hillary Clinton served as honorary chair of the U.S. delegation to the 1995 United Nations Fourth World Conference on Women, held in Beijing, China. With Bill Clinton, she hosted the White House Conference on Early Childhood Development and Learning and the White House Conference on Child Care, both in 1997. She also helped pass the Adoption and Safe Family Act of 1997. She is the author of *It Takes a Village, and Other Lessons Children Teach Us* (1996); *An Invitation to the White House: At Home with History* (2000), and her autobiography, *Living History* (2003).

See also Children's Defense Fund; Congressional Caucus for Women's Issues

References Center for American Women and Politics, "Women in Congress: Leadership Roles and Committee Chairs," Fact sheet, 2005; H. W. Wilson, *Current Biography Yearbook, 1993* (1993); http://clinton.senate.gov; http://www.whitehouse.gov/history/firstladies/hc42.html

Clinton v. Jones (1997)

In *Clinton v. Jones*, the U.S. Supreme Court decided that the Constitution does not prohibit a private citizen from suing a sitting president for acts committed before becoming president. The case developed as a result of Paula Corbin Jones's allegations that in 1991, when she had been an employee of the State of Arkansas and Bill Clinton had been governor of the state, Clinton had made sexual advances to her. She further claimed that after rejecting the advances, her supervisors had punished her. Jones filed her suit in 1994, after Clinton had become president of the United States. Clinton argued that the president has temporary immunity from civil damages litigation resulting from events that occurred before taking office and that the separation of powers requires federal courts to stay private actions until the president leaves office. The Supreme Court rejected both arguments.

Jones's original sexual harassment lawsuit did not go to trial. In November 1998, Clinton agreed to pay Jones $850,000 but did not admit to misconduct and did not agree to apologize to her.

References *Clinton v. Jones*, No. 95–1853 (1997).

Coalition for Women's Appointments

The Coalition for Women's Appointments (CWA) has its roots in a meeting between women leaders and presidential candidate Jimmy Carter. At the meeting, held during the 1976 Democratic National Convention, Carter pledged to appoint a significant number of women to all levels of his administration. After Carter won, women leaders organized CWA to identify women candidates for positions in Carter's administration and to develop the political power to successfully press for the appointments. CWA worked with every administration through Bill Clinton's. It sought women of every racial and ethnic group, of every income level, and from every part of the country.

See also Cabinets, Women in Presidential

References http://nwpc.org.

Coalition of Labor Union Women

Founded in 1974, the Coalition of Labor Union Women (CLUW) works to unify all union women and to develop action programs to address common concerns. The founding conference adopted four goals: organize the unorganized, promote affirmative action, increase women's participation in their unions, and increase women's participation in political and legislative activity. The group elected Olga M. Madar, a leader in creating the organization, its first president.

CLUW's 20,000 members work for full employment, child care legislation, a livable minimum wage, improved maternity and pension benefits, ratification of the Equal Rights Amendment, and protective legislation for all workers. CLUW lobbies for reproductive rights and pay equity and opposes making English the official language of the United States. Its Contraceptive Equity Project works to inform women about bargaining for contraception coverage in health insurance plans and developed a resource packet on the topic. Members also provide leadership in HIV/AIDS awareness, supported by a grant from the Centers for Disease Control. CLUW has helped pass legislation, including the Violence Against Women Act.

CLUW does not endorse candidates, but it urges members to participate in the political process and encourages members to seek public offices at the local, county, state, and national levels. To encourage greater involvement, CLUW offers education and training opportunities and political action programs that include voter registration and education, and member mobilization around CLUW priorities.

The CLUW Center for Education and Research was established in 1979. The center's four program areas are women's health, women's leadership, women's rights, and young women workers.

See also Abortion; Affirmative Action; Equal Rights Amendment; Health Care, Women and; Madar, Olga Marie; Pay Equity; Sexual Harassment; Violence Against Women Office

References CLUW NEWS, March-April 1995, October 1995, March-April 1996, May-June 1996; www.cluw.org.

Code Pink

Founded November 17, 2002, by Medea Benjamin, Jodie Evans, and Gael Murphy, Code Pink describes itself as "a women-initiated grassroots peace and social justice movement." Organized in the months before the pre-emptive strikes against Iraq, the group seeks to end the war, prevent new wars, and invest national resources in health, education, and related activities.

The group's name is a spoof of the Bush Administration's identification of terrorism levels using a color-coded system.

The organization's first public protest was a four-month vigil in front of the White House. During the vigil, Code Pink protestors hung a woman's pink slip from a helium balloon and chanted "Pink Slip George Bush," a reference to the pink slips associated with a person being fired from a job. Several of the women wore pink slips, the undergarment, over their street clothes.

Members go to high schools, concerts, colleges, and military recruiting centers, urging young people not to enlist in the military.

By 2006, Code Pink had groups in over 250 cities in the United States and connections with international peace organizations.

References *The New York Times*, September 4, 2004; *The Washington Post*, March 8, 2004; http://www.codepink4peace.org/article.php?list=type&type=3.

Document "CODEPINK: Women for Peace and Social Justice, Songs of Celebration and Protest"

Coker v. Georgia (1977)

In *Coker v. Georgia*, the U.S. Supreme Court decided that death was a disproportionate penalty for rape, even when the rape was committed in the course of another capital felony, in this case armed robbery. The Court found that the Eighth Amendment prohibits both barbaric and excessive punishments and classified the death penalty in rape cases as excessive. At the time, Ruth Bader Ginsburg, now Supreme Court Justice Ginsburg, filed a brief on behalf of the Women's Rights Project of the American Civil Liberties Union, opposing the death penalty in rape cases. She argued that the death penalty had been imposed in rape cases on the historical view that a woman was a man's property and that the rape violated that property. She further argued that the death penalty often meant that police would not charge men with rape and that juries would not convict them.

References American Civil Liberties Union, "Timeline of Major Supreme Court Decision on Women's Rights (2005); *Coker v. Georgia*, 433 U.S. 584 (1977).

Colautti v. Franklin (1979)

In 1974, Pennsylvania passed the state's Abortion Control Act, requiring every person who performed an abortion to determine whether the fetus was viable, and if evidence indicated that it was, that health care worker was required to try to preserve the life of the fetus. In addition, unless the mother's health or life was at risk, the person performing the abortion had to use the abortion technique most likely to save the life of the fetus. In *Colautti v. Franklin*, the U.S. Supreme Court found the requirement that fetal viability be determined to be void because it was vague. The Court also found the provision regarding the care of the fetus too vague and rejected it, saying that it was unclear whether a physician could make the patient the first priority or whether the law forced the physician to choose between the patient's health and increasing the fetus's chances for survival.

See also Abortion

References *Colautti v. Franklin*, 439 U.S. 379 (1979).

Collins, Barbara-Rose (b. 1939)

Democrat Barbara-Rose Collins of Michigan served in the U.S. House of Representatives from 3 January 1991 to 3 January 1997. After seeking the Democratic nomination for Congress in 1988 and losing, she was successful in 1990. As a member of Congress, Collins worked on economic development for Detroit, legislation to combat stalking, and measures to enhance breast cancer research. She founded and chaired the Congressional Caucus on Children, Youth, and Families in the 103rd Congress. She lost her attempt to return to Congress in the 1996 Democratic primary, at least in part because of a congressional investigation of her use of staff members and of campaign and scholarship funds. In 1997, the House ethics committee announced that it had found reason to believe that Collins had violated laws and House rules. Because Collins was defeated in the 1996 elections, the House did not punish Collins.

Collins served on the Detroit Public School Board from 1971 to 1973. As a school board member, she helped institute community-based parental involvement, establish requirements for homework for students, and improve students' reading material. She served in the Michigan House of Representatives from 1975 to 1981, where she focused on consumer and civil rights, economic development, and women's issues. She helped pass bills for fair housing, to end sexual harassment, and to provide for equality in women's and men's pensions. Elected to the Detroit City Council, she served from 1982 until 1990. Collins led the effort for more rigorous accounting procedures with greater checks and balances in the city's spending and chaired the Detroit City Council's Task Force on Teenage Violence and Juvenile Crime in 1985.

Born in Detroit, Michigan, African American Barbara-Rose Collins attended Wayne State University, majoring in anthropology and political science.

> **See also** Congress, Women in; State Legislatures, Women in
>
> **References** *Congressional Quarterly, Politics in America 1994* (1993); Gill, *African American Women in Congress* (1997).

Collins, Cardiss Hortense Robertson (b. 1931)

Democrat Cardiss Collins of Illinois served in the U.S. House of Representatives from 5 June 1973 to 3 January 1997. After the death of Collins's husband, Congressman George Collins, Chicago Mayor Richard Daley encouraged her to run in the special election to fill the vacancy. A political novice who had only been marginally involved in politics, Cardiss Collins explained: "I guess I must have been in Congress all of 24 hours when I realized that, as the wife of a politician, I had just been a political spectator–not really playing the game. The difference started rolling in, like a sledgehammer." She made the transition and became the longest-serving black woman in Congress at the time of her retirement.

Collins played a significant role in defeating an effort to eliminate school busing for racial integration, passed a measure requiring that 10 percent of all airport concessions be held by minority- and women-owned businesses, and focused attention on public housing and public service jobs. She led an investigation that determined that most airlines hired few black and minority employees; as a result, airlines worked to improve their affirmative action programs. In 1987, she investigated allegations that Eastern Airlines failed to properly maintain its safety equipment, resulting in criminal charges against the airline and some of its managers. An inquiry into gender equity in collegiate athletics led to improved compliance with federal policies. As chair of the congressional Black Caucus, she was a vocal critic of President Ronald Reagan's civil rights policies. She retired from Congress in 1997.

Born in St. Louis, Missouri, Collins graduated from the Detroit High School of Commerce but was unable to find a job and moved to Chicago to work and live with her grandmother. Her first job was as a seamstress in a mattress factory, but she was fired for talking too much. She attended night school at Northwestern University from 1949 to 1950 and worked as a stenographer at the Illinois Department of Labor. As her skills developed, she rose through the ranks of the Illinois civil service, becoming an auditor for the Illinois Department of Revenue.

See also Affirmative Action; Congress, Women in

References Collins and Speace, eds., *Newsmakers 1995 Cumulation* (1995); Kaptur, *Women in Congress: A Twentieth Century Odyssey* (1996); Smith, ed., *Notable Black American Women* (1991).

Collins, Martha Layne Hall (b. 1936)

Democrat Martha Layne Collins was governor of Kentucky from 1983 to 1987. During her campaign, Collins adopted the slogan "Let's Make History" in an effort to combat any resistance voters may have had to electing a woman. As governor, Collins made kindergarten mandatory and established an intern program for beginning teachers. She shepherded remedial education programs and a program that permitted the state to take control of local school districts that failed to meet academic standards. The Collins administration attracted an $800 million Toyota Motor Corporation plant as well as eighty-seven other foreign and domestic businesses. Because the Kentucky state constitution limits governors to one term, Collins did not run for re-election.

Democratic national committeewoman for Kentucky from 1972 to 1976, Collins ran for clerk of the Kentucky Court of Appeals and won the statewide office in 1975. Lieutenant governor from 1979 to 1983, she became the first woman to chair the National Conference of Lieutenant Governors. As chair of the 1984 Democratic National Convention, Collins received national attention, and Walter Mondale considered her for the vice presidential spot on his ticket.

Born in Bagdad, Kentucky, Collins attended Lindenwood College from 1955 to 1956 and received her bachelor of science in education from the University of Kentucky in 1959. She taught home economics and mathematics from 1959 to 1970.

See also Governors, Women

References H. W. Wilson, *Current Biography Yearbook 1986* (1986); Mullaney, *Biographical Directory of the Governors of the United States 1983–1988* (1989).

Collins, Susan Margaret (b. 1952)

Republican Susan Collins of Maine entered the U.S. Senate on 3 January 1997. A deputy whip in the 107th Congress (2001–2002), she chaired the Committee on Governmental Affairs in the 108th Congress (2003–2004) and chaired the Committee on Homeland Security and Governmental Affairs in the 109th Congress (2005–2006). When she became chair of the Committee on Governmental Affairs, she was only the third woman to chair a permanent Senate committee. During the 108th Conngress (2003–2005), at the request of Senate Majority Leader Bill Frist (R-TN), Collins and Senator Joe Lieberman (D-CT) developed the plan that included the creation of a director of national intelligence to oversee the fifteen intelligence agencies and compel them to share information.

Senator Collins supports a constitutional amendment for congressional term limits and has pledged that she will serve no more than twelve years. One of the first Republican senators to call for wide-ranging hearings on both political parties' fundraising methods, her defiance of the Senate majority leader's position gained her national attention. Strongly pro-choice, she was one of only four Republican senators to vote against a ban on partial birth abortions in 1997. Collins opposes capital punishment and cuts in Head Start programs. She supports gay rights, a repeal of the ban on certain semi-automatic assault-style weapons, and the balanced budget amendment. Collins believes that a two-thirds majority vote of Congress should be required to raise taxes. She is critical of burdensome regulations and would like to impose a seven-year expiration date on all new federal regulations.

During her first term, Senator Collins passed a measure calling on the National Institutes of Health to put more emphasis on diabetes research. She also founded the Senate Diabetes Caucus. In the area of consumer protection, she won passage of a measure relating to deceptive practices by small sweepstakes companies. Her advocacy for education resulted in passage of a measure to triple the funding for early reading initiatives. She has also focused attention on phony identifications and credentials available through the Internet, saying that they pose "a serious new threat to government and the integrity of government operations."

Born in Caribou, Maine, Susan Collins comes from a political family: four generations of her family served in the Maine legislature, and her mother was mayor of Caribou and served on the school board and the library board. Collins received her bachelor's degree from Lawrence University in 1975 and then worked as a congressional aide. She served in the Cabinet of Maine's governor from 1987 to 1992, when she became New England administrator for the U.S. Small Business Administration. She unsuccessfully ran for governor of Maine in 1994 and then founded the Husson College Center for Family Business.

While a high school senior, Collins met Senator Margaret Chase Smith (R-ME), whom Collins regards as both a "legend" and a role model. Collins recollects: "We discussed many important issues, she answered my many questions, but what I remember most was her telling me always to stand tall for what I believed, citing her Declaration of Conscience delivered at the height of McCarthyism as an example."

See also Abortion; Congress, Women in; Lesbian Rights

References Rebecca Adams, "Sen. Susan Collins," *CQ Weekly*, 28 December 2002, p. 17o; *Congressional Quarterly, Politics in America 1998* (1998), *Politics in America 2002* (2003), *Politics in America 2006* (2005); Center for the American Women and Politics, "Women in Congress: Leadership Roles and Committee Chairs," Fact sheet (2005); http://collins.senate.gov; *The New York Times*, 20 July 1997; Susan Collins to author, n.d.

Colored Women's League

Founded in 1895, the Colored Women's League has its roots in the Colored Women's League of Washington, D.C. (CWL, DC), which was organized in 1892. Members of CWL, DC tended to be among the city's black elite–dressmakers, hairdressers, and wives of respectable black working men. The impetus for forming a national organization came with the announcement that the United States planned to host the 1893 Columbian Exposition, a world's fair, to be held in Chicago. The Columbian Commission, in charge of the fair, appointed a group of women to organize a women's exhibit but excluded African American women, who petitioned to be allowed to participate and presented a proposal. Their proposal was rejected on the grounds that black women did not have a national organization. CWL, DC responded by trying to call a convention to create a national organization but failed to do it in time for the fair. In 1895, CWL, DC organized the national Colored Women's League, bringing together 113 black women's clubs. The next year, the Colored Women's League merged with the National Federation of Afro-American Women to form the National Association of Colored Women.

> **See also** National Association of Colored Women; National Federation of Afro-American Women
>
> **References** Hine and Thompson, *A Shining Thread of Hope: The History of Black Women in America* (1998).

Comisin Femenil Mexicana - Nacional, Inc.

Organized in 1970, the Comisin Femenil Mexicana Nacional (CFMN) seeks to represent all women's concerns and is dedicated to the political, social, economic, and educational advancement of Latinas. Its public policy priorities include supporting affirmative action, pay equity, and reproductive rights; reducing teenage pregnancy; and improving child care, housing, and education. In 1981, CFMN began a program to encourage women to run for public office. In part due to CFMN's support, Gloria Molina, the organization's first president, became the first Latina to serve in the California legislature.

> **See also** Abortion; Affirmative Action; Child Day Care; Pay Equity

Commissions on the Status of Women

The creation of state and municipal commissions on the status of women was prompted by the President's Commission on the Status of Women (PCSW), created by President John F. Kennedy in 1961. In its 1963 report, the PCSW encouraged states to form commissions and investigate the legal, economic, and political status of women. By the end of 1964, thirty-three states had commissions, all fifty states had some form of commission by 1967, and in the late 1990s more than 270 state and local commissions existed.

As governmental bodies, commissions have authority, provide a link between women's groups and politicians, and institutionalize women's issues in the policymaking process. Cities, counties, states, and other jurisdictions have created commissions, with some receiving public funding and others not, and their structures and authorities vary by location, but some generalizations can be made about them. The creation of a commission makes a political statement that there is a reason to question women's status and that the inquiry warrants the leadership of government. By bringing women together around the issue of their status, the commission heightens their awareness of themselves as a group with common interests and often results in the formation of political networks. As commissioners investigate discriminatory laws and policies, the extent of the barriers to women's full participation and advancement is a disconcerting revelation. When the commissions disseminate their reports through the media and women's organizations, they prompt others to take action.

Commissions have supported the Equal Rights Amendment and have been advocates for child care, displaced homemakers, women's health, welfare reform, and rape law reform. Some commissions focus on women's appointments to public office, and by maintaining data banks of women and their areas of interest, they create a pool of qualified candidates available for consideration. Commissions' effectiveness was enhanced by the Citizens' Advisory Council on the Status of Women, which linked state and local commissions into a national network. Since 1969, the National Association of Commissions for Women has performed that function and offered a range of support services.

> **See also** Child Day Care; Citizens' Advisory Council on the Status of Women;
> Displaced Homemakers; Equal Rights Amendment; Health Care, Women and;
> National Association of Commissions for Women; President's Commission on the
> Status of Women; Rape
>
> **References** Rosenberg, "Representing Women at the State and Local Levels:
> Commissions on the Status of Women" (1982).

Communist Party, USA

Based on the economic and social theories of nineteenth-century German philosopher Karl Marx, Communism is premised upon a rejection of capitalism or private ownership of the means of production. The oppression of poor people and the tyranny of wealthy people will end, Communists argue, only through the common ownership of factories, farms, and other means of production. The Communist Party evolved following the 1917 Russian Revolution, also known as the October Revolution. Communism in Russia included an economy planned by a centralized bureaucracy, the loss of private property, and the denial of human rights.

The Communist Party, USA has its roots in the Socialist Party and emerged from disagreements between factions in 1919. First known as the Communist Party of America, it struggled through a decade of factions splitting from it and merging with it and went through several different names. In the 1920s, the party attempted to attract supporters among union members, form labor unions, and establish coalitions between farmers and laborers. The party adopted the name Communist Party, USA in 1929.

The United States and the Union of Soviet Socialist Republics (Russia and the countries it absorbed) were allies during World War II, but hostilities between the two nations developed after the war, resulting in the Cold War. As tensions between the United States and Soviet republics intensified, U.S. Communists became the targets of congressional investigations and harassment in the 1950s. Communists' power in the

Soviet republics began to diminish in 1989, and two years later the Soviet Union was officially dissolved.

Some notable American women Communists included Ella Reeve Bloor, Angela Davis, and Helen Gurley Flynn.

References Foner and Garraty, eds., *The Reader's Companion to American History* (1991).

Comparable Worth

See **Pay Equity**

Concerned Women for America

Founded in 1979, Concerned Women for America (CWA) supports pro-family Christian policies by opposing the Equal Rights Amendment, abortion, outcome-based education, pornography, and gay rights. CWA founder and chair Beverly LaHaye organized the group in response to feminist Betty Friedan's leadership, arguing that Friedan did not represent all women's views. Intending to protect the American family through prayer and action, CWA claims to be the largest pro-family women's organization in the nation. With 500,000 members organized in forty-eight states, 1,200 prayer/action chapters, and an annual budget of $10 million, CWA works to influence policies at the local, state, and national levels.

CWA identifies six central issues. It defines the family of one man and one woman and their children, their interpretation of the Biblical design of the family. It opposes abortion. It seeks to reform public education by giving parents authority over their children. It fights all forms of pornography and obscenity. It supports religious liberty. CWA also supports national sovereignty, opposing any encroachment on that sovereignty by the United Nations or any other organization.

CWA has used several strategies to press its agenda. Opposed to the proposed federal Equal Rights Amendment, which was passed in 1972, but not ratified, CWA Prayer/Action Chapters fasted and prayed every Wednesday for its defeat, until the ratification deadline passed and the amendment failed. In the mid-1980s, CWA delivered thousands of petitions to Congress, denouncing radio and television advertisements for alcoholic beverages. It has lobbied for the ban on partial birth abortions and for increasing the child tax credit on federal income taxes.

CWA supports a balanced federal budget, prayer in the schools, and sex education programs that are limited to teaching that abstinence is the only way to prevent pregnancy and opposes affirmative action and comparable worth pay plans. To educate and inform the membership on issues affecting families, LaHaye produces a national daily radio program that has an estimated 350,000 listeners. The program focuses on major issues in Congress, provides phone numbers for members of Congress, and encourages listeners to register their opinions. In addition, CWA publishes the monthly magazine *Family Voice*; develops policy papers; and distributes brochures, booklets, and manuals. The Freedom of Choice Act introduced in 1992 provides an example of CWA's ability to respond to proposed legislation. Two hundred fifty thousand signatures on petitions in opposition to the measure were delivered to Congress, and volunteer lobbyists visited every member of Congress.

CWA's Department of Legislation and Public Policy coordinates the lobbying efforts of both the professional staff and volunteer lobbyists. The organization's Project 535, named for the total number of U.S. senators and representatives, is a group of volunteer lobbyists that meets monthly to develop strategies for congressional lobbying efforts. In addition, local and state groups monitor and lobby school boards, state legislatures, and other local policymaking groups.

See also Abortion; Affirmative Action; Equal Rights Amendment; Feminist Movement; Friedan, Betty Naomi Goldstein; Pay Equity

References Burkett, *The Right Women: A Journey through the Heart of Conservative America* (1998); www.cwfa.org.

Congress, Women in

When Jeannette Rankin of Montana took her seat in the U.S. House of Representatives in 1917, she became the first woman member of Congress. In 2006, of the approximately 11,745 people who have served, or are serving in the U.S. House of Representatives and the U.S. Senate, 225 are women, about 2 percent. These women have served terms from as short as one day (Senator Rebecca Latimer Felton, D-GA, from 21 November 1922 to 22 November 1922) to as long as thirty-five years (Representative Edith Nourse Rogers, R-MA, from 30 June 1925 to 10 September 1960). In 1967, fifty years after Jeannette Rankin entered Congress, only one woman served in the U.S. Senate and eleven in the U.S. House. Another twenty-five more years passed before women held 10 percent of the seats; in the 103rd Congress (1993–1995), seven women served in the Senate and forty-seven women served in the House. In the 109th Congress, fourteen women served in the Senate and sixty-six women served in the House, about 15 percent.

Several factors have contributed to the relatively small number of women who have served in Congress. For more than a century, women were not among any definition of the eligible pool of candidates because they could not vote. After women obtained voting rights, political parties sought their votes but did not welcome them in decision-making circles, nor did they nominate women for seats they thought the party could win with a male candidate. In the 1990s, as women were more likely to win their races, increasing numbers of women offered themselves as candidates. In 2004, a record 138 women were major party candidates and in eleven races, both candidates were women. In 2005, California had sent more women to Congress, 29, than any other state. Iowa, Mississippi, New Hampshire, and Vermont have had a woman appointed or elected to the U.S. House of Representatives or the U.S. Senate.

Thirty women of color have served in the U.S. House; twenty of them serve in the 109th Congress (2005–2007). Twenty of them are African Americans, three are Asian Pacific Islanders, and seven are Latinas. Representative Patsy Mink (D-HI) was the first woman of color to serve in Congress, and Representative Shirley Chisholm (D-NY) was the first African American woman. Representative Ileana Ros-Lehtinen (R-FL) is the first Latina elected to Congress and the first Cuban American, male or female. The first sisters to serve in Congress are Representatives Loretta Sanchez and Linda Sanchez, both Democrats from California. Senator Carol Moseley Braun (D-IL) is the only woman of color to serve in the U.S. Senate.

For those women who are recruited to run or who decide to run, the primary and most persistent challenge is financing their campaigns. Women consistently raise less money than their male opponents. To overcome the obstacle, groups like EMILY's List, the WISH List, and other political action committees have developed to provide women candidates with financial support as well as technical advice and other forms of assistance in their campaigns.

Women have traveled several different routes to Congress. Filling a vacancy created by the death of an incumbent was the way for almost a quarter of the women who have entered Congress. The deceased most often was the woman's spouse (in 2006, forty-seven women had succeeded their husbands), but women have been appointed or elected to fill other vacancies. Many of the women who entered Congress by appointment or in a special election to fill a vacancy have had short tenures, notably Rebecca Felton's one-day appointment. Tenures of a year or less are common for these women, but not all of them. Edith Nourse Rogers, who succeeded her husband, served thirty-five years and was responsible for significant legislation.

A second route to Congress is holding state or local public office. The pool of women in those offices has been small. In 1971, women comprised only 4.5 percent of the total membership in state legislatures. As the number of women serving in those bodies has increased, the number of women who have moved from state legislatures to Congress has grown. In the 109th Congress (2005–2006), thirty-eight of the sixty-six women serving in U.S. House of Representatives had first served in their state legislatures and seven of the fourteen women serving in the U.S. Senate had.

Third, some women begin their political careers by working on a congressional staff. Although few women hold or have held high-level positions on congressional staffs and most women hold clerical or secretarial positions, women have used their experience to launch their careers. Some women who succeeded their husbands had earlier worked on their congressional staffs; and Ruth Hanna McCormick (R-IL) had been her father's secretary when he was in Congress.

Representative Carolyn McCarthy (D-NY) entered politics after her husband was killed and her son wounded in the 1993 Long Island Railroad massacre, speaking across the nation on the causes of violence. Senator Patty Murray (D-WA) began her political career organizing 12,000 families in Washington state to save funding for the state's preschool programs. Senator Elizabeth Dole (R-NC) worked in the administrations of Presidents Lyndon B. Johnson, Richard M. Nixon, Ronald Reagan, and George Bush, serving as both Secretary of Transportation and Secretary of Labor, in addition to other positions. Senator Hillary Rodham Clinton (D-NY) was first lady for eight years during her husband Bill Clinton's presidency. Representative Helen Gahagan Douglas (D-CA) was an opera singer and stage and screen actress who became political to focus attention on migrant workers in the 1930s. Two women entered politics because of unsafe playground equipment in their communities.

Political observers declared 1992 the "Year of the Woman" because twenty women entered the House of Representatives and five women entered the Senate, the largest freshman class of women. Several of the women ran for office in response to watching the Senate Judiciary Committee hearings on Clarence Thomas's nomination for the U.S. Supreme Court. The televised hearings resulted from Anita Hill's accusation that

Thomas had sexually harassed her when he was her supervisor. Women across the country and in Congress were outraged as they watched the all-male Senate Judiciary Committee's conduct during the hearings. The image of the panel of men interrogating Hill, challenging the truthfulness of her reported experiences, and demeaning her prompted women to action. The action some women took was to run for office, and a record number of them won their races.

As members of Congress, women raise new issues and offer new perspectives on other issues because their life experiences generally differ from those of men. Several women in Congress have expressed the belief that they have a special responsibility to represent women and their experience. U.S. Senator Barbara Mikulski once explained: "We women speak a different language. We will seek different results. We won't just talk about family values: we'll make sure a mom and dad can stay home from work when a child is sick."

In addition, women's personal experiences add credibility to debate on certain issues. For example, Representative Patsy Mink testified before the House Commerce Committee that when she was pregnant, she had been an unknowing subject in an experiment with DES, a drug thought to prevent miscarriages. Mink described the resulting health problems her daughter, the child she was carrying, has suffered as a result of diethylstilbestrol (DES). Senators Dianne Feinstein's and Carol Moseley Braun's descriptions of being targets of stalkers helped their colleagues understand the realities of the experience and the inadequacies of anti-stalking laws. Representative Margaret Roukema worked for passage of the Family and Medical Leave Act for eight years, watched President George Bush veto it twice, and continued to work for it. Her commitment arose in part from her experience of leaving her graduate studies to care for her son when he was dying of leukemia. She explained that suffering the tragedy and trauma of losing her son was a great enough burden and that she did not know what she would have done if she had been faced with losing a job as well. Representative Constance Morella became an advocate for breast cancer research after her sister died of the disease. When Senator Mary Landrieu's five-year-old son entered preschool, the senator became interested in overhauling the school lunch program.

The differences also extend to voting. On a vote to ban assault weapons, four out of five Republican men in the House opposed it, but three out of five Republican women in the House supported it. The Family and Medical Leave Act of 1993 provides another example. One out of five Republican men in the House, half of the Republican women, and all of the Democratic women voted for it. The Freedom of Access to Clinic Entrances Act, the reauthorization of the National Institutes of Health, and the Hyde Amendment are additional examples of women voting differently from their male colleagues of the same party.

The demonstrated differences between women's and men's voting do not, however, mean that all women in Congress have the same priorities or political beliefs. Just as congressmen differ on issues, so do congresswomen. Those women who have a shared vision on issues related to women, families, and children and other areas began working together in the 1970s to coordinate their efforts and enhance their power. In 1977, women members formed the Women's Congressional Caucus, later reorganized as the Congressional Caucus for Women's Issues, a group that included male members of

Congress. By organizing to exert pressure inside and outside Congress, they focus attention on issues, help bills move forward, and stop bills they believe to be detrimental to women. They also solicit support from influential male congressional leaders, sometimes doing things as simple as explaining a measure's significance to women.

Until the mid-1990s, women held few leadership positions and committee chairs. Senator Hattie Caraway (D-AR) was the first woman senator to chair a committee, enrolled bills, holding the position from 1933 to 1945. The next woman to chair a committee was Senator Nancy Kassebaum (R-KS), chairing the committee on labor and human resources from 1995 to 1997. Senators Susan Collins and Olympia Snowe, both Republicans from Maine, are the other two women who have chaired senate committees. Collins chaired the committee on governmental affairs from 2003 to 2005 and the committee on homeland security and governmental affairs from 2005–2007. Snowe chaired the committee on small business and entrpreneurship from 2003 to 2007. Eleven women senators have held leadership positions. In the 109th Congress: Senator Boxer (D-CA) served as chief deputy whip; Hillary Rodham Clinton (D-KY) as chair of the steering and outreach committee; Elizabeth Dole (D-NC) as chair, National Republican Senatorial Committee; Kay Bailey Hutchison (R-TX) as Republican conference secretary; Blanche Lincoln (D-AR) as chair of rural outreach; and Debbie Stabenow (D-MI) as Democratic Conference secretary.

In the House of Representatives, Representative Mae Ella Nolan (R-CA) was the first woman to chair a committee, Committee on Expenditures in the Post Office Department, from 1923 to 1925. Representative Mary Teresa Norton (D-NJ) chaired the Committee on District of Columbia from 1931 to 1939 and the Committee on Labor from 1939 to 1947. Norton also chaired the Committee on House Administration from 1949 to 1951. Representative Caroline O'Day (D-NJ) chaired the Committee on Election of President, Vice President, and Representatives from 1937 to 1943. Representative Edith Nourse Rogers (R-MA) chaired the Committee on Veterans' Affairs from 1953 to 1955; Representative Leonora Sullivan (d-MO) chaired the Committee on Merchant Marine and Fisheries from 1973 to 1977; and Representative Jan Meyers (R-KS) chaired the Committee on Small Business from 1995 to 1997.

The first woman member of the House of Representatives to hold a leadership position was Representative Chase G. Woodhouse (D-CT), who was secretary of the House Democratic Caucus from 1949 to 1951. Representatives Edna Kelly (D-NY), Leonor Sullivan, Shirley Chisholm, Geraldine Ferraro (D-NY), and Mary Rose Oakar (D-OH) have all held the office. Representatives Nancy L. Johnson (R-CT), Barbarba Vucanovich (R-NV), Deborah Pryce (R-OH), and Barbara Cubin (R-WY) have served as secretary of the House Republican Conference.

Since the 104th Congress (1995 to 1997), women have held increasing numbers of leadership positions in both parties, including deputy whip, assistant whip, and other positions. In the 107th Congress (2001 to 2003), Representative Nancy Pelosi (D-CA) made history in when she was elected House Democratic Whip, the highest position any woman had held in Congress. In the 108th Congress (2003 to 2005), Pelosi again made history when she became the first woman to lead her party, winning election to House Democratic Leader, a position she held in the 109th Congress (2005 to 2007).

References Boxer, *Strangers in the Senate: Politics and the New Revolution of Women in America* (1994); Center for the American Woman and Politics, National Information Bank on Women in Public Office, Eagleton Institute of Politics, Rutgers University; *Congressional Quarterly, Politics in America 1996* (1995); Roberts and Roberts, "When Working Mothers Make the Laws" (1997); www.rci.rutgers.edu.

Congressional Caucus for Women's Issues

Organized in April 1977, the Congressional Caucus for Women's Issues grew out of an informal group that met over lunch to discuss issues before Congress and to develop strategies. In 1977, the group formally organized as the Women's Congressional Caucus because they felt they would have more power to influence legislation as a unified and identifiable group. Margaret Heckler (R-MA) and Elizabeth Holtzman (D-NY) were the first co-chairs of the bipartisan group that included fifteen of the eighteen women serving at the time. After the group changed its name to the Congressional Caucus for Women's Issues (CCWI) and admitted men in 1981, the membership grew to more than 100 at a time when only twenty-five women served in Congress. As the caucus director in 1985 noted: "We can call our friends and members who sit on key committees to promote the legislation [supported by the caucus]."

The caucus's first significant success was obtaining congressional approval for extending the ratification deadline for the Equal Rights Amendment from 1979 to 1982. The caucus next turned its attention to economic issues and introduced the Economic Equity Act in 1981, a set of proposals that addressed a wide range of policies, including taxation, insurance, pensions, child care, and pay equity. Several provisions have been enacted as parts of other bills. In 1990, the caucus introduced the Women's Health Equity Act, a package of bills modeled after the Economic Equity Act. The caucus introduced or influenced the development of the Civil Rights Restoration Act of 1988, the Civil Rights Act of 1991, the Family and Medical Leave Act of 1993, the Violence Against Women Act of 1994, the Congressional Workplace Compliance Act of 1995, and other measures. The caucus avoided taking stands on abortion and related issues because two senior Democratic women, Representatives Lindy Boggs and Mary Rose Oakar, were anti-abortion. After Boggs retired in 1990 and Oakar was defeated in 1992, the caucus voted in favor of supporting abortion rights in 1993.

In 1995, when Congress abolished legislative service organizations and ended the funding for them, the caucus became a congressional members' organization. When Republicans became the majority party in the U.S. House of Representatives in 1995, Congress abolished legislative service organizations (LSO), one of which was the CCWI. The twenty-seven LSOs that had formed since 1959 were caucuses that members of Congress funded by pooling portions of their office funds to finance and hire staff for the LSOs to which they belonged. The Republican leadership explained that they were eliminating the LSOs because they were funded by taxpayers but did not have proper oversight. Congressional staff members meet weekly, and members of Congress meet monthly, keeping each other informed about political developments, discussing legislation, planning caucus activities, and addressing issues. Former staff members created Women's Policy, Inc., which provides information on women's issues in Congress and publishes newsletters and other materials.

> **See also** Abortion; Boggs, Marie Corinne Morrison Claiborne (Lindy); Child Support Enforcement; Congressional Workplace Compliance Act of 1995; Domestic Violence; Economic Equity Act; Education Amendments of 1972, Title IX; Education, Women and; Equal Rights Amendment; Heckler, Margaret Mary O'Shaughnessy; Holtzman, Elizabeth; Mikulski, Barbara Ann; Oakar, Mary Rose; Rape; Spellman, Gladys Blossom Noon; Violence Against Women Act of 1994; Women's Health Equity Act; Women's Policy, Inc.

> **References** Burrell, *A Woman's Place Is in the House: Campaigning for Congress in the Feminist Era* (1994); *Congressional Quarterly Almanac, 103rd Congress, 1st Session . . . 1993* (1994); *Congressional Quarterly Almanac, 104th Congress, 1st Session . . . 1995* (1996); Foerstel and Foerstel, *Climbing the Hill: Gender Conflict in Congress* (1996); Lamson, *In the Vanguard: Six American Women in Public Life* (1979); www.house.gov/lowey/caucus.htm.

Congressional Union

The Congressional Union (CU), organized by Alice Paul and an associate, worked to gain passage of the woman suffrage amendment by attracting attention to it with parades, demonstrations, pickets, and other actions. In addition, the CU adopted the strategy of working to defeat all candidates of the majority party in Congress, regardless of an individual candidate's efforts to pass the amendment. Considered the militant wing of the suffrage movement, the CU rejected seeking suffrage through state constitutional amendments and focused its attention solely on passing a federal amendment.

Alice Paul, who had been involved in the English suffrage movement while studying in London, brought the strategies used in England to the United States. She joined the National American Woman Suffrage Association (NAWSA) in 1912 and later that year became chair of its Congressional Committee. When she accepted the chair, NAWSA leaders explained that she and her committee would not receive any money from the organization and would be responsible for raising any funds they intended to spend. Paul actively solicited financial support from large and small donors across the country and raised thousands of dollars.

In 1913, the Congressional Committee planned its first substantial public action, a parade to coincide with President-elect Woodrow Wilson's arrival in Washington, D.C., for his inauguration. On 3 March 1913, twenty-six floats, ten bands, five squadrons of cavalry, six chariots, and approximately 8,000 women marched through the capital, and about 500,000 people watched the parade instead of Wilson's arrival. The parade observers, however, became unruly and moved into the parade route, but the police along the route did not protect the marchers. About 200 people were treated for injuries, and the Senate investigated the police superintendent's behavior. The press coverage and the investigation that resulted from the parade helped revitalize interest in the suffrage amendment and generated interest in the Congressional Committee.

The committee's actions, however, met with disapproval from some NAWSA leaders who believed that the publicity cast the suffrage movement in an unfavorable light. The Congressional Committee's fundraising success also distressed some NAWSA leaders. They suggested that the committee transfer some of its funds to NAWSA and expressed concern that donors thought their contributions were supporting NAWSA instead of the Congressional Committee. Paul sought to solve the problem by creating the CU, making it an affiliate of NAWSA, and raising money through it. She continued to serve as chair of the Congressional Committee, but tensions between Paul and NAWSA leaders increased. Late in 1913, NAWSA leaders told Paul that she could chair the Congressional Committee or the CU but not both. Paul chose the CU with the understanding that it would continue to be an auxiliary of NAWSA. Early in 1914, NAWSA president Anna Howard Shaw concluded that the CU was a threat to NAWSA and ended its auxiliary status. The CU became an independent organization with a notable national advisory council, including Charlotte Perkins Gilman, Helen Keller, Florence Kelley, Abigail Scott Duniway, and Harriott Stanton Blatch.

Adopting a strategy from her experiences in England, Paul called on women who lived in states that had granted them voting rights to vote against the party in power, regardless of the individual candidate's views on woman suffrage. In 1914, Democrats were the party in power, and Paul campaigned across the country, urging women to vote against Democrats at every level. The strategy was widely criticized by more conservative suffragists because many of the cause's strongest supporters were Democrats, and they feared repercussions from Paul's actions. NAWSA leaders distanced themselves from Paul and the CU and discredited both. The CU, however, had succeeded in making suffrage an issue in several states and claimed that it had defeated five Democrats and that it had contributed to the defeat of an additional twenty-three Democrats.

As the 1916 elections neared, Paul organized the Woman's Party, an organization of enfranchised women that had the sole purpose of promoting the federal suffrage amendment. Members appeared before the resolution committees of both the Republican and Democratic parties asking for support for the amendment. For the first time, both parties supported woman suffrage, but only with regard to state amendments and not the federal amendment. The Republican presidential nominee, however, publicly stated his support for the federal amendment, but incumbent president Woodrow Wilson, the Democratic Party's presidential nominee, remained committed to state amendments. Paul and the Woman's Party organized to defeat Democratic candidates, as in 1914.

The CU continued its program of public actions to attract press attention to woman suffrage. For example, in 1916, while President Wilson spoke to a joint session of Congress, CU members held a banner from the gallery of the U.S. House of Representatives calling for votes for women. The press and members of Congress criticized the display, but it accomplished the organizers' goals by attracting press coverage.

More controversial were the picketers who began demonstrating outside the White House in January 1917. Initially they were ignored, but in June police began arresting picketers for obstructing traffic. The first groups were released, but later groups were tried, found guilty, and fined. When they refused to pay the fines, they were jailed for three days, and President Wilson signed pardons for some of them. When Paul was arrested in an October 1917 demonstration, however, she was sentenced to seven months at a women's prison. After she went on a hunger strike, she was separated from other prisoners; force-fed; placed in a ward for mental patients; and denied visitors, mail, and messages. Stories about her treatment prompted protests that contributed to her release within a month. The CU continued intermittent picketing until early 1918, when Congress began to act favorably on the amendment.

Both houses of Congress passed the Nineteenth Amendment in 1919, and the last needed state ratified it in August 1920. With the CU's goal accomplished, Paul and her followers turned their attention to obtaining equal rights for women. The CU and the Woman's Party formed the National Woman's Party in 1921, and the campaign for a federal equal rights amendment began in 1923.

See also Blatch, Harriot Eaton Stanton; Duniway, Abigail Jane Scott; Equal Rights Amendment; Gilman, Charlotte Perkins; Kelley, Florence; National American Woman Suffrage Association; National Woman's Party; Nineteenth Amendment; Paul, Alice; Shaw, Anna Howard; Suffrage

References Lunardini, *From Equal Suffrage to Equal Rights: Alice Paul and the National Woman's Party* (1986).

Congressional Workplace Compliance Act of 1995

The Congressional Workplace Compliance Act extended coverage of eleven federal labor and anti-discrimination laws to Congress and related offices. With passage of the law, Congress had to comply with the Civil Rights Act of 1964, the Occupational Safety and Health Act of 1970, the Age Discrimination in Employment Act of 1967, the Family Leave and Medical Act of 1993, the Fair Labor Standards Act of 1938, the Americans with Disabilities Act of 1990, the Rehabilitation Act of 1973, the Employee Polygraph Protection Act of 1988, the Worker Adjustment and Retraining Notification Act of 1988, the Veterans Re-employment Act of 1993, and Labor-Management Dispute Procedures. The law permits members of Congress to discriminate based on party affiliation. Some of the offices covered by the law include each member of the House and the Senate, House and Senate committees, joint House and Senate committees, the Capitol police, and the Congressional Budget Office. The law established the Office of Compliance to respond to complaints.

References *Congressional Quarterly Almanac, 104th Congress 1st Session . . . 1995* (1996).

Congresswomen's Caucus

See **Congressional Caucus for Women's Issues**

Consciousness Raising

Consciousness raising (CR) was a technique used by radical feminists in the 1960s to explore the limits that society placed on women and that women placed on themselves. CR groups provided each member the opportunity to examine her experiences and reflect on them with group members. By identifying the personal issues in their lives, including housework, children, and sexuality, women understood the commonalities in their lives. As grassroots radical women's organizations developed in the 1960s, including the Redstockings and New York Radical Women, CR became an important tool for women to understand their status in society. The term was coined by New York Radical Women, but it had been earlier used in the American civil rights movement and by Chinese and Guatemalan revolutionaries.

Through consciousness raising, one early leader explained, women attempted to "awaken the latent consciousness that ... all women have about our oppression." Another saw it as "the political reinterpretation of one's personal life." CR peaked in the 1970s, as women became involved in other feminist activities, including forming women's centers, providing abortion counseling, and opening women-centered bookstores and child day care centers.

See also New York Radical Women; Redstockings; Women's Liberation Movement

References Echols, *Daring to Be Bad: Radical Feminism in America, 1967–1975* (1989); Ferree and Hess, *Controversy and Coalition: The New Feminist Movement across Three Decades of Change* (1994); Freeman, *The Politics of Women's Liberation: The New Feminist Movement across Three Decades of Change* (1975).

Conservatism

Conservatism in the United States began its resurgence in the mid-1960s as Americans began to challenge the liberal agenda that had prevailed since the 1930s. Republican conservative Barry Goldwater's 1964 presidential campaign galvanized many conservatives into action, even though Goldwater lost the election. Opposed to the welfare programs of the 1930s and the civil rights activism of the 1960s, conservatives sought to limit government involvement in citizens' lives, to fight Communism, to strengthen the military, and to reduce taxes.

In the 1970s, conservatism expanded its agenda to include several social issues and attracted the allegiance of fundamentalist Christian groups. For example, conservative Phyllis Schlafly led the fight against ratification of the federal Equal Rights Amendment and against state equal rights amendments, objecting to feminists' goals and the changes they sought through the amendment and other actions. Fundamentalist Christians joined Roman Catholics in their opposition to the U.S. Supreme Court's 1973 decision legalizing abortion in *Roe v. Wade*, to sex education in public schools, and to gays' and lesbians' quest for protection of their civil rights. These themes continued to dominate the conservative agenda throughout the 1990s, when opposition to affirmative action was added. Conservatives achieved one of their goals with the passage of major welfare reform legislation, the Personal Responsibility and Work Opportunity Reconciliation Act of 1996.

See also Affirmative Action; Communist Party, USA; Equal Rights Amendment; Liberalism; Personal Responsibility and Work Opportunity Reconciliation Act of 1996; *Roe v. Wade*; Schlafly, Phyllis Stewart

References Dunn and Woodward, *The Conservative Tradition in America* (1996).

Conway, Kellyanne Fitzpatrick (b. 1967)

Republican pollster Kellyanne Conway is CEO and president of a privately-held, woman-owned polling company founded in 1995. Since beginning her polling career in

1988, Conway has advised clients in 46 states, including former Speaker of the House Newt Gingrich (Republican, Georgia), former senator Fred Thompson (Republican, Tennessee), and former Vice President Dan Quayle. Other clients have included Microsoft Corporation, Unilever, *New York Magazine*, and Wyeth-Ayerst Laboratories.

Conway has provided commentary on ABC, CBS, NBC, CNN, and other television network shows, as well as on radio and in print.

With Democratic pollster Celinda Lake, Conway wrote *What Women Really Want: How American Women Are Quietly Erasing Political, Racial, Class, and Religious Lines to Change the Way We Live* (2005). She earned a bachelor's degree in political science from Trinity College in 1989 and a law degree from George Washington University Law Center in 1992.

References "Paradox," *American Demographics*, 31 May 2004, pp. 26–31; www.pollingcompany.com; http://www.trinitycd.edu/news_events/capgown_02/conway2.htm

Corning Glass Works v. Brennan (1974)

In *Corning Glass Works v. Brennan*, the first equal pay case to reach the U.S. Supreme Court, the Court found that Corning Glass Works' pay policies violated the Equal Pay Act of 1963 by paying a higher base wage to male night shift inspectors than it paid to female inspectors performing the same tasks on the day shift. Some of the pay differentials had developed in the 1930s when protective labor legislation had prohibited women from working night shifts. All inspection work during the night was performed by men, and all daytime inspection work was performed by women, who were paid less than men, an arrangement that a 1944 collective bargaining agreement had formalized. After the passage of the Equal Pay Act, Corning opened night shift jobs to women as vacancies occurred. The company's 1969 collective bargaining agreement gave women and men the same rates, but not if they had been hired before the agreement. The Court concluded: "On the facts of this case, the company's continued discrimination in base wages between night and day workers, though phrased in terms of a neutral factor other than sex, nevertheless operated to perpetuate the effects of the company's prior illegal practice of paying women less than men for equal work."

See also Employment Discrimination; Equal Pay Act of 1963

References *Corning Glass Works v. Brennan*, 417 U.S. 188 (1974).

Costanza, Margaret (Midge) (b. 1932)

The first woman to hold the title of assistant to the president, Democrat Margaret Costanza advised President Jimmy Carter from 1977 to 1978. Costanza's political involvement included working in W. Averell Harriman's 1954 gubernatorial campaign and Robert F. Kennedy's 1964 senatorial campaign, holding local and regional positions in the Democratic Party, and becoming Democratic national committeewoman for New York in 1972. In 1973, Costanza won a race for member-at-large on the Rochester, New York city council and unsuccessfully ran for Congress in 1974. Through her congressional campaign, Costanza met Jimmy Carter, who had campaigned for her and who was preparing to run for president. Costanza was among the first New York politicians to endorse him, and she co-chaired his New York campaign in 1976. After his election, Carter invited Costanza to join his administration.

Costanza had an office next to the Oval Office, an indication of the importance Carter placed on her duties as liaison with organized special interest groups, including business, women, Native Americans, minorities, senior citizens, environmentalists, and dozens of other interests. Described as "the president's window to the nation," Costanza was valued by President Carter for her opinions and recommendations, but she also created controversies within the administration. She supported amnesty for Vietnam deserters and draft dodgers, publicly criticized the director of the Office of Management and Budget, and orchestrated an attempt to change the president's anti-abortion views. Following these and other conflicts with the administration, Costanza resigned on 1 August 1978.

Born in LeRoy, New York, Margaret Costanza began her career following graduation from high school. She held several clerical and administrative positions and was active in the community.

References H. W. Wilson, *Current Biography Yearbook 1978* (1978).

Coulter, Ann (b. 1961)

Conservative political commentator and bestselling author Ann Coulter is the legal correspondent for the conservative magazine, *Human Events,* and writes a weekly syndicated column for Universal Press Syndicate, which is printed in more than 100 newspapers nationwide and linked to several conservative websites.

Born in New Canaan, Connecticut, Coulter earned a bachelor's degree from Cornell University in 1985 and a JD degree from the University of Michigan Law School in 1988. Before her career as a political commentator, Coulter was a litigator for the Center for Individual Rights and worked for United States Senator Spencer Abraham (R-Michigan).

Coulter has written five *New York Times* bestselling books: *High Crimes and Misdemeanors: The Case Against Bill Clinton*(1998); *Slander: Liberal Lies About the American Right* (2002); *Treason: Liberal Treachery from the Cold War to the War on Terrorism* (2003); *How to Talk to a Liberal (If You Must)* (2004); and *Godless: The Church of Liberalism* (2006).

She began her career as a political commentator in 1996, when she worked for MSNBC. She has been a controversial figure, losing her job at MSNBC in October 1997 after she told, on air, a disabled Vietnam veteran: "No wonder you guys lost the war," in response to his statement that "in 90% of the cases that U.S. soldiers got blown up ... they were our own mines." Coulter later said that she did not know the man was disabled during the war. She subsequently made numerous guest appearances on other television shows, including *Larry King Live, Politically Incorrect, Crossfire, CNN* and *Fox News Channel.*

Coulter provoked another controversy in 2006, during an interview on NBC's *Today Show* that focused on comments made in her latest book, *Godless: The Church of Liberalism.* During the interview she repeated her accusation that some of the widows of the 9/11 terrorist attacks were "enjoying" their husbands deaths and benefiting financially from the deaths. She further questioned whether or not the widows were improperly compensated for the deaths, asking: "how do we know their husbands weren't planning to divorce these harpies?"

References H.W. Wilson, *Current Biography Yearbook 2003*(2003); John Cloud, "Ms. Right: Ann Coulter," *Time*, 25 April 2005, p. 32; Sara Nelson, "Shameless," *Publishers Weekly*, 12 June 2006, p. 4.

Council of Presidents

Organized in 1985 by Sarah Harder and Irene Natividad to further a feminist legislative agenda, the Council of Presidents (CP) comprises presidents of more than eighty national women's organizations. CP sponsors the Women's Agenda, an annual list of legislative priorities that has included support for child care, family and medical leave, reproductive rights, civil rights, pay and educational equity, and opposition to violence against women. Although every member organization may not support every item in the Women's Agenda, all of them pledge that they will not work against any item. Member organizations include the American Association of University Women, Business and Professional Women/USA, General Federation of Women's Clubs, Jewish Women's Caucus, League of Women Voters, National Conference of Puerto Rican Women, National Council of Negro Women, and YWCA of the USA.

See also Abortion; American Association of University Women; Business and Professional Women/USA; Child Day Care; Family and Medical Leave Act of 1993; General Federation of Women's Clubs; League of Women Voters; National Council of Negro Women; National Women's Conference; Natividad, Irene; Pay Equity; YWCA of the USA

References Slavin, ed., *U.S. Women's Interest Groups* (1995).

Council of Women World Leaders

Founded in 1996 by President Vigdis Finnbógadottir of Iceland and American Laura Liswood, the Council of Women World Leaders' mission is "to promote good governance, gender equality and to enhance the experience of democracy globally by increasing the number, effectiveness, and visibility of women who lead at the highest levels in their countries."

The council has sponsored summits of women heads of state, women leaders in finance and economics, and women in justice, law, and equality, as well as other groups of women serving at the ministerial level (comparable to Cabinet level in the United States). The Council also works with the United Nations and other international organizations.

According to Liswood: "The world needs new combinations of leadership." She adds that it will take "overcoming psychological and other barriers to envisioning women as leaders." She believes: "We need to change our fairy tales, our education system, and particularly in the United States, the incumbent system of government."

"Men will someday realize they can't be without women in government," said President Finnbógadottir. "Everything will be richer in flavor and color if more women participated."

The Council resulted from interviews Liswood conducted with 15 women heads of state in the early 1990s.

References *Christian Science Monitor*, 8 October 1997, May 1, 1998; http://www.womenworldleaders.org

County of Washington, Oregon v. Gunther (1981)

In *County of Washington, Oregon v. Gunther*, women guards in the female section of the county jail filed suit under Title VII of the Civil Rights Act of 1964 for back pay, arguing that they had been paid lower wages than male guards supervising male prisoners and that part of the difference was attributable to intentional sex discrimination. Despite the hopes of comparable worth supporters, the claim was not based on comparable worth, a fact the Supreme Court specifically noted. Instead, the question was whether Title VII limited sex-based wage discrimination cases to those that could also be covered by the Equal Pay Act of 1963. The Equal Pay Act only addressed equal pay for equal work, and the female guards acknowledged that their work was not equal to that performed by the male guards supervising male prisoners.

The county had done an evaluation of the worth of the jobs, establishing their comparable worth, and concluded that women guards working in the female section of the county jail should be paid at a rate of 95 percent of the rate paid to male correctional officers working in the male section. However, the county set the women's pay rates at only 70 percent. The Court explained that it was not required to assess the value of the male and female guard jobs and that it did not have to quantify the effect of sex discrimination on wage rates. The Court decided that the female guards could claim they had been undercompensated even though they did not perform work equal to that done by male guards.

See also Civil Rights Act of 1964, Title VII; Employment Discrimination; Equal Pay Act of 1963; Pay Equity

References *County of Washington, Oregon v. Gunther*, 452 U.S. 161 (1981).

Coverture

Articulated by English jurist Sir William Blackstone in his Commentaries on the Laws of England (1765–1769), coverture established women's civil status in common law and became the basis for married women's legal status in the United States. Coverture defined a married woman's legal status as suspended and incorporated into her husband's. In marriage, the man and woman became one, and the law recognized only the husband's existence, a civil death that left married women economically and legally dependent upon their husbands.

The consequences of coverture were wide-ranging. A husband could not give his wife anything or make a contract with her because he would be giving it to himself. A wife, however, could represent her husband as an attorney since that does not imply separation from him. A wife could not sue or be sued, but a husband could be the defendant or sue in his wife's place. A wife could not testify against her husband, was not liable for her own actions, and in some cases was excused from having committed crimes if it could be shown that she acted under her husband's direction. In addition, common law permitted a husband to use physical force to discipline his wife, permitting him to whip her or use his fists as well as restrict her to his home, and married women could not establish their own domiciles. Every married woman's surname was by law that of her husband; a married woman had no right to adopt a different name; and if a man changed his name, his wife's name automatically changed.

Coverture denied women virtually all property rights. The personal property, money, and goods that a woman took into marriage or inherited after it belonged entirely to her husband, to do with as he wished. A wife did not own her clothing, and if she left her husband, she could be charged with theft for the clothes she wore. Any earnings due her belonged to her husband because a woman's services belonged to her husband. In addition, because a wife had no separate legal standing, only the husband could sue for wages due her. At his death, she was entitled to one-third of her husband's real estate and one-third of her personal property, unless he bequeathed his property otherwise. He could will items to her because at his death, coverture ended.

Coverture assigned specific responsibilities to husbands and wives that were reciprocal in nature but not equal. The husband was sole legal guardian of the children, was the preferred legal custodian of children in the event of divorce, and could appoint a guardian other than the mother should he die. A husband assumed any debts his wife had at the time of marriage and those that she acquired while married. In addition, a husband was bound to provide his wife with the necessities of life, even after legal separation or divorce. Wives had a legal obligation to perform domestic chores but had no right to an allowance, wages, or any income.

The civil death created by coverture provided the basis for excluding women from serving on juries, holding public office, and engaging in certain occupations.

Unmarried adult women, known as femme sole, did not have the same constraints on their legal and economic activities. Although they did not have political rights until the Nineteenth Amendment was ratified in 1920, unmarried adult women could own and inherit property, own their earnings, enter into contracts, and sue and be sued.

Eliminating these and other forms of legal discrimination based on sex began with the passage of married women's property acts in the 1840s and continued with some states giving women the ownership of their earnings and other limited property rights. In 1869, Wyoming Territory granted women the right to vote and to hold public office, and women continued the long process of gaining suffrage rights, culminating in the passage of the Nineteenth Amendment in 1920 and the Voting Rights Act of 1965, among other measures. Efforts to obtain the full rights of citizenship, that is, to be an autonomous citizen, to serve on juries, to determine one's name, and to eliminate the barriers of discrimination on the basis of gender, continued throughout the twentieth century.

See also Anthony, Susan Brownell; *Bradwell v. Illinois*; Civil Rights Act of 1964, Title VII; Domestic Violence; Employment Discrimination; Equal Pay Act of 1963; Married Women's Property Acts; Nineteenth Amendment; Sex Discrimination; Stanton, Elizabeth Cady; Suffrage

References Freeman, "The Legal Basis of the Sexual Caste System" (1971); Matthews, *Women's Struggle for Equality* (1997)

Craig v. Boren (1976)

In *Craig v. Boren*, the U.S. Supreme Court found gender-based discrimination in an Oklahoma law unconstitutional under the Fourteenth Amendment. Women eighteen and over were permitted to purchase 3.2 percent beer in Oklahoma, but men had to be twenty-one years old to legally purchase it. Oklahoma cited traffic safety as the reason for the differences, pointing out that in a given period more than 400 men were arrested for driving under the influence of alcohol, but only twenty-four women had been arrested in the same period. In the decision, the Court created an intermediary scrutiny standard, explaining that "classifications by gender must serve important governmental objectives and be substantially related to these objectives."

See also Fourteenth Amendment

References *Craig v. Boren*, 429 U.S. 190 (1976).

Crisp, Mary Dent (b. 1923)

Co-chair of the Republican National Committee (RNC) from 1977 to 1980, Mary Crisp supported reproductive rights and the Equal Rights Amendment (ERA), views that contrasted with those of the party's conservative leaders. Crisp entered politics as a member of the Arizona state central committee in 1962, worked on Republican presidential candidate Barry Goldwater's 1964 campaign, and was elected Republican national committeewoman for Arizona in 1972 and in 1976. Elected RNC secretary after the 1976 Republican National Convention, she was elected co-chairperson in January 1977. During her term as party co-chair, she developed a women's program that included a series of bipartisan seminars and conferences to help women empower themselves. Differences with conservative party members over the ERA and abortion, however, strained their relationships. She believed that her office in the party's headquarters was bugged, an allegation firmly denied by other party leaders. During the party's 1980 platform hearings, Crisp testified against the platform for withdrawing its support of the ERA and for supporting a constitutional amendment banning abortions and resigned as co-chair at the request of conservatives. She chaired independent presidential candidate John Anderson's 1980 campaign. Crisp chaired the National Republican Coalition for Choice from 1989 to 1994.

Born in Allentown, Pennsylvania, Crisp earned her bachelor's degree from Oberlin College in 1946 and her master's degree from Arizona State University in 1975.

References Crisp, "My Journey to Feminism" (1998); Melich, *The Republican War against Women: An Insider's Report from Behind the Lines* (1996); *The New York Times*, 22 June 1980.

Croly, Jane Cunningham (1829–1901)

Journalist Jane Croly's work in the women's clubs movement led to the creation of the General Federation of Women's Clubs. After founding Sorosis in 1868, Croly saw the need for a national organization of similar groups and organized a convention to unite them, resulting in the creation of the federation in 1890. She organized the New York State Federation in 1894.

Born in Market Harborough, Leicestershire, England, Jane Croly moved to the United States with her parents in 1841. Croly began her career in journalism in 1855 at the *New York Tribune* and subsequently wrote for several other newspapers using the pseudonym Jennie June.

Croly wrote *The History of the Woman's Club Movement in America* (1898).

See also General Federation of Women's Clubs

References James, ed., *Notable American Women 1607–1950* (1971); Whitman, ed., *American Reformers* (1985).

Crowley, Candy (b. ca. 1948)

Senior political correspondent for CNN, Candy Crowley began her broadcast journalism career working in the newsroom for WASH, a Washington, D.C. radio station. A stint with Associated Press followed in the early 1980s. A correspondent for NBC News in 1986, she joined CNN in 1987, where she began as a White House and Capital Hill Correspondent. She has covered the presidential campaigns of Pat Buchanan, George H.W. Bush, Bill Clinton, Bob Dole, Jesse Jackson, Edward Kennedy, Ronald Reagan, and Paul Tsongas, among others. Sine the mid-1970s, she has covered every national political convention, except one.

Crowley has also covered the aftermath of Hurricane Katrina (2005) in the Gulf Coast, the impeachment trial of President Bill Clinton, the ceremonies surrounding the 40th anniversary of the World War II invasion of Normanday Beach in 1944, and other national and international events.

Born in Missouri, Crowley graduated from Randolph-Macon Woman's College in 1970.

References http://www.cnn.com/CNN/anchors_reporters/crowley.candy.html; http://www.rmwc.edu/admissions/alumprofiles/ccrowley.asp

Candy Crowley, senior political correspondent for CNN.
(Courtesy CNN)

Cubin, Barbara Lynn (b. 1946)

Republican Barbara Cubin of Wyoming entered the U.S. House of Representatives on 3 January 1995. Cubin held the leadership position of House Deputy Majority Whip, 104th, 105th, and 106th Congresses (1995–1997, 1997–1999, and 1999–2001), and as secretary of the House Republican Conference in the 107th, 108th, and 109th Congresses (2001–2003, 2003–2005, and 2005–2007). Cubin explained that she entered politics "because I wanted my children to have a future, and I thought we were stealing their futures away from them by building a national debt."

An adamant supporter of private property owners' rights, Congresswoman Cubin has fought against restricting development of additional tracts of land, arguing that it would threaten Wyoming residents' economic livelihood. "The last thing we need in Wyoming is more federal land when the government can't adequately manage the property it has now," she has said. A ranch owner, Cubin has objected to the introduction of Canadian gray wolves into Yellowstone National Park, arguing that the wolves injure and kill livestock. She opposes increases in public land grazing fees and has fought to give ranchers more power in determining the management of federal rangeland. Cubin has also advocated permitting states to enforce environmental policies and ending interference by the federal government. Cubin cofounded the Coal Bed Methane Caucus in 2002, reflecting the importance of energy and minerals in her state. Cubin has worked to meet other needs of her rural constituency, including emergency drought relief funding in 2002 and federal funding for airport infrastructure in the 108th Congress (2003–2005). She has sought to ease regulations on wireless telecommunications companies in rural areas.

With three other women members of Congress, Cubin introduced the Heart Disease Education, Analysis and Research, and Treatment (HEART) for Women Act. Cubin explained: "Heart attack, stroke and cardiovascular disease are the number one killer of women in Wyoming. In fact, in Wyoming, almost two women every day die from some type of cardiovascular disease." Balancing the federal budget, providing families with a tax credit of $500 per child, and eliminating the capital gains tax and death taxes are other focuses of her work.

Born in Salinas, California, Cubin received her bachelor of science in chemistry from Creighton University in 1969 and attended Casper College in 1993. She served in

Colorado Representative Barbara Cubin meets with constituents at a town hall meeting in Sundance. (Courtesy Office of Barbara Cubin)

the Wyoming House of Representatives from 1987 to 1991 and the Wyoming Senate from 1992 to 1994. While in the legislature, Cubin was the prime sponsor of a state constitutional amendment permitting judges to impose life sentences without the possibility of parole, which voters ratified. She was vice chair of the energy committee of the National Council of State Legislatures and chaired the research section of the Energy Council, an international organization.

See also Congress, Women in

References Center for American Women and Politics, "Women in Congress: Leadership Roles and Committee Chairs," Fact sheet, 2005; *Congressional Quarterly, Politics in America 1998* (1997), *Politics in America 2006* (2005); http:/www.house.gov/cubin/news/2006/Feb14f.html; "Lawmakers establish Congressional Coalbed Methane Caucus," *Inside Energy*, 9 September 2002, p. 13; *Cubin in Rimm, How Jane Won* (2001).

D

Danner, Patsy Ann (b. 1934)

Democrat Pat Danner of Missouri served in the U.S. House of Representatives from 3 January 1993 to 3 January 2001. Danner's congressional priorities included creating jobs, cutting government waste, and promoting economic development. She opposed gun control measures, efforts to lift the ban on homosexuals in the military, and federal funding for abortions, but she supported safe access to abortion facilities. Danner was co-author of a bill enacted in 1996 that protects donors and distributors of food for the needy from legal liability for illnesses or other problems resulting from the donations. She did not seek re-election in 2000.

Born in Louisville, Kentucky, Pat Danner received her bachelor's degree from Northeast Missouri State University in 1972. From 1973 to 1976, she was district assistant to a congressman and from 1977 to 1981 was federal co-chair of the Ozark Regional Planning Commission. She is the only woman who has chaired a regional commission. Danner served in the Missouri state Senate from 1983 to 1993.

See also Congress, Women in; Reproductive Rights; State Legislatures, Women in

References *Congressional Quarterly, Politics in America 1996* (1995), *Politics in America 1998* (1997).

Daughters of Bilitis

Founded in 1955 by four lesbian couples, Daughters of Bilitis (DOB) seeks to educate the public about homosexuals and conducts research to change public perceptions about lesbians and eliminate discrimination against them. The group's name came from a poem by Pierre Louys, "Song of Bilitis," about a woman believed to have lived on the island of Lesbos during the time of Sappho in the seventh century BCE.

Originating in San Francisco, DOB developed into the first national organization of lesbians. DOB focused on two areas: providing a safe place for lesbians to gather, despite the ongoing threat of police raids, and informing both homosexuals and the general public that gays and lesbians were good citizens. In 1956, DOB began publishing *The Ladder*, a magazine that reported court cases relevant to homosexuals' civil liberties, employment discrimination, and police harassment. In the 1960s, *The Ladder* expanded to include articles by noted feminists, including Kate Millett and May Sarton. In 1970, DOB disbanded as a national organization, but local groups continued to meet.

See also Lesbian Rights; Lyon, Phyllis; Martin, Del

References Slavin, *U.S. Women's Interest Groups* (1995); www.gis.net/~dismith/dob1.html

Daughters of Liberty

Emerging out of the patriotic enthusiasm of the 1760s and 1770s, Daughters of Liberty supported the American revolutionary cause by joining boycotts against British goods. With no formal organization, especially when compared to the Sons of Liberty, groups of American colonial women demonstrated their support for the boycott by spinning wool and flax. To overcome the tedium of the task, they often gathered in large spinning bees and frequently attracted the support and recognition of local newspapers. In addition, some women formed anti-tea leagues. The amount of homespun produced by these groups is unknown, and its direct impact on the economy is equally uncertain, but the meetings made a political statement by focusing attention on the need for frugality and industry in colonial households and by providing a way for American women to contribute to the struggle against Britain.

References Norton, *Liberty's Daughters: The Revolutionary Experience of American Women, 1750–1800* (1980).

Davis, Angela Yvonne (b. 1944)

Radical Angela Davis began participating in civil rights demonstrations as a child in the 1950s and continues to support controversial causes. She gained national attention in 1970, when she was accused of supplying weapons for a raid on the San Rafael, California courthouse and was charged with murder, conspiracy, and kidnapping. Davis had not participated in the raid, although she owned the guns used in it. Placed on the Federal Bureau of Investigation's (FBI's) most wanted list, she went into hiding, was found in New York, and was jailed in California without bail. While she was in jail for sixteen months, the Free Angela campaign grew into an international cause and eventually evolved into the National Alliance Against Racist and Political Repression, for which Davis has worked since 1972, the year she was acquitted of all the charges.

Born in Birmingham, Alabama, Davis earned her bachelor's degree from Brandeis University in 1965, studied at Johann Wolfgang von Goethe University in Frankfurt, Germany, from 1965 to 1967, and earned her master's degree in philosophy from the University of California, San Diego, in 1968. She joined the Communist Party the next year. A member of the faculty at the University of California at Los Angeles from 1969 to 1970, she was dismissed for her membership in the Communist Party and for her public speeches. She had said it was "necessary to unveil the predominant, oppressive ideas and acts of this country" and "begin to develop not only criticism but positive solutions and to carry out these paths in the universities." Davis ran for vice president of the United States in 1980 and 1984 on the Communist Party ticket. Since 1975, Davis has taught at several colleges and universities, including Claremont College,

Civil rights activist Angela Davis speaking at Myer Horowitz Theatre of the University of Alberta, March 28, 2006. (Courtesy Nick Wiebe)

Stanford University, San Francisco State University, Moscow University, Havana University, and the University of California at Santa Cruz.

Among her published books are *If They Come in the Morning* (1971); *Women, Race, and Class* (1983); *Angela Davis: An Autobiography* (1988); *Women, Culture, and Politics* (1989); and *Blues Legacies and Black Feminism* (1998).

See also Affirmative Action; Civil Rights Movement, Women in the; Communist Party, USA

References Hine, ed., *Black Women in America: An Historical Perspective* (1993); *The New York Times*, 5 June 1972; "Still on the Front Line" (1990).

Davis, Jo Ann (b. 1950)

Republican Jo Ann Davis of Virginia entered the U.S. House of Representatives on 3 January 2001. Representative Davis supports strengthening the military, closing gaps in benefits for military personnel, and the U.S. Navy's next generation of aircraft carriers. In 2005, she cofounded the Congressional Shipbuilding Caucus. She has worked to bring attention to the amount of other states' garbage that is hauled into Virginia, arguing for state control over the amount of waste taken into it. Other priorities include reducing redundancy in federal programs and reducing taxes.

Davis served in the Virginia House of Delegates from 1998 to 2000.

Born in Rowan County, North Carolina, Davis attended Hampton Roads Business College in 1971. She became a real estate agent 1984 and a real estate broker in 1988. She owned a management company in 1988 and a real estate agency in 1990.

References *Congressional Quarterly, Politics in America 2004* (2003), *Politics in America 2006* (2005); http://joanndavis.house.gov/HoR/VA01/About+Jo+Ann/; http://www.vote- smart.org/bio.php?can_id=CS040937.

Virginia Congresswoman Jo Ann Davis, speaking about the James River "Ghost Fleet." (Courtesy Office of Jo Ann Davis)

Davis, Susan A. (b. 1944)

Democrat Susan A. Davis of California entered the U.S. House of Representatives on 3 January 2001. A sampling of Davis's priorities includes legislation to encourage highly qualified teachers to teach in low-income schools, to grant the Food and Drug Administration authority to regulate dietary supplements, to increase Veterans Administration home loan guarantees for veterans, and to increase fuel economy standards for trucks and SUVs. She has worked to improve military housing and to keep children of military personnel eligible for free or reduced-cost school lunches.

Before serving in Congress, Davis served on the San Diego City School Board from 1983 to 1992 and served in the California State Assembly from 1994 to 2000.

Born in Cambridge, Massachusetts, Davis earned a bachelor of arts degree in sociology at the University of California, Berkeley, in 1965 and an master of arts degree in social work at the University of North Carolina in 1968.

> **References** *Congressional Quarterly, Politics in America 2004* (2003); http://www.susandavisforcongress.com/pages/2/index.htm; www.house.gov/susandavis/about.htm

Davis v. Monroe County Board of Education (1999)

LaShonda Davis, a fifth-grade student, endured persistent sexual advances from a classmate for five months, despite her mother's protests to school officials that they intervene. When school officials refused to respond, LaShonda's mother called the sheriff, who arrested the boy. The boy pleaded guilty to sexual battery. LaShonda's mother sued the school board for its failure to act. The suit argued that the sexual advances created "an intimidating, hostile, offensive, and abusive school environment" in violation of Title IX of the Education Amendments of 1972. The U.S. Supreme Court found that schools receiving federal financial assistance can be liable for damages when they refuse to act in cases of student-on-student sexual harassment.

Reference *Davis v. Monroe County Board of Education, 526 U.S. 629* (1999)

Day Care Council of America

Founded in 1967, the Day Care Council of America (DCC) sought the passage of federal legislation for universal, publicly funded day care. Working with federal agencies concerned with children's issues, the DCC lobbied members of Congress, testified before congressional committees, and worked with other organizations with common interests. Approximately 6,000 community groups, individuals, and agencies serving children belonged to DCC in 1978. Perhaps because of the success that local day care centers had in securing funding, membership dropped dramatically in the 1980s, falling to 1,000 in 1984. DCC ceased to operate in 1985.

See also Child Day Care

References Slavin, *U.S. Women's Interest Groups* (1995).

Day, Dorothy (1897–1980)

A founder of the Catholic worker movement, the publication *Catholic Worker*, and hospitality houses for poor people, Dorothy Day espoused views that both challenged the Roman Catholic hierarchy and influenced public policy. Day's mission was to comfort the afflicted and afflict the comfortable. Outraged by injustice and opposed to war, Day has been credited with opening the minds of bishops, priests, and laypeople in the Catholic Church to their duty to serve the humblest members of society.

Born in Brooklyn, New York, Dorothy Day attended the University of Illinois from 1914 to 1916. She began her journalism career and her social activism as a writer for socialist and radical newspapers shortly afterward. Her commitment to social issues gained a new dimension after her daughter was born and she began seeking a meaningful faith, leading to her baptism as a Roman Catholic in 1927. Her beliefs led her to seek ways to serve homeless and poor people and contributed to her collaboration

Dorothy Day, radical Socialist and publisher of the Catholic Worker, strived in New York's poorest neighborhoods to feed the hungry and shelter the homeless. Photo from the George H.W. Bush Presidential Library, by Vivian Cherry, 1955.

with French Catholic liberal leader Peter Maurin, with whom she founded the *Catholic Worker*, a liberal newspaper, in 1933. Homeless people began to seek help from the newspaper, prompting Day and Maurin to develop a network of hospitality houses, later known as Catholic worker houses. Following Maurin's death in 1949, Day continued to manage the hospitality houses and publish the newspaper. Day's political influence appears in those who found inspiration in her ideas and acted upon them. Labor leader Cesar Chavez, Vietnam War resister David Miller, Vietnam War opponents Reverends Daniel Berrigan and Philip Berrigan, and others found inspiration in her message and courage from her example.

Day wrote *From Union Square to Rome* (1938), *House of Hospitality* (1939), *On Pilgrimage* (1948), *Therese* (1960), *Loaves and Fishes* (1963), and *On Pilgrimage: The Sixties* (1972). Day spent the last days of her life at one of the hospitality houses she had founded.

References Forest, *Love Is the Measure* (1986); *The New York Times*, 8 November 1972, 30 November 1980.

Declaration of Sentiments and Resolutions (1848)

See **Seneca Falls Convention**

Decter, Midge Rosenthal (b. 1927)

Conservative social critic and writer Midge Decter has condemned modern feminists, arguing that they do not seek freedom from sexual discrimination, but freedom from responsibility. She contends that feminists fear the many options available to them and want to retreat into self-absorption. She believes that modern birth control methods, not the feminist movement, opened career opportunities to women. She criticized parents in the 1970s for tolerating their children's rebellion against society and called on parents to accept their responsibility "to make ourselves the final authority on good and bad, right and wrong."

Decter's career includes editorial positions on several magazines, among them managing editor of *Commentary* from 1961 to 1962, executive editor of *Harper's Magazine* from 1969 to 1971, and book review editor of *Saturday Review/World* magazine from 1972 to 1974. Her books include *The Liberated Woman and Other Americans* (1971), *The New Chastity* (1972), and *Liberal Parents, Radical Children* (1975). A founder of the Committee for the Free World, she was the organization's executive director from 1980 to 1990.

Born in St. Paul, Minnesota, Decter attended the University of Minnesota from 1945 to 1946 and Jewish Theological Seminary from 1946 to 1948.

References H. W. Wilson, *Current Biography Yearbook, 1982* (1982).

Deer, Ada Elizabeth (b. 1935)

Native American Ada Deer became the first woman to head the Bureau of Indian Affairs (BIA) in 1993, serving until 1997. During her confirmation hearings, she told the Senate Committee on Indian Affairs: "Personally, you should know that forty years ago, my tribe, the Menominee, was terminated; twenty years ago we were restored;

and today I come before you as a true survivor of Indian policy." As head of the BIA, Deer administered a budget of $2.4 billion and managed more than 12,000 employees, the largest agency in the Department of Interior. Deer sought to create a federal-tribal partnership to fulfill promises made by the government and to address injustices. She believed that the federal government's role was to support tribal sovereignty and to implement solutions developed by tribes for problems identified by tribes. During her tenure, more than 220 Alaska Native villages received recognition, and the number of self-governance tribes increased, as did the number of tribes contracting for services previously administered by the federal government. In addition, she reorganized the Bureau.

The cause that drew Deer into politics was the restoration of the Menominee tribe. A 1953 law had terminated the Menominee Reservation, and by 1961, federal control over tribal affairs had ended. Without federal involvement, health and education benefits ended, and the ownership of tribal lands was threatened. In the early 1970s, Deer and other leaders formed the Determination of the Rights and Unity for Menominee Shareholders (DRUMS), with the goal of restoring the tribe's recognition. As lobbyist for the group, Deer won passage of an act to restore federal recognition of the Menominees, making them eligible for federal services. Elected chair of the Menominee Restoration Committee in 1974, Deer led the tribe through the process of reestablishing itself; created an administrative structure; oversaw its financial, judicial, and legislative affairs; and helped write its constitution.

Born in Keshena, Wisconsin, on the Menominee Indian Reservation, Ada Deer lived in a one-room log cabin the first twelve years of her life. The daughter of a white mother and Menominee Indian father, she earned her bachelor's degree in social work from the University of Wisconsin in 1957 and a master's degree from the Columbia School of Social Work in 1961. She studied law at the University of Wisconsin and the University of New Mexico and was a fellow at the Harvard Institute of Politics, JFK School of Government, in 1977.

> **References** H. W. Wilson, *Current Biography Yearbook, 1994* (1994);
> www.doi.gov/adabio.html.
>
> **Document** Ada Deer, "Statement before the Joint Hearing of the House Resources Committee and Senate Committee on Indian Affairs," 1997

DeGette, Diana Louise (b. 1957)

Democrat Diana DeGette of Colorado entered the U.S. House of Representatives on 3 January 1997. DeGette held the leadership position of House deputy minority whip in the 106th Congress (1999–2001), floor whip in the 108th Congress (2003–2005) and chief deputy whip in the 109th Congress (2005–2007).

Congresswoman DeGette has focused on expanding health care for children, regulating smoking and tobacco, and protecting the environment. DeGette has worked to expedite the restoration of polluted areas, particularly the Rocky Mountain Arsenal, a Superfund site. During her first term in office, she passed a measure to increase the number of children enrolled in Medicaid. Co-chair of the Congressional Diabetes Caucus, Congresswoman DeGette provided leadership in the passage of legislation increasing the funding for diabetes research and prevention and treatment programs for

Native Americans. She won passage of a measure requiring pediatric experts to review medical devices that will be used on children before they are put on the market. She would like children to have priority on organ transplant lists. In another area of health, she has persistently worked to expand stem cell research. She has also worked to obtain increased funding for research, screening, and education for autism.

DeGette served in the Colorado House of Representatives from 1993 to 1997, where she was instrumental in passing a bill ensuring women unobstructed access to abortion clinics and other medical care facilities. She passed the state's Voluntary Cleanup and Redevelopment Act, considered a model for environmental cleanup programs.

Born in Tachikawa, Japan, Diana DeGette earned her bachelor's degree from Colorado College in 1979 and her law degree from New York University Law School in 1982. She practiced law in Denver, focusing on civil rights and employment litigation, for fifteen years.

See also Congress, Women in; State Legislatures, Women in

References *Congressional Quarterly, Politics in America 1998* (1997), *Politics in America 2004* (2005); "Congresswomen Introduce Combating Autism Act, of 2005," *Life Science Weekly*, 14 June 2005, p.1237; "Special Diabetes Program," Diabetes *Forecast*, 1 April 2003, p. 107; *The New York Times*, 19 May 2005; www.house.gov/degette/about.shtml

DeLauro, Rosa L. (b. 1943)

Democrat Rosa DeLauro of Connecticut entered the U.S. House of Representatives on 3 January 1991. DeLauro has held the leadership positions of House chief deputy minority whip in the 104th and 105th Congresses (1995–1999), assistant to the Democratic leader in the 106th and 107th Congresses (1999–2003), and co-chair of the House Democratic steering committee in the 108th and 109th Congresses (2003–2007).

Connecticut Congresswoman Rosa DeLauro and Senators Kerry, Clinton, and Schumer call for increased funding for the Low-Income Home Energy Assistance Program (LIHEAP) to help Connecticut citizens to meet their energy needs. (Courtesy Office of Rosa DeLauro)

DeLauro has led the fight to increase federal funding for research on breast cancer and cervical cancer. In the 106th Congress (1999–2001), she passed a measure to require health insurers to pay for adequately long hospital stays, at least 48 hours, for women who have undergone mastectomies. She has worked to restrict the development of new weapons systems and to help industries make the transition from defense-related markets to commercial ones.

A co-founder of the Congressional Food Safety Caucus in 2003, DeLauro co-chaired the group, which seeks to identify strategies to secure the food supply. In a related area, DeLauro has introduced legislation requiring chain and fast food restaurants to provide nutritional information on their menus as a way to combat obesity.

DeLauro has received recognition for her efforts to increase funding for psoriasis research and to increase gynecologic cancer education and awareness. She has been an outspoken advocate for Federal Drug Administration (FDA) approval of over-the-counter emergency contraceptives. Regarding the FDA's inaction, DeLauro said: "There is not reasonable medical evidence to support the FDA's delay, only an ideological agenda that undermines science and the public health."

Before entering Congress, DeLauro was executive assistant to the mayor of New Haven in 1976 and 1977 and was executive assistant to the city's development administrator from 1977 to 1979. Chief of staff for Senator Christopher Dodds from 1981 to 1987, she was also executive director of EMILY's List.

Born in New Haven, Connecticut, Rosa L. DeLauro grew up in a political family, the daughter of an alderman and alderwoman. As a child, she attended political gatherings with her parents. She studied at the London School of Economics from 1962 to 1963, received a bachelor's degree from Marymount College in 1964, and earned a master's degree from Columbia University in 1966.

See also Congress, Women in; EMILY's List

References Boxer, *Strangers in the Senate* (1994); *Congressional Quarterly, Politics in America 1996* (1995), *Politics in America 2004* (2003); *Hartford (Connecticut) Courant*, 22 February 2006; "Gynecologic Cancer; Members of Congress Announce National Gynecologic Cancer Awareness Campaign," *Life Science Weekly*, 5 April 2005, p. 800; "Legislative Effort Calls for Nutrition Listing at Restaurants," *Nation's Health*, 1 December 2003, p. 11; www.house.gov/delauro/bio.html.

Delta Sigma Theta Sorority

Founded in 1913 at Howard University, Delta Sigma Theta members have pledged to take "concerted action in removing the handicaps under which we as women and as members of a minority race labor." With more than 200,000 members in over 900 chapters in the United States and eight other nations, Delta Sigma Theta is one of the largest African American women's organizations in the world. Delta Sigma Theta has a five-point agenda: economic development and involvement, educational development, international awareness, physical and mental health, and political awareness and involvement. Its legislative priorities include civil rights, voter registration, education, health, child care, and employment.

The sorority's programs include the Dr. Betty Shabazz Delta Academy, which provides local programs to girls ages 11 to 14, offering them educational support in the areas of math, science, and technology. Leadship skills and the cultivation and maintenance of relationships are also part of the program. Delta Sigma Theta also sponsors Delta Days at the Nation's Capital, an annual legislative conference that includes legislative briefings, issues forums, and advocacy skills development.

Delta Sigma Theta challenged discrimination on college campuses, sent a bookmobile to Georgia in the 1940s, and provided financial support for civil rights actions in the South during the 1960s. The organization lobbied for federal anti-lynching legislation, an end to discrimination in housing, and creation of a permanent Fair Employment Practices Commission. It helped pass the 1964 Civil Rights Act and the 1965 Voting Rights Act.

Among those who have participated in Delta Sigma Theta's leadership training are former congresswomen Shirley Chisholm and Barbara Jordan, as well as Patricia Harris, former secretary of both housing and urban development and health and human services.

> **See also** Alpha Kappa Alpha Sorority; Chisholm, Shirley Anita St. Hill; Civil Rights Movement, Women in the; Evers-Williams, Myrlie Louise Beasley; Harris, Patricia Roberts; Height, Dorothy Irene; Jordan, Barbara Charline; Suffrage; Terrell, Mary Eliza Church
>
> **References** Giddings, *In Search of Sisterhood* (1988); Slavin, *U.S. Women's Interest Groups* (1995); http://www.deltasigmtheta.org

Democratic Party, Women in the

The Democratic Party was the first of the two major parties to have a woman chair its national committee and the only one of the two parties to nominate a woman for vice president of the United States. After women gained suffrage rights in 1920, women leaders in the party began a long crusade to gain a share of the power and a voice in the decision-making process. Several women have emerged as innovative and dynamic leaders in the party and have created opportunities for other women in it.

The first woman went to a Democratic National Convention as a delegate in 1900, and the first woman served on a convention committee (credentials) in 1916, the year the party created a Women's Division. Women's formal entrance into the Democratic National Committee (DNC), the party's governing board, began in 1919, when the party created the position of associate member. Associate members were appointed by each state committee chair, one for each state, comparable to national committeemen. Associate members had no vote but could voice their opinions in DNC meetings. In 1920, the DNC created the voting position of national committeewoman, replacing associate members. National committeewomen, like national committeemen, had full voting rights, were selected by their home state, and served for four-year terms. Women's roles, however, were limited. Men appreciated their work on the party's behalf but resisted giving them substantive roles or rewarding their efforts with the appointments and other benefits granted to men.

One of the party's earliest women leaders was Belle Moskowitz, who was a publicist for Alfred Smith in his three campaigns for governor of New York in 1918, 1920, and 1922 and his presidential bid in 1928. Emily Newell Blair was among the first group of national committeewomen, the first female vice chair of the party in 1921, and the second chair of the Women's Division. As head of the Women's Division, she helped organize hundreds of Democratic women's clubs, conducted training sessions, and called on women to become active in the political party and to run for public office.

In the late 1920s and early 1930s, two women, Eleanor Roosevelt and Molly Dewson, formed a political partnership that significantly changed women's roles and influence in the party. They shared a background in the social reform movement, developed a deep and lasting friendship, and became a powerful political force. Roosevelt recruited Dewson to Democratic Party politics, and the two women successfully organized women to support Franklin Roosevelt's gubernatorial campaigns in 1928 and 1930 and his 1932 presidential campaign. One of their innovations was known as "rainbow fliers," or campaign literature printed on colored paper and used first in the gubernatorial campaigns. They sent millions of the fliers to women during the presidential campaign, a strategy that men in the party later adopted.

Following Franklin Roosevelt's election to the presidency, Eleanor Roosevelt and Dewson worked to enhance women's roles in government and in the party. After agreeing to head the Women's Division of the party, Dewson reportedly arrived in Washington, D.C., with a list of sixty women for top government positions and worked to gain appointments for them. Among her more notable achievements was Franklin Roosevelt's choice for secretary of labor, Frances Perkins, the first woman to serve in a presidential Cabinet. Dewson also won approval of a federal program for unemployed women, a remarkable achievement during the Depression, when women were being moved out of jobs to make them available for men.

In addition to expanding women's roles within the Roosevelt administration, Dewson increased women's effectiveness within the party by training them and then utilizing their skills to benefit the party. For example, Dewson trained women across the country to explain the benefits of the New Deal to voters. With what some have called an avalanche of colored paper, Dewson regularly distributed information to women in the party, notifying them of new programs and projects and the progress of existing ones. Having demonstrated the usefulness of women party members, Eleanor Roosevelt and Dewson gained equal representation for women on the party's 1936 platform committee and won eight slots as party vice chairs for women, the same number as men.

The 1940 convention brought the first debate on the Equal Rights Amendment in the party's Resolutions and Platform Committee. At that time, Eleanor Roosevelt, along with many other women in the New Deal and women in the trade unions, opposed the measure, fearing that it would end protective labor legislation for women. Rejecting the amendment, the committee approved "the principle of equality of opportunity for women."

The 1944 Democratic National Convention changed its position and endorsed the Equal Rights Amendment. Also at that convention, Dorothy Vredenburgh became secretary of the Democratic National Committee, the first female officer in either party. She served until 1989.

By the 1948 convention, Eleanor Roosevelt had shifted her attention to the international arena, and Molly Dewson had retired from politics. India Edwards emerged as a leader, particularly at the 1948 national convention, where she defined inflation as a women's issue and pointed to the problems the escalating costs of food and clothing created for family budgets. Like Dewson before her, Edwards organized women to support the party's candidate, President Harry Truman, and again like Dewson, Edwards recommended women to serve in the administration. Edwards was influential in obtaining several appointments for women, including Georgia Neese Clark as the first female treasurer of the United States and Eugenie Moore Anderson as the United States' first female ambassador, both in 1949. In 1951, Truman offered Edwards the position of chair of the party as a reward for her labors and in recognition of her abilities. She declined, believing that men in the party would not accept a female chairperson.

The party eliminated the Women's Division in 1952, deciding that the time had come to integrate women into the larger party structure. Women protested the change, however, fearing that their role in the party would be diminished rather than enlarged. Women were less visible in the party for the balance of the decade, but a Republican held the presidency and the prevailing climate of opinion encouraged women to find their places in their homes rather than in public life.

At the 1964 Democratic National Convention, African American Fannie Lou Hamer captured the nation's attention during her appeal for justice before the party's committee. In her testimony, Hamer described the indignities and the beatings she had endured as a leader of the civil rights movement in the South. Her televised speech electrified the nation, but the credentials committee seated the white delegation. Four years later, Hamer was one of the twenty-two African American delegates from Mississippi at the 1968 Democratic National Convention.

Following the 1968 convention, the party began a period of reform, including national rules for the selection of convention delegates, and guidelines that called for "reasonable representation" of various groups, including women. As preparations began for the 1972 convention, the National Women's Political Caucus (NWPC) argued that since women comprised more than 50 percent of the population in most states, "reasonable representation" meant that a majority of the delegates from most states would be women. Party leaders interpreted the guidelines less strictly but agreed that state delegations with few women in them would have to show that the imbalance was not the result of discrimination. Some states complied with the guidelines, and delegations from other states faced challenges before the credentials committee, resulting in a significant change in the percentage of women at the 1972 convention. Thirteen percent of the delegates to the 1968 convention had been women; in 1972, women constituted 40 percent of the delegates to the convention. An effort to require equal representation of women at the 1976 convention failed.

At the 1972 Democratic National Convention, Doris Meissner, NWPC executive director, and other staff members set up an office and held informational sessions with delegates throughout the convention. The NWPC wanted four items included in the party platform: reproductive rights, the Equal Rights Amendment, educational equity, and equal pay. The platform did not include the reproductive rights plank, but it did include the other three issues.

The 1972 convention was also notable for two women's efforts to become the party's nominees, one for president and the other for vice president. For the first time in the party's history, an African American woman, Congresswoman Shirley Chisholm of

New York, ran for the presidential nomination. Chisholm's campaign had little promise from the beginning, but she received 152 votes on the first ballot. During the convention a campaign to nominate Frances (Sissy) Farenthold for the vice presidency developed, and NWPC members organized to help her. Farenthold received 404 votes.

Immediately after the convention, Democratic presidential nominee George McGovern proposed a new slate of officers for the Democratic National Committee, including Jean Westwood of Utah for chairperson of the party. When Westwood became the party's chair, she was the first woman to hold the position in either of the two major parties. Following the fall elections and McGovern's defeat, Robert Strauss challenged Westwood for the position of chair and won.

Between the 1972 and 1976 conventions, state party chairpersons expressed their objections to what they described as a quota system for women, minorities, and youth, resulting in a new reform commission. Despite feminists' objections, new rules were implemented that softened the party's policies regarding delegate selection. Only 36 percent of the delegates to the 1976 Democratic National Convention were women.

Women in the NWPC formalized their work within the parties by creating task forces for members of each party. During the 1976 convention, the Democratic Women's Task Force regularly met with delegates, focusing their efforts on passing the equal division rule, which would require 50 percent of the delegates to be women. When likely presidential nominee Jimmy Carter objected to it, the task force members agreed to drop the equal division rule in exchange for his support for the Equal Rights Amendment and a promise that he would appoint women to significant posts in his presidential campaign and administration. Later, the party adopted rules guaranteeing women equal division for the 1980 Democratic National Convention. One of the most compelling moments of the 1976 convention was Texas congresswoman Barbara Jordan's keynote address. The first Democratic woman and the first African American to make an important speech to a national convention, her oratory and her message captivated Americans across the country.

During the Carter administration, the Democratic National Committee resurrected the Women's Division, which had been dissolved in 1952. Iowan Lynn Cutler, who had earlier run for Congress, served as a party vice chair and ran the division. In 1985, the party again closed the division, which meant that it no longer had its own staff or budget. Cutler remained responsible for women's activities in addition to other areas.

At the 1980 Democratic National Convention, Democratic Party feminists established themselves as a force within the party, even though their leaders did not uniformly support the party's nominee, incumbent President Jimmy Carter. Almost 50 percent of the delegates were women, and about 20 percent of the delegates belonged to the NWPC or the National Organization for Women (NOW). The party platform included strong ERA and pro-choice planks.

By the 1984 convention, the Democratic Party had aligned itself with feminist issues, a position that contrasted with that of the Republican Party, which had essentially repudiated feminist issues. With the Democratic Party's allegiance to feminist issues established, feminists turned their attention to nominating a woman for vice president. Before the convention opened, likely Democratic presidential nominee Walter Mondale announced that Congresswoman Geraldine Ferraro would be his running mate. Mondale and Ferraro lost in the November election, but her presence on the ticket gave unprecedented visibility to an American political woman.

The contrasts on women's issues that developed between the two major parties in the 1970s became heightened in the 1980s and by the 1990s were firmly established. The Democratic Party had accepted the feminist agenda, and equal representation within the delegations had become well established. The gender gap–with women more likely to vote for Democrats than Republicans–had become so large in congressional and presidential races that the margins contributed to the elections of members of Congress and of President Bill Clinton. Women continued to favor Democratic presidential nominees in 2000 and 2004, but did not provide a winning margin. Of the 225 women who have served in Congress, 143 have been Democrats and 82 Republicans. In addition, of the 27 women who have served as governors of their states, 17 have been Democrats and 10 Republicans.

> **See also** Abortion; Anderson, Eugenie Moore; Blair, Emily Newell; Chisholm, Shirley Anita St. Hill; Clark Gray, Georgia Neese; Dewson, Mary (Molly) Williams; Education Amendments of 1972, Title IX; Education, Women and; Edwards, India Moffett; Equal Rights Amendment; Ferraro, Geraldine Anne; Hamer, Fannie Lou Townsend; Jordan, Barbara Charline; League of Women Voters; Meissner, Doris Marie; National Organization for Women; National Women's Political Caucus; Nineteenth Amendment; President and Vice President, Women Candidates for; Roosevelt, Eleanor; Westwood, Frances Jean Miles

> **References** Breckenridge, *Women in the Twentieth Century* (1933); Feit, "Organizing for Political Power: The National Women's Political Caucus" (1979); *Freeman*, "Women at the 1988 Democratic Convention" (1988); National Women's Political Caucus, *Democratic Women Are Wonderful* (1980).

Dennett, Mary Coffin Ware (1872–1947)

Birth control advocate and suffragist Mary Coffin Ware Dennett worked to legalize the distribution of contraceptive information by passing legislation ending its designation as obscene material under the Comstock law of 1873. Dennett entered politics through the suffrage movement in 1908, serving as a field secretary for the Massachusetts Suffrage Association. Corresponding secretary for the National American Woman Suffrage Association (NAWSA) beginning in 1910, she became executive secretary in 1912. As her influence in the organization increased, she became openly critical of NAWSA's president, Anna Howard Shaw, and her leadership, resulting in Shaw's resignation in 1914.

Dennett organized the first birth control association in the United States in 1915, the National Birth Control League (NBCL), which sought to change state Comstock laws. When she was unsuccessful in changing state laws, she founded the Voluntary Parenthood League to change the federal Comstock law. As she looked for a member of Congress to sponsor a bill to remove the phrase "prevention of pregnancy" from the Comstock law, Dennett found that some members of Congress were sympathetic, but many were uncomfortable discussing the topic and others feared that young people would engage in immoral behavior if they had birth control information. In 1923, U.S. Senator Albert B. Cummins of Iowa agreed to introduce the provision, as did Congressman William N. Vail of Colorado. Joint hearings were held in 1924, but the bill did not progress, and Dennett resigned as the league's lobbyist. She wrote *Birth*

Control Laws, a history of the Comstock laws and the congressional campaign to change them.

Dennett had written an essay on human sexuality for adolescents titled "The Sex Side of Life: An Explanation for Young People," that was published in *Medical Review of Reviews* in 1918. By 1929, she had been filling orders for "The Sex Side of Life" by sending copies through the mail for more than a decade, but that year she was charged with mailing obscene material, convicted, and fined $300. The case became a cause célèbre, with supporters protesting the charges, the conduct of the trial, and her conviction. A defense committee formed to support an appeal, which Dennett took to the U.S. Court of Appeals. The appeals court reversed the verdict in what became a landmark censorship case by making context a factor in determining obscenity. The contraceptive clause in the 1873 Comstock law was not stricken until 1970.

Born in Boston, Massachusetts, Dennett graduated from the School of Art and Design at the Boston Museum of Fine Arts in 1894 and taught at the Drexel Institute of Art from 1894 to 1897.

See also *Griswold v. Connecticut*; National American Woman Suffrage Association; Sanger, Margaret Louise Higgins; Shaw, Anna Howard; Suffrage

References Chen, *"The Sex Side of Life": Mary Ware Dennett's Pioneering Battle for Birth Control and Sex Education* (1996).

Dewson, Mary (Molly) Williams (1874–1962)

Democratic Party leader Molly Dewson worked with Eleanor Roosevelt to expand women's roles within the party and within President Franklin D. Roosevelt's administration. Regarded as the United States' first female political boss, she developed the campaign strategies to attract women to the Democratic Party that were duplicated throughout the party's organization. As head of the Women's Division of the Democratic National Committee in the 1930s, Dewson had three goals: patronage for women, equal representation for women on all party committees, and providing women with a clear understanding of Roosevelt's New Deal programs. When she retired in 1937, she had succeeded in having Roosevelt appoint the first woman to a presidential Cabinet post and in gaining equal representation for women on all party committees in seventeen states.

Dewson began her career as a social reformer in the late 1890s. She wrote *Twentieth Century Expense Book* (1899), an aid to women purchasing household goods, was superintendent of the parole department for the Massachusetts State Industrial School for Girls, and was executive secretary of the National Consumers League (NCL). While at the NCL, Dewson conducted a statistical study of wage rates for women and girls and reported her findings. The report became the basis for the passage in 1912 of the first minimum wage law in the United States. She also lobbied the Massachusetts legislature for passage of an eight-hour workday for women and children and campaigned for woman suffrage. During World War I, Dewson worked for the Red Cross in France, directing relocation services for displaced refugees, and then returned to the NCL. Through her social reform work, Dewson met Frances Perkins and Eleanor Roosevelt and became close friends of both women.

At Roosevelt's request, Dewson organized women to support Alfred E. Smith's 1928 presidential campaign. When Franklin D. Roosevelt won his campaign for governor of New York that year, Dewson asked him to support a minimum wage bill and to appoint Frances Perkins to the state's industrial commission, and he complied with both requests. In 1930, Eleanor Roosevelt convinced Dewson to work at the New York state women's Democratic committee for Franklin Roosevelt's re-election campaign for governor. During that campaign, Dewson began distributing rainbow fliers, one-page fact sheets on colored paper, an idea originated by someone else but one that Dewson used extensively and effectively. In Franklin Roosevelt's 1932 presidential campaign, Dewson directed the distribution of six million rainbow fliers.

By 1932, Dewson's political acumen was generally recognized within the party, but the party chairman did not support her or her work. At Eleanor Roosevelt's insistence, however, Dewson became head of the Women's Division of the Democratic National Committee (DNC). Dewson developed a nationwide corps of women supporters for the party and for Franklin Roosevelt's presidential candidacy and established committees that addressed the concerns of interest groups, including African Americans, educators, social workers, and writers. Using issues of concern to these and other groups, she reached beyond the party structure and traditional party supporters to create new bases of loyalty.

After Franklin Roosevelt won, Dewson focused on obtaining federal appointments for women to reward and motivate party workers. Through her work, more women obtained jobs at the state and federal levels than in any previous administration. Most notably, Dewson is credited with orchestrating Frances Perkins's appointment as secretary of labor, the first Cabinet position held by a woman. Some of the other women whose appointments resulted from Dewson's work include Mary McLeod Bethune to the National Youth Administration and Nellie Tayloe Ross as director of the U.S. Mint, in addition to the first woman on the U.S. Circuit Court of Appeals and the first woman to represent the United States in a foreign country.

Within the party, Dewson worked for the passage of state laws and party rulings that would require fifty-fifty representation of women in party leadership positions and on all party committees. She initiated training programs to increase women's effectiveness as campaign workers, and she established a paid staff for the Women's Division that worked between and throughout election years. Traditionally, the national parties maintained only a skeleton staff between elections, but Dewson believed that "elections are won between campaigns," an expression she coined. She developed strategies to keep voters informed and interested between elections, including her Reporter Plan, an educational approach to politics that involved women at the county level. Women volunteered to be reporters, chose a federal agency to research, and made presentations about it to civic groups and local clubs, spreading the New Deal message at the grass roots. By 1940, more than 30,000 women were involved in the program.

At the 1936 Democratic National Convention, Dewson obtained passage of two changes in party rules to expand women's roles. One rule required states to appoint the same number of women as men to the platform committee, which guaranteed women places on it. The other change created the same number of female vice chairs as male vice chairs. During the 1936 elections, Democratic women were among the best organized and trained of any group within the party. More than 80 percent of the printed material distributed by the DNC was prepared by women, and more than 80,000 women went door-to-door, canvassing precincts across the country and distributing 83 million rainbow fliers.

Dewson left the DNC in 1937, and President Roosevelt appointed her to the Social Security Board. The board was mired in difficulties with Congress and in its relationships with the states, which Dewson helped ease by encouraging cooperation between federal and state officials and improving relations with Congress. She resigned from the board in 1938 because of poor health. In the last months of the 1940 election campaign, Dewson briefly returned to the Democratic National Committee. Twenty years later, in 1960, she unsuccessfully ran for a seat in Maine's state Senate.

Born in Quincy, Massachusetts, Mary Dewson, generally known as Molly, earned her bachelor's degree from Wellesley College in 1897.

> **See also** Anderson, Mary; Bethune, Mary Jane McLeod; Cabinets, Women in Presidential; Democratic Party, Women in the; Perkins, Frances (Fanny) Corlie; Roosevelt, Eleanor; Ross, Nellie Tayloe; Women's Bureau
>
> **References** Roosevelt and Hickok, *Ladies of Courage* (1954); Ware, *Partner and I: Molly Dewson, Feminism, and New Deal Politics* (1987).

Diaz v. Pan American World Airways, Inc. (1971)

In *Diaz v. Pan American World Airways, Inc.*, Celio Diaz, a man, challenged Pan American's policy of hiring only women as flight cabin attendants, arguing that the policy constituted sex discrimination in violation of the Civil Rights Act of 1964, Title VII. Pan American defended the policy by explaining that being female was a bona fide occupational qualification (BFOQ) for the job because passengers preferred to be served by female flight attendants, and women could better meet passengers' psychological needs. The Fifth Circuit Court of Appeals explained that "allowing the preferences and prejudices of the customers to determine whether the sex discrimination was valid" undermined the purpose of Title VII. The Court found that being female was not a BFOQ for the job of flight cabin attendant and that Pan American's policy violated Title VII.

> **See also** Bona Fide Occupational Qualification; Civil Rights Act of 1964, Title VII; Employment Discrimination
>
> **References** *Diaz v. Pan American World Airways, Inc.*, 442 F.2d 385 (1971).

Displaced Homemakers

A displaced homemaker is a woman whose principal job has been homemaking and who has lost her main source of income because of divorce, separation, widowhood, disability, long-term unemployment of a spouse, or loss of eligibility for public assistance. In 2003, there were 7.3 million displaced homemakers under age 65. Of those women, 48 percent were employed, but 42 percent of all displaced homemakers had incomes below the poverty level and 16 percent were near it. Fifty-eight percent of displaced homemakers had not completed education beyond a high school diploma or GED.

In the 1970s, as the divorce rate escalated, increasing numbers of women found themselves unable to obtain employment, some because they had never been employed in the paid workforce and others because their skills had become outdated. Since then, more than 1,300 programs have been established to offer training and education, assistance in writing resumes, and classes that teach job interview skills.

The idea for displaced homemaker programs originated with two women who identified and named the problem. Tish Sommers, who had been divorced after twenty-three years of marriage, and Laurie Shields, a widow, were both in their fifties and part of a growing number of women needing employment and support to help them make the transition into the workforce. In 1974, using the slogan "Don't agonize, organize," they worked with an attorney to draft the first displaced homemaker legislation. Introduced in the California legislature in 1975, the bill passed, and the first displaced homemaker center opened in Oakland, California, in 1976.

Sommers and Shields established the Alliance for Displaced Homemakers to organize women at the grassroots level, to build coalitions, and to attract media attention for their cause. In 1978, the first national displaced homemakers conference established the Displaced Homemaker Network to lobby for programs and funding. Congresswoman Yvonne Brathwaite Burke (D-CA) passed a measure in 1978 making displaced homemakers eligible for training and services under the Comprehensive Education and Training Act. After Burke's 1978 measure, a variety of services and programs for displaced homemakers was established within several federal agencies and departments. Congress passed the Displaced Homemakers Self-Sufficiency Assistance Act of 1990 to coordinate the many programs and to make them more accessible to displaced homemakers. The measure also provided additional funding to displaced homemaker programs at the state level through federal grants. In 1993, the organization changed its name to Women Work! The National Network for Women's Employment in recognition of the range of economic transitions women confront throughout their lives.

See also Burke, Perle Yvonne Watson Brathwaite; Divorce Law Reform; Women Work! The National Network for Women's Employment

References www.womenwork.org.

DiVall, Linda (b. ca. 1953)

The leading Republican woman pollster, Linda DiVall was introduced to polling by a political science professor at Arizona State University, where she earned her bachelor's degree in 1974. She began her career as a researcher and pollster at the Republican National Committee, moving to the National Republican Congressional Committee, working there until she founded her own polling company in 1985, the first time a Republican woman had started a national survey research company.

A pro-choice feminist, DiVall works for many clients who are neither. She explained: "Abortion is an important issue to me, but there are other things that motivate me equally, if not more." Her clients have included Republican presidential candidate Elizabeth Dole, several members of Congress, corporations, Planned Parenthood, and The White House Project.

DiVall has been a consultant and analyst for CBS News on election nights since 1988.

References "And on the Right…," *Working Woman*, February 1992, p. 69; http://amview.com; "Linda DiVall," *Campaigns and Elections*, August 1998, p. 16; *New York Times*, 23 August 1999.

Divorce Law Reform

Divorce law reform began in 1970 when California passed the nation's first no-fault divorce law. Until then, married people wanting to end their marriage had to engage in an adversarial process that required one of the partners to accuse the other of committing an act that the state recognized as an acceptable reason for divorce. Adultery was a reason recognized in every state, and some states permitted divorces for mental or physical cruelty, desertion, refusal to have sexual relations, or imprisonment. In contrast, a no-fault divorce, also known as dissolution of marriage, could be obtained when irreconcilable differences resulted in the breakdown of a marriage, eliminating the need to assign fault to one of the partners. By 1985, every state had some form of no-fault divorce provision. Even though divorce reform spread across the country as the modern feminist movement developed, women did not seek the changes and had little influence in developing the new policies. The greater ease in obtaining divorces resulted in an increase in them. In 1966, there were 2.5 divorces per 1,000 people, and in 1981, there were 5.3 divorces per 1,000 people. The rate declined to about 4.7 per thousand people in the mid-1980s, and 3.7 in 2004.

See also Child Support Enforcement; Displaced Homemakers; Feminization of Poverty; Pay Equity

References Riley, *Divorce: An American Tradition* (1991); www.cdc.gov.

Dix, Dorothea Lynde (1802–1887)

The first woman lobbyist to gain political influence at the state and national levels, Dorothea Dix sought improved care for homeless people and mentally ill people in the 1840s and 1850s, when little sympathy existed for them and when women had little political influence. Her reform career began in 1841, when she inspected almshouses and other Massachusetts institutions and wrote a report on the conditions in them. Published as a memorial to the state legislature, the report described the human suffering and the horrors she had witnessed and included factual information to support her observations. She argued that mentally ill persons should not be imprisoned and that they needed to be placed in asylums that would provide responsible care for them, noting that the state's asylum facilities were inadequate for the number of people needing space in them. After presenting her report, Dix successfully lobbied legislators, who passed the measures she sought.

She also conducted research, published reports, and lobbied in New York, Vermont, Rhode Island, New Jersey, Pennsylvania, Ohio, Indiana, Maryland, Virginia, Kentucky, Tennessee, and Alabama. She achieved varying degrees of success in different states and developed a range of strategies. In Rhode Island, for example, she convinced a wealthy man to make a large donation toward building an asylum.

By 1848, Dix had concluded that a federal policy was needed and began lobbying Congress. In 1850, she found a sympathetic ally in President Millard Fillmore and through her lobbying efforts, became close to him. In 1852 she won approval for an

Dorothea Dix lobbied state and national legislatures on behalf of homeless and mentally ill people and won major reforms in the conditions of their treatment (Library of Congress Prints and Photographs Division Washington, D.C. 20540 USA LC-USZ62-9797)

appropriation of $100,000 for an asylum in Washington, D.C., and in 1854 Congress approved a federal program to fund mental health care, but President Franklin Pierce vetoed it. In the late 1850s, Dix took her campaign for mentally ill persons to England and Scotland.

During the Civil War, she served as superintendent of nurses in the Union Army, recruiting and training 6,000 nurses to serve with the troops.

Born in Hampden, Maine, Dix was largely self-educated. She taught school, started her own schools when she needed money to support herself, and developed her skills as a writer, publishing a novel and devotional books.

References Gollaher, *Voice for the Mad: The Life of Dorothea Dix* (1995).

Doe v. Bolton (1973)

Decided with *Roe v. Wade*, *Doe v. Bolton* addressed Georgia's abortion law. The U.S. Supreme Court invalidated the state's requirements that abortions must be performed in accredited hospitals, that three physicians must approve a woman's request for an abortion, and that a woman seeking an abortion in Georgia must be a resident of the state.

See also Abortion; *Roe v. Wade*

References *Doe v. Bolton*, 410 U.S. 179 (1973).

Dole, (Mary) Elizabeth Hanford (b. 1936)

Republican Elizabeth Dole of North Carolina entered the U.S. Senate on January 3, 2001. In the 109th Congress (2005–2007), she chairs the National Republican Senatorial Committee. Secretary of transportation in the Reagan administration from 1983 to 1987, Elizabeth Dole was also secretary of labor in the Bush administration from 1989 to 1991. Dole's public service careers began in 1966, in the Department of Health, Education, and Welfare. She also worked as associate director of legislative affairs for President Lyndon B. Johnson's Committee on Consumer Interests and the White House Office of Consumer Affairs. In 1973, President Richard Nixon appointed her to a seven-year term on the Federal Trade Commission.

Elizabeth Dole married U.S. Senator Robert Dole of Kansas in 1975 and changed her party affiliation from Democrat to Republican. When Robert Dole began campaigning for the vice presidential slot on the Republican ticket in 1976, Elizabeth Dole took a leave of absence to campaign for her husband. During that campaign, she first discovered that she had great appeal to voters. After the Ford-Dole ticket lost to Jimmy Carter, Elizabeth returned to her post on the Federal Trade Commission. After serving five and a half years of the seven-year term, she resigned in 1979 to work on her husband's 1980 campaign for the presidency.

When President Ronald Reagan entered the White House in 1981, Elizabeth Dole became assistant to the president for public liaison, building support for the president's programs. Two years later, Reagan appointed her secretary of transportation. Dole made safety her priority and worked with car manufacturers to make improvements, such as requiring a third brake light in autos. Other safety initiatives included increasing seat belt use, raising the legal drinking age to twenty-one, and implementing the first drug-testing procedure in railroad history. She resigned the position in 1987 to work on her husband's 1988 presidential campaign. When Robert Dole decid-

Elizabeth Dole, U.S. Senator from North Carolina.

ed against pursuing the Republican nomination, Elizabeth Dole campaigned for George Bush.

Secretary of labor for President George Bush, Dole negotiated an increase in the minimum wage, improved enforcement of job safety laws and child labor laws, placed more women and minorities in management positions at the Department of Labor, and encouraged private companies to do the same. Dole developed guidelines for school programs to prepare high school graduates for employment and sponsored the first national conference on youth entering the job market out of high school. She received accolades for her role in finding resolutions to a coal miners' strike in the Appalachians. She resigned to accept the presidency of the American Red Cross in 1991.

During her tenure at the American Red Cross, she was credited with developing successful fundraising strategies, cutting costs, instituting more stringent blood-screening tests, and responding to natural disasters. She visited the Persian Gulf after the Gulf War, Croatia, and the famine-stricken countries of Somalia and Mozambique. She led a 1994 humanitarian relief delegation to Rwandan refugee camps in Goma, Zaire. In 1996, Elizabeth Dole took a leave of absence to work on her husband's unsuccessful presidential campaign, returning to the American Red Cross in 1997. Early in 1999, she resigned from the American Red Cross to prepare for her own bid for the presidency of the United States. She later withdrew from the race.

Born in Salisbury, North Carolina, Elizabeth Dole earned her bachelor's degree in political science from Duke University in 1958, studied at Oxford University, and earned her master's degree in 1960 and her law degree in 1965 from Harvard University.

See also Cabinets, Women in Presidential

References *Congressional Quarterly, Cabinets and Counselors: The President and the Executive Branch* (1997), *Politics in America 2004* (2002), *Politics in America 2006* (2005); Dole and Dole, *Unlimited Partners: Our American Story* (1996); H. W. Wilson, *Current Biography Yearbook, 1983* (1983); *The New York Times*, 9 February 1999; *Washington Post*, 9 February 1999.

Document Elizabeth Dole, "Exploratory Committee Announcement Speech," 1999

Domestic Violence

Domestic violence is the serious or repeated injury caused by a person who has family ties or a sexual relationship with the victim. The offenders threaten or use physical or sexual assault to dominate, hurt, and degrade the victim in an effort to control the victim. In 2002, women were 85 percent of the victims of domestic violence, and often in those situations where men are victims, it is the result of women attempting to defend themselves. It is estimated that 8.5 million incidents of intimate partner violence occur each year, with women the victims in 5.3 million incidents and men in 3.2 million. Intimate partner violence results in nearly two million injuries and 1,300 deaths each year. One study noted: "A woman is more likely to be assaulted, injured, raped, or killed by a male partner than any other assailant."

Domestic violence also involves children. An estimated 3.3 million children are exposed to violence by family members against their mothers or female caretakers, and in families where there is partner abuse, children are 1,500 times more likely to be abused than in families without violence between the partners. Between 40 and 60 percent of the men who abuse women also abuse children.

The consequences of domesic violence go beyond a specific occurrence of it, including physical, psychological, and social difficulties. Victims, depending on the frequency and severity of the abuse, may experience central nervous system disorders, gastrointestinal disorders, symptoms associated with post-traumatic stress disorder, and heart or circulatory conditions. Depression, antisocial behavior, suicidal behavior in females, anxiety, the inability to trust men, and low self-esteem are among the psychological consequences of domestic violence experienced by victims.

There are also economic consequences to domestic violence. Medical care for victims costs about $8.3 billion. Victims lose about eight million days of paid work and almost 5.6 million days of household productivity. In addition, women who experience severe aggression by men are more likely to be unemployed, have health problems, and receive welfare.

Laws related to domestic violence have their roots in English common law, which tolerated abusive husbands. English jurist Sir William Blackstone wrote in the 1760s that a husband could beat his wife with a rod no thicker than his thumb. Although the Massachusetts Bay and Plymouth colonies both passed laws against wife beating, in 1824 a Mississippi court permitted "moderate chastisement for domestic discipline," and in 1852 and 1874, North Carolina courts permitted husbands to inflict certain punishments on their wives, including blackened eyes, bruises, and cuts, but no permanent injuries.

As the modern feminist movement developed in the 1960s and 1970s and women began to politicize matters that had previously been considered private, domestic violence became a focus of attention. In the 1970s, the feminist movement publicized domestic violence and developed a new perspective on it, framing it as a social problem. The movement to end domestic violence began when a group in St. Paul, Minnesota, and another in Tucson, Arizona, opened shelters in 1973. Over the next twenty-five years, more than 1,400 hotlines, shelters, and safehouses were established to serve victims of domestic violence. In 1990, however, more than one-half of the counties in the United States had no programs for battered women. To put the number of shelters in perspective, there are nearly three times as many animal shelters in the United States as there are shelters for battered women.

About 50 percent of domestic violence victims leave the abusive relationship. Victims stay in a dangerous environment for a number of reasons: inadequate space in shelters, loss of financial support, and fear of increased violence or death. Some women stay in the relationships because they have experienced indifference from legal authorities or found that the criminal justice system was unable to protect them.

The battered women's movement initially focused on providing emergency services to women, as exemplified by the shelters. Feminists broadened the agenda as they sought greater police protection for victims, more effective responses from the justice system, and safety for victims outside the shelters. Police generally viewed domestic violence as a family disturbance and resisted arresting offenders because the public order was not disrupted. Critics of the police insisted that their inaction implicitly condoned the offender's abuse. In some states, however, police did not have the authority to arrest the offender unless they witnessed the violence, they had a warrant to arrest the offender, or the victim filed a complaint, generally at the police station. Feminist Del Martin's 1976 book *Battered Women* documented police departments' official policies of nonintervention in domestic violence and provided activists with a guide for changing public policies related to domestic violence.

Women began filing lawsuits in the 1980s, asserting that police had failed to protect them and arguing that their rights under the equal protection clause of the Fourteenth Amendment had been violated. In one case, a woman who had repeatedly called for police protection was assaulted and left paralyzed by her estranged husband. She sued the City of Torrington, Connecticut, and was awarded $2.3 million. Other women in similar circumstances followed her example, prompting several jurisdictions to change their policies.

By 1980, forty-five states and the District of Columbia had special civil legal provisions for temporary restraining orders for battered women to help increase police responsiveness in domestic violence cases. More revisions followed in the 1990s, resulting in forty-eight states authorizing arrests without warrants for domestic violence. Some states have laws for mandatory arrests where probable cause suggests domestic violence. In Iowa, which has some of the most rigorous domestic violence laws in the nation, prosecutors' discretion is limited in prosecuting domestic violence.

The federal government first became involved with domestic violence in 1979, when President Jimmy Carter established the Office of Domestic Violence, but President Ronald Reagan closed it in 1981. Congress passed the Family Violence Prevention and Services Act in 1984, providing matching funds for shelters and other services to assist victims of domestic violence and for prevention programs. The Violence Against Women Act of 1994 provided new resources for combating domestic abuse and other forms of violence against women.

> **See also** Fourteenth Amendment; Martin, Del; National Coalition Against Domestic Violence; Violence Against Women Act of 1994
>
> **References** *Congressional Quarterly Almanac, 98th Congress, 2nd Session... 1984* (1985); Halsted, "Domestic Violence: Its Legal Definition" (1992); http://www.abanet.org; http://www.cdc.gov/ncipc/factsheets/ipvfacts.htm.

Dothard v. Rawlinson (1977)

In *Dothard v. Rawlinson*, decided in 1977, the U.S. Supreme Court applied disparate impact to sex discrimination and considered bona fide occupational qualifications (BFOQs). Dianne Rawlinson had been denied a job as a correctional counselor because she did not meet Alabama's minimum weight requirement of 120 pounds and a minimum height requirement. In addition, the state required that guards working in maximum security areas had to be male, claiming that gender was a BFOQ.

In the first part of the case, Rawlinson argued that the minimum height and weight requirements had a different impact on women than on men, that is, a disparate impact. The requirements excluded 41.3 percent of women but only 1 percent of men, policies that Rawlinson claimed were unlawful sex discrimination under Title VII of the Civil Rights Act of 1964. The Court agreed, writing: "It is impermissible under Title VII to refuse to hire an individual woman or man on the basis of stereotyped characteristics of the sexes."

The second part of the case involved Alabama's claim that denying women jobs in certain maximum security areas was legal under the exemptions granted in Title VII's BFOQ section. The Court said that the BFOQ exception should be "extremely narrow" but cited the environment within Alabama's prisons as a legitimate reason for excluding women as guards. The Court said that having women guards posed a security problem "directly linked to the sex of the prison guard" and concluded that being male was a BFOQ for correctional counselors in Alabama's male maximum security prisons.

> **See also** Civil Rights Act of 1964, Title VII; Employment Discrimination
> **References** *Dothard v. Rawlinson*, 433 U.S. 321 (1977).

Douglas, Emily Taft (1899–1994)

Democrat Emily Douglas of Illinois served in the U.S. House of Representatives from 3 January 1945 to 3 January 1947. Congresswoman Douglas was a recognized specialist in foreign affairs, a background she had gained traveling with her family as a child and later with her husband. With another member of Congress, she proposed placing the abolition of atomic weaponry and international arms control under the auspices of the United Nations. She introduced the Library Services Act to make books more available to children in impoverished areas. When her husband Paul Douglas was elected to the U.S. Senate in 1948, he helped pass the measure. Defeated in her effort to win a second term, Douglas was active in the Unitarian Church and began a career as an author.

Born in Chicago, Illinois, Douglas received a bachelor's degree from the University of Chicago in 1920. She studied at the American Academy of Dramatic Arts and was an actress for several years. She later attended graduate school, pursuing an interest in government and political science.

> **See also** Congress, Women in; League of Women Voters; Sanger, Margaret Louise Higgins
> **References** H. W. Wilson, *Current Biography 1945* (1945); Office of the Historian, U.S. House of Representatives, *Women in Congress, 1917–1990* (1991).

Douglas, Helen Mary Gahagan (1900–1980)

Democrat Helen Gahagan Douglas of California served in the U.S. House of Representatives from 3 January 1945 to 3 January 1951. An opera singer and stage and screen actress, Douglas became actively involved in Democratic Party politics as a result of her exposure to the plight of migrants in California. She toured Farm Security Administration camps and raised money for food and gifts for migrant children. President Franklin D. Roosevelt recognized her efforts by appointing her to the National Advisory Commission of the Works Progress Administration.

Elected Democratic national committeewoman for California in 1939, she became state party vice chair and chair of the state party's Women's Division. Through her work in the party, she and her husband, actor Melvyn Douglas, became friends of President Roosevelt. With the encouragement of Roosevelt and Hollywood celebrities, she ran for Congress in 1944. Supported by the Congress of Industrial Organizations

Democratic California Representative Helen Gahagan Douglas, circa 1920

and the International Ladies' Garment Workers Union, she campaigned for the rights of organized labor, full opportunity for private enterprise, taxation based on ability to pay, prevention of unemployment and depression, and the renegotiation of government contracts. Food subsidies for the poor, price controls, and protection for small business were other campaign issues she supported.

Congresswoman Douglas supported New Deal and Fair Deal legislative packages. She introduced an anti-lynching bill and opposed the poll tax. Attacks on African American men, particularly veterans, in the postwar years prompted Douglas to research and write a pamphlet on African American men's military service, one of the earliest examinations of their contributions to the country's war efforts. The first white member of Congress to hire African Americans for staff positions, she nominated African American students who were admitted to West Point military academy and helped desegregate Capitol dining rooms. In 1945, Douglas introduced the Pay Equity Bill, eighteen years before Congress passed the Equal Pay Act of 1963.

Douglas staunchly supported the Reclamation Act of 1902, a policy that created irrigation systems for otherwise untillable land. The act limited landowners to 160 acres of irrigated land, a restriction that Douglas believed protected farmers with smaller landholdings and helped protect the environment. She was also adamant about protecting tidelands from oil development. These two positions first led her to consider running for the U.S. Senate in 1950. They also, however, placed her in direct opposition to large agricultural interests and oil developers.

Richard Nixon, who ran against Douglas in the 1950 Senate race, favored removing the 160-acre limit on the Reclamation Act and developing the oil resources in the tidelands, positions that brought him financial support for his campaign. Nixon's campaign strategy, however, did not focus on those issues. Instead, he accused Douglas of being soft on Communism, labeled her "the pink lady," distorted her voting record, and implied that she was a hero of the Communist movement. The North Korean invasion of South Korea fed the anti-Communist climate, particularly on the West Coast, a region that was more sensitive to events in Asia than were other areas of the United States. The Nixon campaign created an atmosphere of hate that included rocks being thrown at Douglas's car, hecklers disrupting her speeches, and threatening phone calls to her. Douglas failed to take the attacks on her record seriously because she thought that the accusations were absurd. Nixon defeated her.

Born in Boonton, New Jersey, Helen Douglas studied theater from 1920 to 1922 at Barnard College.

See also Congress, Women in; Equal Pay Act of 1963

References Douglas, *A Full Life* (1982); *The New York Times*, 5 January 1971; Office of the Historian, U.S. House of Representatives, *Women in Congress, 1917–1990* (1991); Schoenebaum, ed., *Political Profiles: The Truman Years* (1978).

Douglass, Frederick (1817–1895)

African American Frederick Douglass, born a slave in Tuckahoe, Maryland, became one of the most recognized leaders in the abolitionist movement. After escaping from slavery in 1838, he made his first important anti-slavery speech in 1841 and won the support of abolitionist leaders with his compelling oratory. In 1846, a group of British women paid for his emancipation and later raised money for him to purchase a printing press and start his abolitionist newspaper, *The North Star*.

His support for women's rights became apparent at the 1848 Seneca Falls women's rights convention hosted by Elizabeth Cady Stanton and Lucretia Mott. At the convention, Douglass was the only man who supported Stanton's suffrage resolution, and he helped gain the convention's approval of it. He further demonstrated his support for women's rights by publishing the Declaration of Sentiments and Resolutions, adopted at the convention, in *The North Star*. He regularly attended women's rights conventions and was a featured speaker at the conventions for several years. With their common interests, Douglass and suffragists worked together for more than two decades to end slavery and obtain universal suffrage.

Following the Civil War, Douglass disagreed with Stanton and Susan B. Anthony over strategies for obtaining universal suffrage. When Congress introduced the Fourteenth Amendment to guarantee citizenship rights to former male slaves and the Fifteenth Amendment did not include women, Anthony and Stanton were outraged that women were excluded from the measures. Douglass and others insisted that it was the "Negro's Hour" and that women were not murdered for their gender, whereas blacks were murdered for their race. Stanton and Anthony vigorously and persistently objected to the amendments but ultimately failed, and they were ratified. In 1870, Douglass called for a constitutional amendment enfranchising women.

In 1876, the schism that had grown between Douglass and Anthony and Stanton was overcome when the two women invited him to speak to the National Woman Suf-

Frederick Douglass, famous abolitionist and ally to the suffrage movement (Library of Congress Prints and Photographs Division Washington, D.C. 20540 USA LC-USZ62-15887)

frage Association. Douglass continued to support woman suffrage, but his primary attention was focused on helping African Americans.

See also Abolitionist Movement, Women in the; Anthony, Susan Brownell; Fifteenth Amendment; Fourteenth Amendment; National Woman Suffrage Association; Seneca Falls Convention; Stanton, Elizabeth Cady; Suffrage

References Foner, ed., *Frederick Douglass on Women's Rights* (1992); McFeely, *Frederick Douglass* (1991).

Drake, Thelma Day (b. 1949)

Republican Thelma Drake of Virginia entered the U.S. House of Representatives on 3 January 2005. Drake became a candidate after the Republican incumbent for the district withdrew from the race following the revelation of questionable activities. Only two months before the November elections, a 12-member committee of Republicans selected Drake to fill the ticket.

Drake's campaign had three themes: cut taxes, increase military spending, and support President George W. Bush's strategy for Iraq. As a member of Congress, she has also worked to keep the Chesapeake Bay fishing industry healthy, especially the shellfish industry. She co-founded and co-chairs the Congressional Shellfish Caucus.

Drake served as a delegate to the Virginia state house of delegates from 1996 to 2004. Her strong anti-tax positions as a delegate contributed to her selection as a congressional candidate. A realtor, her other priorities included land and real estate issues, including sponsorship of changes to the Virginia Landlord Tenant Act. She also sought to deny illegal aliens in-state tuition for Virginia colleges and universities.

Born in Elyria, Ohio, Drake graduated from high school in 1967.

References http://drake.house.gov; *Virginian Pilot* (Norfolk, Virginia), 1 September 2004; 3 November 2004; 5 January 2005.

Duniway, Abigail Jane Scott (1834–1915)

Regarded as the single most important suffrage worker in Washington, Oregon, and Idaho, newspaper publisher Abigail Duniway campaigned for woman suffrage for almost forty years. Duniway became active in the suffrage movement in 1871 when she began publishing *The New Northwest*, a newspaper dedicated to woman suffrage, and lecturing on the subject, traveling through the area by riverboat, stagecoach and on horseback.

Duniway led efforts to found the Oregon Equal Suffrage Association in 1873 and was instrumental in gaining the territorial legislature's approval of woman suffrage measures. The electorate, however, defeated the woman suffrage amendment in 1884, 1906, and 1910. The failure in 1906 was particularly difficult because Duniway had become the center of intense conflicts over strategies for passing the amendment, and National American Woman Suffrage Association leader Carrie Chapman Catt and Oregon suffrage leaders faulted Duniway for the loss.

Oregon passed woman suffrage in 1912, but by that time Duniway's health had deteriorated, and her involvement in the campaign was minimal. She was, however, given a significant amount of credit for the achievement, primarily out of respect for her years of dedication to woman suffrage. After its passage, Duniway wrote the suffrage proclamation, signed it with the governor, and became the state's first registered woman voter.

Abigail Scott Duniway was the first woman in Oregon to register to vote, 1912 (Library of Congress Prints and Photographs Division Washington, D.C. 20540 USA LC-USZ61-787)

Born in Tazewell County, Illinois, Abigail Duniway immigrated to Oregon with her family in 1852.

> **See also** Catt, Carrie Clinton Lane Chapman; Congressional Union; Married Women's Property Acts; National American Woman Suffrage Association; Suffrage
>
> **References** Moynihan, *Rebel for Rights: Abigail Scott Duniway* (1983).

Dunn, Jennifer Blackburn (b. 1941)

Republican Jennifer Dunn of Washington served in the U.S. House of Representatives from 3 January 1993 to 3 January 2005. Dunn held the fifth-highest ranking leadership position of vice chair of the House Republican Conference in the 105th Congress (1997–1999). Congresswoman Dunn criticized the Internal Revenue Service's practices, characterized the agency as overzealous, and accused it of trampling on citizens' rights. She sought to close the gender gap by explaining the ways that Republican Party policies affect women. She helped develop the welfare reform package in 1996, sought tax relief for the middle class, and worked to help small and family-owned businesses. She was among the leaders in the repeal of the estate tax in 2001. Congresswoman Dunn did not seek re-election in 2004.

Dunn entered politics as a campaign volunteer and became more active as her children grew up. Chair of the Washington state Republican Party from 1981 to 1992, she chaired the association of Republican state party chairs from 1988 to 1991.

Born in Seattle, Washington, Dunn attended Stanford University in 1959 and the University of Washington from 1960 to 1962, and earned her bachelor of arts in English literature from Stanford University in 1963. Following graduation, she was a systems engineer for IBM from 1964 to 1969. She worked for the King County Department of Assessments from 1978 to 1980.

> **See also** Congress, Women in; Gender Gap; Welfare
>
> **References** *Congressional Quarterly, Politics in America 1994* (1993), *Politics in America 1998* (1997); "Rep. Jennifer Dunn," *CQ Weekly*, 28 December 2002, p. 39 ; www.house.gov/dunn/bio.htm.
>
> **Document** Jennifer Dunn, "What the GOP Does for Women," 1996

Duren v. Missouri (1979)

In Taylor v. Louisiana, decided in 1975, the U.S. Supreme Court had found that a jury selection process that required women to notify the courts of their willingness to serve was unconstitutional. The Court decided in *Duren v. Missouri* that a jury selection process that permitted women to easily decline jury service was also unconstitutional.

The Sixth Amendment requires that jurors be selected from a "fair-cross-section" of the community. In Jackson County, Missouri, the jury selection process began with an annual questionnaire sent to randomly selected voters. The questionnaire included a section addressed to women instructing those who wished to avoid jury duty to complete the section, which would exempt them. Of the potential jurors in this case, less than 10 percent were women.

The Court noted women's traditional responsibilities for children and families, but did not make it gender-based, stating: "We recognize that a State may have an important interest in assuring that those members of the family responsible for the care of children are available to do so. An exemption appropriately tailored to this interest would, we think, survive a fair-cross-section challenge."

References *Duren v. Missouri*, 439 U.S. 357 (1979)

Durr, Virginia Heard Foster (1903–1999)

Called "the white matriarch of the civil rights movement," Virginia Foster Durr began her life as a Southern belle in Alabama, living in the world of contradictions that confronted white women in the racist South of the early twentieth century. After attending Wellesley College for two years, Durr married Clifford Durr, a lawyer who became part of President Franklin Delano Roosevelt's New Deal. Their move to Washington, D.C., led to Virginia Durr meeting Eleanor Roosevelt and joining her in efforts to end the poll tax, a tax that served to disenfranchise African Americans. Virginia Durr also became friends with Mary McLeod Bethune, the most prominent African American in the Roosevelt administration, and Mary Church Terrell, the first president of the National Association of Colored Women. Through these two women, Virginia Durr's acceptance of racism ended and her journey to becoming a civil rights activist began.

The Durrs returned to Alabama in 1951 and Virginia Durr soon joined the only interracial political group in Montgomery, Alabama. Through her activism, Durr met Rosa Parks, who started the Montgomery bus boycott in 1955. The Durrs helped arrange her release on bail, and Virginia Durr began a decade of involvement with the civil rights movement. Over the years, she housed civil rights workers and endured social ostracism by the white community.

Virginia Durr unsuccessfully ran for the United States Senate in Virginia on the Progressive Party ticket in 1948.

See also Bethune, Mary McLeod; Civil Rights Movement, Women in the; Parks, Rosa; Terrell, Mary Church

References *Los Angeles Times*, 26 February 1999; Lynne Olson, *Freedom's Daughters: The Unsung Heroines of the Civil Rights Movement from 1830 to 1970* (2001); *The New York Times*, 26 February 1999; *The Washington Post*, 25 February 1999.

Dworkin, Andrea Rita (1946–2005)

Feminist lecturer and author Andrea Dworkin has worked with lawyer Catharine MacKinnon to enact laws that classify pornography as a form of sex discrimination. They have drafted legislation that has served as a model for measures passed in several cities, but all of them were vetoed or rejected by courts. The only measure that has survived court review was enacted in Canada.

Dworkin's first book, *Woman Hating: A Radical Look at Sexuality* (1974), explored men's dominance of women in Western and Eastern cultures. Its generalizations about men as violent and oppressive created controversies both inside and outside the feminist movement. In her book *Pornography: Men Possessing Women* (1981), she argued that the violence portrayed in pornography leads men to violence against women. The controversy surrounding Dworkin's stand on pornography centers on the limitations that it would place on free speech rights. Among Dworkin's other works are *Pornography Is a Civil Rights Issue for Women* (1986) and the novel *Ice and Fire* (1986).

Born in Camden, New Jersey, Dworkin earned her bachelor's degree from Bennington College in 1968.

> **See also** MacKinnon, Catharine Alice; Pornography
>
> **References** H. W. Wilson, *Current Biography Yearbook 1994* (1994); *The New York Times*, 12 April 2005.

Dwyer, Florence Price (1902–1976)

Republican Florence Dwyer of New Jersey served in the U.S. House of Representatives from 3 January 1957 to 3 January 1973. Dwyer's mother encouraged her to become interested in politics in 1920, the first year of woman suffrage, and Dwyer became active in local and county Republican organizations, served as legislative chair for Business and Professional Women/USA, and worked to get women appointed to government positions. She also lobbied the state legislature for garden clubs and parent-teacher groups.

Secretary to the majority leader of the New Jersey assembly in 1947, she served in the New Jersey House of Representatives from 1950 to 1956. While there, she successfully worked for a measure for equal pay for women and sponsored the first statewide minimum salary schedule for teachers.

In Congress, Dwyer supported consumer rights issues, working with Leonor Sullivan on the Fair Credit Protection Act, an attempt to remove discrimination in lending policies, and was a chief sponsor of the measure that created the Consumer Protection Agency. A leader in the passage of the Equal Pay Act of 1963, Dwyer challenged several provisions in it that she believed subverted the law's intent. She also believed that the bill had too many exclusions because domestic workers, retail workers, and others were not covered by the law. One of the Republican congresswomen who met with President Richard Nixon in 1969, she tried to convince him to help end discrimination against women and lobbied him to establish the Office of Women's Rights and Responsibilities within the Office of the President. Instead, Nixon created a task force, which produced a report that he only reluctantly released because he found it too controversial. She retired from her seat in 1973.

Born in Reading, Pennsylvania, Dwyer attended the University of Toledo and special classes at Rutgers Law School.

> **See also** Congress, Women in; Equal Pay Act of 1963; Equal Rights Amendment; State Legislatures, Women in; Sullivan, Leonor Kretzer
>
> **References** *The New York Times*, 1 March 1976; Office of the Historian, U.S. House of Representatives, *Women in Congress, 1917–1990* (1991); Tomlinson, "Making Their Way: A Study of New Jersey Congresswomen, 1924–1994" (1996).

E

Eagle Forum

Founded in 1975 by Phyllis Schlafly, Eagle Forum seeks to develop and dominate the agenda for conservative women. Eagle Forum works at the local, state, and national levels on a wide range of issues. It opposes equal rights amendments, pay equity, abortion rights, affirmative action, gay rights, bilingual education, and government-sponsored child day care. It also opposes setting national standards for education, teaching evolutionary theories, and educating students about sex and about death. In addition, it opposes the expansion of the North Atlantic Treaty Organization (NATO), the use of U.S. troops in United Nations or NATO actions, and statehood for Puerto Rico and the District of Columbia.

Eagle Forum supports deployment of an anti-ballistic missile defense, establishing English as the official language, and making health insurance tax deductible for individuals. It also supports the right to keep and bear arms, congressional action to "curb the Imperial Judiciary by refusing to confirm activist judges," and congressional action to repeal federal laws that "diminish the Tenth Amendment." In addition, Eagle Forum supports requiring identification for voters, "cleaning up registration rolls," and enforcing ballot security.

With more than 80,000 members, Eagle Forum's strength comes from its extensive grassroots network, including chapters in all fifty states and Australia. The national office is in Alton, Illinois, where Schlafly resides, and the group has an office in Washington, D.C. Eagle Forum participates in congressional and state legislative hearings, monitors votes, makes recommendations to state and federal legislators, and provides information to legislative staffs. Letter-writing campaigns, press releases, and demonstrations are other strategies used.

See also Abortion; Equal Rights Amendment; Reproductive Rights; Schlafly, Phyllis Stewart; Stop ERA

References http://www.eagleforum.org/miscdescript/html.

East, Catherine Shipe (1916–1996)

A federal government researcher and feminist, Catherine East's activism spanned from the President's Commission on the Status of Women (1961–1963), through the founding of the National Organization for Women and the 1977 National Women's Conference, and continued with membership on the board of the National Women's Conference Committee. She worked for the U.S. Civil Service Commission from 1939 to 1963, beginning her career as a junior civil service examiner and advancing to chief of the career service division, and worked for the Department of Labor until 1977. Her position in the Department of Labor gave her access to facts on employment practices and workplace discrimination and other insights into women's status.

East served as a technical adviser to the President's Commission on the Status of Women and helped research and write its report, American Women, released in 1963. Following the completion of the commission's work, President John F. Kennedy established the Interdepartmental Committee on the Status of Women and the Citizens' Advisory Council on the Status of Women in 1963 and appointed East to serve as executive secretary of both groups.

East was part of an informal Washington, D.C. feminist network whose members were mostly women who had long careers in the federal government and who fully realized the limitations placed on them because of their sex. She knew dozens of women who were concerned about sex discrimination and who became involved in the feminist movement. East insisted that women needed an organization comparable to the National Association for the Advancement of Colored People and encouraged Betty Friedan and other women to create one, but she believed that her position as a federal employee prevented her from taking a visible part. As Friedan and others formed the National Organization for Women, East provided the organizers with the information they needed.

Born in Barboursville, West Virginia, East earned her bachelor's degree at Marshall University in 1943 and did post-graduate work at George Washington University from 1942 to 1944.

> **See also** Citizens' Advisory Council on the Status of Women; Equal Rights Amendment; Friedan, Betty Naomi Goldstein; National Association for the Advancement of Colored People, Women in the; National Organization for Women; President's Commission on the Status of Women; Sex Discrimination
>
> **References** Carabillo, Meuli, and Csida, *Feminist Chronicles, 1953–1993* (1993); *The New York Times*, 20 August 1996.

Eastman, Crystal (1881–1928)

Feminist, socialist, peace activist, lawyer, and industrial safety pioneer, Crystal Eastman completed the first in-depth sociological study of industrial accidents ever undertaken. Eastman began her career investigating working conditions and studying more than 1,000 industrial accidents, research that she reported in her book *Work Accidents and the Law* (1910). Arguing that industrial accidents occurred because employers neglected to protect workers' safety and health, she sought to convince policymakers that workers' compensation was a legitimate and reasonable form of economic protection. Appointed in 1909 to the New York State Commission on Employers' Liability and Causes of Industrial Accidents, Unemployment, and Lack of Farm Labor, Eastman

*Crystal Eastman, suffragist, peace activist, and advocate for workers'
rights, receiving a Western Union telegram (Library of Congress Prints
and Photographs Division Washington, D.C. 20540 USA
LC-DIG-ggbain-20386)*

served as secretary of the commission, drafted the state's first workers' compensation
law, and helped pass the measure. Eastman left the commission in 1911. When World
War I began in Europe, Eastman helped organize and chaired the Woman's Peace Party of New York. She was also executive director and a founder of the American Union
Against Militarism (AUAM), a group that sought to keep the United States out of
World War I. AUAM helped avoid war with Mexico in 1917, when the organization
pressured President Woodrow Wilson to seek an alternative, and he appointed a commission that mediated the differences. After the United States entered World War I,
Eastman helped organize the Civil Liberties Bureau of AUAM to protect the rights of
conscientious objectors. Her commitment to civil liberties in a time of war created
tensions within AUAM and contributed to its demise.

A suffragist, Eastman was campaign manager for Wisconsin's failed 1912 campaign,
and she helped organize the Congressional Union in 1913. When the National Woman's Party (NWP) developed out of the Congressional Union in 1920, Eastman strongly supported the equal rights movement championed by NWP, a position that most
social reformers of the era did not share with her. They supported protective labor legislation for women and feared that it would be lost with the adoption of an equal
rights amendment. Eastman, however, maintained that protective labor legislation
protected male unionists who did not want to compete with women for jobs. She also
argued that the legislation supported capitalist power by blocking unity between male
and female workers.

Born in Marlborough, Massachusetts, Crystal Eastman graduated from Vassar College in 1903. She earned her master's degree in sociology from Columbia University in 1904 and her bachelor of law degree from New York University Law School in 1907.

References Cook, ed., *Crystal Eastman on Women and Revolution* (1978); Whitman, ed., *American Reformers* (1985).

Echaveste, Maria (b. 1954)

One of the highest-ranking Hispanics in President Bill Clinton's administration, Maria Echaveste served as assistant to the president and deputy chief of staff from 1998 to 2001. In those positions, she managed policy initiatives, developed legislative and communications strategies for the White House, and coordinated the selection of senior administration appointments. In 1997, she served as director of the U.S. Office of

President Clinton's Latino Appointees. Deputy White House Chief of Staff Maria Echaveste is to the right of President Clinton

Public Liaison, a job she described as being "the eyes and ears of the president." She listened to constituencies' concerns, communicated them to the president, and helped him develop support for his programs among the relevant constituencies. She played an important role in restoring food stamp benefits to legal immigrants, helped pass legislation protecting a group of Guatemalans and Nicaraguans from deportation, and worked to make bankruptcy reform less harmful to women and children. On the importance of having a voice in policymaking, she explains: "If people are trying to make decisions on policy matters, and you're not at the proverbial table saying here's how the constituencies feel about this, you're making policy decisions in a vacuum."

Echaveste began her work in the Clinton administration in 1993 as head of the Wage and Hours Division of the Labor Department, where she sought out and investigated sweatshops operating in the United States. A raid in 1995 on one sweatshop revealed dozens of Thai laborers working in conditions described as near slavery. She pursued the issue of sweatshops and attempted to make major retailers accountable for their suppliers' employment policies. She also enlisted talk show host Kathie Lee Gifford and her husband in the crusade against sweatshops and for garment industry reforms.

Born in Harlingen, Texas, Echaveste grew up in California, the daughter of farm-workers. As a child, she picked strawberries in the fields of the San Joaquin Valley and Ventura County. She earned her bachelor's degree from Stanford University in 1976 and her law degree from the University of California at Berkeley in 1980. She worked in private law practice until she joined the Clinton administration in 1993.

References *Los Angeles Times*, 3 March 1996, 27 April 1997; "The Deputy," *The New Republic*, 20 July 1998, p. 11.

Ecofeminism

With its roots in the words "ecology" and "feminism," ecofeminism identifies a correlation or parallel between the domination of women and the domination of the environment. This definition, however, is inadequate because ecofeminism describes both a philosophy and the basis for groups, both informal and organized, seeking to influence policy.

The philosophical component is multifaceted. Feminists who seek spirituality through nature-based religions, such as paganism and goddess worship, call themselves ecofeminists because these categories of religion often have strong female deities. Another group of ecofeminists equates women and nature, suggesting that in places that women are degraded, nature will also be degraded. Another aspect of it suggests that ecofeminism provides an approach to examining racism.

An international movement, ecofeminism began in the United States in the 1970s. A conference in 1980 by three women involved in the antinuclear, feminist, environmental, and lesbian-feminist movements attracted more than 650 women. Held at Amherst College, the conference included panels on organizing, feminist theory, art, health, militarism, racism, urban ecology, and other topics. Other conferences have followed. Ecofeminists are credited with influencing policy at the 1992 United Nations Conference on Environment and Development, held in Rio de Janeiro.

Reference Noël Sturgeon, *Ecofeminist Natures: Race, Gender, Feminist Theory, and Political Action* (New York: Routledge, 1997), pp. 23–29.

Economic Equity Act

Introduced by the Congressional Caucus for Women's Issues in 1981, the Economic Equity Act is a package of proposals that seeks to improve women's economic status. Revised and reintroduced each session of Congress, the act addresses policies involving insurance, taxes, retirement, child care, access to credit, education, and related issues. Of the more than 100 bills that have been part of the package, several have been enacted, many of them as parts of other bills.

Among the measures that Congress has passed are tax credits for day care programs (1981); the Retirement Equity Act (1984), expanding pension coverage for employees who leave and subsequently return to their jobs, and requiring pension plans to provide survivor benefits to spouses of vested employees, even if they have not reached retirement age; the Child Support Amendments of 1984; child care in public housing (1988); the Women in Apprenticeship and Nontraditional Occupations Act (1992); and the Women and Minorities in Science and Mathematics Act (1992).

See also Child Support Enforcement

References Burrell, *A Woman's Place Is in the House: Campaigning for Congress in the Feminist Era* (1994); *Congressional Quarterly Almanac, 98th Congress, 2nd Session . . . 1984* (1985).

Edelman, Marian Wright (b. 1939)

Marian Wright Edelman is the founder and president of the Children's Defense Fund, the primary federal advocate for the rights of children. She believes that children's issues are "central to the security and well-being of America." A leading congressional adviser on children's and family issues, Edelman has been referred to as "the 101st Senator." She was the first African American woman admitted to the Mississippi bar.

Born in rural Bennettsville, South Carolina, when racial segregation placed formidable barriers in every aspect of life for African Americans, Marian Wright Edelman's family taught her to believe in herself. Raised in a family that cherished education, she attended Spelman College, studied one summer at the Sorbonne in Paris, and spent her junior year at the University of Geneva in Switzerland in preparation for a career in the foreign service.

When she returned to the United States, she became involved in the civil rights movement and was arrested during a sit-in at Atlanta's City Hall in 1960, an experience that made her aware of the need for civil rights lawyers. She decided to become a lawyer and earned her law degree from Yale University in 1963. After training with the National Association for the Advancement of Colored People in New York for a year, she moved to Mississippi to practice. The site of intense civil rights activity, Mississippi had only five African American lawyers and 900,000 black people. Edelman also served on the board of the Child Development Group of Mississippi (CDGM), an organization that ran a Head Start program, offered health programs, and provided other services. When CDGM's funding was threatened, Edelman successfully lobbied Congress for the funds.

Marian Wright Edelman, founder and president of the Children's Defense Fund

In 1973 Edelman launched the Children's Defense Fund (CDF), a research and advocacy organization. CDF has investigated the treatment of institutionalized children, juvenile justice, infant mortality, homelessness, prenatal care, nutrition, the school dropout rate, child abuse, and teen pregnancy. In addition, it has lobbied for foster care reform, child care, and Head Start funding. Edelman once explained: "Everybody loves children. Everybody is for them in general. Everybody kisses them in elections.... But when they get into the budget rooms, or behind closed doors–to really decide how they're going to carve up money–children get lost in the process because they are not powerful." A notable lobbyist, she has enlisted both liberal and conservative members of Congress in her cause.

Edelman is the author of *Families in Peril: An Agenda for Social Change* (1987) and *The Measure of Our Success: A Letter to My Children and Yours* (1992), a collection of personal essays.

> **See also** Children's Defense Fund
>
> **References** Bouton, "Marian Wright Edelman" (1987); H. W. Wilson, *Current Biography Yearbook, 1992* (1992); Viorst, "The Woman behind the First Lady" (1993).
>
> **Document** Marion Wright Edelman, "Educating the Black Child: Our Past and Our Future," 1987

Education Amendments of 1972, Title IX

Title IX of the Education Amendments of 1972 prohibits institutions receiving federal funds from practicing gender discrimination in educational programs or activities. Enforced by the Office for Civil Rights in the U.S. Department of Education, it was the first comprehensive federal law to prohibit sex discrimination against students and employees in these institutions.

Until the passage of the Education Amendments of 1972, the United States had no national policy regarding women and girls in education. Title VI of the Civil Rights Act of 1964 prohibited discrimination in education on the basis of race, color, and national origin but did not include sex. Although Title VII of the act prohibited discrimination on the basis of sex, it applied only to employment. The law's silence permitted public colleges and universities the option of refusing even to admit women. For example, Virginia state law prohibited women from being admitted to the College of Arts and Sciences of the University of Virginia, the most highly rated public institution of higher education in Virginia. It was only under a court order that the college admitted its first woman in 1970.

Married women also experienced legal discrimination in education, regardless of their family's status. One example occurred in 1966, when Luci Baines Johnson, daughter of President Lyndon Johnson, applied for readmission to Georgetown University after her marriage. The university denied her application because the school did not accept married women students.

Institutions of higher education that admitted women had no legal requirements to provide women with educational or program opportunities comparable to those offered to men. Significant differences existed in athletic and sports programs available to women and men at most colleges and universities. For example, men's football and basketball teams held center stage on many campuses, but women's sports programs were neglected, if they existed at all. A Connecticut judge explained in 1971: "Athletic competition builds character in our boys. We do not need that kind of character in our girls."

Feminist leaders objected to this form of legal discrimination on the basis of sex, at least in part because many of them were well-educated, middle-class women who valued education. Bernice Sandler, who was active in the Women's Equity Action League (WEAL), took a leading role in exploring ways to end sex discrimination in education. In 1970, Sandler used President Lyndon Johnson's Executive Order 11375 as the basis for a class action suit that WEAL filed. The executive order prohibited discrimination, including on the basis of sex, by all federal contractors, including educational institutions. In its suit, WEAL asked for reviews of all institutions with federal contracts, filed suit against 260 institutions, and later filed suit against all medical schools in the country. Sandler's actions prompted Congresswoman Martha Griffiths (D-MI) to give the first speech in Congress on gender discrimination in education.

Also in 1970, WEAL advisory board member and Democratic congresswoman Edith Green of Oregon held congressional hearings on sex discrimination in education, the first devoted to the topic. WEAL assisted Green with the hearings by recommending individuals to provide testimony and in other ways. After the hearings, Green asked Sandler to join the committee staff and assemble the written record of the hearings, making Sandler the first person ever appointed to the staff of a congressional committee to work specifically in the area of women's rights. The resulting two volumes, more than 1,000 pages total, concretely established the facts of sex discrimination in education; after Green had thousands of copies printed and distributed, they provided evidence for other activists to use in their advocacy for educational equity. In 1971, members of Congress responded to the hearings by introducing several plans to prohibit sex discrimination in education, but it took several months to negotiate a plan for accomplishing the goal.

The Education Amendments of 1972 apply to all schools from preschool through graduate and professional schools and prohibit any education program receiving federal funds from discriminating on the basis of sex. Educational institutions are prohibited from having different admissions or other standards for women and men and from discriminating against married women, pregnant women, and women with children. Girls and women began gaining access to athletic facilities equal to those granted to men, became eligible for athletic scholarships, and obtained equal opportunities to engage in sports. The law requires schools to have teams for males and teams for females in any given sport, or if there is no girls' team in a sport, they must be permitted to try out for boys' teams.

In 1984, the U.S. Department of Justice sought to enforce the broad scope of Title IX, but in *Grove City College v. Bell* the U.S. Supreme Court ruled that Title IX was program-specific, meaning that only those programs within institutions that received federal funds had to comply with Title IX. With the passage of the Civil Rights Restoration Act of 1988, however, Congress made the institutions, not just directly funded programs, responsible for compliance with Title IX. The U.S. Supreme Court expanded Title IX in *Franklin v. Gwinnett County Public Schools* (1992) by ruling that sexually harassed students could sue for monetary awards.

Some statistics suggest that Title IX has made a difference in women's educational prospects. In 1973, 43 percent of female high school graduates ages sixteen to twenty-four were enrolled in college; in 1994, 63 percent were. In 1972, women earned 1 percent of dental degrees; in 1994, women earned 38 percent of them. In 1972, women comprised 15 percent of college student athletes, compared to 37 percent in 1995. In 1971, 300,000 high school girls (7.5 percent of all high school athletes) participated in athletics; in 1996, 2.4 million girls (39 percent of all high school athletes) participated.

In the late 1990s, female athletes at educational institutions, however, continued to find that their opportunities for scholarships were fewer than those for male athletes, that their coaches were paid less than male athletes' coaches, and that throughout their school's athletic programs they were likely to find substantial differences in the women's athletic programs and the men's athletic programs.

See also Affirmative Action; Civil Rights Act of 1964, Title VII; *Davis v. Monroe County School Board of Education* (1999); Education, Women and; Executive Order 11375; *Franklin v. Gwinnett County Public Schools* (1992); Green, Edith Starrett; *Grove City College v. Bell*; Sexual Harassment; Women's Equity Action League

References Baer, *Women in American Law: The Struggle Toward Equality from the New Deal to the Present* (1996); *Congressional Quarterly Almanac, 92nd Congress, 2nd Session... 1972* (1973); Hankerson, "Courts Have Extended Sex Bias Law's Reach" (1999); Wandersee, *American Women in the 1970s: On the Move* (1988); www.ed.gov; www.edc.org.

Document Secretary Margaret Spellings, "Remarks to the First National Summit on the Advancement of Girls in Math and Science"

Education, Women and

Women have sought to create educational opportunities and to open established institutions to women since the colonial era. Until the 1820s, women's educational opportunities were limited to dame schools that generally taught domestic arts, literature, and languages but not philosophy, higher math, or the sciences. In 1821, Emma Hart Willard (1787–1870) founded the first women's college-level institution in the United States, Troy Female Seminary in Troy, New York. The school gained a strong reputation for developing schoolteachers, one of the few occupations open to women at the time. Another crusader for women's education, Catharine Beecher (1800–1878), opened the Western Female Institute in Cincinnati, Ohio, in 1832 and devoted her life to promoting women's educational opportunity and to training and recruiting teachers for schools on the American frontier.

Mary Lyon (1797–1849) opened Mount Holyoke Female Seminary in 1837 and offered a three-year program. The school became Mount Holyoke College in 1861, when it became a four-year institution. Other four-year women's colleges followed over the next decades, beginning with Vassar College in 1865 and Smith College and Wellesley College in 1875. In addition, most state colleges admitted women. By the 1890s, an influential group of educated women had developed, working as health professionals, social reformers, and teachers.

Several federal programs expanded educational opportunities for women and men in the 1960s, including financial assistance, an increase in vocational education options, and new community college campuses and programs. Other barriers remained. The elite private law schools and medical schools that admitted women often placed quotas on the number of women they accepted, public and private institutions established different admissions standards for women and men, and some schools did not accept married women or women with children.

A fundamental change in women's access to higher education came with passage of Title IX of the Education Amendments of 1972. Its prohibitions against gender discrimination at institutions receiving federal funding gave women equal access to college admissions, enlarged women's educational options, and enhanced women's athletic programs.

See also Affirmative Action; American Association of University Women; Education Amendments of 1972, Title IX; Women's Educational Equity Act of 1974; Women's Equity Action League

References Evans, *Born for Liberty: A History of Women in America* (1989); Mead and Kaplan, eds., *American Women: The Report of the President's Commission on the Status of Women and Other Publications of the Commission* (1965).

Edwards, Elaine Lucille Schwartzenburg (b. 1929)

Democrat Elaine Edwards of Louisiana served in the U.S. Senate from 1 August 1972 to 13 November 1972. When the death of one of Louisiana's senators created a vacancy, Governor Edwin Edwards appointed his wife Elaine Edwards to fill it. She made it clear that she would not run for a full term when she accepted the appointment.

Elaine Edwards was born in Marksville, Louisiana.

See also Congress, Women in

References Office of the Historian, U.S. House of Representatives, *Women in Congress, 1917–1990* (1991).

Edwards, India Moffett (1895–1990)

India Edwards served as executive director of the Women's Division of the Democratic National Committee (DNC) from 1948 to 1952 and then served as a vice chair of the party. One of the few politicians who believed that President Harry Truman would win in 1948, Edwards became part of his political inner circle.

A *Chicago Tribune* writer and editor for more than twenty years, Edwards left the paper in 1942 and moved to Washington, D.C., with her husband. After learning that her son, an Army Air Force flier, had been a passenger on a bomber that exploded in late 1943, Edwards became involved in the war effort, but it was a comment made by Clare Boothe Luce at the 1944 Republican National Convention that moved Edwards into political activism. Luce suggested that if the United States' dead soldiers could vote, they would vote against President Franklin D. Roosevelt. Outraged that Luce would presume to speak for her son, Edwards volunteered at the DNC in 1944 and wrote speeches for the party and for candidates. She joined the DNC staff as executive secretary of the Women's Division in 1945.

When President Harry Truman campaigned on his whistle-stop tour in 1948, Edwards traveled with him, the first woman to travel with a presidential campaign who was not a secretary or a relative of the candidate. She encouraged other women to join the tour as it passed through their areas, an innovation that recognized women's contributions to the campaign and enhanced women's support for Truman, as did her strategy of focusing attention on inflation and blaming it on Republicans in Congress.

After Truman's election in 1948, Edwards brought potential women appointees to Truman's attention. Through an informal network of women across the nation, Edwards learned of qualified women, keeping files on them and their abilities. Through a comparable network of women in government, Washington hostesses, reporters, secretaries, and friends, she learned of potential job openings. By the time a position opened, Edwards often had identified a woman candidate for it, gained the approval of one of the woman's U.S. senators, and prepared to propose her candidacy to Truman. Edwards's influence contributed to the appointment of the first woman ambassador (Eugenie Moore Anderson to Denmark), five women federal judges, Georgia Neese Clark as treasurer of the United States, Perle Mesta as minister to Luxembourg, and Frieda Hennock to the Federal Communications Commission—more women than any other president had appointed to top positions in the federal government. Edwards's self-appointed tasks included following the appointment process through Senate confirmation. When the Senate delayed Hennock's confirmation, Edwards canceled a planned vacation and began making deals with senators. The Senate confirmed Hennock's appointment. Truman asked Edwards to become DNC chair in 1951, but she declined, feeling that the party was not ready for a woman chairman. She later regretted the decision.

In 1952, the party chose a new chairman who announced that the Women's Division would be integrated into the regular party, in what some observers regarded as an attempt to deny Edwards her base of influence. Edwards persevered until October 1953, when the chairman announced her resignation and her replacement.

Edwards's first political experience was marching with her mother in a suffrage parade when she was still a young child in Chicago.

See also Anderson, Eugenie Moore; Clark Gray, Georgia Neese; Democratic Party, Women in the; Luce, Clare Boothe

References Edwards, *Pulling No Punches* (1977); H. W. Wilson, *Current Biography: Who's News and Why, 1949* (1949); Morgan, "India Edwards" (1984).

Eisenhuth Alming, Laura J. Kelly (1858–1937)

The first American woman elected to a statewide office, Laura Eisenhuth served as North Dakota's superintendent of public instruction from 1893 to 1895. Although she was born in Canada, Eisenhuth's family moved to Iowa in 1860. Eisenhuth obtained her education in Iowa and taught in that state's schools for eleven years. She moved to North Dakota in 1887 and in 1889 was elected Foster County superintendent of schools.

Eisenhuth received the Democratic Party's nomination for state superintendent of schools in 1890, but lost in the general election. Nominated again in 1892 by both the Democratic Party and the Independent Party, she won the general election. During her two-year term in office, Eisenhuth sought to professionalize teacher education, recommended that schools in towns with water systems install bath tubs, and advocated improvements in school buildings and grounds, including fencing of school grounds. Nominated by the Democratic and Populist parties in 1894, Eisenhuth lost in the general election to another woman, Emma Bates.

Eisenstadt v. Baird (1972)

In *Eisenstadt v. Baird*, the U.S. Supreme Court invalidated a Massachusetts law that prohibited the distribution of contraceptive drugs, medicines, or devices to unmarried people. The Court said that by treating married and unmarried people differently, the law violated the equal protection clause of the Fourteenth Amendment.

See also *Carey v. Population Services International*; *Griswold v. Connecticut*

References *Eisenstadt v. Baird*, 405 U.S. 438 (1972).

Elders, Joycelyn (b. 1933)

Joycelyn Elders served as U.S. surgeon general from 1993 to 1994, the second woman and the first African American to hold the office. From the time of her nomination, controversy surrounded Elders's appointment. Conservatives objected to her emphasis on sex education, contraception, and abortion and called her the condom queen, but the Senate confirmed her appointment. During her tenure in office, Elders sought to move the nation from sick care to health care by working toward a preventive health care system. She worked to reduce tobacco use and to eliminate drug and alcohol abuse, advocated legalizing the abortifacient RU-486, and renewed efforts to stop the acquired immunodeficiency syndrome (AIDS) epidemic. Pointing to the 135,000 children who take guns to school, Elders worked for gun control. In addition, she advocated sex education and attempted to reduce teen pregnancy.

Her tenure as surgeon general was marked by two controversial comments that she made in response to questions posed to her. Her suggestion that the legalization of drugs might reduce crime and deserved study provoked intense criticism of her. On another occasion, she told a professional conference that the facts about masturbation could be taught in classes on human sexuality. After the press reported her comments, President Bill Clinton asked for and received her resignation.

Born in Schaal, Arkansas, Elders was given the name Minnie Lee Jones at birth and changed it as an adult. She grew up in a poor family that lived on a farm without running water or electricity. Medical treatment for illnesses and injuries involved herbal and folk remedies, and there was no hospital in the area that treated African Americans, nor was there a doctor who would care for them.

Elders graduated from high school when she was fifteen, received a scholarship to attend Philander Smith College, and earned her bachelor of science degree there in 1952. She enlisted in the Army in 1953, viewing the military's educational benefits as a way to pay for medical training, and served until 1956 when she entered medical school. She earned her medical degree from the University of Arkansas School of Medicine in 1960, her master's degree in biochemistry in 1967, and board certification as a pediatric endocrinologist in 1978.

In 1987, then-Governor Bill Clinton appointed Elders chief health director for Arkansas, making her the first woman and the first African American to hold the office. She increased the immunization rate for children, expanded pregnant women's participation in the state's prenatal care program, and thereby reduced the infant mortality rate. In addition, she increased the availability of testing for human immunodeficiency virus (HIV), expanded breast cancer screenings, and provided more home care for frail or terminally ill patients.

As state health director, Elders gained an expanded awareness of the problems of teen pregnancy. She explained that she "saw the massive suffering of so many bright young black women because of having unplanned and unwanted pregnancies. And I began to realize how much they had been exploited, not only by the religious right but also by their own kind with this talk of contraception and genocide." She cast it in terms of slavery: "If you're poor and ignorant, with a child you're a slave. Meaning that you're never going to get out of it. These women are in a kind of bondage to a kind of slavery that the Thirteenth Amendment just didn't deal with." She viewed sex education as a way to help reduce sexually transmitted diseases, domestic violence, and sexual abuse. Elders made teenage contraception use a central theme in the health department and advocated school-based health clinics and comprehensive health education. Her proposals regularly created controversies.

She wrote her memoir, *Joycelyn Elders, M.D.: From Sharecropper's Daughter to Surgeon General of the United States of America* (1996), after leaving the office of the surgeon general.

See also Abortion

References Elders, *Joycelyn Elders, M.D.: From Sharecropper's Daughter to Surgeon General of the United States of America* (1996); H. W. Wilson, *Current Biography Yearbook, 1994* (1994); *The New York Times*, 30 January 1994, 6 June 1996, 24 October 1996.

Emerson, Jo Ann (b. 1950)

Jo Ann Emerson of Missouri entered the U.S. House of Representatives on 5 November 1996, elected as a Republican to fill the vacancy created by the death of her husband, Norvell William (Bill) Emerson, a Republican. Jo Ann Emerson also ran in the general election, but as an Independent because the filing deadline for the 1996 general elections had passed before her husband's death. On 8 January 1997, she changed her party affiliation from Independent to Republican and ran as a Republican in the 1998 and subsequent elections.

In 1996, Jo Ann Emerson campaigned as "Team Emerson," pledging to continue her husband's fight to improve Missouri's highways and to support constitutional amendments to make flag burning illegal, permit voluntary prayer in public schools, impose term limits, and require a two-thirds majority of both chambers of Congress to raise taxes. She favors balancing the budget, saving Medicare from bankruptcy, expanding health care reforms, and expanding U.S. exports. She is pro-life and supports gun owners' rights, private property owners' rights, tax relief, local control of schools, and voluntary school prayer.

Congresswoman Emerson has gained a reputation for reaching across party lines to solve problems. She worked with Democrats to allow the importation of prescription drugs, which often cost less than the same drugs in the United States. With Democrat Eva Clayton of North Carolina, she revived the Congressional Rural Caucus, reflecting the agricultural interests in her district. She fought a proposal by the Bush administration that would have threatened rice sales to Cuba, a significant market for the commodity which Missouri grows.

Born in Washington, D.C., Emerson grew up in a political family in the capital area. Her father Ab Herman was executive director of the Republican National Committee and held advisory positions within the party. Emerson received her bachelor's degree from Ohio Wesleyan University in 1972. Deputy director of communications for the National Republican Congressional Committee, she later worked in public affairs for the American Insurance Association and was director of state relations and grassroots programs for the National Restaurant Association.

> **References** *Congressional Quarterly, Politics in America 1998* (1997); Samuel Goldrich, "Rep. Jo Ann Emerson," *CQ Weekly*, 28 December 2002; Forrest Laws, "Emerson Measure Could Halt OFAC Payment Rule," *Delta Farm Press*, 1 July 2005; www.house.gov/emerson/bio.htm.

EMILY's List

Founded in 1985 by Ellen Malcolm, EMILY'S List is a political action committee (PAC) that works to elect pro-choice Democratic women to congressional and gubernatorial office. EMILY's List has helped dozens of women win races for governor, the U.S. House of Representatives, and the U.S. Senate. EMILY's List identifies and recommends viable, pro-choice Democratic women candidates for the U.S. House of Representatives, U.S. Senate, and for governor, and sends profiles of selected candidates to members. Members of EMILY's List pay $100 to belong, and they agree to contribute at least $100 or more to at least two candidates. EMILY's List recruits candidates, provides campaign staff training and referral, offers candidates technical assistance, and mobilizes women voters on election day. In 2006, it had over 100,000 contributors.

EMILY's List had its first success when Democratic congresswoman Barbara Mikulski of Maryland won her U.S. Senate race in 1986. Between the 1986 and 2004 general elections, the group was instrumental in helping eight women win their races for governor, sixty-one women win their races for the U.S. House of Representatives, eleven women win their races for the U.S. Senate, and 216 women win state and local offices. During the 1985–1986 election cycle, the first in which EMILY's List was involved, the group had about 1,200 members and raised more than $350,000. During the 1995–1996 election cycle, 45,000 members contributed $6.7 million to candidates, $2 million for campaign support, and $3 million to WOMEN VOTE!, the group's get-out-the-vote campaign. In the 2004 election cycle, members contributed more than $10 million to pro-choice Democratic women candidates.

EMILY's List launched its program for state and local office candidates, Political Opportunity Program (POP), after the 2000 general elections. POP trains women running, or considering running, for state legislative seats, constitutional office, and local offices. In 2005, POP held 27 training events in 18 states, with 962 women participating. Its Campaign Corps trains recent college graduates to work on progressive races at the local, state, and national level.

Congresswoman Lynn Rivers of Michigan explained the assistance she received: "EMILY's List helped me make the choices, hire the staff and raise the funds I needed to build–from scratch–an outstanding campaign able to win an incredibly tough election in 1994, an incredibly tough year for Democrats." Congresswoman Eva Clayton of North Carolina agreed that the assistance she received was invaluable: "As a woman running in a rural minority district, I knew few of the experts and donors across the country whose support I needed to win. EMILY's List put me in touch with them, and I was off and running."

See also Abortion; Clayton, Eva McPherson; Malcolm, Ellen Reighley; Rivers, Lynn Nancy

References www.emilyslist.org.

Employment Discrimination

Sex discrimination in employment was legal in the United States until passage of Title VII of the Civil Rights Act of 1964. Employers could lawfully refuse to consider hiring a woman for a position, and if she was hired, her employer could provide her different benefits than a man in the same position. Employers could refuse to offer training, advancement, or partnership to the women they employed. Employers could also legally refuse to consider men for employment. Passage of the Equal Pay Act of 1963 made it illegal to pay different wages to women and men performing the same jobs, but employers could assign women to different job titles and pay them less than men.

The U.S. Supreme Court found sex discrimination in employment constitutional when it decided *Bradwell v. Illinois* in 1873. The case resulted from the Illinois Supreme Court's refusal to admit Myra Bradwell to the bar even though she had fulfilled every requirement to practice law. The U.S. Supreme Court said that states could prohibit women from being admitted to the bar, a precedent that also permitted state regulation of women's participation in other occupations. In 1908, the U.S. Supreme Court again found sex discrimination in employment and in state policies constitutional in *Muller v. Oregon*, a case challenging the constitutionality of an Oregon law that limited the number of hours women could work in factories, mechanical establishments, and laundries to ten hours a day. The decision made legal sex discrimination the law of the land. In a third decision, the U.S. Supreme Court found that a state law prohibiting women from being bartenders, unless the women were the wives or daughters of a bar owner, was constitutional in *Goesaert v. Cleary* (1948).

With the passage of Title VII and the Civil Rights Act of 1964, equal employment opportunity became the policy of the nation. Congress created the Equal Employment Opportunity Commission (EEOC) to enforce the policy by responding to complaints filed by aggrieved employees. The EEOC initially resisted responding to sex discrimination complaints, choosing to focus its efforts on race discrimination, but it developed into a significant resource for women. It interpreted the meaning of Title VII, providing a framework for negotiating settlements between employers and employees and for court challenges to the law.

Title VII included an exemption for sex discrimination, the bona fide occupational qualification (BFOQ). It was intended to permit rational forms of sex discrimination such as might apply to models or actors, and the EEOC concluded that it should be narrowly interpreted. Courts rejected limits on the amount of weight employees could lift, an airline's argument that only women could be flight cabin attendants, and other broad interpretations of the BFOQ. The U.S. Supreme Court considered the BFOQ for the first time in *Dothard v. Rawlinson* (1977) and concluded that being male was a BFOQ to be a guard in the male section of a maximum security prison because of safety. It also considered disparate impact in *Dothard*, finding that minimum height and weight requirements violated Title VII.

The U.S. Supreme Court considered its first gender discrimination case under Title VII in *Phillips v. Martin Marietta Corporation* (1971), finding that Martin Marietta's willingness to hire fathers of preschool-age children and its refusal to hire mothers of preschool-age children constituted sex discrimination. Another aspect of parenthood, pregnancy, has resulted in several decisions and congressional action. In *Geduldig v. Aiello* (1974), *General Electric v. Gilbert* (1975), and *Nashville Gas Co. v. Satty* (1977), the Court decided that employee disability plans did not have to include pregnancy. Congress responded by passing the Pregnancy Discrimination Act of 1978, expanding the definition of sex discrimination to protect pregnant workers. When a California employer challenged a state law requiring unpaid leave for pregnant workers, the Court upheld the law in *Guerra v. California Federal Savings and Loan Association*, decided in 1987. Congress established unpaid leave for pregnancy, adoption, and family illness for both men and women in the Family and Medical Leave Act of 1993. The U.S. Supreme Court decided in *UAW v. Johnson Controls* (1991) that employers cannot bar all fertile women from workplaces where they might be exposed to toxic substances, saying that employers must make workplaces safe for all workers. The total number of sex discrimination charges increased from 21,796 in 1992 to 24,362 in 2003.

One of the most persistent and vexing employment challenges has been overcoming obstacles to women earning living wages. In 2003, white men earned an average $715 per week, Asian/Pacific Islander women earned $598 per week, white women $567, African American women $491, and Hispanic women $410. To put it another way, women must work almost sixteen months to earn as much as men earn in one year.

Women tend to cluster in certain occupations—clerical, teaching, service, and nursing among them—that generally pay less than occupations dominated by men. The Equal Pay Act of 1963 addressed the issue of equal pay for equal work, but it did not alter the relative undercompensation for jobs dominated by women when compared to jobs dominated by men. Comparable worth emerged as a strategy for evaluating jobs and establishing a pay rate based on objective criteria instead of tradition, social prejudices, and gender influences. The U.S. Supreme Court has not ruled on comparable worth, but in *County of Washington, Oregon v. Gunther* (1981), it found that an employer who had performed a comparable worth evaluation of jobs, found that jobs dominated by women were underpaid, and did not make adjustments, had violated Title VII.

An employer's consideration of gender when evaluating an employee for promotion led to the U.S. Supreme Court's decision in *Price Waterhouse v. Hopkins* (1989). The Court decided that if an employer would have reached the same conclusion without considering sex, then considering sex did not violate Title VII. Congress overturned the decision in the Civil Rights Act of 1991 by prohibiting the consideration of race, color, religion, sex, or national origin in employment decisions, even if the decision would have been the same without the consideration of those factors. The Civil Rights Act of 1991 also established the Glass Ceiling Commission to investigate "artificial barriers based on attitudinal or organizational biases that prevent qualified women and minorities from advancing upward into management-level positions."

The Court again considered sex discrimination in *Kolstad v. American Dental Association* (1999), concluding that a woman alleging sex discrimination does not have to show that the employer's conduct was "egregious;" only that the employer acted with malice or reckless indifference to the lawfulness of his action. The next year, in *Reeves v. Sanderson Plumbing Products, Inc.*, the Court found that in some circumstances a jury may find gender discrimination when the reasons the employer gives for his choice in hiring are untrue, even though there may not be direct evidence of discrimination.

Sexually offensive behavior by supervisors and coworkers received the U.S. Supreme Court's attention in *Meritor Savings Bank v. Vinson* (1986), the first sexual harassment case the Court considered. A female employee said that she had performed sexual acts for her supervisor because she believed it was the only way to keep her job. The Court found this form of sexual harassment, quid pro quo, to be in violation of Title VII. In *Harris v. Forklift Systems* (1993), the U.S. Supreme Court ruled that employees do not need to show that the offensive sexual behavior left them psychologically damaged or unable to perform their jobs, creating the second form of sexual harassment, hostile environment. In both *Faragher v. City of Boca Raton* (1998) and *Burlington Industries v. Ellerth* (1998), the Court found that when a supervisor sexually harasses a employee and takes "tangible employment action" against the employee, the employer is responsible for the supervisor's actions.

See also Bona Fide Occupational Qualification; *Bradwell v. Illinois*; *California Federal Savings and Loan v. Guerra*; Civil Rights Act of 1964, Title VII; *County of Washington, Oregon v. Gunther*; *Diaz v. Pan American World Airways, Inc.*; *Dothard v. Rawlinson*; Equal Employment Opportunity Commission; Family and Medical Leave Act of 1993; *Geduldig v. Aiello*; *General Electric v. Gilbert*; Glass Ceiling Commission; *Goesaert v. Cleary*; *Harris v. Forklift Systems*; *Hishon v. King and Spalding*; *Meritor Savings Bank v. Vinson*; *Muller v. Oregon*; *Nashville Gas Co. v. Satty*; Pay Equity; *Phillips v. Martin Marietta Corporation*; Pregnancy Discrimination Act of 1978; *Price Waterhouse v. Hopkins*; Sexual Harassment; *UAW v. Johnson Controls*

References Carleton, "Women in the Workplace and Sex Discrimination Law: A Feminist Analysis of Federal Jurisprudence" (1993); *Congressional Quarterly Almanac, 102nd Congress, 1st Session... 1991* (1992); Hoff-Wilson, "The Unfinished Revolution: Changing Legal Status of U.S. Women" (1987), National Partnership for Women and Families, "Women at Work: Looking Behind the Numbers," Washington, D.C.: The National Partnership for Women and Families (2004); http://www.aclu.org/FilesPDFs/wrp%20timeline.pdf.

English, Karan (b. 1949)

Democrat Karan English of Arizona served in the U.S. House of Representatives from 3 January 1993 to 3 January 1995. English decided to run for Congress after watching the U.S. Senate Judiciary Committee's hearings on Anita Hill's allegations that Supreme Court nominee Clarence Thomas had sexually harassed her. The events surrounding the hearings led her to believe that Congress needed more women members. Women's organizations and environmental groups supported her candidacy, and former Republican Senator Barry Goldwater endorsed her. Congresswoman English supported the presidential line item veto and improved management of natural resources. English lost her bid for a second term in 1994.

Concern about local environmental issues led English into politics, beginning with her election to the Coconino County Board of Supervisors, where she served from 1981 to 1987. That year, she entered the Arizona House of Representatives and served until 1991. Elected to the state Senate in 1990, English chaired the chamber's Environment Committee her freshman year and passed measures establishing regulations for handling hazardous waste and requiring environmental education in elementary and high schools.

Born in Berkeley, California, Karan English earned her bachelor's degree from the University of Arizona in 1973.

See also Congress, Women in; Hill, Anita Faye; State Legislatures, Women in

References *Congressional Quarterly, Politics in America 1994* (1993).

Equal Credit Opportunity Act of 1974

The Equal Credit Opportunity Act of 1974 bans credit discrimination on the bases of sex and marital status. Until passage of the act, women encountered significant barriers to obtaining credit, even when they were the primary wage earners in their families. In the case of divorce or death of the husband, the wife generally lacked a credit history of her own because a married woman's accounts were almost always in her husband's name. For example, Congresswoman Lindy Boggs (D-LA), a wealthy woman in her own right, encountered sex discrimination when she attempted to obtain a credit card in her own name following the death of her husband.

After the Equal Credit Opportunity Act was introduced, women's rights groups, including the National Organization for Women, the Women's Equity Action League, the National Women's Political Caucus, and the Center for Women Policy Studies publicized the issue and mobilized other women's groups that had worked together to pass the Equal Rights Amendment. The organizations encouraged women to write to their members of Congress and describe their attempts to obtain credit in their own names as single women or after being married, widowed, or divorced.

In 1976, the act was amended to cover credit discrimination due to age, race, color, religion, national origin, and receipt of public assistance; in 1988 it was expanded to include commercial credit.

See also Boggs, Marie Corinne Morrison Claiborne (Lindy); Equal Rights Amendment; National Organization for Women; National Women's Political Caucus; Women's Equity Action League

References Costain, "Lobbying for Equal Credit" (1979).

Equal Division Rule
See **Democratic Party, Women in the**

Equal Employment Opportunity Act of 1972

The Equal Employment Opportunity Act of 1972 (EEOA) strengthened the Equal Employment Opportunity Commission's (EEOC's) enforcement powers and expanded coverage of Title VII of the Civil Rights Act of 1964 to include more categories of employers. Under the provisions of the Civil Rights Act of 1964, the EEOC could investigate employment discrimination and could negotiate with employers to remedy the problem but had little enforcement authority. The EEOA established an independent general counsel for the EEOC and gave it the power to file charges of job bias against an employer. The act also extended coverage of Title VII to employers that had been previously exempted, including smaller businesses, smaller unions, state and local governments, and colleges and schools.

See also Civil Rights Act of 1964, Title VII; Equal Employment Opportunity Commission

References *Congressional Quarterly Almanac, 92nd Congress, 2nd Session . . . 1972* (1973).

Equal Employment Opportunity Commission

Created by Title VII of the Civil Rights Act of 1964, the Equal Employment Opportunity Commission (EEOC) is charged with enforcing federal laws prohibiting employment discrimination on the basis of race, color, religion, sex, or national origin. In the years since the EEOC was created, Congress has added enforcement of other measures to its responsibilities, including the Age Discrimination in Employment Act of 1967, the Equal Pay Act of 1963, Title I of the Americans with Disabilities Act of 1990, and the Civil Rights Act of 1991.

The commission initially focused its attention on race discrimination as it affected men and disregarded its mandate to address employment discrimination on the basis of sex. The commission's first director dismissed the sex provision of Title VII, calling it a "fluke" that was "conceived out of wedlock" and saying that "men were entitled to female secretaries." Of the five original members appointed to the commission, only Aileen Hernandez was a woman. She described her appointment as a "20 percent nod to more than 50 percent of the population" and noted that "the Commission was not planning to be an example to industry of the meaning of 'equal opportunity employer'" because no women were hired for the top appointments. Hernandez pointed out: "There was such insensitivity to sex discrimination that a major meeting with employers in California was arranged at a private club which barred women–even though I was scheduled to accompany the Chairman to the meeting."

The commission's disinterest in sex discrimination did not deter complaints. One-third of all the complaints reaching the commission came from women. They dealt with sex-segregated newspaper help-wanted advertisements, state protective legislation that women argued discriminated against them, the definition of bona fide occupational qualifications (BFOQ), and other issues. Protests against sex-segregated help-wanted ads prompted the creation of a special committee to investigate the issue, but it concluded that the sex-segregated ads did not violate Title VII. The issue, however, did not go away. Congresswoman Martha Griffiths (D-MI) wrote to the EEOC: "I assume you will agree that the heading 'white' or 'Negro' or 'Protestant' would be prohibited by the statute, and therefore I have difficulty seeing how advertisements under the headings of 'male' or 'female' could be in compliance with the very clear prohibitions of the law." Two of the commissioners, as well as interested observers, felt that if there were a women's organization comparable to the National Association for the Advancement of Colored People, women's influence would increase. The National Organization for Women (NOW) was created in 1966 to fill that need. NOW successfully challenged several EEOC opinions, including sex-segregated employment advertisements. In 1968, the EEOC banned sex-segregated advertising for jobs in newspapers unless employers could demonstrate that sex was a bona fide occupational qualification, but it was unable to enforce the policy. In 1973, the U.S. Supreme Court ruled that sex-segregated help-wanted ads were not free speech but commercial speech and were not protected by the First Amendment.

Congress strengthened the EEOC with the passage of the Equal Employment Opportunity Act of 1972, giving the commission the power to file suits when negotiation and conciliation failed. The act also expanded the categories of employers covered by Title VII.

The EEOC first addressed the problem of sexual harassment in 1980, finding that it was a form of sex discrimination, and defining it as behavior that interferes with a person's work performance, including "unwelcome sexual advances, requests for sexual favors, and other verbal or physical conduct of a sexual nature." In 1998, the EEOC obtained $34 million in a sexual harassment case against Mitsubishi Manufacturing of America, and the company agreed to change its sexual harassment prevention policy and complaint procedure. The same year, the EEOC also settled a sexual harassment case against Astra USA, Inc., for $10 million and formal apologies to the women involved.

The EEOC receives approximately 15,000 sexual harassment complaints, 24,000 sex discrimination complaints, and 4,000 pregnancy discrimination complaints per year. In addition, it receives complaints related to race, age, and pay discrimination.

> **See also** Bona Fide Occupational Qualification; Civil Rights Act of 1964, Title VII; Equal Employment Opportunity Act of 1972; Griffiths, Martha Edna Wright; Hernandez, Aileen Clarke; *Meritor Savings Bank v. Vinson*; National Association for the Advancement of Colored People, Women in the; National Organization for Women; Sexual Harassment
>
> **References** Carabillo, Meuli, and Csida, *Feminist Chronicles* (1993); Freeman, "Women and Public Policy: An Overview" (1982); www.eeoc.gov.

Equal Pay Act of 1963

The Equal Pay Act of 1963 makes it illegal for private employers to have different rates of pay for women and men doing the same work. It was the first federal law to address sex discrimination. In 1992, women filed 1,186 wage discrimination charges with the Equal Employment Opportunity Commission; and in 2003, women filed 1,026 charges. Men filed 103 wage discrimination charges in 1992 and 120 charges in 2003.

Congresswoman Mary Norton (D-NJ) introduced an equal pay for comparable work bill in 1945, and Congresswomen Frances P. Bolton (R-OH) introduced different versions in 1954. Although President Dwight D. Eisenhower supported the concept, opponents insisted that comparable work could not be defined. Congresswoman Katharine St. George (R-NY) overcame the objection in 1962 when she proposed equal pay for equal work, an approach that Congresswoman Edith Green (D-OR) drafted into a bill and introduced.

Support for equal pay legislation also came from Women's Bureau director Esther Peterson, who made passing it a priority and hired a lobbyist to work with members of Congress on the measure. The measure received further support in 1962, when the President's Commission on the Status of Women endorsed equal pay at its first meeting and commission chair Eleanor Roosevelt declared her support for it at a press conference. The commission's research revealed that in the period from 1955 to 1960, women earned less than two-thirds of what men earned.

When the House debated the bill, St. George said that opposing it "would be like being against motherhood." The Chamber of Commerce of the United States was the bill's most visible opponent. It was supported by the American Association of University Women, Business and Professional Women/USA, the National Consumers League, the National Woman's Party, the American Federation of Labor–Congress of Industrial Organizations, the American Civil Liberties Union, and the Kennedy administration. The bill passed the U.S. House and Senate in 1962 but in different forms, and it ultimately died. Green sponsored the bill again in 1963, when it passed.

The law states that employers subject to the Fair Labor Standards Act of 1938 must pay equal wages for equal work, making exemptions for differences based on seniority, merit, or piece rates. The law specifically excludes women working in restaurants, hotels, laundries, and hospitals; domestic workers; and many small businesses. At the time of the bill's passage, seven million women came under its mandate.

On the anniversary of women's right to vote, feminists march in support of the Equal Right Amendment in Washington DC.1978 Leif Skoogfors/CORBIS

See also American Association of University Women; Bolton, Frances Payne Bingham; Business and Professional Women/USA; Green, Edith Louise Starrett; National Woman's Party; Norton, Mary Teresa Hopkins; Pay Equity; Peterson, Esther; President's Commission on the Status of Women; Roosevelt, Eleanor; St. George, Katharine Delano Price Collier; Women's Bureau

References Congressional Quarterly Almanac, 87th Congress, 2nd Session . . . 1962 (1962); Congressional Quarterly Almanac, 88th Congress, 1st Session . . . 1963 (1964); Harrison, *On Account of Sex (1988);* Linden-Ward and Green, *American Women in the 1960s: Changing the Future (1993);* National Partnership for Women and Families, "Women at Work: Looking Behind the Numbers," Washington, D.C.: The National Partnership for Women and Families (2004).

Equal Rights Amendment

Conceived by Alice Paul of the National Woman's Party, the Equal Rights Amendment (ERA) was first introduced in Congress in 1923. Congress passed the amendment in 1972 and sent it to the states for ratification. The amendment failed in 1982 after only thirty-five states had ratified it, three fewer than needed for it to be added to the U.S. Constitution.

After passage of the Nineteenth Amendment granting woman suffrage in 1920, Alice Paul of the National Woman's Party proposed an Equal Rights Amendment to guarantee women's full equality. The proposed amendment stated: "Men and women shall have equal rights throughout the United States and every place subject to its jurisdiction." Opponents of the amendment included labor, social reformers, the Women's Trade Union League, the American Association of University Women, and the General Federation of Women's Clubs. They rightly feared that the amendment would make unconstitutional the protective labor legislation that they had worked for decades to pass. Paul argued that protective legislation placed women in a subordinate role and that without the amendment, women were legally barred from some of the best colleges and universities.

Introduced in every session of Congress beginning in 1923, it gained the support of several professional women's organizations in the 1930s, including the Osteopathic Women's National Association, the Association of American Women Dentists, the American Alliance of Civil Service Women, the National Association of Women Lawyers, and others. In 1940, the Republican National Convention included support for the amendment in its platform and repeated the endorsement in 1944, the year the Democratic National Convention first included it in its platform.

During World War II, women's contributions to the war effort attracted new supporters for the amendment, including the General Federation of Women's Clubs, Business and Professional Women/USA, and Eleanor Roosevelt. In 1943, Senator Hattie Caraway (D-AR) became the first woman in Congress to sponsor the amendment, and the National Woman's Party formed the Women's Joint Legislative Committee to support it. The next year, opponents formed the National Committee to Defeat the UnEqual Rights Amendment.

In the post-World War II years, the amendment gained the visible support of several notable women, including artist Georgia O'Keeffe, author Pearl Buck, actresses Helen Hayes and Katharine Hepburn, and anthropologist Margaret Mead. Among members of Congress, support came from Republicans who were pro-business and Southern Democrats who were anti-labor. The U.S. Senate voted on the amendment in 1947, but with 38 ayes and 35 nays, it failed to receive the two-thirds majority needed for a constitutional amendment.

The amendment passed the Senate in 1950 and 1953 with the necessary two-thirds majority, but both times it included the statement that "the provisions of this article shall not be construed to impair any right, benefits or exemptions conferred by law upon persons of the female sex." Equal Rights Amendment supporters objected to the exemptions and did not ask the House to debate the amendment.

The President's Commission on the Status of Women refused to endorse the amendment, but it did call for equality under the law. With the emergence of the modern feminist movement, however, the amendment began to receive renewed and intensified attention and support. The National Organization for Women, formed in 1966, became one of the amendment's fiercest and most dedicated supporters.

Democratic Senator Eugene McCarthy of Minnesota introduced the amendment in February 1969 with seventy-nine co-sponsors.

In May 1970, the Senate Judiciary Subcommittee on Constitutional Amendments held three days of hearings on it. During the hearings, Congresswoman Martha Griffiths (D-MI) said that the courts could interpret the Constitution as guaranteeing equal rights for women, but she did not think that would ever happen. Griffiths said: "I seek justice, not in some tomorrow, or by some study commission, but now while I live, and I think the equal rights amendment will help towards the way." Democratic Congresswoman Shirley Chisholm of New York told the subcommittee that the Constitution did not address women's rights because "American institutions were created by white males and ... the freedom, equality, and justice that they mentioned and fought for was intended ... for them and them alone."

The House of Representatives did not hold hearings in 1970. Its chairman of twenty years, Democrat Emanuel Celler of New York, had refused to hold hearings on a constitutional amendment for women's rights throughout his tenure as committee chairman. To get the amendment out of committee, Griffiths succeeded in gaining 218 signatures on a discharge petition for it. On 10 August 1970, the ERA passed the U.S. House of Representatives with 352 ayes and 15 nays.

The Senate responded with more hearings, this time before the full Judiciary Committee. The Senate began debate on the amendment in October 1970 and attached two amendments, one allowing women's exemption from the draft and another permitting non-denominational prayers in public schools. The amendments essentially killed the measure, and the Senate did not vote on the full amendment before the end of the session.

For the first time since 1948, a House Judiciary subcommittee held four days of hearings on the ERA in 1971. The full committee passed a resolution for the amendment, but it had two additions. One allowed Congress to exempt women from the draft, and another permitted different labor standards for men and women, both of which amendment supporters opposed. When the House of Representatives debated the measure, the amendments regarding military service and labor standards were dropped. The House passed the ERA with 354 ayes and 24 nays on 12 October 1971. Democrat Leonor Sullivan of Missouri was the only woman who voted against it.

Even though the unwelcome amendments had been removed, another change had been made in the amendment that set it apart from the version that had passed the House in 1970. The version of the amendment that passed the House in 1971 and that was passed in the Senate in 1972 said:

Resolved by the Senate and House of Representatives of the United States of America in Congress assembled (two-thirds of each House concurring therein), that the following article is proposed as an amendment to the Constitution of the United States, which shall be valid to all intents and purposes as part of the Constitution when ratified by three-fourths of the several States within seven years from the date of its submission by the Congress:

Section 1. Equality of rights under the law shall not be denied or abridged by the United States or by any State on account of sex.

Section 2. The Congress shall have power to enforce, by appropriate legislation, the provisions of this article.

Section 3. This amendment shall take effect two years after the date of ratification.

The seven-year limit for ratifying the amendment received little attention at the time, but it came to be a significant factor in the amendment's ultimate failure.

The chief Senate sponsor was Democrat Birch Bayh of Indiana. Because Bayh's wife was undergoing treatment for cancer, the Senate delayed action on the ERA until 1972. When the Senate considered the measure that year, Democratic Senator Sam J. Ervin, Jr., of North Carolina emerged as the ERA's strongest opponent. He proposed several amendments in efforts to narrow the scope of the ERA. All of them failed. On 22 March 1972, the U.S. Senate passed the ERA with 84 ayes and 8 nays.

To complete the process, three-fourths of the states, or thirty-eight states, had to ratify the amendment. Two hours after Congress sent the amendment to the states, Hawaii ratified it. By the end of the year, twenty-one additional states had ratified the ERA. In addition, six states added ERAs to their state constitutions. The National Organization for Women (NOW), the League of Women Voters (LWV), and Business and Professional Women/USA (BPW/USA), the most active supporters, organized traditional lobbying campaigns as states considered the amendment. They conducted research, testified at hearings, contacted legislators, organized letter-writing campaigns, and supported pro-ERA legislative candidates. Some groups organized rallies and other public events to demonstrate support for ratification. The early successes in 1972 convinced amendment supporters that it would easily be ratified before the seven-year deadline Congress had imposed.

With virtually no organized opposition to the amendment, supporters did not develop long-term strategies for ratification, and they did not allocate significant resources for a lengthy campaign. In addition, the arguments they articulated in its favor addressed feminists' interests and professional women's concerns, but most women did not identify themselves as feminists, and although increasing numbers of women were in the workforce, few of them were professionals. Amendment supporters neglected to consider the amendment's significance from the perspective of homemakers, working-class women, employed women who did not want to be in the labor market, and men. They repeatedly argued that the amendment would end women's second-class citizenship.

Opposition to the amendment, however, was developing. Several local and regional groups with aspirations for national influence formed, but it was Phyllis Schlafly who galvanized opposition to the ERA and ultimately defeated it. Schlafly had begun developing a network of conservative women in 1967 and communicating with them through her monthly newsletter, the *Phyllis Schlafly Report*. She also held training sessions that covered everything from the clothing colors and styles that look best on television to evaluations of their speaking styles and content.

Initially ambivalent about the amendment, Schlafly had not participated in efforts to stop it when Congress had debated it. A friend, however, had urged her to consider the ERA's implications. Schlafly did and found them deplorable. She concluded the amendment would end husbands' financial responsibilities to their wives and would weaken the traditional family. She asserted that the amendment's second section giving Congress the power to enforce the amendment took too much power away from the states and gave it to Congress. She supported protective labor legislation and concurred with supporters and opponents that such measures would become unconstitutional. She also objected to it because she believed that women would be drafted into the military, that same-sex marriages would be lawful, and that abortions would be legal. In October 1972, Schlafly founded and appointed herself national chairperson of Stop ERA. When the U.S. Supreme Court legalized abortion a few months later in *Roe v. Wade* (1973), Schlafly believed that her analysis of the amendment had been confirmed. Schlafly's well-developed public relations skills, organizational ability, compelling speaking style, and forecasts of what the ERA would do brought her national attention and legions of followers.

The amendment, however, gained new support in 1973. The Young Women's Christian Association ended its opposition to the ERA, as did the American Federation of Labor–Congress of Industrial Organizations. The LWV, National Woman's Party, Common Cause, BPW/USA, National Women's Political Caucus (NWPC), and NOW formed the ERA Action Committee, with each member organization accepting responsibility for some aspect of the ratification campaign. For example, the NWPC worked to elect state legislators who supported the amendment, and the LWV trained lobbyists. Eight more states ratified the amendment in 1973. In 1974, three more states ratified it, but the momentum toward ratification had clearly slowed. BPW/USA hired a Republican consulting firm to analyze the seventeen states that had not ratified the ERA and to identify the ten most likely to ratify.

Schlafly had ended feminists' thoughts of a speedy and easy ratification. Her ability to pull hundreds and occasionally thousands of women into state capitols to lobby their legislators overwhelmed feminists. ERA supporters counted votes and lobbied, but not with the effectiveness or the drama Schlafly and her followers demonstrated. In one state capitol, Schlafly draped a casket with a "Bury ERA" banner. In other state capitols, Schlafly and her supporters used skits, costumes, and refreshments in their attempts to gain the attention of legislators and news media. In another state, opponents gave each legislator a loaf of bread with a note begging for a no vote on ERA ratification. Schlafly traveled across the country explaining her objections to the amendment, giving uncommitted legislators and sometimes supporters of the ERA reasons to vote against it. She regularly debated ERA supporters and consistently triumphed.

Other groups also organized to oppose the amendment, including Women Who Want to Be Women; Happiness of Womanhood; American Women Against the ERA; Females Opposed to Equality; and Family, Liberty, and God. The membership of these groups tended to be housewives who feared the changes that could result from the amendment and who worried that the amendment would force them into male roles. Viewing the amendment as an assault on womanhood and the institution of marriage, opponents to the amendment feared losing spousal support or the decriminalization of rape and other sex crimes. Amendment supporters did not address these fears, in part because they discounted them and the women who held them and in part because they did not have responses to them. In addition, some of the tactics amendment supporters used, such as public demonstrations and confrontation, alienated many women and men.

Another state ratified the amendment in 1975, making a total of thirty-four states that had done so, and the push for the last four states began with increased intensity. In 1976, no states ratified the amendment, but one state added an ERA to its constitution. The amendment that had begun with little opposition had stalled. NOW members began daily protests outside the White House, and a national organization, ERAmerica, was formed to channel money and resources to states most likely to ratify. A Harris poll showed that 67 percent of Americans supported the ERA and 27 percent opposed it. In 1976, one state ratified the ERA, but three states had voted to rescind their ratification, actions the U.S. Department of Justice said were illegal and unconstitutional.

To attract publicity to the campaign, NOW called for an economic boycott of states that had not ratified the ERA. More than 200 organizations, in addition to many individuals, supported it by holding their conventions and meetings in states that had ratified and by avoiding travel in other states. The boycott was challenged in court, but the U.S. Circuit Court of Appeals upheld NOW's right to wage it.

As the seven-year deadline for ratification established by Congress approached, two California law students who were also NOW members proposed obtaining an extension deadline. Democratic Congresswoman Elizabeth Holtzman of New York introduced a resolution extending the ratification deadline to March 1986. NOW organized a march in Washington, D.C., that attracted more than 100,000 people who demonstrated their support for the amendment and for extending the deadline. Congress granted an extension to 30 June 1982 but not for the seven years requested.

The extension granted amendment supporters a reprieve that they used to develop a new campaign strategy. They enlarged their focus to a national one in an attempt to convince women across the country that they could influence states to ratify. Fundraising campaigns became more successful. NOW, for example, had raised $150,000 in 1977 and increased that to almost $1 million in 1981. Other groups became increasingly active, creating political action committees to support pro-ERA legislative candidates and recruiting corporate executives to lobby in states that had not yet ratified it. Supporters, however, did not articulate arguments that effectively countered Schlafly's rhetoric against the amendment.

Amendment opponents used President Jimmy Carter's proposal to draft women and men into the military to their advantage by arguing that it affirmed their claims about the ERA. The 1980 Republican National Convention further weakened the amendment's chances when it repudiated its forty-year-long tradition of supporting it.

NOW launched its ERA Countdown Campaign in 1981, with former first lady Betty Ford and actor Alan Alda as honorary co-chairs. Polls showed that 63 percent of Americans supported the amendment and 32 percent opposed it. Massive efforts to raise $15 million for advertising involved door-to-door solicitation and use of Hollywood celebrities and other notables to support the reinvigorated effort. Also, lobbying brigades of women from across the country joined local forces in targeted states to press for ratification.

Early in 1982, attention focused on North Carolina, Florida, and Illinois. The Illinois legislature had considered and rejected the amendment several times, but supporters continued to believe that the state would ratify it. Seven women went on a hunger strike, and seventeen women chained themselves to the door of the Illinois Senate chamber, but none of the targeted states ratified the amendment.

On 30 June 1982, the amendment died, three states short of those needed for ratification. Of the fifteen states that did not ratify, most were in the South, with Illinois being the primary Northern exception. No state had ratified the ERA after 1978. The amendment was reintroduced in the House in 1983 but, with 278 ayes and 147 nays, it needed six more votes in order to have had the required two-thirds majority of those present and voting.

Despite the amendment's failure, Congress passed several measures banning sex discrimination, including the Equal Credit Opportunity Act of 1974, Title IX of the Education Amendments of 1972, the Women's Educational Equity Act of 1974, and the Pregnancy Discrimination Act of 1978. Other measures expanded coverage of Title VII of the Civil Rights Act of 1964, increased the Equal Employment Opportunity Commission's power, added sex to the purview of the U.S. Commission on Civil Rights, and prohibited sex discrimination in state programs funded by federal revenue sharing. In addition, several states added equal rights amendments to their state constitutions and passed a range of laws banning sex discrimination.

See also Abortion; American Association of University Women; Anthony, Susan Brownell; Business and Professional Women/USA; Caraway, Hattie Ophelia Wyatt; Chisholm, Shirley Anita St. Hill; Civil Rights Act of 1964, Title VII; Eagle Forum; Education Amendments of 1972, Title IX; Equal Credit Opportunity Act of 1974; Equal Employment Opportunity Commission; Equal Pay Act of 1963; Equal Rights Amendments, State; ERAmerica; Ford, Elizabeth Ann (Betty) Bloomer; Friedan, Betty Naomi Goldstein; General Federation of Women's Clubs; Holtzman, Elizabeth; League of Women Voters; National Association of Colored Women; National Committee to Defeat the UnEqual Rights Amendment; National Federation of Republican Women; National Organization for Women; National Woman's Party; National Women's Political Caucus; Nineteenth Amendment; Parks, Rosa Louise McCauley; Paul, Alice; President's Commission on the Status of Women; President's Task Force on Women's Rights and Responsibilities; Protective Legislation; Republican Party, Women in the; *Roe v. Wade*; Roosevelt, Eleanor; St. George, Katharine Delano Price Collier; Schlafly, Phyllis Stewart; Seneca Falls Convention; Sex Discrimination; Suffrage; Women's Educational Equity Act of 1974

References Berry, *Why ERA Failed: Politics, Women's Rights, and the Amending Process of the Constitution* (1986); Boles, "Building Support for the ERA: A Case of 'Too Much, Too Late'" (1982); Carroll, "Direct Action and Constitutional Rights: The Case of the ERA" (1986); *Congressional Quarterly Almanac, 91st Congress, 2nd Session . . . 1970* (1970); *Congressional Quarterly Almanac, 92nd Congress, 1st Session . . . 1971*(1972); *Congressional Quarterly Almanac, 92nd Congress, 2nd Session . . . 1972* (1972); *Congressional Quarterly Almanac, 98th Congress, 1st Session . . . 1983* (1984); Felsenthal, *The Biography of Phyllis Schlafly* (1982); Freeman, "From Protection to Equal Opportunity: The Revolution in Women's Legal Status" (1990); Harrison, *On Account of Sex* (1988).

Document Alice Paul, "Should Congress Approve the Proposed Equal Rights Amendment to the Constitution?" 1943; Shirley Chisholm, "Equal Rights for Women," 1969; Ruth Bader Ginsburg, "Let's Have ERA as a Signal," 1977; Phyllis Schlafly, "Eyewitness: Beating the Bra Burners," 1997

Equal Rights Amendments, State

Nineteen states have equal rights sections or provisions in their state constitutions or have added equal rights amendments to their state constitutions, although these provisions vary in their scope and in the ways that state courts have interpreted them. The states with equal rights provisions and the dates of passage are Alaska (1972), Colorado (1972), Connecticut (1974), Florida (1998), Hawaii (1972), Illinois (1970), Iowa (1998), Louisiana (1974), Maryland (1972), Massachusetts (1976), Montana (1972), New Hampshire (1975), New Mexico (1973), Pennsylvania (1971), Texas (1972), Utah (1896), Virginia (1971), Washington (1972), and Wyoming (1890).

Wyoming, the first state to incorporate an equal rights provision, included it in its state constitution in 1890, as did Utah in 1896. Illinois incorporated its provision when it adopted a new constitution in 1970. The other states added constitutional amendments in the 1970s, the exceptions being Florida and Iowa, which added them in 1998.

Some of the provisions cover private and public conduct, and others are limited to public actions only. The standard for determining discriminatory action has varied by state, with some state courts using strict scrutiny and other state courts using less rigorous levels. Legislatures have also differed in their responses to the provisions. For example, after New Mexico added an ERA to its state constitution, the legislature reviewed state laws and changed more than twenty discriminatory laws and proposed two additional constitutional amendments. However, Utah has passed and retained laws that treat women and men differently.

In some states, attorneys general have determined that women could use their birth names and that legal restrictions on female employment are null. The New Mexico State Supreme Court upheld a ban on students visiting the dormitory rooms of the opposite sex, but a Texas court rejected a policy that required women students to live on-campus, whereas men had to live off-campus. The Pennsylvania insurance commissioner prohibited the use of sex in setting automobile insurance rates.

The many differences in states' equal rights provisions, in court interpretations of them, and in legislative responses to them prohibit making generalizations regarding their impact.

See also Equal Rights Amendment

References Altschuler, "State ERAs" (1983); Berry, *Why ERA Failed: Politics, Women's Rights, and the Amending Process of the Constitution* (1986).

ERAmerica

Founded in 1976, ERAmerica was a nationwide, bipartisan political organization that worked for the passage of the federal Equal Rights Amendment (ERA). Business and Professional Women/USA (BPW/USA) initiated creation of ERAmerica after a political consulting firm it had hired recommended that an umbrella organization of associations be formed to coordinate ratification efforts. BPW invited representatives of the League of Women Voters, the National Organization for Women, the National Women's Political Caucus, the Women's Equity Action League, the American Association of University Women, and the National Education Association to join together. Over 200 organizations eventually participated in the coalition.

ERAmerica served as a clearinghouse for information about the amendment, directed congressional testimony, lobbied Congress and state legislatures, held mass demonstrations and rallies, and encouraged letter-writing campaigns and petition drives. Celebrities, including actress Marlo Thomas, actor Alan Alda, columnist Erma Bombeck, and singer Helen Reddy added glamour to the campaign when they made appearances for ERAmerica and helped raise money for it.

ERAmerica disbanded when the deadline to ratify the amendment expired in 1982.

See also American Association of University Women; Business and Professional Women/USA; Carpenter, Mary Elizabeth (Liz) Sutherland; Equal Rights Amendment; League of Women Voters; National Organization for Women; National Women's Political Caucus; Women's Equity Action League

References Slavin, *U.S. Women's Interest Groups* (1995).

Eshoo, Anna Georges (b. 1942)

Democrat Anna Eshoo of California entered the U.S. House of Representatives on 3 January 1993. Reflecting her Silicon Valley constituency with its emphasis on technology, Eshoo has worked to change laws governing investor lawsuits because she believes they hinder the growth of high-technology industry. The House and Senate approved the bill, President Bill Clinton vetoed it, and Eshoo helped lead the House's override of it. It was the first time both the House and Senate overrode one of Clinton's vetoes.

Eshoo supported the North American Free Trade Agreement (NAFTA) despite the opposition of labor unions, human rights activists, and environmentalists, all key groups in her district. Believing that she could lose her congressional seat regardless of her vote on the issue, she commented, "If we vote against NAFTA, we just validate the status quo." Her support for business has appeared in other measures, among them one permitting digital signatures on certain contracts. Among her other priorities are reproductive rights, health care, and services for people living with human immuno-deficiency virus (HIV) and acquired immunodeficiency syndrome (AIDS).

Born in New Britain, Connecticut, Anna Eshoo received her associate's degree from Canada College in 1975. Growing up in a politically active family, Eshoo organized over 800 students to work for John F. Kennedy's 1960 presidential campaign. "Back then," she said, "I really thought I was the one who put him [Kennedy] over the top." Eshoo chaired the San Mateo County Democratic Central Committee from 1978 to 1982, was Democratic national committeewoman for California from 1980 until 1992, and served on the San Mateo County Board of Supervisors from 1983 to 1993. She unsuccessfully ran for Congress in 1988.

See also Congress, Women in

References *Congressional Quarterly, Politics in America 1996* (1995), *Politics in America 1998* (1997), *Politics in America 2006* (2005); www-eshoo.house.gov/bio/html.

Eslick, Willa McCord Blake (1878–1961)

Democrat Willa Eslick of Tennessee served in the U.S. House of Representatives from 4 August 1932 to 3 March 1933. Following the death of her husband, Congressman Edward Eslick, Willa Eslick won the special election to fill the vacancy. She sought to help farmers suffering during the 1930s economic depression by supporting agricultural relief measures and the plans offered by President-elect Franklin D. Roosevelt. Eslick did not run for re-election because her husband's death had occurred after the filing deadline for candidates.

Born in Fayetteville, Tennessee, Willa Eslick attended Dick White College, Milton College, Winthrop Model School, Peabody College, and the Metropolitan College of Music. She was chair of the Giles County Council of Defense during World War I and later was a member of the state Democratic committee.

See also Congress, Women in

References Office of the Historian, U.S. House of Representatives, *Women in Congress, 1917–1990* (1991).

Estrich, Susan (b. 1953)

Susan Estrich became the first woman to manage a major presidential campaign in 1988, when Democratic presidential candidate Michael Dukakis chose her for the position on his staff. She was also the first woman president of the Harvard Law Review. Estrich began her political career in 1979, when U.S. Senator Edward Kennedy asked her to serve as deputy national issues director in his campaign for the 1980 Democratic presidential nomination. Executive director of the Democratic Party's platform committee in 1984, she served as a senior political adviser in the Walter Mondale–Geraldine Ferraro campaign.

Estrich began working in the Dukakis campaign in 1987 as he sought the party's nomination. The campaign for the nomination had stumbled when the former campaign manager resigned after releasing damaging information about another candidate. Estrich directed the campaign's recovery, orchestrated Dukakis's success at the Democratic National Convention, and continued as the Dukakis campaign manager through the general elections. Dukakis lost to George Bush.

Born in Lynn, Massachusetts, Estrich earned her bachelor's degree from Wellesley College in 1974 and her law degree from Harvard University Law School in 1976. Estrich clerked for a U.S. Court of Appeals judge in 1977 and was law clerk for U.S. Supreme Court Justice John Paul Stevens in 1978. Special assistant to the chief counsel of the U.S. Senate Committee on the Judiciary from 1979 to 1980, Estrich returned to Harvard University Law School in 1981 to teach.

See also Democratic Party, Women in the
References *The New York Times*, 6 May 1998.

Evans, Jodie (b. 1954)

A cofounder of Code Pink, Jodie Evans has engaged in political activism for over four decades. She has worked on issues related to the environment, human rights, civil rights, women's rights, and peace. She has produced two documentaries, *Stripped and Teased: Tales of Las Vegas Women* and *Shadow Conventions*, about the gatherings that paralleled the Democratic and Republican 2000 national conventions.

Jodie Evans, co-founder of CODEPINK (Courtesy codepink4peace.org)

From 1973 to 1982, Evans served in California Governor Jerry Brown's campaigns and administration, holding the cabinet position of Director of Administration. She later worked on Brown's 1992 presidential campaign.

She is the co-author, with Medea Benjamin, of *Stop the Next War Now: Effective Responses to Violence and Terrorism* (2005).

In addition to Code Pink, Evans is a cofounder of Unreasonable Women, Bad Babes, and the International Occupation Watch Center. Explaining the connections among her interests, Evans wrote: "The parts of me that fought as a feminist, an environmentalist, anti-war and human rights activist in the 70's, and then continued to be enraged and engaged by new issues, has not let them drop but instead they continue to engage me."

Born in Las Vegas, Nevada, Evans earned her BA degree from Woodbury University in 1975.

References Jodie Evans, email to author, 23 January 2006; http://www.codepink4peace.org/article.php?id=53; http://wholelifetimes.com/2005/wlt2703/codepink2703.html.

Evers-Williams, Myrlie Louise Beasley (b. 1933)

Widow of slain civil rights leader Medgar Evers, Myrlie Evers-Williams chaired the board of the National Association for the Advancement of Colored People (NAACP) from 1995 to 1998. She announced her candidacy for the job at a time when the NAACP struggled with financial and sexual harassment scandals, a lawsuit against the incumbent chair that board members initiated, and substantial debts. Evers-Williams requested the resignation of several board members and instituted a number of reforms within the organization, thereby restoring its integrity. With NAACP president Kweisi Mfume, she overcame its $4 million debt, leaving the organization with a $2 million surplus. She resigned to devote more time to the Medgar Evers Institute.

Myrlie Evers-Williams

Evers-Williams married Medgar Evers in 1950. Five years later, in 1955, he became head of the NAACP Mississippi state office in Jackson. As her husband's secretary, Evers-Williams worked with him to secure voting rights, economic stability, fair housing, equal education, and equal justice and dignity for African Americans. Despite repeated death threats, the couple remained in Jackson, continued their work, and taught their children to fall to the floor if they heard an unusual noise. In the spring of 1963, their home was fire-bombed, and Evers-Williams put out the fire with a garden hose.

On 12 June 1963, Medgar Evers was shot on his front porch. The next night, Evers-Williams attended a mass meeting at Pearl Street Baptist Church. She told the audience: "I am left without my husband and my children without a father, but I am left with the strong determination to try to take up where he left off." Byron de la Beckwith was arrested for Evers's murder, tried, and set free by a hung jury. A second trial also ended without a conviction. Evers-Williams persisted and called for a third trial after allegations of jury tampering in the second trial came to light. On 5 February 1994, Beckwith was found guilty of murder and given a life sentence.

After her husband's murder, Evers-Williams moved her family to Claremont, California, and began classes at Pomona College. While a student, Evers-Williams continued to make public speeches for the NAACP, primarily about her husband's life and work. After graduating in 1968, she worked for the college until 1970. Evers-Williams unsuccessfully ran for Congress in 1970 and for a Los Angeles City Council seat in 1987. She was appointed to the Los Angeles Board of Public Works in 1987.

Born in Vicksburg, Mississippi, Myrlie Evers-Williams attended Alcorn Agricultural and Mechanical College in 1950. She earned her bachelor's degree in 1968 from Pomona College.

Evers-Williams wrote *For Us, the Living* (1967).

> **See also** Civil Rights Movement, Women in the; National Association for the Advancement of Colored People
>
> **References** H. W. Wilson, *Current Biography Yearbook, 1995* (1995); www.naacp.org.

Executive Order 10980

Signed by President John F. Kennedy on 14 December 1961, Executive Order 10980 established the President's Commission on the Status of Women. The order explained that "prejudices and outmoded customs act as barriers to the full realization of women's basic rights which should be respected and fostered as part of our nation's commitment to human dignity, freedom, and democracy." Noting that women had served in every period of national emergency, the order said that after the emergency ended, women had been treated as a marginal group. Stating that women should be allowed to develop their talents and use their skills, the commission's report made recommendations for overcoming employment discrimination on the basis of sex and for services to help women in their roles as wives and mothers.

> **See also** President's Commission on the Status of Women
>
> **References** Mead and Kaplan, eds., *American Women: The Report of the President's Commission on the Status of Women and Other Publications of the Commission* (1965).

Executive Order 11126

Signed by President John F. Kennedy on 1 November 1963, Executive Order 11126 established the Interdepartmental Committee on the Status of Women and the Citizens' Advisory Council on the Status of Women. The two groups were part of the recommendations made by the President's Commission on the Status of Women and were created to provide continuing leadership in the advancement of the status of women. The Interdepartmental Committee's area of responsibility was women employed by the federal government, and the Citizens' Advisory Council oversaw the private sector.

> **See also** Citizens' Advisory Council on the Status of Women; President's Commission on the Status of Women

Executive Order 11246

Signed by President Lyndon Johnson on 24 September 1965, Executive Order 11246 established equal employment opportunity as the policy of the federal government. It prohibited discrimination on the basis of race, creed, color, or national origin. It also required all government contracts to include an equal opportunities clause stating that the contractor would not discriminate on the basis of race, color, or national origin. In addition, the contractor agreed to take affirmative action to prevent discrimination. The affirmative action requirement covered employment, promotion, demotion, recruitment, termination, pay rates, and apprenticeship programs.

> **See also** Affirmative Action; Executive Order 11375
>
> **References** Linden-Ward and Green, *American Women in the 1960s: Changing the Future* (1993).

Executive Order 11375

Signed by President Lyndon Johnson on 13 October 1967, Executive Order 11375 expanded Executive Order 11246 to add sex to the groups covered by the government's equal employment opportunity policy for federal employees. The effort to end sex discrimination in federal employment included the creation of the Federal Women's Program (FWP), which was established to enhance opportunities for women in every area of federal employment. Every federal department and agency had an FWP manager, and some agencies had FWP committees. The Office of Personnel Management administered the program. The Department of Labor used the order to pressure other federal departments to conduct reviews of their compliance and to sue contractors who used unfair hiring practices.

> **See also** Executive Order 11246; Federal Women's Program; Federally Employed Women
>
> **References** www.few.org/fwp/htm.

F

Family and Medical Leave Act of 1993

Passed by Congress and signed by President Bill Clinton in 1993, the Family and Medical Leave Act protects the jobs of workers who take leaves of absence for a range of family responsibilities. The act requires employers to allow employees who have worked for them for at least a year to take up to twelve weeks of unpaid leave during any twelve-month period for the birth or adoption of a child; the placement of a foster child; the serious illness of a child, spouse, or parent; or the employee's own health. The act applies to companies with fifty or more employees, exempting about 95 percent of all employers, but the companies it covers employ about 60 percent of all workers.

Democratic Congresswoman Patricia Schroeder of Colorado and Republican Congresswoman Margaret Roukema of New Jersey led the eight-year campaign to enact the measure. Roukema explained its importance: "This bill represents not only decency, but what is required in the workplace today." She also believed that the bill was a "bedrock family issue," adding: "This is not just symbolism. This is health care. This is job security."

The Family and Medical Leave Act was supported by 9to5, the National Association of Working Women, and other women's groups and opposed by the U.S. Chamber of Commerce and the National Federation of Independent Business. The National Retail Federation withdrew its opposition in 1993, explaining that the proposal had evolved and the association could support it. In addition, Aetna Life and Casualty Company announced that its family leave policy had saved the company $2 million in one year through reduced employee turnover and reduced hiring and training costs.

First introduced in 1985, the bill was killed in 1988 with a Senate filibuster. The bill passed both chambers in 1990, but President George Bush vetoed it, as he did in 1992. That year, the Senate voted to override Bush's veto, but the House was twenty-seven votes short. In 1992, Democratic presidential candidate Bill Clinton made the bill a top campaign issue, and when the bill passed on 4 February 1993, it became his first legislative victory as president.

See also Congress, Women in; 9to5, National Association of Working Women; Roukema, Margaret Scafati; Schroeder, Patricia Nell Scott

References *Congressional Quarterly Almanac, 101st Congress, 2nd Session . . . 1990* (1991); *Congressional Quarterly Almanac, 102nd Congress, 2nd Session . . . 1992* (1993); *Congressional Quarterly Almanac, 103rd Congress, 1st Session . . . 1993* (1994); www.dol.gov/dol/asp/public/programs/ handbook/fmla.htm.

Farenthold, Frances (Sissy) Talton (b. 1926)

The first woman to be nominated for vice president of the United States at a major party convention, Democrat Frances Farenthold entered politics as a volunteer in John F. Kennedy's 1960 presidential campaign. Director of Nueces County Legal Aid from 1965 to 1967 and a member of the Corpus Christi Human Relations Commission, she witnessed the inequities of Texas's welfare system and concluded that state agencies did not meet the needs of poor Texans. Determined to change state policies, Farenthold ran for the state legislature in 1968 on the themes of "Ethics, Efficiency, Education, and Ecology." During her first term, she passed a bill giving the state a portion of the treasures and antiquities found in its waters and coastal areas and attempted to reform welfare programs. She ran for a second term in 1970 and used "Integrity, Courage, and Competence in the 70s" for her campaign theme. When she called for an investigation of a bank scandal that involved the speaker and leadership of the Texas House, the men retaliated. In drawing the new district lines required after the 1970 census, the leadership created a district that left Farenthold without her political base.

In 1972, Farenthold ran for governor but lost. She also worked for George McGovern's nomination at the Democratic National Convention. Congresswoman Shirley Chisholm had earlier declared that she was running for the presidential nomination but then declined to seek a place on the ticket for either the presidential or vice presidential nomination. With Chisholm's withdrawal, several college students circulated a petition for Farenthold's nomination for the vice presidency, and the National Women's Political Caucus joined the campaign and began seeking delegates who would support Farenthold. Gloria Steinem nominated Farenthold from the convention floor, and Fannie Lou Hamer and others seconded the nomination. Farenthold received more than 400 votes, but the nomination went to Thomas Eagleton, who ran with presidential nominee George McGovern. Farenthold campaigned for the McGovern-Eagleton ticket and co-chaired Citizens for McGovern.

Chair of the National Women's Political Caucus from 1973 to 1975, she ran for governor again in 1974 but lost in an underfinanced campaign. She served as president of Wells College from 1976 to 1980.

Born in Corpus Christi, Texas, Farenthold earned her bachelor's degree at Vassar College and her law degree at the University of Texas in 1949.

See also Democratic Party, Women in the; Hamer, Fannie Lou Townsend; National Women's Political Caucus; State Legislatures, Women in; Steinem, Gloria Marie

References Crawford and Ragsdale, *Women in Texas* (1992).

Farrington, Mary Elizabeth Pruett (1898–1984)

Republican Elizabeth Farrington of Hawaii served as territorial delegate to Congress from 31 July 1954 to 3 January 1957. Elected to fill the vacancy created by the death of her husband, Joseph Farrington, she continued his campaigns for statehood for Hawaii and Alaska. Her accomplishments include the establishment of the Geophysics Institute in Hawaii, designating the City of Refuge on the island of Hawaii as a national historical park, and passing a measure to reapportion Hawaii based on population, an achievement that had eluded others for thirty years. She also worked to improve the market for Hawaii's sugar. Farrington lost her re-election attempt in 1956 and returned to Hawaii.

Born in Tokyo, Japan, Farrington graduated from Ward-Belmont Junior College in 1916 and from the University of Wisconsin at Madison in 1918. She did later graduate work at the University of Hawaii. She was a newspaper correspondent from 1918 to 1957.

Active in Republican Party politics, Farrington was president of the League of Republican Women in Washington, D.C., from 1946 to 1948 and president of the National Federation of Republican Women from 1949 to 1953. She was publisher, president, and director of the *Honolulu Star Bulletin* from 1946 to 1967, president and director of the Star Bulletin Printing Company from 1957 to 1963, and president of the Hawaiian Broadcasting System from 1960 to 1963. After serving as director of the Office of Territories in the Department of the Interior from 1969 to 1971, she worked in the congressional liaison office from 1971 to 1973.

See also Congress, Women in

References Engelbarts, *Women in the United States Congress, 1917–1972* (1974); Office of the Historian, U.S. House of Representatives, *Women in Congress, 1917–1990* (1991); Tolchin, *Women in Congress: 1917–1976* (1976).

Fauset, Crystal Dreda Bird (1894–1965)

Crystal Fauset was the first African American woman elected to a state legislature. In the 1930s, Fauset became involved in partisan politics, founding the Philadelphia Democratic Women's League in 1934 and becoming the Democratic National Committee's director of colored women's activities in 1936. Two years later, the Democratic Party recruited her to run for the Pennsylvania legislature. Campaigning on the issues of fair employment, slum clearance, and low-cost housing, Fauset won her race.

Fauset resigned from the legislature in 1939 to become assistant state director of the Pennsylvania Works Progress Administration's (WPA's) Education and Recreation Program and race relations adviser for all of the state WPA programs. In 1941, Fauset became New York City Mayor Fiorella La Guardia's race relations adviser. Later in the year, she joined the national office of Civilian Defense as the special race relations adviser to the director. During this period, she also became a member of President Franklin D. Roosevelt's Black Cabinet, working to end discrimination and serving as an advocate for African Americans.

Early in 1944, Fauset went to work for the Democratic National Committee but left after a few months because she felt that the Democratic Party leadership did not welcome the involvement of African American women. She registered as a Republican.

Fauset turned her attention to international issues in the mid-1940s and helped establish the United Nations Council of Philadelphia, later called the World Affairs

Council. An officer in the World Affairs Council from 1945 to 1950, she traveled extensively in India, the Middle East, and Africa.

Born in Princess Anne, Maryland, Crystal Fauset graduated from Boston Normal School in 1914 and earned her bachelor of science degree from Teachers College at Columbia University in 1931. After teaching from 1915 to 1918, Fauset joined the National Board of the Young Women's Christian Association and traveled across the country as a field secretary for the Girls' Reserves, a program for African American and working girls. In 1927 and 1928, Fauset worked for the Interracial Section of the American Friends Service Committee as a field representative. She made 210 speeches to schools and clubs, speaking to some 50,000 people about the needs and achievements of African Americans and the ways that the races could help each other.

See also State Legislatures, Women in

References Hardy, *American Women Civil Rights Activists* (1993).

Federal Women's Program

The Civil Service Commission of the federal government created the Federal Women's Program (FWP) in 1967 to implement President Lyndon Johnson's Executive Order 11375, prohibiting discrimination on the basis of sex by the federal government and its contractors. FWP sought to enhance women's employment and advancement in the federal government. The program had three objectives: to create a legal and an administrative framework to provide equal job opportunity for federal employees, to eliminate prejudices that limited women to certain jobs, and to encourage women to seek jobs with the federal government and to participate in training programs that offered the possibility of advancement.

The FWP underwent a number of changes in 1969, when President Richard Nixon signed Executive Order 11478. The order integrated the FWP into the Equal Employment Opportunity Program, making agency directors responsible for it and for development of affirmative action plans. The directors were also charged with designating an FWP chair and a committee to provide advice on women's concerns and to monitor progress of the agency's affirmative action program. In 1971, Nixon appointed Barbara Hackman Franklin to identify and recruit women for high-level federal appointments.

See also Affirmative Action; Federally Employed Women; Franklin, Barbara Hackman

References Markoff, "The Federal Women's Program" (1972).

Federally Employed Women

Founded in 1968 to fight sex discrimination in employment by the U.S. government, Federally Employed Women (FEW) grew out of a conference for executive women employed by the federal government. The catalyst for FEW's organization had occurred the year before, when Executive Order 11375 had added sex to the forms of discrimination prohibited within the federal government and by its contractors in Executive Order 11246. Executive Order 11375 also established the Federal Women's Program to enhance women's employment opportunities in the federal government. FEW's organizers believed that the measure had the potential for improving women's opportunities and at the same time believed that implementation and enforcement of its provisions deserved monitoring.

FEW's structure includes chapter, state, and national levels that each have four program areas: legislative, training, compliance, and diversity. The legislative area involves developing an agenda, educating members, lobbying members of Congress, offering testimony, and monitoring legislative action. Legislative priorities have included support for affirmative action, improvements in processing employment complaints, an end to sexual harassment, and protection against discrimination based on sexual orientation. Other priority areas are child care and elder care and access to benefits for women in the military.

In the area of compliance, FEW officers work with departmental and agency management to encourage their enforcement of Executive Order 11375 and to monitor the effectiveness of the Federal Women's Program. Although not a labor union, FEW's representatives help agencies develop goals and objectives to achieve equality of opportunity in the federal workforce. At a 1997 congressional hearing on discrimination in the federal workforce, however, FEW's president testified that most women continued to work in the lowest-paying jobs, that thousands of discrimination complaints were filed annually, and that resolutions of the complaints took too long.

> **See also** Affirmative Action; Child Day Care; Executive Order 11375; Federal Women's Program; Lesbian Rights; Military, Women in the; Sex Discrimination; Sexual Harassment
>
> **References** www.few.org.

Feinstein, Dianne Goldman (b. 1933)

Democrat Dianne Feinstein of California entered the U.S. Senate on 10 November 1992. She first gained national attention in 1978, when she became mayor of San Francisco following the murder of Mayor George Moscone and Supervisor Harvey Milk by a former supervisor.

Born in San Francisco, California, Feinstein received a bachelor's degree in history from Stanford University in 1955. Following graduation, she was a Coro Foundation intern and became familiar with various government agencies through a study of the administration of justice in California. She then worked for the California Industrial Welfare Commission. In the 1960s she served on city, county, and state criminal justice commissions and boards.

Feinstein entered politics as a member of the San Francisco Board of Supervisors, where she served from 1970 to 1978. Because she was president of the board of supervisors and thus next in line, the assassinations of Milk and Moscone resulted in her becoming mayor. Helping the city heal from the tragedy and making the city safe were her first priorities. She introduced and passed a measure banning handguns, but California courts found it unconstitutional. She enlarged the police department, reduced emergency response time from eight minutes to two minutes, and cut the crime rate by 27 percent. To become better acquainted with city residents and to demonstrate her commitment to community service, Feinstein spent Saturday mornings leading neighborhood cleanup patrols, cleaning up trash and painting over graffiti. She retired as mayor in 1987. During her years as mayor, Feinstein was guided by her commitment

Senator Feinstein introducing a 2 year-moratorium on Internet Access Taxes, February 2004. (Courtesy Office of Dianne Feinstein)

to "govern from the center," a philosophy she has followed throughout her political career.

In 1990, Feinstein ran for governor against U.S. Senator Pete Wilson, who won. Wilson resigned from the Senate with four years remaining in his term and appointed John Seymour to serve until 1992, when an election would be held, with two years remaining in the term. Feinstein entered the 1992 Senate race, defeated Seymour, and completed the term that Wilson had begun. During her campaign, Feinstein argued that the Senate needed more than the two women serving in it at the time, saying, "two percent may be good for milk, but it's not good enough for the Senate." When Feinstein and Congresswoman Barbara Boxer won their races for the U.S. Senate in 1992, California became the first state to send two women to the Senate to serve together. In 1994, Feinstein ran for a full six-year term and won.

As a member of the Senate, Feinstein passed the California Desert Protection Act, placing more than three million acres into two national parks, Joshua Tree and Death Valley, and one national preserve, East Mojave, in addition to another three million acres designated as wilderness. The prime mover behind bills banning assault weapons, she explained: "It really comes down to a question of blood or guts–the blood of innocent people or the Senate of the United States having the guts to do what we should do when we take that oath to protect the welfare of our citizens." Co-author of the 1994 Gun-Free Schools Act, she wrote and passed the Hate Crimes Sentencing Enforcement Act. Another measure that she played a key role in, the Comprehensive Methamphetamine Control Act of 1996, created new controls over the manufacture of the drug and increased the criminal penalties for possession and distribution of it. She has proposed a measure to amend the U.S. Constitution by adding a Victims' Bill of Rights and has sought passage of the Federal Gang Violence Act. In addition, she has worked to stop illegal immigration, create harassment-free workplaces, and create new loans for small businesses. She played a pivotal role in the passage of the 2001 campaign finance reform law. During the 107th Congress (2001–2002), she worked with Republicans to reduce opportunities for manipulation of energy markets. The lead sponsor of the Breast Cancer Research stamp, which has raised more than $40 million for breast cancer research, she chairs the Senate Cancer Coalition. She has worked for a constitutional amendment to obtain rights for crime victims.

> **See also** Boxer, Barbara Levy; Congress, Women in; Family and Medical Leave Act of 1993; Sexual Harassment

> **References** Boxer, *Strangers in the Senate: Politics and the New Revolution of Women in America* (1994); *Congressional Quarterly, Politics in America 1994* (1993), *Politics in America 2004* (2003), *Politics in America 2006* (2005); H. W. Wilson, *Current Biography 1979* (1979); Jackie Koszczuk, "Sen. Diane Feinstein," *CQ Weekly*, 28 December 2002, p. 21; Roberts, *Dianne Feinstein: Never Let Them See You Cry* (1994); http://feinstein.senate.gov/biography.html,

Felton, Rebecca Ann Latimer (1835–1930)

Democrat Rebecca Felton of Georgia served in the U.S. Senate from 21 November 1922 to 22 November 1922. She was the first woman to serve in the U.S. Senate and had the shortest term—one day. Felton's first exposure to politics came when her husband served in Congress in the 1870s and she was his campaign manager and press secretary. In the early 1880s, she investigated convict camps, found them appalling, and persuaded the Woman's Christian Temperance Union to join her crusade to house male and female prisoners separately and to house juvenile offenders and adult criminals separately.

By the 1890s, Rebecca Felton had become established as a political leader in her own right, lecturing against convict leasing and liquor. In the early 1900s, she became active in the woman suffrage movement and in efforts to provide vocational training for poor white girls. By that time, she had begun writing a column for the *Atlanta Journal*, articulating her racist, anti-Catholic, and anti-Semitic views and her opposition to child labor laws.

When she was eighty-five years old, she helped elect her old friend Thomas Watson to the U.S. Senate. Watson won, served two years of his term, and died in 1922. The governor of Georgia, who had opposed woman suffrage and wanted a symbolic gesture to appease women voters, appointed Felton to serve between the time of Watson's death and the election of his successor. After the election, Felton convinced the newly elected senator to wait one day to present his credentials, giving her the opportunity to take the Senate seat on 21 November 1922 and to make a speech. After 143 years of an all-male Senate, Felton told her colleagues: "When the women of the country come in and sit with you, though there may be but a very few in the next few years, I pledge to you that you will get ability, you will get integrity of purpose, you will get exalted patriotism, and you will get unstinted usefulness." The following day, she resigned, and the new senator was sworn in. It was almost ten years before another woman, Hattie Caraway, was sworn into the Senate.

Born in DeKalb County, Georgia, Felton attended private schools and graduated from Madison Female College in 1852. The next year she married William Harrell Felton, who was a physician, Methodist clergyman, and farmer. During the Civil War years, the Feltons sought refuge in a farmhouse near Macon, where they experienced the horrors of war when outlaw members of the Union and Confederate armies and freed slaves pillaged their home and terrorized them.

Rebecca Felton wrote *My Memoirs of Georgia Politics* (1911), *The Subjection of Women and the Enfranchisement of Women* (1915), *Country Life in Georgia in the Days of My Youth* (1919), and other works.

See also Caraway, Hattie Ophelia Wyatt; Congress, Women in; Suffrage; Woman's Christian Temperance Union

References Boxer, *Strangers in the Senate: Politics and the New Revolution of Women in America* (1994); James, ed., *Notable American Women, 1607–1950* (1971); Office of the Historian, U.S. House of Representatives, *Women in Congress, 1917–1990* (1991).

The Feminine Mystique

The Feminine Mystique by Betty Friedan, published in 1963, helped launch the modern feminist movement in the United States by exposing the haunting sense of dissatisfaction many women felt and by portraying the experience as one that many women shared. Friedan articulated the social, educational, and economic limits on women's lives that restricted their development as human beings and that hobbled their participation in the full range of human endeavors. Women readers responded by launching projects to change the conditions, laws, relationships, and institutions that hindered them.

The themes in *The Feminine Mystique* emerged from responses to a questionnaire Friedan sent to her former Smith College classmates in preparation for the fifteenth anniversary of their 1942 graduation. Respondents described personal problems, prompting Friedan to investigate further to see if women in the larger population had encountered comparable problems and frustrations. Expanding her research beyond the initial questionnaire, Friedan found that many women yearned for more than making beds, shopping for groceries, caring for their children, and doing the other tasks related to homemaking and mothering. Using birth rates, statistics on age at marriage, cultural images, social norms, and personal experiences, Friedan found that many women shared the "problem that has no name." It was not described in medical or psychological references, but women across the country described feelings of emptiness and desperation.

Friedan concluded that since World War II, a concerted effort had been made to convince women that they could only be happy in their roles as wives, mothers, and homemakers. Friedan called the ideology "the feminine mystique." Friedan wrote: "It is my thesis that as the Victorian culture did not permit women to accept or gratify their basic sexual needs, our culture does not permit women to accept or gratify their basic need to grow and fulfill their potentialities as human beings." Declaring that housework was boring and that the home had become "a comfortable concentration camp," she pointed to several cultural components that encouraged women to limit their world. She included the educational establishment, Freudians, women's magazines, and mass advertising in her indictment and concluded that women should be able to seek equality in both the private and public worlds.

The book prompted women to begin making changes in their lives. Some women questioned their primary roles as wives and mothers and explored new roles in their homes, communities, and the workplace. Women already in the workplace began to question the limits placed on the jobs they could hold and the wages they could earn. They challenged their legal status, their economic status, and their political status and worked to change them.

Friedan used the celebrity and power that she acquired from *The Feminine Mystique* to speak on behalf of women and to encourage women to speak for themselves. The sense of shared fate that the book helped women identify significantly contributed to the emergence of the modern feminist movement.

See also Feminist Movement; Friedan, Betty Naomi Goldstein

References Evans, *Personal Politics: The Roots of Women's Liberation in the Civil Rights Movement and the New Left* (1979); Friedan, *The Feminine Mystique* (1963); Schneir, *Feminism in Our Time* (1994).

Document Betty Friedan, "The Problem That Has No Name," 1963

Feminist Majority Foundation

Founded in 1987, the Feminist Majority Foundation (FMF) recruits women for public office and works for women's equality, reproductive freedom, and increased human services. Organized by Eleanor Smeal, former president of the National Organization for Women, Peg Yorkin, and Katherine Spillar, the Feminist Majority was originally known as the Fund for the Feminist Majority. The group received its initial financial support from Peg Yorkin, who gave $10 million to the Fund for the Feminist Majority, 50 percent of which went to endow the foundation, with the balance supporting the legalization of the abortifacient RU-486 in the United States.

FMF has had several programs to further its goals. The "Feminization of Power Campaign" works to encourage women to seek public office and to assist them as they campaign. The Rock for Choice project reaches out to young people through music to educate and organize them to support abortion rights. The Feminist Majority Foundation educates the public on women's issues, defends women's rights in legal cases, and conducts research. FMF's campaigns in 2006 include the Campaign for Afghan Women and Girls, college campus programs, Get Out Her Vote, and the National Clinic Access Project.

In 2001, FMF acquired *Ms.* magazine.

See also Abortion; Freedom of Access to Clinic Entrances Act of 1994; National Organization for Women; RU-486 (Mifepristone); Sexual Harassment; Smeal, Eleanor Cutri; Violence Against Women Act of 1994

References www.feminist.org.

Feminist Movement

The modern feminist movement, or the "second wave" of feminism, encompasses a wide range of theories and philosophies that hold at their center the quest for women's social, economic, and political equality. The first wave emerged in the mid-1800s, advocated and won woman suffrage rights, and essentially dissolved after ratification of the Nineteenth Amendment. The second wave of feminism began in the 1960s with two primary branches–the women's liberation movement and the feminist movement–that merged into the feminist movement in the 1970s.

Several factors contributed to the emergence of the modern feminist movement, including women's participation in World War II as members of the military and as members of the workforce, the President's Commission on the Status of Women report in the early 1960s, the creation of state commissions on the status of women, and the publication of *The Feminine Mystique* by Betty Friedan in 1963. By identifying and articulating discrimination on the basis of sex, women transformed areas of life that had long been considered family or personal matters into social and political issues. Women formed rape crisis centers, domestic violence shelters, day care centers, and abortion clinics, and they sought to change laws, policies, and society. Existing organizations, such as the American Association for University Women, the League of Women Voters, and others adopted legislative agendas that reflected feminist priorities, and new organizations, including the National Organization for Women and the National Women's Political Caucus, emerged for the purpose of identifying and advocating women's issues. The single most visible solution to sex discrimination that feminists sought was passage and ratification of the Equal Rights Amendment (ERA). The ERA failed in 1982, but the focus on women's status that accompanied it contributed to policy changes in the areas of education, employment, pay, crime, credit, and health.

Feminists have sought to give women greater power over their lives and in business and politics. They have argued that each woman must control her own body, which includes the choice to bear children or not, access to means of birth control and to fertility resources, and availability of abortion services. Other, less controversial forms of power have also been feminist goals. Women have sought power through elective and appointive offices, and other women have supported their efforts by contributing to their campaigns and working in them. The increasing numbers of women in state legislatures and in Congress reflect the successes women have had.

Feminists have challenged and changed an array of social traditions and practices. Homemakers entered the workforce and found that holding the equivalent of two jobs, one at home and one at their employer's, was too much, and they implored their husbands to help with household and child care responsibilities. At the office, women decided that making the coffee, picking up their boss's laundry, and other traditionally female tasks were not in their job descriptions and protested. Vocabulary and word usage came under scrutiny, and the exclusive use of male nouns and pronouns was deemed sexist. For example, "worker" replaced "workman," and "police officer" replaced "policeman." In addition, adult females decided that being addressed or referred to as "girls" was demeaning and objected to it. Women who found sexist jokes offensive concluded that they did not have a social obligation to laugh at them. Feminists sought and obtained changes in their religious denominations to permit the ordination of women. Other women found that Christianity and other male-dominated theologies did not meet their needs and explored ancient, goddess-centered religions and beliefs.

American culture and education have also been affected by the feminist movement. Women writers, artists, and musicians have found greater acceptance and new audiences for their works. Women's studies and women's history courses at colleges and universities have made women's lives, achievements, and contributions more visible to students.

As the feminist movement transformed American politics, society, and culture, a conservative movement developed to stop and reverse the changes. New women's organizations, including Eagle Forum, Concerned Women for America, and other groups, claimed that women belonged at home taking care of their homes and children, that husbands should provide for their families, that abortion was murder and should be illegal, and that women did not need an ERA because they had enough equality. In the 1970s and 1980s, the conservative movement matured, gained increasing power, and slowed or reversed some of the changes feminists had made.

In the 1990s, feminist proposals that had once been considered radical became accepted and were enacted or implemented. The Family and Medical Leave Act of 1993, federal funding for child day care, child support enforcement, and expanded roles for women in the military are a few examples. Although feminists may have been among the first proponents of these measures, they became public policy as a result of broad-based public and congressional support for them.

> **See also** Abortion; American Association of University Women; Civil Rights Act of 1964, Title VII; Displaced Homemakers; Domestic Violence; Equal Rights Amendment; *The Feminine Mystique*; Friedan, Betty Naomi Goldstein; League of Women Voters; National Organization for Women; National Women's Political Caucus; Pay Equity; President's Commission on the Status of Women; Violence Against Women Act of 1994

Feminists for Life of America

Founded in 1972, Feminists for Life of America (FFLA) is a national network with thirty-six state chapters and 3,500 members that opposes abortion, infanticide, capital punishment, and euthanasia. FFLA supports justice, nonviolence, and nondiscrimination, lobbies state legislatures for its agenda, and provides support for women in need. It also supports the Elizabeth Cady Stanton Pregnant and Parenting Students Services Act, introduced in Congress in 2005. The proposal would provide $10 million for 200 grants to encourage higher education institutions to establish a pregnant and parenting student services office, which would begin by evaluating the services available to pregnant students and parenting students, such as housing, child care, maternity coverage, flexible schedules, and related topics. Setting goals for improving services and conducting annual reviews would also be included in the office's responsibilities.

FFLA argues that violence, including abortion, euthanasia, and capital punishment, is inconsistent with core feminist principles of nonviolence, equality, and justice and that abortion physically and psychologically harms women. The organization claims that Susan B. Anthony, Matilda Joslyn Gage, Alice Paul, and other early feminists were pro-life.

> **See also** Anthony, Susan Brownell; Feminist Movement; Gage, Matilda Joslyn; Paul, Alice
>
> **References** http://wwwfeministsforlife.org
>
> **Document** Helen Chenoweth, "Statement to Feminists for Life of America," 1997

Feminization of Poverty

The feminization of poverty describes a phenomenon, recognized in 1978 by a sociologist, that almost one-half of the poor people in the United States lived in households headed by women and that two-thirds of poor U.S. adults were women. Several factors contribute to the feminization of poverty, including teenage motherhood and divorce. Two other factors, sexism and racism, contribute to poverty through the undercompensation of employed women and people of color.

Not only do many women earn less than men, but also they are more likely to have the economic burden of supporting their dependent children. Teenage mothers often have full financial responsibility for their children, and when fathers contribute to their children's support, the payments are small. In addition, teenagers have few resources to support themselves and their children because their education does not prepare them for jobs that provide adequate compensation to raise them above the poverty level.

Divorce affects the financial status of women and their dependent children more negatively than it does men. A year after divorce, on average, men's standard of living increases by 42 percent, whereas that of divorced women and their children decreases by 73 percent. For women who had been full-time homemakers, reentering the workforce poses significant challenges and often requires them to obtain or update job skills.

Alimony and child support can ease the economic difficulties, but the amounts allocated by the courts are often inadequate or not paid. Unable to collect child support, some women and their children become welfare recipients. In response, states and the federal government have incrementally increased child support enforcement laws. Beginning in the 1980s, the federal government implemented several policies to assist in the collection of child support payments and to provide incentives to states to assist custodial parents to whom child support was due.

Sexism contributes to the feminization of poverty in that employed women earn only about 70 percent of the wages that employed men earn. Even though the Equal Pay Act of 1963 requires equal pay for equal work, the gap between women's earnings and men's earnings persists. In addition, the sex-segregated nature of the labor market tends to relegate women to low-paying, low-status jobs with little prospect for advancement. These differences in men's and women's earnings and potential earnings continue throughout women's work lives and into retirement, because retirement benefits, whether private plans or Social Security, are based on earnings.

Racism, like sexism, contributes to the feminization of poverty. People of color experience discrimination in employment, advancement, and pay. For women of color, the combination of racism and sexism works to make them the lowest category of wage earners.

See also Child Support Enforcement; Displaced Homemakers; Divorce Law Reform

References Gimenez, "The Feminization of Poverty: Myth or Reality?" (1990); Riley, *Divorce: An American Tradition* (1991); www.cdc.gov.

Fenwick, Millicent Hammond (1910–1992)

Republican Millicent Fenwick of New Jersey served in the U.S. House of Representatives from 3 January 1975 to 3 January 1983. Fenwick entered politics in the 1930s, working in campaigns and serving on the state Republican committee. She served on the Bernardsville Board of Education from 1938 to 1941, the New Jersey Advisory Committee to the U.S. Commission on Civil Rights in 1957, and the Bernardsville Borough Council from 1958 to 1964, the first woman to serve on it. In 1970, Fenwick won an open seat in the New Jersey legislature, where she passed a bill prohibiting discrimination in hiring on the basis of race, creed, national origin, ancestry, age, marital status, or sex. She also passed measures establishing minimum wages for agricultural workers and requiring toilet facilities for agricultural workers. She worked for equal rights for women, environmental protection, education, and penal reform.

When Fenwick ran for Congress, she refused to accept money from political action committees, reflecting her commitment to honesty and openness in Congress. As a member of Congress, she supported the Equal Rights Amendment, federal funding for abortions, and the food stamp program. Her other interests included securing human rights, promoting the use of synthetic fuels, and ending the "marriage penalty" in tax law. Fenwick was known for her dignity and elegance, for her outspoken comments on the House floor, and for her habit of smoking a pipe. Fenwick unsuccessfully ran for the U.S. Senate in 1982.

Born in New York, New York, Millicent Fenwick interrupted her education when she was fifteen to live in Spain while her father served as ambassador to that country. She attended Columbia University in 1933 and the New School for Social Research in 1942. A model for *Vogue* magazine, she was an associate editor for that and other Condé Nast publications from 1938 to 1948 and wrote *Vogue's Book of Etiquette* in 1948.

See also Abortion; Congress, Women in; Equal Rights Amendment; State Legislatures, Women in

References Office of the Historian, U.S. House of Representatives, *Women in Congress, 1917–1990* (1991); Tomlinson, "Making Their Way: A Study of New Jersey Congresswomen, 1924–1994" (1996).

Ferguson, Miriam Amanda Wallace (1875–1961)

Democrat Miriam "Ma" Ferguson served as governor of Texas from 1925 to 1927 and from 1933 to 1935. She entered politics as a surrogate for her husband James Ferguson, who served as governor from 1915 to 1917. Following impeachment, conviction, and removal from office for mishandling of state funds in 1917, James Ferguson was banned from holding public office. He worked to have the restriction removed but failed and recruited his wife to become a candidate for governor. To emphasize the active role that James Ferguson expected to play if Miriam Ferguson won the election, she used the campaign slogan, "Two Governors for the Price of One." In the course of the campaign, Miriam Ferguson gained a nickname she disliked when a newspaper used her first initials, M(iriam)A(manda), in a headline, but she incorporated it into a campaign slogan, "Me for Ma."

Miriam Ferguson campaigned against the Ku Klux Klan and openly supported tolerance for Catholics and Jews. She promised economy in government, leniency in the administration of Prohibition laws, and improved administration of the state penitentiaries. Elected in 1924, she became the second woman governor in the United States, following Nellie Tayloe Ross of Wyoming, who also began her term in 1925.

Governor Miriam Ferguson targeted the Ku Klux Klan by passing a bill that outlawed the use of masks. She convinced the legislature to restore her husband's political rights, but the state Supreme Court found the act unconstitutional. Although controversy surrounded both of the actions, allegations that her office was selling pardons and paroles actually led to her defeat in 1926. She ran for governor again in 1930 and lost.

In 1932, Ferguson won a second term as governor. Taking office during the depths of the Depression, she declared a bank holiday two days before President Franklin D. Roosevelt's national bank holiday. The legislature passed her requests for congressional redistricting and the legalization of gambling on horse races and prizefighting but refused to approve a sales tax or a corporate income tax. She did not seek re-election in 1934 but tried unsuccessfully in 1940.

Born in Bell County, Texas, Miriam Ferguson attended Baylor Female College. She married James Edward Ferguson in 1899 and devoted herself to raising their children while James Ferguson founded a bank and became active in politics.

See also Governors, Women; Ross, Nellie Tayloe

References Sicherman and Green, eds., *Notable American Women: The Modern Period* (1980).

Ferguson v. City of Charleston (2001)

Medical personnel at the Medical University of South Carolina (MUSC), a public hospital in Charleston, South Carolina, noted an apparent increase in cocaine use by pregnant women seeking prenatal care. Using urine samples from the women as part of their prenatal care, MUSC screened the women for cocaine use. When a woman tested positive, the medical personnel threatened the women with law enforcement if they did not seek substance abuse treatment. Local law enforcement officials believed that the threat encouraged women to seek treatment. After delivery, if a woman tested positive, the hospital contacted the police, who arrested the woman.

Ten women arrested as a result of this policy challenged it, claiming that the drug tests were done without their consent and without warrants, making the arrests unconstitutional.

The U.S. Supreme Court agreed with the women. The Court wrote: "The Fourth Amendment's general prohibitions against nonconsensual, warrantless, and suspicionless searches necessarily applies...."

References *Ferguson v. City of Charleston, 532 U.S. 67* (2001).

Ferraro, Geraldine Anne (b. 1935)

Democrat Geraldine Ferraro of New York served in the U.S. House of Representatives from 3 January 1979 to 3 January 1985. She held the leadership position of secretary of the House Democratic Caucus in the 97th and 98th Congresses (1981–1983 and

Geraldine Ferraro is the only woman, to date, to receive the nomination of the Democratic Party to run for Vice President of the United States.

1983–1985). She was the Democratic candidate for vice president of the United States in 1984, the first woman ever nominated for the office by a major party.

Born in Newburgh, New York, Ferraro received her bachelor's degree in English from Marymount College in 1956 and her law degree from Fordham University in 1960. For the next fourteen years, Ferraro held part-time legal positions and worked in Democratic politics while raising her children. In 1974, she became an assistant district attorney for Queens County, New York, in the Investigations Bureau and the next year became chief of the county's Special Victims Bureau, which handled child abuse, domestic violence, and rape cases. She left after four years to run for Congress.

As a member of Congress, Ferraro was frustrated by her male colleagues' indifference to women's issues, particularly economic ones, including pay rates, health insurance, and pension inequities. Ferraro also supported federal funding for abortions, defended displaced federal workers, worked for increased federal funds for mass transit, supported tuition tax credits, and opposed busing.

At the 1983 National Women's Political Caucus (NWPC) convention, Ferraro met with other women leaders to discuss potential women candidates for president and vice president of the United States. Ferraro told the group that she did not see any good possibility that any of the male contenders for the presidency would select a woman for their vice presidential running mate. Walter Mondale, however, told the convention that he would consider a woman. When he became a leading contender for the Democratic Party's nomination, the NWPC, the National Organization for Women, and other powerful female Democrats pressured him to choose a woman. Mondale selected Ferraro.

When the 1984 Democratic National Convention met, delegates first elected Mondale for their presidential nominee and then Ferraro as their vice presidential candidate. She acknowledged that the nomination came to her in part because she was a woman but insisted she was qualified for it.

Two weeks after receiving the nomination, the first of a series of stories that questioned Ferraro's integrity and her husband John Zaccaro's honesty appeared. Ferraro's handling of congressional financial disclosure statements was questioned, and Zaccaro's real estate transactions as well as other financial dealings were investigated. More damaging stories followed. Zaccaro's initial refusal to release his income tax returns prompted speculation that he was hiding illegal activities. Then, a story about improper loans that family members had made to Ferraro's 1978 congressional campaign appeared, even though she had reported the transactions at the time and paid a fine. The negative media attention diminished after Zaccaro released his tax information and Ferraro held a news conference reviewing the family's finances.

Ferraro's pro-choice stand on reproductive rights became the next issue in the campaign. A Roman Catholic, Ferraro argued that although abortion might not be an option for her, she believed that it should be a protected right for women. Roman Catholic Archbishop John O'Connor of New York attacked her and others who shared her beliefs, pressuring her to change her position on abortion, but she remained firm.

Mondale and Ferraro lost in the general election. Having surrendered her congressional seat to run for the vice presidency, Ferraro became a political commentator. She unsuccessfully sought her party's nomination for the U.S. Senate in 1992 and lost a second bid for the Senate in 1998.

> **See also** Abortion; Congress, Women in; Democratic Party, Women in the; National Organization for Women; National Women's Political Caucus; President and Vice President, Women Candidates for
>
> **References** Ferraro, *Ferraro: My Story* (1985); Office of the Historian, U.S. House of Representatives, *Women in Congress, 1917–1990* (1991).

Fiedler, Roberta (Bobbi) Frances Horowitz (b. 1937)

Republican Bobbi Fiedler of California served in the U.S. House of Representatives from 3 January 1981 to 3 January 1987. A fiscal conservative who generally supported President Ronald Reagan's policies, she disagreed with some of his positions. Most notably, she supported the Equal Rights Amendment and a proposal for women's economic equity. She did not seek a fourth term in the House; instead, she ran for the U.S. Senate but lost in the Republican primary.

After leaving Congress, Fiedler was a government and public affairs consultant. In 1993, she was appointed to the Board of Commissioners of the Los Angeles Community Redevelopment Agency.

Born in Santa Monica, California, Fiedler attended Santa Monica City College and Santa Monica Technical School from 1955 to 1959. She was an interior decorator from 1957 to 1960 and owned a drugstore from 1969 to 1977. Opposed to a busing plan to desegregate Los Angeles schools, she and others organized BUSTOP in 1976, which led to her election to the Los Angeles school board, where she served from 1977 to 1981.

> **See also** Congress, Women in; Economic Equity Act; Equal Rights Amendment
>
> **References** *Congressional Quarterly, Politics in America: Members of Congress in Washington and at Home* (1983); Office of the Historian, U.S. House of Representatives, *Women in Congress, 1917–1991* (1991).

Fifteenth Amendment

The Fifteenth Amendment sought to guarantee suffrage to male former slaves following the Civil War. Congress sent the Fifteenth Amendment to the U.S. Constitution to the states on 27 February 1869, and it was ratified on 30 March 1870. As with the Fourteenth Amendment ratified before it, woman suffragists fought to include women in the Fifteenth Amendment but failed.

The text of the first section of the Fifteenth Amendment is as follows: "The right of citizens of the United States to vote shall not be denied or abridged by the United States or by any State on account of race, color, or previous condition of servitude."

Although some abolitionists insisted that former slaves needed the protection granted by the amendment, woman suffragists opposed the amendment's passage and ratification because it did not include African American women or other women and granted suffrage only to African American males. Republicans who supported the amendment believed that they could depend upon African Americans to vote Republican, but women's votes would not be as reliable.

With the ratification of the Fifteenth Amendment, the woman suffrage movement became increasingly racist. Woman suffrage leaders, including Elizabeth Cady Stanton and Carrie Chapman Catt, began calling for enfranchisement of women to counter African American males' votes. Women gained suffrage rights with the ratification of the Nineteenth Amendment in 1920, but except for a brief period in the 1870s during Reconstruction, no African Americans–women or men–living in the South could fully exercise their rights until passage of the Voting Rights Act of 1965.

See also Catt, Carrie Clinton Lane Chapman; Fourteenth Amendment; Nineteenth Amendment; Stanton, Elizabeth Cady; Suffrage; Voting Rights Act of 1965

Finney, Joan Marie McInroy (1925–2001)

Democrat Joan Finney served as governor of Kansas from 1991 to 1995. Political pundits and her competitors in the 1990 campaign dismissed her low-budget campaign, but she both won the primary election and defeated the incumbent governor. Described as a one-on-one politician, Finney said that she succeeded because she kept in touch with her constituents. During her term as governor, she named an unprecedented number of women to high positions in state government, including her Cabinet and her staff of advisers. She cut property taxes and initiated an investigation of the state prison system. A populist, she sttempted, but failed, to convince the legislature to pass a state constitutional amendment to allow initiatives and referenda.

Finney entered politics as a member of a U.S. senator's staff in 1953, was Kansas commissioner of elections from 1970 to 1972, and was administrative assistant to the mayor of Topeka from 1973 to 1974. An unsuccessful candidate for the U.S. House in 1972, Finney won election as Kansas state treasurer, serving from 1975 to 1991. After serving one term as governor, she did not run for re-election. She ran for the U.S. Senate in 1996, but lost in the primary.

Born in Topeka, Kansas, Joan Finney earned her bachelor's degree from Washburn University in 1974.

See also Governors, Women

References Mullaney, *Biographical Directory of the Governors of the United States 1988–1994* (1994); *The Washington Post*, 30 July 2001.

Flint Auto Workers' Strike

On 30 December 1936, auto workers at the Flint, Michigan General Motors (GM) plant sat down, beginning a strike that spread to 140,000 GM workers and involved more than 50 percent of the company's plants. They demanded recognition of the United Auto Workers (UAW) as their exclusive bargaining agency. On 31 December, fifty women formed the Women's Auxiliary to support the striking men by cooking food for them, establishing a first aid station, and distributing literature. They also established a day care center for striking women, ran picket lines, managed a speakers' bureau, and organized entertainment.

When police attempted to stop women from taking food to the strikers, turned off the heat, and lobbed tear gas into an occupied building, women formed the Women's Emergency Brigade. Armed with rolling pins, brooms, and mops for weapons, members of the brigade formed a line around male pickets, forcing police to shoot at them first. On 11 February 1937, strikers and GM reached an agreement that included recognition of the UAW as the collective bargaining agent and GM's pledge that it would not interfere with employees joining unions.

The Women's Emergency Brigade became a model for union supporters in other automobile manufacturing cities. The Women's Auxiliary and the Women's Emergency Brigade helped sustain strikers' morale and contributed to the success of the strike. In addition, women gained new organizational and leadership skills and developed a sense of power.

See also Coalition of Labor Union Women; Lawrence Textile Mill Strike; Shirtwaist Workers Strike; Triangle Shirtwaist Company Fire

References Foner, *Women and the American Labor Movement: From the First Trade Unions to the Present* (1982); Wertheimer, *We Were There: The Story of Working Women in America* (1977).

Flynn, Elizabeth Gurley (1890–1964)

Elizabeth Gurley Flynn was president of the U.S. Communist Party from 1961 until her death in 1964. Flynn entered the political arena when she was a high school student, giving speeches on soapboxes in New York. Arrested in 1906 during a speech, she was expelled from high school and began organizing for the Industrial Workers of the World (IWW). Between 1908 and 1917, Flynn's work took her across the country as she participated in the IWW's fights for freedom of speech in Montana, Washington, and other Western states and in labor strikes in Massachusetts, New York, and New Jersey, working on behalf of textile and silk workers and cooks and waiters. She left the IWW in 1917 because of a disagreement over strategy.

In the 1920s, Flynn worked to free Nicola Sacco and Bartolomeo Vanzetti, Italian-born anarchists accused of murdering two men during a payroll robbery. She organized mass rallies, raised money for their defense, and engaged lawyers to represent them. Their executions in 1927 convinced Flynn that capitalist justice was no justice.

Elizabeth Gurley Flynn, Communist activist with the Strike leaders at the Paterson silk strike of 1913. From left, Patrick Quinlan, Carlo Tresca, Elizabeth Gurley Flynn, Adolph Lessig, and Bill Haywood.

A founding member of the American Civil Liberties Union (ACLU) in 1920, Flynn's commitment to the organization's importance came from her own experiences. She believed that her civil rights had been violated every time she had been arrested. She served on the ACLU's board until 1940, when she was expelled from it because of her membership in the Communist Party.

Flynn's leadership in the U.S. Communist Party began with her election to its governing board in 1941. She became more visible when she led resistance to the Internal Securities Act, which required all Communist groups to register with the U.S. attorney general. One of the 135 plaintiffs in an unsuccessful lawsuit to have the act declared unconstitutional, she was convicted of conspiracy to overthrow the government in 1951 and was sentenced to three years in prison and fined $6,000.

Elected the first woman president of the U.S. Communist Party in 1961, Flynn successfully challenged the Subversive Activities Control Act of 1950. Flynn's passport was revoked in 1962 for her Communist Party activities. She appealed and won in 1964, when the U.S. Supreme Court found that she had been denied due process of law. She went to Moscow, where she died. A state funeral was held for her in Red Square.

Born in Concord, New Hampshire, Flynn published *I Speak My Own Piece: Autobiography of the "Rebel Girl"* in 1955.

> **References** Camp, *Iron in Her Soul: Elizabeth Gurley Flynn and the American Left* (1995); H. W. Wilson, *Current Biography Yearbook, 1961* (1961).

Fonda, Jane Seymour (b. 1937)

Actress Jane Fonda became a national political figure in the late 1960s and early 1970s. Her vocal support for the Black Panthers and American Indian militants and her outspoken opposition to the war in Vietnam placed her on the Nixon administration's enemies list. Her 1972 trip to North Vietnam and her broadcasts over Radio Hanoi urging U.S. pilots to stop bombing the North earned her the appellation "Hanoi Jane";

some members of Congress introduced measures that called for her to be tried for treason. Describing herself as "a revolutionary woman," Fonda encountered difficulty securing movie roles in the early 1970s. When her popularity was restored, Fonda made several movies in which a woman's consciousness is raised through personal experience.

Born in New York City, Jane Fonda is the daughter of actor Henry Fonda. She attended Vassar College in 1955 and 1956, studied art in Paris, and studied acting under Lee Strasberg. She has worked on the Broadway stage and has made several physical fitness videos.

References H. W. Wilson, *Current Biography Yearbook, 1986* (1986).

Ford, Elizabeth Ann (Betty) Bloomer (b. 1918)

Wife of President Gerald R. Ford, Betty Ford was first lady from 1974 to 1977. The Fords entered the White House following Richard Nixon's resignation from the presidency for his role in the Watergate scandal. Betty Ford's candor in discussing personal and political topics worried her husband's political advisers, embarrassed her children, scandalized some observers, and endeared her to many Americans. She continued her characteristic forthrightness and leadership after she and her husband returned to private life.

Born in Chicago, Illinois, Betty Ford attended the Bennington School of Dance for two summers beginning in 1936 and studied under Martha Graham in New York City. In 1941, she returned to Grand Rapids, Michigan, where she had spent her youth, and formed her own dance group. There, she married Gerald R. Ford in 1948. Two weeks after their wedding, Gerald Ford won election to Congress.

The Fords raised their family in Alexandria, Virginia, where Betty Ford was involved in family activities and Republican women's organizations. In 1973, upon the resignation of Vice President Spiro Agnew, Nixon chose Gerald Ford for vice president. When Nixon resigned in August 1974, Gerald Ford became president of the United States, and Betty Ford became first lady.

Diagnosed with breast cancer in September 1974, Betty Ford told the nation that she had the disease, a matter that she could have kept confidential. Instead, she became an advocate for increased awareness of breast cancer and other women's health concerns and encouraged women to examine themselves for lumps and to regularly get mammograms in order to detect breast cancer early.

Ford's openness during a taped interview for the television news program *60 Minutes* created a flurry of speculation that she had become a political liability for her husband. She had commented that premarital sex might lower the divorce rate, that she favored the U.S. Supreme Court's decision legalizing abortion, that she did not think her children used drugs, and that if her daughter were having an affair, she would want to know the man and to counsel her daughter. The strong initial reaction to the interview concerned the president's advisers until public opinion polls placed her popularity at 75 percent.

During her years in the White House, Betty Ford became an active advocate for feminist issues. A strong supporter of the Equal Rights Amendment, she gave speeches and wrote to and called state legislators, urging them to vote for its ratification. In addition, she encouraged her husband to appoint women to high offices in the federal government and convinced him to decline invitations to the annual Gridiron Club dinner until the group elected a woman member.

In 1978, she entered treatment for dependence on alcohol and prescription medications. Years of suffering from arthritis and a pinched nerve had left her addicted to pain medication, which was complicated by her use of alcohol. As with her experience with cancer, Betty Ford became an advocate for improved awareness, education, and treatment of alcohol and other drug dependencies. She co-founded the Betty Ford Center in Rancho Mirage, California, a facility that helps women, men, and their families recover from the disease. Since the center opened in 1982, Betty Ford has been active as the chair of the board of directors.

The first volume of her autobiography, *The Times of My Life*, chronicled her experience with cancer as well as her life in the White House. The second volume, *Betty: A Glad Awakening*, recounts her recovery from chemical dependence in 1978.

See also Abortion; Equal Rights Amendment; *Roe v. Wade*

References Ford, *The Times of My Life* (1978), *Betty: A Glad Awakening* (1987).

Fourteenth Amendment

The Fourteenth Amendment to the U.S. Constitution was sent to the states on 16 June 1866 and was ratified on 28 July 1868. The amendment includes the first specific statement of equality in the Constitution, which is embodied in its equal protection clause. When it was proposed, the amendment created a schism between abolitionists and suffragists because its second section refers to "male inhabitants" as citizens, the first time the gender qualification appeared in the Constitution. Abolitionists insisted that the newly freed slaves needed the protection that the amendment offered, saying the time was "the Negro's hour," whereas suffragists demanded that the amendment include women. Suffragists lost, but in the 1970s the Fourteenth Amendment became an important tool for fighting sex discrimination.

The text of the first section of the Fourteenth Amendment is as follows:

All persons born or naturalized in the United States, and subject to the jurisdiction thereof, are citizens of the United States and of the State wherein they reside. No state shall make or enforce any law which shall abridge the privileges or immunities of citizens of the United States; nor shall any State deprive any person of life, liberty, property, without due process of law; nor deny to any person within its jurisdiction the equal protection of the laws.

Early decisions made by the U.S. Supreme Court confirmed that the Fourteenth Amendment was not intended to place women on the same political and economic planes as men and confirmed that its intent was to address racial issues. In *Minor v. Happersett* (1875), the Court said that the privileges and immunities clause did not grant any rights that a citizen did not have before the amendment. Courts initially limited the equal protection clause to race but later expanded it to national origin and alienage. The U.S. Supreme Court expanded the amendment to cover sex discrimination for the first time in *Reed v. Reed* (1971) and subsequently decided other sex discrimination cases from that perspective.

See also *Reed v. Reed*; Sex Discrimination

References Baer, *Women in American Law* (1996); Freeman, "From Protection to Equal Opportunity: The Revolution in Women's Legal Status" (1990); Ginsburg, "Gender in the Supreme Court: The 1973 and 1974 Terms" (1976).

Fowler, Tillie Kidd (1942–2005)

Republican Tillie Fowler of Florida served in the U.S. House of Representatives from 3 January 1993 to 2001. She held the leadership positions of House deputy majority whip in the 104th and 105th Congresses (1995–1997 and 1997–1999) and vice chair of the Republican Conference in the 106th Congress (1999–2001). Fowler ran opposed in the 1994, 1996, and 1998 general elections. She supported term limits and pledged to serve only eight years, which she honored. Despite being the highest ranking woman in Congress, she did not seek re-election in 2000. An expert on military issues, her congressional priorities included a strong national defense, support for military personnel, transportation, improving the public works infrastructure, congressional reform, a balanced budget amendment, reproductive rights, and affordable health care.

When allegations of sexual harassment on several military training bases emerged in 1996, Fowler worked with Democrat Jane Harman and Republican Steve Buyer to discover the reasons that Army policies to prevent the problems had failed. Some members of Congress argued that men and women should not be trained together, but Fowler disagreed. She expressed concern that some of the sexual harassment victims had not reported the events and hoped to identify ways to encourage reporting.

Secretary of Defense Donald Rumsfeld appointed her to the Independent Panel to Review Department of Defense Detention Operations in 2004.

Born in Milledgeville, Georgia, Tillie Fowler earned her bachelor's degree in 1964 and her law degree in 1967, both from Emory University. A legislative assistant to a member of Congress from 1967 to 1970, she then worked in the Nixon administration as counsel for the Office of Consumer Affairs in 1970–1971. She changed her party affiliation from Democrat to Republican, moved to Florida, and married. A member of the Jacksonville City Council from 1985 to 1992, she also chaired the Florida Endowment for the Humanities from 1989 to 1991.

See also Abortion; Congress, Women in; Military, Women in the; Sexual Harassment

References *Congressional Quarterly, Politics in America 1994* (1993), *Politics in America 1998* (1997); *The New York Times,* 3 March 2005; www.house.gov/fowler/bio_fowler.html.

Foxx, Virginia Ann (b. 1943)

Republican Virginia Foxx of North Carolina entered the U.S. House of Representatives on 3 January 2005. "I'm a very conservative person," she said, "so I'm looking to sponsor bills that help us with fostering an agenda that will cut spending and uphold our principles."

Representative Foxx introduced legislation to stop tape-recorded political phone calls, fulfilling a campaign pledge she had made after listening to voters' complaints about them. Her bill would allow consumers to register with the National Do Not Call Registry, allowing them to opt out of that category of calls, as well as the other calls already covered. She co-sponsored a bill to deny driver's licenses to illegal immigrants as

North Carolina Representative Virginia Foxx participating in a hearing to investigate claims of exploitation, fraud and ethical problems in Human Cloning and Embryonic Stem Cell Research, March 2006. (Courtesy Office of Virginia Foxx)

a way to improve homeland security. She supports allowing people to put some of their Social Security contributions into private accounts. "The truth has to be told that Social Security is going broke and [President George W. Bush] is trying to fix that," she explained.

Born in Bronx County, New York, Foxx grew up in poverty in the North Carolina mountains. She earned a bachelor of arts in English in 1968, a master's degree in 1972 from the University of North Carolina, Chapel Hill, and a doctorate in 1985 from the University of North Carolina, Greensboro. She held several academic positions, including president of Mayland Community College from 1987 to 1994. A member of the Watauga County board of education from 1967 to 1988, she served in the North Carolina Senate from 1994 to 2004.

> **References** http://www.foxx.house.gov;
> http://bioguide.congress.gov/scripts/biodisplay.pl?index=F000450; Ari Pinkus, "Ban Taped Political Calls? Don't Bet on it," *Campaigns & Elections*, July 2005, p. 10; *The Washington Times*, 14 March 2005.

Frahm, Sheila Sloan (b. 1945)

Republican Sheila Frahm of Kansas served in the U.S. Senate from 11 June 1996 to 5 November 1996. When Bob Dole resigned from the U.S. Senate, Kansas Governor Bill Graves appointed Frahm to the position, which she held until the November election. Frahm entered the primary election to become the Republican nominee to complete the Senate term but lost.

Born in Colby, Kansas, Sheila Frahm received her bachelor of science degree from Ft. Hays State University in 1967 and attended the University of Texas at Austin. She served on the State of Kansas board of education from 1985 to 1988, served in the Kansas Senate from 1989 to 1995, and was Senate majority leader from 1994 to 1995. Lieutenant governor of Kansas from January 1995 to June 1996, she was appointed vice chair of the governor's Cabinet and secretary of the Department of Administration in 1995.

Frahm was appointed executive director of the Kansas Association of Community Colleges in February 1997.

>**See also** Congress, Women in; State Legislatures, Women in
>**References** "Sheila Frahm, R-Kansas" (1996).

Franklin, Barbara Hackman (b. 1940)

Republican Barbara Franklin served as secretary of commerce from 1992 to 1993. She entered government service in 1971 when President Richard Nixon appointed her to direct the first White House program ever developed to recruit women for high-level positions in the federal government. Nixon appointed her to a six-year term on the newly created U.S. Consumer Product Safety Commission in 1973, where she advocated a cost-benefit analysis as part of the regulatory process, worked on child safety, and helped coordinate the federal government's work to control carcinogens and toxic materials.

In 1979 Franklin joined academia as a senior fellow and director of the government and business program at the Wharton School at the University of Pennsylvania, working there until 1988. She formed a consulting firm in 1984, of which she was president and chief executive officer until 1992. President George Bush appointed her an alternate representative to the United Nations before he appointed her secretary of commerce. Her priorities as secretary included advocacy for U.S. business in the areas of international trade and environmental policy. Franklin believed that U.S. business had two advantages in the international market—its creativity and its entrepreneurial spirit.

Born in Lancaster, Pennsylvania, Franklin earned her bachelor's degree from Pennsylvania State University in 1962 and a master's degree in business administration from Harvard University in 1964.

>**See also** Cabinet, Women in; Federal Women's Program
>**References** "Barbara Hackman Franklin, Secretary of Commerce, Advocate for U.S. Business" (1992).

Franklin v. Gwinnett County Public Schools (1992)

Christine Franklin, a student at North Gwinnett High School in Gwinnett County, Georgia, was continually sexually harassed by a teacher, Andrew Hill. Even though administrators and other teachers knew about the harassment, they did nothing to stop it. Instead, they discouraged Franklin from pressing charges against Hill. Hill resigned on the condition that any investigations or charges against him be dropped. The administration accepted the condition and ended the investigation.

Franklin sought damages under Title IX of the Education Amendments of 1972. The question before the U.S. Supreme Court was whether damages could be awarded under Title IX. The Court found that damages could be awarded to enforce Title IX.

>**References** *Franklin v. Gwinnett County Public Schools,* 503 U.S. 60 (1992).

Freedom of Access to Clinic Entrances Act of 1994

Passed in 1994, the Freedom of Access to Clinic Entrances Act was intended to protect women seeking abortions and the physicians performing them by making it a federal crime to obstruct entrances to abortion clinics. The measure came as an attempt to reduce violence at clinics, including 123 arson cases; thirty-seven bombings; and 1,500 cases of stalking, assault, and sabotage between 1982 and 1994. Democratic Congresswoman Patricia Schroeder of Colorado was primarily responsible for the bill's passage.

See also Abortion; Schroeder, Patricia Nell Scott

References Bingham, *Women on the Hill: Challenging the Culture of Congress* (1997).

Friedan, Betty Naomi Goldstein (1921–2006)

Author Betty Friedan's book *The Feminine Mystique*, published in 1963, identified a haunting sense of dissatisfaction that many women shared, motivated women to change their lives, and in the process helped launch the modern feminist movement. A founder of the National Organization for Women and the National Women's Political Caucus, Friedan's leadership in the feminist movement brought her acclaim and criticism both inside and outside the movement she helped create.

Born in Peoria, Illinois, Betty Friedan earned her bachelor's degree from Smith College in 1942 and studied at the University of California at Berkeley, the University of Iowa, and the Esalen Institute. A journalist, Friedan did freelance work following her marriage and the births of her children. In preparation for her Smith College class's fifteenth anniversary reunion in 1957, she wrote and sent a questionnaire to her former classmates. In the hope that she would be able to develop a magazine story from

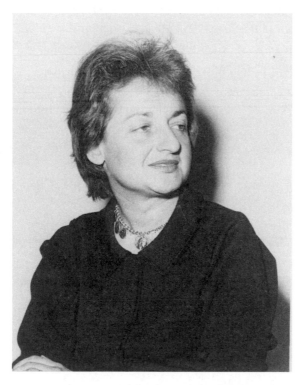

National Organization for Women founder and author of
The Feminine Mystique, Betty Friedan (Library of Congress
Prints and Photographs Division Washington, D.C. 20540 USA LC-USZ62-115884)

the event, she constructed the questions to probe her classmates' experiences since graduation.

The survey responses revealed "the problem that has no name," as Friedan described it. She found that her classmates, like herself, had married well and had successful husbands, talented children, and lives with amenities, but also harbored the aching questions: "Is this all? Is there nothing more in my life?" Friedan wrote an article based on the survey and other research, but magazines rejected it. She expanded the research and wrote a book-length manuscript, *The Feminine Mystique*.

Friedan soon became the leader of a group that had no organization, no structure, and no agenda but nevertheless clamored for changes in women's status. The Equal Employment Opportunity Commission provided a unifying cause when it refused to enforce the ban against sex discrimination in employment contained in Title VII of the Civil Rights Act of 1964, preferring to focus on complaints of race discrimination instead. Friedan and others founded the National Organization for Women (NOW) in 1966 to press the commission to fulfill its mandate and to advocate other legal and social changes. Friedan was founding president of the group, serving until 1970.

Friedan insisted: "This is a two-sex revolution, and when it is completed we will have new and honest patterns of life and profession, where ability and not gender counts." She added: "Man is not the enemy. He is the fellow victim." Her refusal to accept an anti-male ideology and her belief that feminism needed to be more inclusive of family life led to a break between her and the movement she had started. For many women, however, she remained a symbol and leader of the feminist movement.

In the 1980s, Friedan turned her attention to aging, explaining that "now I am in uncharted territory. It isn't that I have stopped being a feminist, but women as a special separate interest group are not my concern anymore." From her research, Friedan concluded in *The Fountain of Age* (1993) that women and men who continued to grow and develop aged the most successfully. She also wrote *It Changed My Life: Writing on the Women's Movement* (1976) and *The Second Stage* (1981).

See also Equal Employment Opportunity Commission; The Feminine Mystique; Feminist Movement; National Organization for Women; National Women's Political Caucus

References *The New York Times*, 29 November 1970, 15 September 1993, 6 February 2006.

Document Betty Friedan, "The Problem That Has No Name," 1963

Frontiero v. Richardson (1973)

In *Frontiero v. Richardson* (1973), the U.S. Supreme Court decided that family members of women in the armed services have the same rights to benefits as the family members of men in the armed services under the due process clause of the Fifth Amendment.

Sharron Frontiero, a lieutenant in the U.S. Air Force, sought to claim her husband as a dependent, which would have granted her a larger housing allowance and provided her husband with medical and dental benefits. The uniformed services automatically granted dependent status to the wives of men in the services, but women in the services had to demonstrate that their husbands were dependents.

The Court noted: "There can be no doubt that our Nation has had a long and unfortunate history of sex discrimination," and "by according differential treatment to male and female members of the uniformed services for the sole purpose of achieving administrative convenience, the challenged statutes violate the Due Process Clause of the Fifth Amendment insofar as they require a female member to prove the dependency of her husband."

In addition, four members, a plurality of the Court, concluded that "classifications based upon sex, like classifications based upon race, alienage, or national origin, are inherently suspect, and must therefore be subjected to strict judicial scrutiny." If one more justice, making a majority, had agreed with the previous statement, the decision would have set a precedent, and sex discrimination would have come under strict scrutiny instead of the intermediate level of scrutiny used in *Reed v. Reed* (1971).

As head of the Women's Rights Project of the American Civil Liberties Union, Ruth Bader Ginsburg, later a U.S. Supreme Court justice, argued the case.

> **See also** American Civil Liberties Union; Ginsburg, Ruth Joan Bader; *Reed v. Reed*; Sex Discrimination
>
> **References** *Frontiero v. Richardson*, 411 U.S. 677 (1973).

Fulani, Lenora Branch (b. ca. 1950)

The first African American and the first woman presidential candidate whose name appeared on the ballots in all 50 states and the District of Columbia, Lenora Fulani ran on the New Alliance Party ticket in 1988. That year, she qualified for federal matching funds, $905,000. She received 240,000 votes, a considerable number for a third-party candidate. When she ran on the ticket in 1992, she received about $1.45 million in federal matching funds, was on the ballot in 45 states, and received 217,000 votes.

Fulani unsuccessfully ran for New York lieutenant governor in 1984 on the New Alliance Party ticket, for mayor of New York City in 1985, and for governor of New York in 1986. Fulani ran in the 1994 New York Democratic primary; she lost, but received 142,000 votes, about 21 percent of those cast. She ran again for lieutenant governor of New York in 1998.

Fulani joined the New Alliance Party in 1980. She described it as "a black-led, multiracial, progressive, third party."

Born in Chester, Pennsylvania, Fulani graduated from Hoftra University in 1971 and earned a master's degree from Columbia University Teachers College in 1972.

> **References** H.W. Wilson, *Current Biography Yearbook 2000* (2001).

Fuller, Margaret (1810–1850)

A major force behind the nineteenth-century American feminist movement, Margaret Fuller called for sexual and social equality for women. Suffrage leader Elizabeth Cady Stanton said that Fuller provided "the vindication of woman's right to think." Fuller's most notable work, *Woman in the Nineteenth Century* (1845), was the beginning of many women's "awakening" to their legal and social status. Fuller demanded equality for women; called for the end of separate spheres of activity; and argued that women needed to develop their intellectual abilities, use their intuitive and creative powers, and become independent before marrying. In her call for women's emotional and fi-

Margaret Fuller, one of the first feminists, advocated women's equality in Woman in the Nineteenth Century *(Library of Congress Prints and Photographs Division Washington, D.C. 20540 USA LC-USZ62-47039)*

nancial independence, Fuller insisted that women must free themselves from men because even the men most sympathetic to women cannot understand women's needs or represent them. She believed that by joining together and forming a sisterhood, women could help each other and take action on social issues, such as opposing the expansion of slavery. To demonstrate women's power, Fuller catalogued the lives of historical and mythological women and offered them as role models.

Born in Cambridgeport, Massachusetts, Fuller received her early education from her father, a member of New England's intellectual elite and the U.S. House of Representatives. Despite her father's disappointment that his firstborn was a daughter, he recognized her intellectual ability and taught her Latin from the time she was six years old. She later attended girls' schools in Boston and Groton, Connecticut.

Fuller taught for a time, but frustration with the classroom led her to develop a series of seminars that leading ladies of Boston paid to attend. Calling the series "conversations," she wrote that they offered "a point of union to well-educated and thinking women ... where many of mature age wish for some place of stimulus and cheer ... and for those younger, a place where they could state their doubts and difficulties, with a hope of gaining aid from the experience or aspirations of others." Begun in 1839, the conversations used Greek mythology to explore the power of human will, sources of creative energy, and development of the arts. The conversations lasted for five years, influencing a nucleus of thinkers who became leaders in the later feminist and abolitionist movements.

Editor of *The Dial*, a Transcendentalist literary and philosophical journal, from 1840 to 1842, she traveled to the Great Lakes, a trip that became the basis for her book *Summer on the Lakes*, in 1843 (1844), and then wrote for the *New York Tribune*. In Europe as the *Tribune*'s foreign correspondent, she wrote thirty-three dispatches on the plight of oppressed people and reported on the 1848 revolution in Italy. During her stay in Italy, Fuller married Giovanni Ossoli and had a son. On the family's return to the United States in 1850, the ship foundered and all three of them drowned.

See also Stanton, Elizabeth Cady; Suffrage

References Matthews, *Women's Struggle for Equality* (1997); Spender, ed., *Feminist Theorists* (1983); von Mehren, *Minerva and the Muse* (1994).

Fulmer, Willa Lybrand (1884–1968)

Democrat Willa Fulmer of South Carolina served in the U.S. House of Representatives from 7 November 1944 to 3 January 1945. Following the death of her husband, Congressman Hampton Pitts Fulmer, Willa Fulmer won the special election to fill the vacancy. Congress adjourned a month after Willa Fulmer took office. She did not receive any committee assignments, nor did she seek another term.

Born in Wagener, South Carolina, Willa Fulmer attended Greenville Female Seminary before marrying Hampton Fulmer.

See also Congress, Women in

References Office of the Historian, U.S. House of Representatives, *Women in Congress, 1917–1990* (1991).

Furse, Elizabeth (b. 1936)

Democrat Elizabeth Furse of Oregon served in the U.S. House of Representatives from 3 January 1993 to 3 January 1999. Furse did not seek a fourth term because she believes in term limits. Co-founder and director of the Oregon Peace Institute in 1985, Furse's motivation to run for Congress was her opposition to the Gulf War. Although she had not been elected to any other office, her years of community activism provided her with a strong network of allies for her candidacy. Furse served on the House Armed Services Committee and worked to cut the defense budget because, she said, the "budget includes every exotic weapon you could possibly think of," but the nation's real enemies are "decaying schools, neglected children, violent streets, too few jobs, disgraceful housing." She passed an amendment that cut the ballistic missile defense program by $150 million and attempted to end funding for the C-17 cargo plane.

Born in Nairobi, Kenya, Furse grew up in South Africa and became a U.S. citizen in 1972. She received her bachelor's degree from Evergreen State College in 1974. A community organizer in Watts in the 1960s, she was director of the Restoration Program for Native American Tribes and lobbied Congress from 1980 to 1986 to pass legislation restoring legal status to three Oregon tribes. In 1982, she managed the successful Oregon ballot measure for a nuclear freeze.

See also Congress, Women in

References *Congressional Quarterly, Politics in America 1996* (1995); www.house.gov/furse/efbio2.htm.

Futrell, Mary Alice Franklin Hatwood (b. 1940)

As president of the National Education Association from 1983 to 1989, Mary Futrell was one of the most powerful African American women in the United States and head of the largest employees' union in the country. Futrell's vision for education included partnerships between business and schools, and programs to reduce high school drop-out rates. She also sought policies to improve and expand Head Start programs, provide child care programs for young families, develop effective drug prevention programs in the schools, ensure adequate resources for schools, and expand the use of computers in teaching. She became president at a time when education was under intense scrutiny and teachers were being criticized for the quality of their work. Futrell countered: "Teachers are easy prey. We're easy people to blame. If we should be blamed for anything, it should be for not standing up to protest against all the burdens that society puts on us."

Born in Alta Vista, Virginia, Futrell earned her bachelor's degree from Virginia State College in 1962, her master's degree in 1968, and her doctorate in education in 1992, the two graduate degrees from George Washington University. She also studied at the University of Virginia from 1978 to 1979 and the Virginia Polytechnic Institute and State University from 1979 to 1980. A high school teacher in Alexandria, Virginia, from 1963 to 1980, Futrell was president of the Virginia Education Association from 1976 to 1978, secretary-treasurer of the National Education Association from 1980 to 1983, and president of the organization from 1983 to 1989.

Futrell became dean of the Graduate School of Education and Human Development at George Washington University in 1995.

References *The New York Times*, 3 July 1983.

Future PAC, The

Founded in 2002 by African American women, The Future PAC seeks to elect more African American women to public office. Through networking and support, The Future PAC raises money, increases awareness of African American women in politics, and is a resource for and about African American women in politics. It also endorses candidates and provides them with financial support. It has endorsed male candidates, Senator Barack Obama (D-IL), for example, and may assist non-African American candidates. Its priority, however, is female African American candidates.

Reference http://thefuturepac.com

G

Gage, Matilda Joslyn (1826–1898)

During the 1800s, Matilda Gage helped develop women's consciousness of their contributions to society through her research and writing. The author of *Woman as Inventor* (1870), Gage illustrated women's contributions to the invention or development of embroidery, bread, the cotton gin, pillow lace, and medical science. In *Woman, Church, and State* (1893), she indicted organized religion for its teachings of women's inferiority and their responsibility for introducing sin into human affairs. Gage also collaborated with Elizabeth Cady Stanton and Susan B. Anthony on *Declaration of the Rights of Women* (1876) and *History of Woman Suffrage*, a multivolume work published from 1881 to 1922. Underlying her work was the belief that the social, political, and economic frameworks created by men needed reconstruction.

Born in Cicero, New York, Gage obtained her education at the Clinton Liberal Institute in New York. She made her first public speech on women's rights at the Third National Women's Rights Convention in Syracuse in 1852. She argued that women did not need to prove their worth to be eligible to vote because they had demonstrated it in the arts, sciences, government, and literature. On another occasion, she described women as political slaves. A member of the first advisory council of the National Woman Suffrage Association (NWSA), Gage wrote for the organization's newspaper, *The Revolution*. She also held several offices in the New York State Woman Suffrage Association and organized education campaigns under its auspices.

Gage founded and was president of the Woman's National Liberal Union in 1890, an organization that criticized social mores and advocated the clear separation of church and state.

See also Abolitionist Movement, Women in the; Anthony, Susan Brownell; National Woman Suffrage Association; Stanton, Elizabeth Cady; Suffrage; Temperance Movement, Women in the

References Spender, ed., *Feminist Theorists* (1983); Whitman, ed., *American Reformers* (1985).

Gasque Van Exem, Elizabeth Mills Hawley (1886–1989)

Democrat Elizabeth Gasque of South Carolina served in the U.S. House of Representatives from 13 September 1938 to 3 January 1939. Following the death of her husband, Congressman Allard Gasque, Elizabeth Gasque won a special election to fill the vacancy. She was not sworn in because Congress did not reconvene that session. She did not run for re-election.

Born on Rice Creek Plantation, Richland County, South Carolina, Elizabeth Gasque attended South Carolina Coeducational Institute and received a degree in expression from Greenville Female College in 1907.

See also Congress, Women in

References Office of the Historian, U.S. House of Representatives, *Women in Congress, 1917–1990* (1991).

Geduldig v. Aiello (1974)

In *Geduldig v. Aiello*, an employed woman argued that California's disability insurance program discriminated against women because it did not cover pregnancy. The insurance program was managed by the state for private employees who contributed 1 percent of their income to it. The U.S. Supreme Court decided that the plan did not violate the Fourteenth Amendment's equal protection clause, explaining: "There is no risk from which men are protected and women are not. Likewise, there is no risk from which women are protected and men are not."

Congress passed the Pregnancy Discrimination Act of 1978, which required employers to include pregnancy and related disabilities in their insurance programs.

See also *California Federal Savings and Loan v. Guerra*; Fourteenth Amendment; *General Electric v. Gilbert*; *Nashville Gas Co. v. Satty*; Pregnancy Discrimination Act of 1978

References *Geduldig v. Aiello*, 417 U.S. 484 (1974).

Gender Gap

The gender gap is the difference between the proportion of women and the proportion of men voting for the winning candidate. Despite suffragists' hopes that women would become a voting bloc, the first hints of that phenomenon did not appear until 1952, thirty-two years after women gained voting rights. In 1952, women voted for successful Republican presidential nominee Dwight D. Eisenhower in greater percentages than men did. Women's hopes that he could end the Korean War, which had begun in 1950, contributed to their support for Eisenhower. Almost another thirty years passed before political observers recognized another appearance of the gender gap. Since 1980, women have tended to vote for Democrats, and men have been more likely to vote for Republicans. Since the 1980 presidential race between Democrat Jimmy Carter and Republican Ronald Reagan, the proportion of women voting for Democratic presidential candidates has grown. In 1996, Democratic presidential candidate Bill Clinton was elected, with 11 percent more women than men voting for him. The gap persisted in the 2000 presidential election, with 53 percent of men and 43 percent of women voting for George W. Bush. Al Gore won 54 percent of women's votes and 42 percent of men's. The gap in the 2004 presidential elections was not as great, with 48 percent of women voting for George W. Bush and 53 percent of men.

The gender gap also appears in senatorial races. For example, in California Democratic candidate Barbara Boxer's 1992 race for the U.S. Senate, 57 percent of the women voted for her and 43 percent for her Republican opponent, whereas 43 percent of the men voted for Boxer and 51 percent of the men voted for her opponent. Women's votes provided the winning margin in dozens of Democratic candidates' congressional and senatorial races in the 1980s and 1990s. The pattern continues even when the Republican candidate is a woman. In Maine's 1996 Senate race, Republican Susan Collins won with 43 percent of women's votes and 56 percent of men's votes. Her Democratic opponent lost with 48 percent of women's votes and 39 percent of men's votes. In the 2000 U.S. Senate races, women provided the margins of victory for the three women who won, all Democrats. In Hillary Rodham's New York Senate race, men voted equally for her and her opponent, but women gave her 60 percent of their votes and only 39 percent for her opponent. Washington Democrat Debbie Stabenow won 54 percent of women's votes and her opponent won 54 percent of men's votes. Washington Democrat Maria Cantwell's race had the same voting distribution as Stabenow's.

See also Democratic Party, Women in the; Republican Party, Women in the

References Center for the American Woman and Politics, Eagleton Institute, Rutgers University; www.feminist.org.

General Electric v. Gilbert (1976)

In *General Electric v. Gilbert*, decided in 1976, the U.S. Supreme Court found that excluding pregnancy from a disability plan does not violate Title VII of the Civil Rights Act of 1964. General Electric provided a disability plan that paid benefits to employees for non-occupational sickness and accidents but excluded pregnancy from the covered disabilities. In its decision, the Court explained: "Pregnancy-related disabilities constitute an *additional* risk, unique to women, and the failure to compensate them for this risk does not destroy the presumed parity of the benefits, accruing to men and women alike" (emphasis in original).

Congress responded to the decision by passing the Pregnancy Discrimination Act of 1978. The measure requires employers to treat pregnancy the same as other temporary disabilities.

See also *California Federal Savings and Loan v. Guerra*; Civil Rights Act of 1964, Title VII; Employment Discrimination; *Geduldig v. Aiello*; *Nashville Gas Co. v. Satty*; Pregnancy Discrimination Act of 1978

References *General Electric v. Gilbert*, 429 U.S. 125 (1976).

General Federation of Women's Clubs

Founded in 1890, the General Federation of Women's Clubs (GFWC) is the oldest nonpartisan, nondenominational women's volunteer organization in the world and, until 1900, was the largest women's organization in the country. It has 6,500 affiliated clubs with more than one million members.

GFWC has its roots in Sorosis, a woman's literary club organized by journalist Jane Cunningham Croly in 1868. After the all-male New York Press Club denied Croly and other women admittance to an 1868 banquet honoring Charles Dickens, Croly formed Sorosis for women only. Sorosis is a Greek word meaning an aggregation: a sweet flavor of many fruits.

Sorosis's founders thought that they were starting a new movement but learned that other independent women's clubs had formed across the country. In 1889, Croly convened a national conference that brought together delegates from sixty-one women's clubs. A constitution and an organizational plan were developed and approved the next year. At the first GFWC conference, the group adopted the motto "Unity in Diversity."

Self-improvement and development were the early focuses of women's clubs, with the agenda expanded to include arts, conservation, education, home life, international affairs, and public affairs. As women's clubs grew in popularity across the country, groups of African American women formed and sought membership in the GFWC. Initially, the GFWC refused to admit clubs dominated by black women, who responded by forming their own federations, including the Colored Women's League and the National Federation of Afro-American Women, which merged into the National Association of Colored Women. Some African American women, however, belonged to local women's clubs that were affiliated with GFWC. When two of these women, Josephine St. Pierre Ruffin and Mary Church Terrell, sought to address GFWC's national convention in 1900, GFWC leaders refused the request and a controversy ensued. Some GFWC member clubs threatened to leave the organization if Ruffin and Terrell were not permitted to speak and others threatened to leave if they were. GFWC resolved the problem at its 1902 convention by declaring that each state affiliate could determine which clubs could belong to it, and that all clubs that belonged to a state affiliate also belonged to the GFWC.

The GFWC established a national model for juvenile courts, and worked to establish the first Forest Reserve in the country in 1899. The GFWC also helped pass the 1906 Pure Food and Drugs Act, and worked for the eight-hour day, the first child labor law, the child labor amendment, the woman suffrage amendment, and independent citizenship for women. Opposed to the Equal Rights Amendment in 1922, GFWC changed its position in 1940 and became a supporter of the ERA. Through its network of grassroots volunteers, the GFWC continues to work for a range of issues, including protecting children from abuse and promoting adoption, implementing tax credits for purchasing health insurance, requiring clothing labels that identify articles made without abusive and exploitative child labor, passing equal pay legislation, requiring child safety locks on handguns, and increasing child literacy.

See also Cable Acts; Child Labor Amendment; Colored Women's League; Croly, Jane Cunningham; Equal Rights Amendment; National Association of Colored Women; Pay Equity; Protective Legislation; Ruffin, Josephine St. Pierre; Suffrage; Terrell, Mary Eliza Church; Women's Joint Congressional Committee

References Lemons, *The Woman Citizen: Social Feminism in the 1920s* (1973); www.gfwc.org.

Gibbs, Florence Reville (1890–1964)

Democrat Florence Gibbs of Georgia served in the U.S. House of Representatives from 1 October 1940 to 3 January 1941. Following the death of her husband, Congressman

Willis Gibbs, she won the special election to fill the vacancy. She did not run for re-election.

Born in Thomson, Georgia, Florence Gibbs graduated from Brenau College.

See also Congress, Women in

References Office of the Historian, U.S. House of Representatives, *Women in Congress, 1917–1990* (1991).

Gibbs, Lois (b. 1951)

Lois Gibbs prides herself on being a good mother, and sending her children to school on land contaminated with toxic chemicals did not fall within her definition of being a good mother. Her children's school in the state of New York was built over 21,800 tons of chemicals, which eventually leaked from their containers and appeared in the schoolyard and in neighbors' basements. Her daughter developed a blood disorder and other children in the area developed illnesses, which Gibbs believed were related to the contamination in the area known as Love Canal. The waste site became Lois Gibbs's catalyst for environmental activism. In 1978, she founded the Love Canal Homeowners' Association to organize neighbors to work out a unified strategy to compel local, state, and federal officials to relocate the families. One of the greatest obstacles Gibbs confronted was that there were no government programs to deal with the problem.

To convince government agencies that a problem existed, Gibbs and her neighbors conducted a health study of area residents. They found that 56 percent of the children were born with birth defects, 22 women had miscarriages, and other health anomalies. Initially, government agencies dismissed their findings. As Gibbs and others continued their fight, they added new strategies to their efforts, demonstrating, meeting with politicians, and attempting to get media attention.

When Gibbs and her followers convinced the Environmental Protection Agency (EPA) to investigate, it was during a time of intense emotions. A confrontation between residents and EPA representatives culminated in the crowd holding the representatives hostage for five hours. The FBI threatened to push through the crowd and free them, but Gibbs intervened and asked the crowd to vote on releasing the hostages. The crowd voted to release the hostages. Three days later, everyone was given the opportunity to temporarily relocate and on 1 October 1980, funding for permanent relocation was offered. A few months later, the first Superfund bill to clean up toxic waste sites passed Congress.

In 1981, Gibbs founded the Center for Health, Environment and Justice (CHEJ), which builds coalitions, provides training, and offers one-on-one technical support. Through its efforts, one company changed the packaging material from one high in toxicity to another less toxic. She believes that by personalizing environmental issues and identifying actions that citizens can take, change occurs. She explained: "If we frame the environmental problem as community and health, as opposed to trees and water, I think we have the ability to really capture the energy of people in communities all across the country."

Gibbs was born in Grand Island, New York.

Reference Sharon M. Livesey, "Organizing and Leading the Grassroots: An Interview with Lois Gibbs, Love Canal Homeowners' Association Activist, Founder of Citizens Clearinghouse for Hazardous Waster, and Executive Director of the Center for Health, Environment and Justice," *Organization & Environment,* December 2003, p. 488.

Document Lois Gibbs, "Green School Initiatives," 2002

Gilman, Charlotte Perkins (1860–1935)

Humanist and feminist intellectual Charlotte Perkins Gilman argued for women's economic independence as the route to their equality with men. Her most influential work, *Women and Economics: A Study of the Economic Relation between Men and Women as a Factor in Social Evolution*, published in 1898, examined the economic relationship between men and women. She concluded that a woman's survival depended upon her ability to attract and keep a husband, making her relationship with her husband into an economic relationship. Claiming that the sexual division of labor stifled and limited women and condemning households as prisons, Gilman asserted that women held the role of servant, even though the work they did was essential to human life.

Gilman believed that each person should be allowed to develop her or his potential and that women should be permitted to pursue the paid employment for which they were best qualified. Her vision included central kitchens that employed cooks to pre-

Charlotte Perkins Gilman argued for economic independence and freedom from domestic servitude for women, ca. 1900 (Library of Congress LC-USZ62-106490)

pare meals for several families, and child care centers that provided supervision and education for children from infancy to school age. She also proposed employing expert housekeepers for cleaning. With household and family chores assumed by paid workers, women whose talents lent themselves to other endeavors would become free to pursue them for wages. By providing her own economic sustenance, a woman could be equal to her husband.

Gilman's theories emerged at least in part from her own experiences. Born in Hartford, Connecticut, she finished private school when she was sixteen and began searching for ways to become economically independent. She attended the Rhode Island School of Design and took correspondence classes. Despite her intention to remain single, she married in 1884 and had a daughter in 1885. Two years later, she found work writing a local newspaper column and selling greeting cards, but those jobs did not last long.

Plagued with depression and unable to care for her home, husband, and daughter, she consulted doctors who recommended enforced rest, passivity, and acceptance of male dominance. She and her husband separated in 1888, and Gilman and her daughter moved to California. She wrote poetry and fiction and, in 1890, began a lecture series on the need for women's economic independence, the importance of collective enterprise, and community effort as the only possibility for solving some problems.

Gilman and her husband divorced in 1894, but he remained one of her closest friends. When he remarried, Gilman sent their daughter to live with him and his new wife, freeing herself from domestic responsibilities. Gilman moved into Chicago's Hull House in 1895 and continued to lecture. In 1900, Gilman married her first cousin, George Houghton Gilman. She wrote *Concerning Children*, published in 1900, and *The Home: Its Work and Influence*, published in 1903. She was popular on the lecture circuit until 1915, but her ideas lost their appeal as war began in Europe and other national and international events contributed to changing the climate of opinion.

See also Congressional Union; National American Woman Suffrage Association; National Woman's Party; Suffrage

References Lane, *To Herland and Beyond: The Life and Work of Charlotte Perkins Gilman* (1991).

Ginsburg, Ruth Joan Bader (b. 1933)

On 10 August 1993, Ruth Bader Ginsburg became the nation's 107th justice and second woman on the U.S. Supreme Court. After earning her law degree at Columbia University Law School in 1959, Ginsburg applied to U.S. Supreme Court Justice Felix Frankfurter to serve as his law clerk, but Frankfurter refused her because she was a woman. Instead, she clerked for a justice in the U.S. District Court in New York from 1959 to 1961. The second woman on the Rutgers University Law School's faculty when she joined it in 1963, she accepted several sex discrimination cases referred to her by the American Civil Liberties Union (ACLU). Despite Frankfurter's refusal to hire her because of her sex, as well as comparable experiences in law school, Ginsburg had not categorized such incidents as sex discrimination. As she worked on the cases referred to her by the ACLU, however, she concluded that gender distinctions affected every

Appointed in 1993, Supreme Court Justice Ruth Bader Ginsburg was only the second woman to serve on the U.S. Supreme Court (Courtesy: U.S. Supreme Court)

aspect of life. She explained: "Once I became involved, I found the legal work fascinating and had high hopes for significant change in the next decade."

In the 1970s, Ginsburg headed the Women's Rights Project of the American Civil Liberties Union, argued six sex discrimination cases before the U.S. Supreme Court, and won five of them. The cases these decisions overturned included an Idaho law that gave precedence to men over women in serving as the administrator of an estate (*Reed v. Reed*, 1971), an Oklahoma law that specified different legal drinking ages for women and men (*Craig v. Boren*, 1976), and a Missouri law that made jury duty optional for women but not for men. She successfully argued that military benefits for husbands of military personnel must be granted on the same basis as those for wives of military personnel (*Frontiero v. Richardson*, 1973). Two years later she persuaded the Court that a Social Security program providing benefits to widows with minor children based upon the deceased husband's contributions should be extended to widowers with minor children (*Weinberger v. Wiesenfeld*, 1975). Sworn in as a member of the U.S. Court of Appeals for the District of Columbia in 1980, she wrote more than 300 opinions in the next thirteen years.

Although she supports reproductive rights, Ginsburg believes that *Roe v. Wade* "went too far in the changes it ordered." During her confirmation hearings for the Supreme Court, Ginsburg said: "[Abortion] is something central to a woman's life, to her dignity. It's a decision she must make for herself. And when government controls that decision for her, she's being treated as less than a fully adult human responsible for her own choices."

As a justice on the Court, Ginsburg has been called a judicial minimalist, restrained, cautious, and non-ideological in her decisions. Perhaps the most visible decision she wrote was *United States v. Virginia*, a sex discrimination case in which the Virginia Military Institute denied admissions to women. Reflecting her work at the Women's Rights Project, she wrote that for a government to discriminate on the basis of sex, "an exceedingly persuasive justification" had to exist, which Ginsburg did not find in Virginia Military Institute's arguments.

Born in Brooklyn, New York, Ginsburg received her bachelor's degree from Cornell University in 1954 and attended Harvard Law School from 1956 to 1958 before transferring to Columbia University Law School.

See also Abortion; American Civil Liberties Union; *Craig v. Boren*; *Frontiero v. Richardson*; *Reed v. Reed*; *Roe v. Wade*; *Weinberger v. Wiesenfeld*

References *Congressional Quarterly Almanac, 103rd Congress, 1st Session... 1993* (1994); Clare Cushman, ed., *Supreme Court Decisions and Women's Rights: Milestones to Equality* (Washington, D.C.: CQ Press, 2001); H. W. Wilson, *Current Biography Yearbook, 1994* (1994); http://supct.law.cornell.edu/supct/justices.bio.html.

Documents Ruth Bader Ginsburg, "Let's Have ERA as a Signal," 1977; Ruth Bader Ginsburg, "The Supreme Court: A Place for Women"

Glass Ceiling Commission

Created as part of the Civil Rights Act of 1991, the Glass Ceiling Commission had twenty-one members appointed by the president and Congress. The commission focused on barriers and opportunities in three areas: selection of candidates for management and decision-making positions, skill development programs, and compensation and reward systems. Chaired by the secretary of labor, the commission completed its work in 1996. It defined "glass ceiling" as "artificial barriers based on attitudinal or organizational biases that prevent qualified women and minorities from advancing upward into management-level positions."

See also Civil Rights Act of 1991

References *Congressional Quarterly Almanac, 102nd Congress, 1st Session... 1991* (1992).

Godwin, Mary Wollstonecraft

See **Wollstonecraft, Mary**

Goesaert v. Cleary (1948)

In *Goesaert v. Cleary*, the U.S. Supreme Court decided in 1948 that discrimination on the basis of sex did not violate the equal protection clause of the Fourteenth Amendment. The case addressed a Michigan law that forbade a female to be a bartender unless she was the wife or daughter of the male owner of a licensed liquor establishment. The Court explained: "The fact that women may now have achieved the virtues that men have long claimed as their prerogatives and now indulge in vices that men have long practiced, does not preclude the states from drawing a sharp line between the sexes, certainly in such matters as the regulation of the liquor traffic." Even though women could be waitresses in bars regardless of their relationship to the owner, the Court wrote: "Michigan evidently believes that the oversight assured through ownership of a bar by a barmaid's husband or father minimizes hazards that may confront a barmaid without such protecting oversight."

Following the passage of Title VII of the Civil Rights Act of 1964, the Court found sex discrimination in employment unconstitutional.

See also Civil Rights Act of 1964, Title VII; Employment Discrimination; Equal Employment Opportunity Commission; Fourteenth Amendment

References *Goesaert v. Cleary*, 335 U.S. 464 (1948).

Goldman, Emma (1869–1940)

Anarchist and feminist Emma Goldman argued that sexual oppression was as important as class oppression in causing human suffering. Born in Kovno, Lithuania, Goldman emigrated to the United States in 1885 to avoid an arranged marriage. After the Chicago Haymarket Square riot in 1886 and the subsequent execution of the Haymarket anarchists, she declared herself an anarchist.

In 1893, Goldman told unemployed workers: "Demonstrate before the places of the rich, demand work. If they do not give you work, demand bread. If they deny you both, take bread. It is your sacred right." Arrested for inciting people to riot, she served one year in prison. She was again arrested in 1901, following the arrest of anarchist Leon Czolgosz for shooting President William McKinley. Authorities believed that she had been involved but were unable to find evidence linking her to the crime, and she was released. Goldman began publishing a monthly anarchist magazine, *Mother Earth*, in 1906 and began a national lecture tour to publicize and support it. She continued publishing *Mother Earth* until 1917, when another prison sentence forced her to abandon the magazine.

A certified midwife and nurse, Goldman worked among poor immigrant women. Repeated pregnancies damaged their health and contributed to a high infant mortality rate. The plight of women bearing unwanted children they could not afford to feed or

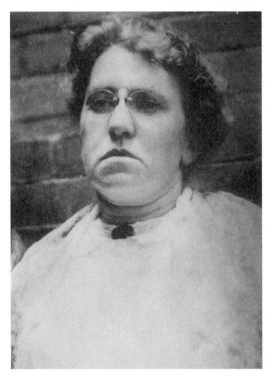

Famous anarchist Emma Goldman s, 1907 (Library of Congress Prints and Photographs Division Washington, D.C. 20540 USA LC-DIG-ggbain-02603)

house and women's attempts to abort their pregnancies convinced Goldman that women needed birth control information. Contraceptive information, however, was classified as obscene under the Comstock law passed in 1873. In 1915, Goldman lectured on contraception and offered pamphlets that gave specific instructions on contraceptive methods. She was arrested at a lecture in New York for selling or advertising contraceptives, even though her lecture dealt with the need to make the materials available and she was not describing contraceptive methods. She used her trial to attract publicity for birth control and the necessity of its availability. She was jailed for two weeks in 1916.

Opposed to U.S. involvement in World War I, Goldman believed that war enslaved workers while enriching masters. She helped men who refused to register for the military, leading to her arrest in 1917 for conspiring against the draft. As she had in her birth control trial, Goldman used the trial to publicize her anarchist views and her opposition to the Selective Service. She was sentenced to two years in prison.

Deported to Russia in 1919, Goldman descried the increasing centralization, bureaucratization, and militarization of the country and moved to England in 1921. She exposed the excesses of the revolution in articles for the *New York World* and wrote *My Disillusionment in Russia* (1923); *My Further Disillusionment in Russia* (1924); and her autobiography, *Living My Life* (1931).

See also Dennett, Mary Coffin Ware; Sanger, Margaret Louise Higgins
References Solomon, *Emma Goldman* (1987); Spender, *Feminist Theorists* (1983).

Goodman, Amy (b. ca. 1957)

Host and executive producer of radio program "*Democracy Now!*," Amy Goodman explores stories and perspectives often marginalized by other media. Called the "voice of the disenfranchised left" by one newspaper, she has reported from Peru, Haiti, Jamaica, Nigeria, Indonesia, and other nations.

While reporting East Timor's battle for independence, she and a colleague, Allan Nairn, witnessed the massacre of 270 East Timorese by Indonesian soldiers. Goodman and Nairn survived, but were beaten by the soldiers. Their documentary on the massacre won several awards.

After graduating from Harvard-Radcliffe in 1984, with a bachelor's degree in anthropology, Goodman began her radio career with Pacifica Radio's New York station WBAI in 1985, producing the station's evening news for 10 years. In 1996, "Democracy Now!" went on the air as a daily election coverage program, which continued after the election and became the network's flagship news and public affairs program.

Goodman's antiwar sentiments have attracted many listeners. Describing her approach to reporting the war in Iraq, she said: "War coverage should be more than a parade of retired generals and retired government flacks posing as reporters."

With her brother David Goodman, she is the author of *Exception to the Rulers: Exposing Oily Politicians, War Profiteers, and the Media That Love Them* (2004).

References *The Los Angeles Times*, April 21, 2004; *The New York Times*, April 22, 1999; *The Washington Post*, March 10, 2003; http://www.democracynow.org/staff.shtml

Goodwin, Doris Kearns (b. 1943)

Presidential historian and author Doris Kearns Goodwin has provided news analysis for NBC News and contributed to Public Broadcasting Service (PBS) documentaries. Goodwin's presidential biographies include *Lyndon Johnson and the American Dream*(1976), The *Fitzgeralds and the Kennedys: An American Saga* (1987), *No Ordinary Time: Franklin and Eleanor Roosevelt; The Home Front in World War II* (1995), and *Team of Rivals: the Political Genius of Abraham Lincoln* (2006).

Goodwin held internships in the U.S. House of Representatives (1965) and the U.S. Department of Labor (1967) and was staff assistant to President Lyndon B. Johnson in 1968.

Born in Brooklyn, New York, Goodwin earned a bachelor of arts degree at Colby College in 1964 and a doctor of philosophy degree at Harvard University in 1968.

References http://www.doriskearnsgoodwin.com/about.php

Governors, Women

In 2006, eight women (six Democrats and two Republicans) served as governor of their states. A total of 28 women have held the office. In 2002, ten women ran for governor of their states and five women won, the most in any single election year. Their successes could be attributed to several factors, perhaps the most significant that several of the women ran for open seats, but the mediocre economy may have contributed, as well as the women candidates' credentials and political experience.

The first woman governor was Democrat Nellie Tayloe Ross of Wyoming. Ross, who followed her husband in office after his death, won a special election and served from 1925 to 1927. Democrat Miriam Ferguson of Texas became governor fifteen days after Ross, serving from 1925 to 1927 and from 1933 to 1935. More than thirty years would pass before Democrat Lurleen Wallace of Alabama would serve as governor from 1967 to 1968.

The first woman governor whose husband had not held the office before her was Democrat Ella Grasso of Connecticut. Grasso took office in 1975 and served until late 1980, when she resigned for health reasons. Three other Democratic women governors were Dixie Lee Ray of Washington (1977–1981), Martha Layne Collins of Kentucky (1984–1988), and Madeleine Kunin of Vermont (1985–1991). Kay Orr of Nebraska (1987–1991) was the first Republican woman to serve as governor and the first female gubernatorial candidate to run against another female candidate. Democrat Rose Mofford of Arizona became governor following the impeachment and conviction of the incumbent governor and served from 1988 to 1991. The first woman to defeat an incumbent governor, Democrat Joan Finney of Kansas, served from 1991 to 1995. Both Ann Richards (D-TX) and Barbara Roberts (D-OR) served from 1991 to 1995. Republican Christine Todd Whitman of New Jersey was elected in 1993, re-elected in 1997, and resigned in 2001 to accept appointment as commissioner of the U.S. Environmental Protection Agency. and Democrat Jeanne Shaheen of New Hampshire began serving in 1997. After another incumbent's removal from office in Arizona (for fraud), Republican Jane Dee Hull became governor in 1997, serving until 2003. Republican Nancy Hollister served as Ohio's governor for eleven days when the incumbent resigned to take another office.

In 2001, three women were elected governors: Republican Jane Swift of Massachusetts after the incumbent accepted another office; Republican Judy Martz of Montana served from 2001 to 2005; and Democrat Ruth Ann Minner of Delaware. Democrat Jennifer Granholm of Michigan, Republican Linda Lingle of Hawaii, Democrat Janet Napolitano of Arizona, and Democrat Kathleen Sebelius of Kansas all took office in 2003. Democrat Kathleen Bianco of Louisiana, Republican M. Jodi Rell of Connecticut succeeded the incumbent who resigned, and Democrat Christine Gregoire of Washington took office in 2004.

> **See also** Collins, Martha Layne Hall; Ferguson, Miriam Amanda Wallace; Finney, Joan; Grasso, Ella Rosa Giovanna Oliva Tambussi; Hull, Jane Dee Bowersock; Kunin, Madeleine May; Mofford, Rose Perica; Orr, Kay Avonne Stark; Ray, Dixy Lee; Richards, Ann Willis; Roberts, Barbara Hughey; Ross, Nellie Tayloe; Roy, Vesta M.; Shaheen, Jeanne; Wallace, Lurleen Burns; Whitman, Christine Todd
>
> **References** Center for the American Woman and Politics, Eagleton Institute of Politics, Rutgers University; Siobhan Gorman, "A 'Tiping Point' for Women Governors?" *National Journal*, 19 October 2002, p. 3082.

Granahan, Kathryn Elizabeth O'Hay (1894–1979)

Democrat Kathryn Granahan of Pennsylvania served in the U.S. House of Representatives from 6 November 1956 to 3 January 1963. Following the death of her husband, Congressman William Granahan, Kathryn Granahan succeeded him as Democratic leader of Philadelphia's Fifty-second Ward and became the party's nominee to complete his term. She won two elections on the same day, one to fill the vacancy and the other to a full term. While in Congress, Granahan worked to eliminate obscenity in literature and in movies, arguing that it contributed to juvenile delinquency and had ill effects on everyone. She was chief sponsor of bills that required mandatory jail sentences for operating a pornographic mail order business and that strengthened the Post Office's power to impound mail addressed to people suspected of mailing pornographic materials. She also asked the U.S. Supreme Court to issue clear guidelines defining pornography.

When Pennsylvania lost a House seat following the 1960 census, Democratic Party leaders decided to sacrifice Granahan's seat, and she retired. Appointed treasurer of the United States by President John F. Kennedy, she served from 1963 to 1966.

Born in Easton, Pennsylvania, Kathryn Granahan attended Mount St. Joseph Collegiate Institute. She was supervisor of public assistance in the Pennsylvania state auditor general's office from 1940 to 1943.

> **See also** Congress, Women in
>
> **References** Engelbarts, *Women in the United States Congress, 1917–1972* (1974); Office of the Historian, U.S. House of Representatives, *Women in Congress, 1917–1990* (1991).

Granger, Kay (b. 1943)

Republican Kay Granger of Texas entered the U.S. House of Representatives on 3 January 1997. She held the leadership position of assistant majority whip in the 105th and 106th Congresses (1997–2001). She began her political career serving on the Fort Worth City Council from 1989 to 1991 and was mayor of the city from 1991 to 1995. To lower the city's crime rate, Granger persuaded the Texas legislature to permit cities to create crime districts, impose a 0.5 percent sales tax, and use the money for crime prevention. By trying a variety of approaches to reduce crime, discarding those that did not work, and expanding the successful ones, Granger and the community reduced crime in Fort Worth by 50 percent. The city's loss of thousands of jobs prompted Granger to develop public-private partnerships that diversified the economy and made it more stable.

Her freshman year, Congresswoman Granger introduced the Higher Education and Learning Promotion Act of 1997 to allow taxpayers receiving the child tax credit to place the money in a tax-free educational savings account. Included in a tax cut bill, it was signed into law. She negotiated a plan to restore funds for manufacturing the F-16 fighter jet, which is built in her district and employs 11,000 workers. Granger supports reproductive rights, a balanced federal budget, and tax cuts for families and small businesses.

Born in Greenville, Texas, Kay Granger received her bachelor of science degree from Texas Wesleyan University in 1965. Before entering politics, she taught school and founded an insurance agency.

> **See also** Abortion; Congress, Women in
> **References** *Congressional Quarterly, Politics in America 1998* (1997); www.pbs.org/newshour/.

Granholm, Jennifer Mulhern (b. 1959)

Michigan Governor Jennifer Granholm wanted to be an actress. After living in Los Angeles for three years and finding little success, she enrolled in the University of California, Berkeley, and earned a bachelor of arts degree in political science in 1984. She earned a JD degree at Harvard University Law School in 1987. A federal prosecutor for the U.S. Department of Justice in Detroit from 1994 to 1996, she had a 98% conviction rate. From 1996 to 1998, Granholm was general counsel for the Detroit and Wayne County Stadium Authority.

Granholm had worked for Independent presidential candidate John Anderson in 1980 and was a field coordinator for Democratic presidential nominee Michael Dukakis in 1988. She became a candidate in 1998, when she ran for Michigan attorney general on the Democratic ticket. In 2002, she successfully ran for governor on the Democratic ticket. Granholm campaigned on curbing urban sprawl, reviving Michigan's cities, enforcing environmental laws, and protecting the state's lakes, waterways, and other natural areas. When she took office, the state faced $4 billion in deficits, which Granholm resolved. She attracted new jobs to the state, expanded health care coverage to include more families, and increased spending for public schools.

Born in Vancouver, British Columbia Granholm moved with her family to southern California when she was three years old.

> **References** "Biographies: Michigan," *National Journal*, 9 November 2002, p. 3310; H.W. Wilson, *Current Biography 2003* (2004); "Michigan's Makeover," *E Magazine*, March/April 2004, pp. 20-22.

Grasso, Ella Rosa Giovanna Oliva Tambussi (1919–1981)

Democrat Ella Grasso of Connecticut served in the U.S. House of Representatives from 21 January 1971 to 3 January 1975 and was governor of Connecticut from 1975 to 1980. She was the first woman to become governor whose husband did not precede her in office.

Grasso's political involvement began when she joined the League of Women Voters (LWV) in 1943. After years of working for other candidates, she ran for the Connecticut House of Representatives, where she served from 1953 to 1957. While in the House, Grasso led a reorganization of state government that eliminated counties, a concept she had worked on as a member of the LWV. After leaving the House, in the late 1950s she was a primary leader in the development of a new state constitution, which went into effect in 1960. Connecticut secretary of state from 1959 to 1971, Grasso became one of the state's best-known politicians and was increasingly visible in the Democratic Party.

As a member of Congress, Grasso worked for the Emergency Employment Act of 1971, the Higher Education Act of 1972, benefits for veterans, assistance for the elderly, and appropriations to fight sickle-cell anemia and Cooley's anemia. She supported an increase in the minimum wage and played a major role in drafting the Comprehensive Employment and Training Act. She opposed reproductive rights.

During her 1974 campaign for governor, she commissioned an investigation that revealed significant overcharges by Connecticut's three major utilities and vowed to reform them. Keeping her pledge once in office, she proposed new financing methods for the utilities' capital improvements, management audit teams, and the creation of an ombudsman's office. When Grasso took office, she discovered that Connecticut had significant financial problems. She reduced state spending and avoided implementing a state income tax. Voters showed their appreciation by re-electing her in 1978. She resigned the governorship on 31 December 1980 because she had ovarian cancer that had spread to other organs.

Born in Windsor Locks, Connecticut, Grasso received her bachelor's degree in economics and sociology in 1941 and her master's degree in 1942, both from Mount Holyoke College.

> **See also** Abortion; Congress, Women in; Governors, Women; State Legislatures, Women in
>
> **References** Engelbarts, *Women in the United States Congress, 1917–1972* (1974); H. W. Wilson, *Current Biography Yearbook, 1975* (1975); *The New York Times*, 6 February 1981.

Gratz et al. v. Bollinger (2003)

Jennifer Gratz and Patrick Hamacher, both white Michigan residents, applied to the University of Michigan's College of Literature, Science, and the Arts (LSA) in the 1990s. After being denied admission, they sued LSA for racial discrimination in violation of the Equal Protection Clause of the Fourteenth Amendment, Title VI of the Civil Rights Act of 1964, and other laws. They based their lawsuit on the racial preference granted every minority applicant. LSA's admissions policy considered high school grades, standardized test scores, curriculum strength, and other factors, granting applicants points in each category. LSA guaranteed admission to applicants with 100 points. In addition to the categories listed above for white applicants, minority students were automatically awarded 20 points. The 20-point advantage given to minority students was the policy that Gratz and Hamacher challenged in their lawsuit.

LSA argued that its goal was to create a diverse student body, but the U.S. Supreme Court found its strategy of granting every minority applicant the 20-point advantage too broad to be constitutional. The Court decided in *Gratz v. Bollinger* that the policy violated the Equal Protection Clause of the Fourteenth Amendment, Title VI of the Civil Rights Act of 1964, and other laws.

References *Gratz v. Bollinger* 539 U.S. 244 (2003)

Graves, Dixie Bibb (1882–1965)

Democrat Dixie Graves of Alabama served in the U.S. Senate from 20 August 1937 to 10 January 1938. When incumbent U.S. Senator Hugo Black was appointed to the U.S. Supreme Court, Alabama Governor Bibb Graves appointed his wife, Dixie Graves, to fill the vacancy until an election could be held. During her brief tenure, Senator Graves made a speech to the Senate tearfully pleading with her colleagues to defeat the anti-lynching bill before them. She argued that the South's law enforcement system could decrease lynching without federal involvement. The extent of her influence on the Senate is unknown, but the speech made her so popular in Alabama that a write-in campaign to make her a candidate for the balance of the term began. She declined, however, and did not run.

Born on a plantation near Montgomery, Alabama, Graves's formal education was limited. As a member of the State Literacy Commission and as chair of the General Federation of Women's Clubs' Commission on Literacy, she worked to end illiteracy. Active in the Alabama Equal Suffrage Association, she served on the state's ratification committee, but Alabama failed to ratify the Nineteenth Amendment. She was president of the Alabama Division of the United Daughters of the Confederacy from 1915 to 1917 and vice president of the Alabama Federation of Women's Clubs in 1929.

See also Anti-lynching Movement; Congress, Women in; General Federation of Women's Clubs; Nineteenth Amendment; Suffrage

References Boxer, *Strangers in the Senate: Politics and the New Revolution of Women in America* (1994); Office of the Historian, U.S. House of Representatives, *Women in Congress, 1917–1990* (1991); Yelverton, *They Also Served: Twenty-Five Remarkable Alabama Women* (1993).

Green, Edith Louise Starrett (1910–1987)

Democrat Edith Green of Oregon served in the U.S. House of Representatives from 3 January 1955 to 31 December 1975. An unsuccessful candidate for secretary of state for Oregon in 1952, Green emphasized education in her successful campaign for Congress in 1954. In her first term, she introduced and passed a bill for a $7.5 million appropriation for library services in rural areas. She played a key role in the passage of the National Defense Education Act in 1958, authored the Higher Education Facilities Act of 1965, and provided leadership in establishing the first federal program for undergraduate scholarships. Her amendments to the 1965 Vocational Rehabilitation Act expanded its scope to include urban youth in vocational training.

Appointed to the President's Commission on the Status of Women and chair of its Civil and Political Rights Committee in the early 1960s, Green authored and introduced the successful Equal Pay Act of 1963, a measure that had been introduced in various forms since the 1940s and that the commission endorsed. The next year, she was the only woman in the House of Representatives who voted against including sex in Title VII of the Civil Rights Act of 1964, saying that it was neither the time nor the place for addressing discrimination on the basis of sex in employment.

A member of the Women's Equity Action League's (WEAL's) advisory board, Green was familiar with the organization's initiatives to end sex discrimination in education. In 1970, Green held the first congressional hearings on the topic and hired Bernice Sandler of WEAL to write a report on them. Green distributed thousands of copies of the report, giving advocates for educational equity a valuable tool as they worked with other activists and members of Congress. In 1971, several members of Congress introduced a variety of plans to prohibit sex discrimination in education, but it took several months to negotiate a plan for accomplishing the goal.

Green declined to run for re-election in 1974. She was a professor of government at Warner Pacific College and in 1979 was appointed to the Oregon Board of Higher Education.

Born in Trent, South Dakota, Edith Green attended Willamette University from 1927 to 1929. She began teaching in 1930 and attended college when she could afford it, receiving her bachelor of science from the University of Oregon in 1939. She left teaching in 1941 and became a radio announcer and a freelance scriptwriter.

See also Civil Rights Act of 1964, Title VII; Congress, Women in; Education Amendments of 1972, Title IX; Equal Pay Act of 1963; President's Commission on the Status of Women; Women's Equity Action League

References Kaptur, *Women of Congress: A Twentieth Century Odyssey* (1996); Office of the Historian, U.S. House of Representatives, *Women in Congress, 1917–1990* (1991).

Green Party USA

The Green Party USA was begun as the Green Committees of Correspondence in 1984 by activists familiar with Green parties in Europe. Organized in forty-six states, the Green Party USA supports ten key values: ecological wisdom, social justice, grassroots democracy, nonviolence, decentralization, community-based economics, feminism, respect for diversity, personal and global responsibility, and future focus/sustainability. Members are guided by the concept of thinking globally and acting locally.

The Green Party USA entered its first presidential campaign in 1996, when Ralph Nader was the party's candidate for president and Winona LaDuke was its vice presidential candidate. The slate attracted more than 700,000 votes, approximately 1 percent of the votes nationwide.

See also LaDuke, Winona

References www.greens.org.

Greene, Enid (b. 1958)

Republican Enid Greene of Utah served in the U.S. House of Representatives from 3 January 1995 to 3 January 1997. Her congressional priorities included the line item veto, the elimination of unfunded mandates to state and local governments, congressional reform, and improvements in the budget process.

Greene ran for Congress and was elected as Enid Greene Waldholtz, but she resumed her family name after divorcing Joseph Waldholtz in 1996. Treasurer for Greene's 1994 campaign, Waldholtz pleaded guilty to making false statements to the

Griffiths, Martha Edna Wright (1912–2003)

Democrat Martha Griffiths of Michigan served in the U.S. House of Representatives from 3 January 1955 to 31 December 1974. Griffiths was one of the foremost congressional leaders for women's rights in the 1960s and 1970s. Through her efforts, Title VII of the 1964 Civil Rights Act included a prohibition against sex discrimination in employment, and Congress passed the Equal Rights Amendment (ERA) in 1972 and sent it to the states for ratification.

Born in Pierce City, Missouri, Martha Griffiths earned her bachelor's degree from the University of Missouri in 1934. She married Hick Griffiths after they had both completed their undergraduate work. He intended to attend law school and wanted Martha to join him. Accepted by Harvard University Law School, Hick Griffiths chose instead to attend law school at the University of Michigan because Harvard University Law School did not accept women and Michigan did. Martha Griffiths received her law degree from the University of Michigan Law School in 1940. Following law school, they worked for the American Automobile Insurance Company. After World War II, they opened a law firm and practiced together.

When Martha Griffiths was recruited to run for the Michigan legislature in 1948, she first declined, but with her husband's encouragement, she agreed to run. She served from 1949 to 1953. After unsuccessfully running for Congress in 1952, she was appointed recorder and judge of Recorders Court in Detroit in 1953. The next year, she again ran for Congress, campaigning on unemployment, education, and high food prices, and won.

A pay increase for postal workers was the first bill Griffiths passed. She supported housing programs, urban renewal, food stamp programs, and increased federal aid to education and hospital construction. Critical of Defense Department spending and its apparent wastefulness, she worked on these issues throughout the 1950s.

In 1962, she became the first woman on the House Ways and Means Committee, where tax bills begin. Seeking simplified and equitable tax laws, she proposed the repeal of the excise tax on automobiles, tax relief for single parents, and a reduction in Social Security taxes for low-income families. With discrimination against women in tax laws her greatest concern, she sought to eliminate the inheritance tax for surviving spouses and to end the inequities of the marriage tax, under which married couples paid higher income taxes than two single people with the same income.

A strong supporter of equality for women and men, she began introducing equal pay bills in the 1950s and helped pass the Equal Pay Act of 1963. When Congress considered the 1964 Civil Rights Act, primarily intended to address race issues, Griffiths believed that if Title VII of the act, prohibiting discrimination in employment, did not include sex as a protected category, then white women would be left without protection. She considered offering an amendment to add sex but encountered opposition from the American Federation of Labor-Congress of Industrial Organizations (AFL-CIO), Assistant Secretary of Labor Esther Peterson, and others who feared that adding sex would threaten passage of the whole act. Then, she explained: "I made up my mind that all women were going to take one giant step forward, so I prepared an amendment that added 'sex' to the bill." When she learned that conservative congressman Howard W. Smith of Virginia intended to offer the amendment, she applauded his decision, believing that under his sponsorship the amendment would attract at least 100 votes that it would not under her sponsorship. She turned her attention to finding the rest of the needed votes.

House debate on the amendment quickly turned into a farce. Smith said that he offered it to correct the "imbalance of spinsters," and another congressman called the amendment "illogical, ill timed, ill placed, and improper." As her colleagues laughed at the amendment, Griffiths entered the debate, reviewed relevant court cases, and said: "A vote against this amendment today by a white man is a vote against his wife, or his widow, or his daughter, or his sister." The amendment passed 168 to 133. She continued to work for the bill's passage in the Senate, where it passed.

The act included the creation of the Equal Employment Opportunity Commission (EEOC) to enforce the provisions. The EEOC's executive director, however, felt that the commission's focus should be on race and dismissed the prohibition against sex discrimination in employment, calling it "a fluke...conceived out of wedlock." Although sex discrimination complaints accumulated, the EEOC mocked the provision. In 1966, Griffiths attacked the commission's disregard for complying with its mandate, asking: "What is this sickness that causes an official to ridicule the law he swore to uphold and enforce?... What kind of mentality is it that can ignore the fact that women's wages are much less than men's, and that Negro women's wages are least of all?"

The other outstanding example of her leadership was the Equal Rights Amendment, first introduced in Congress in 1923. For more than twenty years, it had been locked in the Judiciary Committee by Representative Emanuel Celler, until Griffiths gathered the 218 signatures from her congressional colleagues to bring it to the House floor for debate. On 10 August 1970, the House passed the amendment, 352 to 15, with seventy-four members not voting, but the Senate did not approve it. Griffiths introduced the amendment again in 1971, making two compromises: a seven-year limit on the ratification period and a two-year delay in implementing it following ratification. In 1972, Congress approved the amendment and sent it to the states for ratification, but it failed in the states.

Griffiths decided against running in 1974. She returned to politics in 1982, when she won the race for Michigan's lieutenant governor, serving from 1983 to 1991.

See also Civil Rights Act of 1964, Title VII; Congress, Women in; Equal Employment Opportunity Commission; Equal Pay Act of 1963; Equal Rights Amendment; Peterson, Esther; Smith, Howard Worth; State Legislatures, Women in

References George, *Martha W. Griffiths* (1982); Kaptur, *Women in Congress* (1996); Office of the Historian, U.S. House of Representatives, *Women in Congress, 1917–1990* (1991).

Grimké, Angelina Emily (1805–1879) and Sarah Moore (1792–1873)

The daughters of slaveowners in the South and the only white Southern women leaders in the abolitionist movement, Angelina and Sarah Grimké worked to end slavery. As agents of the American Anti-Slavery Society, the sisters described the horrors of slavery to New England audiences and helped found female anti-slavery societies.

Born in Charleston, South Carolina, the Grimké sisters were educated at home and in private schools to become members of Charleston's society. Sarah Grimké was particularly resentful that her brothers had received a good advanced education, an opportunity denied to her.

In 1819, Sarah Grimké met a prominent Quaker with whom she had extensive conversations during a sea voyage from Philadelphia to Charleston. When she returned home, she continued to study Quakerism. Sarah reported that she heard voices that told her to return to Philadelphia, which she did in 1821, the year she became a Quaker. Angelina joined her sister in Philadelphia in 1828 and also became a Quaker.

By 1836, the sisters had become committed to the abolitionist movement. That year, Angelina Grimké wrote *Appeal to the Christian Women of the South* and Sarah Grimké wrote *An Epistle to the Clergy of the Southern States*, published by the American Anti-Slavery Society. The works were significant for their condemnation of slavery by women who had been part of a slave society. The next year, the women were leaders in a women's anti-slavery convention that has been described as the "first major organizational effort of American women."

As the first female agents of the American Anti-Slavery Society, the Grimké sisters went on several speaking tours between 1837 and 1839. These lectures were among the greater of their contributions to the abolitionist movement, and their public speeches placed them among the pioneers of the women's rights movement. The speeches, however, proved controversial because of social mores that questioned the appropriateness of women speaking in public and because they spoke to audiences of women and men. Of the controversies, Angelina wrote: "We Abolition Women are turning the world upside down." In 1837, the Ministerial Association of the Congregational Churches of Massachusetts issued a public "Pastoral Letter" that was clearly directed at Angelina Grimké, condemning her for speaking before audiences of women and men. In addition, the press attacked her for the same reasons.

The Grimké sisters believed that women and men were equal as moral beings, had equal moral duties as children of God, and had an equal right to fulfill them. In their belief system, if an act was morally right for a man to do, it was also morally right for a woman. Angelina Grimké developed her argument for women's rights from her understanding of her biblical duty to take action in moral areas, which led her to an insistence that women had a right to a voice in all the laws under which they lived and that women had a right to sit in Congress or be president.

In her feminist writings, Sarah Grimké argued that parallels existed between slavery and women's status, explaining that in both situations, one group exerted power over another group—whites over slaves and men over women—and that when power is used in such a way, one group benefits and the other group is exploited. She said that women "ought to feel a peculiar sympathy in the colored man's wrong, for like him, she has been accused of mental inferiority, and denied the privileges of a liberal education." Sarah Grimké believed that men had usurped women's power and that women had accepted the concept of men's superiority. She wrote: "I ask no favors for my sex. All I ask of our brethren is, that they take their feet from off our necks, and permit us to stand upright on that ground which God designed us to occupy." Her development of these concepts made her a major feminist theorist and pioneer, but they aroused opposition to the Grimké sisters both inside and outside the abolitionist movement. Some thought that adding women's issues to the debate would increase opposition to the abolitionist movement.

In 1838, Angelina Grimké married Theodore Weld, one of the leading abolitionists of the time. The two sisters and Weld wrote *American Slavery as It Is: Testimony of a Thousand Witnesses* (1839), considered the most important anti-slavery document written before Harriet Beecher Stowe's *Uncle Tom's Cabin*. They continued to do research, assist local African Americans, and work for women's rights, but their period of intense activity ended in 1839.

See also Abolitionist Movement, Women in the; Public Speaking; Stowe, Harriet Elizabeth Beecher

References Lerner, *The Feminist Thought of Sarah Grimké* (1998); Matthews, *Women's Struggle for Equality: The First Phase, 1828–1876* (1997).

Griswold v. Connecticut (1965)

In its 1965 decision in *Griswold v. Connecticut*, the U.S. Supreme Court expanded the concept of the right to privacy that had been articulated in other cases, but from different perspectives. In its decision, the Court overturned a Connecticut law that prohibited the dissemination and use of contraceptive devices and drugs.

Planned Parenthood had twice tried to take a case to court to overturn the law, but on both occasions, the court invoked procedural grounds to avoid making a decision. In 1961, executive director of the Planned Parenthood League of Connecticut Estelle Griswold and Yale Medical School's department of gynecology and obstetrics professor C. Lee Buxton had established a birth control clinic in New Haven, Connecticut, to provoke another test case. Griswold and Buxton were arrested and convicted of giving birth control information to married women and were fined $100 each.

The Court resisted deciding the case on the basis of the due process clause of the Fourteenth Amendment, choosing instead to explain that within the rights articulated in the Constitution reside peripheral rights without which "the specific rights would be less secure." Noting that "the First Amendment has a penumbra where privacy is protected from governmental intrusion," the Court also found a variety of guarantees creating zones of privacy in the Third, Fourth, and Fifth Amendments. Based upon this reasoning, the Court wrote:

The present case, then, concerns a relationship lying within the zone of privacy created by several fundamental constitutional guarantees. And it concerns a law which, in forbidding the use of contraceptives...seeks to achieve its goals by means having a maximum destructive impact upon that [marital] relationship.... Would we allow the police to search the sacred precincts of marital bedrooms for telltale signs of the use of contraceptives? The very idea is repulsive to the notions of privacy surrounding the marriage relationship.

In 1973, the right of privacy identified in *Griswold v. Connecticut* became fundamental to the Court's decision in *Roe v. Wade*, which ruled that laws prohibiting abortions were unconstitutional.

See also Abortion; Fourteenth Amendment; *Roe v. Wade*

References *Griswold v. Connecticut*, 381 U.S. 479 (1965).

Grove City College v. Bell (1984)

In *Grove City College v. Bell*, the U.S. Department of Education sought to enforce its understanding of Title IX of the Education Amendments of 1972, which prohibits sex discrimination in "any education program or activity receiving federal assistance." The Department of Education understood that to mean that if any program or person received federal funds, the whole institution had to file an assurance of compliance report. Grove City College refused, arguing that it did not directly receive federal funds. The Department of Education replied that because students attending the college received Basic Educational Opportunity Grants, the college's compliance was necessary for the students to continue receiving the financial assistance.

The U.S. Supreme Court decided that the Department of Education could terminate students' grants, that doing so would not be an infringement of their rights, and that institution-wide coverage under Title IX was not required because some students received financial assistance. The decision limited the Department of Education's authority to investigate discrimination complaints, especially in women's athletics. The decision outraged some feminists and women members of Congress, who believed that if any federal funds went to an educational institution, even if it were direct assistance to a student, the whole institution had to comply with Title IX. Congress passed the Civil Rights Restoration Act of 1988 to overturn the decision.

See also Civil Rights Restoration Act of 1988; Education Amendments of 1972, Title IX
References *Grove City College v. Bell*, 465 U.S. 555 (1984).

Grutter v. Bollinger (2003)

When Barbara Grutter, a white Michigan resident, applied to the University of Michigan Law School, the admissions committee initially placed her on a waiting list and later rejected her application. Grutter filed a racial discrimination suit against the law school, claiming that its policies violated the Fourteenth Amendment and Title VI of the Civil Rights Act of 1964, among other provisions. She argued that the law school made race a predominant factor, giving minority applicants an unfair advantage over white applicants with comparable credentials.

The U.S. Supreme Court examined the extent to which the law school used racial preferences. The Court found that the law school focused on students' academic ability while assessing each applicant's talents, experiences, letters of recommendation, application essay, and other relevant materials. The law school asserted that race represented a "potential 'plus' factor" in its admissions process. The law school also asserted that it had a compelling interest in attaining a diverse student body, noting that corporate leaders and military officials contended that exposure to widely diverse people, cultures, and ideas contributed to effective leadership.

The Court decided in *Grutter v. Bollinger* that the law schools' "narrowly tailored use of race in admissions decisions to further a compelling interest in obtaining the educational benefits that flow from a diverse student body is not prohibited by the Equal Protection Clause, Title VI," or other provisions. It upheld the law school's admissions policies.

References *Grutter v. Bollinger* 539 U.S. 306 (2003).

Guinier, Carol Lani (b. 1950)

African American lawyer Lani Guinier's nomination to head the civil rights commission of the U.S. Department of Justice in 1993 evoked strong protests from congressional conservatives who accused her of having dangerously radical views on minority rights. The concepts under attack included a wide range of ways to enhance minority power, such as cumulative voting in elections, which permits voters to concentrate on selected candidates. In legislative bodies, Guinier proposed requiring supermajorities on some votes and permitting minorities veto power on some issues. U.S. Senator Orrin Hatch called her ideas "frightening," and U.S. Senator Bob Dole said: "The key concept has always been access, not proportionality."

Guinier appeared on television news programs to explain her ideas, and her supporters claimed that her views had been distorted, but the attempts to save her nomination failed. President Bill Clinton withdrew Guinier's nomination without permitting her to defend her ideas before the Senate Judiciary Committee, angering members of the Congressional Black Caucus, who viewed the withdrawal as evidence of weak leadership by Clinton.

Born in New York City, Guinier graduated from Radcliffe College in 1971 and received her law degree from Yale Law School in 1975. While in law school, she met Hillary Rodham Clinton and Bill Clinton. In the late 1970s, Guinier worked for the civil rights division of the U.S. Department of Justice, and from 1981 to 1988, she worked for the National Association for the Advancement of Colored People Legal Defense and Education Fund. She was an adjunct professor at the New York University School of Law from 1985 to 1989 and became a law professor at the University of Pennsylvania Law School in 1988. Guinier wrote *The Tyranny of the Majority* (1994). In 1998, she became the first African American woman to receive tenure at Harvard Law School. At the time of her appointment, she said: "What I'm really most excited about is joining a faculty in which other members don't shrink from speaking out publicly, particularly on issues affecting women and people of color."

See also National Association for the Advancement of Colored People, Women in the
References *Congressional Quarterly Almanac, 103rd Congress, 1st Session... 1993* (1994); *The New York Times*, 24 January 1998.

H. L. v. Matheson (1984)

In *H. L. v. Matheson*, the U.S. Supreme Court decided that a Utah law requiring a physician to notify the parents of an immature, dependent minor woman before performing an abortion did not violate her right to privacy. The Court said the law was constitutional because the parents did not have to give their consent to the procedure but only had to be notified. Because the woman in the case did not assert that she was mature, the Court did not rule on the law's constitutionality if a mature minor woman were seeking the procedure.

> **See also** Abortion
>
> **References** *H. L. v. Matheson*, 450 U.S. 398 (1984); www.naral.org.

Hall, Katie Beatrice Green (b. 1938)

Democrat Katie Hall of Indiana served in the U.S. House of Representatives from 2 November 1982 to 3 January 1985. Hall entered politics as a volunteer for Richard Hatcher's campaigns for mayor of Gary, Indiana, beginning in 1967 and through his 1975 campaign. She served in the Indiana House of Representatives from 1973 to 1975 and the state Senate from 1975 to 1982. She focused on education, labor, and women's issues and passed a measure that clarified the state's divorce laws by defining marital property. A strong advocate of the Equal Rights Amendment, she successfully worked for Indiana's ratification of it.

When the incumbent member of Congress died in the fall of 1982, Mayor Hatcher, as chair of the district's party organization, had the power to name the Democratic candidate to fill the vacancy. He named Hall, who ran simultaneously to complete the deceased member's term and for a full term of her own. Hall's campaign issues included support for the expansion of unemployment benefits, job training, and other forms of assistance, and opposition to unlimited military spending, high interest rates, and economic programs that benefited large corporations at the expense of middle-income people.

In Congress, Hall introduced and passed the bill that made Martin Luther King, Jr.'s birthday a federal holiday. Measures for recognizing King's contributions to

American civil rights had been introduced by others for fifteen years, and support for the idea had been steadily building when Hall introduced it. She also worked for programs to alleviate unemployment, which was high in Indiana; to revitalize the steel industry; and to prevent child abuse and family violence. Defeated in the 1984 primary, she also failed in subsequent primaries in 1984 and 1990.

Born in Mound Bayou, Mississippi, African American Katie Hall received her bachelor of science degree from Mississippi Valley State University in 1960 and her master of science degree from Indiana University in 1968. She taught social studies from 1961 to 1975.

See also Congress, Women in; Equal Rights Amendment; State Legislatures, Women in

References Catlin, "Organizational Effectiveness and Black Political Participation: The Case of Katie Hall" (1985); *Congressional Quarterly, Politics in America 1994* (1993).

Hamer, Fannie Lou Townsend (1917–1977)

One of the Deep South's most influential African American civil rights leaders, Fannie Lou Hamer, a sharecropper, went into cotton fields and soybean fields to urge African Americans to register to vote, defying sheriffs, landowners, and tradition. Powerful and compelling when she testified before the 1964 Democratic National Convention's credentials committee, she described her attempts to register to vote and helped the nation understand the cruelty and violence of racism. Hamer's religious faith sustained her through the physical violence she endured and the injuries that resulted. By expressing her faith through hymns of hope, supplication, and praise, she shared her courage and strengthened others.

Born on a Montgomery County, Mississippi, plantation, Fannie Lou Hamer began working in the fields picking cotton when she was six years old. She had about six years of formal education. Her involvement in civil rights began after she attended rallies organized by the Student Nonviolent Coordinating Committee (SNCC) at the Ruleville Baptist Church in 1962. She explained: "They talked about how it was our rights as human beings to register and vote. I never knew we could vote before. Nobody ever told us."

With seventeen others, Hamer attempted to register on 31 August 1962, but she failed to pass the oral examination on a technical legal question regarding de facto laws. As the group returned to Ruleville on a private bus, police stopped the group because the private bus that was transporting them was too yellow and allegedly could be confused with a school bus. The police arrested and jailed them, and a local judge fined them and then released them. When Hamer finally got home, the owner of the plantation on which she lived told her to stop her registration attempts. She explained that she was not attempting to register for his benefit but for her own. The owner evicted her and her family that night. Hamer told the members of the Ruleville Baptist Church her story, saying: "They kicked me off the plantation, they set me free. It's the best thing that could happen. Now I can work for my people." After repeated attempts to register, Hamer learned early in 1963 that she had passed the voter registration test but still could not vote. She had not paid the poll tax the previous two years, which she had been prohibited from paying because she was not a registered voter. Recogniz-

Fannie Lou Hamer, voting rights activist, testified before the credentials committee at the Democratic National Convention, 1964 (Library of Congress LC-U9-12470B-17)

ing the power of Hamer's presence on an audience, her intelligence, and her leadership, SNCC leaders recruited her to be a movement speaker.

On 9 June 1963, Hamer and other civil rights workers were on a bus returning home from a workshop in Charleston, South Carolina, when they attempted to integrate the bus station in Winona, Mississippi. Arrested and jailed, they were beaten by law enforcement officers, who then commanded other inmates to continue the attacks. Hamer was beaten on her head, upper back, lower back, buttocks, legs, and feet. For the rest of her life, Hamer suffered from a blood clot that affected her sight in one eye and damage to her kidneys. The Justice Department filed civil and criminal charges against the officers, but all were found not guilty. The civil rights workers were each convicted of disorderly conduct and resisting arrest and fined.

In 1964, Hamer and other civil rights leaders sought ways to break through the race barriers in Mississippi's Democratic Party. Hamer entered the party's primary as a candidate for Congress, knowing that she would not win. Another strategy was the creation of the Mississippi Freedom Democratic Party (MFDP), an alternative to the white party organization. The MFDP held precinct, county, and state conventions to elect delegates to the Democratic National Convention to be held that summer, intending to challenge the all-white Mississippi delegation's credentials. Throughout the summer, Hamer and her colleagues were kept under surveillance by the Federal Bureau of Investigation.

When Hamer testified before the Democratic National Convention's credentials committee, she told the story of her attempts to register, her work to help other African Americans register to vote, the threats of violence, and the horror of the beating she had endured. She had hoped that her testimony would influence not only the credentials committee but also expose the nation to the injustices under which African Americans lived in the South. She wept in frustration and anger when she learned that President Lyndon Johnson had called an impromptu press conference to preempt her testimony and that the television networks had broadcast his conference instead of her testimony. That evening, however, television networks repeatedly replayed her testimony, and her words electrified the nation as she pleaded for justice.

Excluded from the negotiations that followed the MFDP's testimony, she refused to accept the agreement that male civil rights leaders had reached with Democratic Party officials to seat two MFDP delegates and permit the rest of the delegates to watch the convention. She asked the credentials committee: "Do you think I came here to compromise and to sit in the back seat at this convention? . . . There's got to be a change, not only for the people in the U.S. but all over the world." The convention seated the white delegation in 1964.

In 1968 Hamer was one of the twenty-two African American delegates seated at the Democratic National Convention. At the 1972 convention, Hamer and Gloria Steinem nominated Frances "Sissy" Farenthold for vice president, but the effort failed. In 1975 and 1976, Hamer helped unite the party in Mississippi, resulting in an integrated delegation to the 1976 Democratic National Convention.

Hamer also continued her work on the local level. In 1969, she founded Freedom Farm, a nonprofit effort to help needy families raise food and livestock. The organization also offered social services, minority business opportunities, and scholarships and educational grants. When the county in which she lived refused to develop an effective school desegregation plan, Hamer filed a class action lawsuit in 1970 and won. Hamer unsuccessfully ran for the Mississippi state Senate in 1971.

Despite the injustices she experienced, Hamer refused to hate white people, saying: "I feel sorry for anybody that could let hate wrap them up. Ain't no such thing as I can hate anybody and hope to see God's face."

> **See also** Civil Rights Movement, Women in the; Democratic Party, Women in the; Farenthold, Frances (Sissy) Talton; Steinem, Gloria Marie
>
> **References** Mills, *This Little Light of Mine: The Life of Fannie Lou Hamer* (1993); *The New York Times*, 16 March 1977.

Hansen, Julia Caroline Butler (1907–1988)

Democrat Julia Hansen of Washington served in the U.S. House of Representatives from 8 November 1960 to 31 December 1974. Hansen served on the Cathlamet, Washington City Council from 1938 to 1946 and in the state House of Representatives from 1939 to 1960, where she was speaker pro tempore from 1955 to 1960. She developed expertise in transportation issues and chaired the Western Interstate Committee on Highway Policies from 1951 to 1960.

When the incumbent member of Congress died in office, Hansen ran for and won the seat as well as election for a full term. The first woman to serve on the Appropriations Committee, she was also the first woman to chair an Appropriations subcommittee. As chair of the subcommittee that controlled funding for the Interior Department, she became one of the most influential members of Congress. Her subcommittee dealt with allocations to the National Park Service, the Bureau of Mines, and the Bureau of Indian Affairs. Of the issues addressed in her subcommittee, the plight of Native Americans drew most of her attention, prompting her to travel to observe their living conditions. She declined to run for an eighth term.

Born in Portland, Oregon, Julia Hansen attended Oregon State College from 1924 to 1926. Working as a dietitian and swimming instructor, she supported herself as she pursued her degree at the University of Washington, earning it in 1930. Hansen served a six-year term on the Washington State Toll Bridge Authority beginning in 1975 and chaired the Washington State Transportation Commission from 1979 to 1980.

> **See also** Congress, Women in; State Legislatures, Women in
>
> **References** Office of the Historian, U.S. House of Representatives, *Women in Congress, 1917–1990* (1991); Schoenebaum, ed., *Political Profiles: The Nixon/Ford Years* (1979).

Harden, Cecil Murray (1894–1984)

Republican Cecil Harden of Indiana served in the U.S. House of Representatives from 3 January 1949 to 3 January 1959. Harden became involved in Republican Party politics in 1932, serving as a precinct vice committeewoman. She chaired the Fountain County Republican Party from 1938 to 1950 and was Republican national committeewoman for Indiana from 1944 to 1959 and from 1964 to 1972. Congresswoman Harden obtained congressional approval for flood control and recreational projects in her district. After losing her attempt for a sixth term, Harden was the special assistant for women's affairs to the postmaster general from 1959 to 1961. She served on the National Advisory Committee for the White House Conference on Aging in 1970.

Born in Covington, Indiana, Harden attended the University of Indiana and taught in public schools from 1912 to 1914.

> **See also** Congress, Women in
>
> **References** Office of the Historian, U.S. House of Representatives, *Women in Congress, 1917–1990* (1991); H. W. Wilson, *Current Biography: Who's News and Why, 1949* (1949).

Harman, Jane Frank (b. 1945)

Democrat Jane Harman of California served in the U.S. House of Representatives from 3 January 1993 to 3 January 1999. After an unsuccessful race for governor of California in 1998, Harman won her 2000 campaign to return to the House. In the two-year interim, she served on the congressionally mandated National Council on Terrorism. Following the September 11, 2001 terrorist attacks on the United States, Congresswoman Harman focused on protecting the United States from international terrorism. She advocated appointing a federal homeland security adviser before President George W. Bush began his push to create the position. She also advocated the creation of a new department of homeland security, again before President Bush made it a priority. Protecting American ports has been one of her priorities, especially the Port of Los Angeles, which is in her congressional district.

She began her political career as chief legislative assistant to a senator and then served as chief counsel and staff director to the Senate Judiciary Committee on constitutional rights from 1975 to 1977. She was hired as deputy secretary to the White House Cabinet from 1977 to 1978 and special counsel to the Department of Defense until 1979, when she went into corporate law. Harman was counsel for the Democratic Platform Committee in 1984 and chaired the Democratic National Committee's National Lawyers' Counsel from 1986 to 1990.

Congresswoman Harman introduced and successfully managed an amendment to fully fund the C-17 cargo plane and secured funding for the F/A-18 Milstar satellite, measures important to her district's aerospace industry. She led the fight to keep the Los Angeles Air Force Base open and supported innovative defense conversion, reinvestment, and transition projects.

The daughter of immigrants and a member of a House task force on immigration, Harman successfully fought reductions in the number of legal immigrants admitted to the United States each year, saying that "legal immigration is the lifeblood of the country, enriching it both economically and culturally."

She co-sponsored the Freedom of Choice Act and the Freedom of Access to Clinic Entrances Act of 1994 and played a leading role in the investigations of sexual misconduct in the military. She has supported deficit reduction, term limits, tough crime laws, and investments in technology and children. In 1998, Harman was a candidate for governor of California but lost in the primary election.

Born in New York City and raised in Los Angeles, Jane Harman received her bachelor's degree from Smith College in 1966 and her law degree from Harvard University in 1969.

See also Abortion; Congress, Women in; Freedom of Access to Clinic Entrances Act of 1994; Military, Women in the

References *Congressional Quarterly, Politics in America 1994* (1993), *Politics in America 1998* (1997), *Politics in America 2004* (2003); Brian Nuttig, "Rep. Jane Harman," *CQ Weekly*, 28 December 2002, p. 45; http://www.house.gov/harman/.

Harriman, Pamela Beryl Digby Churchill Hayward (1920–1997)

A devoted Democrat who helped rebuild her party in the 1980s, Pamela Harriman served as U.S. ambassador to France from 1993 to 1997. A wealthy socialite first known for her ability to entertain, Harriman developed a base of power and influence through her willingness to contribute money to the Democratic Party and related groups and through her skill for raising funds for those interests.

Born in Kent, England, Harriman was the daughter of a baron. She received her education at a finishing school in Paris. In 1939, Harriman married Randolph Churchill, one of Winston Churchill's sons. Through her father-in-law, Pamela gained access to the inner circles of British politics and became acquainted with U.S. political and military leaders who were frequent visitors during World War II. Entertaining international leaders became a part of her life when she was a young woman. Divorced in 1945, she married Leland Hayward in 1959. A Broadway producer, Hayward introduced Pamela Harriman to U.S. entertainment figures, and again she was an active hostess.

She married former New York Governor W. Averell Harriman in 1971, became a naturalized U.S. citizen, and through her husband became active in the Democratic Party. After President Jimmy Carter and several Democratic members of Congress lost their races in 1980, Pamela Harriman sought ways to rejuvenate the party. She held a series of issues dinners to discuss and develop strategies and started a political action committee (PAC) named "Democrats for the 80s," raising $1.3 million in its first two years. When she disbanded the PAC in 1990, she had raised $12 million with it. The party rewarded her with an invitation to address its 1984 national convention. Gloria Steinem introduced her at the convention as "the woman who proved that all feminists don't have to wear combat boots," a reference to Harriman's elegance and grace. In 1986, Averell Harriman died, but Pamela Harriman continued her interest in party politics and renewed her interest in foreign policy.

When Bill Clinton, who had attended one of her issues dinners, ran for president in 1992, she gave him her support, primarily by raising money for his campaign. Clinton showed his appreciation by appointing her ambassador to France. Harriman dealt in international trade issues, North Atlantic Treaty Organization (NATO) expansion, and the General Agreement on Tariffs and Trade (GATT) negotiations. When disagreements over farm and audiovisual trade matters created uncommonly high levels of irritation between the United States and France, Harriman's familiarity with French life and culture helped resolve the differences. She described her role: "I was a sort of messenger going back and forth, explaining to Washington why the French think and argue the way they do and also in the other direction, telling the French why our farmers are just as important to us as theirs are to them."

See also Democratic Party, Women in the; Steinem, Gloria Marie

References *The New York Times*, 2 March 1977, 1 October 1982, 6 February 1997; Smith, *Reflected Glory: The Life of Pamela Churchill Harriman* (1997).

Harris, Katherine (b. 1957)

Republican Katherine Harris of Florida entered the U.S. House of Representatives on 3 January 2003. Harris gained national attention, however, in 2000 when she was Florida secretary of state and oversaw the state's 36-day recount of ballots in the presidential election. Lauded by some for following Florida laws, she was castigated by others for her decisions in the recount. In the end, fellow Republican George W. Bush was declared the winner.

Harris began her political career as a state senator, serving from 1994 to 1998. In the Florida senate, she worked for economic development, increased teacher salaries, and gained stiffer penalties for white collar crimes and crimes against elderly persons. As Florida secretary of state from 1998 to 2002, Harris held responsibility for international trade with the state, as well as elections, historic preservation, and other areas.

During her first term, Congresswoman Harris obtained passage of $200 million over two years to help first-time homebuyers with their down payments and closing costs. An enthusiastic supporter of the arts, Harris helped obtain $1 million to rebuild the planetarium in Bradenton, Florida, which had been destroyed in a fire.

Born on Key West, Florida, Harris earned a bachelor of arts degree from Agnes Scott College in 1979 and a master's in public administration from Harvard University in 1996. She also attended the University of Madrid in Spain in 1978. Before her political career, Harris was a real estate broker. She wrote *Center of the Storm: Practicing Principled Leadership in Times of Crisis* (2002).

References Congressional Quarterly, Politics in America 2006 (2005); http://harris.house.gov/biography; "Katherine Harris," *National Journal*, 9 November 2002, p. 3295.

Harris, LaDonna (b. 1931)

An advocate for Native Americans, LaDonna Harris founded Americans for Indian Opportunity in 1970. She advocates the development of policies that recognize the government-to-government relationship between federal agencies and Native American tribes. Through a leadership program that she developed, Harris uses traditional tribal values to prepare a new generation of tribal leaders.

Harris became politically active when her husband Fred Harris entered the Senate in 1965. She organized the first intertribal organization in Oklahoma, Oklahomans for Indian Opportunity, bringing together sixty tribes for economic development. The first U.S. senator's wife to testify before a congressional committee, she helped return Blue Lake to the people of Taos Pueblo and helped the Menominee Tribe regain federal recognition. President Lyndon Johnson appointed LaDonna Harris to the National Council on Indian Opportunity in 1968, but she resigned, saying that federal agencies were not responding quickly enough to proposals to assist Native Americans.

Disillusioned with President Jimmy Carter's social policies, she accepted the Citizens Party's nomination for vice president in 1980. Harris shared the party's positions on environmental protection and social and economic justice. Realizing that her candidacy and that of her running mate, Barry Commoner, had little chance for success, Harris said: "You do things symbolically so people become used to seeing women in these positions."

Harris was born in Temple, Oklahoma, and raised by her Comanche grandparents. She was a founder of the National Women's Political Caucus and served on its national board for several years. She also served on the National Commission on the Observance of International Women's Year.

See also Deer, Ada Elizabeth; National Women's Political Caucus

References Bataille, ed., *Native American Women* (1993); *The New York Times*, 11 July 1970, 27 October 1980.

Harris, Patricia Roberts (1924–1985)

Patricia Roberts Harris served as secretary of the Department of Housing and Urban Development and as secretary of the Department of Health and Human Services. She began her public service career as ambassador to Luxembourg from 1965 to 1967, the first female African American ambassador to represent the United States.

In 1977, President Jimmy Carter appointed her secretary of the U.S. Department of Housing and Urban Development. During her confirmation hearings, Democratic Senator William Proxmire of Wisconsin questioned whether she would be able to defend the interests of the poor. Harris responded:

I am one of them. You do not seem to understand who I am. I am a black woman, the daughter of a dining car worker. I am a black woman who could not buy a house eight years ago in parts of the District of Columbia. I didn't start out as a member of a prestigious law firm, but as a woman who needed a scholarship to go to school. If you think that I have forgotten that, you are wrong.

She served as head of the department until 1979. When the U.S. Department of Health, Education, and Welfare was reorganized as the Department of Health and Human Services, Harris became its first secretary, serving from 1979 to 1981.

Born in Mattoon, Illinois, Patricia Harris earned her bachelor's degree from Howard University in 1945, did postgraduate work at the University of Chicago from 1945 to 1947 and at American University from 1949 to 1950, and received her law degree from George Washington University in 1960. Program director at the Chicago Young Women's Christian Association from 1946 to 1949, Harris was also assistant director for the American Council of Human Rights from 1953 to 1959 and a research associate at George Washington University from 1959 to 1960. After working as a trial attorney for the U.S. Department of Justice from 1960 to 1961, she taught law at Howard University from 1961 to 1965 and from 1967 to 1969, the year she became dean of the university's law school.

See also Cabinets, Women in Presidential

References H. W. Wilson, *Current Biography 1965* (1965); *The New York Times*, 14 October 1971, 24 March 1985; Smith, ed., *Epic Lives* (1993).

Harris v. Forklift Systems (1993)

The U.S. Supreme Court decided in *Harris v. Forklift Systems* that an employee does not need to show serious psychological damage or other injury to prove sexual harassment as prohibited by Title VII of the Civil Rights Act of 1964. The decision made it easier to prove the hostility, abusiveness, or offensiveness of a workplace.

Teresa Harris claimed that her employer asked women employees to retrieve items from his front pants pocket, dropped items on the floor and asked women to pick them up, and called a female employee "a dumb ass woman." In addition, her employer insulted Harris because of her gender and subjected her to sexual comments. Harris did not claim that she suffered psychological damage or was unable to perform her job, but she did insist that the employer's behavior created a hostile environment. The Court agreed, saying that "Title VII comes into play before the harassing conduct leads to a nervous breakdown."

See also Civil Rights Act of 1964, Title VII; Sexual Harassment

References Fallon, "Sexual Harassment" (1995); *Hoff, Law, Gender, and Injustice* (1991).

Harris v. McRae (1980)

In *Harris v. McRae*, the U.S. Supreme Court ruled that Medicaid does not require states to pay for medically necessary abortions. The case resulted from passage of the Hyde Amendment of 1976, which prohibited the use of Medicaid funds to pay for abortions except to save the life of the mother or for victims of rape or incest. The constitutionality of the prohibition was challenged on the grounds that it violated the due process clause of the Fifth Amendment and the religion clauses of the First Amendment.

The Court found that the Hyde Amendment does not place governmental obstacles before a woman seeking an abortion and that a woman's freedom of choice does not include a constitutional entitlement to financial resources to exercise her right. The statutory issue was whether the Medicaid Act requires a state to fund the cost of medically necessary abortions for which federal reimbursement is unavailable under the Hyde Amendment. The constitutional issue was whether the Hyde Amendment, by denying public funding for certain medically necessary abortions, interferes with the equal protection guarantees of the due process clause of the Fifth Amendment or the religion clauses of the First Amendment. The Court decided that the Hyde Amendment does not violate the establishment clause of the First Amendment, even though the funding restrictions reflect the religious tenets of the Roman Catholic Church.

See also Abortion

References *Harris v. McRae*, 448 U.S. 297 (1980).

Hart, Melissa Anne (b. 1962)

Republican Melissa Hart of Pennsylvania entered the U.S. House of Representatives on 3 January 2001. She was the chief sponsor of the Unborn Victims of Violence law. If a federal crime of violence is committed against a pregnant woman and her unborn child is harmed, the perpetrator may be charged with two crimes against two victims, giving federal legal status to fetuses for the first time. She sponsored an amendment to increase funding for victims of crime, which also passed. She also introduced a measure to withhold federal funds from schools that offer the "morning after" birth control pill to students. Hart also introduced legislation that would require alerts on unsolicited e-mails that contain sexually explicit material.

In other areas, Hart passed legislation that improves medical benefits for black lung disease victims. She introduced legislation to encourage redevelopment of former industrial sites. One measure would give tax-exempt status to bonds used for environmental remediation, and another would permit tax exempt savings accounts for use in environmental cleanup.

Hart served in the Pennsylvania state senate from 1991 to 2000.

Born in Pittsburgh, Pennsylvania, she earned a bachelor of arts degree from Washington and Jefferson College in 1984 and a JD degree from the University of Pittsburgh in 1987.

References Congressional Quarterly, Politics in America 2004 (2003), Politics in America 2006 (2005); http://hart.house.gov/bio.asp; *Pittsburgh Post-Gazette*, 8 March 2004; *Washington Post*, 27 February 2004.

President Ronald Reagan, at his desk in the Oval Office, speaking with Republican senator Paula Hawkins of Florida. Washington, D.C., 1987, LC-DIG-pplot-13557-00719 (digital file from LC-HS505-56)

Hawkins, Paula Fickes (b. 1927)

Republican Paula Hawkins of Florida served in the U.S. Senate from 1 January 1981 to 3 January 1987. Hawkins focused much of her attention on issues related to children. After conducting a Senate investigation on missing children, she passed the Missing Children Act of 1982 and the Missing Children's Assistance Act in 1984. Hawkins brought national attention to the issue of child abuse when she disclosed that she had been a victim of it. Saying that the administrative and judicial systems were inadequate to deal with child abuse, she sponsored a bill to provide remedies. The Senate passed her bill, but the House did not. She lost her re-election attempt in 1986.

Born in Salt Lake City, Utah, Hawkins attended Utah State University from 1944 to 1947. Appointed to the Florida Governor's Commission on the Status of Women in 1968, she served until 1971. She served on the Florida Public Service Commission from 1973 to 1979, leaving to become vice president of consumer affairs for Air Florida. She is the author of *Children at Risk*, published in 1986.

See also Congress, Women in

References Boxer, *Strangers in the Senate* (1994); H. W. Wilson, *Current Biography Yearbook, 1985* (1985); Office of the Historian, U.S. House of Representatives, *Women in Congress, 1917–1990* (1991).

Health Care, Women and

The history of women's health as a political issue has its roots in the early nineteenth century, when states began to make abortion illegal. Although women's reproductive health has persisted as a political issue, other aspects of women's health, from health insurance coverage to funding for medical research and the characteristics of the human participants, have also entered the political arena.

Women's reproductive health has easily been the most political and controversial area of women's health, one that has been surrounded by intense moral debates. Social reformer Anthony Comstock played an early role in establishing the federal and state governments' regulation of women's health. In 1873, Comstock persuaded Congress to pass an "Act for the suppression of trade in, and circulation of, obscene literature and articles of immoral use." Known as the Comstock law, the measure made it a crime to send obscene material and any "article or thing designed or intended for the prevention of conception or procuring of abortion." Over the next forty years, most states enacted comparable measures. This criminalization of the use of the postal system for the distribution of birth control and abortion information and devices effectively limited women's access to controlling their reproductive lives. Birth control pioneers Mary Ware Dennett, Margaret Sanger, and others lobbied state legislatures and Congress for decades to remove the classification, but it was the federal appeals court 1936 decision in *United States v. One Package of Japanese Pessaries* that removed birth control from the list of obscene materials. Since the U.S. Supreme Court's 1973 decision legalizing abortion in *Roe v. Wade*, abortion has been the most politicized women's health issue, generating fierce moral and ethical debates.

Another reproductive health concern emerged when the oral contraceptive Enovid, also known as the Pill, was introduced to the U.S. market in 1960. As women taking the Pill experienced increased rates of thromboembolism (blood clotting), stroke, arterial dysfunction, and other health hazards, concerns about the drug's risk grew. Some medical authorities advised against using it, whereas others argued that it was safe. The Pill, unpleasant experiences with physicians, and other factors contributed to women's wanting explanations of medical terms and procedures and more information about their bodies and health care alternatives. Women read medical journals and other medical sources, formed discussion groups to share their knowledge, and established clinics. The Boston Women's Health Clinic published *Our Bodies, Ourselves* in 1969 and gave new energy to women's quest to understand and control their own bodies.

A variety of women's health issues emerged as visible political issues in 1986 when the Congressional Caucus for Women's Issues (CCWI) challenged health research priorities and practices and sought remedies for the exclusion of women and minorities from clinical studies of drugs and other medical treatments. In 1990, the CCWI introduced the Women's Health Equity Act, parts of which passed Congress that year and in subsequent years.

The National Breast Cancer Coalition emerged as a powerful lobby in the early 1990s, dramatically increasing research funding for the disease. In 1991, the group sought to generate 175,000 letters to Congress and the president, choosing the number because it represents the number of women annually diagnosed with breast cancer. They surpassed their goal, and 600,000 letters supporting breast cancer research went to members of Congress and the president. The letters of support helped increase funding to $145 million for 1992, about $52 million more than in 1991, or a 55 percent increase. In 1993, the coalition succeeded in increasing the appropriation by $325 million, an increase of 160 percent over 1992. In addition, several groups, including the Breast Cancer Fund and the Susan G. Komen Breast Cancer Foundation, support research and education.

See also Abortion; Congressional Caucus for Women's Issues; Dennett, Mary Coffin Ware; *Roe v. Wade*; Sanger, Margaret Louise Higgins; Women's Health Equity Act

References Bingham, *Women on the Hill: Challenging the Culture of Congress* (1997); *Congressional Quarterly Almanac, 103rd Congress, 1st Session… 1993* (1994); Linden-Ward and Green, *American Women in the 1960s: Changing the Future* (1993).

Heckler, Margaret Mary O'Shaughnessy (b. 1931)

Republican Margaret Heckler of Massachusetts served in the U.S. House of Representatives from 3 January 1967 to 3 January 1983. Heckler was secretary of health and human services from 1983 to 1985 and ambassador to Ireland from 1985 to 1989. As a member of Congress, Heckler worked for federal funding of child day care for low-income families, sought to protect the pension rights of employed women on maternity leave, and advocated establishing shelters for victims of domestic violence. A leading proponent of the Equal Rights Amendment, she co-sponsored the measure to extend the deadline for its ratification. With Congresswoman Elizabeth Holtzman (D-NY), she founded the Congresswoman's Caucus, later known as the Congressional Caucus for Women's Issues, in 1977 and served as its co-chair for five years. Heckler lost the race for a ninth term.

President Ronald Reagan appointed her secretary of health and human services in 1983. In that office, Heckler established new guidelines for Social Security disability programs, campaigned to increase funding for research and patient care for people with acquired immunodeficiency syndrome (AIDS) and Alzheimer's disease, and supported tax credits for day care.

Born in Flushing, New York, Heckler studied at the University of Leiden in the Netherlands in 1952, earned her bachelor's degree from Albertus Magnus College in 1953, and received her law degree from Boston College Law School in 1956. Heckler entered politics as a member of the Wellesley Town Meeting, serving from 1958 to 1966.

See also Abortion; Cabinets, Women in Presidential; Congress, Women in; Congressional Caucus for Women's Issues; Equal Rights Amendment; Holtzman, Elizabeth

References H. W. Wilson, *Current Biography Yearbook, 1983* (1983); Office of the Historian, U.S. House of Representatives, *Women in Congress, 1917–1990* (1991).

Height, Dorothy Irene (b. 1912)

President of the National Council of Negro Women (NCNW) for more than forty years, Dorothy Height has been an advocate for women's rights and African American rights. An adviser to Eleanor Roosevelt and a civil rights strategist, Height's leadership extended from the neighborhood to the international levels.

Born in Richmond, Virginia, Height earned a college scholarship by winning a national oratorical contest sponsored by the Elks Club. Height applied to Barnard College, but the school told her that it already had two African American students and that she would have to wait a term for admission. Accepted at New York University, she earned her bachelor's and master's degrees there and later studied at the New York School of Social Work.

In 1937 Height joined the Young Women's Christian Association's (YWCA's) staff at its Harlem branch and NCNW, two associations that worked together to enhance her effectiveness as a civil rights advocate. A leader in both organizations, she became a member of the YWCA's national board in 1944. Height led the YWCA's campaign to integrate public swimming pools in the early 1960s, helped develop and was director of the YWCA's Center for Racial Justice, and directed a voter registration drive sponsored by the YWCA and a New York City radio station. She worked to bring black and white women together in several Alabama communities, hoping that talking to each other might help them work together. Height retired from the YWCA in 1977.

Elected NCNW president in 1957, she gained tax-exempt status for the organization, a change that helped it attract large foundation grants. Also, under her leadership, NCNW established the Mary McLeod Bethune Museum and Archives for Black Women's History and led the campaign to erect the Bethune statue in Washington, D.C., the first memorial to an African American in that city. Height organized Black Family Reunion celebrations to affirm the importance of strengthening black families and expanded NCNW programs to include child care centers in urban and rural areas, housing initiatives, health care, and career education for girls. She retired from the NCNW presidency in 1997.

Height has testified before congressional committees in a wide range of areas, including the Economic Opportunity Act of 1964, the war on poverty, the Economic Opportunity Act Amendments of 1967, housing legislation, Social Security and welfare proposals, extension of the ratification deadline for the Equal Rights Amendment, teen pregnancy, and racism in National Football League field management, recruitment,

Dorothy Height, social activist and educator.

and hiring practices. National president of Delta Sigma Theta sorority from 1947 to 1956, Height was a founder of the National Women's Political Caucus in 1971.

In 2004, she received the Congressional Gold Medal, the highest recognition Congress gives individuals.

See also Bethune, Mary Jane McLeod; Delta Sigma Theta Sorority; Equal Rights Amendment; National Council of Negro Women; National Women's Political Caucus; YWCA of the USA

References Hardy, *American Women Civil Rights Activists* (1993); Hine, ed., *Black Women in America* (1993); *The New York Times*, 13 August 1979, 5 December 1997; *The Washington Post*, 25 March 2004; www.ncnw.com.

Henderson, Hazel Mustard (b. 1933)

Economist Hazel Henderson has been a leader in creating a sustainable economic model that includes environmental costs and human costs of production. She advocates corporate social responsibility, renewable energy, and the triple bottom line, which is respecting people and the environment while making a profit. She developed the Calvert-Henderson Quality of Life Indicators, which examine education, employment, energy, environment, health, human rights, income, infrastructure, national security, public safety, recreation, and shelter to measure a nation's well-being.

Henderson created and co-produces *Ethical Markets*, a financial lifestyle magazine television program that looks at assets and wealth in a nontraditional way. It shows viewers examples of companies that reflect the values of the triple bottom line. Shown

Dr. Hazel Henderson is a world renowned futurist, evolutionary economist, a worldwide syndicated columnist, consultant on sustainable development, and author of Beyond Globalization, and seven other books. (Courtesy Hazel Henderson)

on PBS (Public Broadcasting System), the program reaches 44 million homes each week.

Born in Bristol, England, Henderson immigrated to the United States in 1957 and became a naturalized citizen in 1962. Two years later, concerned about the impact of pollution on her daughter, Henderson cofounded Citizens for Clean Air. With 20,000 members in a few months, the group launched an antipollution media campaign. Henderson, however, was dismissed by the group's leaders because she did not have a background in economics. She studied economics and over the next decade developed the sustainable model she now advocates.

References H.W. Wilson, *Current Biography Yearbook 2003* (2004); http://www.calvert-henderson.com; http://www.ethicalmarkets.com; Jim Motovalli, "Visionary Thinking: Women Shape the Environmental Movement's Theoretical Base," *E Magazine*, 11 January 1997, p. 30.

Herman, Alexis Margaret (b. 1947)

Alexis Herman served as secretary of labor from 1997 to 2001, the first African American to hold the position and the highest-ranking African American woman in President Bill Clinton's Cabinet. Secretary Herman started the Youth Opportunity Movement, a program designed, she said: ". . . around our young people to reclaim them, to make sure they are part of this economic mainstream, going forward." She believed the program was particularly important to at-risk young African American males. The $1 billion training program worked with private-sector businesses, not-for-profit groups, and community- and faith-based organizations. Herman also made enforcing anti-discrimination laws and equal pay laws a priority.

Secretary of Labor Alexis Herman was the first African American to hold the position, 1997 (Associated Press AP)

She began her public service career as director of the Women's Bureau in 1977, making her the senior black woman in the Labor Department. She was also the youngest director in the bureau's history. Herman focused her efforts on eliminating discrimination based on gender, age, and race. She believed that the problems facing women included limited marketable job skills, the availability of child care, and rigid work schedules. After Ronald Reagan's election, she left government service and in 1981 started her own consulting firm to help businesses comply with affirmative action training programs.

She worked in Jesse Jackson's 1984 and 1988 presidential campaigns, coordinating his activities at each Democratic National Convention (DNC). DNC chairman Ron Brown appointed her his chief of staff in 1989 and then deputy party chairwoman, a position she held until 1991. As chief executive officer of the 1992 DNC Committee, Herman's management of the convention contributed to Bill Clinton's increased popularity immediately after he received the party's presidential nomination.

Following Clinton's election in 1992, Herman became deputy director of the Clinton-Gore Presidential Transition Office. Appointed assistant to the president, director of the Public Liaison Office, she provided a link between the White House and the public and worked with several special interest groups. Herman's ability to work with disparate groups and to bring them together on issues contributed to her selection as secretary of labor in 1997. Her priorities include increasing the number of job-retraining programs, welfare-to-work programs involving businesses, and company-based child day care centers as well as implementing pension reform and new initiatives in job safety.

Born in Mobile, Alabama, Herman attended Heart of Mary Roman Catholic High School, a school for African Americans. During her sophomore year, she confronted a diocesan official and asked him to explain the reasons her school did not have the same annual religious pageant that was held at the white schools in the diocese. The school suspended her for the question but readmitted her after parents of other African American students protested. Herman earned her bachelor's degree from Xavier University in 1969 and did graduate work at the University of South Alabama from 1970 to 1972. After graduating from college, Herman returned to Mobile and helped desegregate the city's parochial schools.

See also Affirmative Action; Cabinets, Women in Presidential; Women's Bureau

References H. W. Wilson, *Current Biography Yearbook, 1998* (1998); *The New York Times*, 31 August 1994, 21 December 1996; Marjorie Whigham-Desir, "The Magnolia Mediator: Secretary of Labor Alexis Herman Speaks Out on the Changing Dynamics of the 21st Century Workplace," *Black Enterprise*, May 2000, p. 143.

Hernandez, Aileen Clarke (b. 1926)

The first woman appointed to the Equal Employment Opportunity Commission (EEOC), African American Aileen Hernandez was a founder and the second president of the National Organization for Women (NOW) and a founder of the National Women's Political Caucus. Hernandez began her civil rights activism in the mid-1940s, picketing the National Theater, Lisner Auditorium, and a restaurant chain to protest segregation. From 1951 to 1961, she worked for the International Ladies' Garment Workers Union (ILGWU) as an organizational assistant, assistant educational director, and director of public relations and education. She was assistant chief of the California Fair Employment Practices Commission from 1962 to 1965.

In 1965, President Lyndon Johnson appointed Hernandez to the EEOC, created the year before as part of Title VII of the Civil Rights Act of 1964 to enforce prohibitions against employment discrimination on the basis of race, color, religion, national origin, or sex. She played a pivotal role in changing airline companies' policy of firing stewardesses when they married, but she privately acknowledged that the EEOC was weak and that women needed an organization comparable to the National Association for the Advancement of Colored People. She explained: "Behind the scenes, I was actively involved in getting women's organizations protesting some of the things that were not happening at the commission." After eighteen months, Hernandez left the commission out of frustration with the poor progress made in enforcing laws against discrimination.

A founding member of NOW, Hernandez served as executive vice president of the organization from 1966 to 1970 and as president from 1970 to 1971. She was elected executive vice president, effective after the date of her resignation from the EEOC. She saw the repeal of abortion laws, free day care centers, equal employment opportunities, and passage of the Equal Rights Amendment (ERA) as the organization's priorities. In 1970 and 1971, Hernandez appeared before congressional committees in support of the ERA and in 1973 offered testimony on women's economic problems.

Hernandez said that NOW had an "embarrassingly elitist and middle-class image," one that she hoped to change by addressing problems confronting low-income women and women in menial jobs. After leaving the presidency, she created the Minority Women's Task Force in 1972 and organized a minority women's survey. The survey highlighted the sense of isolation felt by minority women that she had articulated.

Born in Brooklyn, New York, Hernandez earned her bachelor's degree in political science and sociology from Howard University in 1947 and graduated from the ILGWU labor college in 1951. She also attended the University of Oslo in Norway, New York University, the University of California at Los Angeles, and the University of Southern California, receiving her master's degree from Los Angeles State College in 1959.

See also Civil Rights Act of 1964, Title VII; Equal Employment Opportunity Commission; Equal Rights Amendment; National Organization for Women; National Women's Political Caucus

References H. W. Wilson, *Current Biography Yearbook, 1971* (1971); Hardy, *American Women Civil Rights Activists* (1993); *The New York Times*, 2 May 1970.

Herseth, Stephanie (b. 1970)

Democrat Stephanie Herseth of South Dakota entered the U.S. House of Representatives on 3 June 2004. She first ran for Congress in 2002, in a contest for an open seat. That year, her opponent was Republican Bill Janklow, who sought the congressional office after serving as South Dakota's governor from 1979 to 1987 and from 1994 to 2002. Janklow won the 2002 congressional race, but vacated the seat in January 2004, after being convicted of vehicular manslaughter.

Representative Herseth talks with farmers from central South Dakota about the severe drought, July 2006. (Courtesy Office of Stephanie Herseth)

Herseth won the special election for South Dakota's at-large congressional seat and won re-election in the 2004 general election. She is the first woman member elected to Congress from South Dakota. Gladys Pyle was appointed to the Senate in 1938, after the death of the incumbent, but was not sworn in. Vera C. Bushfield was appointed in 1948 following the death of her husband and completed his term.

As a member of Congress, Herseth advocates labeling the country of origin of beef products. "The evidence keeps mounting that opening the border presents a real and serious risk to our food supply and cattle producers," she explained.

In the 109th Congress (2005-2006), Congresswoman Herseth introduced legislation to increase payments to two American Indian tribes, both in South Dakota. Native Americans comprise about 8 percent of her state's population, making their interests among her priorities.

Born near Houghton, South Dakota, Herseth earned a bachelor of arts degree in government at Georgetown University in 1993 and a juris doctor degree at Georgetown University Law School in 1997. A member of the Georgetown University Law Center faculty, she also taught American government classes in the Czech Republic. Herseth had a private law practice at the time of her election.

References *American News* (Aberdeen, South Dakota), 17 May 2002, 22 July 2004, 28 October 2005; *Congress Daily*, 5 August 2002; Congressional Quarterly, Politics in America 2006 (2005); "South Dakota Elects a Democrat," *National Journal*, 5 June 2004, p.1780.

Hicks, (Anna) Louise Day (1923–2003)

Democrat Louise Hicks of Massachusetts served in the U.S. House of Representatives from 3 January 1971 to 3 January 1973. Hicks started her political career as a member of the Boston School Committee in 1961, where she opposed busing to integrate public schools. From 1963 until a court-ordered plan went into effect in 1974, Hicks led Boston's anti-busing supporters, insisting that she favored neighborhood schools. An unsuccessful candidate for mayor of Boston in 1967, she was later elected to the Boston City Council, serving from 1969 to 1971. As a member of Congress, Hicks continued her opposition to school busing. She supported voluntary school prayer and tax credits for students attending private schools and worked for proposals to allow direct federal aid to low-income students and to allow tax credits to parents of students attending non-public schools. When her district was redrawn after reapportionment, she lost her attempt for a second term.

Born in South Boston, Louise Hicks graduated from Wheelock Teachers' College in 1938 and taught elementary school for two years. She completed her bachelor of science degree in education in 1955 at Boston University and earned her law degree from Boston University School of Law in 1958.

See also Congress, Women in

References Schoenebaum, ed., *Political Profiles: The Nixon/Ford Years* (1979).

Hill, Anita Faye (b. 1956)

Law professor Anita Hill became a national figure in October 1991 when she accused U.S. Supreme Court nominee Clarence Thomas of sexually harassing her when he was her boss. Her televised testimony before the U.S. Senate's Judiciary Committee brought sexual harassment to the nation's attention in unprecedented ways. In addition, the image of the committee of white men questioning an African American woman about the experience outraged many women across the nation, motivating some of them to become candidates for public office and resulting in record numbers of women serving in Congress following the 1992 elections.

Hill's accusations stemmed from the years she had been Thomas's assistant, beginning in 1981, when he was assistant secretary for civil rights in the U.S. Department of Education. Three months after they began working together, Thomas suggested a social relationship, but Hill declined because she did not want to mix her personal and professional lives and she was not attracted to him. Thomas then began scheduling lunch meetings with Hill and turned the topic to his sexual interests, topics that Hill explained she did not want to discuss. Eventually, Hill had fewer personal conversations with Thomas, and his objectionable behavior stopped.

By 1982, Hill was concerned that the Department of Education would be abolished and that her job would end. When Thomas was appointed head of the Equal Employment Opportunity Commission (EEOC), he offered Hill a position as his assistant, and she accepted it. Hill's responsibilities included reviewing the commission's position on sexual harassment in the workplace as part of its antidiscrimination enforcement mandate. In the process, Hill realized that the EEOC had pursued cases involving behavior similar to what she had endured. She did not discuss the matter with Thomas because it embarrassed her. She did not file a charge against him, believing that the outcome was uncertain. (The U.S. Supreme Court did not decide that sexual harassment was sex discrimination until 1986.) Later in 1982, Thomas resumed making comments containing sexual innuendo to Hill.

When Hill received a job offer to teach at Oral Roberts University, it appealed to her because it offered her an escape from Thomas. In 1986, Hill accepted a teaching position at the University of Oklahoma College of Law.

When President George Bush nominated Thomas to the U.S. Supreme Court in 1991, one of Senator Howard Metzenbaum's aides received a tip that Thomas had sexually harassed Hill when she had worked for him in the 1980s. In response to an inquiry and because she had been told that her response would be confidential, Hill prepared a statement that was part of a report sent to Senate Judiciary Committee members.

During the Judiciary Committee's hearings on Thomas's nomination, Hill's allegations were not considered. The committee voted seven to seven on Thomas's nomination and sent its report with no recommendation to the Senate. During Senate debate, Hill's name and other material were leaked to *Newsday* and to National Public Radio. On 6 October 1991, when both news agencies made the information public, some observers believed that President Bush would withdraw Thomas's name after learning of the sexual harassment allegations Hill had made. Instead, Thomas's confirmation procedure continued.

On Tuesday, 8 October 1991, three Democratic senators used their one-minute speeches to challenge and protest Thomas's pending confirmation. Congresswoman Patricia Schroeder (D-CO) organized a group of seven Democratic women members of the House to go to the Senate to explain to senators their concerns regarding Thomas's potential confirmation and their belief that the charges against him were serious.

Anita Hill, Professor of Law, Social Policy Women's Studies of the Heller Graduate School, Brandeis University, at NYSE. Najlah Feanny/CORBIS SABA

Television cameras and newspaper photographers recorded the women's march on the Senate and sent the image across the nation. Their action, along with public pressure, led to the Senate's reopening of Thomas's hearings.

From Friday, 11 October 1991, to Sunday, 13 October 1991, the Senate hearings on Hill's allegations of Thomas's sexual harassment captured both the media's and the public's attention. Throughout the hearings, the committee focused its questions on Hill's integrity, her recollections, and her veracity rather than on Thomas's behavior or the general issue of sexual harassment. Even though three other women had been identified as targets of sexual harassment by Thomas, the committee refused to call them or an expert on sexual harassment as witnesses. The committee members' seeming intent to discredit Hill outraged women across the country, who viewed the committee's questions as unwarranted attacks on Hill.

In unprecedented ways, however, the nation focused on the question of sexual harassment, what constituted it, and what the consequences of it should be. In the months following the hearing, the number of formal sexual harassment complaints filed with the EEOC increased more than 50 percent. Women's political organizations gained new members and received increased financial support following the hearings. Several women ran for and won political office, among them Carol Moseley Braun, who became the first African American woman to serve in the U.S. Senate, and Cynthia McKinney, for whom Hill provided "a moral context" for her decision to run for the U.S. House of Representatives.

Hill returned to teaching at the University of Oklahoma College of Law, but she experienced a great deal of backlash from other professors and even from the Oklahoma legislature, which tried to revoke her position. She was a visiting professor at the University of California at Berkeley and eventually moved on to Brandeis University.

Born near Morris, Oklahoma, Anita Hill earned her bachelor of science from Oklahoma State University in 1977 and her law degree from Yale Law School in 1980. She was in private practice from 1980 to 1981.

> **See also** Congress, Women in; Equal Employment Opportunity Commission; McKinney, Cynthia Ann; Moseley Braun, Carol; Schroeder, Patricia Nell Scott; Sexual Harassment
>
> **References** Boxer, *Strangers in the Senate* (1994); Hill, *Speaking Truth to Power* (1997).
>
> **Document** Anita Hill, "Sexual Harassment: The Nature of the Beast," 1992

Hill, Julia "Butterfly" (b. 1974)

For 738 days, Julia Butterfly Hill lived on a six-foot-by-eight-foot platform perched 180 feet above the ground in a 1,000-year-old redwood tree named Luna. Through terrifying winds, cold, rain, and isolation, Hill remained in the tree, determined to protect it from loggers. Her vigil began on December 10, 1997, and ended on December 18, 1999. She descended from Luna only after reaching an agreement that protected Luna and the area surrounding her.

Luna grows on land owned by a logging company, making Hill's residency in the tree, conducted without the permission of the logging company, an action of illegal trespassing. The local sheriff refused to arrest Hill, saying that he would not jeopardize

Julia Butterfly Hill, co-founder of the Circle of Life Foundation. Hill lived in a 1,000-year-old redwood tree to protest the logging of old growth forests. (Courtesy Vermont Law School)

a deputy by asking him to climb the tree. He further stated that Hill did not pose a public hazard.

To protect her identity, she used a childhood nickname, Butterfly, as her "forest name."

Tree-sitting was a strategy initiated by Humboldt County, California environmentalists attempting to protect giant redwood forests. Several people had done it for a day or two at a time, but when organizers sought a volunteer to spend a week in a tree, Hill stepped forward and spent more than two years in it. She said: "I gave my word to the forest, to Luna, that until I felt I'd done everything I could to help make people aware, I could not come down." Supported by a ground crew of environmental activists, Hill gained media attention after spending six months tree-sitting, a record at the time.

While living in Luna, Hill founded Circle of Life, a group that advocates peace, justice, and environmental sustainability. She has written *The Legacy of Luna: the Story of a Tree, a Woman, and the Struggle to Save the Redwoods* (2000) and *One Makes the Difference: Inspiring Actions That Change Our World* (2002).

References *Los Angeles Times*, October 22, 1998; *Washington Post*, September 22, 2004; www.circleoflife.org.

Hills, Carla Helen Anderson (b. 1934)

Carla Hills served as U.S. secretary of housing and urban development from March 1975 to January 1977 and as special trade representative from 1989 to 1993. Hills began her public service career in 1974 as assistant attorney general in charge of the civil division of the Department of Justice, the highest-ranking woman in the department. President Gerald Ford appointed her secretary of housing and urban development in 1975, making her the third woman to hold a Cabinet-level position. A fiscal conservative, she focused on rehabilitating existing housing for low- and moderate-income families rather than on new construction. Hills generally opposed public housing, characterized it as wasteful and expensive, and supported rent subsidies instead. She served until 1977 and then went into a private law practice.

Hills returned to public life in 1989 when President George Bush appointed her U.S. trade representative. As President Bush's principal adviser on international trade policy and the nation's chief trade negotiator, she helped negotiate the North American Free Trade Agreement, the General Agreement on Tariffs and Trade, and agreements with Japanese companies to open their markets to U.S. imports. During negotiations to limit European governments' assistance to farmers, the talks came to a stalemate and Hills threatened to impose prohibitive tariffs on French wines and other products. Instead of the international trade war that observers predicted, Hills negotiated an agreement acceptable to both the European Community and the United States.

Born in Los Angeles, California, Hills studied at St. Hilda's College in Oxford, England, in 1954 and earned her bachelor's degree from Stanford University in 1955 and her law degree from Yale University in 1958.

See also Cabinets, Women in Presidential

References H. W. Wilson, *Current Biography Yearbook, 1993* (1993); *The New York Times*, 14 February 1975, 7 December 1988, 18 December 1992; Schoenebaum, ed., *Political Profiles: The Nixon/Ford Years* (1979).

Hishon v. King and Spalding (1984)

Elizabeth Hishon worked for King and Spalding, a large law firm that had more than fifty partners and about fifty associate attorneys. The firm had never had a woman partner in 1980, when Hishon filed her lawsuit accusing the firm of sex discrimination in violation of Title VII of the Civil Rights Act of 1964. When she had been recruited in 1972 by the law firm, she had been led to believe that, after five or six years, advancement to partner was a matter of course for associates whjuose work was satisfactory. After working for the firm for twelve years as an associate, she had not been invited to become a partner, prompting the lawsuit. The district court dismissed her lawsuit on the ground that Title VII did not apply to the selection of partners in a partnership. The U.S. Supreme Court disagreed with the district court and said that Title VII covers partners in a partnership and bans discrimination on the basis of race or sex.

See also Civil Rights Act of 1964, Title VII; Employment Discrimination

References *Hishon v. King and Spalding*, 467 U.S. 69 (1984).

Hobby, Oveta Culp (1905–1995)

The first secretary of the U.S. Department of Health, Education, and Welfare, Democrat Oveta Culp Hobby was also the first director of the Women's Auxiliary Army

Corps. Hobby began her public service career as a dollar-a-year executive with the War Department in the women's interest section of the Bureau of Public Relations. The next year, she developed plans for the newly created Women's Auxiliary Army Corps and became the first director of the corps in 1942, holding the rank of colonel. The corps ended its auxiliary status in 1943 and became the Women's Army Corps (WAC) with full military status. Many of Hobby's initial duties involved establishing policies and procedures for military women, recruiting them, and integrating them into the armed forces. She dealt with both substantive and trivial issues. African Americans questioned how a Southerner such as Hobby would deal with training and appointing officers, prompting Hobby's announcement that African American women would be appointed officers in proportion to the number of African American women in the general population. She appeared before Congress's Military Affairs Committee to gain approval for the positions women could hold in the army and obtained its consent on 239 job classifications. Throughout her tenure as head of the Corps, Hobby fought sex biases. For example, the military proposed dishonorable discharge for women who became pregnant without prior approval, but Hobby objected by proposing that men who fathered children out of wedlock should also receive a dishonorable discharge. Hobby won her point, and pregnant WACs received honorable discharges. The press questioned her on whether or not women would be able to wear makeup. Hobby concluded that they could wear modest amounts of it. At the end of World War II, about 100,000 women had served in the Corps. In 1945, Hobby resigned and returned to Houston.

Although Hobby considered herself a conservative Democrat, she supported Republican Governor Thomas E. Dewey's unsuccessful 1948 presidential campaign. As coeditor and publisher of the *Houston Post*, she announced her support for Republican General Dwight D. Eisenhower's 1952 presidential candidacy and spent several months in New York working in the Citizens for Eisenhower headquarters. After winning the election, Eisenhower appointed Hobby to head the Federal Security Agency, which became the Department of Health, Education, and Welfare (HEW). As secretary of HEW, Hobby supervised the development of nurse-training programs and a hospital reinsurance program. Her most important contribution was likely her decision to license six drug companies to manufacture the Salk vaccine for polio in 1955.

Born in Killeen, Texas, Hobby studied law at Mary Hardin–Baylor College and completed her studies at the University of Texas Law School. In 1919, when she was in high school, Hobby's father was elected to the Texas legislature, and she went with him to Austin to work for him. In 1925, she became parliamentarian of the Texas legislature, holding the position for six years, and served in the position again in 1939 and 1941. She wrote *Mr. Chairman*, a textbook on parliamentary procedure, in 1937.

Married to former Texas governor and newspaper owner William Pettis Hobby, Oveta Hobby was an editor and executive vice president of the newspaper as well as executive director of a radio station her husband owned. Following her retirement from government service, Hobby returned to Houston and resumed her role in the newspaper and the family's other business enterprises.

See also Cabinets, Women in Presidential; Military, Women in the; Rogers, Edith Frances Nourse

References Crawford and Ragsdale, *Women in Texas* (1992); H. W. Wilson, *Current Biography: Who's News and Why, 1942* (1942), *Current Biography: Who's News and Why, 1953* (1953); *The New York Times*, 17 August 1995; Schoenebaum, ed., *Political Profiles: The Eisenhower Years* (1977).

Hodgson v. Minnesota (1990)

Hodgson v. Minnesota challenged a 1981 Minnesota law requiring that the parents of a female child under eighteen years of age be notified before she could obtain an abortion. Under the law, both parents of the minor female seeking an abortion had to be given notice forty-eight hours before the procedure could be performed. The law included a judicial bypass procedure, which meant that if the young woman did not wish to notify her parents, she could go to a judge for notification. To obtain a court order, the minor female had to prove that she was mature and capable of giving informed consent. The law also specified exceptions to the two-parent notification, including divorce; emergency treatment to save the woman's life; and sexual or physical abuse, in which case the proper authorities had to have been notified.

Abortion clinics, physicians, pregnant minors, and others filed suit, claiming the law violated the due process and equal protection clauses of the Fourteenth Amendment. The Court invalidated the two-parent notification without a judicial bypass procedure, saying that it had no rational basis. The Court upheld the forty-eight-hour waiting period and the two-parent notification that included a procedure for a judicial waiver.

See also Abortion; Fourteenth Amendment

References *Hodgson v. Minnesota*, 497 U.S. 417 (1990).

Hoff, Joan (b. 1939)

Presidential and contemporary affairs historian and author Joan Hoff regularly provides commentary on the public television program *NewsHour*. She became a research professor in the history and philosophy department at Montana State University in 2001.

Hoff wrote *American Business & Foreign Policy, 1920-1993* (1971); *The Hoover Presidency: A Reappraisal* (1974); *Ideology and Economics: U.S. Relations with the Soviet Union, 1918-1933* (1974); *Herbert Hoover: Forgotten Progressive* (1975); *Without Precedent: The Life and Career of Eleanor Roosevelt* (1984); *Rights of Passage: The Past and Future of the ERA* (1986); *Law, Gender, and Injustice: A Legal History of U.S. Women* (1991); and *Nixon Reconsidered* (1994). In addition to other works she has written, Hoff has co-authored several books.

Born in Butte, Montana, Hoff earned a bachelor of arts degree at the University of Montana in 1957, a master of arts degree at Cornell University in 1960, and a doctor of philosophy degree at the University of California in 1966.

References http://www.montana.edu/news/1070315112.html

Hollister, Nancy P. (b. 1949)

Nancy Hollister became governor of Ohio on 31 December1998 and served until 11 January 1999. After Governor George Voinovich won election to the U.S. Senate, he resigned to prepare for his new office. Hollister, then Ohio's lieutenant governor, assumed the office of governor until the newly elected governor took office.

Hollister began her political career in 1980 as a Marietta, Ohio city council member, serving until 1984, when she won election as the city's mayor, an office she held until 1991. She served as lieutenant governor from 1995 to 1998. She unsuccessfully ran for the U.S. House of Representatives in 1998.

In 1999, she was first appointed and later elected to the Ohio House of Representatives, serving there until 2005.

Born in Evansville, Indiana, Hollister attended Kent State University.

References *The Post* (Athens, Ohio) 7 January 1999;
http://www.ohiohistorycentral.org/entry.php?rec=1758

Holt, Marjorie Sewell (b. 1920)

Republican Marjorie Holt of Maryland served in the U.S. House of Representatives from 3 January 1973 to 3 January 1987. Holt entered Congress with an agenda of reducing non-military spending and increasing military spending, and in 1978 she introduced an alternative budget and came within five votes of passing it. Holt continued to regularly develop and introduce her Republican version of the budget, which became part of her party's national political strategy. She adamantly opposed school busing, introduced measures to end it, and gained House approval for a constitutional amendment to ban it.

Born in Birmingham, Alabama, Marjorie Holt earned her bachelor's degree from Jacksonville University in 1945 and her law degree from the University of Florida in 1949. After several years in private law practice, Holt was circuit court clerk for Anne Arundel County Court from 1966 to 1972. She served on the Maryland Governor's Commission on Law Enforcement and Administration of Justice from 1970 to 1972.

See also Congress, Women in

References *Congressional Quarterly, Politics in America: Members of Congress in Washington and at Home* (1983); Office of the Historian, U.S. House of Representatives, *Women in Congress, 1917–1990* (1991).

Holtzman, Elizabeth (b. 1941)

Democrat Elizabeth Holtzman of New York served in the U.S. House of Representatives from 3 January 1973 to 3 January 1981. When Holtzman entered the 1972 Democratic primary, she challenged incumbent Congressman Emanuel Celler, who had represented the district for fifty years. Celler, whose campaign was well financed and whose campaign organization was far more sophisticated than Holtzman's, dismissed her candidacy. She conducted a grassroots campaign, emphasized her opposition to the war in Vietnam, argued that Celler had become removed from his constituency, and pointed to the amount of time he was absent from Congress. Her victory in the primary election all but ensured her election to Congress.

Shortly after Holtzman entered Congress, President Richard Nixon ordered the bombing of Cambodia, and she filed suit in U.S. district court to stop the bombings. The court ordered them to stop, but the decision was overturned on appeal. She took the matter to the U.S. Supreme Court, but her request for a hearing was denied.

In 1979, Holtzman discovered that fifty alleged Nazi war criminals resided in the United States, and she began a crusade to have them deported. For years, she challenged the Immigration and Naturalization Service to respond to her demands for deportation action, and eventually more than 100 Nazi war criminals were expelled from the United States.

A feminist, Holtzman was one of the organizers and one of the first co-chairs of the Congresswomen's Caucus, later known as the Congressional Caucus for Women's Issues, created to bring women members of Congress together to discuss matters of common interest. Holtzman served on the President's National Commission on the Observance of International Women's Year, the group that planned the 1977 National Women's Conference. A strong Equal Rights Amendment supporter, Holtzman told one group: "Sooner or later, inevitably and inexorably, our Constitution will embody the principle of women's equality under the law." In 1978, she passed a bill that helped protect the privacy of rape victims by preventing cross-examination into their prior sexual experience.

Holtzman entered the 1980 Democratic primary for the U.S. Senate instead of running for a fifth term. She won the primary but lost the general election. In 1981, Holtzman won the race for district attorney of Brooklyn, where she served until 1989, the year she was elected comptroller of New York City. After serving from 1990 to 1994, she returned to private law practice. In 2000, President Bill Clinton appointed Holtzman to the The Nazi War Crimes and Japanese Imperial Government Records Interagency Working Group (IWG), which has as its mission declassifying documents related to World War II.

Born in New York, New York, Holtzman received her bachelor's degree from Radcliffe College in 1962 and her law degree from Harvard Law School in 1965. While in law school, she spent the summer of 1963 in Georgia working with the Student Nonviolent Coordinating Committee, a civil rights organization. The next summer she worked for the National Association for the Advancement of Colored People Legal Defense and Education Fund.

See also Congress, Women in; Congressional Caucus for Women's Issues; Equal Rights Amendment; Heckler, Margaret Mary O'Shaughnessy; National Women's Conference

References Holtzman, *Who Said It Would Be Easy: One Woman's Life in the Political Arena* (1996); Office of the Historian, U.S. House of Representatives, *Women in Congress, 1917–1990* (1991).

Honeyman, Nan Wood (1881–1970)

Democrat Nan Honeyman of Oregon served in the U.S. House of Representatives from 3 January 1937 to 3 January 1939. Honeyman strongly supported New Deal policies and was accused of subordinating her district's needs to President Franklin D. Roosevelt's national political concerns. She was defeated in her attempt for a second term in 1938 and in 1940. She was senior representative for the Pacific Coast of the Office of Price Administration in 1941 and 1942 and collector of customs for Portland, Oregon, from 1942 to 1953.

Born in West Point, New York, Nan Honeyman graduated from St. Helens Hall in 1898 and later attended Finch School in New York to study music. Honeyman served in the Oregon House of Representatives from 1935 to 1937 and filled a vacancy in the Oregon Senate in 1942.

See also Congress, Women in; State Legislatures, Women in

References Office of the Historian, U.S. House of Representatives, *Women in Congress, 1917–1990* (1991).

Hooks, Bell (b. 1952)

African American intellectual bell hooks has criticized the feminist movement for its racism and has argued that it must recognize that women have a variety of backgrounds and experiences and that race and class affect women's lives as much as gender. She seeks to understand race, gender, and class biases by beginning with her own experiences and the experiences of other women and developing theories from them. She further seeks to use her theories to alter the ways people live their lives, which she calls the practical phase of her work. To involve a larger audience than academics, hooks uses popular culture to link familiar movies or books to theory, providing a base from which to engage students and readers and then move them to considering theory.

College professor and mentor, hooks has published several works, including *Ain't I a Woman: Black Women and Feminism* (1981); *Feminist Theory from Margin to Center* (1984); *Yearning: Race, Gender, and Cultural Politics* (1990); *Breaking Bread: Insurgent Black Intellectual Life* (1991); *Teaching to Transgress: Education as the Practice of Freedom* (1994); *We Real Cool: Black Men and Masculinity* (2003); and *Teaching Community: A Pedagogy of Hope* (2003).

Born in Hopkinsville, Kentucky, bell hooks was given the name Gloria Jean Watkins, taking her maternal great-grandmother's name when she began her writing career. She uses lowercase letters instead of capital letters because she believes that who has written something is less important than what she or he has written. hooks completed her undergraduate studies at Stanford University in 1973 and earned her master's degree from the University of Wisconsin in 1976 and her doctoral degree from the University of California at Santa Cruz in 1983. She has taught at various California universities, Yale University, Oberlin College, and the City College of New York.

See also Feminist Movement

References H. W. Wilson, *Current Biography Yearbook, 1995* (1995); hooks, with Mckinnon, "Sisterhood: Beyond Public and Private" (1996).

Hooley, Darlene (b. 1939)

Democrat Darlene Hooley of Oregon entered the U.S. House of Representatives on 3 January 1997. During her congressional campaign, Hooley pledged to work for income tax deductions for college tuition and for improved vocational programs for people needing professional retraining. Hooley's congressional priorities include protecting funding for early childhood education, preserving Social Security and Medicare, and protecting abortion rights.

Congresswoman Hooley led the effort to obtain adequate body armor for soldiers in Iraq and to secure armored Humvees for them. She passed legislation allowing consumers to see their credit reports annally from all three major credit bureaus at no cost, and another providing additional funding for schools in rural areas affected by declining logging revenues. She has introduced measures to protect consumers from identity theft and, with Republican Congresswoman Mary Bono of California, to require country of origin labeling for meat products and fresh produce.

A former teacher, Hooley became an activist for safer playgrounds in the 1970s, served on the park district board, and then served on the West Linn City Council from 1977 to 1981. While in the Oregon State House of Representatives from 1981 to 1987, she passed welfare reform legislation that moved people from welfare to work. She authored the state's first recycling laws, rewrote the state's land use laws, and wrote and passed equal pay laws.

Hooley accepted an appointment to fill a vacancy on the Clackamas County Commission in 1987 and then won re-election to it until 1996. On the Commission, she worked to improve county roads, implement welfare reform, increase the number of police, and create new jobs in the private sector. She helped establish a pilot project in which welfare recipients received counseling to reduce the number of people on welfare assistance.

Born in Williston, North Dakota, Darlene Hooley attended Pasadena Nazarene College from 1957 to 1959 and received her bachelor's degree from Oregon State University in 1961.

See also Congress, Women in

Darlene Hooley listens intently to testimony during the Hearing on Social Security: The Long-Term Budget Implications, 107th Congress. (Courtesy U.S. House of Representatives)

References *Columbus (Ohio) Dispatch*, 22 July 2005; *Congress Daily*, 18 March 2004; *Congressional Quarterly, Politics in America 1998* (1997); *Congressional Quarterly Weekly Report*, 4 January 1997; *Education Daily*, 1 November 2000; http://hooley.house.gov.

Horn, Joan Kelly (b. 1936)

Democrat Joan Horn of Missouri served in the U.S. House of Representatives from 3 January 1991 to 5 January 1993. Horn was active in the Democratic Party, the Missouri Women's Political Caucus, and the Freedom of Choice Council, connections that provided her with an important network when she sought a seat in Congress, her first political office. In addition, she and her husband were partners in a research and polling firm, which gave her additional political experience. She lost re-election attempts in 1992 and 1996.

Born in St. Louis, Missouri, Joan Horn earned her bachelor's degree in 1973 and her master's degree in 1975 from the University of Missouri at St. Louis.

See also Congress, Women in

References *Congressional Quarterly, Politics in America 1992* (1991).

Howe, Julia Ward (1819–1910)

Best known for writing "Battle Hymn of the Republic," Julia Ward Howe provided leadership in the areas of woman suffrage, women's education, and peace. Married in 1843 to social reformer Dr. Samuel Gridley Howe, she bore six children in the next sixteen years. In addition to caring for them, she attended lectures; studied foreign languages, religion, and philosophy; and wrote poetry and dramas, interests she developed because her husband did not want her involved in public life.

Julia Howe's entrance into public life began when she anonymously published *Passion-Flowers*, a collection of poems in 1854, and a second collection, *Words for the Hour*, in 1857. She wrote "The Battle Hymn of the Republic" in 1861, *Atlantic Monthly* published it in 1862, and it became a Civil War anthem. With its success, Julia Howe actively engaged in her literary career, publishing a literary magazine in 1867.

She also became active in the woman suffrage movement. In 1868, she was a founder and the first president of the New England Woman Suffrage Association, serving until 1877 and again from 1893 to 1910. She became a leader in the newly organized American Woman Suffrage Association in 1869. President of the Massachusetts Woman Suffrage Association from 1870 to 1877 and from 1891 to 1893, she founded a weekly woman suffrage magazine, *Woman's Journal*, in 1870, and edited it for twenty years.

Also in 1870, she wrote "Appeal to Womanhood throughout the World," a call to women to become active in peace issues. She organized the Woman's Peace Conference in London in 1872.

Howe's husband died in 1876 and with her new freedom, she went on her first speaking tour that year, advocating the development of a national women's club movement. A founder of the New England Women's Club in 1868, she was its president for most of the rest of her life, beginning in 1870. She was also a founder of the General Federation of Women's Clubs in 1890.

In addition to her commitments to woman suffrage and the women's club movement, Howe continued her literary career, publishing collections of her lectures, a biography of Margaret Fuller, and her memoirs.

> **See also** American Woman Suffrage Association; General Federation of Women's Clubs; Peace Movement; Suffrage
>
> **References** Garraty and Carnes, eds., *American National Biography* (1999).

Hoyt v. Florida (1961)

The U.S. Supreme Court decided in *Hoyt v. Florida* that being judged by an all-male jury did not violate an accused person's Fourteenth Amendment rights. At the time, women could not serve on state juries in three states, and in twenty-six states and the District of Columbia women could claim exemptions not available to men. In Florida, women who wanted to serve on a jury had to register with the clerk of the circuit court, which few did.

In Hoyt, a woman convicted of killing her husband appealed on the grounds that she had been denied her Fourteenth Amendment rights because Florida's law unconstitutionally excluded women from jury service. The woman argued that her case demanded women on the jury because women would have been more sympathetic than men in considering her temporary insanity defense.

The Court rejected her appeal, saying first that "woman is still regarded as the center of home and family life. We cannot say that it is constitutionally impermissible for a State, acting in pursuit of the general welfare, to conclude that a woman should be relieved from the civic duty of jury service unless she herself determines that such service is consistent with her own special responsibilities." From that perspective, the Court said that it was reasonable "for a state legislature to [assume] that it would not be administratively feasible to decide in each individual instance whether family responsibilities of a prospective female juror were serious enough to warrant an exemption."

In 1975, the Court overturned this decision in *Taylor v. Louisiana*.

> **See also** Fourteenth Amendment; Juries, Women on; *Taylor v. Louisiana*
>
> **References** Getman, "The Emerging Constitutional Principle of Sexual Equality" (1973); *Hoyt v. Florida*, 368 U.S. 57 (1961).

Huck, Winifred Sprague Mason (1882–1936)

Republican Winifred Huck of Illinois served in the U.S. House of Representatives from 7 November 1922 to 3 March 1923. The daughter of Congressman William Mason, who died in office, Winifred Huck won the special election to fill the vacancy. She introduced legislation to grant independence to the Philippine Islands, to grant self-government to Cuba and Ireland, and to require a direct popular vote before U.S. armed forces could be involved in an overseas war. She was denied the party's nomination for the full term that began in 1923.

In 1925, Huck investigated the criminal justice system and prisons. With the cooperation of Ohio's governor, she was arrested for a minor crime, convicted, incarcerated for a month, and pardoned by the governor. She then began a trip to New York, seeking employment as an ex-convict along the way and writing a series of syndicated articles about her experiences. In 1928 and 1929, she was an investigative reporter for the *Chicago Evening Post.*

Huck was born in Chicago, Illinois.

See also Congress, Women in

References James, ed., *Notable American Women 1607–1950* (1971); *The New York Times*, 26 August 1936.

Huerta, Dolores Clara Fernandez (b. 1930)

Dolores Huerta has sought economic and employment justice for Hispanic American agricultural workers since the early 1960s, when she and Cesar Chavez co-founded the National Farm Workers Association (NFWA). A folk hero in the Mexican American community for her work as a contract negotiator, strike organizer, lobbyist, and boycott coordinator, Huerta has been arrested more than two dozen times and has experienced harassment and violence.

Huerta entered the migrant labor movement in part out of frustration at teaching migrants' children because, she later explained: "I couldn't stand seeing kids come to class hungry and needing shoes. I thought I could do more by organizing farm workers than by trying to teach their hungry kids." In 1955, she met a representative of the Community Service Organization (CSO), a Mexican American self-help association that sought to empower Latinos through political action. A founding member of the Stockton, California CSO, Huerta served as the group's lobbyist to the California legislature in the late 1950s and early 1960s. She helped pass more than a dozen bills, including measures requiring businesses to provide pensions to legal immigrants and allowing farmworkers to receive public assistance, retirement benefits, and disability and unemployment insurance regardless of their status as U.S. citizens.

Through the CSO, Huerta worked with Chavez, who proposed creating a union for farmworkers. In 1962, they formed the NFWA, went into fields, and explained the anticipated benefits of organizing to farmworkers. Chavez and Huerta endured threats from landowners and law enforcement officers. When the American Federation of Labor-Congress of Industrial Organizations (AFL-CIO) initiated a strike against California grape growers, the NFWA joined the effort in 1965. The AFL-CIO group and the NFWA merged into the United Farm Workers Organizing Committee (UFWOC) in 1966. For her involvement in the strike as an organizer, Huerta was repeatedly arrested and placed under surveillance by the Central Intelligence Agency.

Huerta was named chief negotiator for UFWOC, even though she was not a lawyer, had no experience as a labor negotiator, and had never read a union contract before the strike began. By 1967 she had negotiated contracts that gave workers an hourly raise, health care benefits, job security, and protection from pesticide poisoning. Despite the success with some growers, the majority resisted the UFWOC, and the organization called for a national boycott of table grapes in 1968. As director of the boycott, Huerta moved to New York and mobilized unions, political activists, Hispanic associations, community organizations, and others in support of the boycott, one of the most successful boycotts in the United States. In 1970, Huerta negotiated collective bargaining agreements with more than two dozen growers and obtained many new benefits for grape workers. The success attracted new members to UFWOC, and membership reached 80,000. In 1972, the UFWOC became an independent affiliate of the AFL-CIO and was renamed the United Farm Workers of America, AFL-CIO (UFW).

More boycotts followed in the 1970s, with Huerta managing the lettuce, grape, and Gallo wine boycotts. One of the successes of the boycotts was the passage of the Agricultural Labor Relations Act in 1975, the first law that recognized collective bargaining rights of California farmworkers.

Huerta described the achievements of the organizing efforts: "I think we brought to the world, the United States, anyway, the whole idea of boycotting as a nonviolent tactic. I think we showed the world that nonviolence can work to make social change.… I think we have laid a pattern of how farm workers are eventually going to get out of their bondage. It may not happen right now in our foreseeable future, but the pattern is there and farmworkers are going to make it."

From 1991 to 1993, she took a leave of absence from the UFW to work on the Feminist Majority's Feminization of Power campaign, a project that encourages Latinas to run for public office. She then returned to the UFW and began organizing the 20,000 workers in California's strawberry industry.

Born in Dawson, New Mexico, Huerta earned her associate's degree from Stockton College.

See also The Feminist Majority

References Felner, "Dolores Huerta" (1998); H. W. Wilson, *Current Biography Yearbook, 1997* (1997); Garcia, "Dolores Huerta: Woman, Organizer, and Symbol" (1993).

Document Dolores Huerta, "Dolores Huerta Talks," 1972

Huffington, Arianna Stassinopoulos (b. 1950)

Political columnist and author Arianna Huffington created The Huffington Post, a blog with over one million visitors per month. "I am obsessive and the Internet rewards obsession," she said about her successful site. Huffington, who was initially a conservative pundit, became increasingly moderate in her political views, criticizing President George W. Bush and his administration.

Huffington entered the Washington, D.C. political scene in the early 1990s, when her former husband, Michael Huffington, served in Congress. Following their divorce, Arianna Huffington became increasingly visible as a frequent talk show guest, columnist, and author. She had written two biographies and other works prior to becoming a political columnist. She has since written political satires and commentaries, including *Greetings from the Lincoln Bedroom* (1998) and *How to Overthrow the Government* (2000). Arianna Huffington was an unsuccessful Iindependent candidate for governor of California in 2003.

Born in Athens, Greece, Huffington earned her master in arts degree at Cambridge University in England.

References *The New York Times*, 15 May 2006; *San Jose Mercury News*, 22 September 2003; *Washington Post*, 11 August 2003.

Hufstedler, Shirley Ann Mount (b. 1925)

The first secretary of the U.S. Department of Education, Shirley Hufstedler served from 1979 to 1981. Creating the department had been one of President Jimmy Carter's pledges in his 1976 campaign and Congress had authorized establishing the Department of Education in September 1979. Confirmed by the Senate on 30 November 1979, Hufstedler's initial task was to bring together 152 federal education programs previously administered by the Defense Department and the Department of Health, Education, and Welfare. She explained: "The federal government cannot simply 'set policy' in terms of what should be done to help school systems. The most we can do is to help them help themselves and to try to create a climate in which people can begin to think in cooperation terms instead of confrontation terms." The department officially opened on 4 May 1980.

Born in Denver, Colorado, Shirley Hufstedler earned her bachelor's degree in business administration in 1945 and her law degree from Stanford University in 1949. In private law practice from 1950 to 1960, she was special legal consultant to the California state attorney general. Appointed to fill an unexpired term as judge on the Los Angeles Superior Court in 1961, she was elected to a full term the next year and served until 1966, when she was appointed to the California State Court of Appeals for the Second District. In 1968, President Lyndon Johnson appointed Hufstedler to the U.S. Court of Appeals for the Ninth Circuit, the second woman to serve on the federal appellate bench.

Hufstedler chaired the U.S. Commission on Immigration Reform, which was created by Congress in 1990 and dissolved in 1997.

> **See also** Cabinets, Women in Presidential
>
> **References** H. W. Wilson, *Current Biography Yearbook, 1980* (1980).

Hughes, Karen Parfitt (b. 1967)

Among President George W. Bush's most trusted advisers, Karen Hughes served his administration as Counselor to the President from 2001 to 2002 and as Undersecretary of State for Public Diplomacy and Public Affairs beginning in 2005.

Born in Paris, France, Hughes spent her childhood in the United States, Canada, and Panama Canal Zone. Following her graduation from Southern Methodist University in 1977 with a BA in English and a BFA in journalism, Hughes began her career as a reporter for a Fort Worth, Texas television station, working there until 1984. That year, Hughes began her political career when she became the Texas media coordinator for President Ronald Reagan's successful re-election campaign.

In 1985, Hughes served as a consultant to the Republican Party of Texas, joining its staff as executive director in 1991. When George W. Bush ran for governor of Texas in 1994, he recruited Hughes to be the director of communications for his campaign. Following his election, she joined his administration, again as director of communications. Hughes held the same position during Bush's campaign for the presidency in 2000. She added a new dimension to presidential campaigns when she took her son Robert, then a teenager, with her on the campaign trail, home schooling him.

As Counselor to the President, Hughes noted that the most difficult task was conducting the press briefings following the September 11, 2001 terrorist attacks.

Karen Parfitt Hughes is a Republican bureaucrat from Texas. She currently serves as the Under Secretary for Public Diplomacy and Public Affairs in the U.S. Department of State with the rank of ambassador.

The New York Times wrote: "The rule of thumb in any White House is that nobody is indispensable except the president. But Karen Hughes has come as close to that description as any recent presidential aide." Hughes's decision to leave the White House in 2002 to spend more time with her family in Austin, Texas, surprised many political observers. She remained involved with the White House, however, traveling regularly to Washington, DC, to advise President Bush.

Hughes rejoined the Bush Administration in mid-2005 to serve as Undersecretary of State for Public Diplomacy and Public Affairs, with the rank of ambassador. Early in her tenure, she initiated her Engage, Exchange, Educate, and Empower program. Through it, she intends to present the United States' views on major issues, to increase the number of people in foreign exchange programs, to encourage Americans to learn foreign languages and residents of other nations to learn English, and to empower people, especially women in the Arab world.

Hughes wrote her memoir, *Ten Minutes from Normal*, published in 2004.

References Hughes, Karen, *Ten Minutes from Normal* (2004); *The New York Times*, April 24, 2002; *Newsweek* November 14, 2005.

Hull, Jane Dee Bowersock (b. 1935)

Republican Jane Dee Hull served as governor of Arizona from 5 September 1997 to 6 January 2003. She believes that her legacy as governor is education, increasing funding for the classroom, and constructing school buildings in poor areas and fast-growing ones.

Hull entered politics in 1965 as a precinct committeewoman, worked in Republican campaigns, and served in the Arizona House of Representatives from 1979 to 1993. In 1989, she served as the state's first female speaker of the House and was Arizona secretary of state from 1995 to 1997. Her tenure as secretary of state ended when incumbent Arizona Governor Fife Symington III was convicted of fraud and resigned from office. The state constitution provides that the secretary of state becomes governor when the office is vacant. Hull was elected governor in 1998 for a full term, making her the first woman elected governor in Arizona. Rose Mofford had succeeded an incumbent governor in 1988, but was not elected. Hull was not a candidate in 2002.

Born in Kansas City, Missouri, Jane Hull earned her bachelor of science degree from the University of Kansas, did postgraduate work in political science and economics at Arizona State University, and graduated from the Josephson Ethics Institute.

See also Governors, Women; State Legislatures, Women in
References *Arizona Republic*, 22 December 2002.

Humphrey Brown, Muriel Fay Buck (1912–1998)

Democrat Muriel Humphrey of Minnesota served in the U.S. Senate from 25 January 1978 to 7 November 1978. Her life as a political wife began in 1943, when her first husband, Hubert Humphrey, ran for mayor of Minneapolis, Minnesota. She campaigned for him during his many races for the U.S. Senate as well as his campaign for vice president of the United States in 1964, which he won, and for president in 1968, which he lost. When he died in office in 1978, Muriel Humphrey was appointed to fill the vacancy.

In office, Muriel Humphrey passed an amendment to enhance the job security of federal employees who expose waste or fraud and co-sponsored the resolution to extend the ratification deadline of the Equal Rights Amendment. After a granddaughter was born mentally disabled, Humphrey worked for people with mental disabilities. Humphrey declined to run in the special election to complete the term. She remarried in 1981 and remained vocal in the political arena. When liberalism and liberal ideas came under attack in the late 1980s, Muriel Humphrey announced: "I'm a liberal and I'm proud of it. In fact, I was probably a little more liberal than Hubert was."

Born in Huron, South Dakota, Humphrey attended Huron College in the 1930s, leaving when she married Hubert Humphrey in 1936. She worked as a bookkeeper in a utility company to put her husband through college. A shy woman, she strove to overcome her shyness as her husband's political career developed. After he received the Democratic Party's nomination for president, she explained: "I just wanted to be a housewife. I didn't even know how I'd be a mother. I would have been horrified to have thought of this."

See also Congress, Women in; Equal Rights Amendment
References *The New York Times*, 21 September 1998; Office of the Historian, U.S. House of Representatives, *Women in Congress, 1917–1990* (1991).

Hurley, Ruby (1909–1980)

African American Ruby Hurley was known as "the queen of civil rights" for her work with the National Association for the Advancement of Colored People (NAACP) in the 1950s and 1960s. Appointed youth secretary of the NAACP in 1943, she directed the organization of youth councils and college affiliates across the country. Assigned to Birmingham, Alabama, in 1951 when the organization opened a southeastern regional office, she left when the state banned the organization and reopened the regional office in Atlanta, Georgia. She helped investigate bomb threats made to an NAACP field secretary in Florida in 1951 and the murder of the Reverend George W. Lee, who was registering African American voters. She monitored the trial of two white Mississippians accused of murdering Emmett Till, a young African American. Hurley was involved in the desegregation of the University of Alabama, the University of Georgia, and the University of Mississippi.

During a sit-in demonstration at a lunch counter in Greensboro, North Carolina, Hurley cited the Constitution as the basis for her actions and then explained: "What we're saying, Mr. White Folks, is this: 'You wrote it and all we want you to do is live by it!'"

Born in Washington, D.C., Ruby Hurley graduated from Miner Teachers College and attended the Robert H. Terrell Law School.

> **See also** Civil Rights Movement, Women in the; National Association for the Advancement of Colored People, Women in the
>
> **References** *The New York Times*, 15 August 1980.

Hutchinson, Anne Marbury (1591–1643)

Puritan Anne Hutchinson was born in Alford, Lincolnshire, England; became a member of Puritan minister John Cotton's congregation in Boston, England; and with her husband, William Hutchinson, and their children followed Cotton to colonial Boston in 1634. Cotton preached the covenant of grace, a belief that redemption came from God's grace and that faith provided the basis for salvation. The covenant of works was the opposing belief, one that espoused that obedience to moral law was the way to salvation and that one's outward behavior indicated that one had been redeemed. Hutchinson interpreted the covenant of grace to mean that the spirit of Christ lived within each person, leading her to argue that men and women were equal. People who shared her beliefs were called antinomians and were charged with heresy by the Church.

A midwife and respected woman in the community, Hutchinson was sought by other women for her advice. Through their conversations, Hutchinson realized that some women had accepted the covenant of works rather than the covenant of grace, in which she believed. To offer women an opportunity to speak openly and freely about their beliefs, Hutchinson organized weekly meetings in her home to discuss, criticize, and interpret the week's sermon. So many people, men and women, attended that she initiated a second weekly meeting. As her following grew, one minister attacked her in his sermons, and she responded by criticizing his theology.

Hutchinson's challenge to ministerial authority led to her famous trial, although she was not charged with any specific crime. Her offense was that she had not accepted the limits placed on women at the time. She was tried in civil court in 1637 for sedition for leading discussions on sermons and on her theological ideas, found guilty, and banished. Hutchinson was tried again before an ecclesiastical court in early 1638 for heresy and was excommunicated. Anne and William Hutchinson and their children joined another religious dissident, Roger Williams, in Rhode Island, living there until 1642 when William died and they moved to New York. Hutchinson and all but one daughter were killed by Native Americans in 1643.

References Cameron, *Anne Hutchinson, Guilty or Not? A Closer Look at Her Trials* (1994).

Hutchison, Kathryn (Kay) Ann Bailey (b. 1943)

Republican Kay Hutchison of Texas entered the U.S. Senate on 14 June 1993. When incumbent Texas Senator Lloyd Bentsen left office to join President Bill Clinton's Cabinet, Hutchison won the special election to complete the term. She won election to a full six-year term in November 1994. Hutchison held the leadership positions of Senate deputy majority whip in the 104th, 105th, and 106th Congresses (1995–2001), vice chair of the Senate Republican Conference in the 107th and 108th Congresses (2001–2005), and Republican conference secretary in the 109th Congress (2005–2007).

Senator Hutchison has passed a measure creating the homemakers' individual retirement account. Before passage of the measure, only employed persons could establish individual retirement accounts, leaving homemakers who are not employed in the labor market without the opportunity to take advantage of the tax savings associated with the accounts. With passage of the measure, a married person not employed in the labor market can establish an account and the homemaker and wage-earning spouse can save for retirement at the same rate as two-income families. Hutchison also passed a measure that makes stalking across state lines a federal offense. In another measure, Senator Hutchison passed legislation creating the Overseas Basing Commission to review American preparedness for the twenty-first century.

Following the September 11, 2001 terrorist attacks on the United States, Hutchison pressed for several new security measures, including aviation security and increased air cargo security. With Texas and Mexico sharing a border, Hutchison has focused her attention on reducing illegal immigration and the movement of drugs across the border. She has worked for campaign finance reform, military preparedness and a strong defense budget, simplification of the process for small businesses to become government suppliers, congressional term limits, cuts in personal income taxes, and a balanced budget.

A political and legal affairs correspondent for a Houston television station from 1969 to 1971, Hutchison then went to Washington, D.C., to serve as press secretary to Republican Party co-chair Anne Armstrong. Hutchison returned to Texas and served in the state House of Representatives from 1973 to 1977, where she co-sponsored rape reform legislation with Sarah Weddington. President Gerald Ford appointed her vice chair of the National Transportation Safety Board in 1976, where she served until 1978, when she moved to Dallas. She was senior vice president and general counsel of Republic Bank Corporation and later co-founded Fidelity National Bank of Dallas and owned McCraw Candies. She ran unsuccessfully for Congress in 1982. Hutchison served as Texas state treasurer from 1991 to 1993.

Born in Galveston, Texas, Hutchison attended the University of Texas from 1961 to 1964 and earned her bachelor of laws degree in 1967 from the University of Texas Law School and her bachelor of arts degree in 1992 from the University of Texas.

See also Congress, Women in; Stalking; State Legislatures, Women in; Weddington, Sarah Ragle

References *Congressional Quarterly, Politics in America 1996* (1995); Mike Sherry, "Sen. Kay Bailey Hutchison," *CQ Weekly*, 28 December 2002, p.25; http://hutchison.senate.gov

Hyde, Henry John (b. 1924)

Republican Henry Hyde of Illinois entered the U.S. House of Representatives on 3 January 1975. During his first term in office, Hyde passed an amendment prohibiting federal funding for abortions except to save the life of the mother. He has succeeded in attaching the amendment to every subsequent annual appropriations bill. After the amendment was challenged in the courts, the U.S. Supreme Court found it constitutional in *Harris v. McRae* (1980). One of the most ardent abortion opponents in Congress, Hyde seeks a constitutional amendment banning abortions except to save the life of the mother. Criticized for his exclusion of abortion funding for pregnancies resulting from rape or incest, Hyde has explained: "The fetus has committed no crime. Killing the unborn child would be an admission that there are values superior to human life and I don't recognize any value superior to human life."

Born in Chicago, Hyde earned his bachelor of science degree from Georgetown University in 1947 and his law degree from the Loyola University School of Law in 1949. An unsuccessful candidate for Congress in 1962, Hyde served in the Illinois House of Representatives from 1967 to 1975.

See also Abortion; *Harris v. McRae*

References H. W. Wilson, *Current Biography Yearbook, 1989* (1989).

Ifill, Gwen (b. 1955)

The first African American woman to host a major political talk show, Gwen Ifill moderates the PBS weekly news program *Washington Week in Review*. She is also a senior political correspondent for *The Newshour with Jim Lehrer*. Ifill earlier worked in print media, writing for the *Washington Post*, and *The New York Times*, among other newspapers, before moving to broadcast media covering Congress for NBC. She joined PBS in 1999, saying: "PBS told me I could have my own program plus still be a reporter. I couldn't turn down the combination."

Born in New York, New York, Ifill earned a bachelor of arts degree at Simmons College in 1977.

References Paige Albiniak, "A Nose for News and Politics," *Broadcasting & Cable*, 7 August 2000, p. 55 ; *The Washington Post*, 1 October 1999.

Independent Women's Forum

Founded in 1992 to provide an alternative female voice in political debates, the Independent Women's Forum (IWF) began informally to support Clarence Thomas's nomination to the U.S. Supreme Court. With about 500 members, IWF espouses conservative views on social issues and bases its positions on the belief that the family is the foundation of society and is the center of most women's lives. IWF works to "counter the dangerous influence of radical feminism in the courts," and "combat corrose feminist ideology on campus."

IWF members include businesswomen, economists, lawyers, teachers, and homemakers who support individual responsibility, strong families, and less government. IWF has supported the Virginia Military Institute's attempt to remain all-male, Paula Jones's sexual harassment suit against President Bill Clinton, welfare reform, single-sex educational programs, and mandatory testing for human immunodeficiency virus (HIV) and disclosure of the results. It opposes affirmative action and worked against the Violence Against Women Act. IWF has campus programs, works through the courts, and sponsors work/family projects.

Independent Women's Voice is the lobbying arm of IWF.

See also Affirmative Action; Hill, Anita Faye; Sexual Harassment; *United States v. Virginia*; Violence Against Women Act of 1994

References Burkett, *The Right Women* (1998); www.iwf.org.

Ireland, Patricia (b. 1945)

Patricia Ireland was president of the National Organization for Women (NOW) from 1991 to 2001. Ireland became involved in the feminist movement through a personal experience. A flight attendant for Pan American World Airlines from 1967 to 1975, Ireland learned that the company's health insurance policy covered male employees' families but not female employees' families. She protested the company policy and contacted NOW for advice. Following NOW's recommendations, she successfully challenged the policy, but only for women who were heads of households. The company later granted women the same insurance coverage as men. Years later, Ireland noted: "The vice president of the labor task force at Dade County NOW is now the dean of women lawmakers in the Florida legislature. I am the president of NOW. And Pan Am is bankrupt."

Ireland discovered that she could create change; that although laws existed to protect women's rights, they were not consistently enforced; and that NOW's feminist agenda related to her. She also found satisfaction in having power. Increasingly dissatisfied with the control that Pan Am exercised over her life as well as that of other flight attendants, Ireland sought new avenues to gain status and power. She entered law school while still working for Pan Am to support herself and her husband. Following graduation in 1975, she joined a private law firm, where she worked for twelve years. During those years, she also did pro bono work for women and through that work learned how legal barriers limited women's options and prohibited women from fully exercising their human rights. Her exposure to the inequities of divorce laws and inheritance laws, the crimes of violence permitted under marriage laws, and the economic travesties perpetuated by businesses and governments contributed to her growing commitment to the feminist agenda.

Ireland's continued involvement in NOW led to her election as vice president of the organization in 1987 and her appointment to the presidency in 1991, when incumbent president Molly Yard resigned because of illness. Controversy over her personal life immediately accompanied Ireland's move to the president's office. A gay rights magazine article revealed that Ireland, who had been married for twenty years, also had a woman companion. Questions of her sexual orientation surrounded her, but Ireland resisted engaging in a battle or even fully responding. She explained: "This is how I live my life and I'm not ashamed. Here I am. Here's my whole set of skills. You get the parts of me you like and also the parts that make you uncomfortable. You have to understand that other people's comfort is no longer my job. I am no longer a flight attendant."

During her tenure as president of NOW, Ireland had its members in the Women-Friendly Workplace Campaign and called on corporations to end sexual harassment and other workplace discrimination. Through her leadership, NOW initiated an innovative lawsuit using racketeering laws to stop attacks on abortion clinics. The case, *NOW v. Scheidler*, went to the U.S. Supreme Court and was decided in NOW's favor.

Ireland developed NOW's Elect Women for a Change campaign in 1992 and the organization's Victory 2000 campaign to elect 2,000 new feminists to office by the turn of the century. She also enhanced NOW's involvement in international issues by nurturing its Global Feminist Program, working with African women to end genital mutilation and with other groups to end the gender apartheid imposed by the Taliban in Afghanistan.

After completing her term as president of NOW, Ireland was briefly president of the YWCA in 2003.

Born in Oak Park, Illinois, Patricia Ireland earned her bachelor's degree in German from the University of Tennessee in 1966 and her law degree from the University of Miami Law School in 1975. Ireland wrote her memoir, *What Women Want*, in 1996.

See also Feminist Movement; National Organization for Women; *NOW v. Scheidler*
References Ireland, *What Women Want* (1996); *The New York Times*, 3 March 1992, 21 October 2003; www.now.org.

Ivins, Molly Tyler (b. 1944)

Syndicated political columnist Molly Ivins described herself in 1991 as "dripping-fangs liberal," lampooning Republicans with glee. In her 16 May 2006 column on President George W. Bush's proposals for dealing with illegal Mexican immigrants, she wrote: "I hate to raise such an ugly possibility, but have you considered lunacy as an explanation? Craziness would make a certain amount of sense. I mean, you announce you are going to militarize the Mexican border, but you assure the president of Mexico you are not militarizing the border. You announce you are sending the National Guard, but then you assure everyone it's not very many soldiers and just for a little while."

She has called politics the "world's most fascinatin' poker game," and says that it should be covered "as a celebration of heroes and villains." The title of one her books suggests the approach to her work: *Molly Ivins Can't Say That, Can She?* (1991). Ivins is also the author of *Shrub: The Short But Happy Life of George W. Bush* (2000); *Bushwhacked: Life in George W. Bush's America* (2003); and *Who Let the Dogs in? Incredible Political Animals I Have Known* (2004), among others.

After graduating from Smith College in 1966 and earning an master of arts degree at Columbia University School of Journalism in 1967, Ivins worked on several newspapers, including the *Houston Chronicle*, the *Minneapolis Tribune,* and *The New York Times.* She became an independent columnist in 2001. She has provided commentary on National Public Radio, as well as appearing on talk shows.

Born in Monterey, California, she grew up in Houston, Texas.

References Giselle Benatar, "Good Golly Miss Molly! Six Feet of Killer Journalist," *Entertainment Weekly,* 27 September 1991, p. 34;
http://www.creators.com/opinion_show.cfm?next=2&ColumnsName=miv; Michelle Green, "Pages: The Mouth of Texas: Tart of Tongue, Rapier of Wit, Molly Ivins Skewers Wayward Pols," *People*, 9 December 1991, p. 99.
Document Molly Ivins, "I Will Not Support Hillary Clinton for President," 2006

Jackson Lee, Sheila (b. 1950)

Democrat Sheila Jackson Lee of Texas entered the U.S. House of Representatives on 3 January 1995. Elected president of the Democratic freshman class, Jackson Lee helped found the bipartisan Congressional Children's Caucus during her second term. She has introduced and passed legislation relating to adoption, jobs for public housing residents, and research grants for historically black colleges and universities as well as those serving Hispanics. Flood control and support for the National Aeronautics and Space Administration (NASA) are two areas important to her constituents that she has also worked on.

Jackson Lee has supported affirmative action programs, saying that, as an African American, she would not have attended Yale University without them. She explained: "It is so intensely personal, I have trouble containing myself when I debate this issue." When Congress considered the crime bill, she offered an amendment to use money normally reserved for building prisons for building boot camps for offenders. The amendment passed, but the funds became part of block grants that allowed states to determine their use. Believing that block grants contributed to segregationist policies, Jackson Lee voted against the bill. Her achievements included an amendment to provide adequate funding for the African Development Foundation, a U.S. federal agency that supports community-based self-help initiatives to alleviate poverty and promote sustainable development in Africa.

Homelessness, gun safety and responsibility, welfare reform emphasizing back-to-work programs, and science and technology issues are among Jackson Lee's legislative priorities. She advocates funds for anti-violence programs in schools, full funding for Head Start, and increased support for school lunch programs.

Born in Jamaica, New York, Sheila Jackson Lee earned her bachelor's degree in political science from Yale University in 1972 and her law degree from the University of Virginia Law School in 1975. She worked for the U.S. House of Representatives Select Committee on Assassinations as staff counselor from 1977 to 1978. She moved to Houston, Texas, and entered into private law practice for the next several years.

Appointed an associate judge on the Houston Municipal Court in 1987, Jackson Lee later served on the Houston City Council from 1990 to 1994. As a council member, she sponsored and won passage of a gun safety law containing penalties for adults who do not have their guns locked away from children. She expanded the summer hours for city parks and recreation areas as a way to discourage gang activity, and she created a city-authorized committee on homelessness.

See also Affirmative Action; Brady, Sarah Jane Kemp; Congress, Women in; Lesbian Rights

References *Congressional Quarterly, Politics in America 1996* (1995); Doherty, "Surface Racial Harmony on Hill Hides Simmering Tensions" (1998); Gill, *African American Women in Congress* (1997); www.house.gov/jacksonlee/bio.

J.E.B. v. Alabama ex rel T.B. (1994)

The U.S. Supreme Court ended the question of sex discrimination in the selection of jurors in *J.E.B. v. Alabama ex rel T.B. In the case,* lawyers on both sides had excluded all of the male potential jurors and selected only women. The Court wrote: "The Equal Protection Clause [of the Fourteenth Amendment] prohibits discrimination in jury selection on the basis of gender, or on the assumption that an individual will be biased in a particular case solely because that person happens to be a woman or a man." Earlier cases had addressed the topic from other perspectives, but in this decision, the Court specifically found sex discrimination in jury selection unconstitutional.

Justice Sandra Day O'Connor concurred with the decision, but she added: "[O]ne need not be a sexist to share the intuition that, in certain cases, a person's gender and resulting life experience will be relevant to his or her view of the case." She cautioned that the decision could have unforeseen consequences. She wondered if the effort to fight gender discrimination could work to women's disadvantage. She posed the situation of a battered wife on trial for wounding her abusive husband and questioned whether the Supreme Court decision would prevent her from having as many women jurors as possible. O'Connor expressed the hope that it would not be the result of the decision, but assumed that it would be.

Reference *J.E.B. v. Alabama ex rel T.B.* 511 U.S. 127 (1994)

Jenckes, Virginia Ellis (1877–1975)

Democrat Virginia Jenckes of Indiana served in the U.S. House of Representatives from 4 March 1933 to 3 January 1939. Jenckes based her congressional campaign on ending Prohibition, arguing that because alcohol used grain in its manufacture, legalizing it would improve the market for the grain raised by her constituents. As a member of Congress, flood control legislation was her chief concern, but she did not serve on a committee that dealt with the issue, which limited her ability to use her expertise in the area. She ran for a fourth term but lost in the general election.

During her tenure in Congress, Jenckes was a U.S. delegate to the 1937 Paris meeting of the Interparliamentary Union, a world organization of parliaments that provides forums for international dialogues between nations with peace as its primary goal. In 1956, she gained attention for her role in helping five priests escape from

Hungary during the 1956 uprising in that country. She later worked for the American Red Cross.

Born in Terre Haute, Indiana, Jenckes became a farmer in 1912. She was a founder and secretary of the Wabash Maumee Valley Improvement Association, serving from 1926 to 1932.

See also Congress, Women in

References Breckenridge, *Women in the Twentieth Century* (1933); Engelbarts, *Women in the United States Congress, 1917–1972* (1974); Office of the Historian, U.S. House of Representatives, *Women in Congress, 1917–1990* (1991).

Johnson, Claudia Alta (Lady Bird) Taylor (b. 1912)

Lady Bird Johnson was first lady from 1963 to 1969, the years her husband Lyndon Baines Johnson was president of the United States. As first lady, Johnson promoted her husband's Great Society programs, making three or four national tours annually to bring attention to them. A strong supporter of its education components, she served as honorary chair of Head Start. An environmentalist, she organized the 1965 White House Conference on Natural Beauty, played a significant role in the passage of the Highway Beautification Act of 1965, and led a national beautification project that included recruiting friends to help plant thousands of tulip and daffodil bulbs in Washington, D.C. Through Project Green Thumb, Johnson enlisted retired farmers who volunteered to improve highway borders. After leaving the White House, she continued her environmental work, serving on national boards and founding the National Wildlife Research Center.

Born in Karnack, Texas, Lady Bird Johnson's given name is Claudia Alta Taylor, but when a nurse caring for her as a baby said that she was as "pretty as a lady bird," it became her name. Johnson earned her bachelor's degree in history in 1933 and a jour-

First Lady Claudia "Lady Bird" Johnson (Library of Congress LC-USZ62-25816B)

nalism degree in 1934, both from the University of Texas. She married Lyndon Johnson in 1934.

Lady Bird Johnson campaigned for her husband throughout his career, including his congressional, senatorial, vice presidential, and presidential campaigns. During World War II, she managed his congressional office after he enlisted in the military and directed many of the couple's financial investments, including the purchase of a radio station in the 1940s and other property. During the years that Lyndon Johnson was vice president, Lady Bird Johnson traveled more than 120,000 miles and visited thirty foreign countries on behalf of the United States. Lady Bird Johnson was riding in the Dallas, Texas, motorcade the November 1963 day that President John Kennedy was assassinated. Her husband became president of the United States a few hours after the shooting. Johnson wrote *A White House Diary* (1970) and co-authored *Wildflowers across America* (1988).

> **References** Crawford and Ragsdale, *Women in Texas* (1992); Gould, "First Lady as Catalyst: Lady Bird Johnson and Highway Beautification in the 1960s" (1986).

Johnson, Eddie Bernice (b. 1935)

Democrat Eddie Bernice Johnson of Texas entered the U.S. House of Representatives on 5 January 1993. Johnson held the leadership position of Democratic deputy whip in the 106th Congress (1999–2001). She chaired the Congressional Black Caucus in the 107th Congress (2001–2003), having held every leadership position in it. As chair, Congresswoman Johnson focused on comprehensive election reform, making technology available to all, and expanding minority access to capital, as well as other issues. She also organized a meeting of the Asian, Black, and Hispanic caucuses to discuss strategies for working together to achieve common goals. Regarding the caucus, Johnson said: "We work together almost incessantly; we are friends and, more importantly, freedom fighters."

Johnson's first career was in nursing, as chief psychiatric nurse at a Veterans Administration hospital from 1956 to 1972. Congresswoman Johnson's dominant concerns are unemployment and the attendant social concerns. She believes that education and job training are the keys to solving those problems. She explained: "I'm not opposed to cracking down on crime and eliminating violence in the country, but I've always believed that education and job training are the best crime fighters around." She has worked to establish a federal grant program to encourage children to study math and science. She has also sponsored measures encouraging women to enter scientific and technical professions and doubling funding for the National Science Foundation.

Her other congressional priorities include the economy, the environment, accessible health care, and job opportunities for minorities. She has sponsored measures for expanded research on osteoporosis and related bone diseases, to protect access to reproductive health care services, to expand health care services under Medicare, and to reform tax policies related to deducting health insurance costs. In addition, she has sponsored a measure to impose stricter jail terms on those convicted of serious crimes that also involve acts of hate based on a victim's race, religion, gender, or sexual orientation. Congresswoman Johnson founded A World of Women for World Peace, which seeks to develop leaders for building a peace culture.

A member of the Texas House of Representatives from 1973 to 1977, Johnson passed legislation for age-appropriate public education programs for self-reliance and preventive health care, and she and Sarah Weddington passed a bill prohibiting school districts from firing pregnant teachers. She held hearings to examine and expose racism in city and state hiring and contracting.

In 1977, President Jimmy Carter appointed Johnson regional director for the Department of Health, Education, and Welfare (HEW), where she served until 1979. She became executive assistant to the HEW administrator for primary health care in 1979 and held the office until 1981. She resumed her political career in 1987, when she entered the Texas Senate, and served until 1993.

Born in Waco, Texas, African American Eddie Johnson earned her nursing diploma at St. Mary's College at the University of Notre Dame in 1955, her bachelor of science degree from Texas Christian University in 1967, and her master's degree in public administration from Southern Methodist University in 1976.

See also Abortion; Congress, Women in; Weddington, Sarah Ragle

References *Congressional Quarterly, Politics in America 1996* (1995), *Politics in America 2006* (2005); Gill, *African American Women in Congress* (1997); "Johnson Unites Three Minority Caucuses to Develop New Agenda," *Jet*, 13 May 2002, p. 4; "Representative Eddie Bernice Johnson Voted New Chair of Congressional Black Caucus," *Jet*, 25 December 2000, p.4; http://www.house.gov/ebjohnson/ bio.htm.

Johnson, Lady Bird

See **Johnson, Claudia Alta (Lady Bird) Taylor**

Johnson, Nancy Lee (b. 1935)

Republican Nancy Johnson of Connecticut entered the U.S. House of Representatives on 3 January 1983. Congresswoman Johnson co-authored the law adding prescription drug benefits to Medicare, wrote the law that created the children's health insurance program, and introduced a comprehensive bill to provide universal access to care and to control costs. Johnson also developed a comprehensive child care package that would have provided vouchers to pay the fees. Other interests include improving outdated public schools and constructing news ones and encouraging stem cell research. She has been involved in developing trade export policies and assisting the ball-bearing and roller-bearing industry, an important employer in Connecticut.

As chair of the House Committee on Standards of Official Conduct, Johnson led the two-year investigation of Speaker Newt Gingrich's fundraising activities, organizations in the fundraising activities, and the financing of the college course he taught. Accused by Democrats of attempting to protect Gingrich, Johnson also underwent intense pressure from Republicans who wanted her to avoid a vendetta against Gingrich. In December 1996, Gingrich admitted that he had failed to properly manage the financing of his political activities and that he had given the ethics committee misleading information. In January 1997, the House voted to reprimand Gingrich and to impose a penalty of $300,000 against him. Johnson held the leadership position of secretary of the Republican Caucus in the 103rd Congress (1993–1995).

Born in Chicago, Illinois, Nancy Johnson earned her bachelor's degree from Radcliffe College in 1957 and attended the University of London from 1957 to 1958. Before entering politics, Johnson was a community activist and an adjunct professor of political science at Central Connecticut State University. She served in the Connecticut Senate from 1977 to 1983.

See also Congress, Women in; Reproductive Rights; State Legislatures, Women in

References *Bond Buyer*, 21 April 2005; *Congressional Quarterly, Politics in America 1994* (1993), *Politics in America 1998* (1997); http://www.house.gove/nancyjohnson; "Federal Cash Needed to Repair Schools," *NEA Today*, 1 November 2001, p. 19.

Johnson v. Transportation Agency of Santa Clara County (1987)

In *Johnson v. Transportation Agency*, the legality of an affirmative action plan for women was the issue. The U.S. Supreme Court decided in 1987 that the plan was permissible under Title VII of the Civil Rights Act of 1964.

In 1978, the Santa Clara County Transit District Board of Supervisors adopted an affirmative action plan and included sex as one of the factors to be considered in deciding among qualified applicants for a position. When the job of road dispatcher opened, Diane Joyce, the county's first female road maintenance worker, applied for it. She and six men were certified eligible for the position, with Joyce receiving a seventy-three on the qualifying interview and Paul Johnson, another qualified applicant, receiving a score of seventy-five on the interview. After a second interview, Johnson was recommended for the job, but the agency director, who ultimately made the decision, chose Joyce. The Court found the affirmative action plan and the decision to hire Joyce acceptable.

See also Affirmative Action; Employment Discrimination

References Becker, "Prince Charming: Abstract Equality" (1988); *Johnson v. Transportation Agency of Santa Clara County*, 480 U.S. 616 (1987).

Jones, Elaine R. (b. 1944)

One of the nation's outstanding civil rights lawyers, Elaine Jones was the first woman president and director-counsel of the NAACP Legal Defense and Educational Fund (LDF), serving from 1993 to 2004. She made the commitment to become a lawyer when she was eight years old, knowing at that young age the injustices of racial discrimination. "[W]e were sitting in the back of the bus, going to segregated schools, living a life mapped out by signs that said 'colored only,'" she said later, describing growing up in Norfolk, Virginia.

After earning her AB degree in political science at Howard University, Jones volunteered with the Peace Corps, teaching English in Turkey. After returning to the U.S., she earned her LLB degree at the University of Virginia School of Law, becoming the first black woman to enroll in and graduate from the law school.

After graduating, Jones received an offer from a prestigious law firm, but declined, instead accepting a position with the NAACP's LDF. With a team of lawyers, she traveled throughout the South defending indigents facing the death penalty. During one trial, the Ku Klux Klan surrounded the courthouse. "They were out there in full regalia," she recollected. She won the case.

Only two years after receiving her law degree, Jones was the counsel of record in the U.S. Supreme Court case *Furman v. Georgia* (1972), which abolished the death penalty in 37 states.

In the mid-1970s, Jones served as special assistant to the U.S. Secretary of Transportation, focusing much of her attention on opening the U.S. Coast Guard to women. She returned to LDF after two years, helping the organization establish its Washington, DC lobbying office, where she worked until 1993, when she began her tenure as LDF's president.

After retiring from LDF in 2004, Jones said: "[O]ne thing I'll always be passionate about is changing the prison industrial complex and overturning the mandatory sentencing law that puts so many brothers and sisters in jail." She continued: "Most of these prisons are in rural White communities, and the economy of those areas depends on having Black and brown inmates. This is as racist as it gets." She intends to use the networks and associations she has developed to educate and mobilize citizens in her cause.

References Jones, "Second Acts," *Essence*, August 1, 2004, p. 129; *The Washington Post*, June 23, 2003.

Jones, Stephanie Tubbs (b. 1949)

Democrat Stephanie Tubbs Jones of Ohio entered the U.S. House of Representatives on 3 January 1999. When Tubbs Jones entered Congress, her priorities included using budget surpluses to fund Social Security, making child day care more available and less expensive, and increasing funding for Head Start and similar programs. During her first term, Congresswoman Tubbs Jones passed the Child Abuse Prevention and Enforcement Act. She has introduced legislation to fund research and education on uterine fibroids, a bill to require certification of mortgage brokers, and another to equip college dorms, fraternities, and sororities with fire suppression devices. During the 108th Congress, Tubbs Jones became the first black woman to serve on the House Ways and Means Committee. Tubbs Jones opposes mandatory sentencing, explaining that she believes it takes away the need for a judge. The former county judge and county prosecutor was elected to the Cleveland Municipal Court when she was thirty-one years old.

Born in Cleveland, Ohio, Tubbs Jones earned her bachelor's degree in 1971 and her law degree in 1974, both at Case Western Reserve University. After serving on the municipal court, Jones was the first black woman in Ohio history to serve on the Court of Common Pleas, holding the position from 1983 to 1991. She was then Cuyahoga County prosecutor from 1991 until her election to Congress in 1998.

See also Congress, Women in

References "Stephanie Tubbs Jones" (1998); http://house.gove/tubbjones/biography; "Rep. Stephanie Tubbs Jones Becomes First Black Woman on House Ways and Means Committee, *Jet*, 3 February 2003, p.6.

Jordan, Barbara Charline (1936–1996)

Democrat Barbara Jordan of Texas served in the U.S. House of Representatives from 3 January 1973 to 3 January 1979. Throughout her public career, Jordan reminded Americans of their nation's highest ideals and the need to include all citizens in attaining them, using language so simple and direct that she carried her audiences with her.

Born in Houston, Texas, Barbara Jordan attended Houston's segregated public schools and earned her bachelor of arts degree in political science and history from Texas Southern University in 1956 and her law degree from Boston University in 1959. Following her admission to the bar, she opened a private practice. She entered politics in 1960, working in Harris County, Texas, on John F. Kennedy's presidential campaign. Organizing precincts to identify Kennedy supporters, she began speaking before increasingly larger groups and learned that her speaking style and message resonated with voters.

With her interest in politics sparked, Jordan ran for the Texas House of Representatives in 1960 but lost in the primary. She lost again in 1962, but reapportionment in 1966 placed her in a new district, and she won her race for the state Senate. When she took office in 1967, Jordan became the first African American woman to serve in the Texas legislature. Despite her status as an elected state official, racism continued to interfere in her life. For example, she could not eat at the segregated private clubs where her colleagues gathered for meetings, conversation, and meals.

In the legislature, Jordan sponsored and passed measures that created the Texas Fair Employment Commission, improved workers' compensation, and expanded minimum wage provisions to cover employees not included in the federal law. She introduced the state's first Fair Housing Act and chaired the Senate's Reapportionment Committee. She wrote and passed legislation that created the Texas Department of Community Affairs, developed programs for education and training programs for handicapped persons, and reformed the workers' compensation program. Jordan served in the state Senate until 1972, when she ran for Congress.

While campaigning for Congress, Jordan said: "All blacks are militant in their guts. But militancy is expressed in different ways." Jordan expressed her militancy with an elegance and intellectual clarity that compelled listeners to respond to her message. After winning her seat in the U.S. House of Representatives, Jordan sought the counsel of former president Lyndon B. Johnson, a fellow Texan, who advised her to seek a seat on the prestigious Judiciary Committee and used his influence to help her obtain it.

Americans came to recognize Jordan's intelligence and powerful oratory during the 1974 House Judiciary Committee's deliberations on the impeachment of Richard Nixon. In a memorable speech, she decried the Constitution's drafters' omission of black Americans: "'We the people'—it is a very eloquent beginning. But when the Constitution of the United States was completed on the seventeenth day of September in 1787, I was not included in that 'We the people.' I felt for many years that somehow George Washington and Alexander Hamilton just left me out by mistake. But through the process of amendment, interpretation and court decisions, I have finally been included in 'We, the people.'" She continued: "My faith in the Constitution is whole, it is complete, it is total. I am not going to sit here and be an idle spectator to the diminution, the subversion and the destruction of the Constitution." After making her case against

Nixon, she said that if the committee did not impeach Nixon, "then perhaps the eighteenth-century Constitution should be abandoned to a twentieth-century paper shredder." The authority and confidence with which she spoke camouflaged her concern about voting to impeach a president. She wept after casting her vote.

Jordan worked to develop national programs to combat disease, to increase the minimum wage, and to improve the standard of living of impoverished Americans. She passed an amendment to the Law Enforcement Assistance Act that denied funds to jurisdictions that discriminated and an amendment to a revenue-sharing bill that created a civil rights provision in it. In addition, she was instrumental in passing the Extended Voting Rights Act in 1975, which added other people of color to the African Americans included in the 1965 Voting Rights Act.

At the 1976 Democratic National Convention, Jordan once again captivated listeners with her beautiful and resonant voice and her extraordinary thoughts. She electrified the convention hall by saying: "We are a people in search of a national community, attempting to fulfill our national purpose, to create and sustain a society in which all of us are equal. I have the confidence that the Democratic Party can lead the way. We cannot improve on the system of government handed down to us by the founders of the Republic, but we can find new ways to implement that system and to realize our destiny." She did not seek a fourth term in Congress.

Jordan was diagnosed with multiple sclerosis in 1973, and by 1977 a second attack of the disease had significantly reduced her mobility. Initially, Jordan had managed to camouflage the effects of the disease, which became increasingly difficult after the second attack, but she steadfastly refused to reveal the disease from which she suffered until 1988. When she announced her retirement, she had no career plans.

In 1979, Jordan was named to the Lyndon B. Johnson Chair in National Policy at the Lyndon B. Johnson School of Public Affairs at the University of Texas at Austin. For the next five years, she retreated from public life and devoted herself to teaching.

She emerged from her self-imposed seclusion to actively campaign for presidential candidate Walter Mondale and vice presidential candidate Geraldine Ferraro, as well as for other Democratic nominees in the 1984 general elections. In 1987, Jordan gained increased visibility as she raised her voice in opposition to Judge Robert Bork's nomination for the U.S. Supreme Court. Because he had opposed civil rights cases, she joined others in mounting a significant campaign against Bork, who was not confirmed. When Ann Richards ran for governor of Texas in 1990, Jordan helped in the campaign, serving as Richards's ethics counsel. After Richards's election, Jordan met with the people Richards appointed to state government positions and discussed ethics in government with them.

Once again, at the 1992 Democratic National Convention, Jordan delivered a keynote address. She held the delegates' attention by saying:

We can change the direction of America's engine and become proud and competitive again. The American dream is not dead. True, it is gasping for breath, but it is not dead. However, there is no time to waste because the American dream is slipping away from too many. It is slipping away from too many black and brown mothers and their children; from the homeless of every color and sex; from the immigrants living in communities without water and sewer systems. The American dream is slipping away from the workers whose jobs are no longer there because we are better at building war equipment that sits in warehouses than we are at building decent housing.

As chair of the Commission on Immigration Reform from 1993 to 1996, she objected to a proposal to deny automatic citizenship to children born in this country whose parents are illegal immigrants. She told Congress: "To deny birthright citizenship would derail this engine of American liberty." Jordan wrote her autobiography, *Barbara Jordan: A Self-Portrait*, in 1979.

See also Congress, Women in; Democratic Party, Women in the; Ferraro, Geraldine Anne; Richards, Ann Willis; Voting Rights Act of 1965

References H. W. Wilson, *Current Biography Yearbook 1993* (1993); Jordan and Hearon, *Barbara Jordan* (1979); Rogers, *Barbara Jordan: American Hero* (1998).

Document Barbara Jordan, "A New Beginning: A New Dedication," 1976

Jumper, Betty Mae (b. 1923)

The first woman to serve as chair of the Seminole Tribal Council, Betty Mae Jumper worked to help the tribe move toward economic self-sufficiency. In 1957, when the Seminole tribe formally organized, Jumper was elected to the tribal council for a two-year term and then served on its board of directors for four years. She was elected chairperson of the Seminole Tribal Council in 1967, serving a four-year term, and was the first woman to chair any tribe in North America. As chair, Jumper worked to improve health, employment, education, welfare, and housing conditions for Seminoles. During her tenure, the tribe entered into land-lease and other agreements to help it move toward economic self-sufficiency. Active in the National Tribal Chairman's Association, Jumper was a founder of United Southeastern Tribes.

Born at Indiantown, Florida, Betty Mae Jumper completed a one-year nursing program at Kiowa Indian Hospital in Oklahoma. She returned to the Seminole reservation and worked with the public health nurse.

She wrote her memoir, *...And with the Wagon Came God's Word*, in 1980.

References Bataille, ed., *Native American Women* (1993); www.seminoletribe.com.

Juries, Women on

The English common law heritage that formed the basis of American colonial law persisted in several aspects of women's status, including their service on juries. During the American colonial period, jury duty was a responsibility reserved for white men, and women's role on juries was limited to determining if a defendant was pregnant in two situations: when the defendant made a request to have a stay of execution until after the birth of her child, and when a widow made the request to delay the disposition of her deceased husband's estate until after childbirth. The question of guilt or innocence was reserved for male jurors. By the end of the colonial period, even this restricted role was removed when male medical practitioners began deciding whether or not the defendant was pregnant and replaced the women.

The ratification of the Sixth Amendment to the U.S. Constitution, providing that "the accused shall enjoy the right to a speedy and public trial, by an impartial jury of the State," did little to change women's roles on juries. In addition, state constitutions written after the Revolution adopted common law practices of trial by jury, but they did not specifically include women jurors, policies upheld by the courts.

In *Stauder v. West Virginia* (1879), the Supreme Court held that excluding African Americans from juries denied blacks equal protection and due process under the Fourteenth Amendment, but the decision clearly stated that women could be excluded. Afterward, women's rights activists continued to point out that women suffered a disability because women had never been judged by a jury of their peers.

In Wyoming, women served on juries after the state constitution was ratified in 1890, but their service did not last long. An 1892 court decision found that women had no right to sit on juries unless specifically permitted by state statute. In 1898, women in Utah became the first U.S. women to qualify for jury service without subsequently losing the right.

With the passage of the Nineteenth Amendment granting women suffrage rights in 1920, a few states made women automatically eligible for jury service. The Illinois state Supreme Court decided that because women had not been voters at the time the state's statutes on jury service had been written, women could not serve on juries. The Illinois state legislature defeated bills granting women the right to serve on juries in 1923, 1925, 1927, and 1929 and then sent the issue to the voters in 1930. The state Supreme Court, however, ruled the referendum unconstitutional. Not until 1939 could Illinois women finally serve on juries. Connecticut women lobbied the state's legislature from 1921 to 1937, when they succeeded. In other states, women argued to serve on juries as a right and began organizing state legislative campaigns to remove the word male from jury statutes.

Opponents to women's jury service believed that women's obligations to their husbands and children should take precedence over their obligations to the state. Some states, however, permitted women to serve on juries if they went to the county courthouse and registered their willingness to be jurors, making jury service a right but not an obligation. Feminists opposed this permissive approach because if women were to be judged by a jury of their peers, then other women had to be willing to serve as jurors.

The permissive approach survived a challenge in the U.S. Supreme Court in 1961, when a Florida woman convicted of murder appealed the verdict on the basis of the all-male jury that decided her case. In arguing the case, *Hoyt v. Florida*, before the Court, the Florida assistant attorney general explained that women could not be required to serve on juries because they have "to cook the dinners!" The Court said that "woman is still regarded as the center of the home and family life" and found permissive jury duty constitutional.

Some changes, however, had occurred. The Civil Rights Act of 1957 made women eligible to serve on all federal juries. In 1921, thirty-seven states excluded women from jury service, but in 1965, only Alabama, Mississippi, and South Carolina prohibited women from serving on juries. By 1973, women could serve on juries in every state, but in nineteen states special exemptions for women remained.

In 1975, the U.S. Supreme Court reconsidered state policies that required women to register before becoming eligible for jury duty and found them a violation of Sixth

Amendment and Fourteenth Amendment rights in *Taylor v. Louisiana*, ending different policies for jury service for women and men.

See also Fourteenth Amendment; *Hoyt v. Florida*; League of Women Voters; Nineteenth Amendment; Suffrage; *Taylor v. Louisiana*

References Lemons, *The Woman Citizen: Social Feminism in the 1920s* (1973); Mead and Kaplan, eds., *American Women: The Report of the President's Commission on the Status of Women and Other Publications of the Commission* (1965); Sachs and Wilson, *Sexism and the Law* (1978); Schweber, "But Some Were Less Equal... the Fight for Women Jurors" (1979).

Document Burnita Shelton Matthews, "The Woman Juror"

Kahn, Florence Prag (1868–1948)

Republican Florence Kahn of California served in the U.S. House of Representatives from 2 February 1925 to 3 January 1937. Married to Congressman Julius Kahn, Florence Kahn gained political experience working with him. After he died in office, she won election to fill the vacancy. When she entered the House, she was assigned to the Committee on Indian Affairs but refused to accept it, saying: "the only Indians in my district are in front of cigar stores and I can't do anything for them." She received an assignment to the committee on education and then to military affairs, her first choice. She was the first woman to serve on the House Appropriations Committee.

Kahn sought to end Prohibition because she was convinced that it could not be enforced. A supporter of enlarging the military and establishing military bases in California, she was also instrumental in obtaining congressional authorization for $75 million to build the San Francisco Bay Bridge connecting San Francisco and Oakland. She lost her attempt for a seventh term and returned to private life.

Born in Salt Lake City, Utah, Florence Kahn graduated from the University of California at Berkeley in 1887. She then taught high school English and history.

> **See also** Congress, Women in
>
> **References** Office of the Historian, U.S. House of Representatives, *Women in Congress, 1917–1990* (1991).

Kaptur, Marcia (Marcy) Carolyn (b. 1946)

Democrat Marcy Kaptur of Ohio entered the U.S. House of Representatives on 3 January 1983. The senior Democratic woman in the House, she has focused on revitalizing the economy of industrial Ohio and promoting international trade issues relating to her district's interests. In addition to arguing for workers' rights and labor and environmental standards in nations that trade with the United States, she has opposed granting China most-favored-nation status because she believes that Chinese workers are exploited by their government and has worked to pass legislation prohibiting government officials from representing foreign interests for one year after they leave government. Her other priorities include technology, energy and the environment; child care in public housing; home ownership; agriculture; and protecting individuals' bank deposits. Kaptur worked for seventeen years for the construction of the national World War II Memorial, dedicated in 2004.

Born in Toledo, Ohio, Kaptur earned her bachelor of arts degree in history from the University of Wisconsin in 1968 and her master's degree in urban planning in 1974. From 1969 to 1975, Kaptur worked as an urban planner in addition to completing her graduate degree. Director of planning for the National Center for Urban Ethnic Affairs from 1975 to 1977, she was assistant director for urban affairs in the Carter administration from 1977 to 1979. While she was pursuing a doctorate in urban planning at the Massachusetts Institute of Technology, local party officials recruited her to run for Congress.

Kaptur is the author of *Women of Congress: A Twentieth-Century Odyssey* (1996).

See also Congress, Women in

References *Congressional Quarterly, Politics in America 1994* (1993); http://www.kaptur.house.gov.

Kassebaum Baker, Nancy Landon (b. 1932)

Republican Nancy Kassebaum of Kansas served in the U.S. Senate from 23 December 1978 to 3 January 1997. She was the first woman elected to the U.S. Senate who was not the widow of a congressman. As chair of the Foreign Relations Subcommittee on African Affairs, Kassebaum led the fight for economic sanctions on South Africa as a strategy to help end apartheid. She encouraged the United Nations to reform itself by reducing its bureaucracy and advocated reducing the United States' financial support to it. The first woman to chair a major Senate committee, the Labor and Human Resources Committee (104th Congress, 1995 to 1997), she influenced the development of legislation involving education, labor relations, minimum wages, collective bargaining, health insurance reform, and welfare reform. For example, the Kassebaum-Kennedy Health Insurance Reform Act of 1996 allows workers greater portability in transferring their benefits from one job to another. She also passed legislation to fund research and production of pharmaceuticals for uncommon diseases.

A moderate Republican, Kassebaum co-founded the Republican Majority Coalition to counter the religious right in the party. Pro-choice, she supported international family planning programs. Kassebaum retired from the Senate in 1997.

Born in Topeka, Kansas, Nancy Kassebaum earned her bachelor's degree in political science from the University of Kansas in 1954 and her master's degree in diplomatic history from the University of Michigan in 1956. Kassebaum grew up in a political family. Her father was Alf Landon, governor of Kansas from 1933 to 1937 and Republican presidential candidate in 1936. Following her marriage in 1956, Kassebaum was involved in the family's radio stations and served on the Kansas Governmental Ethics Commission from 1975 to 1976 and the Kansas Committee on the Humanities from 1975 to 1979. She served on the Maize (Kansas) School Board from 1973 to 1975.

See also Abortion; Congress, Women in

References *Congressional Quarterly, Politics in America 1994* (1993); Kaptur, *Women of Congress: A Twentieth-Century Odyssey* (1996).

Kee, Maude Elizabeth Simpkins (1895–1975)

Democrat Maude Kee of West Virginia served in the U.S. House of Representatives from 26 July 1951 to 3 January 1965. Following her husband John Kee's election to Congress in 1932, she became his executive secretary, a position she held until his death. Maude Kee won the special election to fill the vacancy. While in Congress, her investigation into veterans' hospitals resulted in improved conditions in them. As representative of the largest bituminous coal-producing district in the nation, she worked with the United Mine Workers, the National Coal Association, and the Appalachian Electric Power Company to gain federal support for using coal to produce electricity. She also helped attract new industry to the area and passed measures to establish centers to train coal miners for new jobs. She declined to seek an eighth term because of ill health. Her son James Kee, who had been her administrative assistant, won the seat.

Born in Radford, Virginia, Maude Kee graduated from Roanoke Business College and then was a secretary in the Roanoke Times business office. She later wrote a syndicated weekly newspaper column.

See also Congress, Women in

References Engelbarts, *Women in the United States Congress, 1917–1972* (1974); Office of the Historian, U.S. House of Representatives, *Women in Congress, 1917–1990* (1991); Tolchin, *Women in Congress: 1917–1976* (1976).

Kelley, Florence (1859–1932)

Social reformer Florence Kelley played pivotal roles in the passage of wage and hours laws to protect women workers, in the creation of the Children's Bureau of the U.S. Department of Labor, and in developing public support to prohibit child labor. As secretary of the National Consumers League, she organized dozens of local affiliates and two international conferences.

Born in Philadelphia, Kelley graduated from Cornell University in 1882. She began studies at the University of Zurich in 1883, became a socialist, and translated Friedrich Engels's *The Condition of the Working Class in England* in 1844 into English; it was published in New York in 1887. Over the next few years, she married, bore three children, and returned to New York. In 1891, Kelley and her children moved to Illinois, and she divorced her husband.

An investigator for the Illinois Bureau of Labor Statistics in 1892, she reported the conditions in about 1,000 garment industry sweatshops. Based on that research and her participation in a survey of city slums, Kelley developed a group of proposals to limit the hours women could work in factories to eight hours per day and forty-eight hours per week, ban child labor for children under fourteen years old, regulate the labor of children fourteen to sixteen years old, and create a state factory inspector's office. Kelley lobbied the Illinois legislature for the package of proposals, and in 1893, the legislature passed it. Appointed Illinois's chief factory inspector in 1893, Kelley used the position to publicize the deplorable conditions in which children worked. Removed from office in 1897 for political reasons, Kelley traveled widely, speaking around the country on improving working conditions and advocating labor legislation.

Kelley became the general secretary of the National Consumers League in 1899 and continued to work on behalf of women and children in the labor force. When an Oregon law limiting the number of hours that women could work was challenged in the U.S. Supreme Court, Kelley helped recruit Louis D. Brandeis as counsel for the case and helped compile the research included in the famous Brandeis brief. In *Muller v. Oregon* (1908), the Court decided in favor of protective labor legislation for women. Kelley continued to take her protective labor legislation message around the country, drafted the model minimum wage law adopted by Massachusetts in 1912, and contributed to nine states' decisions to enact minimum wage legislation.

To address the problems of child labor, Kelley and Lillian Wald had organized the New York Child Labor Committee in 1902 and the National Child Labor Committee in 1904. Wald and Kelley sought the creation of a federal children's commission and developed support for it among settlement house workers and other social reformers. Congress established the Children's Bureau in 1912 to gather information about children in the labor force. After Congress passed a bill limiting child labor and the U.S. Supreme Court found it unconstitutional, Kelley turned her attention to passing a child labor amendment.

Kelley was a founding member of the National Association for the Advancement of Colored People and worked in the suffrage movement.

See also Child Labor Amendment; Children's Bureau; Congressional Union; *Muller v. Oregon*; National Association for the Advancement of Colored People, Women in the; National Consumers League; Protective Legislation; Suffrage; Wald, Lillian D.; Women's International League for Peace and Freedom

References Sklar, *Florence Kelley and the Nation's Work* (1995); Trattner, *Crusade for the Children: A History of the National Child Labor Committee and Child Labor Reform in America* (1970).

Document Florence Kelley, "Child Labor and Woman Suffrage," 1905

Kelly, Edna Patricia Kathleen Flannery (1906–1997)

Democrat Edna Kelly of New York served in the U.S. House of Representatives from 8 November 1949 to 3 January 1969. Kelly entered politics following her husband's death in 1942. With the encouragement of a political leader who had been a friend of her husband's, Kelly revived the women's auxiliary of the Madison Democratic Club and joined the staff of the Democratic Party delegation in the New York legislature. The Democratic Party chose her for its nominee to fill a vacancy created by an incumbent's death. In her campaign, Kelly pledged to work for issues she believed to be important to women, including an investigation of milk prices, opposition to excise taxes, and the creation of day care centers.

An expert in foreign policy, particularly on the Soviet bloc, she supported the North Atlantic Treaty Organization (NATO) as a defense against Communism and helped write the legislation that created the Peace Corps. She consistently opposed any programs that would provide aid to Communist nations, particularly Yugoslavia, and successfully passed amendments that excluded those nations from aid programs. She passed a measure leading to an international effort that resettled more than 1.5 million displaced persons, primarily of Eastern European and Russian descent, following World War II. She was also instrumental in sponsoring measures that provided financial assistance to educational and health institutions in Israel. She held the leadership position of secretary of the Democratic Caucus in the 83rd, 84th, and 88th Congresses (1953–1955, 1955–1957, and 1963–1965) and was Democratic national committeewoman for New York from 1956 to 1968. Redistricting in 1968 placed her and another incumbent in the same congressional district, and despite a spirited primary campaign, Edna Kelly lost the election.

Born in East Hampton, New York, Edna Kelly earned her BA from Hunter College in 1928.

> **See also** Congress, Women in; Democratic Party, Women in the
> **References** Engelbarts, *Women in the United States Congress, 1917–1972* (1974); H. W. Wilson, *Current Biography: Who's News and Why, 1949* (1949); *The New York Times*, 17 December 1997; Tolchin, *Women in Congress: 1917–1976* (1976).

Kelly, Sue W. (b. 1936)

Republican Sue Kelly of New York entered the U.S. House of Representatives on 3 January 1995. Congresswoman Kelly has worked to balance the budget, create opportunities for small businesses, and eliminate the capital gains tax. She supports reproductive rights, capital punishment, a presidential line item veto, and Meals on Wheels. Active in environmental issues, she helped pass legislation to protect the Sterling Forest on the border between New York and New Jersey. She has taken leadership roles in corporate reform legislation, the Women's Health and Cancer Rights Act, a measure addressing the shortage of nurses, and measures against identity theft.

Before entering Congress, Kelly had several careers, among them biomedical researcher, rape crisis counselor, emergency room patient advocate, and ombudsman for nursing homes. She has owned a florist business, taught junior high school science and math, and was adjunct professor of health advocacy at Sarah Lawrence College from 1987 to 1992. Kelly was a co-founder of the Bedford League of Women Voters and a founding member of the Town of Bedford Recreation Committee.

Born in Lima, Ohio, Sue Kelly earned a bachelor's degree in botany and bacteriology in 1958 from Denison University. She later attended Pace Law School and earned a master's degree in health advocacy from Sarah Lawrence College in 1988.

> **See also** Congress, Women in; Reproductive Rights; Women's Health and Cancer Rights Act
> **References** *Congressional Quarterly, Politics in America 1996* (1995); http://suekelly.house.gov; Melissa A. Fitzpatrick, "Thankfully, We Reinvested," *Nursing Management*, 1 November 2002, p. 6.

Kennedy, Claudia J. (b. 1947)

Retired three-star General Claudia Kennedy is one of only three women to reach the rank of three-star general and the only woman to reach it in the U.S. Army. The Army's former deputy chief of staff for intelligence, Kennedy joined the army in 1968. She worked in several areas until 1973, when she was assigned to the electronic warfare staff in Korea. She spent the balance of her career in intelligence areas.

In 2000, when General Larry G. Smith was appointed deputy inspector general, a position that included responsibility for investigating sexual harassment accusations, Kennedy filed a complaint accusing him of improper sexual conduct. After an investigation, the army concluded that Kennedy had been harassed and assaulted. A letter of reprimand was placed in Smith's file.

Kennedy told an audience: "Our army is filled with women and men who care and are in a position to change and improve the conditions in which we serve." She encouraged other women to tell a friend when sexually harassed and then to tell "people in authority who care."

Born in Frankfurt, Germany, the daughter of an American government employee, Kennedy earned a bachelor of arts degree from Rhodes College in 1968.

References "MI Corps Hall of Fame," *Military Intelligence Professional Bulletin*, 1 April 2004, p. 64; Gregory Vistica, "Kennedy's Story of Her Assault," *Newsweek*, 8 May 2000, p. 47.

Kennedy, Florynce Rae (1916–2000)

A founder of the National Organization for Women, African American Florynce Kennedy was an outspoken feminist and civil rights leader beginning in the 1960s. A flamboyant dresser, often wearing Western boots and hat, she once described herself as "radicalism's rudest mouth." Born in Kansas City, Missouri, Kennedy earned her bachelor's degree in 1948 and her law degree in 1951, both from Columbia University. Initially denied admission to Columbia Law School, Kennedy believed it was because of her race. She threatened to sue the school, but the university relented and admitted her. In 1954, Kennedy opened a private law practice that initially struggled financially. At one point she worked in a department store to pay the rent.

Feminist attorney Flo Kennedy at the National Organization for Women (NOW) national convention. Image: Najlah Feanny/CORBIS SABA

As lawyer for the estates of deceased African American performers Billie Holiday and Charlie Parker, Kennedy successfully fought record companies to recover money from royalties and sales due to the estates. The experience, however, prompted her to question the legal system. She wrote in her memoir: "Handling the Holiday and Parker estates taught me more than I was really ready for about government and business delinquency and the hostility and helplessness of the courts. Not only was I not earning a living, there began to be a serious question in my mind whether practicing law could ever be an effective means of changing society or even of simple resistance to oppression." Kennedy believes that "the courts are so racist and bigoted. As a lawyer, you're looking for justice for people, but if you know there's no justice, what are you going to go looking there for? There's absolutely no justice for anybody I'd want to defend."

Kennedy founded the Media Workshop in 1966 to combat racism in the media and advertising. When a large advertising agency refused to provide her with information about its hiring and programming practices, Kennedy led a group of pickets. Eventually, she met with the agency. After her success with it, she said: "When you want to get to the suites, start in the streets." It was a tactic she also used successfully with television networks and other media corporations.

A founder of the National Organization for Women (NOW), Kennedy left the organization in 1970, saying that it "got to be so boring and scared." Out of frustration, she founded the Feminist Party in 1971, which supported Shirley Chisholm's unsuccessful 1972 candidacy for president of the United States.

See also Chisholm, Shirley Anita St. Hill; Civil Rights Movement, Women in the; National Organization for Women; Steinem, Gloria Marie

References Kennedy, *Color Me Flo* (1976); *Los Angeles Times*, 28 December 2000.

Kennedy, Jacqueline Bouvier

See **Onassis, Jacqueline Bouvier Kennedy**

Kennelly, Barbara Bailey (b. 1936)

Democrat Barbara Kennelly of Connecticut served in the U.S. House of Representatives from 12 January 1982 to 3 January 1999. Kennelly held a number of firsts in Congress: she was the first woman to serve on the House Committee on Intelligence, the first woman to serve as a chief deputy majority whip, and the first woman vice chair of the House Democratic Caucus in the 104th and 105th Congresses (1995–1999). She also held the leadership position of House democratic chief deputy whip in the 102nd and 103rd Congresses (1991–1995).

Kennelly began her political career on the Hartford Court of Common Council, where she served from 1975 to 1979. She was Connecticut secretary of state from 1979 to 1982. When the incumbent member of Congress died in office, she won the special election to fill the vacancy. Once in Congress, Kennelly passed a measure in 1984 that provided assistance in collecting court-ordered child support, worked on energy and mass transportation policies, and sponsored a balanced budget measure. She supported child protection programs, foster care, and health care for children. She championed the earned income tax credit, which increases take-home pay for low-income families. An increase in the standard deductions for the elderly and the blind and the Hate Crimes Statistics Act are based upon legislation Kennelly introduced.

Instead of seeking another congressional term, Kennelly ran for governor of Connecticut in 1998 and lost. She served in President Bill Clinton's administration as counselor at the Social Security Administration. She became president and CEO of the National Committee to Preserve Social Security and Medicare in 2002.

Born in Hartford, Connecticut, Kennelly grew up in a political family. Her father was John Bailey, a Connecticut party boss and chairman of the Democratic National Committee in the 1960s. She earned her bachelor's degree in economics from Trinity College in Washington, D.C., in 1958; a certificate in business administration from Harvard Business School in 1959; and her master's degree in government from Trinity College in Hartford, Connecticut, in 1973.

See also Child Support Enforcement; Congress, Women in

References *Congress Daily*, 8 April 2002; *Congressional Quarterly, Politics in America 1996* (1995); *The New York Times*, 14 February 1999; www.house.gov/kennelly/bio.htm.

Keys, Martha Elizabeth Ludwig (b. 1930)

Democrat Martha Keys of Kansas served in the U.S. House of Representatives from 3 January 1975 to 3 January 1979. Keys entered politics as Kansas coordinator for George McGovern's 1972 presidential campaign. McGovern lost the election, but Keys had proven her effectiveness and became her party's nominee for Congress in 1974. As a member of Congress, her priorities included election reform, energy policy, and improvement of national health care programs. While in Congress, Keys divorced her husband and married Indiana Congressman Andrew Jacobs, making them the first wife and husband to serve together in Congress. Keys lost her attempt for a third term. A special adviser to the secretary of health, education, and welfare from 1979 to 1980, she was also assistant secretary of education from 1980 to 1981 and a consultant from 1981 to 1984. She directed the Center for a New Democracy from 1985 to 1986.

Born in Hutchinson, Kansas, Martha Keys attended Olivet College from 1946 to 1947 and received her bachelor of arts degree from the University of Missouri at Kansas City in 1951.

See also Congress, Women in

References Office of the Historian, U.S. House of Representatives, *Women in Congress, 1917–1990* (1991).

Kilpatrick, Carolyn Cheeks (b. 1945)

Democrat Carolyn Kilpatrick of Michigan entered the U.S. House of Representatives on 3 January 1997. After serving in the Michigan House of Representatives from 1979 to 1997, Kilpatrick challenged incumbent Congresswoman Barbara-Rose Collins, who was the subject of investigations into ethical and financial misconduct. Kilpatrick won the primary with 51 percent of the vote compared to Collins's 31 percent. Kilpatrick won the general election with 81 percent.

Representing the poorest district in Michigan, the city-center neighborhoods of Detroit, Kilpatrick believes that the federal government should help remedy the problems in her district. Among the problems: high infant mortality, high unemployment, blighted neighborhoods, and substandard housing. Congresswoman Kilpatrick's legislative priorities include promoting economic development, creating new jobs, increasing the wages of working families, and improving the access and affordability of health care. In addition, she has worked to develop a transportation strategy that includes mass transit. She has also brought attention to minority-owned media outlets and the discrimination they confront in obtaining advertising from major advertisers.

Born in Detroit, Michigan, African American Carolyn Kilpatrick received her associate of arts degree from Ferris State College in 1965, her bachelor of science degree from Western Michigan University in 1972, and her master of science degree in education from the University of Michigan in 1977. Kilpatrick taught high school from 1972 to 1978.

See also Congress, Women in; State Legislatures, Women in

References *Congressional Quarterly, Politics in America 1998* (1997); *Politics in America 2006* (2005); http://www.house.gov/kilpatrick/bio.shtml.

King, Coretta Scott (1927–2006)

African American Coretta Scott King's civil rights activism began in the early 1950s, after she married Martin Luther King, Jr., and helped him organize the bus boycott in Montgomery, Alabama. Violence and threats of violence surrounded them, a bomb exploded on the family's front porch in 1956 but injured no one, and the next year another bomb was found on their front porch. They continued their work, and Coretta Scott King helped her husband organize the Southern Christian Leadership Confer-

Coretta Scott King, widow of Martin Luther King, Jr.

ence (SCLC) in 1957. In 1959, Coretta Scott King, a vocalist, performed in India and studied Mahatma Gandhi's nonviolent strategies with her husband. In the 1960s, she performed freedom concerts of song, recitation, and poetry to raise money and to develop support for the SCLC.

On 4 April 1968, Martin Luther King, Jr., was assassinated in Memphis, Tennessee. Over the next months, Coretta Scott King fulfilled her husband's speaking commitments, calling on U.S. women to "unite and form a solid block of woman power" to fight racism, poverty, and war. In 1974, Coretta Scott King became the founding president of the Martin Luther King, Jr. Center for Nonviolent Social Change in Atlanta, Georgia, serving until 1989. Through her work, the twenty-three-acre neighborhood around her husband's birthplace was declared a National Historic Site by the National Park Service. She chaired the Martin Luther King, Jr., Federal Holiday Commission. The annual celebrations began in 1986 and are held on the anniversary of her husband's birthday. In 1969, Coretta Scott King published *My Life with Martin Luther King, Jr.*

Born in Marion, Alabama, Coretta Scott King earned her bachelor's degree in education and music from Antioch College in 1951 and her doctorate in music from the New England Conservatory of Music in 1971. She held her concert debut in 1948, performing as a soloist with the Second Baptist Church in Springfield, Ohio.

See also Civil Rights Movement, Women in the

References Hardy, *American Women Civil Rights Activists* (1993); Hine, ed., *Black Women in America* (1993); Smith, ed., *Epic Lives* (1993).

King, Mary (b. 1940)

Civil rights activist and feminist pioneer Mary King joined the civil rights movement after graduating from college in 1962. Assistant director of communications for the Student Nonviolent Coordinating Committee (SNCC) from 1963 to 1965, she participated in sit-ins in Atlanta, Georgia, and was arrested and jailed for four days. Male dominance in the organization led King and Casey Hayden to write a letter outlining their observations and to circulate it at a SNCC meeting. Their anonymous letter on the position of women in SNCC prompted Stokely Carmichael to comment: "The position of women in SNCC is prone." King and Hayden later wrote "Sex and Caste: A Kind of Memo from Casey Hayden and Mary King to a Number of Other Women in the Peace and Freedom Movements," exploring parallels "between the treatment of Negroes and treatment of women in our society as a whole." Unaware that women in the North were launching the feminist movement, they wrote: "Objectively, the chances seem nil that we could start a movement based on anything as distant to general American thought as a sex-caste system." The memo became one of the founding documents of the radical women's liberation movement of the mid-1960s.

In late 1964 and early 1965, African American leaders in SNCC concluded that the participation of white people no longer served its purposes, and King, one of the few white leaders in the organization, left. She became a program officer for the U.S. Office of Economic Opportunity from 1968 to 1972, when she established a consulting firm. Impressed by Jimmy Carter in 1971, she began helping to develop his campaign strategy the next year and worked with him through his election to the presidency in

1976. Carter appointed her deputy director of ACTION, a federal agency that oversaw the Peace Corps, Volunteers in Service to America (VISTA), and other volunteer programs. A Middle East specialist, she later conducted research on conflict resolution, ethnic diversity, and related issues.

Born in New York, King earned her bachelor of arts degree at Ohio Wesleyan University in 1962 and her doctoral degree from the University of Wales at Aberystwyth in 1998. King wrote *Freedom Song: A Personal Story of the 1960s Civil Rights Movement* (1987).

See also Civil Rights Movement, Women in the; Women's Liberation Movement

References Hayden and King, "Sex and Caste: A Kind of Memo from Casey Hayden and Mary King to a Number of Other Women in the Peace and Freedom Movements" (1966); *The New York Times*, 8 July 1976; http://www.upeace.org/faculty/mking.cfm.

Kirchberg v. Feenstra (1981)

In *Kirchberg v. Feenstra*, the U.S. Supreme Court decided in 1981 that sex discrimination is unconstitutional unless the discrimination furthers an important governmental interest. In this case, Joan Feenstra filed a criminal complaint against her husband Harold Feenstra, charging him with molesting their daughter. Her husband hired attorney Karl Kirchberg and signed a promissory note to prepay him. Then Harold Feenstra took out a mortgage on the home that he owned with Joan Feenstra, who was not told about the mortgage and whose consent was not required. At the time, Louisiana law gave her husband exclusive control over community property under its head and master provisions. She dropped the charges against her husband, they separated, and he left the state. She learned about the mortgage on her home when Kirchberg demanded the balance due on the promissory note and threatened to foreclose on the mortgage on her home unless she paid the note.

Kirchberg argued that his case differed from *Craig v. Boren* (1976) and *Orr v. Orr* (1979), cases that the Court had earlier decided, because the Louisiana Civil Code provided a way for wives to protect their property. By making a "declaration by authentic act," Joan Feenstra could have prevented her husband from leasing, selling, or mortgaging their home. Because she did not take advantage of the procedure, Kirchberg contended that she had become the "architect of her own predicament." The Court disagreed, saying that the first question was the constitutionality of Louisiana's head and master law. The Court found that the law's gender-based discrimination violated the equal protection clause of the Fourteenth Amendment.

During the time that this case was making its way through the appeals process, Louisiana revised its code provisions relating to community property, eliminated the head and master concept, and implemented a policy giving both spouses equal control over community property.

See also *Craig v. Boren*, Fourteenth Amendment; *Orr v. Orr*

References *Kirchberg v. Feenstra*, 450 U.S. 455 (1981).

Kirkpatrick, Jeane Duane Jordan (b. 1926)

Political scientist Jeane Kirkpatrick served as U.S. representative to the United Nations from 1981 to 1985, the first woman to hold the position. When President Ronald Rea-

U.S. ambassador to the United Nations Jeane Kirkpatrick

gan appointed Kirkpatrick to the ambassadorship, she became the highest-ranking woman in the history of U.S. foreign policy. Reflecting on her experience, Kirkpatrick said: "I never really thought about it until I found myself participating in the arenas in which the big decisions were being made in foreign policy and security policy. It occurred to me all of a heap that I might very well be the first woman in American history who had ever been what is called 'at the table' at such decisions by serving on the National Security Planning Group." Part of her responsibilities included serving on the National Security Planning Group and the National Security Council.

Born in Duncan, Oklahoma, Jeane Kirkpatrick earned her associate's degree from Stephens College in 1946, her bachelor of arts degree from Barnard College in 1948, and her master of arts degree in 1950 and her doctoral degree in 1968 from Columbia University. She did postgraduate work at the Institut de Science Politique of the University of Paris on a French government fellowship from 1952 to 1953.

A professor at Georgetown University and a senior fellow at the American Enterprise Institute, Kirkpatrick's published work includes dozens of scholarly articles and books, including *Political Woman* (1974), *The New Presidential Elite* (1976), *Dismantling the Parties: Reflections on Party Reform and Party Decomposition* (1978), *Dictatorships and Double Standards: Rationalism and Reason in Politics* (1982), *The Reagan Phenomenon* (1983), and *The Withering Away of the Totalitarian State and Other Surprises* (1990).

See also Cabinets, Women in Presidential

References H. W. Wilson, *Current Biography Yearbook, 1981* (1981); *The New York Times*, 23 December 1980, 17 August 1994.

Kissling, Frances (b. 1943)

Frances Kissling became president of Catholics for a Free Choice (CFFC) in 1982. She believes that controversies in the Catholic Church that surround reproductive rights, family planning, and women's ordination are not spiritual matters but are political issues and are efforts to control women.

Born in New York, New York, Frances Kissling attended St. John's University in New York from 1961 to 1964 and received her bachelor of arts degree from the New School for Social Research in 1966. A Roman Catholic, Kissling entered a convent and prepared to join the Sisters of Saint Joseph but left after several months because she disagreed with many of the Church's teachings, including those on birth control and human sexuality. At the same time, she left the Catholic Church. She began running an abortion clinic in New York in 1970.

In the late 1970s, Kissling combined her early religious training with the knowledge that she had gained in her work to create a new vision of a Church more sensitive to all powerless people. Her vision of a transformed Church includes access to safe, legal reproductive health care for all women. To further her vision, she became president of CFFC in 1982. That year, CFFC became the first pro-choice group to hold congressional briefings on abortion and family planning, a strategy now used by many pro-choice organizations.

Kissling co-authored *Rosie: The Investigation of a Wrongful Death* (1979).

> **See also** Abortion; *Doe v. Bolton*; *Harris v. McRae*
> **References** Stan, "Frances Kissling: Making the Vatican Sweat" (1995); www.cath4choice.org.

Knutson, Coya Gjesdal (1912–1996)

Democrat Coya Knutson of Minnesota served in the U.S. House of Representatives from 3 January 1955 to 3 January 1959. The first woman to serve on the House Agriculture Committee, she promoted agricultural exports and worked to preserve family farms. She advocated increasing price supports for agricultural products, expanding the food stamp program, and establishing a federally supported school lunch program. She passed the sections of the National Defense Education Act that created a federal college student loan fund. During her campaign for a third term, her husband publicly protested her candidacy and asked her to return home. After his letter was published in a newspaper, the publicity that surrounded it led to her defeat. She ran again in 1960 but lost. She divorced her husband in 1962. Knutson was a liaison officer for the Office of Civil Defense from 1961 to 1970.

Born in Edmore, North Dakota, Coya Knutson received her bachelor of science degree from Concordia College in 1934 and did postgraduate work in library science at State Teachers College in Moorhead and at the Juilliard School of Music. She taught in North Dakota and Minnesota high schools and then worked for the Red Lake County Welfare Board from 1948 to 1950. She served in the Minnesota House of Representatives from 1951 to 1954.

> **See also** Congress, Women in; State Legislatures, Women in
> **References** *The New York Times*, 12 October 1996; Office of the Historian, U.S. House of Representatives, *Women in Congress, 1917–1990* (1991); Tolchin, *Women in Congress: 1917–1976* (1976).

Koontz, Elizabeth Duncan (1919–1989)

Director of the Women's Bureau of the U.S. Labor Department from 1969 to 1973, the first African American to hold the post, Elizabeth Koontz was named deputy assistant secretary of labor and special counselor to the secretary of labor for women's affairs in 1972. In those positions, Koontz worked for the Equal Rights Amendment, equal opportunities for women, equal pay, and enforcement of protective labor laws. She also worked to improve household workers' skills and to have them included in minimum wage laws. Koontz brought together a group of union women to discuss their common interests and responsibilities, a group which later evolved into the Coalition of Labor Union Women.

Born in Salisbury, North Carolina, Elizabeth Koontz earned her bachelor's degree in English and elementary education from Livingstone College in 1938 and her master's degree in education from Atlanta University in 1941. Koontz later did further graduate work at Columbia University and Indiana University and earned a certificate in special education for the mentally retarded at North Carolina State College.

Koontz held offices in local and state affiliates of the National Education Association (NEA) beginning in the 1950s. President of the Department of Classroom Teachers from 1965 to 1966, she also served on President Lyndon B. Johnson's National Advisory Council on Education of Disadvantaged Children from 1965 to 1968 and was NEA national vice president in 1967 and 1968. President of the NEA in 1968, Koontz advocated job and retirement security, contracts to protect teachers, and larger roles in decision-making and policy development for teachers. Koontz resigned the presidency after six months to accept the appointment at the Women's Bureau.

> **See also** Coalition of Labor Union Women; Equal Rights Amendment; Women's Bureau
>
> **References** H. W. Wilson, *Current Biography 1969* (1969); Hardy, *American Women Civil Rights Activists* (1993); *The New York Times*, 8 January 1989.

Kreps, Juanita Morris (b. 1921)

U.S. secretary of commerce from 1977 to 1979, Juanita Kreps advocated redefining the balance between work and leisure throughout a person's life, including more leisure during one's working life and extending one's working years beyond age sixty-five. She helped assemble the Carter administration's urban package, including a Commerce Department program to maintain and restore the economic viability of cities. Her department was the first to propose setting aside 10 percent of its contracts for minority businesses.

Born in Lynch, Kentucky, Juanita Kreps earned her bachelor's degree from Berea College in 1942 and both her master's (1944) and doctoral degrees (1948) from Duke University. A college teacher and administrator, Kreps became a nationally recognized economist specializing in the area of aging. She wrote *Sex in the Marketplace: American Women at Work* (1971), dealing with problems women confront in the workforce.

The first woman to serve on the board of J. C. Penney Company, she also became the first woman to serve on the New York Stock Exchange board in 1972.

> **See also** Cabinets, Women in Presidential
>
> **References** Lamson, *In the Vanguard: Six American Women in Public Life* (1979); *The New York Times*, 8 May 1977.

Kuhn, Margaret (Maggie) E. (1905–1995)

A founder and the convening president of the Gray Panthers, Maggie Kuhn became an advocate for older Americans after her forced retirement when she was sixty-five years old. As she searched for a way to continue working, she met with other social activists who had been or were soon to be forced into retirement. In 1970, the Gray Panthers emerged from those gatherings. Kuhn advocated "fundamental social change that would eliminate injustice, discrimination and oppression in our present society." She sought a legal prohibition against mandatory retirement, supported publicly owned and democratically controlled utilities, and advocated health insurance paid totally by the government. She led efforts for regulation of the hearing aid and nursing home industries, presented position papers to the American Medical Association, and testified before congressional committees on the fragmentation of services for the elderly. Regarding a welfare reform bill, she told a congressional committee: "Public welfare in this country does not need reforming; it needs radicalization. To merely rearrange the outdated, unworkable concepts of the Elizabethan Poor Laws is not a solution."

Born in Buffalo, New York, Kuhn earned her bachelor of arts degree from Flora Stone Mather College of Case Western Reserve University in 1926. She continued to write, travel, and lecture until her death at the age of eighty-nine.

References H. W. Wilson, *Current Biography Yearbook, 1978* (1978); *The New York Times*, 23 April 1995.

Kunin, Madeleine May (b. 1933)

Democrat Madeleine Kunin was governor of Vermont from 1985 to 1991, served as deputy secretary of the U.S. Department of Education from 1993 to 1996, and served as U.S. ambassador to Switzerland from 1996–1999. Her political journey began in 1972 with an unsuccessful campaign for alderman in Burlington, Vermont, but later that year she won election to the Vermont House of Representatives. Her platform included educational, environmental, and poverty issues. After serving three terms in the legislature, Kunin was elected lieutenant governor in 1978. She won in 1978 and was re-elected in 1980.

Kunin ran for governor in 1982, lost, and then won when she tried again in 1984. With her success, she became Vermont's first woman governor and only its third Democratic governor in 130 years. After being re-elected in 1986 and in 1988, she became the first woman governor in the nation to win three terms in office. When Kunin began her first term, the state had a deficit, but after eighteen months in office, she announced that the state budget was in the black. She also equalized education spending across the state, obtained an increase of 25 percent in the education budget, expanded child care subsidies, and passed a measure for kindergarten for all Vermont children. In other areas, she improved groundwater protection, established a state mini-Superfund, and created a new rural enterprise zone and a state venture capital corporation.

Following Bill Clinton's 1992 election as U.S. president, Kunin served as a member of his transition team. In 1993, President Clinton appointed her deputy secretary of education. Her responsibilities included serving as the Education Department liaison with the White House and other agencies.

Born in Zurich, Switzerland, Kunin had fled to the United States with her brother and widowed mother in 1940 to escape the Nazi regime and its threats to Jews. She earned her bachelor of arts degree from the University of Massachusetts in 1956, her master of science degree from Columbia University in 1957, and her master of arts degree from the University of Vermont in 1967.

Kunin published *Living a Political Life* in 1994.

See also Governors, Women; State Legislatures, Women in

References H. W. Wilson, *Current Biography Yearbook, 1987* (1987); Kunin, *Living a Political Life* (1994); *The New York Times*, 7 April 1993.

L

Lachance, Janice Rachel (b. ca. 1952)

Janice Lachance served as director of the Office of Personnel Management, a Cabinet-level position in the Clinton administration, from 1997 to 2000. The Office of Personnel Management provides support to federal agencies to ensure their compliance with the federal merit system and personnel laws and regulations.

Lachance began her career in public service working on the staffs of members of Congress and as a legal counsel for a congressional subcommittee, as well as the U.S. Small Business Administration. She next served as director of communications and political affairs for the American Federation of Government Employees, AFL-CIO from 1987 to 1993. Lachance was director of communications for the Office of Personnel Management from 1993 to 1996 and chief of staff for the office from 1996 to 1997.

Born in Biddeford, Maine, Lachance earned a BA degree from Manhattanville College in 1974 and a JD degree from Tulane University in 1978.

> **References** http://clinton4.nara.gov/WH/EOP/First-_Lady/teens/lachance.html;
> http://www.opm.gov/news/janice-r-lachance- to-head-opm-communication,786.aspx

La Flesche, Susette (1854–1903)

The first woman to speak for Native Americans' rights, Susette La Flesche's Native American name was Inshta Theumba, or "Bright Eyes." Born in an Omaha Indian village in Nebraska, she graduated from the Elizabeth Institute in about 1873 and returned home to teach.

La Flesche became involved in Native American rights in the late 1870s, after federal policies forced Ponca Indians to leave their homeland and move to Oklahoma, where almost one-third of them died. Initially, La Flesche served as an interpreter for Ponca Indian Chief Standing Bear when he toured the Eastern United States to develop public support for his tribe's plight. Wearing Native American clothing and using her native name, La Flesche created a dramatic presence and emerged as an articulate and eloquent speaker. Her descriptions of the injustices inflicted upon Native Americans inspired others, including Helen Maria Fiske Hunt Jackson and Mary L. Bonney, to begin their work for Native Americans' rights.

The most widely known Native American woman of her time, La Flesche provided testimony at U.S. Senate hearings regarding the Ponca Indians in 1879 and 1880. She continued to lecture in the United States and in England throughout the 1880s. Toward the end of the decade, her lectures contributed to the passage of the Dawes Act of 1887, authorizing the allotment of land to individual Native Americans. Native Americans who accepted individual allotments of tribal or public lands immediately became citizens. The allotments, however, were controversial because they were burdened with several restrictions on their use and ultimately made it easier for non-Indians to acquire the land. Congress passed the Indian Citizenship Act in 1924, granting all Native Americans United States citizenship.

In 1902, La Flesche moved to an area near Bancroft, Nebraska, living on the land allotted her as a tribal member. She died there in 1903.

See also Bonney, Mary Lucinda; Bonnin, Gertrude Simmons

References Hardy, *American Women Civil Rights Activists* (1993).

LaDuke, Winona (b. 1959)

One of the most prominent Native American environmental activists in North America, Anishinabeg tribal member Winona LaDuke believes that the primary native women's issues are the survival of indigenous communities and preservation of the environment. To further those goals, LaDuke founded the White Earth Land Recovery Project in Minnesota, a multifaceted endeavor. The project purchased and holds in trust 1,300 acres of land, a minuscule part of the original 836,000 acres of the White Earth Reservation pledged to Anishinabeg Indians in an 1867 treaty. The project has also been involved in economic development, setting up a marketing collective that encourages local processing of wild rice as well as a diaper service. That has alleviated the need for disposable diapers, saved users money, and reduced the sanitation problems in the local dump. The project also sponsors a literacy program in the Ojibwe language of the Anishinabeg, with the goals of making the language more commonly used and of gaining its recognition as an official state language by the State of Minnesota.

LaDuke founded the Indigenous Women's Network (IWN) in 1985, a coalition of 400 native women activists and groups. The IWN advocates the revitalization of indigenous languages and cultures, sponsors international forums, and supports local projects.

In 1996 and 2000, LaDuke was the Green Party's candidate for vice president. During the 2000 campaign, she said: I'd like to see a country where diversity is valued, not admonished. Where Indian nations are valued for who we are and our integrity is cherished."

Born in Los Angeles, California, Winona LaDuke earned her bachelor of arts degree from Harvard University in 1982 and her master of arts degree from Antioch College in 1989.

References Paul and Perkinson, "Winona LaDuke" (1995); "Winona LaDuke: Fighting the Good Fight," *News from Indian Country*, 15 November 2000, p. 9A.

Document Winona LaDuke, "The Indigenous Women's Network: Our Future, Our Responsibility," 1995

Lake, Celinda (b. 1953)

Among the nation's foremost experts on electing women to public office, Celinda Lake made her reputation specializing in pro-choice Democratic women and groups. Her clients include U.S. Senators Carol Mosely-Braun, Blanche Lincoln, and Mary Landrieu, Washington Governor Gary Locke, EMILY's List, Sierra Club, the Human Rights Campaign, and the PEW Foundation.

Born in Bozeman, Montana, to a Republican family, Lake's interests in politics led her to attend a Republican summer camp when she was a teenager. In her freshman year at Smith College, she worked for Republican President Richard Nixon's 1972 re-election campaign. By her junior year in college, she realized that her views had changed and became a Democrat.

While spending her junior in college in Switzerland, Lake met a group of Americans conducting research on voting behavior and discovered survey research. After graduating from Smith College in 1975, Lake earned her master's degree at the University of Michigan in 1980, examining gender differences in voting for her thesis. Her reason for choosing polling as her profession, she wrote, is "Love of politics and desire to listen to people and know how they think."

In 1996, Lake predicted that a woman would be president in the next 16 years.

She is the coauthor of Public *Opinion Polling: A Handbook for Public Interest and Citizen Advocacy Groups* (1987) and *What Women Really Want: How American Women are Quietly Erasing Political, Racial, Class, and Religious Lines to Change the Way We Live* (2005).

Celinda Lake, acknowledged as one of the Democratice Party's leading political strategists, and founder of Lake Research Partners. (Courtesy Celinda Lake)

References Howard Kurtz, "Capitol Gains," *Working Woman*, February 1992, pp. 66–69; Celinda Lake, "What Do Women Want?" in Nancy M. Neuman, ed., *True to Ourselves: A Celebration of Women Making a* Difference (San Francisco: Jossey-Bass Publishers, 1998), pp. 171–181; "Movers and Shakers," *Campaigns & Elections*, September 1996, p. 14.

Lampkin, Daisy Elizabeth Adams (ca. 1884–1965)

African American Daisy Lampkin was national field secretary for the National Association for the Advancement of Colored People (NAACP) in the 1930s and 1940s. She helped establish chapters all over the United States, increased membership to the highest levels of the time, and raised money for the organization's anti-lynching campaign. Lampkin entered politics as president of Pittsburgh's Negro Women's Suffrage League in 1915. She became active in civil rights issues through the National Association of Colored Women, serving as its national organizer and chairing its executive board. She was also active in the Republican Party, working for the Women's Division in the 1920s.

Lampkin's work with the NAACP began in Pittsburgh in the 1920s, when she served on its executive committee and headed a membership campaign that attracted 2,000 new members and revitalized the branch. She joined NAACP's staff in 1930 as a regional field secretary until 1935, when she was appointed national field secretary. She resigned from the post in 1947 because of fatigue. She continued to serve on the NAACP board of directors and to conduct local fundraising and membership drives, until she collapsed after giving a speech in 1964.

Born in Washington, D.C., Lampkin attended public schools in Reading, Pennsylvania. She was a partner in and vice president of the *Pittsburgh Courier*.

See also Anti-lynching Movement; Civil Rights Movement, Women in the; National Association for the Advancement of Colored People, Women in the; National Association of Colored Women; Suffrage

References Hines, *Black Women in America* (1993); Sicherman and Green, eds., *Notable American Women: The Modern Period* (1980).

Landes, Bertha Ethel Knight (1868–1943)

The first female mayor of a large U.S. city, Bertha Landes was mayor of Seattle, Washington, from 1926 to 1928. Landes, who had initially opposed woman suffrage, came to believe that cities were similar to families and that the details of municipal housekeeping required women's influence. During her tenure as mayor, she worked to reduce lawlessness and to provide services to the community.

Born in Ware, Massachusetts, Landes graduated from Indiana University in 1891 and married two years later. She and her husband moved to Seattle in 1895, and she became actively involved in the city's women's clubs. As president of the Seattle Federated Women's Clubs from 1920 to 1922, her duties included managing an exhibit of Washington manufacturers, which gained her recognition throughout the business community and expanded her visibility.

After winning a seat on the city council in 1922, Landes worked for the elimination of fire hazards, liquor law enforcement, greater efficiency in government, and regulation of dance halls. Elected president of the city council in 1924, she was then required to serve as acting mayor in the mayor's absence. When Mayor Edwin Brown left Seattle for an extended period of time, Landes went into action. She told the police chief to remove corrupt police officers, but he refused, and she replaced him with a police chief who raided lotteries, closed speakeasies, and confiscated slot machines.

Using law and order as her campaign theme, Landes challenged Brown in the 1926 mayoral election. After defeating Brown, Mayor Landes hired a new police chief, brought area law enforcement officials together, and negotiated jurisdictional disputes in order to reduce crime. She replaced corrupt members of the Civil Service Commission and the Public Works Board. She implemented traffic safety measures and expanded the city's parks and its power and water systems. Landes lost her re-election bid in 1928, but the publicity from her one term as mayor created a demand for her as a speaker, and she went on several national speaking tours.

See also Public Offices, Women Elected to

References Haarsager, *Bertha Knight Landes of Seattle* (1994).

Landrieu, Mary (b. 1955)

Democrat Mary Landrieu of Louisiana entered the U.S. Senate on 3 January 1997. Following the destruction caused by Hurricane Katrina in 2005, Senator Landrieu focused her efforts on obtaining funding and services for rebuilding New Orleans, Louisiana, and the surrounding coastal area. In addition, Senator Landrieu gained national attention for her criticism of President George W. Bush and the federal government for their delayed responses to the devastation.

Before the hurricane, Senator Landrieu's primary legislative priority was education, including full funding for Head Start, more federal money for classroom computers, and tax credits for college tuition. She supports greater enforcement of equal pay laws

*Senator Mary Landrieu (D-LA) in 1996 became the first woman
elected to the Senate from Louisiana (Associated Press AP)*

and improved access to job training programs. Landrieu wants to establish a research and technology partnership between the federal government and the private sector to help farmers. She has also worked to develop a national energy policy that will increase domestic production while protecting eroding coastal regions.

In the 106th Congress (1999–2001), Landrieu worked to pass the Conservation and Reinvestment Act, which sought to guarantee $3 billion in offshore drilling revenues for federal and state conservation programs. She achieved a partial victory when Congress agreed to annual appropriations of some of the revenues for conservation. In the 108th Congress (2003–2005), Landrieu forced the Senate to stay in session until it approved giving companies $2 billion in tax credits for keeping National Guard members and military reservists fighting in Afghanistan and Iraq on company payrolls.

Senator Landrieu made an uncommon pledge in 2000: that she would not campaign against the women in the Senate at that time, whether they were Democrats or Republicans. Some observers believed that her decision reflected the importance she placed on her female colleagues.

Mary Landrieu served in the Louisiana House of Representatives from 1980 to 1988 and was state treasurer from 1988 to 1996. An unsuccessful candidate for governor in 1995, Landrieu won the 1996 Senate race with a margin of 5,788 votes. Her Republican opponent alleged that widespread voter fraud was involved and petitioned the Senate for a new election. The Senate Rules and Administration Committee investigated the election and reported that there had been isolated incidences of fraud, some election irregularities, and improper record-keeping, but those matters had not affected the election outcome. The committee ended its investigation on 1 October 1998, concluding there was not enough evidence that further investigation was warranted.

Born in Arlington, Virginia, Landrieu grew up in a political family: her father, Moon Landrieu, was mayor of New Orleans and U.S. secretary of housing and urban development in the Carter administration. She received her bachelor of arts degree from Louisiana State University in 1977.

> **See also** Congress, Women in; State Legislatures, Women in
>
> **References** *Chicago Tribune*, 16 September 2005; *Congressional Quarterly, Politics in America 1998* (1997), *Politics in America 2002* (2001); *Politics in America 2006* (2005); http://landrieu.senate.gov; "Lack of Evidence Brings Probe of Senate Election to an End" (1997); "Sen. Landreieu Pushes D.C. for Help Bringing N.O. Residents Home," *New Orleans CityBusiness*, 9 February 2006, p. 1.

Langley, Katherine Gudger (1888–1948)

Republican Katherine Langley of Kentucky served in the U.S. House of Representatives from 4 March 1927 to 3 March 1931. Langley entered politics as vice chairperson of the Kentucky State Central Committee, serving from 1920 to 1922, and was the first chair of the Kentucky Woman's Republican State Committee in 1920. Her husband John Langley was a member of the U.S. House of Representatives from 1907 until he was convicted of conspiring to transport and sell liquor and sentenced to a federal penitentiary in 1926. After he forfeited his congressional seat, Katherine Langley sought to vindicate her husband by running for it.

As a member of Congress, Katherine Langley passed legislation responsive to the social and economic needs of her low-income constituency, advocated the creation of a Cabinet-level department of education, and supported women's issues. She convinced President Calvin Coolidge to grant her husband clemency on the condition that John Langley never again seek public office. Within a short time and without telling his wife, however, John Langley announced his intention to run in 1930 for the congressional seat that she held. Having already filed for re-election, Katherine Langley refused to withdraw from the election. The notoriety surrounding the family cost her a third term. From 1939 to 1942, Katherine Langley was a railroad commissioner for the State of Kentucky.

Born in Madison County, North Carolina, Katherine Langley graduated from Woman's College in Richmond and then attended Emerson College of Oratory in Boston. She taught expression at Virginia Institute until she left to become her father's congressional secretary.

See also Congress, Women in; Willebrandt, Mabel Walker

References James, ed., *Notable American Women, 1607–1950* (1971); Office of the Historian, U.S. House of Representatives, *Women in Congress, 1917–1990* (1991).

Lathrop, Julia (1858–1932)

The first woman to head a major federal agency, Julia Lathrop was appointed head of the Children's Bureau by President Howard Taft in 1912. Lathrop entered politics as a social reformer, moving into Chicago's Hull House in 1890. The governor of Illinois appointed her to the state's Board of Charities in 1893, a position she used to investigate the state's 102 county farms. She resigned from the board in 1901, was reappointed in 1905, and remained on it until 1909. The office gave her the opportunity to develop support for the first juvenile court in the United States.

After Congress passed legislation creating the Children's Bureau in 1912 and Lathrop became its head, she directed investigations of infant mortality, maternal mortality, child labor laws, and related issues. She explained that she wanted to make the bureau "a great national clearinghouse for information regarding the welfare of children." She helped pass the Sheppard-Towner Maternity and Infancy Protection Act of 1921, and then poor health forced her retirement.

Born in Rockford, Illinois, Lathrop earned her bachelor's degree from Vassar College in 1880.

See also Addams, Jane; Children's Bureau; Sheppard-Towner Maternity and Infancy Protection Act of 1921

References Lindenmeyer, "A Right to Childhood": *The U.S. Children's Bureau and Child Welfare, 1912–1946* (1997).

Lawrence Textile Mill Strike

The Lawrence, Massachusetts, textile mill strike of 1912 began as an unorganized walkout that quickly involved almost 25,000 workers. The catalyst for the strike was a Massachusetts law that reduced children's work weeks from fifty-six hours to fifty-four hours and that became effective on 1 January 1912. The mill decided to reduce all employees' work weeks to fifty-four hours, a decision that concerned adult employees because they feared that their pay would also be reduced. When employees received their pay on 11 January, they discovered that their wages had been reduced and began walking out. They demanded a pay increase of 15 percent, the fifty-four-hour week, and double pay for overtime, as well as that strikers be rehired without discrimination. The strikers appealed to the American Federation of Labor's United Textile Workers Union for assistance, but it refused. They next called on the Industrial Workers of the World (IWW), which sent them organizers and strategists, including Elizabeth Gurley Flynn. The IWW leadership placed women in positions of authority, and women had equal votes with men when making decisions regarding the strike.

Scattered skirmishes between strikers and police escalated into violence, resulting in the militia's involvement and more violence. Strike leaders sought to protect women and children from the militia's attacks and recommended that they remain home and stay out of the picket lines. Instead, a pregnant striker announced that police were less likely to attack women and children, and she encouraged women to remain on the picket lines and men to stay home. Her assumptions proved to be wrong. When she and other women picketed, they were beaten. The pregnant woman's child was later delivered stillborn, a death attributed to the beating.

As the strike continued, strikers worried about their children's safety and struggled to provide them with food and other necessities. To alleviate the problems, union members and supporters in New York City agreed to house the children until the end of the strike. When the first group of children arrived in New York, newspapers publicized their plight, providing attention that angered employers. As a way to support employers, Lawrence city officials declared that no further evacuations would be permitted. When a group of mothers defied the order and prepared to place their children on a train, police arrested and beat some of the women and children.

The continued publicity prompted mill owners to settle the strike in mid-March 1912. The agreement included wage increases and other pay concessions, a fifty-four-hour work week, and time-and-a-quarter for overtime. Strikers were rehired.

Women were given primary credit for the strike's success. Their courage, commitment, discipline, and leadership helped sustain the effort until their points had been won. Women also gained a new sense of power and new experiences as leaders by holding positions of authority.

See also Flynn, Elizabeth Gurley; Shirtwaist Workers Strike

References Foner, *Women and the American Labor Movement: From the First Trade Unions to the Present* (1982); Wertheimer, *We Were There: The Story of Working Women in America* (1977).

League of Women Voters

Founded in 1919 through the leadership of suffragist Carrie Chapman Catt, the League of Women Voters (LWV) emerged from the National American Woman Suffrage Association (NAWSA) as ratification of the Nineteenth Amendment appeared imminent. A non-partisan organization with a strong emphasis on education and research, LWV works at the local, state, and national levels to influence public policy in four areas: good government, social policy, civil rights, and natural resources.

The LWV's early leaders sought to educate new women voters through citizenship schools that offered classes in marking ballots and held political education institutes. In addition to providing political education, the LWV soon became involved in lobbying state legislatures and Congress for a wide range of public policy issues. The League's initial agenda included support for protective labor legislation for women, maternal and infant medical care, independent citizenship for women, an end to discriminatory governmental policies, tariff revision, enforcement of antitrust laws, creation of a federal department of education, and U.S. membership in the League of Nations.

Working with the Women's Joint Congressional Committee in 1921, the LWV had its first legislative success with passage of the Sheppard-Towner Maternity and Infancy Protection Act, which provided federal aid for maternal and infant care. Other early successes included passage of the Cable Acts giving women independent citizenship, the Packers and Stockyards Control Act, and the Civil Service Reclassification Act; the creation of the Women's Bureau in the Department of Labor; and the construction of a federal women's prison. In the 1920s, LWV affiliates succeeded in passing laws on the state level that granted women equal guardianship over their minor children, gave married women the right to make contractual agreements without their husbands' consent, and gave women the right to hold public office.

Also in the 1920s, the LWV led several local campaigns supporting city governments in attempts to rid communities of corruption and bossism and to foster more efficient and orderly government. League members often brought other groups together in coalitions to support the changes in municipal government. Although men often held visible roles in the campaigns, League members frequently did most of the work.

In the 1930s, the LWV supported U.S. participation in the World Court. During the early 1940s, LWV members undertook a massive educational program to support U.S. involvement in World War II, offering reasons for its belief that the United States could not remain isolationist in its policies. As the war drew to a close, the LWV strongly supported the creation of the United Nations. The League focused on good government issues and provided leadership in state reapportionment advocacy during the 1960s. As national leaders worked for reapportionment, the League was involved in lobbying efforts and lawsuits to achieve equal representation in state legislative bodies and in Congress.

From 1921 until the 1950s, the LWV had opposed the Equal Rights Amendment, concerned that it would make protective labor legislation for women unconstitutional. As the LWV became an advocate for civil rights, it expanded its activism to include women's rights and the Equal Rights Amendment and vigorously supported ratification efforts in the 1970s. Other areas in which the LWV has provided leadership include passage of the Federal Water Pollution Control Act of 1972, the Pregnancy Discrimination Act of 1978, Title IX of the Education Amendments of 1972, the Voting Rights Act of 1982, and the Family and Medical Leave Act of 1993.

LWV positions on issues result from nationwide study and consensus among the members. To gather information, LWV members employ a variety of sources, including interviews with technical experts and public officials, public meetings, surveys, and the organization's own resources. After gathering information and developing a position on a topic, such as national health care policy, statewide school formulas, or local recycling policies, the League works to shape public policy. Grassroots lobbying, the primary tool in the LWV's strategy, is supported by Washington-based volunteers, national board members, and staff.

The LWV's priorities include enacting campaign finance reform, civil liberties, election reform, lobby reform and ethics, redistricting reform, the Voting Rights Act, the Arctic National Wildlife Refuge, clean air, and voting rights for the residents of the District of Columbia. The LWV has provided information to voters about candidates since 1928, when it hosted *Meet the Candidates*, the first national radio broadcast of a candidate forum. In 1976, the League sponsored televised debates between presidential candidates Gerald Ford and Jimmy Carter, for which it won an Emmy award.

The LWV has state organizations in every state, the District of Columbia, Hong Kong, and the Virgin Islands and more than 1,000 local groups. The LWV opened its membership to men in 1974.

> **See also** Cable Acts; Catt, Carrie Clinton Lane Chapman; Coverture; Education Amendments of 1972, Title IX; Equal Rights Amendment; Family and Medical Leave Act of 1993; National American Woman Suffrage Association; Nineteenth Amendment; Pregnancy Discrimination Act of 1978; Protective Legislation; Public Offices, Women Elected to; Sheppard-Towner Maternity and Infancy Protection Act of 1921; Suffrage; Willebrandt, Mabel Walker; Women's Bureau

> **References** Breckenridge, *Women in the Twentieth Century: A Study of Their Political, Social and Economic Activities* (1933); Lemons, *The Woman Citizen* (1973); www.lwv.org; Young, *In the Public Interest* (1989).

Lease, Mary Elizabeth Clyens (1850–1933)

A compelling orator, Mary Elizabeth Lease supported a range of social causes and became a leader of the Populist Party in the late 1890s. Lease began her reform work in 1883, when she joined the Woman's Christian Temperance Union and began giving speeches. In the mid-1880s, she became involved in the suffrage movement and wrote a series of newspaper articles titled "Are Women Inferior to Men?" She served as the president of the Wichita Equal Suffrage Association and joined the Knights of Labor and the Kansas Farmers' Alliance.

In 1885, Lease began appearing as a paid lecturer, conducted a fundraising tour for the Irish National League, and helped form a group to assist small farmers. As a severe drought, high shipping costs, and mortgage foreclosures took their toll on farmers in 1889, Lease encouraged them to organize the People's Party, which became the Populist Party. She toured Kansas in 1890 and made more than 160 speeches for the party. Her fiery speeches and her deep voice resonated with discontented farmers as she admonished them to "raise less corn and more hell." Controversy surrounded her—supporters called her Queen Mary, and detractors called her the Kansas Pythoness.

In the 1890s, Lease helped extend the party's efforts into Missouri, the West, and the South and became a national leader. A delegate to the party's 1892 Kansas convention, she successfully worked for a suffrage plank in the platform. Lease campaigned with the party's presidential candidate James B. Weaver and helped the party win several races in Kansas. In recognition of her efforts, Lease was appointed president of the State Board of Charities, but her inability to compromise led to her removal. She challenged it and sought reinstatement. The Kansas Supreme Court ruled in her favor after a thirty-year-long battle.

Lease campaigned in 1896 for Populist presidential nominee William Jennings Bryan, but the party had begun to lose its base. Following the election, Lease lectured on woman suffrage and Prohibition, but her public influence declined. From 1908 to 1918, she occasionally gave lectures for the New York City Board of Education. She retired from public life in 1918.

Born in Ridgway, Pennsylvania, Mary Elizabeth Lease graduated from St. Elizabeth's Academy in Allegheny, New York, in 1868 with a teaching certificate. After studying law at home, Lease was admitted to the Kansas bar in 1889. She moved to Kansas in 1870 to teach at a Catholic girls' school in Osage Mission, marrying two year later. After she and her husband struggled as farmers, they moved to Wichita, where he was a pharmacist and she became involved in civic organizations. Lease and her husband divorced in 1902.

In her book *The Problem of Civilization Solved* (1895), Lease advocated nationalization of railroads, free trade, high tariffs, the initiative and referendum, and other reforms.

See also Suffrage; Woman's Christian Temperance Union

References Hardy, *American Women Civil Rights Activists* (1993); James, ed., *Notable American Women 1607–1950* (1971).

Lee, Barbara (b. 1946)

Democrat Barbara Lee of California entered the U.S. House of Representatives on 7 April 1998. Lee, who had been an aide for Congressman Ronald V. Dellums for twelve years, ran for his seat when he retired. She campaigned on the theme "carrying the baton." Congresswoman Lee's priorities include increased funding for education and cleanup of toxic waste sites, urban issues, and affordable housing. She has also advocated divestment from companies doing business in Sudan, citing the Sudanese government's campaign of violence, displacement, and genocide in the Darfur region.

She gained national attention when she cast the only vote against the resolution authorizing a military response to the September 11, 2001 terrorist attacks. In her remarks before the vote, Lee said: "I have agonized over this vote. But I came to grips with it in the very painful yet beautiful memorial service today [15 September 2001] at the National Cathedral. As a member of the clergy said, 'As we act, let us not become the evil that we deplore.'" She later opposed the pre-emptive invasion of Iraq, saying that it would set "a dangerous precedent."

In other areas, Lee passed an amendment permitting domestic violence victims to stay in public housing, instead of being evicted with their attackers. She has advocated the creation of a Cabinet-level Department of Peace. She is a leader on the national and international levels in fighting for attention to the AIDS epidemic, drafting several of the provisions included in a law signed by President George W. Bush in 2003. Lee has served as co-chair of the Congressional Progressive Caucus.

Born in El Paso, Texas, Barbara Lee earned her bachelor of arts degree from Mills College in 1973 and her master's degree in social work from the University of California at Berkeley in 1975. A college course assignment to work for a political campaign led Lee to Congresswoman Shirley Chisholm's 1972 campaign for the Democratic Party's presidential nomination. Before working for Dellums, she co-founded a community health center in Berkeley, California.

Lee served in the California Assembly from 1990 to 1996 and in the California Senate from 1996 to 1998. While in the California legislature, Lee successfully sponsored legislation to redevelop closed military facilities and open a California trade office in Johannesburg, South Africa.

See also Congress, Women in; State Legislatures, Women in

References "Barbara Lee, D-Calif." (1998); *Congressional Quarterly, Politics in America 2002* (2001), *Politics in America 2004* (2003), *Politics in America 2006* (2005); "Congresswoman Barbara Lee Calls for Start to Sudan Divestment," *Finance Wire*, 30 January 2005; http://lee.house.gov; "The Extraordinary Conscience of Barbara Lee," *Peacework*, 1 October 2001, p. 17.

Lesbian Rights

Lesbian rights activists seek to end discrimination based on sexual orientation in several areas, including housing, employment, family relationships, criminal law, and threats and acts of violence. From the 1950s until the acquired immunodeficiency syndrome (AIDS) epidemic in the 1980s, lesbian activists generally supported their own organizations, but in the 1980s many joined forces with gay men to seek funds for AIDS research and to pursue their political and civil rights.

For many lesbians the potential disclosure of their sexual orientation posed a significant threat because exposure could result in the loss of employment or of custody of their children. In the 1950s, gathering with other lesbians in bars or other public places exposed them to police raids and the possibility that their names would appear in the newspaper. A group led by Del Martin and Phyllis Lyon formed Daughters of Bilitis in 1955 to provide a safe place for lesbians to gather and later expanded its mission to educating the public about homosexuals.

As the modern feminist movement emerged in the 1960s, several leaders, including Rita Mae Brown, Ti-Grace Atkinson, and Kate Millett, attempted to explain lesbianism to their feminist colleagues but were met with confusion and condemnation. Feminist leader Betty Friedan publicly referred to lesbians as "the lavender menace" and attempted to have lesbians removed from the National Organization for Women's (NOW's) leadership. In 1971, however, NOW passed a resolution recognizing "the double oppression of women who are lesbians" and acknowledging "the oppression of lesbians as a legitimate concern of feminism."

A dozen women, including Rita Mae Brown, formed the Furies in 1971 and developed a feminist lesbian political view that argued that heterosexuality was the problem. Calling lesbianism a political choice, they based their analysis on the belief that relationships between women and men involved power and dominance. Rejecting power relationships, the Furies described themselves as radical, separatist, and opposed to the patriarchy. The group disbanded in 1973, unable to overcome differences in class. Other lesbian groups published poetry, novels, and newspapers, formed collectives, and opened businesses, creating a lesbian feminist counterculture.

A benchmark in gay activism resulted from a police raid in 1969 on a gay and lesbian bar in New York City, the Stonewall Inn. As the police attempted to close the bar and arrested its patrons, an angry riot erupted that lasted three days. The events convinced many that as long as gays and lesbians continued to conceal their sexual orientation, that is, to "stay in the closet," they would remain politically powerless and unable to claim their civil rights as citizens.

In the 1970s, lesbians and gays began to realize some of their goals. About thirty cities passed civil rights ordinances banning discrimination against lesbians and gays, and anti-discrimination lawsuits were filed for employment and housing rights, for the right to serve in the military, and on behalf of lesbian mothers for custody of their children. By the late 1990s, ten states and 165 communities had laws protecting lesbians and gays from workplace discrimination, but a backlash developed. Colorado provides an example of a state in which several communities had enacted ordinances banning discrimination based on sexual orientation in several areas, including public accommodations, employment, and education. In 1992, Colorado voters approved a state constitutional amendment prohibiting all legislative, executive, or judicial action at any level of state or local government intended to protect gays and lesbians. The U.S. Supreme Court, however, found that the state amendment violated the equal protection clause of the Fourteenth Amendment.

Among the groups that advocate civil rights for lesbians and gays is the Human Rights Campaign (HRC), the largest national lesbian and gay political organization in the United States. HRC lobbies the federal government on gay, lesbian, and AIDS issues; educates the public; and participates in election campaigns. The American Civil Liberties Union's Lesbian and Gay Rights Project takes cases to court that have a significant effect on the lives of lesbians, gay men, and bisexuals and promotes laws and policies to help achieve equality and fairness for them.

Before the 1970s, lesbians and gay men had held public offices, but they had not revealed their sexual orientation. In 1974, two lesbians ran for public office and became the first openly gay people to win, Elaine Noble to the Massachusetts House of Representatives and Kathy Kozachenko to the Ann Arbor, Michigan, City Council. In 1998, Democrat Tammy Baldwin became the first lesbian who had made public statements about her sexual orientation to be elected to Congress.

The legal status of same-sex relationships gained increasing attention beginning in the 1990s. One strategy that has been used since the early 1970s is legal challenges of state laws that limit marriage to one man and one woman. A sampling of lawsuits offers an overview of this approach. The first lawsuit was in 1971 filed in Hawaii, when the exclusion of lesbian and gay couples from civil marriage was first challenged. Before the case reached the state Supreme Court, however, voters passed a state constitutional amendment in 1998 permitting the legislature to limit marriage to different-sex couples. A similar lawsuit filed in Alaska met the same fate: voters passed a state constitutional amendment, also in 1998, defining marriage as the union of one man and one woman. A lawsuit filed in Vermont, however, reached the state Supreme Court. In 1999, the Vermont Court found that denying same-sex partners the same benefits and privileges as married couples violated the state's constitution. The Vermont legislature passed a measure permitting same-sex couples to enter into civil unions. Under civil unions, however, couples are not covered by federal rights and benefits. The Massachusetts state Supreme Court found in 2003 that civil unions did not meet the standards of the state's constitution. Massachusetts began granting marriage licenses to same-sex couples in 2004. In addition to recognizing same-sex marriages and civil unions, other states recognize domestic partnerships.

In 2004, opponents of same-sex marriages passed state constitutional amendments in thirteen states limiting marriage to the union of a man and a woman. The states are: Arkansas, Georgia, Kentucky, Louisiana, Michigan, Mississippi, Missouri, Montana, North Dakota Ohio, Oklahoma, Oregon, and Utah. In 2004, President George W. Bush supported a constitutional amendment the United States Constitution banning same sex marriages.

At the federal level, Congress passed the Defense of Marriage Act in 1996, stating that no state has to recognize a same-sex marriage performed by another state. President George W. Bush supports a federal constitutional amendment banning same-sex marriages.

> **See also** American Civil Liberties Union; Atkinson, Ti-Grace; Baldwin, Tammy; Bowers v. Hardwick; Brown, Rita Mae; Cammermeyer, Margrethe; Daughters of Bilitis; Friedan, Betty Naomi Goldstein; Millett, Katherine (Kate) Murray; National Organization for Women; Radicalesbians
>
> **References** Cavin, "The Invisible Army of Women: Lesbian Social Protests, 1969–1988" (1990); *Congressional Quarterly Almanac, 104th Congress, 2nd Session… 1996* (1997); Davis, *Moving the Mountain* (1991); "For Better or for Worse? As More Gays Say 'I do,' Bush Calls for a Constitutional B an," *Time*, 8 March 2004, pp. 26–27; www.aclu.org; www.nclr.org. www.aclu.org.

Lewis, Ann Frank (b. 1937)

Democratic Party strategist Ann F. Lewis was counselor to President Bill Clinton from 1999 to 2000. She served as White House director of communications from 1997 until her appointment as counselor. She served as deputy campaign manager and director of communications in the 1996 Clinton-Gore Re-election Campaign. She was an advisor in Democrat Al Gore's 1996 presidential campaign and John Kerry's 2000 presidential campaign. She has also been an adviser to Democratic Senator Hillary Rodham Clinton of New York.

Lewis entered politics in 1968 as an assistant to Boston's mayor, working for him until 1975. A congressional aide from 1976 to 1981, she was political director for the Democratic National Committee from 1981 to 1985, when she became national director for Americans for Democratic Action. She wrote a column for *Ms.* magazine from 1988 to 1992 and was vice president of public policy for Planned Parenthood Federation of America before joining the Clinton-Gore campaign in 1996.

Born in Jersey City, New Jersey, Lewis attended Radcliffe College from 1954 to 1955. She is a founding member of the National Women's Political Caucus. Her brother is Barney Frank, a member of Congress.

> **See also** Democratic Party, Women in the; *Ms. Magazine*; National Women's Political Caucus; Planned Parenthood Federation of America
>
> **References** *The New York Times*, 28 September 1987.

Liasson, Mara (b. 1955)

National political correspondent for National Public Radio (NPR), Liasson's stories are aired on two of the network's shows, *All Things Considered* and *Morning Edition*.

Liasson also reports for FOX News, appearing on the network's Sunday news program. From 1989 to 1992, Liasson covered Congress, becoming NPR's White House correspondent from 1993 to 2001. She has covered four presidential elections: 1992, 1996, 2000, and 2004.

Before joining NPR in 1985, Liasson was a freelance reporter in San Francisco, worked for a California public radio station, and worked in print media. Born in New York, New York, Liasson earned a bachelor's degree at Brown University in 1977 and attended Columbia University from 1988 to 1989.

References http://foxnews.com; http://npr.org;

Liberalism

American liberalism gained its contemporary meaning through President Franklin D. Roosevelt's New Deal programs in the 1930s. Roosevelt's New Deal liberalism changed ideas about government's duty and responsibility in the nation's economic life by developing federal welfare programs, redistributing wealth, and enhancing the potential for equal opportunity. New Deal legislation gave trade unions new protections and encouraged their growth, altering the balance of power between employers and employees.

In the mid-1960s, liberal policies included the expansion of government health, education, and other social programs for poor and low-income families. Unlike New Deal programs, President Lyndon Johnson's Great Society programs addressed racism through the Civil Rights Act of 1964 and the Voting Rights Act of 1965 and included African Americans in the social programs. The civil rights movement, which had created pressure for passage of legislation promoting racial justice, inspired women, gays and lesbians, Hispanics, Native Americans, and other groups to press for recognition of their causes and for legislation to protect them. The proposed Equal Rights Amendment serves as one example of an attempt to define and guarantee a group's rights. The U.S. Supreme Court also participated in the liberal agenda through its 1954 decision desegregating schools in *Brown v. Board of Education* and its 1973 decision legalizing abortion in *Roe v. Wade.*

The liberal agenda came under increasingly intense scrutiny in the 1970s as citizens evaluated the financial costs of social programs and changes in social relationships and found the first too high and the second too unsettling. Voters expressed their frustration with liberal policies by electing conservatives Ronald Reagan and George Bush to the presidency. By the 1988 presidential elections, the word liberal had become a pejorative term and was referred to as the "L" word.

See also Civil Rights Act of 1964, Title VII; Voting Rights Act of 1965

References Foner and Garraty, eds., *The Reader's Companion to American History* (1991).

Liliuokalani (1838–1917)

The last sovereign queen of the Hawaiian Islands, Liliuokalani took the throne in 1891, during a turbulent time in the islands' history. Born in Honolulu, Liliuokalani attended a missionary school, where she learned English. She inherited the throne from her brother King David Kalakaua, who had ruled the islands from 1874 until his death in 1891. In 1887, he had accepted a new constitution, demanded by American interests, that forfeited much of the power of the monarchy to a Cabinet controlled by Americans. When Queen Liliuokalani ascended to the throne, she sought to restore some of the monarchy's power by issuing a new constitution, which was her historic right as monarch. Native Hawaiians supported her plan, but Americans who had financial interests in the islands' sugar plantations wanted the United States to annex the islands. Her attempt to balance the interests of native islanders and of foreigners was interpreted as a capricious act by the Americans on the islands.

Lawyer Sanford Ballard Dole, who was the son of missionaries and who had grown up on the islands, led a group that responded to Liliuokalani's new constitution by establishing a republic in 1893 and deposing Liliuokalani. They hoped to convince the United States to annex the islands. President Grover Cleveland sent a representative to attempt to negotiate a solution to the problem, but was unsuccessful. Cleveland sent another representative who offered to support the queen if she would grant amnesty to the annexationists, but she hesitated and the opportunity was lost.

On 4 July 1894, Sanford Dole and his followers announced that he had become president of the Republic of Hawaii and the United States government recognized the new government. Hawaiian royalists protested the action and were jailed. Early in 1895, Liliuokalani formally abdicated the throne in exchange for the freedom of the royalists. She was imprisoned for misprision of treason, that is, knowing that a treasonous act was planned by someone else. Tried and convicted, she was imprisoned in Iolani Palace until February 1896. The United States annexed Hawaii in 1898.

> **See also** Mink, Patsy Matsu Takemoto
>
> **References** Allen, *The Betrayal of Liliuokalani: Last Queen of Hawaii, 1838–1917* (1982); Garraty and Carnes, eds., *American National Biography* (1999).
>
> **Document** Queen Liliuokalani, "Appeal to President Grover Cleveland," 1893

Lincoln, Blanche Lambert (b. 1960)

Democrat Blanche Lambert Lincoln of Arkansas served in the U.S. House of Representatives from 3 January 1993 to 3 January 1997 and entered the U.S. Senate on 3 January 1999. Lincoln started her political career as a receptionist and congressional aide to Representative Bill Alexander (D-AR), working for him from 1982 to 1984. She was a researcher and lobbyist for the next six years.

In late 1991, while discussing problems in politics with a friend, Lincoln decided to run for the U.S. House of Representatives to help remedy them. In the Arkansas primary in 1992, she challenged Bill Alexander, who had been involved in questionable activities, including 487 overdrafts at the House of Representatives' bank. The scandal gave political novice Lincoln the break she needed, and she easily defeated Alexander in the primary and her Republican opponent in the general election. Once in Congress, she worked to enhance rural development, cut the federal budget, reform welfare programs, and improve rural water and health care access.

After becoming pregnant with twins in 1996, Lincoln did not seek a third term. When Democratic Senator Dale Bumpers announced his retirement, Lincoln entered the race, saying: "Nearly one of every three senators is a millionaire, but there are only five mothers." She based her campaign on making the nation better for her children, improving education, and using the federal budget surplus for the benefit of Social Security and Medicare. Senator Lincoln has introduced legislation to exempt family-owned business from the estate tax and another measure to expand eligibility for the child tax credit. Lincoln explained to her constituents that she wanted to watch her children grow up and that she would be moving her family to Washingon, D.C., with her. Before her twins entered school, she pled with Senate leaders to allow members time with their families, and she limited weekend business trips.

In 2001, she fought for the child tax credit by withholding her support for President George W. Bush's 2001 tax cut package until it allowed the credit partially refundable. Two years later, she again fought for the credit when it was initially removed from the 2003 tax bill. After successfully keeping the credit in the bill, she said: "I am continually astounded that some members of Congress don't understand how challenging it is to raise a family in today's economy." In 2005, Lincoln sought to expand eligibility to an additional one million lower-income families.

The daughter of a family that has farmed in northeast Arkansas for seven generations, Lincoln has steadfastly advocated agricultural issues. When President George W. Bush sought her support for the 2001 tax cuts during a trip on Air Force One, Senator Lincoln gave him two letters describing her requests for disaster relief for Arkansas farmers and for increased anti-poverty programs for the Mississippi Delta. Explaining her commitment to farmers, she said: "Agriculture is my base, not only for my state's economy but also my heritage."

She founded and chairs the Senate Hunger Caucus and holds the leadership position of Chair of Rural Outreach in the Democratic Caucus. Following the 2004 elections, Lincoln joined two other senators in forming the Third Way, a legislative lobbying group designed to advocate moderate Democrats' proposals.

Born in Helena, Arkansas, Lincoln earned a bachelor of arts degree from Randolph-Macon Woman's College in 1982 and attended the University of Arkansas and the University of London.

See also Congress, Women in

References "Blanche Lincoln" (1998); *Congress Daily*, 27 April 2005, 6 October 2005; *Congressional Quarterly, Politics in America 1996* (1995), 2002 (2001), 2004 (2003), 2006 (2005); "Ex-Rep. Lincoln to Seek Bumpers' Senate Seat" (1997); http://lincoln.senate.gov.

Lingle, Linda Cutter (b. ca. 1953)

Elected Hawaii's first woman governor in 2002, Linda Cutter Lingle also became the state's first Republican governor in 40 years. In her campaign, she pledged to lower taxes, maintain the state's hurricane relief fund, and improve public education.

Born in St. Louis, Missouri, Lingle moved with her family to California when she was 12. After earning a bachelor's degree in journalism from California State University in 1975, she moved to Hawai'i, where her father and uncle lived. The next year, she founded and served as publisher of the *Moloka'i Free Press,* a community newspaper.

While reporting on local government for her newspaper, Lingle became interested in local politics. She won a seat on the Maui County Council in 1980, serving until 1990. During her county council service, she created a zoning and planning commis-

*Hawaii Governor Linda Lingle welcomes women to the 3rd annual
International Women's Leadership Conference, August 2006.
(Courtesy Office of the Governor of Hawaii)*

sion for Molokaʻi. Elected mayor of Maui in 1990 and re-elected in 1994, Lingle changed the county's budgeting system, allowing the public to track the county's expenditures.

Lingle ran for governor in 1998, but narrowly lost. For the next four years, she chaired the state's Republican party and honed her message in preparation for another campaign for governor. After winning the position in 2002, she has worked to diversify the state's economy and reduce business regulations.

References "Biographies: Hawaii," *National Journal*, 9 November 2002, p. 3302; Cathy S. Cruz, "Feminine Phenomenon," *Hawaii Business*, 1 October 2002, p. 26; http://www.hawaii.gov/gov/gov/gov/biography.html.

Liswood, Laura (b. 1950)

A study about the differences between men and women legislators led Laura Liswood to think, "What would it be like if a woman were president of the United States?" She embarked on a journey that took her around the world, interviewing women presidents and prime ministers in the Philippines, Sri Lanka, Pakistan, Norway, Nicaragua, Lithuania, and nine other countries. She concluded: "Women must play an integral role in all the world's issues or else humanity's challenges will never be solved." She wrote *Women World Leaders: Fifteen Great Politicians Tell Their Stories* (1995) and with Judy Woodruff created a documentary with the same title in 1996.

During the interviews, Liswood learned that several of the female heads of state had not met each other and that they were enthusiastic about that possibility, leading Lis-

Laura A. Liswood, cofounder and secretary-general of the Council of Women World Leaders.

wood to cofound the Council of Women World Leaders with Iceland's President Vigdis Finnbogadottir in 1996. Liswood serves as secretary general of the organization.

Liswood cofounded The White House Project in 1997, inspired by her work with the female heads of state. The White House Project seeks to elect a woman president of the United States by changing opinions of women as leaders.

Owner and publisher of *Seattle Woman*, Liswood was commissioner of the City of Seattle Women's Commission and founded May's List, a political donor network emphasizing women's leadership in the political arena. The secretary of defense appointed her to a three-year term on the Defense Advisory Committee on Women in the Services (DACOWITS) in 2000.

Named in 2001 managing director, Global Leadership and Diversity, for Goldman Sachs, a global investment banker, Liswood is a senior advisor to the company.

Born in Sacramento, California, Liswood earned her AB degree at San Diego State University in 1971, her JD degree at the University of California School of Law in 1974, and her MBA at Harvard Business School in 1976.

> **References** Laura Liswood, email to author January 12, 2006;
> http://www.womenworldleaders.org/; *Wall Street Journal*, June 14, 2005.

> **Document** Laura Liswood, "We Don't Need to be Perfect. We Just Need to Make the Run."

Lloyd Bouquard, Rachel Marilyn Laird (b. 1929)

Democrat Marilyn Lloyd of Tennessee served in the U.S. House of Representatives from 3 January 1975 to 3 January 1995. Lloyd served under the name Marilyn Lloyd Bouquard in the 96th through 98th Congresses (1979–1985). She entered politics after her husband, who was a candidate for Congress, died during the campaign. Democratic Party officials recruited her to fill the vacancy on the ballot.

Congresswoman Lloyd worked to keep the Clinch River nuclear breeder reactor a viable project in her district, but Congress killed it in 1983. She succeeded in convincing Congress to complete construction of the Tellico Dam after progress had stopped to protect snail darters, an endangered fish species. Lloyd also wrote and passed a bill in 1982 to build nuclear waste test facilities. Considered a conservative Southern Democrat, Lloyd changed her position on abortion from being pro-life to pro-choice. She also joined Congresswomen Patricia Schroeder and Beverly Byron in their strong criticism of the Navy's responses to the Tailhook convention scandal involving naval officers' sexual assaults on several women. Lloyd retired in 1995.

Born in Fort Smith, Arkansas, Marilyn Lloyd attended Shorter College in 1960.

> **See also** Abortion; Congress, Women in; Military, Women in the; Schroeder, Patricia Nell Scott; Sexual Harassment
>
> **References** *Congressional Quarterly, Politics in America 1994* (1993); Office of the Historian, U.S. House of Representatives, *Women in Congress, 1917–1990* (1991).

Lockwood, Belva Ann Bennett McNall (1830–1917)

An advocate for women's rights and woman suffrage, Belva Lockwood was the first woman admitted to practice before the U.S. Supreme Court and U.S. Court of Claims. Born in Royalton Township, New York, Belva Lockwood attended Gasport Academy from 1853 to 1854 and earned her bachelor of science degree from Genesee College in 1857. She worked in education for most of the 1860s.

After being denied admission to three law schools because she was a woman, Lockwood entered National University Law School in 1871 and completed the curriculum

Belva Lockwood, the first American woman to graduate from law school and to practice before the U.S. Supreme Court, 1885 (Library of Congress LC-DIG-cwpbh-04374)

in 1873. When male students resisted graduating with her, she was denied her law school diploma. After appealing to President Ulysses S. Grant, who was the school's ex-officio president, she received the degree. She was the first American woman to complete a course of study at a university law school.

Three years later, Lockwood again encountered gender barriers. The federal Court of Claims refused to permit her to plead before it, as did the U.S. Supreme Court. She drafted a law to overcome the courts' refusal to admit women, lobbied Congress for it, publicized the issue with the help of Myra Bradwell and her newspaper, and succeeded in getting it passed. In 1879, she became the first woman admitted to practice before the nation's highest court and the U.S. Court of Claims. The next year she sponsored the first Southern African American admitted to practice before the U.S. Supreme Court.

A suffragist, Lockwood had helped found the Universal Suffrage Association, and in the 1870s and 1880s, she was active in the National Woman Suffrage Association. She addressed the Platform Committee of the Republican National Convention in 1884 to ask for woman suffrage. Believing that publicity could benefit women's causes, in 1884 she accepted the National Equal Rights Party's nomination for president of the United States. Her platform included equal rights for all, reduction of the liquor traffic, uniform marriage and divorce laws, and peace. Lockwood received 4,149 votes in six states. She ran again in 1888, when she received fewer votes but had increased visibility.

Lockwood was one of the attorneys representing Eastern Cherokee Indians in a 1906 case against the United States. The case resulted from violations of the 1838 treaty that involved the relocation of thousands of Cherokees from Georgia and Tennessee to Oklahoma. The relocation became known as the Trail of Tears because about 4,000 Cherokees died on the way. Arguing the case before the U.S. Supreme Court, she won a settlement of $5 million for them.

> **See also** Anthony, Susan Brownell; National American Woman Suffrage Association; Suffrage

> **References** Hardy, *American Women Civil Rights Activists* (1993); Morello, *The Woman Lawyer in America: 1638 to the Present* (1986).

Lofgren, Zoe (b. 1947)

Democrat Zoe Lofgren of California entered the U.S. House of Representatives on 3 January 1995. Lofgren's service to her congressional district began in the 1970s, when she worked for Congressman Don Edwards in his Washington, D.C., and district offices. When Edwards retired, she ran for his seat. Early in her campaign, Lofgren gained national attention for a dispute with state election officials. She had stated that her occupation was county supervisor/mother. State election officials said that motherhood was a status, not an occupation, and that she could not use the description. Lofgren responded that officials' objections were typical of the ways in which the law does not recognize women's unpaid work. The controversy provided her with a framework for discussing her key campaign issues: reducing violent crime and increasing federal support to help families and children.

With Silicon Valley just west of her congressional district, Lofgren has worked on several high technology issues. Educating her colleagues about the issues has been one of her continuing contributions to the debate on them. She fought with the Clinton administration over foreign sales of encryption software, ultimately convincing the administration to ease restrictions on the sales.

Lofgren's congressional priorities have included health care, housing, children and families, and education. She has introduced legislation to accelerate the development of fusion as an energy source, passed her proposal to make Internet access more affordable for schools, libraries, and rural health centers, and has sought to abolish the Electoral College. When Democrats held the majority in the U.S. House of Representatives, she passed a measure to double the number of highly skilled foreign workers who could obtain visas to work in the United States.

As a member of the minority party, Lofgren has focused her efforts on revising Republican proposals to reflect more of her philosophy. She has passed amendments that restored protections for battered spouses and children in an immigration bill and that provided affordable Internet access for public schools in a telecommunications bill. Even though Lofgren has had success amending Republican proposals, she has found the House's work deficient, saying: "I'm frustrated by the sheer volume of stupid things we've done."

Born in Palo Alto, California, Zoe Lofgren received her bachelor's degree in political science from Stanford University in 1970 and her law degree from the University of Santa Clara Law School in 1975. She has had a private law practice and has taught classes in immigration law, legal research, and writing at the University of Santa Clara Law School. A trustee on the San Jose–Evergreen Community College District from 1979 to 1981, she then served on the Santa Clara County Board of Supervisors from 1981 to 1995. As a supervisor, Lofgren worked to improve and expand the county's highways system.

See also Congress, Women in

References *Congressional Quarterly, Politics in America 1998* (1997), *Politics in America 2002* (2001), *Politics in America 2004* (2003); *Politics in America 2006* (2005); http::/zoelofgren.house.gov; *San Francisco Chronicle*, 26 November 2000; *San Jose Mercury News*, 4 October 2000.

Long, Catherine Small (b. 1924)

Democrat Catherine Long of Louisiana served in the U.S. House of Representatives from 30 March 1985 to 3 January 1987. After her husband's death in office, she won the special election to fill the vacancy. Congresswoman Long co-sponsored legislation that secured pension and health benefits for women and restricted race and sex discrimination in insurance. She did not run for a second term.

Born in Dayton, Ohio, Catherine Long earned her bachelor of arts degree from Louisiana State University in 1948. After serving as a pharmacist's mate in the U.S. Navy, she worked on two congressional staffs. She developed her political skills by working for the state party's finance council and the party's state central committee.

See also Congress, Women in

References Office of the Historian, U.S. House of Representatives, *Women in Congress, 1917–1990* (1991).

Long, Rose McConnell (1892–1970)

Democrat Rose Long of Louisiana served in the U.S. Senate from 31 January 1936 to 2 January 1937. Following the assassination of her husband, U.S. Senator Huey Long, Rose Long was first appointed and then elected to fill the vacancy. While in office, she worked to enlarge Chalmette National Historic Park but did not run for a full term. Her son Russell Long was also a U.S. senator.

Born in Greensburg, Indiana, Rose Long was a secretary at a hardware store before her marriage.

See also Congress, Women in

References Office of the Historian, U.S. House of Representatives, *Women in Congress, 1917–1990* (1991).

Long Thompson, Jill Lynnette (b. 1952)

Democrat Jill Long Thompson of Indiana served in the U.S. House of Representatives from 28 March 1989 to 3 January 1995. After her congressional service, Long Thompson was appointed undersecretary of agriculture for rural development in President Bill Clinton's administration.

Born in Warsaw, Indiana, Long Thompson received her bachelor of science degree from Valparaiso University in 1974, and a master's degree in business administration in 1978 and a doctoral degree in 1984, both from Indiana University. Before running for Congress, she was a professor of business at both universities. From 1983 to 1986, she was a member of the Valparaiso City Council. She ran unsuccessfully for the U.S. Senate in 1986 and the U.S. House of Representatives in 1988.

When the House seat was vacated in 1989, Long Thompson ran once again, this time successfully. A Democrat in a strong Republican district, she found a balance between her party's interests and those of her district. For example, she supported pro-choice legislation and increasing the minimum wage while taking more conservative positions on some fiscal votes.

In 1990, Long Thompson gained passage of amendments to the farm bill, including one to give farmers planting flexibility and another to give incentives to farmers who used conservation techniques. She also passed measures for expanded hospice care services for terminally ill veterans and for counseling for women veterans who were sexually harassed or assaulted during their military service.

Defeated in her 1994 re-election attempt, Long Thompson became a fellow at the Institute of Politics at the John F. Kennedy School of Government at Harvard University and a member of the board of directors of the Commodity Credit Corporation. She served as undersecretary for development in the U.S. Department of Agriculture from 1995 to 2001. She was an unsuccessful candidate to the U.S. House of Representatives for the 108th Congress in 2002.

See also Congress, Women in; Reproductive Rights; Sexual Harassment

References *Congressional Quarterly, Politics in America 1994* (1993); www.usda.gov/agencies/gallery/thompson.htm.

Los Angeles Department of Water and Power v. Manhart (1978)

In this class action suit, Marie Manhart and other female employees of the Los Angeles Department of Water and Power claimed the department discriminated against them on the basis of sex, in violation of Title VII of the Civil Rights Act of 1964. Because women statistically live longer than men and their pensions would cost more than men's pensions, the department required women to make larger contributions to the pension fund than men. The women wanted their contributions reduced and the excess contributions refunded to them.

The U.S. Supreme Court found that the policy discriminated against women in violation of Title VII and said that the higher contributions could no longer be required of women. At the same time, the Court decided against refunding the excess the women had contributed to the pension fund, explaining that it could jeopardize the fund's solvency.

> **References** Clare Cushman, *Supreme Court Decisions and Women's Rights: Milestone to Equality*, 2001, pp. 148–150; *Los Angeles Department of Water and Power v. Manhart, 435 U.S. 702* (1978)

Louchheim, Kathleen (Katie) Scofield (1903–1991)

A Democratic Party leader in the 1940s and 1950s, Kathleen Louchheim was the first woman to obtain an appointment in the higher levels of the U.S. State Department, serving as deputy assistant secretary of state from 1962 to 1968. Louchheim began working as a volunteer with the Democratic National Committee in 1938 and worked in Franklin D. Roosevelt's 1940 presidential campaign. In 1941, she became assistant to the director of public information in the Office of Foreign Relief and Rehabilitation Operations in the State Department. In 1945 and 1946, she was a displaced persons specialist and worked in Germany.

After working in Adlai Stevenson's unsuccessful 1952 presidential campaign, Louchheim became assistant chairperson of the Democratic National Committee, with responsibilities in the labor division. Director of women's activities for the party from 1953 to 1960, she sought to make politics more interesting for women, to identify women who could raise money on the national level, and to encourage women to serve in the party's leadership. She also was a party vice chair from 1956 to 1960.

With John F. Kennedy's election in 1960 and her party's return to the White House, Louchheim was appointed special assistant and consultant on women's activities in the State Department in 1961. She said her duties were to greet foreign women visitors and diplomats' wives. Appointed deputy assistant secretary of state in 1962, she was the first woman to hold the position. Deputy assistant secretary of state for public affairs for a short time, she then served as deputy assistant secretary of state for community advisory services from 1963 to 1966 and for educational and cultural affairs until 1968. The next two years, she was the U.S. ambassador to the United Nations Educational, Scientific, and Cultural Organization.

Born in New York City, Louchheim attended Columbia University from 1926 to 1927. She wrote *With or Without Roses* (1966), *By the Political Sea* (1970), and *The Making of the New Deal—The Insiders Speak* (1983).

See also Democratic Party, Women in the; Edwards, India Moffett

References Louchheim, *By the Political Sea* (1970).

Lowey, Nita Melnikoff (b. 1937)

Democrat Nita Lowey of New York entered the U.S. House of Representatives on 3 January 1989. Her political career began with a neighborhood gathering in 1974 to help the Democratic candidate for lieutenant governor, Mario Cuomo. He lost that election but was appointed New York secretary of state, and he appointed Lowey to the anti-poverty division of his office, where she served from 1975 to 1985. She then became assistant secretary of state, a position she held until 1987.

Lowey was among the congresswomen who marched to the U.S. Senate in October 1991 to discuss Anita Hill's accusations that U.S. Supreme Court nominee Clarence Thomas had sexually harassed her. The action contributed to the U.S. Senate holding additional hearings before confirming Clarence's appointment.

Lowey supported the Freedom of Access to Clinic Entrances Act of 1994 and Medicaid funding for abortions for poor women. She opposed a rule that prohibited abortion counseling and referrals in federally funded planning clinics and also opposed legislation to make partial birth abortion illegal. In 1998, Lowey succeeded in gaining House and Senate approval for a measure providing contraceptive coverage for federal workers whose health insurance included pharmaceuticals, but the conference committee deleted it. In a compromise, Lowey proposed exempting physicians who oppose contraceptive coverage for religious or moral reasons and obtained its approval.

Education, child care, health, and nutrition have also been priorities for Lowey, particularly as they relate to poor people, women, minorities, and the elderly. She successfully worked for a bill that provided funding for drug education and counseling services for students. As a minority member of Congress, she passed a measure that requires food allergen labeling identifying the eight most common food allergies.

When Republican leaders threatened to eliminate the Public Broadcasting System (PBS), Congresswoman Lowey invited Bert and Ernie, two of the muppets from the educational program *Sesame Street* to a congressional hearing. The publicity that followed helped save the network.

Lowey co-founded the Hudson River Congressional Caucus in 2004. Also that year, she obtained $500,000 for the Hudson River National Heritage Area.

In the 104th, 105th, and 106th Congresses (1995–2001), she held the leadership position of minority whip at large. In the 107th Congress (2001–2003), she chaired the Democratic Congressional Campaign Committee, which raises funds for congressional candidates, and set fundraising records during her term. Lowey also co-chaired the Congressional Caucus for Women's Issues in the 105th Congress (1997–1999).

Born in Bronx, New York, Lowey received her bachelor of arts degree from Mount Holyoke College in 1959.

> **See also** Congress, Women in; Congressional Caucus for Women's Issues; Freedom of Access to Clinic Entrances Act of 1994; Hill, Anita Faye; Reproductive Rights; Sexual Harassment

> **References** *Congressional Quarterly, Politics in America 1994* (1993), *Politics in America 1998* (1997); *CQ Weekly*, 28 December 2002; http://www.house.gov/lowey.

Luce, Clare Boothe (1903–1987)

Republican Clare Boothe Luce of Connecticut served in the U.S. House of Representatives from 3 January 1943 to 3 January 1947. A playwright, author, and journalist, Luce became a celebrity with the Broadway productions of *The Women* (1936), which was made into a movie, and *Kiss the Boys Goodbye* (1938), several years before she ran for Congress.

Born in New York, New York, Clare Boothe Luce attended St. Mary's School and Miss Mason's School, graduating in 1919. Editor of *Vanity Fair* magazine in the early 1930s, she helped her husband Henry Luce create *Time* magazine, for which she was a newspaper correspondent during World War II. She also wrote *Europe in the Spring* (1940), based on four months she spent observing the war in Europe. When she returned to the United States, she campaigned for unsuccessful Republican presidential candidate Wendell Wilkie.

Congresswoman Luce sponsored a bill to create a department of children's welfare, which would have included health, educational, and welfare services; another to establish a department of science and research; and a measure to require equal pay for equal work regardless of sex or color. During both of her terms in office, she offered resolutions for racial equality in the armed services. She decided against running for a third term in 1946.

President Dwight Eisenhower appointed her ambassador to Italy in 1953, making her the second woman to hold the office. She served in it until 1957, and was given the Presidential Medal of Freedom. She was appointed ambassador to Brazil in 1959 and confirmed, but a bitter confrontation during the confirmation hearing led her to resign three days after she was confirmed. Luce served on the President's Foreign Intelligence Advisory Board from 1973 to 1979 and from 1982 to 1987. She remained active in Republican politics, working for presidential candidates until the mid-1980s.

See also Congress, Women in; Edwards, India Moffett; Equal Pay Act of 1963

References Morris, *Rage for Fame* (1997); Office of the Historian, U.S. House of Representatives, *Women in Congress, 1917–1990* (1991).

Lusk, Georgia Lee Witt (1893–1971)

Democrat Georgia Lusk of New Mexico served in the U.S. House of Representatives from 3 January 1947 to 3 January 1949. She supported federal aid to education, improved school lunch programs, and creation of a Cabinet-level department of education. Her other legislative interests included increasing benefits for veterans, providing military assistance for Turkey and Greece, and strengthening foreign aid programs. She ran for re-election in 1948 but lost in the primary.

Born in Carlsbad, New Mexico, Georgia Lusk graduated from New Mexico State Teachers College in 1914. The next year she married rancher-banker Dolph Lusk. She had two sons and was pregnant with her third child when her husband died in 1919. To support her family, Georgia Lusk managed the family's ranch and returned to teaching.

Elected county school superintendent in 1924, Lusk moved to the state level in 1930, when she ran for state superintendent of schools, holding the office from 1931 to 1935, 1943 to 1947, and 1955 to 1960. During her first two terms, Lusk guided the legislature's recodification of school laws and convinced legislators to increase teacher salaries, fund school construction, implement a retirement program for teachers, and provide students with free textbooks. After her term in Congress, President Harry Truman appointed her to the War Claims Commission in 1949, where she served until 1953.

See also Congress, Women in

References H. W. Wilson, *Current Biography: Who's News and Why, 1947* (1947); Office of the Historian, U.S. House of Representatives, *Women in Congress, 1917–1990* (1991); Sicherman and Green, eds., *Notable American Women: The Modern Period* (1980).

Lyon, Phyllis (b. 1924)

Feminist and lesbian activist Phyllis Lyon and her life partner Del Martin founded Daughters of Bilitis in 1955, the first national lesbian organization. They created the organization's publication, *The Ladder*, which began publishing in 1956, with Lyon as its first editor. In 1964, Lyon and Martin, along with three other members of Daughters of Bilitis, met with Methodist clergy, eventually forming the Council on Religion and the Homosexual (CRH). Lyon became the de facto staff member for CRH and through it, later co-founded the National Sex and Drug Forum. Lyon became a sex educator, and with others founded The Institute for Advanced Study of Human Sexuality. After earning a doctorate in education in human sexuality at the Institute for Advanced Study of Human Sexuality, she taught at the institute from 1976 to 1987.

Lyon and Martin helped lead the National Orgnization for Women's adoption of resolutions that connected discrimination against lesbians with feminism in the early 1970s. Lyon co-authored with Martin *Lesbian/Woman* (1972) and *Lesbian Love and Liberation* (1973), two of the earliest books written by and about lesbians. Lyon served on the San Francisco Commission on the Status of Women from 1976 to 1979 and on the San Francisco Human Rights Commission from 1976 to 1987. Lyon and Martin were the first same-sex couple to obtain an official marriage license in San Francisco, in March 2004.

See also Daughters of Bilitis; Lesbian Rights; Martin, Del

References DeLeon, ed., *Leaders from the 1960s: A Biographical Sourcebook of American Activism* (1994); http://www.lgbtran.org

MacKinnon, Catharine Alice (b. 1946)

Feminist scholar and lawyer Catharine MacKinnon has reframed questions of sexual harassment and pornography, opening new legal arguments for women seeking justice. She has been described as "the law's most prominent feminist legal theorist." An intellectual and legal leader in the feminist movement, MacKinnon became involved with the issue of sexual harassment in 1975, after learning the story of a woman who had left her job because she was sexually harassed. Denied unemployment benefits on the basis that she had left voluntarily, the woman appealed but lost. Although MacKinnon was not a lawyer at the time, she used the case as the basis for her thesis, which redefined sexual harassment as a form of sex discrimination. The thesis became part of her first book, *Sexual Harassment of Working Women: A Case of Sex Discrimination* (1979). In 1986, MacKinnon was co-counsel in the first sexual harassment case heard by the U.S. Supreme Court. In *Meritor Savings Bank v. Vinson,* MacKinnon successfully defined a hostile environment as a form of sexual harassment that was illegal under Title VII of the Civil Rights Act of 1964.

In the 1980s, MacKinnon turned her attention to developing a campaign against pornography, calling it a form of sex discrimination that harms women. Working with feminist theorist Andrea Dworkin, MacKinnon met Linda Marchiano, who was known as Linda Lovelace in pornographic movies. Marchiano claimed that she had been imprisoned, tortured, raped, and coerced into making pornographic movies, claims that MacKinnon helped publicize, even though she could not recover damages for Marchiano.

With Dworkin, MacKinnon drafted anti-pornography legislation for states and ordinances for cities and lobbied for them across the nation. When they have been enacted, they have been rejected on appeal in the courts. Controversy has surrounded MacKinnon's theories on pornography, with feminists both applauding and condemning them. In 1987, MacKinnon published a collection of her lectures on several topics, including pornography, in *Feminism Unmodified: Discourses on Life and Law.* The next year, she and Dworkin co-authored *Pornography and Civil Rights: A New Day for Women's Equality,* which focuses more narrowly on the topic of pornography. *Toward a Feminist Theory of the State* (1989) continued the development of her ideas on pornography, as did *Only Words* (1993).

MacKinnon participated in writing the brief for a case heard by the Canadian Supreme Court, which upheld the obscenity provisions of its criminal law. MacKinnon noted: "This makes Canada the first place in the world that says what is obscene is what harms women, not what offends our values."

MacKinnon earned her bachelor of arts degree from Smith College in 1969, her law degree from Yale University Law School in 1977, and her doctoral degree from Yale University in 1987.

> **See also** *Meritor Savings Bank v. Vinson*; Pornography; Sexual Harassment

> **References** H. W. Wilson, *Current Biography Yearbook, 1994* (1994); *The New York Times*, 6 October 1991.

Madar, Olga Marie (1916–1996)

Union leader Olga Madar was the first woman elected to the International Executive Board (IEB) of United Auto Workers (UAW), serving on it from 1966 to 1974, and was the founding president of the Coalition of Labor Union Women (CLUW). Madar's commitment to the labor movement came from a personal experience while working on Chrysler Corporation's assembly line in 1933. Hired for her skill as a softball player, she was unable to keep up with the assembly line and had nightmares about it. However, she kept her job, while others were being laid off during the Depression, because of her athletic ability. She later explained: "There was no union then and the fact that they would hire me when other workers were being laid off—just because I could play softball—was incredible. It was my first indication that a union was badly needed."

In 1947, Madar became the director of the UAW Recreation Department. Eliminating racism in professional bowling was her first assignment, which she accomplished in 1952 when the American Bowling Congress and the Women's International Bowling Congress ended their white-only rules.

Efforts to elect a woman to the IEB had begun in 1937 but had failed until Madar and others began to campaign in 1964 to create a place for a woman by changing IEB's constitution and adding an at-large position with the intent that a woman would fill it. In 1966, Madar won the election for the office and became the first woman vice president of UAW and the first woman elected an international vice president of the union. After her election to the board, the UAW became more active in women's issues.

As women became dissatisfied with their lack of power within unions, Madar led the founding of the Coalition of Labor Union Women (CLUW) in 1974. The CLUW's first president, Madar worked to eliminate all forms of discrimination against women. Following her retirement, Madar continued to be active in the retirees' programs.

Born in Sykesville, Pennsylvania, Madar graduated from Eastern Michigan University in 1938.

> **See also** Coalition of Labor Union Women

> **References** *CLUW News*, May–June 1996; *The New York Times*, 18 May 1996.

Maher v. Roe (1977)

In *Maher v. Roe*, the U.S. Supreme Court considered the constitutionality of a Connecticut regulation limiting Medicaid payments for first-trimester abortions to those considered medically necessary. The Court found that the Connecticut policy did not interfere with a woman's right to an abortion. The Court concluded that the state could pay for childbirth while refusing to pay for non-therapeutic abortions because it had the power to encourage actions deemed to be in the public interest—in this case, childbirth. The Court concluded that Connecticut's policy was constitutional and emphasized that the decision did not proscribe government funding of non-therapeutic abortions.

> **See also** Abortion; *Beal v. Doe*
>
> **References** *Maher v. Roe,* 432 U.S. 464 (1977).

Majette, Denise L. (b.1955)

Democrat Denise Majette of Georgia served in the U.S. House of Representatives from 3 January 2003 to 3 January 2005. She defeated Representative Cynthia McKinney in the 2002 Democratic primary and easily won the general election. Representative Majette was not a candidate for re-election in 2004, but was an unsuccessful candidate that year for the United States Senate.

Majette pressed for increases in Head Start funding, opposed granting the gun industry immunity from lawsuits, and introduced legislation to make a mountain in Georgia a protected preserve.

Before running for Congress, Majette was a judge on the Georgia state court of Dekalb County from 1993 to 2002.

Born in Brooklyn, New York, Majette earned a bachelor of arts degree at Yale University in 1976 and a juris doctor degree at Duke University in 1979. She has had a private practice and was on the faculty at Wake Forest Law School.

> **References** *Atlanta Business Chronicle,* 27 June 2003; http://bioguide.congress.gov.

Malcolm, Ellen Reighley (b. 1947)

Ellen Malcolm founded EMILY's List, a political action committee (PAC) to support pro-choice Democratic women gubernatorial and congressional candidates, in 1985. Malcolm had concluded that a new funding strategy was needed to support women candidates after working for Missouri Democrat Harriet Woods's campaign for the U.S. Senate, a race Woods lost by 27,000 votes because she could not raise enough money to keep her television advertisements on the air. Malcolm has since developed the skills and strategies to raise millions of dollars in an election cycle, convincing donors to give to both EMILY's List and other Democratic groups. Her strategy has been called "ingenious" by one political conservative.

Malcolm enrolled in George Washington University's master's of business administration program to develop the management and marketing skills she needed to make her proposed PAC successful. She also sought a distinctive name for the PAC and put together the acronym EMILY, which stands for "Early Money Is Like Yeast" (it raises the dough). Malcolm explained: "I want women to be powerful players in the middle, not just a fringe element." To reach that goal, Malcolm set EMILY's annual membership fee at $100 with the agreement that each member would also contribute at least $100 to two candidates on the organization's list. She used the language of the corporate world to describe her mission: "We've created a product, if you will, that is tailored to women like us, who are over 35, involved in politics. We are political venture capitalists. You'll rarely hear me give the typical 'we're-mad-at-the-world' feminist dogma."

Born in Hackensack, New Jersey, Malcolm earned her bachelor of arts degree from Hollins College in 1969 and her master's degree in business administration from George Washington University in 1984. From 1971 to 1976, Malcolm worked for Common Cause, serving as an issues coordinator and then as the Southern states coordinator. She became public information coordinator for the National Women's Political Caucus in 1978 and its project director the next year.

See also Abortion; Congress, Women in; EMILY's List; National Women's Political Caucus

References *The New York Times*, 2 May 1993; 13 May 2004.

Maloney, Carolyn Bosher (b. 1948)

Democrat Carolyn Maloney of New York entered the U.S. House of Representatives on 3 January 1993. In her first campaign, Maloney told voters that there were too many millionaires and not enough women in Congress. During her early service in Congress, Maloney's congressional priorities included improving the foster care system, reforming campaign finance laws, protecting Capitol Hill employees from sexual harassment, and providing full funding for Head Start programs. Following the September 11, 2001 terrorist attacks on the United States, Maloney, who represents Manhattan and Queens, New York, fought for federal funding for recovery programs for New York City.

Maloney passed the Debt Collection Bill, a measure establishing a computerized tracking system to help uncover wrongdoing in government contracting, and a measure to permit elderly people living in public housing to own household pets. Maloney has supported a constitutional amendment to balance the budget, and new taxes on gasoline.

After she sponsored the Northern Rockies Ecosystem Protection Act, classifying 16 million acres in five states as wilderness, some Western members of Congress mockingly proposed a countermeasure to designate Manhattan as a natural wilderness.

Co-chair of the Congressional Caucus on Women's Issues in the 106th Congress (1999–2001), Maloney has worked for several issues concerning women. Beginning with 105th Congress (1997–1999), she has introduced the Equal Rights Amendment every session. In 1999, she obtained passage of a law permitting women to breastfeed on federal property.

The 2000 census was another issue of great concern to Congresswoman Maloney. Calling it the "civil rights issue" of the 1990s, she sought to grant the Census Bureau the option of statistical sampling because she believed, along with others, that minority groups were undercounted. She lost the battle on sampling in both Congress and the courts, but she did convince Congress to provide funding for extra census takers.

Born in Greensboro, North Carolina, Carolyn Maloney earned her bachelor of arts degree from Greensboro College in 1968. From 1970 to 1977, Maloney was a teacher and an administrator for the New York City Board of Education. She then held senior staff positions in the New York state assembly and the New York state Senate from 1977 to 1979 and served on the New York City Council from 1983 until 1993. While on the city council, she was the principal author of the New York City Campaign Finance Act.

> **See also** Abortion; Congress, Women in; Congressional Workplace Compliance Act of 1995; Sexual Harassment
>
> **References** Congressional Quarterly, *Politics in America 1994* (1993), *Politics in America 1998* (1997), *Politics in America 2002* (2001), *Politics in America 2004* (2005; http://www.house.gov/maloney.

MANA, a National Latina Organization

Organized in 1975 as the Mexican American Women's National Association, MANA developed when a group of Chicanas living in Washington, D.C., began gathering for weekend brunches to discuss their exclusion from the feminist movement's agenda and their relative invisibility in policymaking meetings. The founders, many of whom held jobs in the federal government, in Congress, or with private policymaking groups, concluded that Chicanas needed an organization comparable to those formed by white and African American women.

In 1975, the organization installed its first elected officers and defined MANA's goals, which included advocating for issues important to Chicanas, developing leadership opportunities, creating a national awareness of Chicana concerns, and developing a national communications network for Chicanas. Later that year, MANA hosted the first national conference for and by Chicanas.

When the number of unnecessary sterilizations performed on Chicanas dramatically increased, MANA convinced policymakers to change federal regulations to ensure that Mexican American women understood the surgical process and its consequences and that they received the information in their primary language. MANA has called for pharmaceutical labeling in Spanish and in English, worked for employment opportunities, and sought appointments to governmental boards and commissions for Hispanics.

MANA representatives have testified before Congress on domestic violence and child support enforcement. MANA supports affirmative action, reproductive rights, the Equal Rights Amendment, pay equity, and welfare reform to change policies that hinder women attempting to become economically independent. In 2005, MANA focused on health care, lack of health insurance among Hispanics, and creating ways to access both.

> **See also** Abortion; Affirmative Action, Equal Rights Amendment; Pay Equity
>
> **References** Crocker, *MANA: One Dream, Many Voices* (1991), MANA, press release, 1 November 2005.

Mankiller, Wilma P. (b. 1945)

Wilma Mankiller served as chief of the Cherokee Nation from 1985 to 1995, the first female chief of a major tribe. Born in Rocky Mountain, Oklahoma, the daughter of a

Caucasian mother and Cherokee father, Mankiller's early years were spent in Oklahoma. When she was twelve years old, her family moved to San Francisco as part of a Bureau of Indian Affairs relocation program, which sought to end Native Americans' status as wards of the federal government. In 1969, she became active in the Native American rights movement when a group of Native Americans took over the former Alcatraz prison to protest their treatment by the federal government. By then married and a mother, Mankiller did not feel that she could join the demonstrators, but she raised money for them and visited them. She explained: "Those college students who participated in Alcatraz articulated a lot of feelings I had that I'd never been able to express."

Mankiller attended Skyline College in 1973 and San Francisco State College from 1973 to 1975 and received her bachelor of arts degree from Union College in 1977. She did postgraduate work in community planning at the University of Arkansas in 1979. In 1977, Mankiller and her husband divorced, and she returned to Oklahoma to claim land that her grandfather had owned as part of a settlement with the U.S. government. She worked for the Cherokee Nation as economic stimulus coordinator, becoming the tribe's program development specialist in 1979. An automobile accident that year left Mankiller badly injured, resulting in an extended hospitalization and a lengthy period of recovery. Her full resumption of her work responsibilities was further delayed when she was diagnosed with systemic myasthenia gravis, requiring surgery and another period of recuperation.

With her health restored, Mankiller founded the Community Development Department of the Cherokee Nation in 1981 and then directed it. Through grants, Mankiller obtained money for a number of projects, including rehabilitating housing, installing a sixteen-mile-long water line, and developing Cherokee Gardens, a horticultural operation.

In 1983, Ross Swimmer, the incumbent principal chief of the Cherokee Nation, asked Mankiller to be his running mate for deputy chief in the tribal elections. During the campaign, Mankiller encountered overt sexism that included hate mail, death threats, and having the tires of her car slashed. When the ticket won, she became the first woman to serve as deputy chief of the Cherokee Nation. In 1985, Swimmer left to head the Bureau of Indian Affairs in Washington, D.C., and Mankiller was sworn in as principal chief, becoming the first woman to hold the office.

Mankiller explained the significance of a woman holding the office: "Early historians referred to our government as a petticoat government because of the strong role of the women in the tribe. Then we adopted a lot of ugly things that were part of the non-Indian world and one of those things was sexism. This whole system of tribal government was designed by men. So in 1687 women enjoyed a prominent role, but in 1987 we found people questioning whether women should be in leadership positions in the tribe." Mankiller won the election for a full term in 1987 and re-election in 1991.

As principal chief, Mankiller protected the traditions and heritage of her tribe. While overseeing a budget of $76 million and managing a workforce of almost 1,000 employees, she focused on reducing the unemployment rate, raising education levels, and improving health care in addition to her continuing concerns with economic development. Under her leadership, the tribe built a hydroelectric generating facility; obtained funds to help Cherokee women on welfare become more self-sufficient; and developed plans for a job corps center, an alcohol treatment facility, and new health clinics.

The name *Mankiller* is an old term of respect for Indian warriors who guarded tribal villages and has been in her family for generations. When asked about it, she explained: "Some people do earn their names in native culture. I didn't, but I don't always tell people that. Sometimes I just say that Mankiller is my name, I earned it, and I let 'em wonder." Her memoir, *Mankiller: A Chief and Her People,* was published in 1993.

See also Bonney, Mary Lucinda; Deer, Ada Elizabeth; Jumper, Betty Mae

References H. W. Wilson, *Current Biography Yearbook, 1988* (1988); Mankiller and Wallis, *Mankiller* (1993); *The New York Times,* 15 December 1985, 4 November 1993.

Mankin, Helen Douglas (1894–1956)

Democrat Helen Mankin of Georgia served in the U.S. House of Representatives from 12 February 1946 to 3 January 1947. Mankin entered politics as chief of Georgia's Child Labor Committee, a group that sought to ratify the proposed Child Labor Amendment. After unsuccessfully lobbying the Georgia legislature in 1935, she decided to work on the amendment from inside the legislature and ran for a seat in it, serving from 1937 to 1946. During those years, she worked to repeal the poll tax, change registration laws, improve teachers' salaries, reform prisons, and adopt the secret ballot. She helped pass a bill permitting women to serve on juries and another allowing women to be appointed their children's guardians.

When the incumbent congressman resigned, Mankin won the seat in a special election. In the first election since the end of the poll tax in Georgia, Mankin, who had actively sought the support of African American voters, was quietly endorsed by that community. Her winning margin came from predominantly black precincts. Mankin ran in the July 1946 primary for a full term and won the majority of votes, but the state's county unit system for determining the victor denied her the nomination. She began a write-in campaign, but white supremacy groups intimidated her supporters and she lost the general election. Mankin filed a lawsuit challenging the county unit system. Her case went to the U.S. District Court, which ruled against her in 1950, as did the U.S. Supreme Court. The ruling was reversed in 1962.

Born in Atlanta, Georgia, Helen Mankin earned a bachelor of arts degree from Rockford College in 1917. During World War I, she joined the American Women's Hospital Unit, was attached to the French army, and for thirteen months drove an ambulance in France. She returned to the United States, earned her bachelor of laws degree from Atlanta Law School in 1920, and joined the family law firm.

See also Child Labor Amendment; Congress, Women in; State Legislatures, Women in

References H. W. Wilson, *Current Biography: Who's News and Why, 1946* (1946); Spritzer, *The Belle of Ashby Street* (1982).

Margolies-Mezvinsky, Marjorie (b. 1942)

Democrat Marjorie Margolies-Mezvinsky of Pennsylvania served in the U.S. House of Representatives from 3 January 1993 to 3 January 1995. A group of Democratic women recruited Margolies-Mezvinsky to run in a district that had not elected a Democrat in seventy-six years. Her support for reproductive rights and for more sensitivity for families in the workplace contributed to her success.

As Congress worked its way through Democratic President Bill Clinton's budget in 1993, Margolies-Mezvinsky was the only freshman Democrat who voted against it. She opposed the plan because she thought that it cut too little spending and had too many tax increases. She intended to vote against the conference committee bill reconciling the House and Senate bills because it included essentially the components she had opposed. Observers questioned where President Clinton would get the votes needed to pass the bill, and pressure was placed on Democratic members of Congress to vote for the conference committee bill. Anticipating pressure to vote for it, she considered her options and concluded that if she voted for it, her political career would be over. When President Clinton telephoned Margolies-Mezvinsky just before the House voted on the bill, she told him that she would vote for it only if hers were the deciding vote. At the time she cast her vote, she decided that her vote would end either her political career or the president's. She voted for the conference committee bill. Margolies-Mezvinsky was defeated in her attempt for a second term.

In 1998, Margolies-Mezvinsky founded Women's Campaign International to help female candidates around the world. She explained: "I spend about three months a year traveling sometimes with a team of twenty people. We train women to run for office and get involved in politics."

Born in Philadelphia, Pennsylvania, Margolies-Mezvinsky attended Skidmore College from 1959 to 1961 and received her bachelor of arts degree from the University of Pennsylvania in 1963. A local television reporter in the early 1960s, Margolies-Mezvinsky is also a bestselling author and has won five Emmy Awards. She wrote *They Came to Stay* (1970) about her experience as the first single woman in the United States to adopt a foreign-born child, a Korean. In 1974, she adopted a Vietnamese child.

See also Abortion; Congress, Women in

References Campaigns & Elections, May 2005; *Congressional Quarterly, Politics in America 1994* (1993); Margolies-Mezvinsky, *A Woman's Place… the Freshmen Women Who Changed the Face of Congress* (1994).

Married Women's Property Acts

Until the passage of married women's property acts in the mid–nineteenth century, marriage essentially resulted in a woman's civil death, which included the denial of her right to own property. In 1839, Mississippi became the first state to grant married women the right to own property. The law, like those passed in Maryland in 1843 and Arkansas in 1846, sought to protect family property given to married daughters through gifts or inheritance, but the measures did not expand women's economic autonomy. Their husbands maintained control of the property and any earnings from it.

The first Northern state to pass a married women's property law, Michigan in 1844, established a separate estate for the wife that included personal and real property that she acquired both before and after her marriage. Other states passed more limited acts that protected a wife's real estate from seizure to pay for her husband's debts.

In the late 1830s, Ernestine Rose, a Polish immigrant, began circulating petitions in New York for equal property rights for women. Elizabeth Cady Stanton and other women's rights advocates joined her in circulating petitions, educating the public, and talking to legislators for passage of a bill. In 1848, the State of New York passed a Married Women's Property Act, the broadest of the acts passed by any state at the time. New York's law gave a married woman separate ownership and control of the property she brought into a marriage and any property she inherited after it. Rose and Stanton were joined by Susan B. Anthony in the 1850s in their work to further expand married women's property rights, resulting in the 1860 Married Women's Earning Act, which gave married women ownership of their earnings. Another measure passed that year gave married women a role in determining their children's guardianship, power that husbands had formerly exclusively held. In 1862, the legislature addressed the issue again and generally returned women's legal rights to the status they had been before the 1860 measure.

In the 1840s, Maine, Massachusetts, Iowa, Ohio, Indiana, Vermont, and Rhode Island passed similar legislation. These property rights laws for married women were the primary legal change in women's status in the nineteenth century. Both women's rights activists and those opposed to women's rights supported property reform as a matter of justice. Opponents to women's rights did not anticipate extending the concept of married women's property rights to political or other rights of citizenship. The acts, however, fueled the debate on women's rights.

See also Anthony, Susan Brownell; Coverture; Stanton, Elizabeth Cady; Suffrage

References Matthews, *Women's Struggle for Equality: The First Phase, 1828–1876* (1997).

Martin, Del Taliaferro (b. 1921)

Feminist and lesbian activist Del Martin and her life partner Phyllis Lyon founded Daughters of Bilitis in 1955, the first national lesbian organization, of which she was president from 1957 to 1960. Martin and Lyon also founded the organization's publication, *The Ladder,* which Martin edited from 1960 to 1962. The two women were instrumental in founding the Council on Religion and the Homosexual and both served on its board of directors. Martin and Lyon wrote *Lesbian/Woman* (1972) and *Lesbian Love and Liberation* (1973), two of the earliest books written by and about lesbians. Martin wrote *Battered Wives* in 1977, the first book on domestic violence published in the United States, and became a nationally recognized speaker on the topic. The first openly gay woman to serve on the National Organization for Women's national board of directors, Martin chaired the organization's National Task Force on Battered Women/Household Violence in the 1970s. Martin also was a leader in the campaign calling on the American Psychiatric Association to declare that homosexuality was not a mental illness.

Born in San Francisco, Martin was married to a man for four years. She later changed her first name to Del. Martin studied journalism at the University of California at Berkley and at San Francisco State College.

See also Daughters of Bilitis; Lesbian Rights; Lyon, Phyllis; National Organization for Women

References DeLeon, ed., *Leaders from the 1960s: A Biographical Sourcebook of American Activism* (1994); http://wwwlgbtran.org.

Martin, Judith Lynn Morley (b. 1939)

Republican Lynn Martin of Illinois served in the U.S. House of Representatives from 3 January 1981 to 3 January 1991. She held the leadership position of vice chair of the House Republican Conference in the 99th and 100th Congresses (1985–1989). President George Bush appointed her secretary of labor, a position she held from 1991 to 1993.

Martin entered politics in 1972, when she won a seat on the Winnebago County Board, and served on it until 1977, when she entered the Illinois House of Representatives. Two years later, she won a seat in the state Senate and served until 1981, the year she entered Congress.

A fiscal conservative, Congresswoman Martin supported reproductive rights, equal rights for women, and parental leave. She supported an increase in the minimum wage and voted to override Bush's veto of the bill. After conducting a survey of congressional office employees and staff that demonstrated that women staffers were generally relegated to the lowest positions, Martin unsuccessfully sought to remedy the problem by including congressional employees under the Civil Rights Act of 1964, from which they had been specifically excluded. Martin became the first woman member of the House Republican leadership in 1984, when she won election as vice chair of the House Republican Conference. She made her reputation in Congress as an adroit budget negotiator in 1986, when she was the acting ranking minority member substituting for an ailing congressman. Martin ran unsuccessfully for the U.S. Senate in 1990.

Secretary of the Department of Labor from 1991 to 1995, Martin sought to expand the options for pension portability, to strengthen enforcement of child labor laws and worker safety laws, to end discrimination in the workplace, and to improve job training. With the goal of creating a model workplace, department employees received sexual harassment training and diversity training. The Glass Ceiling Initiative, a program begun by Martin, sought to identify barriers to women's promotion and development within the workplace. The report from the initiative led Congress to establish the Glass Ceiling Commission to examine the issue on a larger scale.

Born in Chicago, Illinois, Lynn Martin earned her bachelor of arts degree from the University of Illinois in 1960. She taught high school English, government, and economics before entering politics.

See also Abortion; Cabinets, Women in Presidential; Civil Rights Act of 1964, Title VII; Congress, Women in; Congressional Workplace Compliance Act of 1995; Equal Rights Amendment; Glass Ceiling Commission; State Legislatures, Women in

References *Congressional Quarterly, Cabinets and Counselors: The President and the Executive Branch* (1997); H. W. Wilson, *Current Biography Yearbook, 1989* (1989).

Martin, Marion E. (1900–1987)

Founder of the National Federation of Republican Women (NFRW), Marion Martin began her work for the Republican National Committee (RNC) in 1936, when she became Republican national committeewoman for Maine as well as assistant chair of the RNC from 1936 to 1946. She served in the Maine legislature from 1931 to 1938, two terms each in the Maine House of Representatives and the Maine Senate.

In her role as assistant chairperson, Martin toured the United States in the fall of 1937 to assess the many independent Republican women's clubs in the country. She concluded that they were "frequently misguided and utterly ineffectual" at supporting the party's candidates and recommended forming a national umbrella organization. She envisioned creating a political machine out of the existing clubs and using them to organize more clubs. To appeal to women, she designed a program that combined social activities with political education, using materials developed in her Washington, D.C., office. She organized the first meeting in 1937, convinced uncertain delegates of the merits of unifying under the NFRW, and officially launched the organization in 1938.

Martin also worked to increase women's visibility in the party, offering party leaders the names of women qualified to hold positions in it. She sought passage of fifty-fifty rules that would require all state and national party committees to have equal numbers of women and men on them. She encouraged the party's leadership to select women for political appointments and to support their candidacies for elected offices.

Born in Kingman, Maine, Martin attended Wellesley College for a year and a half before withdrawing because she had contracted tuberculosis. She received her bachelor of arts degree from the University of Maine in 1935. After leaving the RNC, Martin served as commissioner of labor and industry for the State of Maine.

See also National Federation of Republican Women; Republican Party, Women in the

References *The New York Times,* 11 January 1987; Rymph, "Marion Martin and the Problem of Republican Feminism, 1937–1947" (1996).

Martz, Judy (b. 1943)

Governor of Montana from 2001 to 2005, Republican Judy Martz was the state's first woman to hold the office. Martz served as lieutenant governor from 1997 to 2001. During her term as governor, Martz hosted three summits on health care and one on reducing the production, distribution, and use of methamphetamine. She aso appointed commissions to study taxes, school funding and health care. Her term in office was marred by ethics questions, which were investigated and dismissed. Martz did not seek re-election in 2004.

Born in Big Timber, Montana, Martz was a speed skater on the 1964 U.S. Olympic team.

Reference http://mt.gov/gov2/; http://asp.usatoday.com/news/politicselections/CandidateProfile.aspx?ci=1 778&oi=G

Matalin, Mary Joe (b. 1953)

Republican political consultant and strategist Mary Matalin was political director for President George Bush's unsuccessful 1992 campaign for re-election. Matalin entered politics in 1980 when a former college professor asked her to work with him on a U.S. Senate campaign. Her candidate lost, but she had found a career as a political organizer. She joined the staff of the Republican National Committee (RNC) in 1981 as executive assistant to the party's deputy chairman. Matalin entered law school in 1983 but left a year later and returned to the RNC to run its voter contact program. Appointed chief of staff to the party's co-chairman in 1985, she next joined George Bush's 1988 presidential campaign staff to organize support for him in the Iowa and Michigan caucuses. After Bush won the party's presidential nomination, Matalin managed the party's Victory '88 voter mobilization program. Chief of staff for the RNC's chairperson from 1989 to 1991, she joined the Bush campaign in late 1991 as political director.

During Bush's 1992 campaign for re-election, Matalin attracted press attention for her criticism of Democratic candidate Bill Clinton. Bush had directed his campaign staff to refrain from questioning Clinton's morality, limiting Matalin's ability to accuse Clinton of being morally unfit to be president. She ignored Bush's policy and told a reporter that the Bush campaign had "never said that [Clinton's] a philandering pot-smoking draft dodger." She also issued a press release alleging that Clinton had extramarital relationships and referred to news stories about the relationships as "bimbo eruptions."

Matalin's personal life also attracted press attention because she had a romantic relationship with James Carville, who was chief political director for Clinton. Although their political attacks on each other's candidate and their romance provided sidebars to the campaign, Matalin's loyalty to Bush was unquestioned. The couple married in 1993 and wrote *All's Fair: Love, War, and Running for President* (1994), a memoir of their separate recollections of the 1992 campaign. Matalin was co-host of CNN's *Crossfire*.

An analyst for MSNBC, Matalin initially considered a position in Robert Dole's 1996 campaign, but withdrew over concerns that the MSNBC position could hinder Dole's campaign. Matalin worked in President George W. Bush's 2000 campaign as an adviser. Vice President Dick Cheney named her counselor to the vice president and she also served as assistant to the president from 2001 to 2003. In 2006, Matalin became treasurer for Senator George Allen of Virginia's 2006 re-election campaign. Allen was expected to become a candidate for the Republican nomination for president.

Born in Chicago, Matalin attended Western Illinois University for a year, dropped out and worked at a steel mill, returned to the university, and earned her bachelor of arts degree in 1978. After the 1992 campaign, she was a television talk show co-host and then became a radio talk show host.

See also Republican Party, Women in the

References Collins, "The Fall and Rise of Mary Matalin" (1994); H. W. Wilson, *Current Biography Yearbook, 1996* (1996); *The New York Times*, 21 April 2000; "Office of the Vice President, *National Journal*, 23 June 2001, p. 1898; *Washington Post*, 9 April 2006.

Matsui, Doris Okada (b. 1944)

Democrat Doris Matsui of California entered the U.S. House of Representatives on 8 March 2005. Following the death of her husband, Representative Robert Matsui, Doris Matsui declared her candidacy to succeed him. She is the forty-fifth widow to assume her husband's seat in Congress. Representative Doris Matsui's priorities include federal support for stem cell research and opposition to President George W. Bush's plans to create private accounts within Social Security.

California Representative Doris Matsui meets with local leaders to dicuss preparing students for the workforce, August 2006. (Courtesy Office of Doris Matsui)

Doris Matsui served as one of eight board members of President-Elect Bill Clinton's 1992 presidential transition team, helping develop early policy initiatives and assisting in the formation of his Cabinet. During the Clinton administration, she worked in the White House as deputy assistant to the president and deputy director of public liaison. She left public service in 1998 and joined a law firm as a senior advisor.

Born in Poston Internment camp in Arizona, Matsui grew up in Dinuba, California. She earned a BA degree at the University of California, Berkeley.

References http://matsui.house.gov/aboutdoris.asp; http://www.matsuiforcongress.com/about; *San Francisco Chronicle*, 17 November 2005; *The Desert Sun* (Palm Springs, California), 9 March 2005.

May Bedell, Catherine Dean Barnes (1914–2004)

Republican Catherine May of Washington served in the U.S. House of Representatives from 3 January 1959 to 3 January 1971. Congresswoman May represented a rural district and served on the Agriculture Committee, where she generally supported agricultural producers over consumers. She promoted domestic production of beet sugar, an important industry in her area, and advocated establishing a U.S. world food study and coordinating commission. May was defeated in her attempt for a seventh term. She served on the U.S. International Trade Commission from 1971 to 1981 and was appointed a special consultant to the president on the Fifty States Project in 1982.

Born in Yakima, Washington, May graduated from Yakima Valley Junior College in 1934, received her bachelor of arts degree in 1936, and completed a five-year degree in education in 1937, both from the University of Washington. She studied speech at the University of Southern California in 1939. A high school English teacher from 1937 to 1940, May was a journalist and radio news broadcaster in the 1940s and 1950s. She served in the Washington legislature from 1952 to 1958.

See also Congress, Women in; State Legislatures, Women in

References Office of the Historian, U.S. House of Representatives, *Women in Congress, 1917–1990* (1991).

McCabe, Jewell Jackson (b. 1945)

Jewell Jackson McCabe was chair of the National Coalition of 100 Black Women from 1981 to 1991. An active volunteer for the New York Urban Coalition, the National Association for the Advancement of Colored People, the United Way, and other organizations, McCabe was a member of the New York Coalition of 100 Black Women, founded by her mother, Julia Jackson. In 1978, McCabe became president of the New York Coalition and developed plans to make it a national group. By 1981, she had organized chapters in twenty states, and by 1996, the National Coalition of 100 Black Women had 7,000 members in sixty-two chapters. In 1991, McCabe resigned the presidency of the coalition but remained chair of its board of directors.

Born in Washington, D.C., McCabe attended Bard College from 1963 to 1966. Public relations officer for New York City's Special Services for Children, she became associate public information director for the Women's Division of the Office of the Governor in 1975.

See also National Association for the Advancement of Colored People, Women in the; National Coalition of 100 Black Women

References Mabunda, ed., *Contemporary Black Biography*, Vol. 10 (1996).

McCarthy, Carolyn (b. 1944)

Democrat Carolyn McCarthy of New York entered the U.S. House of Representatives on 3 January 1997 to 3 January 2005. A tragedy launched her political activism. Her husband was killed and her son was injured in the 1993 Long Island Railroad massacre. McCarthy began a public campaign against gun violence, speaking around the country on the causes of violence. In 1994, she asked her congressman to oppose efforts to repeal the ban on assault weapons, but he refused her pleas and supported the repeal. McCarthy challenged him in the next election and won. She believes that providing children with a good education, creating safe and drug-free schools, reducing drug use, creating opportunities to attend college, and creating more job opportunities will reduce violence.

Having had personal experience with dyslexia as a child, McCarthy has worked to obtain increased funding for children with learning disabilities. Congresswoman McCarthy supports health care reform, environmental protection, assistance for crime victims, and tax cuts for working families.

Born in Brooklyn, New York, McCarthy received her degree in licensed practical nursing from Glen Cove Nursing School in 1964. She was a nurse for more than thirty years.

See also Congress, Women in

References *Congressional Quarterly, Politics in America 1998* (1997), *Politics in America 2006* (2005).

McCarthy, Karen (b. 1947)

Democrat Karen McCarthy of Missouri served in the U.S. House of Representatives from 3 January 1995 to 3 January 2005. She supports the balanced budget amendment and welfare reform, although she objected to some provisions of the measure enacted in 1996. She has criticized Republican priorities, saying: "If you are a poor, hungry child in America, then you have to wait in line behind the space station and tax breaks for the wealthy before you can receive a nutritious meal."

She introduced a bill in 2002 to keep independent film production in the United States. It offers tax-incentives to investors, if 95 percent of wages related to the film are earned in this country.

McCarthy's first career was teaching high school English. She served in the Missouri state House of Representatives from 1977 to 1995. In the legislature, she focused on environmental issues, health care, welfare reform, and crime control policy. She was the first woman president of the National Conference of State Legislatures, a position she held in 1994.

Born in Haverhill, Massachusetts, Karen McCarthy received her bachelor of science degree from the University of Kansas in 1969, her master of arts degree from the University of Missouri in 1976, and her master's degree in business administration from the University of Kansas in 1986. She attended the John F. Kennedy School of Government, Harvard University in 1982.

See also Congress, Women in; State Legislatures, Women in

References *Congressional Quarterly, Politics in America 1998* (1997); *Variety*, 12 July 2004.

McCarty v. McCarty (1980)

Richard McCarty was a colonel in the army who had served eighteen of the twenty years required for retirement with pay when he obtained a divorce in California from his wife Patricia McCarty. Under California's dissolution of marriage laws, each partner retains her or his separate property, and community and quasi-community property is equally divided. Richard McCarty wanted the court deciding the dissolution of marriage to confirm that his retirement benefits were his separate property, but the court refused, saying that it was quasi-community property and awarding Patricia McCarty approximately 45 percent of the retirement pay. The U.S. Supreme Court said that retirement pay is the personal entitlement of the retiree and that a state court could not allocate a portion of it to Patricia McCarty because all of it belonged to Richard McCarty. The Court noted that retirement pay was intended to encourage an orderly promotion of younger members by having senior members of the military retire, and without that incentive senior members might stay. In addition, the Court said that Congress had determined the amount necessary for a retired member of the military, and if it were reduced, then the congressional intent could be frustrated.

Congress passed the Uniformed Services Former Spouses' Protection Act in 1982 to overturn the decision. The measure also created a mechanism to assist former spouses in collecting property that the court allocated to them in a divorce.

See also Divorce Law Reform

References *McCarty v. McCarty*, 453 U.S. 210 (1980).

McCollum, Betty (b. 1954)

Democrat Betty McCollum of Minnesota entered the U.S. House of Representatives on 3 January 2001. Congresswoman McCollum became interested in politics after her daughter was hurt on a city park slide and the city did nothing to fix the problem,

Minnesota Congresswoman Betty McCollum hosting a town hall meeting in St. Paul to discuss the future of Social Security, 2005. (Courtesy Office of Betty McCollum)

making her the third woman to enter politics and ultimately serve Congress for that reason. Representative Darlene Hooley (Democrat, Oregon) and Senator Patty Murray (Democrat, Washington) preceded McCollum. McCollum lost her first bid for the city council, but won on her second attempt. She served on the North St. Paul city council from 1987 to 1992. She next served in the Minnesota House of Representatives from 1993 to 2000, where she was an environmental advocate.

As a member of Congress, McCollum has worked for greater leadership by the United States in combating the AIDS pandemic and to reduce poverty and hunger in Africa. She has criticized the federal government's inadequate funding for special education and has introduced legislation to normalize trade relations with Laos, a controversial issue among Hmong people, who argue that the Laotian government is persecuting Hmong people.

Born in Minneapolis, Minnesota, McCollum earned her bachelor's degree from the College of St. Catherine in 1987.

References "Betty McCollum," *Carroll's Federal Directory,* Carroll Publishing, 2005; Congressional Quarterly, Politics in America 2006 (2005). http://minnesota.publicradio.org/collections/special/2004/campaign/conger ss/mccollum/index.php?offset=20; http://www.mccollum.house.gov

McCormack, Ellen (b. 1926)

Motivated to run by her opposition to abortion, homemaker Ellen McCormack ran for the Democratic Party's presidential nomination in 1976. After the State of New York reformed its abortion law in 1970, making it easier to obtain the procedure, McCormack helped organize a pro-life group on Long Island. Four years later, she worked on a pro-life candidate's unsuccessful campaign for the U.S. Senate. As a presidential candidate, McCormack acknowledged that her campaign had only one issue, abortion, and that she entered the race to attract attention to it.

McCormack's campaign became controversial after she applied for matching funds from the Federal Election Commission (FEC). The National Abortion Rights Action League challenged the request, but the FEC approved the application, and McCormack's campaign received more than $200,000 in federal matching funds. McCormack's name was placed in nomination at the 1976 Democratic National Convention, and she received twenty-two delegate votes.

McCormack ran for lieutenant governor of New York in 1978 on the Right to Life ticket, attracting 3 percent of the votes in the general election.

See also Abortion; President and Vice President, Women Candidates for

References *The New York Times*, 9 February 1976; Schoenebaum, ed., *Political Profiles: The Nixon/Ford Years* (1979).

McCormick Simms, Ruth Hanna (1880–1944)

Republican Ruth McCormick of Illinois served in the U.S. House of Representatives from 15 April 1929 to 4 March 1931. In 1930, she entered the Republican primary for the U.S. Senate and won, becoming the first woman nominated by a major party for the Senate. She lost in the general election.

Born in Cleveland, Ohio, Ruth McCormick attended Hathaway School and Miss Porter's School. Despite her family's wishes that she attend college, she became personal secretary to her father, Republican Party leader Marcus Alonzo Hanna, when he became a U.S. senator in 1899. She married Medill McCormick of the *Chicago Tribune* in 1903 and moved to Chicago, where she became involved in women's clubs and the labor reform movement. In 1913, Ruth McCormick chaired the Congressional Committee of the National American Woman Suffrage Association and developed an effective lobbying program for woman suffrage.

McCormick's activism in the Republican Party gained national recognition when she was named chair of the Republican Women's National Executive Committee in 1918 in anticipation of ratification of the Nineteenth Amendment. Appointed an associate member of the Republican National Committee (RNC) from 1919 to 1924, she began working for equal representation of women on RNC committees in 1923. She was elected the first national committeewoman for Illinois in 1924 and served until 1928. Medill McCormick died in 1925.

When Ruth McCormick ran for Congress in 1928, she was her own campaign manager, but she had a man oversee the men's division of her campaign. Most of her campaign support came from the Republican women's clubs that she had worked with for several years. Although surprised by the depth of the resistance to a woman's candidacy, she won both the primary and general elections.

After reapportionment in 1931, it became apparent that the at-large seat she held would be eliminated, and she ran for the U.S. Senate. She won the 1930 Republican primary but lost the general election in that year's Democratic landslide. McCormick married retired Congressman Albert Simms in 1932 and moved with him to New Mexico.

See also Congress, Women in; National American Woman Suffrage Association; Nineteenth Amendment; Republican Party, Women in the; Suffrage

References Miller, *Ruth Hanna McCormick* (1992); Office of the Historian, U.S. House of Representatives, *Women in Congress, 1917–1990* (1991).

McKinney, Cynthia Ann (b. 1955)

Democrat Cynthia McKinney of Georgia served in the U.S. House of Representatives from 3 January 1993 to 3 January 2003. Defeated by Denise Majette in the 2002 primary, McKinney ran for and won her old seat in 2004, when Majette made an unsuccessful run for the U.S. Senate. In 2005, she called for the immediate withdrawal of American troops from Iraq.

McKinney became a candidate following Anita Hill's testimony accusing U.S. Supreme Court nominee Clarence Thomas of sexual harassment. McKinney said that Hill gave her "a moral context" for her decision to run for Congress. Her campaign issues included improving education, health care, and economic development opportunities for poor and disenfranchised people. Her campaign had the usual intensity associated with congressional races, but it also had another factor. Racism and threats of violence made it unsafe for her to enter some parts of the district that she wanted to represent.

In 1995, the U.S. Supreme Court declared Georgia's Eleventh Congressional District, the district McKinney represented, a "racial gerrymander" and ordered that it be redrawn. In 1996, McKinney easily won election from the redrawn district and became the first African American woman to win a congressional seat from a Southern district with a white majority. She introduced legislation permitting states to create multi-member districts. Voters would vote for several seats, an approach she believed would "help heal the racial division created by current legal battles over districts drawn to ensure minorities comprise a majority."

McKinney worked with the Environmental Protection Agency to designate a polluted neighborhood in her district as a "hazard to public health," with the goal of having it restored. She convinced the Department of Justice to help with a fraud investigation of landowners in her district. Some of her other legislative priorities included gift and lobby reform, tax fairness, voting rights, and electoral reform.

In late 2000, McKinney held a press conference announcing her intention to ask the Government Accounting Office to investigate the U.S. military's connections to Burnese sweatshops. She objected to the military selling clothing made in the sweatshops through its stores on military installations. Within hours of the press conference, the Pentagon said it would no longer import clothing from Burma.

Following the September 11, 2001 terrorist attacks, McKinney criticized President George W. Bush, alleging that the administration had not attempted to stop the attacks because the president's friends stood to profit. Congresswoman McKinney was criticized for the comments, as well as for her support of Palestinian causes and her opposition to American sanctions against Iraq before the war in that country.

Born in Atlanta, Georgia, McKinney earned her bachelor of arts degree in international relations from the University of Southern California in 1978, attended Tufts University, and was a diplomatic fellow at Spelman College in 1984. She taught political science at Clark Atlanta University and then at Agnes Scott College.

McKinney ran for the Georgia legislature in 1986 with the encouragement of her father J. E. McKinney, a Georgia state representative. She lost that race but won when she ran again in 1988. From 1989 to 1993, she served in the Georgia House of Representatives, where she focused on civil rights, economic opportunities for businesses owned by women and minorities, environmental justice, and fair reapportionment. She gained national attention when she announced her opposition to the Gulf War on the floor of the Georgia House of Representatives. Two-thirds of the members left the chamber during her speech, but her father listened and defended her.

> **See also** Congress, Women in; Hill, Anita Faye; Sexual Harassment; State Legislatures, Women in

> **References** Bingham, *Women on the Hill: Challenging the Culture of Congress* (1997); *Congressional Quarterly, Politics in America 1994* (1993), *Politics in America 1998* (1997), *Politics in America 2006* (2005); Gill, *African American Women in Congress* (1997); *The New York Times*, 11 April 2004; Matthew Rothschild, "Closed Down in Burma," *The Progressive*, February 2001, p. 31.

McLaughlin, Ann Dore Lauenstein (b. 1941)

Ann McLaughlin served as U.S. secretary of labor from 1987 to 1989. As secretary of labor, McLaughlin focused attention on gaps in child care services, established the first blue-ribbon commission to address workforce competitiveness issues, and stressed economic growth to enhance the welfare of U.S. workers. She helped negotiate a bill requiring companies planning large employee layoffs to provide sixty days' notice and another measure limiting employers' use of polygraph tests. She addressed issues related to drugs in the workplace, unemployment insurance, apprenticeship training, older workers, and labor market shortages.

Born in Chatham, New Jersey, McLaughlin studied at Marymount College from 1959 to 1961, studied at the University of London from 1961 to 1962, received her bachelor of arts degree from Marymount College in 1963, and did postgraduate work at the Wharton School in 1987. A supervisor of network commercial scheduling for the American Broadcasting Company in New York from 1963 to 1966, she returned to Marymount College in 1966 to become the college's director of alumnae relations. In 1969, she became an advertising account executive with a public relations firm. She joined the Committee to Re-elect the President in 1971, and following Richard Nixon's re-election she worked on the Presidential Inaugural Committee. Director of public affairs for the Environmental Protection Agency in 1973, she left office in August 1974 when Nixon resigned the presidency.

McLaughlin returned to government service from 1981 to 1984 as an assistant secretary at the Department of the Treasury. McLaughlin moved to the Department of the Interior, where she served until 1987.

> **See also** Cabinets, Women in Presidential

References H. W. Wilson, *Current Biography Yearbook, 1988* (1988).

McMillan, Clara Gooding (1894–1976)

Democrat Clara McMillan of South Carolina served in the U.S. House of Representatives from 7 November 1939 to 3 January 1941. McMillan filled the vacancy created by her husband's death but declined to run for a full term. After her brief tenure in Congress, McMillan held positions in the National Youth Administration, the Office of War Information, and the Department of State. She retired in 1957.

Born in Brunson, South Carolina, Clara McMillan attended the Confederate Home College and Flora MacDonald College.

See also Congress, Women in

References Office of the Historian, U.S. House of Representatives, *Women in Congress, 1917–1990* (1991).

McMorris, Cathy (b. 1969)

Republican Cathy McMorris of Washington entered the U.S. House of Representatives on 3 January 2005. Congresswoman McMorris's priorities include identifying economic opportunities for her district, improving access to quality health care, developing an affordable health care program, and keeping cities and the nation safe. She supports limiting medical malpractice lawsuits and limiting the amount that juries can award for pain and suffering. Increasing Medicaid reimbursement rates for rural hospitals is another priority. McMorris served in the Washington House of Representatives from 1994 to 2004 and was minority leader from 2002 to 2003.

Born in Salem, Oregon, McMorris earned a bachelor of arts degree at Pensacola Christian College in 1990 and a master's of business administration at the University of Washington in 2002.

References Congressional Quarterly, *Politics in America 2006* (2005); http://www.mcmorris.house.gov

Washington Representative Cathy McMorris hosting a Homeland Security Roundtable with Washington Congressman Dave Reichert, May 2006 (Courtesy Office of Cathy McMorris)

Meek, Carrie Pittman (b. 1926)

Democrat Carrie P. Meek of Florida served in the U.S. House of Representatives from 3 January 1993 to 3 January 2003. She did not run for re-election in 2002; her son Kendrick Meek succeeded her in office. Congresswoman Meek was a leader in efforts to obtain an accurate count in the year 2000 national census. Arguing that the 1990 decennial census failed to count about four million people, she introduced a bill permitting the Census Bureau to hire low-income residents in particular neighborhoods to count the people in that area, which would have neighbors counting neighbors and presumably would lead to a more accurate count. Another part of the bill would restrict the amount of sampling that could be done, again in an effort to gain a more accurate census.

As her district attempted to recover from the devastation of Hurricane Andrew in 1992, Congresswoman Meek worked to obtain more than $100 million in federal assistance to help rebuild Dade County. In another area of particular interest to her district, Meek passed and President Bill Clinton signed in 1998 a measure making 50,000 Haitian immigrants eligible for green cards (lawful permanent residency). The law "shows that the cry for justice of Haitians in this country is real and cannot be ignored," Meek said.

When Congress considered raising the annual pay level at which employees participated in Social Security from $50 a year to a higher level, Meek entered the debate. Noting that she, her mother, her sister, and her neighbors had done domestic work, she explained: "Families that employed [domestics] would express much affection and gratitude towards them, but they did nothing for their employees' future economic security." She recommended that the level should be $300 annual pay, but $1,000 was the level in the bill that passed.

In 1995, Meek criticized Republican attempts to cut Head Start funding, arguing: "It is one of the few programs, federal programs, which has succeeded over the years. But now to cut it is a dangerous thing, because what we are doing on one hand is giving a big tax cut to the rich and we are cutting off at the pass these poor children who need Head Start." She also fought efforts to reduce the growth of Medicaid and to end sugar price supports (sugar is a major Florida commodity). Meek has obtained appropriations for a marine research center at the University of Miami and for a medical training facility at Homestead Air Force Base.

Born in Tallahassee, Florida, Carrie Meek is the granddaughter of slaves. As a child she was a domestic worker. She earned her bachelor of arts degree from Florida A&M University in 1946, and her master of science degree from the University of Michigan in 1948. She completed the course work for a doctorate in 1979 but has not written a dissertation.

A women's basketball coach at Bethune-Cookman College from 1949 to 1958, she worked with Mary McLeod Bethune, who greatly influenced her. Meek also taught biological sciences and physical education there and at Florida A&M University from 1958 to 1961. Associate dean of Miami Dade Community College from 1968 to 1979, she was special assistant to the school's vice president from 1979 to 1982.

Meek served in the Florida House of Representatives from 1979 to 1983 and the Florida Senate from 1983 to 1993. As a state legislator, Meek developed much of the state's housing finance policy, including legislation that helped working-class people own their homes and another measure that assisted with the construction of affordable rental units.

See also Bethune, Mary Jane McLeod; Congress, Women in; State Legislatures, Women in

References *Congressional Quarterly, Politics in America 1994* (1993); National Women's Political Caucus, *National Directory of Women Elected Officials 1995* (1995); "Rep. Carrie Meek Wins Approval of Bill to Help Haitian Immigrants," *Jet*, 30 November 1998, p. 8; www.house.gov/meek/bio.htm.

Meissner, Doris Marie (b. 1941)

Doris Meissner served as commissioner of the Immigration and Naturalization Service (INS) from 1993 to 2000. During her tenure, she improved the professionalism at the INS, reduced the amount of time required for naturalization, and oversaw the doubling of the number of INS employees. She began her political career in 1971 as a founding member and the first executive chair of the National Women's Political Caucus (NWPC). During the 1972 Democratic and Republican National Conventions, she and groups of volunteers worked to change party rules to mandate larger roles for women in the parties. A White House fellow and special assistant to the attorney general from 1973 to 1974, she was assistant director of the Office of Policy and Planning in 1975. Executive director of the Cabinet Committee on Illegal Aliens in 1976 and deputy associate attorney general from 1977 to 1980, she was acting commissioner of the INS in 1981 and executive associate commissioner from 1982 to 1985.

Born in Milwaukee, Wisconsin, Doris Meissner earned her bachelor of arts degree in 1963 and her master of arts degree in 1969 from the University of Wisconsin. The daughter of German immigrants, Meissner grew up during World War II amid the xenophobia of the time, especially toward Germans. As her career in immigration developed, she understood and sympathized with the fears and anxieties that many immigrants experience.

See also Democratic Party, Women in the; National Women's Political Caucus; Republican Party, Women in the

References *The New York Times*, 20 June 1993; *Washington Post*, 20 November 2000.

Meritor Savings Bank v. Vinson (1986)

In *Meritor Savings Bank v. Vinson,* the U.S. Supreme Court agreed with the Equal Employment Opportunity Commission that workplace sexual harassment is illegal and that a hostile or abusive work environment violates Title VII of the Civil Rights Act of 1964.

Mechelle Vinson worked for Meritor Savings Bank, beginning as a teller in 1974 and gaining promotions to the position of assistant branch manager at the time she was dismissed in 1978 for excessive use of sick leave. She filed suit against her supervisor, accusing him of sexually harassing her from 1974 to 1977, repeatedly demanding sexual intercourse, fondling her in front of other employees, exposing himself to her, and raping her. In addition, after refusing him several times, she had sexual intercourse with him, events that she did not describe as rape. Vinson did not report the harassment because she feared her supervisor and would have had to make the report to him.

Before *Meritor,* only sexual harassment that included an economic threat (quid pro quo), such as loss of employment or employment benefits, had been recognized, but after *Meritor,* a hostile work environment became the second classification under which action could be taken. Because hostile work environment harassment is the more common type of harassment, the Court's decision provides working women with another avenue for litigation. The decision also stated that compliance with sexual demands does not necessarily mean that sexual harassment did not occur, but it did state that the woman's dress and speech could be admitted as evidence.

See also Civil Rights Act of 1964, Title VII; Employment Discrimination; Equal Employment Opportunity Commission; Sexual Harassment

References Fallon, "Sexual Harassment" (1995); Hoff, *Law, Gender, and Injustice* (1991); *Meritor Savings Bank v. Vinson,* 477 U.S. 57 (1986).

Meyers, Jan (b. 1928)

Republican Jan Meyers of Kansas served in the U.S. House of Representatives from 3 January 1985 to 3 January 1997. President of the Shawnee Mission League of Women Voters from 1961 to 1965, Meyers entered elective politics when she ran for the Overland Park City Council, beginning her tenure in 1967 and serving as president from 1970 to 1972. She served in the Kansas Senate from 1972 to 1984. As a member of Congress, Meyers passed a bill to study improvements in firefighter safety and obtained funding for a federal building and courthouse in Kansas City, Kansas. An unsuccessful candidate in the 1978 Kansas Republican House primary (she lost to Nancy Kassebaum), she won an open seat in the House in 1984. Meyers chaired the House Committee on Small Business in the 104th Congress (1995–1997). Her priorities included family planning, health care, welfare reform, budget reform, drug abuse prevention, and energy conservation. Meyers retired in 1997.

Born in Lincoln, Nebraska, Jan Meyers earned her associate of fine arts degree from William Woods College in 1948 and her bachelor of arts from the University of Nebraska in 1951.

See also Congress, Women in; State Legislatures, Women in

References *Congressional Quarterly, Politics in America 1994* (1993).

Meyner, Helen Day Stevenson (1929–1997)

Democrat Helen Meyner of New Jersey served in the U.S. House of Representatives from 3 January 1975 to 3 January 1979. When the Democratic candidate for Congress was disqualified in 1972, women leaders in the Democratic Party recruited Meyner as a last-minute replacement. She accepted the challenge but lost in a close race. She ran again in 1974 and was successful. In Congress, Meyner was committed to peace issues and proposed establishing a national academy of peace and conflict resolution. She was instrumental in keeping open the Army's Picatinny Arsenal in her district by having the Armament Research and Development Command transferred there. She also sought to reduce defense spending. She worked for the Equal Rights Amendment and for appropriations for the National Women's Conference. Meyner was defeated in her attempt for a third term.

Born in New York, New York, Helen Meyner earned her bachelor of arts degree from Colorado College in 1950. An American Red Cross field-worker in Korea from 1950 to 1952, she was a guide at the United Nations from 1952 to 1953 and an airline consumer adviser from 1953 to 1956. She was a special assistant to Adlai Stevenson during his 1956 presidential campaign. In 1957, she married New Jersey Governor Robert Meyner. Helen Meyner wrote a twice-weekly newspaper column from 1957 to 1969, conducted a television interview program from 1965 to 1968, and was an active volunteer in the community.

See also Congress, Women in; Equal Rights Amendment; National Women's Conference

References *The New York Times,* 3 November 1997; Office of the Historian, U.S. House of Representatives, *Women in Congress, 1917–1990* (1991); Tomlinson, "Making Their Way" (1996).

RU-486 (Mifepristone)

Fomerly known as RU-486, mifepristone is a nonsurgical abortion pharmaceutical developed by a French company in 1980. Used in Great Britain, France, and Sweden, it was banned for personal use in the United States in 1989 at the urging of pro-life groups and pro-life members of Congress. Studies of it proceeded in the United States, however, and researchers concluded that it was a safe and effective emergency contraceptive and also useful as a method for early abortions. Scientists also encouraged further research on mifepristone as a possible treatment for endometriosis, some types of breast cancer, uterine fibroids, and other medical conditions. In 1995, the pharmaceutical company that developed mifepristone donated the U.S. patent rights for the drug to the Population Council, which began clinical trials. In 1996, the Food and Drug Administration gave limited approval for the use of the product, but in 1997 the drug manufacturer ended its relationship with the Population Council. In 2000, mifepristone became available under the name Mifeprex.

See also Abortion
References http://www.naral.org.

Mikulski, Barbara Ann (b. 1936)

Democrat Barbara Mikulski of Maryland served in the U.S. House of Representatives from 3 January 1977 to 3 January 1987. She entered the U.S. Senate on 6 January 1987 and is the senior woman in it. A social worker for a local Catholic Charities organization and for the Baltimore City Welfare Department, Mikulski entered politics at the grassroots level. She once said: "When I was a social worker, I wanted to help people, but it was difficult to do because I didn't have all of the resources I wanted. Now, I am a social worker with power." A proposal for a highway that would have gone through historic Fells Point of Baltimore, cutting through the city's first black home-ownership neighborhood, prompted Mikulski to organize her neighbors to stop it. The network of community groups succeeded and at the same time provided Mikulski with a political base when she ran for the city council. Mikulski served on the Baltimore City

Council from 1971 to 1977. During those years, she gained increasing visibility and power within the Democratic Party, especially as chair of the Commission on Delegate Selection and Party Organization in 1973.

As a member of the U.S. House and the Senate, Mikulski has been a strong advocate for women's issues, including the Equal Rights Amendment and reproductive rights. She has worked for investigations of sexual harassment, encouraged federal agencies to develop personnel policies on discrimination and sexual harassment, promoted the implementation of a comprehensive women's health package, and argued for increased funding for breast and cervical cancer screening. She has fought domestic violence by supporting the Violence Against Women Act. She wrote the Spousal Anti-Impoverishment Act to protect older Americans from bankruptcy to pay for a spouse's nursing home care and the law requiring federal standards for mammograms.

Mikulski has worked to maintain funding for NASA's space station, a source of thousands of jobs in Maryland, and has argued that medical research with life-saving possibilities could be performed on the station. An author of the 1984 Child Abuse Act and an advocate for unisex insurance rates, Mikulski also focuses on education, aging, health insurance, the National Service Program, the rights of working people, and job creation. She has worked to expand math and science educational opportunities.

Noted for her sense of humor, Mikulski once described the challenges of being a political woman, saying: "If you're married, you're neglecting him; if you're single, you couldn't get him; if you're divorced, you couldn't keep him; and if you're widowed, you killed him!" On another occasion, she said: "Some women stare out the window waiting for Prince Charming. I stare out the window waiting for more women senators!" She held the leadership positions of assistant Senate Democratic floor leader in the 103rd Congress (1993–1995) and secretary of the Senate Democratic Conference in the 104th through 108th Congresses (1995–2005).

Born in Baltimore, Maryland, Barbara Mikulski received her bachelor of arts degree from Mount Saint Agnes College in 1958 and her master's degree in social work from the University of Maryland in 1965.

See also Abortion; Congress, Women in; Equal Rights Amendment; Sexual Harassment; Violence Against Women Act of 1994; Women's Health Equity Act

References Boxer, *Strangers in the Senate* (1994); *Congressional Quarterly, Politics in America 1994* (1993), *Politics in America 2004* (2003); H. W. Wilson, *Current Biography Yearbook, 1985* (1985); http://mikulski.senate.gov.

Military, Women in the

Women have fought in combat since the Revolutionary War, but it was through their services as nurses that women began to be integrated into the military. During the Civil War, Dorothea Dix recruited and trained 6,000 nurses to serve with the Union Army, but they were not a continuing part of the military organization. The military appointed women to serve as civilian nurses during the Spanish-American War, but they were not uniformed members of the military. Congress created the Army Nurse Corps in 1901 and the Navy Nurse Corps in 1908, but they had no military rank, retirement, or veterans' benefits.

Women's roles expanded in 1917 during World War I, when the Navy enrolled women in the Naval Coastal Defense Reserve with the rank of yeoman to provide combat support as clerks, draftsmen, fingerprint experts, translators, and similar positions. The Marine Corps followed suit in 1918. For the first time, women held full military rank and status, received the same pay as men, wore uniforms, and had the other benefits and obligations that their male counterparts had. The Army employed women as civilians to perform comparable tasks, and the Army Nurse Corps continued to have its auxiliary status. When the war ended, all women in the armed forces were discharged except those in the nursing auxiliaries.

With the advent of World War II and the personnel shortages that accompanied it, Congresswoman Edith Nourse Rogers (R-MA) passed legislation creating the Women's Army Auxiliary Corps (WAAC) in 1942. The auxiliary structure did not provide women the same legal protection men had, nor did they receive the same benefits as men if they were injured, have military rank, or receive equal pay. In 1943, the Women's Army Corps (WAC) replaced the WAAC, and women gained full military status. In 1942, Congress created the Navy Women's Reserve (also known as Women Accepted for Voluntary Emergency Service, or WAVES), the Marine Corps Women's Reserve (Women Marines), and the U.S. Coast Guard Women's Reserve (SPARS, from the Coast Guard motto "Semper Paratus—Always Ready"). When the Air Force became a separate branch of the military after World War II, it created Women in the Air Force (WAF).

Congress integrated women into the armed forces in 1948 but banned them from combat planes and ships, limited them to no more than 2 percent of personnel in any one service, and made lieutenant colonel or Navy commander the highest rank they could hold. In addition, if they became pregnant, adopted children, or married someone with children, they were automatically discharged.

Personnel shortages during the Korean War prompted the establishment of the Defense Advisory Committee on Women in the Services (DACOWITS) in 1951. Initially a public relations group of fifty women, DACOWITS has evolved into an advocacy group for women in the military, playing a key role in passing the Women Officers Act of 1967. The act permitted women to hold the ranks of general and admiral. The measure also removed the 2 percent limit on women's participation in the military, but it gave each of the branches of the military the authority to establish its own limit and effectively the limit remained.

In the 1970s, all of the services allowed pregnant women to stay in the military, required the military academies to accept women, and permitted women to serve on all noncombat Navy ships and to serve temporary duty on warships not on combat missions. In addition, the U.S. Supreme Court decided in *Frontiero v. Richardson* (1973) that the dependents of women in the military are eligible for the same benefits as the dependents of men in the military.

Through the 1980s and 1990s, the military opened almost every job to women except ground combat and service on submarines. Women, however, cite their exclusion from combat as a barrier to gaining full equality and respect. Retired Air Force Major General Jeanne Holm wrote that the bans on women's participation in combat "automatically excluded [them] from participation in the primary mission of the armed forces, and their second-class status was thus assured." In 1993, Congress repealed legislation that had prevented women from serving on combat ships and the secretary of defense ordered the military services to allow women aviators to compete for assignments as combat pilots. Both the Navy and the Air Force had women pilots trained for combat at the time, but the Army and the Marines did not have women pilots with comparable training.

Sexual harassment has been recognized as a problem at least since the 1970s, when DACOWITS members became aware of it. In 1980, a naval officer was court-martialed for sexual harassment, but it was the Tailhook scandal that brought national attention to the problem. In 1991, during the Tailhook Association's convention at a Las Vegas hotel, 117 officers were participants, observers, or aware of incidents of sexual assault, indecent exposure, conduct unbecoming an officer, and failure to provide proper leadership. A Pentagon report on the event said that 83 women and 7 men had been subjected to assault during the convention. In 1996, the Army revealed that a captain and two sergeants training auto mechanics at Aberdeen Proving Ground in Maryland had coerced young recruits into having sex. One sergeant was convicted of rape and sent to prison, and twelve others were relieved of their duties. U.S. Senator Olympia Snowe (R-ME) said that "women in the armed services today deserve to know right now that this problem is going to be taken care of" and that sexual harassment in the military "is absolutely a failure of leadership." Scandals at other bases continued to be revealed as Congress and the military sought to find ways to end sexual harassment.

In 2006, Congress continued to refuse to allow women in combat, passing a measure requiring the department of defense to file a notice with Congress before opening new positions to women and observe a thirty-day waiting period. The military and some members of Congress object to the policies, saying that it makes it difficult for women to integrate themselves into mostly male military units. Tens of thousands of women served in Afghanistan and Iraq. In 2006, women comprised about 15 percent of the active-duty members of the military.

See also Dix, Dorothea Lynde; Rogers, Edith Frances Nourse; Schroeder, Patricia Nell Scott; Sexual Harassment; Snowe, Olympia Jean Bouchles

References *Congressional Quarterly Almanac, 103rd Congress, 1st Session . . . 1993* (1994); Devilbiss, *Women and Military Service: A History, Analysis, and Overview of Key Issues* (1990); Franke, *Ground Zero: The Gender Wars in the Military* (1997); Freeman, "Women and Public Policy: An Overview" (1982); Gruenwald, "Women in the Military: Mission in Progress" (1997); *Washington Post,* 27 February 2006.

Millender-McDonald, Juanita (b. 1938)

Democrat Juanita Millender-McDonald of California entered the U.S. House of Representatives on 26 March 1996. She began her political career as a member of the Carson City Council, where she served from 1990 to 1992. From 1993 to 1996, she served in the California legislature. She ran for Congress after the incumbent was convicted of extortion and tax evasion and resigned from office in December 1995. An African American, Congresswoman Millender-McDonald has introduced legislation to create a select congressional committee to investigate allegations that the Central Intelligence Agency was involved in cocaine trafficking in inner-city neighborhoods. She supports abortion rights, bilingual education, and job training. Her work also includes legislation to increase diabetes research in minority and female populations, preserve records of former African American slaves, and end the sale of alcohol to minors over the Internet.

During the 107th Congress (2001–2003), she co-chaired the Congressional Caucus for Women's Issues. She has worked to increase Small Business Administration funding for women's business centers and worked to assure that women have equal access to federal vocational education funds.

Following the September 11, 2001 terrorist attacks, Millender-McDonald has sought to increase transportation security. She introduced bills to increase maritime security projects and to mandate the use of explosive-proof containers.

Born in Birmingham, Alabama, Millender-McDonald earned her bachelor of science degree from the University of Redlands in 1981, her master of arts degree from California State University in 1988, and also attended the University of Southern California.

See also Abortion; Congress, Women in; State Legislatures, Women in

References *Congressional Quarterly, Politics in America 1998* (1997), *Politics in America 2006* (2005); http://house.gov/Millender-mcdonald

Miller, Candice S. (b. 1954)

Republican Candice Miller of Michigan entered the U.S. House of Representatives on 3 January 2003. Miller's political career began in 1979, when she served as a trustee for the Harrison Township Board for two years. Harrison Township supervisor from 1980 to 1992, Miller next served as treasurer for Macomb County, Michigan, from 1992 to 1994. As Michigan secretary of state from 1994 to 2002, Miller increased the number of registered organ donors, reformed the state's voter file, and developed a model program for interactive services with the Michigan department of state via the Internet.

Congresswoman Miller supports a constitutional amendment that would limit the classification of people counted in the decennial census to citizens, instead of counting every person living in the country.

Miller first ran for Congress in 1986, losing to incumbent David Bonior.

Born in Detroit, Michigan, Miller attended Macomb County Community College and Northwood Institute for Business Management.

References *Detroit Free Press*, 14 December 2005; Crain's Detroit Business, 7 June 1999; http://candicemiller.house.gov

Miller, Laura (b. 1958)

Mayor of Dallas, Texas, since 2002, Laura Miller led the effort to provide housing and other needs to Hurricane Katrina (2005) evacuees relocated to her city. In partnership with Dallas's religious community, Miller raised $2.7 million in private funds that paid for rent, utilities, and furniture. In other areas, Miller led the revitalization of the Dallas downtown area, worked with the city council to pass an anti-discrimination ordinance and banned smoking in restaurants, and developed a plan to reduce homelessness.

A journalist before entering politics, Miller primarily covered city hall. In 1998, she wrote that she was "tired of watching a small number of overly influential people manipulate the system to their own advantage" and announced her candidacy for the city council, where she served until her election as mayor.

Born in Baltimore, Maryland, Miller graduated from the University of Wisconsin-Madison.

References: http://www.dallascityhall.com/pdf/mcc/LauraMillerBiography.p df; Ana Mantica, "The Ultimate City Hall Beat," *Editor & Publisher*, 28 January 2002, p. 25.

Millett, Katherine (Kate) Murray (b. 1934)

Author of *Sexual Politics* (1970), Kate Millett developed the first feminist theories on the origins of the patriarchy. A pioneer in feminist criticism, she linked literature to larger trends in society, politics, and culture. Millett became a national figure in 1970 with the publication of *Sexual Politics*, in which she used literature as the basis for her examination of gender roles and patriarchy in society. Millett argued that gender is a function of social construction rather than biological differences and provided one of the first feminist examinations of patriarchy. She described men's power over others as the last caste system and a remnant of feudalism, calling chivalry a substitute for respect and equal rights for women. The celebrity that accompanied the success of *Sexual Politics* led to a public confrontation in which Millett, a married woman, was forced to declare herself a lesbian. The event marked the first public confrontation between feminism and lesbianism, and *Time* magazine made it a cover story. Ti-Grace Atkinson, Gloria Steinem, Florynce Kennedy, and other feminists rallied to Millett's support and held a "Kate Is Great" press conference.

Born in St. Paul, Minnesota, Millett earned her bachelor of arts degree from the University of Minnesota in 1956, studied at St. Hilda's College at Oxford University in England in 1958, and received her doctorate from Columbia University in 1970. After studying in England, Millett held a variety of jobs to support herself as she worked to

Kate Millett, famous for her book Sexual Politics (1970), which analyzed the effects of the patriarchy on women's status.

develop her skills as an artist. Her silkscreen prints and sculptures have been exhibited in galleries on both the East and West Coasts and in Germany.

Millett's other written works include *The Prostitution Papers* (1973), *Flying* (1974), *Going to Iran* (1980), *The Loony Bin Trip* (1990), and *$A.D.$* (1995).

See also Atkinson, Ti-Grace; Kennedy, Florynce Rae; Lesbian Rights; Steinem, Gloria Marie

References H. W. Wilson, *Current Biography Yearbook, 1995* (1995); Linden-Ward and Green, *American Women in the 1960s: Changing the Future* (1993).

Mink, Patsy Matsu Takemoto (1927–2002)

Democrat Patsy Mink of Hawaii served in the U.S. House of Representatives from 3 January 1965 to 3 January 1977 and served again in the House from 22 September 1990 to 28 September 2002. She was the first non-Caucasian woman elected to Congress. She unsuccessfully sought the Democratic nomination for president in 1972. In the 1960s and 1970s, she concentrated on education, a bill to construct schools in the U.S. Pacific territories, a measure to expand the federal student loan program, and another to help teachers pursue advanced degrees or take refresher courses. She passed a measure to create an economic development program and remove inequities against Pacific Islanders in the Immigration and Nationality Act. After unsuccessfully seeking the Democratic nomination for the U.S. Senate in 1976, she was assistant secretary of state for oceans and international environmental and scientific affairs from 1977 to 1978 and president of Americans for Democratic Action from 1978 to 1981. She served on the Honolulu City Council from 1983 to 1987.

When the incumbent member of Congress resigned in 1990, Mink won his seat in a special election. In 1995 Mink described her experience as an involuntary and unknowing subject in an experiment to determine the effectiveness of diethylstilbestrol

Representative Patsy Mink the first non-white woman to serve in Congress.

(DES) in preventing miscarriages. While pregnant with her daughter in 1951, she had been given DES even though she was not at risk for miscarriage. Because of the drug, her adult daughter has dealt with repeated occurrences of a precancerous condition. In 1978, Mink and other women sued the manufacturer and won a settlement. Their daughters also sued, but because they did not have cancer at the time, they did not receive an award. Congresswoman Mink's revelation of her experience with DES provides an example of ways that women bring an additional perspective to policy debates.

Mink sponsored the Family Stability and Work Act in 1995 as an alternative welfare reform bill. It emphasized combining monetary assistance with job training, job search assistance, and child care. In presenting the bill, Mink said: "Best of all it demeans no one because they are poor, and it protects children and legal aliens by refusing to segregate their rights and privileges because of status, and assures eligibility of federal support while allowing maximum flexibility to the states to provide for jobs, job training, and child care." She worked for the Family and Medical Leave Act of 1993 and worked for increased funding for ovarian cancer research, educational equity for girls and women, and the expansion of Head Start.

Congresswoman Mink died while in office. A candidate for the 108th Congress, she was posthumously elected to it in 2002.

Born in Paia, Hawaii, Patsy Mink attended Wilson College in 1946 and the University of Nebraska in 1948, earned her bachelor's degree in zoology and chemistry from the University of Hawaii in 1948, and received her law degree from the University of Chicago in 1951.

She went into private law practice in Hawaii and lectured on business law at the University of Hawaii from 1952 to 1956 and from 1959 to 1962. She was attorney for the Hawaii House of Representatives in 1955. Mink served in the Territory of Hawaii House of Representatives from 1956 to 1958, the Territorial Senate from 1958 to 1959, and the Hawaii state Senate from 1963 to 1964.

> **See also** Congress, Women in; Family and Medical Leave Act of 1993; State Legislatures , Women in
>
> **References** *Congressional Quarterly, Politics in America 1994* (1993), *Politics in America 2002* (2003); *Congressional Record,* 24 March 1995; H. W. Wilson, *Current Biography Yearbook, 1968* (1968); Office of the Historian, U.S. House of Representatives, *Women in Congress, 1917–1990* (1991).
>
> **Document** Patsy Mink, "Seeking a Link with the Past," 1971

Minner, Ruth Ann Coverdale (b. 1935)

The first female governor of Delaware, Ruth Ann Minner dropped out of high school when she was 16 to help support her parents and siblings. She married when she was 17. Her introduction to politics came through a part-time job in the Delaware House of Representatives. Her husband died when she was 32, leaving her with three children to support. She took a job with a crop reporting service and attended classes to obtain a GED.

She intended to become a classroom teacher, but in 1973 took a job as the receptionist for Delaware's governor. Her grasp of issues prompted the state Democratic party to convince her to run for an open legislative seat the next year. Minner served in the state House from 1974 to 1982 and in the state Senate from 1982 to 1992. As a member of the legislature, Minner passed a measure that funded purchases of green space, and built walkways and bike trails. She also passed laws that established educational courses against drunk driving, instituted campaign finance reform, and established income tax credits for child care expenses.

Lieutenant governor from 1992 to 2000, Minner worked with the state's governor to reorganize state government and to stimulate economic development. Elected governor in 2000, Minner developed programs for technical education and created the Livable Delaware Advisory Council to encourage city planning.

References *Bond Buyer,* 9 March 2001 ; *Delaware State News,* 24 December 2005; Elaine Stuart, "From Dropout to Doer," *State Government News,* January 1995, p. 38.

Minor v. Happersett (1875)

In *Minor v. Happersett,* Virginia Minor attempted to gain suffrage rights by arguing that the State of Missouri had violated her First, Thirteenth, and Fourteenth Amendment rights when it prohibited her from registering to vote in 1872. The U.S. Supreme Court found that the U.S. Constitution does not grant the right of suffrage to anyone and the states' decisions to limit voting to men were not unconstitutional.

Minor contended that the First Amendment provided voting rights as a form of free expression, that under the Thirteenth Amendment being denied the vote was a form of involuntary servitude, and that the Fourteenth Amendment made voting for federal officials a privilege of citizenship. The U.S. Supreme Court refused to consider the first two arguments and focused on the Fourteenth Amendment argument. Although agreeing that women were citizens and that women were persons because they were counted as part of the total population, the Court found that the Fourteenth Amendment did not add to the privileges and immunities of citizens but only added a guaranty of protection for those already in place. In addition, the Court noted that for ninety years, citizenship had been conferred without the right of suffrage and that historically women were a special category of citizens and their inability to vote did not infringe on their rights as citizens.

See also Suffrage

References Sachs and Wilson, *Sexism and the Law* (1978).

Mississippi University for Women v. Hogan (1982)

In *Mississippi University for Women v. Hogan,* the question was whether a state law excluding men from a state-supported professional nursing school violated the equal protection clause of the Fourteenth Amendment. In 1979, Joe Hogan applied for admission to Mississippi University for Women School of Nursing's baccalaureate program, and even though he was qualified, the school denied him admission because of his sex. The U.S. Supreme Court said that denying qualified males the right to enroll violated the equal protection clause of the Fourteenth Amendment.

See also Fourteenth Amendment

References *Mississippi University for Women v. Hogan,* 458 U.S. 718 (1982).

Mofford, Rose Perica (b. 1922)

Democrat Rose Mofford served as governor of Arizona from 5 April 1988 to 6 March 1991. Mofford became governor through the state's constitutional provision for filling the governor's office if the incumbent governor vacates the office: the secretary of state becomes governor. In February 1988, Arizona Governor Evan Mecham was impeached by the state House of Representatives for high crimes, misdemeanors, and malfeasance in office. From that day until the state Senate convicted Mecham on 4 April 1988, Mofford served as acting governor. With Mecham's conviction, Mofford became governor. She saw helping to heal the trauma of the Mecham years and returning public trust to the governor's office as her primary goals. She became known as the grandmother of Arizona.

During her tenure, Mofford became the subject of an investigation regarding her investments, loans, and related financial matters and was cleared of any wrongdoing. Deeper criticism resulted from her commutation of the sentences of two murderers without knowing the full circumstances. She reversed the orders, but she suffered politically. In 1990, Mofford announced her plans to retire.

Born in Globe, Arizona, Mofford attended Lams Business College and Phoenix College and graduated from U.S. Industrial Defense College. She began her career in state government as secretary to Arizona's state treasurer from 1941 to 1943, when she became secretary to the state tax commissioner. She next served as business manager of *Arizona Highways Magazine* from 1954 to 1955. In 1955, Mofford became assistant secretary of state. From 1975 to 1977, she was assistant director of the department of revenue. When Arizona Secretary of State Wesley Bolin became governor in 1977, he appointed Mofford secretary of state. She ran for and won the office in 1978 and continued to serve until 1988.

See also Governors, Women

References Mullaney, *Biographical Directory of the Governors of the United States 1988–1994* (1994); *The New York Times,* 7 February 1988.

Molinari, Susan (b. 1958)

Republican Susan Molinari of New York served in the U.S. House of Representatives from 20 March 1990 to 2 August 1997. She held the leadership position of vice chair of the House Republican conference in the 104th Congress (1995–1997) and in the 105th Congress (1997) until her retirement from office. Molinari, who grew up in a political family, resigned from her seat to become a television news anchor, which had been her dream job and one for which she had sought opportunities throughout the years she had been in politics.

Born in Staten Island, New York, Susan Molinari received her bachelor of arts degree in 1980 and her master of arts degree in political communications in 1982, both from the State University of New York. She began her career as a financial assistant for the Republican Governor's Association from 1981 to 1983, the year she joined the Republican National Committee as its ethnic community liaison.

Molinari served on the New York City Council from 1986 to 1990, where she focused on environmental and transportation issues. She was particularly concerned with the responsible disposal of garbage and hospital waste, which was dumped in the ocean and then washed onto the Staten Island shore, creating significant health hazards. In addition, she helped improve local recycling programs.

When her father Guy Molinari resigned his seat in Congress to become Staten Island Borough president, Susan Molinari ran for and won his seat in a special election. After taking office, she discovered that a military port for Staten Island, for which commitments had been previously made, was in danger of being abandoned by Congress. Saving the port quickly became her first priority, one in which she was successful.

Although Molinari considers herself a conservative Republican, she holds views that sometimes place her in conflict with her party, her support for the Family and Medical Leave Act of 1993 providing one example. President George Bush and the Republican Party leadership opposed the act, but Molinari explained: "Republicans are supposed to care about families, and I could think of no more dramatic way to demonstrate that kind of caring than to support the Family and Medical Leave Act." Following her comments during debate on the bill, one Republican member of Congress did not speak to her for a year. Her support for reproductive rights was another area in which she and her party disagreed.

Molinari's occasional policy differences with her party, however, did not alienate her from her partisan colleagues. In 1995, she was elected vice chair of the Republican Conference, making her the highest-ranking woman in the House of Representatives. In 1996, she delivered the keynote address at the Republican National Convention.

Other policy areas important to Molinari included protection of wetlands, other environmental issues, and the rights of crime victims. She worked to pass judicial reforms to toughen laws dealing with repeat rapists and child molesters and helped increase funding for the Violence Against Women Act of 1994. As chair of the Transportation and Infrastructure Subcommittee on Railroads, she has focused on increasing rail safety and advocated reforming Amtrak to meet its budget targets. In the international arena, Molinari has worked for the U.S. government to recognize Croatia as a republic and to facilitate aid efforts.

While in Congress, Molinari married Representative Bill Paxon, another New York Republican member of Congress. In May 1997, Molinari announced her planned resignation from the House to become a network television co-anchor.

See also Congress, Women in; Reproductive Rights; Violence Against Women Act of 1994

References *Congressional Quarterly, Politics in America 1994* (1993), *Politics in America 1998* (1997); Molinari, *Representative Mom* (1998); www.house.gov/ molinari/bio.htm.

Moore, Gwendolynne S. (b. 1951)

Democrat Gwendolynne Moore of Wisconsin entered the U.S. House of Representatives on 3 January 2005. Congresswoman Moore began her political career in the Wisconsin state assembly in 1989, serving until 1992. She then served in the Wisconsin state Senate from 1993 to 2003. "Too many people feel that where you start out dictates where you should end up. I was on welfare and just shy of 19 when my first daughter was born, but I was encouraged to take advantage of my ability and drive and remained in school," Moore said. After eight years, Moore earned her bachelor of arts degree at Marquette University in 1978. Following her graduation, she was a VIS-TA (Volunteers in Service to America) worker. Through VISTA, she helped organize a community credit union and worked to improve housing in Milwaukee.

Born in Racine, Moore earned a certificate for senior executives in state and local government from Harvard University in 2000.

References Robyn D. Clarke, "Striving for More: Gwen Moore Worked Her Way from Welfare to Washington, *Black Enterprise*, June 2005, p. 290; http://house.gov/gwenmoore

Moore, Minyon (b. 1958)

Political consultant Minyon Moore began her career working for Harold Washington's 1983 campaign for mayor of Chicago. She worked on Jesse Jackson's 1984 and 1988 campaigns for the Democratic Party's presidential nomination, serving as his deputy field director in the 1988 campaign. After Michael Dukakis won the party's nomination in 1988, Moore became his national deputy field director. She also worked as a director of Jackson's Rainbow Coalition. Beginning in 1992, Moore worked for the Democratic National Committee, where she held several positions, including voter project director, deputy chief of staff and director of public liaison from 1993 to 1995, and national political director from 1995 to 1997. In President Bill Clinton's administration, she was deputy assistant to the president and director of public liaison from 1997 to 2001.

Born in Chicago, Moore attended the University of Chicago.

References "People," *National Journal*, 20 July 2002, p. 2192; Gregg Sangillo, "Image-Makers," *National Journal*, 26 February 2005, p. 627; *Washington Post*, 30 June 1996.

Morella, Constance Albanese (b. 1931)

Republican Constance Morella of Maryland served in the U.S. House of Representatives from 3 January 1987 to 3 January 2003. Legislation introduced and passed by Morella includes the Women in Apprenticeship and Nontraditional Occupations Act of 1992, which provides grants to community-based groups that help private employers recruit, train, and retain women in apprenticeships or jobs traditionally held by men. Morella's Battered Women's Testimony Act of 1992 increases the use of expert testimony in trials of battered women accused of killing their abusers. A third bill related to women's issues that she introduced and passed is the Judicial Training Act of 1992, a policy that provides training for judges and other court personnel dealing with child custody cases in families that have experienced domestic violence. In addition, Morella has been a strong advocate for breast cancer research, at least in part because her sister died of the disease. Morella co-chaired the Congressional Caucus for Women's Issues in the 104th Congress (1995–1997).

Some of Morella's other priorities include the federal workforce, scientific research and development, educational and economic equity, women's health, prevention of domestic violence, and acquired immunodeficiency syndrome (AIDS) research and prevention. In addition, she has provided leadership in the areas of clean air and water, green technology, and population stabilization.

Morella sought re-election to the House in 2002, but lost. In 2003, President George W. Bush appointed her ambassador to the Organization for Economic Cooperation and Development.

Born in Somerville, Massachusetts, Constance Morella received her bachelor of arts degree from Boston University in 1954 and her master's degree in English from American University in 1967. She taught at Montgomery College in Rockville, Maryland, from 1970 to 1985 and served in the Maryland House of Delegates from 1979 to 1987.

See also Congress, Women in; Congressional Caucus for Women's Issues; State Legislatures, Women in

References *Congressional Quarterly, Politics in America 1996* (1995); *Washington Post*, 26 October 2003.

Moseley Braun, Carol (b. 1947)

Democrat Carol Moseley Braun of Illinois served in the U.S. Senate from 3 January 1993 to 3 January 1999. She was the first African American woman elected to the U.S. Senate. After her unsuccessful re-election in 1998, Moseley Braun was a consultant on school construction for the Department of Education for a brief period. Later in 1999, President Bill Clinton appointed her ambassador to New Zealand. She was an unsuccessful candidate for the Democratic nomination for president in 2004.

Born in Chicago, Illinois, Carol Moseley Braun began her political activism when she was a high school student. She staged a one-woman sit-in at a restaurant that denied her service because of her color, had stones thrown at her while visiting a beach previously used exclusively by whites, and marched with the Reverend Martin Luther King, Jr. Moseley Braun earned her bachelor of arts degree in political science from the University of Illinois in 1967 and her law degree from the University of Chicago in 1972.

Moseley Braun began her career in a private law practice in 1972. She served as an assistant U.S. attorney from 1974 to 1977. She ran for the Illinois House of Representatives in 1977 and served until 1988. While in the legislature, Moseley Braun worked for educational reform and legislative redistricting. She also opposed investments in South Africa and discrimination by private clubs. She next served as Cook County recorder of deeds from 1988 to 1992. During her tenure as recorder, she turned an outdated office into a modern operation.

Moseley Braun decided to run for the U.S. Senate for two reasons. First, she had become bored with her job as recorder. The second reason was the spectacle of the Senate Judiciary Committee hearings on the confirmation of Clarence Thomas for the U.S. Supreme Court in which Anita Hill testified that Thomas had sexually harassed her. Moseley Braun became convinced that the mostly white, all-male Senate was unaware of most citizens' lives. Outraged by Illinois Senator Alan Dixon's vote to confirm Thomas, Moseley Braun became a candidate in the primary election and defeated Dixon. Few observers believed that Moseley Braun could win either the primary or the general elections. Following her successes, questions arose about her campaign finances, personal life, staff changes and misjudgments, and her actions as a state legislator, which complicated her early days in the Senate.

*Senator Carol Moseley Braun (D-IL), the first African American
woman elected to the U.S. Senate, defended herself against
accusations of campaign finance abuse in 1992; she was defeated
in her bid for re-election in 1998 (Associated Press AP)*

During her first session in the Senate, Moseley Braun objected to North Carolina Senator Jesse Helms's proposal to renew a patent for the United Daughters of the Confederacy's (UDC) insignia. The patent has permitted the UDC to use the seal of the U.S. Senate since the Civil War and was routinely renewed every fourteen years. Offended by the insignia's inclusion of the national flag of the Confederate States of America, Moseley Braun threatened to filibuster the issue "until this room freezes over." She told the Senate: "I have to tell you this vote is about race, it is about racial symbolism. It is about racial symbols, the racial past, and the single most painful episode in American history." She continued: "On this issue there can be no consensus…. It is absolutely unacceptable to me and to millions of Americans, black or white, that we would put the imprimatur of the U.S. Senate on this kind of idea." Moseley Braun won, and the UDC's patent was not renewed.

Senator Moseley Braun's committee assignments included a position on the Judiciary Committee, the same body that held hearings on U.S. Supreme Court nominee Clarence Thomas's confirmation. In the Senate, Moseley Braun was a strong civil rights advocate, supporting gays in the military and as nominees for appointments. Her achievements included passing the Education Infrastructure Act to repair and renovate school facilities and libraries. Moseley Braun was also involved in child support issues, support for small business, and the Violent Crime Control and Law Enforcement Act of 1994.

See also Congress, Women in; Hill, Anita Faye; State Legislatures, Women in

References *Christian Science Monitor*, 20 November 2003; *Congressional Quarterly, Politics in America 1996* (1995), *Politics in America 1998* (1997); H. W. Wilson, *Current Biography Yearbook, 1994* (1994); *Jet*, 25 January 1999, 27 December 1999; Smith, *Powerful Black Women* (1996); www.senate.gov/~Moseley Braun/bio.htm.
Document Carol Mosely-Braun, "Getting Beyond Racism," 1993

Moskowitz, Belle Lindner Israels (1877–1933)

Belle Moskowitz was among the earliest female political advisers in the Democratic Party. Her skills as a publicist and strategist led to her becoming a trusted consultant to Alfred E. Smith, beginning with his candidacy for governor of New York in 1918. After he won, Moskowitz coined his administration's slogan during the post–World War I era, naming him the Reconstruction Governor. At her recommendation, Smith established New York's Reconstruction Commission, which sought to address the state's short-term and long-term problems. Smith appointed Moskowitz executive secretary of the commission, a position she used to focus attention on Smith's abilities to solve problems, filming him at work and distributing the footage across the state. She also oversaw the publication of twelve reports on labor and industry, the rising cost of living, public health, education, and government reorganization. Smith lost re-election in 1920, and Moskowitz moved into public relations.

Moskowitz worked again with Smith in 1922 during his second successful campaign for governor. Employed by the New York Democratic State Committee, Moskowitz was Smith's public relations counselor, writing his speeches, recommending appointees, and monitoring legislation for him.

During Smith's 1928 campaign to be the Democratic presidential nominee, Moskowitz's role centered on publicity, maintaining a wide correspondence with newspaper reporters across the country. A trusted member of the campaign, she also helped develop strategy. After Smith won the nomination, Moskowitz held the same responsibilities in Smith's presidential campaign that she had held earlier. Under Eleanor Roosevelt's leadership, Moskowitz also directed the women's division of the campaign. After Smith's defeat, Moskowitz opened a public relations firm.

Born in New York City, the daughter of East Prussian immigrants, Moskowitz attended a teachers' college in 1894, leaving to study dramatic reading. Beginning in 1900, Moskowitz did social work in a Jewish neighborhood settlement, wrote articles on social reform, and organized a committee to study working girls' leisure activities. Between 1913 and 1916, she was a negotiator between labor and management in the garment industry.

See also Democratic Party, Women in the; Roosevelt, Eleanor
References Perry, *Belle Moskowitz: Feminine Politics and the Exercise of Power in the Age of Alfred E. Smith* (1987).

Motley, Constance Baker (1921–2005)

Civil rights lawyer Constance Baker Motley was the first African American woman appointed a federal judge. As a lawyer for the National Association for the Advancement of Colored People (NAACP) Legal Defense and Education Fund, she argued and won dozens of cases from the 1940s through the mid-1960s. She once said: "You can have twenty-seven degrees from twenty-seven different universities, but if your skin is different, you're still forced to use the door marked 'colored.' We want an end to that—and everything like it."

Born in New Haven, Connecticut, Constance Baker Motley worked in the National Youth Administration after graduating from high school in 1939. Despite childhood dreams of being a lawyer, her family's poverty did not make a college education a realistic goal. She was president of the New Haven Negro Youth Council and involved in Dixwell Community House, a gathering place for African Americans. At a meeting about the center's programs and facilities with the center's governing board, Motley pointed out that no African Americans served on the board and explained that African Americans did not have a sense of ownership in the center. In the audience was a philanthropist who provided financial support to Dixwell. Impressed by Motley's comments, he later contacted her and asked her the reasons why she was not in college. When she explained that she could not afford it but that she wanted to be a lawyer, he told her that he would pay for her education. Motley earned her bachelor's degree in economics from New York University in 1943 and her law degree from Columbia School of Law in 1946.

While she was a law student, Motley volunteered at the NAACP Legal Defense and Education Fund beginning in 1945 and joined the staff after graduating. The NAACP had turned its attention to racial segregation in education, the area in which Motley was first involved. Much of Motley's work was in the South, where racism reigned, danger stalked civil rights workers, and neither whites nor African Americans were accustomed to black professionals. For example, when Motley and a colleague served as counsel in a Mississippi case to equalize black teachers' salaries in 1949, they were the first African Americans to try a case in the state in the twentieth century.

From 1950 to 1954, she participated in the landmark *Brown v. Board of Education* of Topeka, Kansas school desegregation case. In that case, the U.S. Supreme Court decided that the equal protection clause of the Fourteenth Amendment prohibits states from maintaining racially segregated public schools. According to Motley, the decision began a period of the greatest social upheaval since the Civil War: "The *Brown* decision was the catalyst which changed our society from a closed society to an open society and created the momentum for other minority groups to establish public interest law firms to secure their rights." Over the next years, Motley played a significant role in almost every major school integration case, including cases in Alabama, Florida, Georgia, Ohio, and other states.

Motley became associate counsel for the NAACP Legal Defense and Education Fund in 1961, the first woman to hold the position, the second-highest in the organization. That year, she argued a case before the U.S. Supreme Court, probably the first African American woman to do so.

In 1961 and 1962, she successfully represented James Meredith in his effort to gain admission to the then all-white University of Mississippi. Motley persisted despite the opposition displayed by the state's judicial, executive, and university officials, including their defiance of appeals courts' decisions. Motley was a member of the team who represented Martin Luther King, Jr., throughout his Birmingham, Alabama campaign and successfully fought the suspension of over 1,000 African American students from Birmingham who participated in the demonstrations that accompanied King's campaign. In 1963, she defended four civil rights workers convicted of breaking a Georgia insurrection law, which was punishable with the death penalty. She won the case in federal court, which declared the law unconstitutional.

A summary of the U.S. Supreme Court cases in which Motley participated includes three related to the exclusion of blacks from juries, fourteen involving lunch-counter sit-ins, twenty school desegregation cases, and eighteen other discrimination cases. Of the ten Supreme Court cases in which she was the lead counsel, Motley successfully argued nine of them, with the tenth decided without argument. In addition, she participated in seventy-three cases that went to the U.S. Court of Appeals.

In 1964, Motley became the first African American woman elected to the New York Senate. From 1965 to 1966, she served as borough president of Manhattan, the first woman to hold the position. She also became the first woman to sit on the New York City Board of Estimates.

In 1966, President Lyndon Johnson appointed Motley federal judge of the Southern District of New York State, making her the first African American woman named a federal judge. In 1982, Motley was appointed federal district court judge. She was named a senior federal judge in 1986.

> **See also** Civil Rights Movement, Women in the; Fourteenth Amendment; National Association for the Advancement of Colored People, Women in the; State Legislatures, Women in

> **References** H. W. Wilson, *Current Biography Yearbook, 1964* (1964); Motley, *Equal Justice under Law* (1998); *Washington Post*, 29 September 2005.

Mott, Lucretia Coffin (1793–1880)

Quaker minister, abolitionist, and suffragist Lucretia Coffin Mott organized the first anti-slavery convention of U.S. women and helped launch the nineteenth-century women's rights movement. Throughout her life, Mott worked for equality for African Americans, women, Native Americans, immigrants, and poor people.

Born on Nantucket Island, Massachusetts, Mott attended a local grammar school and then a Quaker boarding school, where she developed her commitment to abolitionism. After completing the curriculum, Mott joined the teaching staff and occasionally taught after her marriage in 1811. Mott was formally recognized as a Quaker minister in 1821, but her relationship to the Quaker faith would be repeatedly challenged as she became increasingly involved in social reform issues.

Mott decided in the early 1820s to boycott all products made by slave labor, including cotton, cane sugar, and molasses. Although her boycott did not provoke controversy, her repeated discussions during Meeting (the Quaker expression for corporate worship) attracted criticism. She furthered her involvement in the abolitionist effort in 1833 when she organized a gathering that led to the formation of the Philadelphia Female Anti-Slavery Society. Mott organized the first Female Anti-Slavery Convention of American women in 1837, but it was the second convention the next year that proved dramatic and dangerous. A mob of thousands of people gathered outside the convention hall, posing so great a threat that the mayor asked those gathered at the convention to leave. Mott, demonstrating the courage that characterized her, invited the women to leave quietly in pairs, one white woman accompanying each black woman through the crowd. Later that night, a mob of 17,000 burned the convention hall. The third convention, in 1839, proceeded without violence. That year, Mott became an officer in the Pennsylvania Anti-Slavery Society.

The society named Lucretia Mott and her husband James Mott delegates to the World Anti-Slavery Society convention in London in 1840. Lucretia Mott was one of several U.S. women delegates to the convention, all of whom learned upon arriving in London that the convention organizers did not want to seat the women. The Motts and others protested the exclusion, but the English abolitionists remained adamant, and the women were relegated to a balcony.

Also seated in the balcony was Elizabeth Cady Stanton, the wife of a delegate, who became an admirer and friend of Lucretia Mott. The two women spent hours together, not only on the perimeter of the convention hall but also walking the streets of London. They discussed women's low status and possible remedies and decided to hold a women's rights convention when they returned to the United States.

Eight years later, in July 1848, while visiting a mutual friend of hers and Stanton's, Mott received an invitation to a tea that Stanton also planned to attend. Over cups of tea on 13 July 1848, Mott, Stanton, and a few other women wrote a call to a women's rights convention for publication the next day in the Seneca Falls newspaper. In less than a week, they drafted resolutions based upon the Declaration of Independence for the convention's consideration. One of the resolutions Stanton proposed distressed Mott because it called for woman suffrage. Mott believed that it would make the women appear ridiculous, but she came to see that it was important and consented to its introduction.

Lucretia Mott's husband James presided over the convention, the women believing it improper for one of them to chair it. The resolutions, including the one for suffrage, were accepted by the convention on 20 July 1848, but after the convention, some of the women in attendance asked to have their names removed from the document because their husbands opposed it. The convention launched the nineteenth-century women's rights movement and with it the demand for woman suffrage. In addition to political rights, Mott believed that professional opportunities should be opened to women. For example, despite the opposition of the American Medical Association, she worked to help women obtain training and gain acceptance as doctors.

By the 1850s, Mott had become a national figure, widely known and respected for her work in the abolitionist movement and as a minister. She continued to advocate boycotting products made by slaves as the best way to end slavery. In the 1860s, she opposed the Civil War, as she opposed all war. President Abraham Lincoln's 1863 Emancipation Proclamation did not alter her view of the war, nor did it appeal to her as a first step toward ending slavery because it only freed slaves in areas controlled by Confederates, areas over which the Union government had no control.

After the Civil War and the introduction of the Fourteenth Amendment, Mott joined feminists in opposing it. The amendment included the word *male* in its definition of citizens, outraging Stanton and others who believed that it would make woman suffrage even more difficult to obtain. Although Mott opposed the amendment's wording, she did not focus great attention on it. Instead, she became an advocate for peace, preaching against war and working with the Universal Peace Movement.

*Lucretia Mott, suffragist and abolitionist, was one
of the five women who called the Seneca Falls Convention
that began the women's rights movement in the United States
(Library of Congress LC-USZ62-42559)*

See also Abolitionist Movement, Women in the; Fourteenth Amendment; Seneca Falls Convention; Stanton, Elizabeth Cady; Suffrage

References Bacon, *Valiant Friend: The Life of Lucretia Mott* (1980).

Ms. Foundation for Women

Founded in 1972, the Ms. Foundation for Women (MFW) is a national, multi-issue, public women's fund that works to change public consciousness, the law, philanthropy, and social policy. By directing its resources to projects that endeavor to overcome racial, class, age, disability, sexual orientation, and cultural barriers, MFW supports women's and girls' efforts to govern their own lives and influence the world around them. To meet its goals, MFW focuses on economic security, health and safety, and girls, young women, and leadership. The foundation may be best known for Take Our Daughters to Work® Day, an annual public education program begun in 1993.

The Ms. Foundation for Women was established because at the time there were no foundations that gave money to women as a category. Founded the same year as *Ms.* magazine, the foundation's funding was to come from the magazine's profits, but the magazine struggled financially and did not produce the anticipated revenues. In 1973, Marlo Thomas created an NBC-TV special, *Free to Be... You and Me* to benefit the foundation, and other fundraising projects followed.

In 1984, Marie Wilson joined the foundation as its president, and under her leadership, the foundation has expanded its financial resources and its programs. The annual budget has grown from $400,000 to $6.2 million since 1984. In addition, Wilson established an endowment fund for the foundation and raised $10 million for it.

The foundation's program areas include support for groups that seek economic justice and that foster economic development through job creation, constituency building, public policy advocacy, welfare reform, pay equity, child care, and related projects. In the area of women's health and safety, the foundation supports programs that address gender bias in health care; protect reproductive rights; and increase resources to end domestic violence, incest, child sexual abuse, rape, and sexual assault and harassment. The foundation makes grants to leadership programs for girls and young women, including those related to improving girls' health; ending violence against girls; creating non-sexist, non-violent curricula; and reducing teen pregnancy rates.

In 1993, MFW created Take Our Daughters to Work Day to focus the attention of policymakers, the media, and the general public on the needs and concerns of girls. Held on the fourth Thursday in April, Take Our Daughters to Work Day encourages employers to permit girls ages nine to fifteen to spend the day at work with a parent or other adult. The project, which has involved companies across the country, has been more successful than its creators imagined, involving millions of girls and adults, with some employers offering special programs for the girls and the adults they accompany. The President's Interagency Council on Women, for example, sponsored Take Our Daughters to Work Day, providing opportunities for high school students to meet federal officials, including former Secretary of State Madeleine Albright and others. The program evolved into Take our Daughters and Sons to Work® Day in 2003.

In 2002, MFW sponsored the research for *Raise the Floor: Wages and Policies That Work*, which proposes a national minimum needs budget for adults and families; a realistic federal minimum wage; and policies to supplement wages so that people can meet their basic needs.

See also Abortion; Domestic Violence; *Ms.* Magazine; Rape; Sexual Harassment

References www.ms.foundation.org.

Ms. Magazine

Founded in 1972 by Gloria Steinem, *Ms.* magazine quickly gained the loyalty of many women in the developing feminist movement and attracted the criticism of many other feminists who objected to its moderate tone. Steinem once called it the "how-to magazine for the liberated human female—not how to make jelly, but how to seize control of your life." *Ms.* has its roots in the Women's Action Alliance, which was created by Steinem to help women at the grassroots level fight the barriers in their lives. Women responded to the alliance with inquiries and requests, prompting Steinem to start a newsletter as a way of communicating with the large number of women wanting more information. Plans for a modest newsletter evolved into a magazine format that Steinem believed had potential for success independent of the alliance.

A trial edition of *Ms.* appeared as a supplement in the 20 December 1971 edition of *New York* magazine, and in the spring of 1972, the preview issue was published. The magazine received more than 20,000 letters in response to the preview issue, giving

Steinem and publisher Pat Carbine hope for its success and confidence in proceeding. The first regular issue was published in July 1972.

The magazine quickly became part of the feminist movement and a source for women seeking new ways to understand and interpret the world around them. It served as a catalyst, a communication tool among feminists, and a guide for many women. Some of its articles became famous among feminists. For example, Jane O'Reilly wrote a piece about the "clicks" in a feminist's mind that connect seemingly innocuous statements with the sexism that underlies them.

Although readership grew, advertising revenues did not keep pace with the magazine's costs. Some advertisers feared the controversial editorial material, others demanded articles about their products, and still others questioned whether women purchased their products. *Ms.* sales staff worked to convince advertisers that women purchased cars, stereos, and other consumer items, but marketers believed that women's purchases were limited to cosmetics, clothing, and domestic household items. Financial difficulties resulted in the sale of *Ms.* to an Australian media firm in 1987. The magazine underwent various transformations and was owned by other groups until 1998, when Steinem and others purchased it. Published bimonthly, it no longer has any advertising and features international and national women's news, investigative reports, personal narratives, fiction, poetry, and humor. In 2001, the Feminist Majority Foundation assumed ownership of *Ms.*

See also Feminist Movement; Ms. Foundation for Women; Steinem, Gloria Marie

References Heilbrun, *The Education of a Woman: The Life of Gloria Steinem* (1996); http://www.msmagazine.com.

Muller v. Oregon (1908)

In 1908, the U.S. Supreme Court decided in *Muller v. Oregon* that discriminating on the basis of sex in employment and in state policies was constitutional. The case challenged a 1903 Oregon law that limited the number of hours that women could work in factories, mechanical establishments, and laundries to ten hours a day. The policy was one of many that social reformers had worked to pass to protect female and child laborers from the health hazards and dangers in the workplace.

In *Lochner v. New York*, the Court had rejected a New York law that limited the number of hours that laborers in bakeries could work on the basis that it was an illegitimate use of the state's police power and an arbitrary interference in the right to contract. The Court explained that the Oregon law differed in that it applied only to women.

In this case, Carl Muller, a laundry operator, required a female employee to work more than ten hours a day, and for breaking the ten-hour limit, he was tried, convicted, and fined. He appealed, basing his arguments on the *Lochner* decision.

The State of Oregon received significant assistance in its defense from Louis Brandeis (later a Supreme Court justice) and Josephine Goldmark, who was active in the National Consumers League, an organization that supported protective legislation for workers. Goldmark researched and Brandeis wrote a brief that featured the innovation of offering anecdotal and statistical evidence that supported the arguments relating to women's health and the state's interest in protecting it. Of the 104 pages in the brief, only two dealt with legal precedents and logic; the social and economic information formed the balance. Known as the Brandeis brief, it changed legal procedures before the Court.

The Court upheld the Oregon law, explaining that when a woman stands on her feet day after day, it "tends to [have] injurious effects upon the body, and as healthy mothers are essential to vigorous offspring, the physical well-being of woman becomes an object of public interest and care in order to preserve the strength and vigor of the race."

See also Employment Discrimination; Progressive Party, Women in the; Protective Legislation

References *Muller v. Oregon*, 208 U.S. 412 (1908).

Murkowski, Lisa (b. 1957)

Republican Lisa Murkowski of Alaska entered the U.S. Senate on 20 December 2002. After her father, Senator Frank Murkowski became governor of Alaska in 2002, he appointed his daughter, Lisa Murkowski, to fill the remaining two years of his term. She

Alaskan Senator Lisa Murkowski stands with a group of medical students in support of efforts to increase access to health care (Courtesy Office of Lisa Murkowski)

is the first senator's daughter ever in the Senate, the first person appointed by a parent, and the first native-born Alaskan to represent the state in the U.S. Senate. After winning election in 2004 to a full six-year term, she became the first woman to win statewide office in Alaska.

Senator Murkowski supports opening Alaska's Arctic National Wildlife Refuge to oil and gas exploration, a position widely supported by her constituents. She succeeded in passing legislation that provides federal loan guarantees for a 3,500-mile pipeline to carry natural gas from Alaska to the Midwestern states. She has also worked to transfer 89 million acres of land from federal to state ownership. In addition, she would like restrictions on logging in the Tongass National Forest removed.

Born in Ketchikan, Alaska, Murkowski attended Willamette University from 1975 to 1977. She earned a bachelor of arts degree in economics at Georgetown University in 1980 and earned a juris doctorate degree from Willamette College of Law in 1985. An Anchorage district attorney from 1987 to 1989, she had a private practice from 1989 to 1996. She served in the Alaska House of Representatives from 1999 to 2002.

> **References** Congressional Quarterly, *Politics in America 2004* (2003), *Politics in America 2006* (2005); http://murkowski.senate.gov; *The New York Times*, 21 December 2002

Murray, Patty Johns (b. 1950)

Democrat Patty Murray of Washington entered the U.S. Senate on 5 January 1993. Murray's motivation to run for the U.S. Senate came from watching U.S. Supreme Court nominee Clarence Thomas's confirmation hearings on television. The Senate Judiciary Committee's treatment of Anita Hill during the hearings outraged Murray and convinced her to run for the Senate. As she campaigned, she described herself as a "mom in tennis shoes," creating a distinction between herself and her primary and general election opponents, whom she characterized as Washington insiders.

When the Senate debated the question of issuing a subpoena for the personal diaries of Republican Senator Robert Packwood, who was accused of sexual harassment, Senator Murray argued that the Senate's focus needed to be on a substantive discussion of sexual harassment. She warned against sending U.S. women a message that said: "If you are harassed, keep quiet, say nothing; the cards are stacked against your ever winning."

Senator Murray has supported family leave legislation, health care reform, tax relief for the middle class, reproductive rights, and reinvestment in the infrastructure. She passed legislation making surplus government computers available to schools and has worked to connect schools to the Internet, protect and rebuild salmon runs, and provide assistance to veterans. She won re-election to the Senate in a close race in 1998.

In her second term, Murray led the passage of a measure to require regular inspections of oil and gas pipelines. She has introduced legislation requiring insurance companies that cover Viagra to also cover contraception. Improved access to health care for veterans, high-speed Internet for rural areas, and setting aside a new wilderness area were among her other interests.

Senator Murray chaired the Democratic Senate Campaign Committee, the first woman to hold the position, in the 107th Congress (2001–2003). She held the leadership position of assistant floor leader in the 109th Congress (2005–2007).

Born in Seattle, Washington, Patty Murray earned her bachelor of arts degree in recreational therapy from Washington State University in 1972. She entered politics when she organized 12,000 Washington state families to save state funding for preschool programs. From 1977 to 1984, she was a parent volunteer at the Shoreline Community Cooperative School, and she was a parent education instructor at Shoreline Community College from 1984 to 1987. Murray also served on the Shoreline School District board of directors from 1983 to 1989. Lobbying the state legislature for education and environmental issues in the mid-1980s convinced Murray to run for the state Senate, where she served from 1989 to 1993.

See also Congress, Women in; Hill, Anita Faye; Sexual Harassment; State Legislatures, Women in

References *Congressional Quarterly, Politics in America 1994* (1993); H. W. Wilson, *Current Biography Yearbook, 1994* (1994); http://murray.senate.gov.

Murray, Pauli (1910–1985)

A leader in the civil rights and women's rights movements, African American lawyer Pauli Murray played pivotal roles in the President's Commission on the Status of Women and the inclusion of sex in Title VII of the 1964 Civil Rights Act. Part of an informal underground network of women in the early 1960s, Murray was a founding member of the National Organization for Women.

Born in Baltimore, Maryland, Murray grew up in Durham, North Carolina, having moved there following her mother's death, and was raised by an aunt and her maternal grandparents. She graduated from Hunter College in 1933, earned her law degree from Howard University Law School in 1944, and her master of law degree from Boalt Hall of Law at the University of California at Berkeley in 1945. She earned her doctor of juridical science degree from Yale Law School in 1965, the first African American to receive the degree. She received her master of divinity degree from the General Theological Seminary in 1976.

Murray began protesting racial segregation when she was a child, walking several miles to school rather than ride the city's segregated buses, and as a young adult she refused to attend a segregated college for her undergraduate work. In 1938, she applied to the graduate school of the University of North Carolina, which had never admitted an African American student. Denied admission because of her race, she considered suing the university, but leaders in the black community counseled against it, and she accepted the defeat. Her attempt, however, received wide publicity, and other African American students began applying to Southern universities. In 1951, several black students gained admission to the University of North Carolina's Law School, actions that Murray saw as evidence of her role as a pioneer in the struggle for equality of opportunity in higher education.

In 1940, Murray and a friend were arrested and charged with disorderly conduct for refusing to sit on a broken seat in a Greyhound bus. Jailed for three days, they were found guilty and fined. She lost the case on appeal, but she later wrote that the experience "convinced me that creative nonviolent resistance could be a powerful weapon in the struggle for human dignity." These and other civil rights experiences led Murray to law school. While attending law school, Murray helped integrate two Washington, D.C. restaurants through sit-ins.

It was also during this time that she became conscious of sex bias, which she labeled "Jane Crow." She encountered it more fully after receiving her law degree, when she won a fellowship for graduate study at Harvard University. After the announcement that she was to receive it, the fellowship was withdrawn because of her gender. She instead attended Boalt Hall of Law.

Before the modern feminist movement emerged, Murray participated in one of the catalysts that prompted it, serving on the Committee on Civil and Political Rights of the 1961 President's Commission on the Status of Women. Among the committee members there was disagreement on the Equal Rights Amendment, with some of the members strongly supporting it and others equally adamant in their rejection of it. At the committee's request, Murray prepared a memo, "A Proposal to Reexamine the Applicability of the Fourteenth Amendment to State Laws and Practices Which Discriminate on the Basis of Sex *Per Se*," which considered the Fourteenth Amendment as an alternative to the Equal Rights Amendment. The memo provided the means for negotiating a compromise that urged litigation under the Fourteenth Amendment without rejecting the possibility that an Equal Rights Amendment could be necessary. In addition, through her work on the committee, Murray became part of an informal network of feminists that developed as the commissioners and committee members discovered common interests.

After the U.S. House of Representatives passed the Civil Rights Act of 1964 with a prohibition against sex discrimination in employment (in Title VII), the U.S. Senate considered removing sex from the protected classifications. Murray wrote a memorandum supporting the inclusion of sex in the bill. The memo was widely distributed, particularly among senators, and was crucial to the Senate's retaining sex in the bill. She later worked to encourage the Equal Employment Opportunity Commission, created by the act, to enforce its provisions. Her efforts included co-authoring a law review article on Title VII showing that it and the Fifth and Fourteenth Amendments could be interpreted to give women equal rights.

Murray's life took another direction after she ministered to a dying friend. Because of the experience, Murray felt called to the service of the Church. After graduating from General Theological Seminary, she was ordained to the Holy Order of the Deacons of the Episcopal Church, USA. In 1977, she was ordained an Episcopal priest, the first black woman ordained in that denomination.

Murray's first book, *States' Laws on Race and Color* (1951), became an important resource for civil rights lawyers fighting segregation laws. Her second book, *Proud Shoes: The Story of an American Family* (1956), was a biography of her grandparents that established a new genre of American literature: the African American family history. In 1960, she went to Ghana to teach, and while there, she co-authored *The Constitution and Government of Ghana* (1961). Murray's autobiography, *Song in a Weary Throat: An American Pilgrimage*, was published posthumously in 1987.

See also Civil Rights Act of 1964, Title VII; Civil Rights Movement, Women in the; Equal Employment Opportunity Commission; Equal Rights Amendment; National Organization for Women; President's Commission on the Status of Women

References Murray, *Song in a Weary Throat* (1987).

Colorado Congresswoman Marilyn Musgrave (D-CO) meets with border sheriffs during a tour of the U.S.-Mexico border on 2 June 2006.

Musgrave, Marilyn N. (b. 1949)

Republican Marilyn Musgrave of Colorado entered the U.S. House of Representatives on 3 January 2003. During her first term in office, Congresswoman Musgrave founded the Congressional Second Amendment Caucus. She has proposed an amendment to the U.S. Constitution that would define marriage as the union of one woman and one man, an idea that gained additional support when President George W. Bush endorsed it. She opposes allowing the courts define marriage. She led the fight against an eight-cent-per-gallon increase in the federal gasoline tax, which Republican leaders sought. When she subsequently requested additional money for projects in her district, leaders refused because she had not supported the gasoline tax increase, but she enlisted the help of other Republicans and succeeded. Her other priorities include cutting taxes, promoting fiscal discipline, improving education, and supporting agriculture.

A member of the Fort Morgan, Colorado school board from 1990 to 1994, Musgrave advocated increased academic rigor and discipline for students. She served in the Colorado state House of Representatives from 1994 to 1998, and in the Colorado state Senate from 1998 to 2002.

Born in Greeley, Colorado, Musgrave earned a bachelor of arts degree at Colorado State University in 1972.

> **References** Congressional Quarterly, *Politics in America 2006* (2005); http://musgrave.house.gov; National Journal, 22 May 2004.

Myers, Margaret Jane (Dee Dee) (b. 1961)

The first woman and, at the time of her appointment, the youngest person to serve as White House press secretary, Dee Dee Myers held the post from 1993 to 1994. She entered politics in 1984 as a volunteer in Democratic presidential candidate Walter Mondale's 1984 campaign, performing menial tasks, but ended the campaign as assistant press secretary for California. Deputy press secretary for Los Angeles Mayor Tom Bradley from 1985 to 1988, she was also California press secretary for Michael Dukakis's 1988 presidential campaign and spokeswoman for Dianne Feinstein's 1990 unsuccessful campaign for governor of California. Her job as press secretary for Bill Clinton's 1992 presidential campaign was made unusually difficult by reports that Clinton had had extramarital affairs and by unfavorable stories about the reasons he had avoided the draft.

After leaving the White House, Myers was a consultant for the television drama *The West Wing* and a political analyst for NBC and MSNBC.

Born in Quonset Point, Rhode Island, Myers was given her nickname "Dee Dee" by an older sister. She earned her bachelor of science degree at Santa Clara University in 1983.

> **References** Kathleen Doane, "Wing Woman," *Cincinnati*, February 2005; H. W. Wilson, *Current Biography Yearbook, 1994* (1994).

Myrick, Sue (b. 1941)

Republican Sue Myrick of North Carolina entered the U.S. House of Representatives on 3 January 1995. A breast cancer survivor, Congresswoman Myrick passed a measure in 2000 permitting states to provide Medicaid coverage for low-income women with breast or cervical cancer. Co-chair of the House Cancer Caucus beginning with the 107th Congress (2001–2003), she worked to double the National Cancer Institute's funding. In another area, she passed a measure providing grants for a national database on missing adults, similar to the one for missing children.

She has supported "comp time," in which employees do not receive overtime wages but receive time off from their job instead. She explained: "Comp time is pro-family, pro-worker, and when we really think about it, a pro-child approach to provide relief to the hard-working men and women across our nation who struggle daily to support their families." Myrick's priorities include streamlining government bureaucracy, privatizing many components of the federal government, and cutting the federal budget deficit.

Born in Tiffin, Ohio, Sue Myrick attended Heidelberg College from 1959 to 1960. She is the former president and chief executive officer of Myrick Advertising and Myrick Enterprises. Myrick served on the Charlotte City Council from 1983 to 1985 and was mayor from 1987 to 1991, years in which she was active in the U.S. Conference of Mayors. She also served on President George Bush's Affordable Housing Commission and the Strengthening America Commission.

> **See also** Congress, Women in
> **References** *Congressional Quarterly, Politics in America 1998* (1997) *Politics in America 2006* (2005); www. house.gov/myrick/bio.htm.

Napolitano, Grace Flores (b. 1936)

Democrat Grace Napolitano of California entered the U.S. House of Representatives on 3 January 1999, the fifth Latina elected to Congress. Chair of the Congressional Hispanic Caucus in the 109th Congress (2005–2007), Napolitano intended to work with the Congressional Black Caucus and the Congressional Asian Pacific Caucus to share priorities. She founded the Congressional Mental Health Caucus in the 108th Congress (2003–2005), and co-chaired it in the 109th Congress.

She began her political career as the first Latina member of the Norwalk, California city council, serving from 1986 to 1992. Elected to the California State Assembly in 1992, she led the effort to preserve 1,400 acres of open land for parks and wilderness, one of the largest new areas of its kind in southern California, and sought to enhance California's international trade by promoting the state in China, Thailand, Mexico, and other countries. She served in the assembly until her election to Congress in 1998. As a member of Congress, Napolitano has focused on helping small businesses participate in international markets, obtaining federal assistance for environmental cleanup projects in her district, and identifying new water resources for the Los Angeles area. In the 107th Congress (2001–2003), she won approval of a measure requiring the Energy Department to clean up 10 million tons of waste from uranium mining, believed to be contaminating the Colorado River with radioactive uranium and other toxins. She also won funding that session for water recycling projects in California. In addition, she obtained funds to clean up ground water in the San Gabriel Basin in California.

Born in Brownsville, Texas, Napolitano completed her formal education at Brownsville High School in 1954.

See also Congress, Women in; State Legislatures, Women in

References *Congressional Quarterly, Politics in America 2006* (2005); http://www.napolitano.house.gov; "Grace F. Napolitano" (1998).

Napolitano, Janet Ann (b. 1957)

Democrat Janet Napolitano became governor of Arizona in 2003, the first woman governor to follow another woman governor in office. She campaigned on improving education and the state's child protective services, developing a homeland security plan, and creating a prescription drug plan for low-income Arizonans. At the time, Arizona faced a $300 million deficit for 2003 and another $1 billion for 2004. Napolitano led the state through its financial problems without raising taxes or cutting funding for public schools.

She has led the state in phasing in voluntary all-day kindergarten and reformed the state's child protective services. In other areas, she has worked to improve the state's ability to fight fires, helped create a new medical school, and initiated a program for reduced-cost prescription drugs.

Napolitano served as attorney general of Arizona from 1999 to 2002. She was U.S. district attorney for Arizona from 1993 to 1997.

Born in New York, Napolitano earned a bachelor of science degree at the University of Santa Clara in 1979 and a juris doctorate from the University of Virginia in 1983.

References *Arizona Republic*, 5 January 2003; http://azgovernor.gov.

NARAL Pro-Choice America

Founded in 1969, NARAL Pro-Choice America promotes reproductive freedom through its twenty-eight state affiliates. Initially known as the National Association for the Repeal of Abortion Laws, the organization changed its name to National Abortion Rights Action League in 1973 after the U.S. Supreme Court's decision in *Roe v. Wade* legalizing abortion. Its second name change came in 1994, when NARAL expanded its mission to include the prevention of unwanted pregnancies and advocacy for healthy pregnancies and children. It changed its name again in 2003 to the current one as part of a marketing and mobilization campaign.

NARAL Pro-Choice America is a nonprofit organization that develops political strategies, organizes grassroots campaigns, and lobbies Congress and state legislatures. Through its political action committee, the organization supports pro-choice candidates with paid media advertising, financial contributions, and get-out-the-vote projects on election days. The NARAL Foundation supports research and legal work, publishes policy reports, conducts public education campaigns, and provides leadership training.

NARAL Pro-Choice America successfully worked with other groups to remove the 1980s gag rule that prevented abortion counseling at federally funded family planning clinics, to lift the ban on federally funded medical research on fetal tissue transplants, and to permit abortions at military hospitals. It also helped pass the Freedom of Access to Clinic Entrances Act of 1994. NARAL supports testing and marketing the abortifacient RU-486, health reform that includes a full range of reproductive health services for women, and the proposed Freedom of Choice Act.

See also Abortion; Freedom of Access to Clinic Entrances Act of 1994; *Roe v. Wade*; RU-486 (Mifepristone)

References www.pro-choiceamerica.org

Nashville Gas Co. v. Satty (1977)

In *Nashville Gas Co. v. Satty*, the U.S. Supreme Court considered two of the company's employment policies related to pregnant women. Nashville Gas Company required pregnant women to take a leave of absence without receiving sick pay, even though the company provided it for non-occupational disabilities other than pregnancy. In addition, when women returned to work, they lost their seniority, even though employees who took sick leave for other non-occupational disabilities retained their seniority.

The Court decided that denying sick pay for pregnancy did not violate Title VII of the Civil Rights Act of 1964, unless it was a pretext for discriminating against one sex or the other, and remanded the case for consideration of that point. The Court decided that denying seniority to employees returning from pregnancy leave violated Title VII, saying that the policy imposed a substantial burden on women.

> **See also** *Geduldig v. Aiello*; *General Electric v. Gilbert*; Pregnancy Discrimination Act of 1978
>
> **References** *Nashville Gas Co. v. Satty*, 434 U.S. 136 (1977).

National Advisory Committee for Women

Created in 1978 by President Jimmy Carter's Executive Order 12050, the National Advisory Committee for Women (NACW) was established to monitor the progress of the National Plan of Action passed at the 1977 National Women's Conference. Carter appointed thirty-eight women and men to the commission and designated former Congresswoman Bella Abzug and Carmen Delgado Votaw to be its co-chairs. The executive order also created an interdepartmental task force and directed it to review the impact of agency programs and regulations on women. Before it had completed its work, the committee issued a press release criticizing Carter's economic policies, saying the policies placed a disproportionately unfair burden on women. The White House fired Abzug from the committee, and several committee members then resigned in protest. The President's Advisory Committee for Women replaced the NACW in mid-1979 and operated until December 1980.

> **See also** Abzug, Bella Savitzky; National Women's Conference
>
> **References** East, *American Women: 1963*, 1983, 2003 (1983).

National American Woman Suffrage Association

The National American Woman Suffrage Association (NAWSA) was created in 1890, when the National Woman Suffrage Association (NWSA) and the American Woman Suffrage Association (AWSA) merged. For thirty years the organization served as the primary advocate for woman suffrage, educating the public, seeking congressional support, and assisting in campaigns for state amendments. It was the largest suffrage association in the nation when the Nineteenth Amendment was ratified in 1920.

Veteran women's rights advocate Elizabeth Cady Stanton was the NAWSA's first president, serving from 1890 to 1892. Her longtime political partner Susan B. Anthony followed her in the presidency, guiding the organization until 1900. By that year, four Western states had granted women full suffrage: Wyoming, Colorado, Idaho, and Utah. Anthony chose Carrie Chapman Catt, a less well-known suffrage leader who was a generation younger than her predecessors, to succeed her. During the four years that

Lawyer Inez Boissevain, wearing white cape, seated on white horse at the National American Woman Suffrage Association parade, March 3, 1913, Washington, D.C (Library of Congress LC-DIG-ppmsc-00031)

Catt served as NAWSA president, several states conducted campaigns, but none of the amendments passed. The federal suffrage amendment had even less success. Congressional supporters of the amendment regularly introduced the amendment but were unable to obtain significant action on it.

Under Anna Howard Shaw's presidency, from 1904 to 1915, seven states adopted constitutional amendments granting women suffrage rights, and one state, Illinois, gave women presidential suffrage through legislation, but lobbying efforts at the congressional level failed to result in substantive action. A new force entered the campaign in 1913 when Alice Paul, who had worked with British suffragists, brought new energy and ideas to the association. As chair of the NAWSA's congressional committee, she organized a suffrage parade in Washington, D.C., that competed with President-elect Woodrow Wilson's arrival for his inauguration. The parade and other actions she orchestrated attracted publicity, provoked debate, and gained her the reputation of being a militant. Paul proved to be too controversial for the more staid and conservative NAWSA leadership, who objected to her strategies. Paul formed the Congressional Union, left NAWSA, and remained a visible force in the suffrage effort, frustrating NAWSA leaders with her actions, which they believed hindered the amendment's progress.

Catt returned to the NAWSA's presidency in 1915 with a new strategy, called the "Winning Plan." The plan had three aspects to it. Women living in suffrage states were to work for political candidates who supported woman suffrage. The NAWSA would no longer participate in every state campaign but would limit itself to working only in those campaigns that leaders thought could be won. Every available resource would be devoted to congressional passage of a federal amendment. The plan was a political strategy that contrasted with the educational campaigns that association had traditionally conducted. Catt presented it to the NAWSA's 1915 convention and obtained the convention's approval of it. She also worked to gain President Woodrow Wilson's support for the amendment, keeping communications open between them.

When the United States entered World War I, the NAWSA financed several hospitals in Europe and at home, and the association's leaders held visible roles in federal war agencies. NAWSA members volunteered for the Red Cross, canvassed their neighborhoods for food conservation programs, participated in the war service census, and worked on the Liberty Loan drives. President Woodrow Wilson rewarded these patriotic efforts in 1918 with his announcement that the war could not have been conducted without women's contributions and that he supported woman suffrage.

The U.S. House of Representatives passed the amendment in January 1918, but the Senate defeated it in February 1919. The House again passed the amendment in May 1919, and the Senate followed in June 1919. The NAWSA turned its focus to ratifying the amendment, reaching the goal on 20 August 1920, when Tennessee became the last state needed to add the Nineteenth Amendment to the U.S. Constitution.

At the NAWSA's 1920 convention, Catt had suggested the creation of an educational organization to provide newly enfranchised women with information about citizenship, voting, and related matters. The League of Women Voters emerged from her proposal.

> **See also** American Woman Suffrage Association; Anthony, Susan Brownell; Catt, Carrie Clinton Lane Chapman; Congressional Union; League of Women Voters; National Woman Suffrage Association; Paul, Alice; Shaw, Anna Howard; Stanton, Elizabeth Cady; Suffrage
>
> **References** Flexner and Fitzpatrick, *Century of Struggle: The Woman's Rights Movement in the United States* (1996).

National Association for the Advancement of Colored People, Women in the

Founded in 1909, the National Association for the Advancement of Colored People (NAACP) is the oldest and largest civil rights organization in the United States, with more than 500,000 members in 2,200 branches located in every state, the District of Columbia, Japan, and Germany. The NAACP has used legal actions as its primary strategy to end discrimination and to gain full citizenship for African Americans. The organization also lobbies state legislatures and Congress to ensure and protect the rights of minority citizens.

A 1908 race riot in Springfield, Illinois, prompted black and white Americans to join together to fight racism. W. E. B. Du Bois, Ida B. Wells-Barnett, Henry Moscowitz, Oswald Garrison Villard, William English Walling, and Mary White Ovington issued a call to form the organization. In its early years, several women, including Ida B. Wells-Barnett, Mary McLeod Bethune, and Mary Church Terrell, made significant contributions to the development and effectiveness of the organization, especially in its anti-lynching campaigns and its attempts, though unsuccessful, to pass anti-lynching legislation.

The NAACP worked against racial discrimination in New Deal programs and in the military during World War II. During the civil rights movement of the 1950s and 1960s, Daisy Lampkin, Ella Baker, Ruby Hurley, and Daisy Bates were among the notable activists in the organization. The NAACP provided leadership in developing coalitions for civil rights legislation, including the Civil Rights Acts of 1957, 1960, and 1964; the Voting Rights Act of 1965; and the Fair Housing Rights Act of 1968.

In addition to its leadership in Congress, the NAACP has developed numerous court cases and provided legal support to civil rights activists. In 1954, the NAACP's lawyers argued *Brown v. Board of Education* of Topeka, Kansas, the landmark case that ended legal racial segregation in public education. The next year, the organization's Montgomery Branch secretary, Rosa Parks, refused to surrender her bus seat to a white man, prompting the city's bus boycott. Among the many lawyers working for the NAACP, Constance Baker Motley assisted in and argued several of the civil rights cases of the 1950s and 1960s, including defending Martin Luther King, Jr., and other notable civil rights leaders.

> **See also** Baker, Ella Josephine; Bates, Daisy Lee Gatson; Bethune, Mary Jane McLeod; Civil Rights Movement, Women in the; Hurley, Ruby; Lampkin, Daisy Elizabeth Adams; Motley, Constance Baker; Simmons, Althea T. L.; Terrell, Mary Eliza Church; Wells-Barnett, Ida Bell
>
> **References** www.naacp.org.

National Association of Colored Women's Clubs, Inc.

Founded in 1896, the National Association of Colored Women's Clubs (NACWC) brought together black women's clubs across the country into the first national communications network among African American women. As the Progressive reform movement emerged in the 1890s, African American women began to form local service and education clubs in several cities. When the General Federation of Women's Clubs refused to accept the Woman's Era Club, an organization of African American women, black women's clubs became affiliated with either the National Federation of Afro-American Women (NFAAW) or the National Colored Women's League (NCWL). In 1896, the NFAAW and NCWL merged to form the NACWC. The organizing committee elected Mary Church Terrell the group's first president.

With the motto "Lifting as We Climb," NACWC members participated in local projects including kindergartens, day nurseries, orphanages, jail and settlement work, and girls' homes. Mothers' clubs, hospitals, and the needs of black women domestic workers were other areas in which members worked. The NACWC also supported equal rights for blacks, work opportunities for black women, and changes in the criminal justice system. These areas of concern represented the priorities of members who sought racial uplift as the NACWC's primary focus. The association also worked for woman suffrage, particularly to include provisions in the woman suffrage amendment to protect Southern black women's suffrage rights.

After World War I, the number of lynchings increased dramatically, and the NACWC responded by mobilizing women to distribute information about the crime and to raise money for the National Association for the Advancement of Colored People's national campaign to end it. In 1922, Mary Talbert formed the Anti-lynching Crusaders in an effort to unite one million women against lynching and to pass a federal anti-lynching bill. The NACWC published reports on the crime that refuted the myths surrounding it, particularly that white men lynched black men in retribution for black men raping white women. Anti-lynching legislation did not pass, but the

Harriet Tubman, one of the founders of the National Association of Colored Women, ca. 1860. (Library of Congress LC-USZ62-781)

publicity and other organizational efforts to end the crime contributed to a reduction in the number of instances of it.

By 1920, the NACWC had 300,000 members and had paid the $5,000 mortgage on abolitionist Frederick Douglass's home in Anacostia, which it continues to maintain. When Mary McLeod Bethune became president in 1924, she led efforts to purchase a building for the organization's national headquarters. When she founded the National Council of Negro Women in 1935 to work for national policy changes, the association became less politically involved and more social. By the 1980s, its membership had dropped to 45,000, where it has remained relatively stable.

In 2006, the NACWC sponsored GrandParents Academy, providing leadership skills development, as well as other educational opportunities. It also has an AIDS (aquired immunodeficiency syndrome) educational program.

> **See also** Bethune, Mary Jane McLeod; Civil Rights Movement, Women in the; National Council of Negro Women; National Federation of Afro-American Women; Ruffin, Josephine St. Pierre; Suffrage; Talbert, Mary Morris Burnett; Terrell, Mary Eliza Church
>
> **References** Kendrick, "'They Also Serve': The National Association of Colored Women, Inc." (1990); Slavin, ed., *U.S. Women's Public Interest Groups* (1995); http://www.nacwc.org.

National Association of Commissions for Women

Founded in 1969, the National Association of Commissions for Women (NACW) is a non-partisan membership organization of government-created regional, state, and local commissions that works to improve the status of women. With equality and justice for all women as its mission, the NACW provides leadership on the national level, taking policy positions on national issues. The NACW provides 220 state and local commissions for women with technical advice and support.

> **See also** Commissions on the Status of Women; President's Commission on the Status of Women
> **References** www.nacw.org.

National Center for Lesbian Rights

Established in 1977, the National Center for Lesbian Rights (NCLR) is a multicultural legal center focused on the rights and safety of lesbians and their families. Using litigation and advocacy, NCLR has projects devoted to family law, youth, immigration and asylum, older citizens, and sports. It also publishes material on parenting, adoption, youth in foster care and the juvenile justice system, school safety, employment, marriage, and other topics. Each year, NCLR serves more than 4,500 individuals in all 50 states.

> **Reference** http://nclrights.org
> **Document** Kate Kendall, "It's the Family, Stupid!" 1999.

National Coalition Against Domestic Violence

Founded in 1978, the National Coalition Against Domestic Violence (NCADV) seeks to end violence in the lives of women and children through a national network of state coalitions and local organizations serving battered women and their children. The coalition provides technical assistance to member groups, conducts community awareness campaigns, and develops public policy recommendations. It sponsors a national lobby day, providing state and local advocates with assistance in meeting with their members of Congress to dicuss anti-violence legislation. NCADV sponsors Domestic Violence Awareness Month every October to focus attention on the problem and a national registry, called "Remember My Name," of women killed as a result of domestic violence.

> **See also** Domestic Violence
> **References** www.ncadv.org.

National Coalition of 100 Black Women

Founded in 1981, the National Coalition of 100 Black Women (NCBW) develops programs to empower African American women. The organization has sixty-two chapters in twenty-three states and the District of Columbia. The organization's roots are in a 1970 gathering of African American women in New York City to address the needs of black women, including the black family, career advancement, and political and economic empowerment. Through the coalition's programs, members developed leadership skills and sought ways to use them. The membership grew beyond the 100 in its name, and through the leadership of president Jewell Jackson McCabe, it expanded into a national organization in 1981.

The coalition's areas of interest in public policy include affirmative action, pay equity, equal opportunity, foreign aid, reproductive health rights, welfare reform, and support for federal appointees. Among the projects NCBW has sponsored are a program to match pregnant teenagers with role models, a career exploration program for high school students, and a model mentoring program. In 1986, NCBW held a colloquy examining the leadership values of prominent black women, and in 1989 it launched a health rights education program.

See also Abortion; Affirmative Action; McCabe, Jewell Jackson; Pay Equity

References www.womenconnect.com/ncbw/history.htm.

National Commission on the Observance of International Women's Year, 1975

Created by President Gerald Ford's Executive Order 11832 on 9 January 1975, the National Commission on the Observance of International Women's Year, 1975, was later charged by Congress with organizing and convening a National Women's Conference (NWC). The congressional action, signed by the president on 24 December 1975, was sponsored by Congresswoman Bella Abzug (D-NY) and constituted U.S. recognition of the United Nations' project to focus attention on the problems of women throughout the world.

Among those appointed to the commission were presiding officer Jill Ruckelshaus, actor Jean Stapleton, former Congresswoman Clare Boothe Luce, and Republican National Committee chair Mary Louise Smith, all active feminists. The commissioners appointed committees to review the progress women had made since the issuance of the 1963 report by the President's Commission on the Status of Women and to make recommendations. In addition, an interdepartmental task force was created to ensure that agencies prepared analyses of the impact of federal programs on women. The commission made its report in "To Form a More Perfect Union...," which included 115 recommendations for policy changes to improve women's status. The report became an integral part of the planning for the 1977 National Women's Conference.

After the passage of Abzug's bill, the commission's tasks changed from performing research and making recommendations to developing plans for a national convention, organizing fifty-six state and territorial preliminary conventions, and providing support to them. In addition, with the election of President Jimmy Carter, several of the commission members were replaced with his appointees.

Congress gave the commission a feminist mandate, directing it to involve groups "which work to advance the rights of women," to "recognize the contributions of women to the development of our country," and to "assess the progress that has been made to date by both the private and public sectors in promoting equality between men and women in all aspects of life in the United States." The women and men appointed to the commission generally had strong feminist credentials, and some of them were feminist leaders, including commission co-chair Abzug, *Ms.* magazine editor Gloria Steinem, Liz Carpenter, National Women's Political Caucus chair Audrey Rowe Colom, former Congresswoman Martha Griffiths, former first lady Betty Ford, and others. The topical areas that the commission drafted for the conference's attention reflected feminist priorities: child care, reproductive rights, employment, the Equal Rights Amendment, and related issues.

The commission's duties included appointing state coordinating committees to organize and convene a state meeting. At the state meetings, the public participated by choosing delegates to the national conference, commenting on draft resolutions prepared by the national commission, and proposing resolutions for the national commission's consideration. Although the state meetings were free to select delegates of their choice, Congress specifically directed the commission to ensure that low-income women; members of diverse racial, ethnic, and religious groups; and women of all ages were represented in the delegations. The commission accomplished the goal by reserving some delegate assignments to itself and creating the required balance after the states had selected their delegates.

Congress appropriated $5 million to fund the commission. Some of the funds were allocated to the states for their meetings, and the balance was used to provide financial assistance to delegates who could not pay their own expenses, to prepare and distribute background information and the final report, to hire staff, and to pay for the conference and its related expenses.

The National Women's Conference was held in November 1977, and the commission submitted its report, The Spirit of Houston, to President Jimmy Carter on 22 March 1978. The commission dissolved on 31 March 1978 as mandated by Congress. Carter established the National Advisory Committee for Women in April 1978, but its effectiveness was limited by a disagreement between Abzug, its chair, and Carter. Ultimately, a group of volunteers formed the National Women's Conference Committee to continue the NWC's work.

> **See also** Abortion; Abzug, Bella Savitzky; Carpenter, Mary Elizabeth (Liz) Sutherland; Employment Discrimination; Equal Rights Amendment; Ford, Elizabeth Ann (Betty) Bloomer; Griffiths, Martha Edna Wright; Luce, Clare Boothe; National Advisory Committee for Women; National Women's Conference; National Women's Conference Committee; Smith, Mary Louise; Steinem, Gloria Marie
> **References** Bird, *What Women Want* (1979); East, *American Women: 1963, 1983, 2003* (1983).

National Committee on Pay Equity

Founded in 1979, the National Committee on Pay Equity is a coalition of more than 55 organizations and coalitions working to end sex-based and race-based wage discrimination. The organization provides leadership, information, and technical assistance to pay equity advocates, public officials, employers, the media, and the public. The organization supports the proposed Paycheck Fairness Act and the proposed Fair Pay Act.

According to the committee, the wage gap costs the average American full-time woman worker between $700,000 and $2 million over her lifetime.

> **See also** Pay Equity
> **References** http://www.pay-equity.org

National Committee to Defeat the UnEqual Rights Amendment

Organized in 1944, the National Committee to Defeat the UnEqual Rights Amendment (NCDURA) was a coalition of twenty-seven groups, including labor unions, the National Consumers League, the League of Women Voters, the National Council of

Catholic Women, and the National Council of Negro Women. The organization emerged as the Equal Rights Amendment (ERA) and attracted increasingly favorable attention during World War II. NCDURA advocated "specific bills for specific ills" instead of the ERA because the ERA would invalidate protective labor legislation for women. The organization first proposed an equal pay act as an alternative to the ERA but was unable to gain congressional approval for the measure.

In 1947, under the leadership of Women's Bureau director Mary Anderson, NCDURA changed its name to the National Committee on the Status of Women and proposed the Status Bill. The bill stated that "no distinctions on the basis of sex shall be made except such as are reasonably based on differences in physical structure, biological or social function." The measure also included a provision to create a Commission on the Legal Status of Women to study sex discrimination, but Congress did not pass it. The committee dissolved without passing legislation. President John F. Kennedy, however, created the President's Commission on the Status of Women in 1961 by executive order.

See also Anderson, Mary; Equal Rights Amendment; League of Women Voters; National Consumers League; National Council of Negro Women; President's Commission on the Status of Women

References Freeman, *From Protection to Equal Opportunity: The Revolution in Women's Legal Status* (1990).

National Congress of Black Women

Founded in 1984 as the National Political Congress of Black Women, the National Congress of Black Women (NCBW) provides a political forum for African American women. Its primary mission is the political empowerment of African American women. The NCBW encourages black women to register to vote, trains them in the political process, and encourages them to seek both elective and appointive offices at all levels of government. In addition, it has identified black women who were qualified for appointment to high levels of policymaking within President Bill Clinton's administration, contributing to the greater number of African American women serving in his administration than in any previous administration. It also develops and advocates public policy. Other areas of interest include preparing African American women under 18 for political involvement and protesting "gangsta rap" and misogynistic lyrics in that music genre.

The NCBW has worked for affirmative action, access to non-traditional jobs, economic development, housing and urban development, and other issues. Through its hearings on housing market discrimination against African Americans, it has prompted legislative action. The NCBW continues to work on job discrimination, health care, drug abuse, single parenting, education, and the availability of child day care.

See also Chisholm, Shirley Anita St. Hill

References www.npcbw.org.

National Consumers League

Formed in 1899, the National Consumers League (NCL) sought to improve women's and children's working conditions through consumer pressure and protective labor legislation. At the end of the twentieth century, the NCL stated that its mission was "to protect and promote the economic and social interests of America's consumers." It operates the National Fraud Information Center and the Internet Fraud Watch and manages the Alliance Against Fraud in Telemarketing, the Child Labor Coalition, and a public service campaign to teach young children what to do in case of a fire.

The NCL began as a local effort in New York to help retail saleswomen obtain relief from long hours and low wages. In 1890, a group of philanthropists, social reformers, and settlement house leaders established the Consumers League of New York (CLNY). The group developed a list of minimum working conditions, including minimum pay at $6 per week, a ten-hour day, a six-day week, a locker room, a lunch room, and no children under the age of fourteen. CLNY investigated local retailers, identified those that met the minimum conditions, and published the results as its White List. Only eight stores made the first White List, but CLNY leaders encouraged consumers to limit their purchases to merchants on its list. In addition, the CLNY encouraged and helped women retail workers organize unions despite the resistance of male union leaders. As the league expanded into other cities, it identified sweatshops and the products they made and encouraged consumers to avoid purchasing items produced by them.

As more cities organized consumers' leagues, they joined together as the National Consumers League in 1899. By that time, it had become apparent that voluntary efforts had only limited success, and the organization entered a period of professionalization. A key part of the transformation was the decision to hire Florence Kelley as the first general secretary. Kelley organized leagues in sixty cities in twenty states and launched a series of investigations and reports. First, the league investigated workplaces where women's and children's stitched cotton underwear was produced and documented low wages, long hours, forced speed-ups, and poor working conditions. The second investigation probed home work and revealed filthy tenements, people with contagious diseases working on clothing, starvation wages, and child labor. The third researched child labor, disclosing the 1.7 million children under sixteen years old working in New England and Southern textile mills.

Kelley kept the NCL's focus on child labor for the rest of her tenure as the organization's executive secretary. In 1904, the NCL published a handbook on child labor that included a state-by-state report on child labor laws. She helped organize the National Child Labor Committee and, with Lillian Wald, proposed the creation of a federal commission on children. President Theodore Roosevelt's 1909 White House Conference on Child Health and Welfare provided a forum for the two women to advocate their proposal. In 1912, Congress created the Children's Bureau, and the NCL provided the bureau with information that guided the formation of its legislative agenda. The NCL advocated passing federal child labor laws and twice succeeded, but the U.S. Supreme Court found both of them unconstitutional. Proponents next gained congressional approval of a child labor amendment, but the states did not ratify it. New Deal legislation, however, prohibited most child labor.

The NCL's 1907 study of self-supporting women's wages and standards of living led to the organization's effort to pass minimum wage laws. Kelley drafted a model minimum wage law that Massachusetts passed in 1912, and she traveled the country, speaking on the law and playing a significant role in nine additional states' passing similar policies within the year.

The NCL also played significant roles in defending protective labor legislation in the courts. The most visible case was *Muller v. Oregon* (1908), a challenge to the state's law limiting women's workday to ten hours. Kelley persuaded Louis D. Brandeis, who donated his services, to defend the law before the U.S. Supreme Court. The NCL gathered much of the research for what became known as the Brandeis brief, an innovation that presented more than 100 pages of social and economic research to support the defense. The NCL raised funds to print the brief and to pay other expenses. The court decided in favor of Oregon's law limiting women's workday. The NCL took thirteen more cases to the courts, and eight of them went to the U.S. Supreme Court.

In the 1930s, New Deal legislation addressed many of the issues that the NCL had raised, including minimum wage legislation that covered both women and men, maximum working hours, and child labor. During World War II, the NCL turned its attention to advocacy in state legislatures, and in the 1950s and 1960s, it worked to include migrant workers under state and federal employment laws. Consumer protection and efforts to reduce child labor were the NCL's focus in the 1990s. In 2006, privacy, food safety, and medication were added to its priorities.

> **See also** Employment Discrimination; Kelley, Florence; *Muller v. Oregon*; Protective Legislation

> **References** National Consumers League, *Roots of the Consumer Movement: A Chronicle of Consumer History in the Twentieth Century* (1979); www.nclnet.org.

National Council of Jewish Women

Founded in 1893, the National Council of Jewish Women (NCJW) emerged from the desire to preserve Judaism by teaching Jewish women their religious duties. It soon became an advocacy organization addressing a wide range of social, health, environmental, and peace issues. Its more than 90,000 members in more than 500 affiliates seek to ensure individual and civil rights, improve the status of women, further the quality of Jewish life, improve day care and public schooling, and promote the well-being of children and families.

Early projects included founding a religious school for Jewish immigrant girls in Chicago and a synagogue in Indiana. Described as a "conduit through which Progressive ideology entered the Jewish community," the NCJW provided aid to single immigrant women, meeting them as they entered the country, offering them housing, and providing other services to help prevent them from becoming prostitutes. The success of the programs caused the federal government to seek the NCJW's assistance with immigrants. In 1904, the council established a permanent immigrant aid station at Ellis Island to receive Jewish women. Other early programs included programs for the blind and assistance to delinquent children.

In the early 1900s, the NCJW's advocacy work began with its support for the 1906 Pure Food and Drug Act and Meat Inspection Act and continued with advocacy for child labor laws and protective labor legislation for women. In 1920, the NCJW joined the Women's Joint Congressional Committee and helped pass the Sheppard-Towner Maternity and Infancy Protection Act of 1921 and the Cable Acts, among other measures. The council supported civil rights legislation, beginning with the anti-lynching bill in 1938, continuing through the Civil Rights Acts of 1957, 1964, and 1985; and placing particular emphasis on the Voting Rights Act of 1965. The organization supports the Equal Rights Amendment, reproductive rights, an end to domestic violence, and development of safe, affordable, quality child day care.

> **See also** Abortion; Cable Acts; Civil Rights Act of 1964, Title VII; Domestic Violence; Equal Rights Amendment; Protective Legislation; Sheppard-Towner Maternity and Infancy Protection Act of 1921; Voting Rights Act of 1965; Women's Joint Congressional Committee
>
> **References** Rogow, *Gone to Another Meeting: The National Council of Jewish Women, 1893–1993* (1993); www.ncjw.org.

National Council of Negro Women

Founded in 1935 by Mary McLeod Bethune, the National Council of Negro Women (NCNW) was the first national coalition of black women's organizations. The National Association of Colored Women (NACW), founded in 1896, had brought together women's clubs and national associations of women's clubs, and the NCNW created an umbrella organization that included the NACW, African American women's college-based professional sororities, and other professional, religious, and political organizations. The NCNW's mission is "to advance opportunities and the quality of life for African American women, their families and communities," and it seeks to "extend the collective power and leadership of African American women."

When she organized the NCNW, Bethune believed that bringing black women's organizations together would "harness the great power of nearly a million women into a force for constructive action." After serving as president of the National Association of Colored Women from 1924 to 1928, Bethune was convinced that a national coalition of women's groups was needed to gain the full representation of African American women in national public affairs. By bringing national African American women's organizations together, Bethune believed that coordination of the organizations' efforts would reduce duplication among them and increase their effectiveness.

Ending segregation and other forms of racism has been an NCNW priority since its beginning. In the 1940s, the organization exposed discriminatory practices that excluded African Americans from government training programs and employment opportunities at plants producing materials for World War II. The NCNW worked for the admission of black women into the women's divisions of the Army, Navy, and Air Force, and Bethune recruited many of the first black women to join the Women's Army Corps. Through the NCNW's advocacy, African American women gained positions in the War Manpower Commission, the Women's and Children's Bureaus, the Department of Labor, and other federal agencies. By the end of Bethune's tenure as president of the council in 1949, the organization was recognized as the major advocate for black women.

Another African American woman with strong leadership ability, Dorothy Irene Height, became president in 1957. Height had served the NCNW in several posts and brought a strong understanding of the issues before the organization, particularly the emerging civil rights movement. In the 1960s, the NCNW worked with the Student Nonviolent Coordinating Committee on voter registration projects by sending volunteers, money, and other resources. In 1965, the NCNW recruited Northern white female professionals to work in Freedom Schools that offered classes in voting and other related areas.

Under Height's leadership, the NCNW focused attention on youth, employment opportunities, housing, health, hunger, civil rights, women's issues, family issues, and related areas. With a grant from the U.S. Agency for International Development, the NCNW established an international division to work with women in Africa, the Caribbean, and other areas of the world. The NCNW dedicated the Mary McLeod Bethune Memorial in 1974, the first monument to an African American or to a woman of any race on public land in Washington, D.C., and the Mary McLeod Bethune Museum and National Archives for Black Women's History was also dedicated in 1974.

In 1986, Height began the Black Family Reunion celebrations, annual cultural events that focus on the strengths and values of the African American family. The Black Family Reunion Cookbook was published in 1992, the first of three volumes that document the diversity and heritage of African American cuisine.

The Dorothy I. Height Leadership Institute held its first programs in 1997. The institute provides three kinds of leadership training—for affiliate organizations' members, community volunteers, and college students. The fourth component of the institute is the African American Women's Critical Issues Research and Development, a think-tank approach to developing positions on current issues and the subsequent dissemination of the information to members and affiliates.

The NCNW's membership includes thirty-seven affiliated national organizations, 250 community groups in forty-two states, and 45,000 individuals. The national affiliates include sororities, professional associations, and civic and social clubs.

See also Alpha Kappa Alpha Sorority; Baker, Ella Josephine; Bethune, Mary Jane McLeod; Civil Rights Movement, Women in the; Height, Dorothy Irene; National Association of Colored Women; Tubman, Harriet

References Fitzgerald, *The National Council of Negro Women* (1985); Hine, *Black Women in America* (1993); www.ncnw.com.

National Federation of Afro-American Women

Formed in 1895, the National Federation of Afro-American Women (NFAAW) was organized "to teach an ignorant and suspicious world that our [black women's] aims are identical with those of all good aspiring women." African American leader Josephine Ruffin wrote those words as part of her call to create a group to counter a journalist's assertion that black women were "prostitutes, thieves, and liars." Ruffin called on African American women to work together to teach the world the truth. Twenty clubs founded the NFAAW, a number that grew to thirty-six clubs from twelve states. The NFAAW merged with the Colored Women's League in 1896 to form the National Association of Colored Women.

See also Colored Women's League; National Association of Colored Women

References Hine and Thompson, *A Shining Thread of Hope: The History of Black Women in America* (1998).

National Federation of Republican Women

Founded in 1938, the National Federation of Republican Women (NFRW) is the largest women's partisan organization in the United States, with about 100,000 members in 1,800 local groups based in every state, the District of Columbia, Puerto Rico, and the Virgin Islands. NFRW members work to elect Republicans to every level of public office through educational programs, fundraising efforts, and volunteer work.

Republican women had begun forming local groups in the 1870s to support the party's efforts, particularly in election years. Often, these groups organized on an ad hoc basis and dissolved after the election. Hundreds of clubs existed by the late 1930s; Indiana, for example, had more than 100 Republican women's organizations. Some of the groups caused Republican Party leaders concern because they tried to establish party policy, endorsed candidates in the primary elections, or worked for Democratic candidates. In addition, by the 1930s the Democratic Party had developed a national network of women volunteers and held firm majorities in Congress; a majority of the nation's governors were Democrats; and Democratic President Franklin D. Roosevelt was in the White House.

Party leaders decided that they could impose discipline on the groups, coordinate their programs, and utilize the volunteer resources by bringing them together under an umbrella. In 1938, Republican National Committee (RNC) assistant chairperson and director of women's activities Marion E. Martin called a meeting to unite the groups into a national organization. Eleven states joined as charter members, representing eighty-five clubs and 95,000 members. Martin became executive director of the NFRW and developed political education programs, organized affiliates, and provided leadership. By 1940, the federation had 350,000 members.

At the 1967 NFRW biennial convention, a controversy developed over the election of the group's leadership. Generally, the organization's vice president is elected president for the next two-year term. Phyllis Schlafly had held the vice presidency for the 1965–1967 term, but some NFRW and Republican Party leaders believed that she was too conservative for the good of the party and influenced the nominating committee to endorse NFRW board member Gladys O'Donnell and leave Schlafly off the ballot. Amid charges of unfair voting procedures, O'Donnell won the presidency. Outraged, Schlafly called for the creation of a conservative women's organization and launched the *Phyllis Schlafly Report*, a monthly newsletter.

The NFRW seeks to advance the power of women through political access and participation and to develop leaders for the future. Its current programs include recruiting women candidates for local and state office, lobbying, training women in campaign management, and organizing leadership development seminars.

See also Eagle Forum; Martin, Marion E.; National League of Republican Colored Women; Republican Party, Women in the; Schlafly, Phyllis Stewart

References Rymph, "Marion Martin and the Problem of Republican Feminism" (1996); Williams, comp., *The History of the Founding and Development of the National Federation of Republican Women* (1963); www.nfrw.org.

National Gender Balance Project USA

Founded in 1988, the National Gender Balance Project USA (NGBP) works to increase the number of women serving on state boards and commissions by passing legislation requiring governors to appoint women to the positions. In 1988, Iowa became the first state in the nation to require gender balance on all state boards and commissions, committees, and councils. Iowa feminist Kappie Spencer founded the NGBP to encourage replication of Iowa's law in other states. By bringing the concept to the attention of other feminist groups, the project has enlisted the support of several groups, including the American Association of University Women, the Women's Agenda Conference, the National Association of Commissions for Women, and the National Women's Political Caucus. Several states have adopted variations of Iowa's law, with Florida expanding it to include ethnic representation. The NGBP argues that attaining gender balance better utilizes women's talents and provides a broader perspective for developing policy. In addition, serving on policymaking bodies provides a route to elective office for women and men.

> **See also** American Association of University Women; National Association of Commissions for Women; National Women's Political Caucus

National League of Republican Colored Women

The National League of Republican Colored Women (NLRCW) developed from the National Association of Colored Women (NACW) in 1924, when Republican national committeewomen Mamie Williams of Georgia and Mary Booze of Mississippi united black women's Republican clubs. Among the group's officers was treasurer Mary Church Terrell, the first president of the NACW. With the slogan "We are in politics to stay and we shall be a stay in politics," the group worked to gain African American women's support for the Republican ticket in the 1924 elections.

In 1928, NLRCW president Nannie Burroughs of Washington, D.C., was appointed to the Republican National Committee's Speakers Bureau and was a popular and sought-after speaker. The group celebrated Republican presidential candidate Herbert Hoover's success, and several NLRCW members went to Washington for his inauguration. When they arrived, however, Burroughs was asked to retrieve inauguration tickets accidentally sent to the African American women who had worked in the campaign. In addition, the inaugural ball was segregated.

Over the next four years, an accumulation of racial offenses and the Hoover administration's inaction on civil rights prompted many African American women to leave the Republican Party and give their allegiance to the Democratic Party. By 1932, the NLRCW had dissolved.

> **See also** National Federation of Republican Women; Republican Party, Women in the; Terrell, Mary Eliza Church
>
> **References** Higginbotham, *In Politics to Stay: Black Women Leaders and Party Politics in the 1920s* (1990).

National Organization for Women

Founded in 1966, the National Organization for Women (NOW) has more than 500,000 members and 500 chapters, making it the largest organization of feminist activists in the United States. NOW was founded out of frustration with the Equal Employment Opportunity Commission's (EEOC's) resistance to enforcing the prohibitions against sex discrimination in Title VII of the Civil Rights Act of 1964. Feminist leaders Betty Friedan, Pauli Murray, EEOC commissioner Aileen Hernandez, Catherine East, and others concluded that a civil rights organization for women was needed to advocate for women's concerns. Their idea was to create a group for women comparable to the National Association for the Advancement of Colored People. Twenty-eight women each contributed $5, and NOW was born. The founders stated NOW's purpose as follows: "To take action to bring women into full participation in the mainstream of American society now, assuming all the privileges and responsibilities thereof in truly equal partnership with men." NOW's first action was sending a telegram to the EEOC, urging the commissioners to end sex-segregated help-wanted newspaper ads. Challenging the EEOC was a primary focus of NOW's efforts for several years.

In late October 1966, an organizing conference elected Friedan president, Karen Clarenbach chair of the board, and Hernandez executive vice president. In 1967, task forces on women in poverty, legal and political rights, equal opportunity in employment, the image of women in mass media, and other groups gathered information and stated NOW's position on the issues. NOW's first priorities included federal aid for child care centers and full income tax deductions for child care services. In addition that year, support for the Equal Rights Amendment (ERA) and the repeal of all abortion laws became and continue to be the group's most publicized, most ardently supported, and most controversial issues.

Support for the ERA had a divisive effect on NOW. Several of its leaders and followers came from organized labor, particularly the United Auto Workers (UAW). In 1967, the UAW opposed the ERA, and although the UAW members active in NOW supported the amendment, they felt that they had to withdraw from NOW when the organization endorsed it. Two years later, after the UAW decided to support the ERA, women UAW members rejoined NOW and resumed their active participation.

NOW's support for the repeal of abortion laws also caused division. Some feminists who supported the Equal Rights Amendment believed that adding abortion to the organization's agenda made it unnecessarily controversial and held the potential for alienating feminists who did not want abortion decriminalized. In 1968, one of NOW's founding members left and organized the Women's Equity Action League. Despite the controversy, NOW continued its work for reproductive rights by organizing clinic defense, lobbying Congress for the Freedom of Access to Clinic Entrances Act, and winning a major lawsuit against Operation Rescue under the Racketeer Influenced and Corrupt Organizations (RICO) statute.

Attracting and effectively using press attention were among the leadership's greatest strengths. Members picketed men-only restaurants, demonstrated on Mother's Day for "Rights, Not Roses," and protested laws against abortion. NOW initiated and largely organized the Women's Strike for Equality on 26 August 1970, an event that included demonstrations in more than ninety major cities in forty-two states and involved more than 100,000 women nationwide. In another demonstration supporting child care tax deductions, a baby carriage brigade included signs asking: "Are children as important as martinis?" referring to the tax deductions allowed for business entertaining. Other examples of NOW-sponsored marches include the 1978 march for the Equal Rights Amendment, which drew more than 100,000 people to Washington,

D.C., and the March for Women's Lives in 1992, which drew 750,000 abortion rights supporters to Washington, D.C., the largest protest ever in the nation's capital.

Through the NOW Legal Defense and Education Fund (LDEF), founded in 1970, NOW also gained publicity for the lawsuits it filed. For example, in 1970 NOW filed a sex discrimination complaint under Executive Order 11375 against 1,300 corporations that had failed to file affirmative action plans for hiring women. Beginning in 1971, NOW protested the discriminatory practices of AT&T in hiring, promotions, fringe benefits, and executive appointments. In the agreement reached among the Department of Labor, the EEOC, and AT&T, the corporation agreed to a lump-sum payment of $15 million to 15,000 workers, wage adjustments, and new hiring practices, including giving more women craft jobs and broadened management opportunities. In the 1990s, the NOW LDEF won major settlements in sex discrimination lawsuits against the Mitsubishi Corporation and Smith-Barney.

In addition to its controversial stands on abortion and equal rights, NOW added a third issue: lesbianism as a concern of feminism. Initially, Friedan had rejected including lesbian issues in NOW's agenda and had referred to lesbians as the "lavender menace." At its 1971 convention, however, NOW passed a resolution stating that lesbianism was a concern of feminism.

After congressional approval of the Equal Rights Amendment in 1972, NOW committed much of its resources to its ratification. The early successes of the amendment in 1972—twenty-two states ratified that year—lulled some leaders into believing that the amendment would easily be ratified by the necessary thirty-eight states. After Phyllis Schlafly organized Stop ERA in 1973 and defeated ratification attempts in several states, it became clear that a more organized and better-funded effort would be required for ratification. In 1978, NOW announced a boycott of unratified states, an effort that other organizations joined. NOW helped extend the ratification deadline and intensified its efforts, but the amendment failed in 1982.

Although the ERA consumed many of the organization's resources for several years and remains one of the organization's platforms, it continued to support and develop other issues related to obtaining women's equality. NOW works to end sexual harassment and sexual and physical violence against women. It also works to elect feminists to public office, to end racism, to protect abortion rights and reproductive freedom, for constitutional equality, for economic justice, and to secure civil rights for lesbians.

> **See also** Abortion; Affirmative Action; Civil Rights Act of 1964, Title VII; Equal Employment Opportunity Commission; Equal Rights Amendment; Feminist Movement; Friedan, Betty Naomi Goldstein; Hernandez, Aileen Clarke; Murray, Pauli; National Association for the Advancement of Colored People, Women in the; *NOW v. Scheidler*; Suffrage; Women's Equity Action League
>
> **References** Carabillo, Meuli, and Csida, *Feminist Chronicles 1953–1993* (1993); Freeman, *The Politics of Women's Liberation* (1975); www.now.org.
>
> **Document** "The National Organization for Women's Bill of Rights for Women," 1967

National Organization of Black Elected Legislative Women

Founded in 1985, the National Organization of Black Elected Legislative Women (NOBEL/Women) trains African American women to prepare them for elective and appointive office. Founded by former state legislator Diane Watson, NOBEL/Women works to increase the number of African American women elected to every level of government and to increase the number of black women appointed to private and public boards and commissions. In 2001, NOBEL/Women and the Center for American Women and Politics (CAWP) formed the NOBEL/Women and CAWP Leadership Institute. NOBEL/Women also sponsors forums and other educational programs. NOBEL/Women focuses on public policy issues, promotes black women's participation in the development of public policy, and develops policy proposals.

NOBEL has lobbied for programs to help black youth, pressed for the rights of political refugees in South Africa, and sponsored a symposium on the black community and diseases affecting women.

See also National Political Congress of Black Women; National Women's Political Caucus

References Hine, ed., *Black Women in America* (1993); http://nobelwomen.org.

National Right to Life Committee

Founded in 1973 by the Roman Catholic Church, the National Right to Life Committee (NRLC) later became a non-sectarian group. With 3,000 chapters in all 50 states, the NRLC is the largest pro-life organization in the United States. The NRLC was organized in response to the 1973 U.S. Supreme Court decision in *Roe v. Wade* that legalized abortions. The committee coordinates lobbying efforts at the state and federal levels, involves its membership in letter-writing campaigns and other forms of citizen advocacy to enact restrictions on abortions and to end legal abortions, and employs professional lobbyists.

The NRLC has supported a human life amendment to declare the personhood of the fetus from the moment of conception. Although the NRLC and other pro-life groups have not succeeded in passing the amendment, they have helped to pass restrictive laws in most states, including measures that required parental notification before a minor could obtain an abortion and mandatory waiting periods.

The NRLC's departments include a general counsel which defends pro-life legislation in the courts, the NRL Political Action Committee which identifies and supports pro-life candidates, and outreach which works with churches, college students, and other groups.

See also Abortion

References Blanchard, *The Anti-Abortion Movement and the Rise of the Religious Right: From Polite to Fiery Protest* (1994); http://www.nrlc.org

National Welfare Rights Organization

Founded in 1967, the National Welfare Rights Organization (NWRO) educated welfare recipients about their rights and lobbied Congress. In the 1960s, the presence of poverty in the midst of affluence led President Lyndon Johnson to discuss the possibility of eliminating poverty in the United States. As Congress passed several anti-poverty measures, welfare recipients created networks to educate themselves and others about the programs and their rights within them.

Initially, local groups used protest strategies such as occupying welfare offices and demanding resolution to their grievances. Later, the NWRO lobbied Congress for a guaranteed national income and for resources to allow welfare recipients to manage their own lives, and they protested policies that invaded welfare recipients' privacy. The organization's successes included an increase in the benefit level of the food stamp program and the addition of a cost-of-living provision in the program. NWRO also won cases in the U.S. Supreme Court, including one that gave welfare recipients the right to a hearing before the termination of their benefits. Bankruptcy in 1975 forced the closing of the national headquarters.

References Slavin, ed., *U.S. Women's Interest Groups* (1995).

National Woman Suffrage Association

Founded in 1869 by Elizabeth Cady Stanton and Susan B. Anthony, the National Woman Suffrage Association (NWSA) resulted from a conflict between the abolitionist and women's rights movements over the Fifteenth Amendment. Conflicts had first emerged over the Fourteenth Amendment's inclusion of the word male in its identification of citizens. When the Fifteenth Amendment was proposed, it limited its guarantees for voting rights to former slaves and did not include women. Suffragists Anthony and Stanton supported providing voting rights to former slaves, but they wanted the amendment to also include women. They appealed to the abolitionists and Republicans with whom they had long been allied but to no avail, and the amendment was introduced and ratified without including women in its provisions. To organize opposition against the amendment and to organize support for a woman suffrage amendment, Anthony and Stanton formed the NWSA. In response, women's rights advocates who supported the Fifteenth Amendment, even though it did not include women, organized the American Woman Suffrage Association. The two groups merged into the National American Woman Suffrage Association in 1890.

See also American Woman Suffrage Association; Anthony, Susan Brownell; Fifteenth Amendment; National American Woman Suffrage Association; Nineteenth Amendment; Stanton, Elizabeth Cady

References Flexner and Fitzpatrick, *Century of Struggle: The Woman's Rights Movement in the United States*, enlarged edition (1996).

National Woman's Loyal League

See **Woman's National Loyal League**

National Woman's Party

The National Woman's Party (NWP), founded by Alice Paul, initiated the concept of the Equal Rights Amendment in the early 1920s and continues to support passage and ratification of it. For decades, the NWP was the only active advocate of the amendment and was regularly in conflict with many women's organizations, leaving it isolated from them. In addition, the NWP membership was an elite group of women, and its leaders made no attempt to become a mass membership organization.

The NWP has its roots in two organizations founded to further the suffrage cause. The first, the Congressional Union, sought to obtain congressional approval of a suffrage amendment. In 1916, Paul began organizing the second organization, the Woman's Party, in states that had granted women suffrage. Through the Woman's Party,

Paul hoped to elect congressional candidates who would support the suffrage amendment. After passage of the Nineteenth Amendment granting women suffrage, the Woman's Party and the Congressional Union dissolved, and the NWP emerged in its place.

NWP viewed woman suffrage as the first step in women achieving full equality, noting that the vote had not eliminated sex discrimination. The NWP conducted a survey of state laws and identified policies that discriminated against women, including limits on women's rights to their earnings, to own property, to serve on juries, and to hold public office. In addition, child custody and divorce laws favored men. Based upon its research, the NWP announced its goal to gain complete equality for women.

In 1923, on the seventy-fifth anniversary of the Seneca Falls, New York, women's rights convention, the NWP approved the Lucretia Mott Amendment, also known as the Equal Rights Amendment. The amendment stated: "Men and women shall have equal rights throughout the United States and every place subject to its jurisdiction."

Social feminists and several women's organizations, including the National Women's Trade Union League, the League of Women Voters, the American Association of University Women, and the General Federation of Women's Clubs, opposed the amendment, fearing that it would make protective labor laws for women unconstitutional. They proposed the alternative of passing laws that removed the discriminatory policies, one law at a time, one state at a time. The NWP acknowledged that the ERA would likely outlaw protective labor legislation. In addition, some members believed

No more messenger boys for the National Woman's Party–from president to messenger all the members of the staff are feminine. This is in accordance with the stipulation of Mrs. Belmont when she donated the National Women's [i.e., Woman's] Party headquarters. Photo of Julia Obear, messenger 1922. (Library of Congress LC-USZ6-1841)

that the protective legislation kept women out of higher-paying jobs and generally reduced their opportunities. They rejected the alternative, saying that it would take too long. By insisting on the amendment, the NWP became alienated from other women's organizations.

Through the efforts of the NWP, the ERA was introduced in the U.S. Congress every session beginning in 1923. Occasionally, hearings were held on it, but there was no substantial action on it. With the advent of World War II, the NWP launched a massive publicity campaign to pass the ERA. It obtained endorsements for the ERA from celebrities, including novelist Pearl Buck, artist Georgia O'Keeffe, and actresses Helen Hayes and Katharine Hepburn, but the NWP remained unable to overcome labor and women's groups' objections to the amendment. After World War II, organizational turmoil and disputes diminished the group's effectiveness, and by the mid-1950s, its membership had declined from old age and death.

Although the NWP was able to have the amendment introduced in Congress, it was unable to move it beyond that initial step. In the 1960s, as the modern feminist movement developed and the ERA gained the support of the newly formed women's political organizations, the NWP participated in congressional hearings. However, leadership in the ratification campaign that followed congressional approval of the ERA came from the National Organization for Women, the National Women's Political Caucus, and other groups.

> **See also** American Association of University Women; Congressional Union; Equal Rights Amendment; General Federation of Women's Clubs; Juries, Women on; League of Women Voters; National American Woman Suffrage Association; National Organization for Women; National Women's Political Caucus; Nineteenth Amendment; Paul, Alice; Suffrage; Women's Trade Union League
>
> **References** Cott, "Feminist Politics in the 1920s: The National Woman's Party" (1984); Freeman, "From Protection to Equal Opportunity: The Revolution in Women's Legal Status" (1990); Lemon, *The Woman Citizen* (1973).

National Women's Conference

Held in Houston, Texas, from 19 to 21 November 1977, the National Women's Conference (NWC) brought together thousands of U.S. women delegates and observers to debate and approve the National Plan of Action. The NWC was the brainchild of Congresswoman Bella Abzug (D-NY), who successfully sponsored legislation authorizing the National Commission on the Observance of International Women's Year, 1975, to call the conference and to provide federal funding for it.

Congress provided the commission with clear directions regarding conference delegates, purposes, and processes. Public Law 94–167, which mandated the conference, overtly stated feminist goals, including recognition of "the contributions of women to the development of our country"; an assessment of "the progress that has been made to date by both the private and public sectors in promoting equality between men and women in all aspects of life in the United States"; an identification of "the barriers that prevent women from participating fully and equally in all aspects of national life"; and development of "recommendations for means by which such barriers can be removed." The feminist predisposition of the commission becomes apparent from some of those appointed to it: commission co-chair Abzug, *Ms.* magazine editor Gloria

Rosalynn Carter attends the National Womens Conference , 11/19/1977 Jimmy Carter Library (NLJC), 441 Freedom Parkway, Atlanta, GA 30307-1498 PHONE: 404-865-7100, FAX: 404-865-7102, EMAIL: carter.library@nara.gov NLC-WHSP-C-03425-30A

Steinem, former Congresswoman Martha Griffiths (D-MI), California Assemblywoman and later Congresswoman Maxine Waters (D-CA), National Organization for Women president Eleanor Smeal, and other feminist leaders. Although the law also called for racial, ethnic, age, and religious diversity and the purposeful inclusion of low-income women, it did not require political diversity.

Congress mandated state meetings in every state and the six territories (the District of Columbia, the Commonwealth of Puerto Rico, Guam, American Samoa, the Virgin Islands, and the Trust Territory of the Pacific Islands), and in compliance fifty-six state conferences were held before the November NWC. At the state meetings, which were open to the public, attendees debated the draft resolutions proposed by the commission and proposed their own resolutions. Attendees also selected delegates to the NWC, an open process that resulted in considerable consternation among conference organizers when conservative groups such as the Eagle Forum, the John Birch Society, the Ku Klux Klan, and the Mormon Church began packing state meetings to elect sympathetic delegates. After Utah, Mississippi, and other states elected conservative delegates, NWC organizers began to fear confrontations between feminists and conservatives and the ultimate defeat of their agenda.

After states had chosen their delegations, 1,403 women had been selected. In addition, 186 alternates, forty-seven commissioners, and 370 delegates-at-large had official standing at the NWC. The status of delegate-at-large had been created as a way for the commission to establish the required diversity. The states, however, had successfully reached out to groups that had historically been underrepresented, resulting in 64.5 percent of the delegates being white, compared to 84.4 percent of the general female population, leaving some of the delegate-at-large positions to be filled by white, middle-class women.

The NWC opened on 19 November 1977, featuring the presentation of a lighted torch that more than 2,000 women runners had relayed 2,610 miles from Seneca Falls, New York, the site of the first women's rights convention, to Houston. After first lady Rosalynn Carter and former first ladies Betty Ford and Lady Bird Johnson spoke to the convention, deliberations on the resolutions began. Using microphones placed throughout the convention hall, delegates addressed the convention, supporting, attempting to amend, and speaking against the proposed resolutions. The confrontations between feminists and conservatives did not develop in any significant way. Delegates held signs and wore buttons that announced their support of or opposition to issues such as abortion and the Equal Rights Amendment.

The NWC approved twenty-six resolutions that became the National Plan of Action. The resolutions called for the end of violence in the home, prevention of child abuse and treatment for abused children, expanded legislation recognizing the needs of disabled women, an increase in the number of women in elective and appointive public offices, ratification of the Equal Rights Amendment, support for displaced homemaker programs, improved services for older women, and changes in criminal codes to correct inequities against rape victims. Among the other topical areas were arts and humanities, business, child care, credit, education, minority women, offenders, rural women, and welfare and poverty.

NWC organizers had known that the two most controversial resolutions were on reproductive freedom and sexual preference. As debate began on the reproductive freedom resolution, which included abortion rights, supporters stepped to the microphones and made their points, but there were only a few brief comments from the opposition to the resolution, despite the chair's request that an opponent comment. Delegates approved the resolution.

The resolution to eliminate discrimination on the basis of sexual preferences had not been among the recommendations drafted by the commission, but thirty state meetings had approved the issue in their agendas. The commission responded by adding a resolution barring discrimination on the basis of sexual preferences for consideration by the NWC. Both feminists and conservatives struggled with the resolution, with one feminist calling it "an albatross" for the feminist agenda and saying that it would make ratification of the Equal Rights Amendment more difficult. Feminist Betty Friedan told the convention: "I am known to be violently opposed to the lesbian issue" but added: "I believe we must help the women who are lesbians" and supported the resolution. After the conference approved the resolution, delegates from Mississippi turned their backs to the podium, bent their heads as if praying, and held signs saying "Keep Them in the Closet."

The last resolution approved by the conference related to establishing a committee of the conference with the responsibility to call another NWC, as required by Public Law 94–167. In April 1978, President Jimmy Carter established the National Advisory Committee for Women (NACW), appointed forty people to it, and named Bella Abzug and Carmen Delgado Votaw its co-chairs. The NACW's effectiveness was interrupted by a dispute between Abzug and Carter, resulting in Carter's dismissal of Abzug and several committee members' resignations in protest.

Ultimately, a group of volunteers formed the National Women's Conference Committee, which coordinated efforts to implement the National Plan of Action.

See also Abortion; Abzug, Bella Savitzky; Domestic Violence; Education, Women and; Equal Rights Amendment; Friedan, Betty Naomi Goldstein; Griffiths, Martha Edna Wright; Lesbian Rights; National Advisory Committee for Women; National Commission on the Observance of International Women's Year, 1975; National Women's Conference Committee; Rape; Schlafly, Phyllis Stewart; Smeal, Eleanor Cutri; Steinem, Gloria Marie; Waters, Maxine Moore

References Bird, *What Women Want* (1979); East, *American Women: 1963, 1983, 2003* (1983).

Document "The National Women's Conference Plan of Action," 1977

National Women's Conference Committee

The National Women's Conference Committee (NWCC) works through existing organizations to implement the National Plan of Action approved by the National Women's Conference in 1977. Created in 1978 as the International Women's Year Continuing Committee, the NWCC is a private, nonprofit corporation that is supported by paid memberships and a volunteer corps.

The NWCC has its roots in the 1977 National Women's Conference held in Houston, Texas. The National Commission on the Observance of International Women's Year, 1975, which had planned and organized the conference, dissolved in early 1978 as required by the law that had authorized the conference. Among the resolutions in the National Plan of Action was one for a continuing committee, which had also been a provision of the legislation authorizing the conference. Within a short time, President Jimmy Carter had created the National Advisory Committee for Women, but its work was abandoned after Carter and committee co-chair Abzug disagreed and Carter fired her, prompting several committee members to resign. Carter appointed another committee, but it dissolved at the end of his administration in 1980.

A group of women who had been involved in the National Women's Conference organized the NWCC to pursue the goals it had outlined. The NWCC has helped organize advocacy networks in thirty-four states, developed strategies for international networks of women, and convened annual national meetings to assess progress on the National Plan of Action. It has published materials on the Equal Rights Amendment and on the National Plan of Action.

See also Abzug, Bella Savitzky; National Advisory Committee for Women; National Commission on the Observance of International Women's Year, 1975; National Women's Conference

References Bird, *What Women Want* (1979); East, *American Women: 1963, 1983, 2003* (1983).

National Women's Law Center

Established in 1972, the National Women's Law Center (NWLC) seeks to expand opportunities for women and girls through advocacy, research, education, technical assistance, and litigation. NWLC has formed coalitions, worked with state and federal agencies, and lobbied Congress to promote policies that protect and advance women's equality. Reproductive rights, women's education, women's health, and women's economic opportunities and sustenance are among the areas in which NWLC has been involved.

In the area of women's reproductive lives, NWLC stopped the coercive use of an experimental contraceptive on poor and institutionalized women in 1973, secured new regulations to protect poor women from involuntary sterilization, and played a leading role in the passage of the Pregnancy Discrimination Act of 1978. It also helped obtain Federal Food and Drug Administration approval of RU-486.

Enforcement of Title IX of the Education Acts of 1972 has been another area of NWLC's efforts. In 1980, NWLC challenged Temple University's intercollegiate athletic program, resulting in a precedent-setting, court-ordered settlement that expanded the women's sports program. Seventeen years later, NWLC filed charges against colleges and universities alleging sex discrimination in athletic scholarships and secured millions of dollars in scholarships for women students. In a third effort to gain equity for women students, NWLC exposed a $6.5 million scholarship gap for female athletes at just 30 colleges and universities. In another area of education, NWLC won the U.S. Supreme Court case *Davis v. Monroe County Board of Education* to make schools accountable for student harassment by other students.

In the early 1980s, NWLC helped pass expansion of the Dependent Care Tax Credit, making it more valuable to low-income families. NWLC later persuaded the Internal Revenue Service to add the credit to the 1040A (short form) income tax form, increasing the number of taxpayers who took advantage of the credit by almost 1.4 million taxpayers. In 1985, NWLC organized the first Coalition on Women and Taxes, contributing to the passage of important benefits for women in the 1986 Tax Reform Act.

NWLC had its origins as a women's rights project of the Center for Law and Social Policy (CLASP). Female administrative staff presented the male lawyers of CLASP with four demands: better pay, the hiring women staff attorneys, the creation of a women's rights project, and no more serving of coffee. NWLC became an independent group in 1981.

> **References** National Women's Law Center, "Expanding the Possibilities for Thirty Years," (Washington, D.C.: National Women's Law Center, 2002).

National Women's Political Caucus

Founded in 1971, the National Women's Political Caucus (NWPC) is a national grassroots organization dedicated to increasing the number of pro-choice women in elected and appointed positions at every level of government. Through its work, the NWPC has helped raise women's awareness of themselves as a political interest group and has helped gain politicians' recognition of women as a constituency.

Feminist leader Betty Friedan conceived the idea of forming the NWPC and founded the organization with some of modern feminism's most notable leaders, including Gloria Steinem, Fannie Lou Hamer, Olga Madar, LaDonna Harris, Liz Carpenter, Dorothy Height, and Congresswomen Shirley Chisholm and Bella Abzug, among many others. They shared a belief that a multipartisan women's organization was needed to promote the election and appointment of women to political offices.

At the time, the number of women serving in political leadership roles and public office had not become an issue in the public consciousness. There were no national campaign funds for women candidates and only random efforts to obtain political appointments for women. In the year the NWPC was founded, less than 3 percent of the members of Congress were women, and 4.5 percent of the members of state legislatures were women. Caucus members believed that increasing the number of women would enhance the potential for passage of the Equal Rights Amendment and other feminist legislative priorities.

The NWPC identifies, recruits, trains, and supports women seeking elected and appointed office. In one campaign cycle in the 1990s, the NWPC trained more than 2,500 women, teaching them how to raise money, develop a campaign message and strategy, motivate volunteers, and work with the news media. It also endorses candidates and raises money for endorsed candidates.

Increasing the numbers of women delegates to the Democratic National Convention and the Republican National Convention was an early priority for the NWPC. In 1972, it established training programs to assist women interested in becoming delegates and to teach them the process of becoming delegates. The NWPC also sent representatives to both parties' conventions, meeting with women delegates, explaining the NWPC's priorities, organizing networks, and providing support in the forms of information and strategy suggestions. The Republican Women's Task Force and the Democratic Women's Task Force emerged from the 1972 efforts and continued to work for feminist platform proposals at subsequent national conventions.

The NWPC's legislative priorities have included the Equal Rights Amendment, abortion rights, child care, economic equity, welfare reform, fair housing, and the Pregnancy Discrimination Act of 1978. In 2006, its priorities also included long-term care insurance, equality of insurance benefits, sex education, and international human rights for women.

The NWPC sponsors the EMMAs (Exception Merit in Media Awards) in recognition of the importance of media in their coverage of women and women's issues.

See also Abzug, Bella Savitzky; Carpenter, Mary Elizabeth (Liz) Sutherland; Chisholm, Shirley Anita St. Hill; Congress, Women in; Democratic Party, Women in the; Equal Rights Amendment; Friedan, Betty Naomi Goldstein; Hamer, Fannie Lou Townsend; Height, Dorothy Irene; Madar, Olga Marie; Meissner, Doris Marie; Pregnancy Discrimination Act of 1978; Republican Party, Women in the; State Legislatures, Women in; Steinem, Gloria Marie

References Feit, "Organizing for Political Power: The National Women's Political Caucus" (1979); http://www.nwpc.org.

Natividad, Irene (b. 1948)

Irene Natividad was chair of the National Women's Political Caucus from 1985 to 1989. Under Natividad's leadership, the NWPC established the Minority Women Candidates' Training Program, analyzed factors affecting success and defeat in women's congressional races, and held training workshops for political candidates and their staffs. In addition, Natividad explained: "One of our missions [at the NWPC] is to transfer the political experience we have developed on a national level to the state and local level. We want to train women to run for local offices because if we don't feed that pipeline we won't have winners." Interested in helping women obtain federal appointments, she met with President George H.W. Bush to discuss potential women appointees in his administration.

After the end of her second term as chair of the NWPC in 1989, Natividad's interests turned to international issues. She worked on the 1992 Global Forum of Women and the 1994 Taiwan Forum for Women. In 2001, she was president of the Global Summit of Women, an annual international gathering of women leaders. She co-chairs Corporate Women Directors International, which seeks to increase the number of women on corporate boards. Natividad offers political commentary on cable and broadcast news networks.

Born in Manila, the Philippines, Irene Natividad moved with her family to Okinawa, Japan; Iran; Greece; and India because of her father's work. Natividad graduated from high school in Greece. She earned her bachelor's degree in 1971 from Long Island University and a master's degree in American literature in 1973 and another master's degree in philosophy in 1976, both from Columbia University. She completed the course requirements for a doctoral degree but has yet to complete her dissertation for it.

Natividad became involved in politics during Eugene McCarthy's unsuccessful campaign for president in 1968. She held college faculty and administrative positions from 1974 to 1985. Founder and president of Asian American Professional Women in 1980, she also founded the National Network of Asian-Pacific American Women and the Child Care Action Campaign. From 1982 to 1984, Natividad chaired the New York state Asian Pacific Caucus of the Democratic Party and was deputy vice chair of the Asian Pacific Caucus of the Democratic National Committee. During Democratic vice presidential nominee Geraldine Ferraro's 1984 campaign, Natividad served as Asian American liaison for it.

See also National Women's Political Caucus

References Claudine Kolle, "Breaking into the Boys' Club," *Asian Business*, November 2001, p. 44; *The New York Times*, 18 November 1987; Zia and Gall, eds., *Notable Asian Americans* (1995).

Neuberger, Maurine Brown (1907–2000)

Democrat Maurine Neuberger of Oregon served in the U.S. Senate from 9 November 1960 to 3 January 1967. Her political career began shortly after she married Richard L. Neuberger in 1945. In 1948 Richard Neuberger won a seat in the Oregon state Senate, and in 1950 Maurine Neuberger won a seat in the Oregon House of Representatives. When the session began in 1951, Maurine and Richard Neuberger were the first married couple in the nation to serve simultaneously in both houses of a state legislature. They wrote *Adventures in Politics: We Go to the Legislature* (1954) about their experiences.

While in the legislature, Maurine Neuberger co-sponsored the bill that created the Oregon Fair Employment Practices Act. She contributed to the passage of bills that made it unlawful to discriminate in employment, housing, public accommodations, and education based upon race, color, national origin, religion, sex, marital status, handicap, or age. Maurine Neuberger served in the Oregon House of Representatives through the 1955 session, when she decided to join her husband in Washington, D.C. In 1954, Richard Neuberger had won election to the U.S. Senate.

In Washington, Neuberger became her husband's political partner, worked in his office, researched bills, wrote a monthly constituent newsletter, and prepared a weekly radio program. When Richard Neuberger unexpectedly died on 9 March 1960, two days before the filing deadline for the primary elections, Maurine Neuberger became a candidate to fill the vacancy and to serve for the full term beginning in 1961. She won both contests.

As a member of the U.S. Senate, Maurine Neuberger supported the regulation of billboards along federal highways, higher soybean price supports, and reform of immigration laws to end national origins quota systems. She wrote *Smoke Screen: Tobacco and the Public Welfare* (1963), calling for stronger controls on cigarette advertising and warning labels on cigarette packages. In addition, she advocated education of adolescents and adults about the health problems related to smoking.

Elected when few women held political offices, Neuberger said: "In politics, the woman intruder is most effective when she is seen but rarely heard. This does not mean she must be a cipher, but she must make every verbal missile count." She declined to run for a second full term. She later taught at Boston University, Radcliffe Institute, and Reed College.

Born in Multnomah County, Oregon, Maurine Neuberger graduated from high school in 1923 and two years later earned a teaching certificate from Oregon College of Education. After teaching in public schools for a few years, she returned to college and earned a bachelor's degree in English and physical education from the University of Oregon. She later attended graduate school at the University of California at Los Angeles.

See also Congress, Women in; State Legislatures, Women in

References H. W. Wilson, *Current Biography Yearbook, 1961*; Office of the Historian, U.S. House of Representatives, *Women in Congress, 1917–1991* (1991); *Los Angeles Times*, 24 February 2000; *The Washington Post*, 25 February 2000.

New York Radical Women

Formed by Pam Allen and Shulamith Firestone in 1967, New York Radical Women (NYRW) was one of the earliest radical women's liberation groups. The group's most publicized demonstration occurred outside the 1968 Miss America beauty pageant in Atlantic City, New Jersey. Two hundred women carried picket signs saying: "Women are people, not livestock" and "Can makeup cover the wounds of our oppression?" They designated a large container "the freedom trash can" and invited participants to toss items of "female torture" into it. Hair curlers, girdles, bras, and high heels went into the can, acts that attracted media attention. Reports that women burned their bras at the event are untrue, but from those reports feminists were given the derogatory appellation of "bra burners." The media attention alerted the nation that a new feminist movement was emerging in this country. The group dissolved in 1969.

References Echols, *Daring to Be Bad: Radical Feminism in America, 1967–1975* (1989)

News Media, Women Politicians and

The U.S. news media plays a substantial role in shaping the public's appraisals of political candidates and politicians, female and male. The media has a long tradition of reporting on political women differently than it has reported on political men, encouraging the perception that women do not belong in the political arena and perpetuating stereotypes of women. The information news outlets offer about female candidates may be accurate, but it also may emphasize matters of little consequence or use prejudicial language.

Women's physical appearance and attire have attracted undue attention, with descriptions of a woman's height, weight, and hairstyle appearing regularly. In 1982, for example, the *Des Moines Register* concluded that Iowa Democratic gubernatorial nominee Roxanne Conlin's changing hairstyles over several years deserved space in its news section and displayed several photos of her with different hairstyles. Other political women have objected when their clothing received more space than their accomplishments. In 1974, after President Richard Nixon resigned as a result of the Watergate scandal, Mary Louise Smith became chair of the Republican National Committee (RNC). At a time when the Republican Party was mired in controversy, reporters asked Smith if she planned to dye her hair and if she purchased her clothes from designers or off the rack. Such practices trivialize political women and minimize their accomplishments.

The adjectives used to describe political women provide an example of the news media's tendency to stereotype women. Female members of Congress have been described as "plucky," "perky," "spunky," and "feisty," words that would not be used to describe a male member of Congress. U.S. Senator Kay Bailey Hutchison (R-TX) was once described as an "aging cheerleader" and U.S. Representative Bella Abzug (D-NY) was called "aggressive" and "abrasive." Abzug noted that if she were a man, the words courageous and dynamic would more likely have been used. RNC chair Smith was consistently referred to as a gray-haired grandmother from Iowa, which was true, but reporters did not characterize Democratic National Committee chairman Robert Strauss as a gray-haired grandfather from Texas.

Sex-role stereotyping in the news media takes several forms. Political women are asked about their homemaking, sewing, and cooking skills, questions that political men are spared. In addition, men are not asked about their abilities to repair an automobile, build a house, or mow a lawn. Reporters frequently question political women about how it feels to be a woman officeholder, a question that men are not asked to address.

See also Abzug, Bella Savitzky; Hutchison, Kathryn (Kay) Ann Bailey; Public Offices, Women Elected to; Smith, Mary Louise

References Braden, *Women Politicians and the Media* (1996).

9to5, National Association of Working Women

Founded in 1973 by Karen Nussbaum and nine other women, 9to5, National Association of Working Women seeks to end workplace discrimination and to help women make the transition from welfare to work. The organization and its 15,000 members work on several levels, from providing information to working women seeking advice to lobbying state legislatures and Congress. Its bill of rights for working women includes fair pay, family-friendly policies, pro-rated benefits for part-time work, a voice in job design, job security, safe and healthful workplaces, and workplaces free from all forms of discrimination and harassment. In 2006, the organization's priorities also included expanding family and medical leave benefits and increasing access to child care.

Through its Job Survival Hotline, staff members answer as many as 25,000 phone calls a year from women wanting advice on job security, sexual harassment, workers' rights, maternity leave, and discrimination. Because ending sexual harassment in the workplace is a priority for 9to5, the association's former director, Ellen Bravo, and Ellen Cassedy wrote *The 9to5 Guide to Combating Sexual Harassment: Candid Advice from 9to5, the National Association of Working Women* in 1992. The book defines sexual harassment, provides statistics about it, offers advice on how to deal with harassers, and includes information on filing complaints.

9to5's public policy priorities include tax benefits for family-friendly companies, withholding government contracts from those companies that are not family-friendly, increasing the minimum wage, increasing child care options, and requiring benefits for part-time employees. The organization supported the Family and Medical Leave Act of 1993, the Civil Rights Act of 1991, the 1990 child care legislation, and state laws on workplace health and safety and sexual harassment.

The organization inspired the 1980 movie and song *Nine to Five*.

> **See also** Bravo, Ellen; Child Day Care; Civil Rights Act of 1991; Family and Medical Leave Act of 1993; Nussbaum, Karen; Pay Equity; Sexual Harassment
>
> **References** http://www.9to5.org.

Nineteenth Amendment

The Nineteenth Amendment guarantees women the right to vote. Passed by Congress on 4 June 1919, it was ratified and added to the U.S. Constitution on 26 August 1920 after more than seventy years of lobbying, organizing, and campaigning for it.

The text of the Nineteenth Amendment reads:

The right of citizens of the United States to vote shall not be denied or abridged by the United States or by any State on account of sex.

Congress shall have power to enforce this article by appropriate legislation.

> **See also** American Woman Suffrage Association; Anthony, Susan Brownell; Catt, Carrie Clinton Lane Chapman; Mott, Lucretia Coffin; National American Woman Suffrage Association; National Woman Suffrage Association; National Woman's Party; Paul, Alice; Seneca Falls Convention; Stone, Lucy; Suffrage

Nixon, Pat Ryan (1912–1993)

Pat Nixon was first lady from 1969 to 1974, the years her husband Richard Nixon was president of the United States. Her life as a politician's wife began in 1946, the year her husband ran for Congress, and continued until he resigned from office as a result of the Watergate scandal. Throughout Richard Nixon's political career, Pat Nixon steadfastly stood by her husband, campaigning for him, entertaining political supporters and other guests, and traveling with him on international trips, especially during the years he was vice president and president. During Richard Nixon's first term as presi-

Suffragists standing around a table in the office of Missouri Governor Frederick Gardner as he signs the resolution ratifying the 19th constitutional amendment; Missouri became the 11th state to ratify the "Anthony Amendment." (Library of CongressLC-USZ62-132969)

President and Mrs. Nixon strolling beneath the cherry blossoms at the Tidal Basin in Washington D.C. , 04/14/1969 Nixon Presidential Materials Staff (NLNS), National Archives at College Park, 8601 Adelphi Road, Room 1320, College Park, MD 20740-6001 PHONE: 301-837-3290, FAX: 301-837-3202, EMAIL: nixon@nara.gov ARC: 194622

dent, she sought but did not identify a special project by which she would become known. Although she continued to explore possibilities during his second term, the turmoil created by the Watergate scandal overwhelmed her search. After Richard Nixon resigned from the presidency, the couple returned to California.

Born in Ely, Nevada, Pat Nixon was named Thelma Catherine Ryan, which she changed to Pat Ryan in 1931. After graduating from the University of Southern California in 1937, she taught school in Whittier, California, and met Richard Nixon when they both had roles in a community theater production. They married in 1941, and she ended her teaching career.

References Eisenhower, *Pat Nixon* (1986).

Nolan, Mae Ella Hunt (1886–1973)

Republican Mae Nolan of California served in the U.S. House of Representatives from 23 January 1923 to 3 March 1925. She won the election to fill the vacancy created by the death of her husband, John Nolan. As chair of the Committee on Expenditures in the Post Office Department, Mae Nolan was the first woman to chair a House committee. She introduced a measure for a minimum daily wage of $3 for federal employees, which passed the House but failed in the Senate. She passed legislation that transferred the Palace of Fine Arts from the federal government to the City of San Francisco and that authorized the construction of a federal building. She declined to run for a second term, saying politics was "entirely too masculine to have any attraction for feminine responsibilities."

Born in San Francisco, California, Mae Ella Nolan attended Ayres Business College in San Francisco.

See also Congress, Women in

References Chamberlin, *A Minority of Members* (1973); Engelbarts, *Women in the United States Congress, 1917–1972* (1974).

Norrell, Catherine Dorris (1901–1981)

Democrat Catherine Norrell of Arkansas served in the U.S. House of Representatives from 18 April 1961 to 3 January 1963. She entered politics through her husband, Congressman William Norrell, serving as his staff assistant. After her husband died in office, she won the election to fill the vacancy. Congresswoman Norrell sought to protect Arkansas' clay, textile, and lumber industries through tariffs and other government regulation. She declined to run for a second term.

Born in Camden, Arkansas, Catherine Norrell attended Ouachita Baptist College and the University of Arkansas. She then taught music and was director of the Arkansas A&M music department.

After leaving Congress, Norrell was appointed deputy assistant secretary of state for educational and cultural affairs by President John Kennedy and served from 1963 to 1965. She was director of the State Department's reception center in Honolulu from 1965 to 1969.

See also Congress, Women in

References Office of the Historian, U.S. House of Representatives, *Women in Congress, 1917–1990* (1991).

Northup, Anne Meagher (b. 1948)

Republican Anne Meagher Northup of Kentucky entered the U.S. House of Representatives on 3 January 1997. Among her congressional priorities is the construction of a bridge over the Ohio River near Louisville. Northup has worked to increase accountability in federal programs and seeks local government control of programs and the reduction of government regulations to help small businesses. Northup has also worked on health care reform, focusing on making health care both affordable and accessible. She introduced legislation creating the National Reading Panel, which researched the ways children most effectively learn to read. To publicize the panel's findings, she founded the bipartisan House Reading Caucus in 1998. As co-chair of the Congressional Coalition on Adoption, Northup traveled to China in an effort to reduce the increasing number of obstacles confronting Americans seeking to adopt Chinese orphans.

Born in Louisville, Kentucky, Anne Northup earned her bachelor's degree in economics and business from St. Mary's College in 1970. Northup served in the Kentucky House of Representatives from 1987 to 1996.

> **See also** Congress, Women in; State Legislatures, Women in
>
> **References** *Congressional Quarterly, Politics in America 1998* (1997); http://northup.house.gove/bio.asp

Norton, Eleanor Holmes (b. 1937)

Democrat Eleanor Holmes Norton of the District of Columbia entered the U.S. House of Representatives on 3 January 1991. As representative for the district, Norton is a delegate and does not have a vote in House business. She is the first African American woman elected to Congress from the District of Columbia.

Born in Washington, D.C., Eleanor Holmes Norton earned her bachelor of arts degree from Antioch College in 1959 and her master of arts degree in 1963 and her law degree in 1964 from Yale Law School. Norton clerked for a federal judge following law school and then was assistant legal director of the American Civil Liberties Union (ACLU). Representing a white supremacist group that had been denied permission to hold a rally in Maryland, she argued and won her first case before the U.S. Supreme Court in 1968.

Norton headed the New York City Human Rights Commission from 1971 to 1977. She convinced several companies to provide maternity benefits, helped change workers' compensation policies, and won a woman sportswriter the right to sit in the press box at hockey games, in addition to other successes. From 1977 to 1981, Norton chaired the Equal Employment Opportunity Commission (EEOC). When she began her work there, the commission had a backlog of almost 100,000 worker complaints. Norton changed the arbitration system and reduced the backlog to 32,000 cases. Her work with the EEOC contributed to her decision in 1991 to urge the Senate to hold hearings after Anita Hill alleged that she had been sexually harassed by U.S. Supreme Court nominee Clarence Thomas. One of the women who marched to the U.S. Senate in October 1991, Norton explained: "As a black woman I identified with Anita Hill; as the former chair of the EEOC and because I wrote the guidelines, I had a special obligation, and I believe if we didn't walk the hearing would not have been held." She walked for "black women who have had their sexuality trivialized and scandalized; black women who have had their sexuality demeaned just as Clarence Thomas had done to Anita Hill."

Congresswoman Norton has worked for civil rights, women's rights, law enforcement, education, and economic development and political independence for the District of Columbia. A unique situation exists in the district. Residents pay taxes, but their congressional representative does not have a constitutional right to vote on the floor of the House. In 1993, Norton persuaded her colleagues to grant the district's representative that privilege, but when Republicans gained the majority for the 104th Congress in 1995, the privilege was withdrawn. Her first priority is full congressional voting representation for the District. Norton relies on her persuasive abilities perhaps more than other members of Congress as she works to represent the district's needs for infrastructure maintenance and improvements, additional federal funds, and an adequate tax system.

In 2000, Delegate Norton introduced legislation to address the problem of binge drinking among college students by increasing the federal taxes on beer and wine to rates comparable to those on hard liquor. In 2004, she co-authored legislation to increase security on public transportation, including buses, Amtrak, subways, and ferries.

See also Congress, Women in; Equal Employment Opportunity Commission; Hill, Anita Faye; Sexual Harassment

References Boxer, *Strangers in the Senate* (1994); Charles Dervarics, "New Legislation Targets Binge Drinking Among Students," *Black Issues in Higher Education*, 20 June 2002, p. 9; http://www.norton.house.gov;

Norton, Gale (b. 1954)

The first woman Secretary of the Interior, Gale Norton held the post from 2001 to 2006. She named the cornerstone of her tenure the Four C's: "communication, consultation, cooperation, all in the service of conservation." She believes that for conservation to be effective, the process of making policy must include the people who live on and work the land. To that end, she consulted with states, Native American tribes, businesses, conservation organizations, and private citizens.

She said that the biggest challenge she faced as secretary was the Indian Trust Fund. "We have had to make some substantial changes in a system that has been criticized for 100 years."

Assistant to the deputy secretary of the U.S. Department of Agriculture from 1984 to 1985, Norton was associate solicitor for the U.S. Department of the Interior from 1985 to 1987. She was attorney general for the state of Colorado from 1991 to 1999.

Born in Wichita, Kansas, Norton earned a bachelor of arts degree in 1975 and a juris doctorate degree in 1978, both at the University of Denver.

References http://www.doi.gov/secretary/biography.html; "The Nation's Low-Profile Landlady," *National Journal*, 25 January 2003, p. 260.

Norton, Mary Teresa Hopkins (1875–1959)

Democrat Mary Teresa Norton of New Jersey served in the U.S. House of Representatives from 4 March 1925 to 3 January 1951, making her the dean of congresswomen at the time of her retirement. Norton's political career emerged from her efforts to assist working women through a day nursery she founded. Seeking financial support from Jersey City, she appealed to Mayor Frank Hague, who facilitated the city government's making a financial commitment to the nursery. In return, Norton permitted Hague and the state Democratic committee to use her name on its list of members.

After the woman suffrage amendment was ratified in 1920, both Democrats and Republicans sought women's votes and organizational skills. Democrat Hague, one of the most powerful political bosses in U.S. history, enlisted Norton's help attracting women to the party and helped her develop her political skills. For three years, she recruited and organized women voters. In 1923, Hague persuaded Norton to run for the Hudson County Board of Freeholders. On the county board, she worked for the construction of a maternity hospital that the county would build and support, an effort that resulted in the only facility in the country financed that way. Her experience on the board exposed her to the inadequate services and assistance available for disabled or elderly people.

At Hague's urging, Norton resigned from the board in 1924 to run for the U.S. House of Representatives. With the help of Hague and the mothers who had known Norton through the day nursery, she won the election. She was the first Democratic woman elected to Congress who had not followed her husband into the office and the first woman elected from the East. After her election, a reporter asked her to pose for photographs: one hanging clothes on the line and the other cooking in her kitchen. She refused, saying: "I do not expect to cook, and I do not expect to wash any clothes in Congress."

In 1925, Congresswoman Norton sponsored legislation that funded construction of the first veterans' hospital in New Jersey. By 1928, Norton had become part of a circle of Democratic women activists that included Eleanor Roosevelt, Belle Moskowitz, and Molly Dewson, all of whom worked to involve more women in party politics. During the 1930s, Norton worked with Dewson to enhance the status of women working for the party at the local level and sought to highlight their contributions to the party and reward them.

When Democrats gained the majority in Congress in 1931, Norton became the second woman to chair a congressional committee, the District of Columbia Committee. At the time, Congress governed the district. Norton worked for home rule for the district, to improve slum areas in the city, to give women the right to serve on juries, and to permit women to be police officers. She helped improve the district's public transportation, made progress in improving its slums, passed the district's first old-age pension, and obtained an appropriation to build a hospital for tubercular children. Her diligent attention to the district earned Norton the nickname "Mayor of Washington." She chaired the committee until 1937.

She next chaired the Labor Committee, making her the first woman to chair a major legislative committee, beginning in 1937 and holding the post until 1946. A strong supporter of President Franklin D. Roosevelt's New Deal legislation, she had been instrumental in the passage of the National Labor Relations Act of 1935. As chair of the Labor Committee, her most outstanding work was the Fair Labor Standards Act of 1938, which took a full year to pass. Secretary of Labor Frances Perkins and Norton shared a commitment to establish a minimum pay provision based upon occupation and not sex, but the American Federation of Labor (AFL) opposed the wages and hours sections of the bill and wanted it killed. At the request of the AFL, Hague asked Norton to kill the bill, a power she had as committee chair, but she refused and took the bill to the House floor, where it failed. In 1938, Norton negotiated a compromise with AFL and brought out a new bill, but the Rules Committee buried it. Norton obtained the necessary 218 signatures on a discharge petition to move the bill out of the Rules Committee and onto the floor for debate. The bill passed with its provision that maximum hours and minimum wages be the same for men and women. The act established a minimum wage of twenty-five cents an hour, a forty-hour work week, and overtime wages at time and a half. In addition, it prohibited child labor. After the bill's passage, Norton said: "I am prouder of getting that bill through the House than anything else I've ever done in my life."

Her interest in the area of pay continued, and she was instrumental in raising the minimum wage, eventually to seventy-five cents an hour. In 1945, she introduced the Women's Equal Pay Act, but a measure enacting the policy did not pass until 1963. As committee chair, Norton encountered the resentment of some of her male colleagues, who sabotaged some legislation originating in her committee. In addition, important labor legislation that was within the purview of her committee sometimes went to other committees because a woman chaired the Labor Committee.

In 1941, Norton enlisted the help of eight of the nine women in Congress to develop bipartisan support for a $6 million appropriation for federal nursery schools for the children of women working in war industries. During the years of World War II, the appropriation rose to $75 million.

Since the 1920s, when Norton had recruited women to join the ranks of the Democratic Party, she had continued her efforts to encourage women to become politically active. Her interests included displaced homemakers, maternity leave, and equal pay for equal work for women. She wrote: "I think women should first of all be interested in other women, interested in other women's projects, their dreams, and their ambitions. It's up to women to stand for each other." She had intended to run for another term in 1950, but while she was in the hospital with pneumonia, she decided against it. She served as a consultant to the Labor Department until 1953.

Born in Jersey City, New Jersey, Norton's formal education ended when she was fourteen years old.

> **See also** Congress, Women in; Displaced Homemakers; Equal Pay Act of 1963; Family and Medical Leave Act of 1993
>
> **References** Kaptur, *Women of Congress* (1996); Mitchell, "Women Standing for Women: The Early Political Career of Mary T. Norton" (1978); Tomlinson, "Making Their Way: A Study of New Jersey Congresswomen, 1924–1994" (1996).

Novello, Antonia Coello (b. 1944)

Antonia Novello was the first woman, the first Puerto Rican, and the first Hispanic surgeon general of the United States, serving from 1990 to 1993. Before appointing her surgeon general, President George Bush confirmed that Novello shared the administration's opposition to abortion. Novello, who was born with an abnormally large and malfunctioning colon that required several surgical operations, explained: "Having been born with a congenital defect makes me think that everything has a chance to live." She added: "Women have to move a little bit away from abortion as the only issue to tackle."

As surgeon general, Novello campaigned against teen smoking and called on R. J. Reynolds Tobacco Company to stop using ads featuring Joe Camel, a cartoon character that had more appeal to children than to adults. She also asked beer and wine companies to end advertising campaigns directed at children and teenagers, saying: "The ads have youth believing that instead of getting up early, exercising, going to school, playing a sport or learning to be a team player, all they have to do to fit in is learn to drink the right alcohol." Novello also focused attention on domestic violence, the number of children not vaccinated against common infectious diseases, and the high rates of injury and death experienced by farm families.

Born in Fajardo, Puerto Rico, Novello earned her bachelor of science degree in 1965 and her medical degree in 1970, both from the University of Puerto Rico. She completed her internship in pediatrics at the University of Michigan and subspecialty training in pediatric nephrology at the University of Michigan Medical Center from 1973 to 1974 and at Georgetown University Hospital from 1974 to 1975. She earned her master's degree in public health from Johns Hopkins University in 1982.

Novello opened a private practice in Springfield, Virginia, in 1976, but left it two years later, saying, "when the pediatrician cries as much as the parents [of the patients] do, then you know it's time to get out." She joined the U.S. Public Health Service and was a project officer in the artificial kidney and chronic uremia program at the National Institutes of Health (NIH). A staff physician at NIH in 1979 and 1980, she was executive secretary of the Division of Grants at NIH from 1981 to 1986 and deputy director of the National Institute of Child Health and Human Development from 1986 until 1989. While at NIH, Novello also held a legislative fellowship and worked with the Senate Committee on Labor and Human Resources. During her fellowship, she made significant contributions to the drafting and enactment of the National Organ Transplant Act of 1984 and helped draft the warning used on cigarette packages.

From 1993 to 1996, Novello was the special representative for health and nutrition with UNICEF. In 1999, New York Governor George Pataki appointed her commissioner of health for the state of New York.

> **References** H. W. Wilson, *Current Biography Yearbook, 1992* (1992);
> http://www.health.state.ny.us/commissioner.

NOW v. Scheidler (1994) (2003) (2006)

In this series of three U.S. Supreme Court cases, the National Organization for Women sought to use the Racketeer Influenced and Corrupt Organizations Act (RICO) to sue anti-abortion groups that harassed, threatened, or used violence against reproductive health clinics. In *NOW v. Scheidler* (1994), the U.S. Supreme Court found that RICO applied to a coalition of anti-abortion groups. The case arose from a lawsuit brought by the National Organization for Women (NOW) and abortion clinics, alleging that the Pro-Life Action League Network (PLAN); Operation Rescue; and several individuals, including Joseph Scheidler, who was named in the lawsuit, were part of a nationwide conspiracy that sought to close abortion clinics. NOW contended that the violent actions that had occurred at abortion clinics, including trespass, threats, physical attacks, arson, theft of fetuses, and other acts, were coordinated events. The question that the Court had to decide was whether RICO applied only to enterprises with an economic motive, and the Supreme Court concluded that the law could be applied more broadly.

In the 2003 version of *NOW v. Scheidler*, the court found that since the anti-abortion groups did not acquire property, the actions were not extortion under RICO. In the 2006 version, the Court found that acts and threats of violence that did not involve extortion were not covered by RICO.

See also Abortion; National Organization for Women; Operation Rescue; Pro-Life Action League

References Bradley, "*NOW v. Scheidler*: RICO Meets the First Amendment" (1995); http://www.plannedparenthood.org/pp2/portal/files/portal/medicalinfo/abortion/fact-abortion-rulings.xml.

Nussbaum, Karen (b. 1950)

Karen Nussbaum was a co-founder of 9to5, National Association of Working Women and served as its first executive director from 1973 to 1993. She was director of the Women's Bureau of the Department of Labor from 1993 to 1996.

When she worked as a clerk-typist at Harvard University, Nussbaum found the low pay and lack of benefits and vacation time unacceptable and resented the lack of respect with which secretaries were treated. Discussing the issues with other women secretaries, she found several of them shared her grievances. With a few of her colleagues, Nussbaum called a meeting that about fifty women attended. The group expanded from Harvard University to include Boston in 1973. The Boston group joined similar groups that had formed in other cities to create 9to5, National Association of Working Women.

The organization seeks to improve its members' working conditions, wages, and promotion opportunities. Nussbaum led the formation of a national union in 1982, District 925 of the Service Employees International Union, a sister organization for those workers who want to belong to a union.

In 1993, President Bill Clinton appointed Nussbaum director of the Women's Bureau. She focused the bureau's attention on average working women and initiated the Working Women Count! survey of working women and the challenges they face in the workplace. She created programs to inform working women of their rights regarding sexual harassment, pregnancy discrimination, and the Family and Medical Leave Act of 1993. In 1996, Nussbaum became the first head of the Working Women's Department of the American Federation of Labor–Congress of Industrial Organizations.

Born in Chicago, Illinois, Karen Nussbaum attended the University of Chicago.

See also Family and Medical Leave Act of 1993; 9to5, National Association of Working Women; Women's Bureau

References http://dol.gov/dol/opa/public/media/press/wb/wb96066.htm; www.dol.gov/dol/wb/public/edu/gallery.htm.